# Organised Crime

A Catalyst in the Europeanisation of National
Police and Prosecution Agencies?

Edited by

## Monica den Boer

© 2002, European Institute of Public Administration /
Institut européen d'administration publique
Maastricht, the Netherlands / Pays-Bas
http://www.eipa.nl

The revision of these texts was done externally.

Organised Crime: A Catalyst in the Europeanisation of
National Police and Prosecution Agencies?

**ISBN 90-6779-162-8**

© 2002, European Institute of Public Administration.
EIPA's website: http://www.eipa.nl

Typeset and printed by the Publications Service, EIPA, the Netherlands.

# Table of Contents

# List of Authors

**Didier Bigo**

Professor of Politics, Institut d'Etudes politiques, Paris, France

**Monica den Boer**

Associate Professor of Public Administration, Centre for Law, Public Administration and Informatisation, Tilburg University; Visiting Professor, EIPA, The Netherlands

**Patrick Doelle**

Administrator, Legislation and Legal Affairs Unit, European Anti-Fraud Office (OLAF), Brussels

**Janne Flyghed**

Associate Professor, Department of Criminology, Stockholm University, Stockholm, Sweden

**Franziska Hagedorn**

PhD student, London School of Economics, London, United Kingdom

**Tuija Hietaniemi**

Associate Professor, University of Helsinki; Researcher, National Bureau of Investigation, Vantaa, Finland

**Peter Kruize**

Research fellow, Faculty of Law, University of Copenhagen, Denmark

**Hans-Heiner Kühne**

Professor of Criminal Law, Law Faculty, Universität Trier, Trier, Germany

**Oscar Jaime-Jimenez**

Professor of Politics, University of Pamplona, Spain

**Effi Lambropoulou**

Associate Professor, Panteion University of Social and Political Science, Department of Sociology, Section: Criminology, Athens, Greece

**Francesca Longo**

Researcher, Department of Political Studies, University of Catania, Catania, Sicily, Italy

**Laia Moreno**             Assistant, Universidad de Burgos, Spain

**Kurt Schmoller**          Professor of Criminal Law, Universität Salzburg, Institut für Strafrecht, Strafprozessrecht und Kriminologie, Salzburg, Austria

**Armand Schockweiler**     Lieutenant-Colonel, Member of the General Inspectorate of the Luxembourg Police, Luxembourg

**James Sheptycki**         Lecturer, Department of Sociology, University of Durham, Durham, United Kingdom

**Gert Vermeulen**          Professor of Criminal Law, University of Ghent, Ghent, Belgium

**Dermot Walsh**            Professor of Law, Law Department, University of Limerick, Limerick, Ireland

# Foreword

In the months following the terrorist attacks in the USA on 11 September 2001, numerous EU decisions were taken within the arena of cooperation in Justice and Home Affairs. In many EU Member States, there is now an active debate about the extent to which EU decisions have an impact on domestic legal systems and criminal justice infrastructures. Many of the organisations and agencies highlighted in this publication bear overall responsibility for the coordination of investigations into international terrorism. Hence, this book could not have been published more timely, as it lays down an updated geography of police and judicial cooperation between EU Member States in the fight against international organised crime and terrorism.

Except for thanking the authors for revising their reports for the purposes of publication, I would like to thank three persons in particular. First of all, many thanks to Veerle Deckmyn, who – as Head of EIPA publications – supported the publication of this book and argued our case in the Academic Council. Secondly, an inexpressible amount of gratitude to Denise Grew, who demonstrated endless patience and accuracy throughout the revision process. Thirdly, many thanks to Patrick Doelle, who – as a former research assistant on the project – was responsible for the editorial process when this book first appeared as a report in May 2000. Finally, I would like to thank the EIPA team for hosting this successful research project and for assisting the authors and myself as editor with the translation, revision and publication of the reports.

Tilburg, 4 January 2002

# Converge or Not to Converge...That's the Question: A Comparative Analysis of Europeanisation Trends in Criminal Justice Organisations

*Monica den Boer and Patrick Doelle*

## 1. INTRODUCTION

During the past few years, justice and home affairs cooperation between the EU Member States has expanded considerably. Cross-border cooperation in the criminal justice area has gained more importance as internal border controls have gradually been lifted and as criminal agents have had more opportunities to exploit loopholes in national laws and policies.

The murder of the Italian judge Giovanni Falcone on 23 May 1992 increased awareness among the governments of the EU Member States and the general public of the threat posed by organised crime to European democratic societies. One of the consequences has been that, since the beginning of the 1990s, a vast body of measures has been introduced at national and EU level to combat organised crime. One of these measures is the Joint Action adopted on 19 March 1998 by the Council of the European Union which established the so-called *Falcone* funding programme – a tribute to the famous Italian judge and Mafia-investigator. The objective of this programme is to finance activities such as exchanges, seminars, training or research projects which enhance initiatives in the control of organised crime. The funding which the European Institute of Public Administration (EIPA) has obtained from the Falcone programme provided the main financial support for the research project 98/FAL/145 (below referred to as the "Falcone" project). The Research and Documentation Centre of the Dutch Ministry acted as co-sponsor of the project. This prepared the ground for a project which embraces the synthesis report and 15 reports concerning the national criminal justice systems in the EU Member States with regard to the control of organised crime.

Starting from the assumption that the criminal justice systems of the EU Member States are increasingly converging as a consequence of the internationally coordinated fight against organised crime, the "Falcone" project had the principal objective of identifying, analysing and evaluating the recent organisational changes in relevant departments of the national law enforcement and public prosecution bodies.

The general overture to this volume has a number of additional objectives, namely:

- First, to provide a broad account of the underlying rationale of (expected) criminal justice reforms which are meant to counter the upsurge of international organised crime;
- Second, to give an overview of the frameworks and (legal) instruments that have been adopted by relevant decision-making fora of the European Union, which we assume have had and will have an organisational impact on the national criminal justice systems of the EU Member States;
- Third, to draw on leading theoretical perspectives which have assisted us in deepening key research notions, such as "convergence", "systemic interaction", and "Europeanisation";
- Fourth, to provide an overview of the underlying research hypotheses, which were tested by means of a common questionnaire (see Appendix);
- Fifth, and central to this synthesis report, to give a cross-comparative account of the principal findings, based on horizontal analysis of the national reports;
- Finally, to revisit the research hypotheses and to list the core findings of the research project.

Before going into the substantive aspects of our research, a number of issues concerning the research methodology are presented in Section 2. Section 3 discusses the threat of international organised crime as it is perceived by the EU Member States, and the legal, policy-oriented or operational definitions which are employed nationally. A presentation of the EU frameworks and legal instruments which are expected to fuel organisational changes within the national police and prosecution services follows in Section 4. Section 5 contains an outline of selected theoretical perspectives on reforms and convergence. Section 6 revisits the research hypotheses. Section 7, which presents the body of the empirical data, contains a cross-comparison of the principal research findings of the national reports. An overall analysis can be found in Section 8. The chapter concludes with Section 9, which provides a quick summary of the main findings, and puts forward some observations that may be dealt with in possible future research.

## 2. RESEARCH PROCESS AND METHODOLOGY

Carrying out comparative research at an international level is an illuminating learning exercise. Our account below seeks not only to describe the essential parts of the research process and methodology, but also to evaluate it in order to benefit future international research projects.

### 2.1 The Research Network

At the core of our research project was the formation of an international research network, which was responsible for carrying out the bulk of the research. Without the expertise and professional insight of the contributors to the research network, our empirical findings would no doubt have been less detailed and comprehensive.

A choice was made during the design stage of the research proposal to identify one experienced and specialised researcher in each EU Member State. The establishment of the network was partly based on an existing international network linked to the research coordinator, Dr Den Boer, but for some EU Member States we had to draw upon contacts of employees of the European Institute of Public Administration (EIPA) to identify the right people. The research network was established during the first months of the project, and gained momentum during the First Round Table, which was convened on 3 and 4 June 1999 at EIPA, Maastricht (see chapter 2.3 for a more detailed account of the Round Tables).

The participation of national researchers had a number of benefits, such as access to respondents and documents via native speakers, the availability of academic and/or professional knowledge of the national criminal justice system and – in most cases – a rapid and flexible access to the key respondents. This allowed us to obtain a maximum amount of information for the comparative analysis of the reforms.

The combination of authors from different academic backgrounds – law, politics, public administration and sociology – gave the research a strongly multidisciplinary character, which resulted in some controversial debates.

### 2.2 Professional Referees

Three professional referees were invited to participate in the project as consultants and to monitor its progress:
- *Dr Willy Bruggeman*, Deputy Senior Director of Europol
- *Mr Glenn Audenaert*, Head of the Belgian Europol National Unit,

towards the end of our project appointed as Commissioner of the Judicial Police for the Greater District of Brussels
- *Mr Wil van Gemert*, Director of the Dutch Criminal Intelligence Department.

The referees were particularly helpful in delineating the research project. Together with the researchers, they discussed the relevance of the research hypotheses and the design of the questionnaire. Furthermore, their expertise, authority and access to networks made it possible to take account of the most recent developments. Some referees have guaranteed their continued advice after completion of the research project, particularly with a view to purposefully disseminating the research findings among law enforcement professionals.

## 2.3 Round Tables

The researchers and referees met during two Round Tables organised by EIPA in Maastricht. The first Round Table, which was convened on 3 and 4 June 1999, had the objective of familiarising contributors with one another. A discussion paper was prepared for the first Round Table, which contained a description of the project, the main research hypotheses and the methodology. During the Round Table, each individual researcher introduced him/herself and gave a concise account of the current organisational arrangements *vis-à-vis* organised crime in his/her EU Member State. The second day was devoted to a discussion about the methodology (in particular the questionnaire), and to the establishment of procedural agreements, such as a deadline for the first drafts.

The second Round Table was held on 3 and 4 February 2000, and was again hosted by EIPA, Maastricht. The objective of this Round Table was twofold. On the one hand, the researchers were requested to give a detailed account of their research findings, which allowed for some cross-referencing between the researchers. On the other hand, the researchers established a consensus on the final title of the research report, the individual and collective responsibilities for authorship, and the publication of the synthesis report in combination with the national reports.

## 2.4 Questionnaire

In order to achieve optimal comparability between the research findings, a joint standard questionnaire[1] was designed. One of the main reference points in the questionnaire was a series of EU legal instruments, which have been adopted in the field of justice and home affairs cooperation (Title VI Treaty on European Union). In particular the recommendations of the 1997 High Level Group Action Plan on Organised Crime – which pertain to the creation of national contact points and national coordination centres – offered both a functional and comparative perspective on the adaptation of national law enforcement structures to the threat of organised crime.

The questionnaire covered the following fields:
- General characteristics of the national criminal justice systems, in particular the organisational structures of the police service and the prosecution service;
- Reorganisation or structural adaptation flowing from or related to the EU legal instruments (e.g. the 1997 EU Action Plan on Organised Crime, the 1991 EC Money Laundering Directive);
- Reorganisation relevant to the control of organised crime, but not directly related to European influences (e.g. flowing from national parliamentary inquiries);
- Main structures for international cooperation, in particular the organisation of international information and intelligence flows;
- Multidisciplinary cooperation structures with bodies other than police or prosecution (e.g. customs service, intelligence service, special investigation services, financial intelligence units, private investigation departments, and private security companies);
- Accountability systems and authorisation procedures relating to the investigation of organised crime cases;
- The rationale, the acceptance and the expected effectiveness of the reorganisation or reforms within the police and/or prosecution service.

The researchers were urged to use the questionnaire as the leading methodological tool for the execution of their research. However, they were free in the application of it: some used it as a list of questions for respondents, others used the questionnaire as a grid to structure the information they obtained. The researchers were also free to employ complementary research methods, such as interviews with key persons and documentary research.

Throughout the research project, it turned out that the questionnaire was a little ambitious: in particular the questions concerning accountability structures and the acceptance of reforms could not always be taken into consideration. Nevertheless, the current national reports represent a lot more than just a scoreboard about the implementation of EU instruments, as they offer background analysis about the latest developments in the Member States.

## 2.5 Comparative Analysis

In order to establish what planning and implementation of reforms have been carried out in the national police and justice organisations, comparative (empirical) research has been of quintessential importance in our project. The authors who have contributed to this book have not only endeavoured to provide a description of the structure, function and task of the relevant organisations, but also to look into reform processes and their rationales. Cross-national empirical research is undeniably tricky, however, mainly because, as is widely acknowledged within the academic community, national definitions in respect of laws, mandates, and discretionary powers can be very different. Comparative research tends to "over-compress" variations within national cultures.[2] Fijnaut, an expert in comparative policing studies, observes in relation to the UK and France that:[3]

> "Even this brief comparison of four neighbouring police systems shows the difficulty of finding a common denominator with which to analyse the changes that have occurred in these systems in recent years. While integration and centralisation are appropriate concepts by which to define the changes in the Dutch and Belgian police services and may, with due caution, also be applied to the British situation, they are wholly unsuitable for any analysis of developments in French policing, except in a negative manner (no centralisation of command, no integration of police forces....) if more countries were to be included in the comparison ... the final result would be more varied still."

The authors who have contributed to this volume have tended to be more optimistic about the possibility of undertaking such cross-national comparative research, perhaps also because we did not start off with the objective of developing common categories. Nevertheless, it became clear that concepts such as "centralisation", "authority", "privatisation", "specialisation" all carry their own specific meaning within their own national context.

In the context of our research, we analysed organisations that are embedded within a wide array of administrative structures. Some states emphasise regional or provincial autonomy, which has considerable effects on the functioning of police and justice organisations; it may imply a considerable margin of manoeuvre to determine crime-control strategies, selection of personnel, choice of information systems, training priorities, and so on. Other states embrace centralised structures, which usually result in hierarchically organised police and justice organisations and a noticeably higher level of uniformity.

Most public administration systems can be considered as hybrids that incorporate centralised and decentralised features alike, which further complicates the analysis of organisational evolution and changes.[4] Moreover, the near-exclusive focus on national coordination facilities for the fight against organised crime implies that we automatically turn a blind eye to the many differentiations within the organisation at large.

The heterogeneity of research findings was reduced by initially achieving consensus about the content and structure of the research questionnaire, and by agreeing on a common reporting structure. Furthermore, the reports exclusively focus on the policing and prosecutorial functions of the criminal justice systems, and do not devote attention to the adjudicatory and correctional functions.[5] The research network has primarily concentrated their attention on the state police and state prosecution services, and not on other public or private authorities that may carry out related tasks.

A final source of heterogeneity concerns the definitions and concepts of (international) organised crime in the criminal law (or administrative law) codes of the Member States.[6] Similarly, the recording of offences may be different in each individual Member State, and this will be reflected in the statistics.

Despite the many objections that may be levelled against cross-national comparative research, the national reports have generated a wealth of information, and have contributed to an improved understanding of the national criminal justice systems. Furthermore, comparative research can provide a better insight into the problems that are encountered in achieving further integration of national criminal justice systems in Europe. In a similar fashion, an international research network coordinated by Dutch and British academics, observed:

> "One of the fascinating aspects of comparative studies is that we each view the information that we have gained through the lens of our own culture. It is a salutary experience to see systems and procedures which have become reified in our minds from a perspective which finds it hard to believe that things could be done this way."[7]

## 2.6 Dissemination

The material presented in this volume may be of great interest and benefit to agents who are involved in European police and judicial cooperation in criminal matters, in particular within the field of organised crime control. Some Member States expressed interest in disseminating the results for the benefit of the professional community (e.g. by publication of a national report on a police web site). Moreover, the research findings may be further exploited within the academic community at large, the European Judicial Network, Europol, the imminent Eurojust and the future European Police College.


## 3.   ORGANISED CRIME IN THE EU

### 3.1  A Challenge for the EU Member States

The liberalisation of the economic and financial markets and significant migratory flows are generally considered as the two chief elements that have contributed to the expansion of international organised crime in the past years.[8] According to this analysis, criminal organisations have exploited the abolition of trade barriers and border controls to increase their mobility and expand their illegal activities in the fields of drug trafficking and drug production, arms trafficking, the smuggling of illegal immigrants, car/vehicle theft, etc. Sharp contrasts in the economic and financial welfare between countries or regions[9] seem to pave the way for criminal entrepreneurs to establish profitable illegal businesses that operate in the niches of legal markets. The contrasts in economic welfare and payment form an ideal breeding ground for the corruption of public officials and the recruitment of members of the criminal organisation. Moreover, (international) organised crime thrives in weak states and environments which exercise a minimal regulatory power.

Meanwhile, technological innovations such as mobile telecommunications and the Internet facilitate various operational activities of criminal organisations: the speed of financial transactions benefits the money laundering industry, mobile telephony undermines the control of national authorities because of the anonymity of the telecommunications and the absence of legislation regarding cyberspace.[10] In short, international organised crime is seen as a potent danger to the internal security of Member States, with a vicious capacity to undermine the integrity of the public sectors and politics of nation states, to circumvent and even exploit the regulatory power of these states, and to use their economies and their infrastructures as a lever for their own illegal activities.

The area of the European Union with its four freedoms of movement (goods, services, capital and people), which have been progressively achieved, is often mentioned as a strong incentive for criminal organisations to expand their activities. Following a study carried out in 1997 in Italy, their annual turnover in Europe is estimated at 600,000 billion Lire (more than 300 billion euro), which is equal to 4.2% of the GNP of all European countries (ex-URSS countries included), or equal to the turnover of the top five European companies (Royal Dutch Shell, Daimler-Benz, Siemens, Volkswagen, ENI).[11] It would be a rather fruitless exercise to determine to what extent the opening of the borders and the liberalisation of exchange have actually contributed to an increase of transnational organised crime in the EU.[12] Rather than the abolition of border controls, the presence of the borders themselves are enormously advantageous to criminal organisations, because they can benefit from the heterogeneity of legislation and administrative structures in the EU Member States.[13]

The surging awareness of the security challenge posed by organised crime has culminated in a number of systemic and/or organisational changes in the criminal justice systems of the Member States. At national level, police and prosecution services have been subjected to reforms in order to rationalise and coordinate the international exchange of information. At the same time, the control of international organised crime has popularised the employment of innovative criminal investigation methods (the so-called "proactive" or "undercover" methods), which potentially infringe deeply into the personal lives of suspects, or which may have a significant impact on the diplomatic relations between states. The sensitivity of these undercover methods has forced most EU Member States to design new regulatory frameworks, new legislation and revised accountability systems that provide for checks and balances.[14]

These developments in the EU Member States have not taken place in splendid isolation. They should be seen in the context of an acknowledgement that only a common approach in the control of international organised crime can be successful. While the general anti-organised crime efforts undertaken at EU and national level are presented in the next sections, we will first examine the definitions of (international) organised crime within the individual EU Member States.

## 3.2 Defining Organised Crime: Why So Difficult?

The colourful range of definitions and constitutive criteria which have been proposed by the academic world and agencies involved in the fight against organised crime reveal how difficult it is to define a phenomenon which tends to be characterised by heterogeneous elements, organisational and logistical variety, as well as differing activities and objectives.[15] In spite of this enormous complexity, several attempts have been undertaken at EU level to agree upon common definitions and criteria.

9

First, we should mention the Joint Action that the Council of the European Union adopted on 21 December 1998, which provides for a definition of a "criminal organisation".[16] According to Article 1 of the Joint Action:

> "a criminal organisation shall mean a structured association, established over a period of time, of more than two persons, acting in concert with a view to committing offences which are punishable by deprivation of liberty or a detention order of a maximum of at least four years or a more serious penalty, whether such offences are an end in themselves or a means of obtaining material benefits and, where appropriate, of improperly influencing the operation of public authorities."

The purpose of the Joint Action is to criminalise the participation in a criminal organisation in the legislation of all EU Member States. Even if a Joint Action is a binding instrument, it has no direct effect and there is no mechanism to enforce its implementation in national law. Hence, until now, only a few EU Member States have adopted the measures required to act in conformity with the provisions of the Joint Action.

On the other hand, the Council agreed on the establishment of a common mechanism for the collection and systematic analysis of information on international organised crime.[17] This mechanism is to be used by the EU Member States and Europol for the elaboration of the national and the EU situation reports on organised crime. One important element of the mechanism is a list of 11 characteristics of organised crime which assist Member States in preparing their reports:[18]

(1) Collaboration of more than 2 people;
(2) Each with own appointed tasks;
(3) For a prolonged or indefinite period of time (this criterion refers to the stability and (potential) durability of the group);
(4) Using some form of discipline and control;
(5) Suspected of the commission of serious criminal offences;
(6) Operating at an international level;
(7) Using violence or other means suitable for intimidation;
(8) Using commercial or businesslike structures;
(9) Engaged in money laundering;
(10) Exerting influence on politics, the media, public administration, judicial authorities or the economy;
(11) Determined by the pursuit of profit and/or power.

The table below shows – as far as information was available – whether the EU Member States use the EU definitions and characteristics or whether they have adopted their own criteria. While no EU Member State has adopted a legal definition for the term "organised crime", some have recently introduced new provisions which define criteria or aggravating circumstances falling under the scope of organised crime. Several EU Member States decided to criminalise the membership and participation in a "criminal organisation", but not all of them adopted the definition of the 1998 EU Joint Action literally. The latter seems mostly due to the fact that some Member States changed their Criminal Code before the adoption of the Joint Action. As far as definitions and criteria, other than legal ones, are concerned, especially those for police use, the EU does not seem to have a determining influence. Even if one supposes that the 11 abovementioned criteria are used in drawing up the situation reports, their general use by the police forces does not always seem to be accepted.

A tentative conclusion may be that the impact of the European Union has thus far been limited regarding the adoption of legal rules and practical criteria aimed at defining organised crime. The next section deals with EU-wide instruments and frameworks that may have had an influence on organisational structures and procedures of the law enforcement organisations and public prosecution services of the Member States.

## 4.  EU FRAMEWORKS AND INSTRUMENTS

Title VI of the Maastricht Treaty on European Union (the so-called "Third Pillar") has laid down the foundations and framework for cooperation in justice and home affairs at EU level. Among the different initiatives that have been taken and the instruments that have been adopted in the field of organised crime, the most relevant for the present research project have undoubtedly been Europol and – as a follow-up with a broader perspective – the 1997 Action Plan to Combat Organised Crime. But other instruments, like the first EC Money Laundering Directive of 1991 and several Joint Actions, have also been of interest to the study and should therefore be briefly mentioned. Finally, even if it was not adopted in the framework of the EU and does not have the control of organised crime as its main objective, the Schengen Implementing Convention (SIC) should also be taken into consideration. Meanwhile, however, the domain of justice and home affairs cooperation within the EU has been very dynamic. Hence, new developments have been continuous, including the establishment of reporting and monitoring mechanisms to oversee the implementation of EU instruments in this field. The present chapter briefly introduces these latest developments in JHA which may trigger organisational changes at the national level in the near future, like the creation of UCLAF (now OLAF), and also proposals made as part of the conclusions of the Tampere summit, the follow-up of the 1997

## *Figure 1:*
## *Organised Crime Definitions and Criteria in the EU Member States*[19]

|  | Legal definition (legislation) | Other definitions/criteria (policy/ operational) |
|---|---|---|
| **Austria** | No definition of "organised crime", but of a "criminal organisation" (§ 278a Criminal Code) | List of indicators used by the law enforcement authorities |
| **Belgium** | No definition of "organised crime", but of a "criminal organisation" (according to the EU Joint Action) | Definition of "organised crime" of the German Federal Criminal Police Office (BKA) used for operational purposes |
| **Denmark** | No definition | EU criteria used for the situation report |
| **Finland** | Draft text under discussion at the Parliament, defining "organised crime" and "criminal organisation" (according to the EU Joint Action) | |
| **France** | No definition of "organised crime", but various expressions and definitions which refer to collective behaviour aimed at committing serious offences with the help of an organised structure | – definition for legal practice<br>– list of five elements for police practice |
| **Germany** | No definition of "organised crime", but the constitution and membership of a "criminal association" punishable (Article 129 Criminal Code) | Definition of the Federal Criminal Police Office (BKA) for the police use |
| **Greece** | No definition of "organised crime", but the constitution and membership of a criminal gang punishable (Article 187 Criminal Code) | EU criteria used by the police, i.e. for the situation report |
| **Ireland** | No definition of "organised crime", but common law offence of "conspiracy" | |
| **Italy** | No definition of "organised crime", but of a "Mafia-type association" (Article 416 bis Criminal Code) | |
| **Luxembourg** | No definition of "organised crime", but of a "criminal organisation" (according to the EU Joint Action) | |
| **Netherlands** | No definition of "organised crime", but criminalisation of the membership of a criminal organisation (Article 140 Criminal Code) | List of five characteristics and rating system for organised crime |
| **Portugal** | No definition of "organised crime", but of a "criminal association" (Article 299 Criminal Code) | |
| **Spain** | No definition of "organised crime", but specific criteria for organised crime (Article 282 bis 4 of the Criminal Prosecution Code) | |
| **Sweden** | No definition | List of eleven criteria adopted by the EU |
| **United Kingdom** | No definition | Definition of the National Criminal Intelligence Service (NCIS) for police use |

12

Action Plan to Combat Organised Crime and the EU Convention on Mutual Assistance in Criminal Matters.

## 4.1 Europol

The European Drugs Unit (EDU) was first established as a forerunner of Europol in 1993. Its purpose was to facilitate the exchange of information and coordination of police investigations, in a limited field of competence, through a network of liaison officers based in The Hague.[20] The functioning of the EDU required that each Member State create a National Drugs Unit in order to channel intelligence between the EDU and the competent national authorities. The Europol Convention was adopted by the Council on 26 July 1995 and entered into force on 1 October 1998. The creation of Europol no doubt reinforces the effect of central coordination through the establishment of a central computerised system of data collection and analysis, which is expected to improve the information position of Europol and the Europol National Units.[21]

Except for the creation or designation of national units, Europol will have other – less apparent but no less important – harmonising side effects on the organisation of police and public prosecution services in the Member States. An example is the establishment of a common mechanism for the collection and analysis of information with a view to providing Europol with comparable data for the development of an annual Organised Crime Situation Report.[22] Another example is a series of rules regarding the exchange of intelligence which require common classifications for the assessment of information and its source or for the confidentiality of information.[23] Finally, Article 24 of the Europol Convention demands that each Member State designate a national supervisory body which should monitor the handling of personal data; this legal provision has resulted in the creation of national data protection boards in countries that previously did not have such an institution (e.g. Italy, Greece).[24]

In addition, the rules that were agreed on in the 1997 Treaty of Amsterdam, which entered into force on 1 May 1999, will contribute to the centralisation and harmonisation of national organisations. Article 30, par. 2 (a) and (b) of the Treaty provides for instance for the creation of joint investigation teams comprising representatives of Europol and for the possibility for Europol to request the competent authorities of the Member States to conduct and coordinate their investigations in specific cases. These new rules may reinforce the role of national or central authorities in the Member States. In the meantime, discussions are being held at EU-Presidency level about a global revision of the Europol Convention in order to deal with the new semi-operational powers.[25] In a recent speech at a conference organised by the Dutch Senate, Commissioner Vitorino for Justice and Home Affairs advanced the thesis that further parliamentary control with regard to Europol should be stepped up given its evolving powers; he has in mind a kind of 'joint venture' between the national Parliaments and the European Parliament, and the establishment of a joint committee which should comprise representatives of both national and European Parliaments.[26]

## 4.2 Action Plan to Combat Organised Crime

The Action Plan to Combat Organised Crime was elaborated by a High Level Group and adopted by the Council on 28 April 1997. The Plan formulates 30 recommendations which should be implemented in accordance with various timetables.[27] Some of these recommendations directly concern the organisational structures and procedures of police and prosecution services in the Member States, and have therefore provided the basis for a number of questions in the questionnaire.

*Recommendation 1* asks the Member States to "examine whether it would be appropriate... to designate a body at national level which would have an overall responsibility for the coordination of the fight against organised crime."

Several Member States had already created such a coordinating body before this recommendation was launched. The most striking example is probably the Italian National Anti-Mafia Directorate (*Direzione nazionale antimafia/* DNA), which was created in 1991 to play the role of a central prosecution service for the coordination of investigations in the field of organised crime.[28] The head of the DNA, the *Procuratore nazionale antimafia*, directs the 26 Anti-Mafia district prosecution services, and is served by the *Direzione investigativa antimafia* (DIA), an inter-force law enforcement agency with national competence.

A document issued by the Council of the EU in 1998 on the implementation of some recommendations of the Action Plan also mentions the creation of other bodies like the Coordinating Committee on Serious Crime at the Public Prosecutor's Office in the Netherlands. In the UK, an Organised Crime Strategy Group was established at the Home Office, which bears overall responsibility for coordination but has no direct competence with regard to operational activities. According to the Council document, the creation of a national coordinating body was at that time in progress (Finland) or seriously taken into consideration (Spain), while others did not consider it necessary at this stage to designate a separate body for the coordination function (Germany, Ireland).[29]

***Recommendation 19*** underlines the necessity to designate central national contact points "in order to speed up the exchange of information and the completion of application procedures for law enforcement cooperation.... With regard to the Europol convention, the central national unit referred to therein should be the contact point on behalf of all law enforcement authorities in the Member States. It is advisable that existing contact points, such as the Interpol NCB, SIRENE bureaux, etc. should be brought together in this central contact point, or at least, that close relations between such units should be established."

This recommendation illustrates the efforts made at EU level to centralise and harmonise anti-organised crime bodies within the national police organisations by means of integrating different cooperation structures. Almost every Member State has already established a central national contact point for Europol, Interpol and SIRENE.[30] However, according to the abovementioned Council document, only four Member States (the Netherlands, Finland, the United Kingdom and Germany) had designated a single contact point at that time.[31]

***Recommendation 20*** considers the creation of multidisciplinary integrated teams at national level which "should have sufficient insight into national criminal investigations to be able to contribute to the development of national policies in the fight against organised crime."

As well as bringing together representatives of various law enforcement agencies under Europol (Member States are supposed to send liaison officers from each national agency), this recommendation also seeks to improve effectiveness by circumventing traditional inter-organisational rivalry and conflicts, and aims to increase multidisciplinary intelligence gathering. Some EU Member States already had multidisciplinary integrated teams in place prior to the Action Plan. In Italy, the Italian Anti-Mafia Investigation Directorate (*Direzione investigativa antimafia*/DIA) is an inter-force organism under the authority of the Ministry of Interior, which has the function of collecting intelligence and of conducting investigations in the field of organised crime. All three Italian law enforcement agencies (*Polizia di Stato, Carabinieri, Guardia di Finanze*) are represented in the DIA.[32] According to the abovementioned Council document, the Netherlands created several permanent teams, while the United Kingdom established them on an *ad hoc* basis.[33]

*Recommendation 21* suggests the creation of a European Judicial Network (EJN), and "in order to develop this network, each Member State should designate a central contact point permitting the exchange of information between national judicial authorities." The EJN was established on the basis of a Joint Action adopted on 29 June 1998.[34] The development of such a network needs to be considered in relation to the problem of accountability in relations between police and prosecution services. The setting up of a European Police Office without a parallel European Prosecution Service to which the former is accountable has been criticised by some authors.[35] The recommendation takes this fact into account, asking for an examination of whether the EJN "should in the long term be transformed into a more permanent structure, which could become an important interlocutor of Europol."

Unlike the abovementioned recommendations which encourage changes in the organisational structures of police and prosecution services, *Recommendation 2* is more concerned with organisational procedures as it recommends the setting up or identification of "a mechanism for the collection and analysis of data which is so construed that it can provide a picture of the organised crime situation in the Member State and which can assist law enforcement authorities in fighting organised crime." The Contact and Support Network, together with Europol, has developed a common methodology for the elaboration of the organised crime situation report which is produced annually by Europol on the basis of the national reports. The use of a common methodology may have a harmonising effect on the cultures and mentalities of the different law enforcement agencies, especially in their perception of organised crime.

## 4.3 Other Relevant Legal Instruments

Among the other legal instruments adopted under Title VI of the TEU which may have an impact on organisational structures and procedures, the following should be mentioned:[36]

- Joint Action of 15 October 1996 concerning the creation and maintenance of a directory of specialised counter-terrorist competences, skills and expertise to facilitate counter-terrorist cooperation among the Member States of the EU;[37]

- Joint Action of 29 November 1996 concerning the creation and maintenance of a directory of specialised competencies, skills and expertise in the fight against international organised crime, in order to facilitate law enforcement cooperation between the Member States;[38]

- Resolution of 29 November 1996 on the drawing up of police/customs agreements in the fight against drugs;[39]

- Joint Action of 17 December 1996 concerning the approximation of the laws and practices of the Member States of the EU to combat drug addiction and to prevent and combat illegal drug trafficking;[40]

- Joint Action for the refining of targeting criteria, selection methods and collection of customs and police information;[41]

- Joint Action of 29 June 1998 on good practice in mutual legal assistance in criminal matters.[42]

Crucially, relevant initiatives also evolve from communitarian cooperation. One important initiative was the creation in 1989 of the Anti-Fraud Unit of the European Commission (UCLAF) with a view to protecting the financial interests of the European Communities. UCLAF – now called OLAF – plays a coordinating role in the complex investigations in the Member States and may therefore have propelled organisational changes in the national services concerning the prosecution of this form of serious crime. Furthermore, the 1991 EC Money Laundering Directive[43] obliged the Member States to create financial intelligence structures which collect and analyse information from financial institutions on irregular and/or suspicious transactions.

Finally, it must be stressed that the Schengen *acquis*, in particular the Schengen Implementing Convention, which was signed in 1990, has had a major impact on police and judicial cooperation in Europe. Although the Schengen Convention was originally negotiated and adopted outside the EU framework, it has had a pioneering role in the introduction of measures to compensate for the security deficit resulting from the abolition of internal border controls. Moreover, "Schengen" only allowed accession by EU Member States, which implies that the expertise and operational practices have always resided within the EU. At the time of writing, 13 EU Member States are partners to Schengen; for the time being, this excludes UK and Ireland, while Norway and Ireland have implemented Schengen and carry the status of associate members. The Schengen *acquis* was incorporated into the EU by virtue of a protocol attached to the Amsterdam Treaty.[44]

Because of the particular relevance of several Schengen instruments – particularly those on police cooperation, judicial cooperation and information

– we have tried to include them in the research as much as possible. Even though the Schengen framework was not designed with the purpose of controlling international organised crime, the creation of the National Schengen Information Systems (NSIS) caused the creation of national SIRENE bureaux, which are also useful for international cooperation in cases of organised crime. This is why Recommendation 19 of the Action Plan to Combat Organised Crime calls for the unification (or at least close relations) of the SIRENE bureaux and the Europol national units.

## 4.4 New Developments: OLAF, Tampere, a Follow-Up Action Plan and the Mutual Assistance Convention

Several new and exciting developments took place since the start of the research project. First, we should mention the developments around UCLAF/OLAF, the anti-fraud office of the European Commission. As a consequence of the first report of the Committee of Independent Experts[45] and the following resignation of the "Santer" Commission, UCLAF was transformed into OLAF, with a more independent status and more extensive powers.[46] In the framework of the Committee for the coordination of the fight against fraud (Cocolaf), OLAF and the EU Member States discuss ways to improve cooperation between the competent authorities.[47]

Several Member States decided or planned to create special units for the fight against fraud, which directly cooperate with UCLAF/OLAF. While France set up special teams at the level of police and customs, and a coordination unit at ministerial level (ICLAF), Ireland announced the creation of the "Criminal Assets Bureau" (CAB), a multidisciplinary unit composed of police, customs and tax officers.[48] Denmark, Greece and Portugal have also decided to set up offices with the specific task of protecting the Community's financial interests.[49] The cooperation with UCLAF/OLAF may not only encourage an approximation between the organisational structures of the Member States, but also between their working methods, i.e. the exchange of information and joint operations. At the time of writing, OLAF was concluding formal bilateral agreements with national authorities – as was done with the Italian *Guardia di Finanza* – with a view to establishing a legal basis for their cooperation.[50]

The special EU summit on Justice and Home Affairs, which was held on 15 and 16 October 1999 in Tampere (Finland), was also included in our research as several relevant recommendations were adopted.[51] One crucial recommendation in the area of police and justice cooperation in criminal matters called for the strengthening of Europol's powers. Another important recommendation – which hints at further institutionalisation – called for the creation of Eurojust, a unit with the task of coordinating the cooperation between national prosecution authorities. Meanwhile, a "pro-Eurojust" has been set up and the Belgian Presidency of the EU has made it one of its top priorities in the Justice and Home Affairs domain to conclude a legal instrument providing for its official establishment. Other recommendations concerned the creation of joint investigation teams to combat the trafficking of drugs and human beings as well as terrorism, and the establishment of a European Police Chiefs operational Task Force and of a European Police College. Moreover, the establishment of a scoreboard was agreed on with the purpose of keeping "under constant review progress made towards implementing the necessary measures and meeting the deadlines" agreed on at Amsterdam and Tampere for the progressive creation of an area of freedom, security and justice.[52]

Furthermore, at the summit in Helsinki on 10 and 11 December 1999, the European Council approved the report on the finalisation and evaluation of the High Level Group Action Plan on Organised Crime.[53] This report provides an overview of the implementation of the 1997 Action Plan, which officially ended on 31 December 1999.[54] At the time, the recommendations were at different stages of implementation. While Recommendation 19, on the creation of national contact points for law enforcement cooperation, had been completely implemented, the establishment of multidisciplinary integrated teams (Recommendation 20) required further long-term activity. Regarding Recommendation 1 on national coordination bodies, the report only states that the appropriateness of the designation of such bodies in the Member States has been examined. In general, the report stresses the results achieved so far, but also mentions the difficulties and delays in the implementation.

This prepared the ground for a follow-up to the Action Plan, which led to the adoption of a new programme called *"The Prevention and Control of Organised Crime: a European Union Strategy for the beginning of the new Millennium"*.[55] This programme covers the period until 30 June 2005, and contains 39 recommendations which enlarge and deepen many of the recommendations of the 1997 EU Action Plan. Only a few recommendations are expected to have a direct impact on the organisational structures and procedures of the EU Member States. Hence, only three recommendations of particular relevance have been singled out for further analysis:

- As regards the national structures, Recommendation 17b of the new action programme calls for the establishment of units "specifically dedicated to the process of tracing, seizure and confiscation of assets... taking into account the experience of such units operating successfully in some Member States." An illustrative example of such a unit is the Irish Criminal Assets Bureau (CAB) created in 1996.

- Recommendation 23 concerns the establishment of Eurojust on the basis of a legal instrument which would also determine the general framework of its relations with national prosecuting authorities, Europol, OLAF and the European Judicial Network.
- Instead, Recommendation 10 may have a noticeable impact on organisational procedures in the special field of illegal immigration networks, as it states that "Member States shall undertake, in close cooperation with Europol, the Commission and the European Judicial Network, to ensure that clear rules on the coordination of investigations into such networks are laid down at both the law enforcement and the judicial level."

Finally, we should mention the Convention on Mutual Legal Assistance in Criminal Matters. The Convention was subject of negotiation for several years, but was adopted by the JHA Council on 29 May 2000. Article 13 of the Convention provides for the possibility to create joint (operational) teams to conduct criminal investigations in one or more Member States. A specific legally binding instrument allowing for the establishment of such teams was also recently proposed by some Member States. As other Member States criticised this initiative on the ground that duplication of legislation should be avoided, the Council working groups have been discussing which solution seems most appropriate.[56]

The developments sketched above can be considered as building blocks in an emerging "European Police Governance". Walker observes an incrementalist logic which prevails within the professional community and which, in the near future, will be used to argue that Europol should be granted executive powers alongside intelligence and operational coordination.[57]

## 5. THEORETICAL PERSPECTIVES ON REFORMS AND CONVERGENCE

### 5.1 Administrative Reforms: Organisations and Change

Traditionally, police organisations and public prosecution services are well-established organisations with a relatively long life cycle. Like all other organisations, national law enforcement organisations are primarily characterised by stability, continuity and predictability. Their long-term existence is secured by means of a relatively fixed structure, composition and mission. At the same time, however, a contrary current[58] dictates change, fluidity, contingency, and an organic sensitivity to internal and external impulses.

As organisations seek to create responses to old problems, new problems arise: "Nothing is more permanent than change".[59] There are several indications that organisations are in perpetual flux: new organisations are constantly being created and others disappear; organisations expand or become smaller, or dispose of parts of the organisation; organisations change considerably under the influence of new technological developments; work processes are constantly adapted to improve effectiveness, efficiency or quality; staff are hired or fired, promoted, transferred or given a new task.[60]

Organisations can also have a self-learning dynamic that may propel organisational change. Open-textured and well-networked organisations, but also organic organisations, "adhocracies" and professional organisations, tend to have a high degree of flexibility and reflexivity. These organisations perceive their environment as rather diffuse, patchy or fragmented, culminating in differentiated images of the functioning of the organisation, or even in perceived contradictions between internal and external images and expectations.[61]

In a similar fashion, police and justice organisations are becoming increasingly less immune to external influences, for the following reasons:

- As public organisations principally financed from tax funds, police and justice organisations are subjected to communal inspection and various accountability procedures, ranging from official crime clearance statistics, to parliamentary debate and evaluation by the media; displays of unsatisfactory performance may, in turn, trigger incentives for (new) reform;[62]

- Their status as public organisations subjects police and justice organisations to an array of new public management (NPM) reforms that have also affected other public sectors such as social security, health insurance and public housing;[63]

- The exclusive monopoly of the police and justice organisations is becoming more relative in view of the steady expansion of the private security industry; this puts the traditional organisation of law enforcement in a competitive position, and forces it to reconsider investigation practices and surveillance methods;[64]

- The fast-developing internationalisation of regulatory mechanisms and crime markets forces police and justice organisations to look beyond the borders of their own organisation; formal and informal contacts may lead to comparative learning and "cross-fertilisation";[65]

- The wide-scale application of new information and communication technologies (ICT) facilitates cross-organisational and cross-national networking, leading to the "horizontalisation" of bureaucratic hierarchies, and hence touches upon the traditional organisational patterns, such as command structures, knowledge-sharing and information exchange;[66]

- The upsurge of multidisciplinary, cross-sector or "integral security" approaches to crime problems forces police and justice organisations to take account of different organisational perceptions, images and cultures.[67]

Internationalisation (also referred to as "Europeanisation" or "globalisation") is to be regarded as one of many facets leading to organisational reform. Hence, it may be difficult – if not impossible – to prove positive cause-effect relationships between, on the one hand, the Europeanisation of regulatory mechanisms or the internationalisation of organised crime markets, and, on the other hand, organisational reforms in the national law enforcement systems of the EU Member States. At the same time, it should be observed that notions such as "Europeanisation" and "globalisation" are too vague and indeterminate, and that these mechanisms ought to be further differentiated and refined.[68]

## 5.2 Differentiating Elements of Reform Processes

Before we go into the details of convergence trajectories, we should again point out that reform processes in national politico-administrative systems potentially show an enormous variety. The following differentiating elements of reform processes should be taken into account:[69]

(1) The *reasons* to initiate reform within national public administration systems and/or criminal justice systems may differ greatly, e.g. political decision, legal regulation, exposure in the media, public opinion.
(2) The *objectives* the agents of reform seek to realise may be different, e.g. increases in efficiency and/or effectiveness, quality improvement, cost reduction, symbolic or legitimacy benefits.
(3) The *reform trajectories*, or the "solution models", may vary from specialisation, coordination, and centralisation or de-centralisation, to adaptation of scale.
(4) The *methods of implementation* may show considerable variation, e.g. in terms of finance, personnel, kind of organisation, performance measurement. Also the processes of implementation may be different (bottom-up versus top-down, legal regulation, task allocation, etc.).

In the course of our research project, we established that these four components of administrative or organisational reform cannot be clearly discerned. A reason for this may be that traditionally, police and justice organisations tend to be rather introverted, and do not make much of an attempt to announce organisational changes in public. Moreover, the reforms that we are discussing in the context of this research project are neither systemically profound nor large scale in scope and size: their implementation may hence be an almost subterraneous, internal process.

One reform component is highlighted more often than the other components, namely reform trajectories in the form of specialisation, coordination, (de-)centralisation and scale. Reforms, reorganisations and innovations are rarely homogeneous in nature, and are paralleled by processes which look – on the surface – contradictory. With regard to organisational changes in order to facilitate international law enforcement cooperation and to improve the control of organised crime, some Member States have simultaneously implemented a mixture of organisational schemes, varying from the creation of single-purpose units (e.g. units for synthetic drugs or hormone Mafia) to the creation of (horizontal) coordination units that should guarantee the coherence of policy and services.[70]

## 5.3 Theoretical Perspectives on Convergence

The following theoretical perspectives on convergence provide some guidance in the understanding of processes of organisational reform that may entail or cause convergence. We have selected three paradigms, namely: a) the pooling of knowledge and resources; b) mimesis, and c) Europeanisation. The paradigms are inspired by different theoretical assumptions; none of them have – to our knowledge – been extensively applied to a comparative organisational analysis of police and justice organisations in the EU Member States (see Figure 2 below).

### 5.3.1   *Pooling of knowledge and resources*
Organised crime is a relatively infrequent (but high profile) phenomenon. Hence, criminal investigation minimally requires:
a)  specialist law enforcement expertise (e.g. accountancy, chemical production processes);
b)  networking and contacts with national and foreign law enforcement organisations;
c)  knowledge of the employment and regulation of special investigative techniques (e.g. interception of telecommunications, infiltration, controlled delivery, store fronts);
d)  usage of rare and costly devices (tracking devices, scanners, etc.); and
e)  synthesis of forensic and criminal intelligence.

This set of requirements forces law enforcement agencies at local and regional level to pool their resources at national and international level. Europol is the embodiment of these pragmatic ambitions by making itself

23

*Figure 2:*
*Theoretical perspectives on convergence*

|  | Theoretical perspective | Application advantage | Application drawback |
|---|---|---|---|
| **Pooling Knowledge and Resources** | Administrative functionalism | Organisational superstructure only; best practices; interoperability and search for most effective means; optimalisation objective | Not embedded in regulatory or politico-administrative context |
| **Mimesis** | Organisational studies; contingency theory | Emphasis on environmental factors; organisational adaptation; socialisation assumption | Can only be applied to interdependent organisations; requires identification of success factors |
| **Europeanisation** | Legal theory; comparative law; international relations | Provides tool for identifying regulatory incentive | Vague category, requires differentiation; different theoretical views on role of convergence |

available as a centre of expertise, strategic knowledge, coordination of operational activities and intelligence analysis. The pooling of resources, which can be related to principles of subsidiarity and proportionality, may be regarded as a functionalist response, which leaves the fundamental characteristics of national criminal justice systems unaltered. Hence, "pooling" demands convergence from the Member States only to the extent that it seeks to guarantee their joint (political and financial) commitment and contribution to supranationally coordinated intelligence processes.

The interpretation of models of coordination is usually a matter for professional, bureaucratic and political élites within the EU Member States. Their views may be dominated by national organisational traditions. Moreover, newly created national coordination structures are either embedded or accommodated within the existing structure, or superimposed on the existing national criminal justice system without fundamentally altering its characteristics.

### 5.3.2 Mimesis

A second theoretical perspective on (organisational) convergence is that organisations with a similar professional mission participate in a game of "copying". In monitoring their "competitors", they select aspects of the other organisation and introduce them into their own. DiMaggio and Powell call this "isomorphism",[71] and they define it as "a constraining process that forces one unit in a population to resemble other units that face the same set of environmental conditions."[72] It seems that this definition is too tight to apply to our subject of research: "constraint" and "the same set" are variables that are obviously not present in our research context, because police and public prosecution organisations are deeply embedded within their own national criminal justice systems. As they are nationally segregated, they are exposed to a variety of other constraints and stimuli than "just" international organised crime and EU initiatives.

However, when we look at the definitions of the three distinct types of isomorphism (coercive, mimetic and normative), it may be the case that "coercive isomorphism" applies to some extent, as it "results from both formal and informal pressures exerted on organizations by other organizations upon which they are dependent and by cultural expectations in the society in which organizations function"; "The existence of a common legal environment affects many aspects of an organization's behaviour and structure."[73] These definitions are rather vague, however, and within the distinctive criminal justice systems we can certainly not speak of a "common" legal environment. Mimetic processes, meanwhile, may be propelled by "symbolic uncertainty", which may prompt organisations to model themselves on other organisations.[74] The question whether copying actually takes place across the national criminal justice systems in Europe cannot be answered until we have compared the reports in relation to organisational changes more closely. Reorganisation processes are complex and are usually implemented over longer periods of time. At the same time, organisations may try to change constantly,[75] as they learn from their own errors and from organisations in their environment. Hence, mimesis can also be seen as a by-product of learning processes.

Following some of the organisational-level predictors of DiMaggio and Powell,[76] isomorphism between the national criminal justice systems is unlikely, because: a) they are not mutually dependent, except for certain aspects of international cooperation (information, intelligence pooling, mutual legal assistance); b) the organisations do not depend on the same sources for funding, personnel and legitimacy; c) an organisation will model itself after organisations it perceives to be successful, but this requires a systematic analysis of the organisational features of that successful organisation.

If there is a certain degree of isomorphism at all between the national coordination structures of the EU Member States, it depends on what criteria, features and (invisible) powers are taken into account.

### 5.3.3 *Europeanisation*
The globalisation of criminality through increased mobility and advanced technology may be regarded as a change in the environment of law enforcement organisations. On the one hand, law enforcement organisations are expected to respond to this challenge (organisational adaptation to changes in the environment); on the other hand, they are the (co-)enunciators of the crime discourse and may be the (co-)producers of a climate that is ready for change.

25

The European Union provides a political and regulatory vehicle for national law enforcement authorities to explore the enlargement of scale and to strengthen international cooperation. One of the effects of EU legislation – whether this is based on communitarian or intergovernmental legal instruments – may be that organisational structures and working mechanisms will slowly converge because the systems receive stimuli from 'Brussels':

"Whatever the future may bring, Member States of the Council of Europe and those of the European Union must ensure that their criminal justice systems operate in accordance with the requirements of what may be termed European law. First, on the basis of the European Convention on Human Rights a distinct European rule of law is emerging that affects both adversarial and inquisitorial systems to an ever increasing extent. Secondly, despite the perception in the 1960s and 1970s that criminal law would not be affected by the Treaty of Rome, European Community law also has had a considerable impact and that impact, too, increases in scope and depth. Two powerful courts, the European Court of Human Rights and the Court of Justice of the European Communities are there to ensure compliance. Finally, within the Council of Europe, within the framework of political cooperation envisaged by the Treaty on European Union, and within some other forums, notably that of Schengen, international cooperation in criminal matters is being developed and intensified to a point where harmonization of criminal policies is contemplated, and a first European law enforcement agency, that of Europol, is being created. There is hardly any area of criminal justice left that has not, in some way or another and to a greater or lesser extent, been touched by Europeanisation. This development is of crucial importance to comparative studies. At the present time comparative studies of criminal justice systems in Europe inevitably have to become comparative studies of how Europeanisation affects these systems and in what ways they respond to it. Inevitably too, in its own way Europeanisation contributes to a process of convergence of national systems of justice."[77]

To date, the compulsory creation of a Europol national unit in each EU Member State (according to Article 4 of the Europol Convention) is the best illustration of an external organisational impulse which has been dictated by intergovernmental EU decision making. Even though a Europol unit or Europol desk is diffusely embedded within the systems of the EU Member States, it may be employed as a model for similar national structures for the coordination of intelligence flows on organised crime.

It may be worthwhile to view European regulations and policy instruments as a normative framework that may be superimposed on national organisational structures. However, most likely, the Member States experience a certain margin of freedom within this normative framework, for the following reasons: a) during the negotiations on Title VI instruments, they enjoy considerable space for bargaining and they can seize the opportunity to ensure that the essential characteristics of their criminal justice systems remain unaffected by the implementation of the relevant EU instrument; b) most Title VI instruments are not directly binding; and c) failure to implement Title VI instruments cannot be sanctioned by the European Court of Justice.

Although there are no legal rules which impose harmonisation (no coercion), there are plenty of policy instruments that may have the effect of an indirect or bottom-up type of systemic approximation. In the latter sense, the EU recommendations may have the effect of facilitation or "structuration".[78] Facilitation means – in the context of this research project – the interaction structures that have been created by the European Union (or are a side-effect of EU activities) which facilitate direct contact between police and judicial organisations. Examples are: Title VI working groups (police cooperation, organised crime, etc.), EU conferences (Tampere on JHA issues), EU-Presidency conferences (e.g. "Intellex" during the Dutch EU Presidency in 1997 on intelligence exchange; and "Integrated Security", under the Belgian EU Presidency in 2001), training and exchange programmes (Falcone, Oisin, cooperation with the AEPC), professional conferences (Europol, EULEC), and operational contacts (Europol, Schengen, Interpol). These contacts and exchanges of experience lie at the heart of a complex networking model, which has a bearing on informal processes of systemic interaction.[79]

In respect of the Europeanisation thesis, it may be instructive to consider Rometsch and Wessels,[80] who developed three hypothetical phases concerning institutional activity in the European integration processes, namely:

(1) the *"Europeanisation"* of national institutions, i.e. the shift of attention of all national institutions and their increasing participation – in terms of the number of actors and the intensity – in the EC/EU decision-making cycle;

(2) the *"fusion"* of national and European institutions in the policy cycle, i.e. the common sharing of responsibilities for the use of state instruments and the increasing influence of the EC arena on the vertical and horizontal interaction of national and European institutions;

(3) the *"convergence"* of the constitutional and institutional set-up in the Member States, i.e. as a result of Europeanisation and "fusion", institutions undertake similar innovations and adaptations which lead towards one common model and, as a result, to the disappearance of pre-existing differences among Member States.

None of these hypothetical steps was specifically tested in the field of the police and judiciary, but Rometsch and Wessels observed an "increasing intensive interaction between both national and European institutions." Moreover, they note that the latter hypothesis concerning the convergence of political systems is hardly true, whilst the first two hypotheses on Europeanisation and fusion are valid. Applied to institutions such as the national parliaments, the outcome of the research is that [parliaments] "will try to keep their independence and will participate in the system as long as it seems useful for the fulfilment of their own tasks and their own survival."[81]

The abovementioned Dutch-British comparative research on Europeanisation and convergence of national criminal justice systems concludes that convergence tends to be selective and hence that it does not affect the various components of criminal justice systems to the same extent.[82]

More cautionary notes can however be found elsewhere in the literature on Europeanisation. Harmsen[83] concludes that while there has unquestionably been a growing range and frequency of contacts between national administrations and the EU system, there is little evidence of the expected convergence towards a common institutional model. Moreover, as Pollitt and Bouckaert seem to be indicating in their book on public management reform, there are distinctive national patterns of institutional adjustment, and thus one could speak of an uneven "Europeanisation process". Interestingly, Harmsen observes:[84]

"More striking than the absence of any generalized pattern of convergence, however, is the relative **absence of convergence** (emphasis added by authors mdb and pd) as regards even those structures and processes within the member states devised specifically to deal with the developing European Union politico-administrative system.

"Contradicting the conclusions of Rometsch and Wessels, there is considerable evidence to suggest that even a minimal convergence, produced by a shared search for best practice in the face of common pressures, does not appear to be taking place in any systematic or generalized fashion."

Perhaps it is too early to judge whether EU legal instruments have had a harmonising influence on the organisational structures of police and public prosecution systems in the Member States. In a decade or so, the criminal justice landscape might look very different from now.

## 5.4 Intermediate conclusion

In the end, two important questions remain. The first question is whether the types of administrative reforms we discussed can be considered as genuine or not. Do they merely concern a cosmetic adaptation of the administrative superstructure, or do they actually imply more profound transformations of culture, categorisations, working styles, and ideological belief systems? Although it may be a premature conclusion, the organisational changes in the police and justice organisations that are subject of this research do not seem to create a sense of "shock" or "crisis", and do not establish a break with the organisational antecedent. Instead, the creation of national infrastructures for the facilitation of international law enforcement cooperation and the control of organised crime can be characterised as a functional-pragmatic adaptation of existing organisational structures. In the words of Pollitt and Bouckaert, these reforms amount to "small adaptations or extensions of existing structures."[85]

The second question is whether these functional-pragmatic adaptations contribute to systemic convergence between national police and justice organisations. When one develops the argument of the preceding paragraph, the answer would logically be "no". If – on the basis of the empirical research carried out in the 15 Member States – one could indeed draw the conclusion that the organisational changes which are inspired by EU rules and regulations cannot be considered as profound systemic changes, there can be no integral systemic convergence. But although the law enforcement systems continue to show a rather differentiated organisational set-up, their national structures (national criminal intelligence services, national information desks, national coordination units, etc.) may gradually begin to adopt similar shapes and functions.

## 6.  CONVERGENCE: FICTION OR EMERGING PATTERN?

On the basis of theoretical perspectives outlined above, we have selected several domains for further analysis. These are:
(1) Organisational convergence
(2) Centralisation
(3) Enlargement of scale
(4) Decentralisation and specialisation
(5) Informal processes
(6) Accountability
(7) Organisational interaction
(8) Competition

## 6.1 Convergence

There is a perception that national structures for international police and justice cooperation are slowly beginning to converge.[86] Moreover, although harmonisation between criminal justice systems is remote, there are various indications that the traditional differences between Anglo-Saxon and continental models of policing are fading.[87] The emphasis on structural differences between these systems can only be made in genealogical terms;[88] the central directive character that seemed to be the core characteristic for most continental systems has become more diffuse due to a growing emphasis on locally and regionally determined intervention ("autonomisation"). Meanwhile, the decentralised character of the English and Welsh police system[89] has been challenged by the reinforcement of the position of the Home Secretary, the introduction of performance tables, and the establishment of a national crime squad. A difference which remains a rather divisive factor is the supervisory role of the prosecution service in criminal investigations.[90]

## 6.2 Centralisation

Centralisation seems to be a particular feature which has been (re-)emphasised in criminal justice systems in the belief that the central coordination of international information exchange benefits the efficiency and transparency of the contacts with foreign law enforcement organisations. The Dutch Parliamentary Inquiry Committee for instance came out with the recommendation that there should be more central management of the criminal justice system.

Within the research project, structures with central competences have been scrutinised in particular detail. Examples include: national crime squads with operational competences at the national level; national intelligence centres which have a nation-wide mandate to collect, coordinate, analyse, and channel intelligence; national prosecution boards which are given an exclusive mandate to supervise or coordinate serious and/or international organised crime cases; national platforms for the notification, collection and storage of information, such as on irregular financial transactions.[91] In this context, (policy or government) proposals in the EU Member States are compared to review the management mandate of relevant ministers (Minister of Justice; Minister of the Interior).[92]

The apparent sensitivity of the term "centralisation" has been taken into account; our model of analysis allows us to incorporate both superordinate structures, such as the German *Bundeskriminalamt*, and coordinate structures, such as the twenty-sixth police force in the Netherlands which is vested with national competences.

## 6.3 Enlargement of Scale

Another particular facet that has been introduced in an increasing number of police systems is enlargement of scale. Very often it is the case that complex or serious crime cases cannot be investigated at the local or regional level, as there is a shortage of human resources or technical means to do so. These situations have contributed to the rationalisation and pooling of certain resources (knowledge, expertise, technical equipment, information systems), very often again at a national level, or at the level of a *Land* (Germany) or a group of counties (England and Wales). Law enforcement organisations show a tendency to adapt the scale of their organisation to that of the problem they seek to tackle. As criminality seems to be adopting an increasingly transnational dimension, law enforcement organisations shift the level at which they seek to control crime.

## 6.4 Decentralisation and Specialisation

Centralisation and the enlargement of scale have not necessarily been introduced to the detriment of local (municipal, community) or regional (county, province, region) level. In fact, it may well be the case that a) central and decentralised law enforcement structures are perfectly complementary as they operate in tandem; and b) that centralisation tendencies have propelled "satellites", "nodes" or working modules at the sub-central level in order to facilitate and streamline the contacts between the local and national or even supranational level.

Similarly, the establishment of national coordination centres for the flow of criminal intelligence and national operational squads, seems to be paralleled by a process of task division and fragmentation ("functionalist delocalisation"). This process can be illustrated by the creation of special synthetic drugs or financial crime units. Hence, we seem to be witnessing a bifurcation process, with centralisation tendencies on the one hand, and delocalisation tendencies on the other. Also subject of analysis is whether the mandate of these deconcentrated, specialised units is a national one, and to which authorities they are accountable.

## 6.5 Informal Processes

The convergence between criminal justice systems seems very much a product of informal, bottom-up processes, rather than European or superimposed policy decisions. International contacts within bilateral or multilateral joint ventures have had a pragmatic effect on learning. It remains to be seen to what extent law enforcement cooperation in the EU context is more bureaucratic or political in nature and may be regarded as a legislative-driven process. However, the future competence of Europol to provide support (e.g. meeting or interpreting facilities, expertise) to multinational operational task forces, may help to shorten the distance to Europol that is being experienced by law enforcement practitioners.

The inventory which was undertaken in 1998 by the EU Multidisciplinary Group on Organised Crime indicated that relatively few Member States had installed at that time a central coordination service for the notification of organised crime cases and/or centrally guided information exchange.[93] The location of Interpol NCBs, SIRENE Bureaux and Europol satellites within (existing) central criminal intelligence services may well be the by-product of a process of gradual accumulation and rationalisation (based on efficiency arguments), rather than a rational stepwise implementation process. Another – socio-organisational – argument that would support the strength of bottom-up processes is that large-scale reforms are more difficult to implement than small reorganisations, as they usually meet with considerable resistance from the members of the organisation.

The weakening political and professional support for the reform of the Belgian police services (now completed) illustrates the mobilisation of such resistance. Hence, some questions in the questionnaire dealt with the way in which reforms are being introduced, and what the acceptance level of these reforms has been. One other subsidiary question is whether and to what extent national crises (e.g. Dutroux in Belgium; the IRT scandal in the Netherlands; the killing of judges Falcone and Borsellino in Italy) are responsible for organisational change.

## 6.6 Accountability

The need for a more effective control of organised crime has also made the employment of undercover policing methods and the employment of intelligence. From the perspective of constitutional integrity and civil liberties, this development has been controversial, as can be demonstrated by the political consternation in the Netherlands after the collapse of an interregional crime squad (which gave rise to the resignation of two ministers and an extensive parliamentary inquiry), and the resignation of a German minister over the adoption of legislation concerning the bugging of private homes.[94]

Although it is not the aim of this particular research project to study the convergence of the national legislation on undercover methods,[95] the sensitive and controversial nature of methods such as controlled delivery, the use of infiltrators, and the establishment of storefronts, has required most Member States to reflect on their accountability systems. There are indications that accountability systems have been made more transparent, particularly in view of authorisation procedures, the delegation of mandates, and reporting rules. One of the normative criteria formulated by the Dutch Parliamentary Inquiry Committee for instance was "the more encroaching the investigation method, the more senior level the authorisation level should be."[96] This recommendation has been reflected in the reorganisation of the Dutch Public Prosecution Service, which now accommodates a National Board of Procurators General and a National Public Prosecutor's Office.

## 6.7 Organisational Interaction

The increase of supranational initiatives against international organised crime seems to have resulted in a more lively interaction between operational law enforcement (police, customs, immigration service) and the public prosecution bodies, particularly in view of complex investigations. Moreover, as law enforcement organisations do not always have sufficient capacity or expertise to generate intelligence about the activities of internationally active criminal groups, there is more pressure on the interaction between criminal justice bodies and the private sphere; this applies particularly to multinational companies that have their own "inhouse" investigation bureaux (examples are insurance companies or credit card companies, such as Eurocard). Police organisations may eventually face stiff competition from non-state policing initiatives in the private and the public domain.[97]

## 6.8 Competition

International cooperation in the fight against organised crime may have led to the pooling of resources on the one hand but it may also have resulted in more intensive competition between national law enforcement organisations.[98] In this process, police organisations monitor the latest developments in befriended or neighbouring countries and "borrow" features they consider useful in the control of international organised crime.[99] Some EU initiatives may also indirectly create competition between the Member States, as the Joint Action of 1997 establishing a mechanism for evaluating the application and implementation at national level of international undertakings in the fight against organised crime.[100]

## 7.   A CROSS-COMPARISON BETWEEN THE EU MEMBER STATES

The findings presented in the national reports facilitate a comparative overview of the impact of EU legal instruments and frameworks on national reform processes. Hence, the chapter below makes an inventory of the reorganisation or reform which has been undertaken in areas relevant to the control of organised crime. The inventory is tentative and descriptive, rather than analytical in character, and draws heavily upon the questionnaire (Appendix). The cross-comparative tables[101] provide an overview of all bodies foreseen or recommended by relevant EU legal instruments, as well as some other relevant services.

### 7.1 Central Coordination Bodies

It appears that a central body with overall responsibility for the coordination of the fight against organised crime, as mentioned by Recommendation 1 of the 1997 EU Action Plan, has not been created or designated in any of the EU Member States. However, many EU Member States have central coordination bodies at the level of the law enforcement agencies and of the prosecution service, some of which have been created in recent years as a consequence of the control of organised and/or serious crime.[102]

At the level of the prosecution service, one can distinguish Member States where the body is directly located at the Ministry of Justice,[103] and those where it is an office of the prosecution service itself with national competence.[104] It may be the case that the coordination is shared between two bodies, as happens in the Netherlands with the National Prosecution Bureau, which is competent for the prosecution of organised crime, and the Board of Procurators General, which focuses more specifically on the formulation of general and binding policy guidelines. In some cases, there is no general body of coordination, but a national prosecution service responsible for a specific field of crime, like in Denmark and Sweden.

At the level of the law enforcement agencies, the situation is even more heterogeneous because of the different organisational systems existing in the Member States. While only Italy has a coordination body which comprises officers of all the law enforcement agencies,[105] most of the Member States only have coordination bodies at the level of each law enforcement agency. Sometimes this function is even split between several services which are responsible for specific fields of crime (i.e. drug trafficking, terrorism)[106] or respectively for the policy and the operational activities.[107]

## 7.2 Central National Contact Points

Most of the Member States have followed Recommendation 19 of the 1997 EU Action Plan and designated a central national contact point for the law enforcement agencies, which embraces the Europol National Unit (ENU), the Interpol National Central Bureau (NCB) and the SIRENE desk. As in general these three services are distinct units, but operating in the same department, the implementation of the Recommendation to create a "single" central contact point has been rather successful. The implementation may have been supported by the necessity to ensure close relations and effective coordination between these three units which have convinced the EU Member States to adopt this solution. Whatever the rationale may be behind these changes, it is obvious that this development contributes in a significant way to the centralisation tendencies in the law enforcement agencies.

At the level of the prosecution service, it seems that most of the Member States designated a central contact point, which is a prerequisite for the establishment of the European Judicial Network (EJN) foreseen by Recommendation 21 of the Action Plan.[108] Here again, one can distinguish between Member States where the central contact point is located at the level of the Ministry of Justice, and those where it is part of the national prosecution office.[109]

## 7.3 Multidisciplinary Integrated Teams

Recommendation 20 of the 1997 EU Action Plan, which suggests the setting up of national multidisciplinary integrated teams, specifically in the area of organised crime, does not provide a clear definition of this term.[110] For that reason, the present report applies a rather general definition: a multidisciplinary team is composed of officials from different Ministries or agencies. We have not taken into account if the team has a coordinating and/or an operational role.

Consequently, in EU Member States which have only one single national police force, special teams which are composed of police officers and public prosecutors are considered as multidisciplinary integrated teams. Such a team, the Special Economic Crime Squad (SØK), has already been in existence since 1973 in Denmark. A similar team, the Economic Crime Authority (EBM), was set up in 1998 in Sweden. Some Member States with a plural police system have created teams drawing officials from the different law enforcement agencies. These teams are either independent bodies, which is the case in Greece, Ireland and Italy,[111] or they are located within one of the agencies, which is generally the police service.[112] Many Member States have

35

## Figure 3:
## Central Coordination Bodies

| | At the level of the prosecution service | At the level of the law enforcement agencies |
|---|---|---|
| **Austria** | Federal Ministry of Justice | Federal Ministry of Interior, Directorate General for Public Security, Group II/D Criminal Police – Interpol, Division II/8 (1995) |
| **Belgium** | – Board of Prosecutors-General (1997)<br>– Federal Public Prosecutor's office (planned) | – General Police Support Service (1994)<br>– Gendarmerie, Central Bureau of Investigations<br>– Judicial Police, General Commissariat |
| **Denmark** | – No general body<br>– Special Economic Crime Squad (SØK) | National Commissioner's Office, Department A |
| **Finland** | Prosecutor's General Office (1997) | National Bureau of Investigation (NBI) |
| **France** | Ministry of Justice, Central Office for the Fight Against Organised Crime (1995) | – National Police General Directorate (DGPN), Anti-Mafia Investigation and Coordination Unit (UCRAM) (1993)<br>– Criminal Investigation Central Directorate (DCPJ), Central Investigation and Organised Crime Section (SCICO) (1995) |
| **Germany** | | Federal Criminal Police Office (BKA), Organised and General Crime Division, Unit OA 11 (Organised Crime Coordination) |
| **Greece** | | Ministry of Public Order (MPO):<br>– Public Security Division (DDA), for general affairs<br>– State Security Division (DKA), for terrorism and crimes against interstate and international relations<br>– Central Anti-Drug Agency (SODN) (1997) |
| **Ireland** | Director of Public Prosecution (DPP) | – Garda Siochana, National Bureau of Criminal Investigation (NBCI) (90s)<br>– Garda Siochana, National Drugs Unit (90s) |
| **Italy** | National Anti-Mafia Directorate (DNA) (1991) | Ministry of Interior, Directorate of Anti-Mafia Investigations (DIA) (1991) |
| **Luxembourg** | General Public Prosecutor | |
| **Netherlands** | – Board of Procurator's General<br>– National Public Prosecutor's Office (1999) | National Police Agency (KLPD) (1993) |
| **Portugal** | General Public Prosecutor | – Ministry of Interior, Security Intelligence Services (SIS)<br>– Ministry of Justice, Judicial Police |
| **Spain** | | – Ministry of Interior, Coordination Cabinet of the Security Secretariat<br>– National Police Agency (CNP), Technical Secretariat of the Central Division of the Judicial Police |
| **Sweden** | | National Criminal Investigation Department (RKP), National Criminal Intelligence Service (KUT) (1995) |
| **United Kingdom** | Crown Prosecution Service | National Criminal Intelligence Service (NCIS) (1992) |

(at least) temporary teams, which are set up on an *ad hoc* basis,[113] or they have multidisciplinary teams at local level.[114]

## 7.4 Financial Intelligence Units

Except for the creation of a Europol National Unit, the Financial Intelligence Unit (FIU) is the only body which the EU Member States were obliged to create. Article 6 of the 1991 EC Money Laundering Directive did not however prescribe at which level this body had to be located. Therefore, the Member States adopted a variety of solutions regarding their FIUs. While most of them located it at the level of the law enforcement agencies,[115] some Member States created the FIU at the level of the public prosecution service,[116] a Ministry[117] or the National Central Bank,[118] or even created an independent body.[119] If the FIU is located at the level of the law enforcement agencies or the public prosecution service, it is often part of a service which is responsible for the fight against organised and/or financial crime.

## 7.5 OLAF

The national law enforcement bodies with a specific competence in the field of economic and financial crime generally cooperate on a permanent basis with OLAF – the European Anti-fraud Office (formerly UCLAF) – which belongs to the European Commission, or even second a representative to the office in Brussels. More and more, the national competent bodies conclude formal agreements with OLAF, which may have the effect of streamlining their policies and working methods in the long term. Thus, in this particular field of (organised) crime, we can see a clear process of specialisation in the criminal justice systems of the EU Member States. However, in general these special bodies have been set up for national reasons and not so much with the objective of improving the cooperation with OLAF or the protection of the EU's financial interests. The transformation of UCLAF into OLAF may have put the Member States under more pressure in this field.

## 8.   CORE FINDINGS

In this chapter, the main findings which we generated from the various national reports are presented in line with the hypotheses outlined above.

## Figure 4:
### Central national contact points at the level of the law enforcement agencies

|  | Europol National Unit | NCB Interpol | SIRENE Bureau (Schengen) |
|---|---|---|---|
| **Austria** | Group II/D Criminal Police – Interpol, Division II/8/a | Group II/D Criminal Police – Interpol, Division II/9 and Division II/10 | Group II/D Criminal Police – Interpol, Division II/10/a |
| **Belgium** | Directorate Operational Police Cooperation | Directorate Operational Police Cooperation | Directorate Operational Police Cooperation |
| **Denmark** | National Commissioner's Office, Department A | National Commissioner's Office, Department A | National Commissioner's Office, Department A |
| **Finland** | National Bureau of Investigation (NBI), Criminal Intelligence Division | NBI, Criminal Investigation Division | NBI, Criminal Investigation Division |
| **France** | Criminal Investigation Central Directorate (DCPJ), Sub-Directorate of External Relations (SDLE) | SDLE | SDLE |
| **Germany** | Federal Criminal Police Office (BKA), Central Services Division, Group 3 | BKA, Central Services Division, Group 3 | BKA, Central Services Division, Group 3 |
| **Greece** | Ministry of Public Order, Central Anti-Drugs Unit (SODN) (soon: Ministry of Public Order, Division of International Police Cooperation (DDAS)) | DDAS | DDAS |
| **Ireland** | Garda Siochana, Liaison and Protection Service |  | Garda Siochana, Liaison and Protection Service |
| **Italy** | Ministry of Interior, Central Criminal Police Directorate | Ministry of Interior, Central Criminal Police Directorate | Ministry of Interior, Central Criminal Police Directorate |
| **Luxembourg** | Bureau of International Police Cooperation | Bureau of International Police Cooperation | Bureau of International Police Cooperation |
| **Netherlands** | National Police Agency, National Criminal Intelligence Department | National Criminal Intelligence Department | National Criminal Intelligence Department |
| **Portugal** | Ministry of Justice, Judicial Police | Ministry of Justice, Judicial Police | Ministry of Interior |
| **Spain** | National Centre for International Communications (CENCI) | CENCI | General Police Directorate |
| **Sweden** | National Criminal Investigation Department, National Criminal Intelligence Service (KUT), National Liaison Office (NSK) | NSK | NSK |
| **United Kingdom** | National Criminal Intelligence Service (NCIS) | NCIS | NCIS (planned) |

*Figure 5:*
## Multidisciplinary integrated teams/Financial Intelligence Units

| | Multidisciplinary integrated teams | Financial Intelligence Unit |
|---|---|---|
| **Austria** | – Temporary ad hoc teams<br>– Local task force in Vienna to combat organised crime (1991) | Federal Ministry of Interior, Directorate General for Public Security, Group II/D Criminal Police – Interpol, Division II/8 |
| **Belgium** | Several specialised units (e.g. Multidisciplinary hormone unit, multidisciplinary unit for combating meat fraud, interdepartmental coordination unit for combating international trafficking in human beings) | Ministry of Justice and Ministry of Finance, Financial Information Processing Unit (1993) |
| **Denmark** | – Special Economic Crime Squad (SØK)<br>– Temporary task forces (i.e. Task Force Rocker Crime) | SØK, Information and Analytical Section (1993) |
| **Finland** | Ad hoc teams | National Bureau of Investigation, Money Laundering Clearing House (1998) |
| **France** | Criminal Investigation Central Directorate (DCPJ), several offices dealing with aspects of organised crime | Ministry of Economics and Finance, Financial intelligence and action unit (TRACFIN) (1990) |
| **Germany** | Several joint teams (police and customs) at federal and state level for the fight against drug trafficking | Federal Criminal Police Office (BKA), Organised and General Crime Division, Unit OA 14 (Money Laundering Clearing House) |
| **Greece** | – Ministry of Public Order, Central Anti-Drug Coordination Unit (SODN)<br>– Money Laundering Committee (1995) | Money Laundering Committee (1995) |
| **Ireland** | Criminal Assets Bureau (1996) | Garda Siochana, Garda Bureau of Fraud Investigation (GBFI) |
| **Italy** | – Ministry of Interior, Directorate of Anti-Mafia Investigations (DIA) (1991)<br>– Central Drug Enforcement Agency (1996)<br>– Witness Protection Service | Custom and Revenue Police, Central Investigation Service on Organised Crime (SCICO) (1991) |
| **Luxembourg** | Temporary teams | Public Prosecutor of the judicial district of Luxembourg |
| **Netherlands** | – 7 Interregional Core Squads<br>– Synthetic Drugs Unit | Ministry of Justice, central notification point for unusual transactions (MOT) (1994) |
| **Portugal** | Ad hoc teams | Ministry of Justice, Judicial Police |
| **Spain** | Ad hoc teams at the judicial level | National Central Bank, Executive Service for the Prevention of Money Laundering (SEPBLAC) |
| **Sweden** | Economic Crimes Authority (EBM) (1998) | National Criminal Investigation Department, National Criminal Intelligence Service, Criminal Intelligence Collection (1998) |
| **United Kingdom** | National Criminal Intelligence Service (NCIS) | NCIS |

## Figure 6:
### Central contact points for the prosecution service/bodies cooperating with OLAF

| | Central contact point for the Public Prosecution Service | Cooperation with UCLAF/OLAF |
|---|---|---|
| **Austria** | Federal Ministry of Justice, Division IV/1 | Federal Ministry of Finance, Division III/8 |
| **Belgium** | – National magistrates (1997)<br>– Ministry of Justice, Individual Judicial Assistance Service | Judicial Police, General Commissariat, Central Unit for Combating Economic and Financial Delinquency |
| **Denmark** | Ministry of Justice, International Office | Serious Economic Crime Squad (SØK) |
| **Finland** | Ministry of Justice | |
| **France** | Ministry of Justice, European and International Affairs Unit | |
| **Germany** | | |
| **Greece** | | Ministry of Finance, Customs Services, Financial and Economic Crimes Office (SDOE) |
| **Ireland** | | Garda Siochana, Garda Bureau of Fraud Investigation (GBFI) |
| **Italy** | National Anti-Mafia Directorate (DNA) (1991) | Custom and Revenue Police, Central Investigation Service on Organised Crime (SCICO) (1991) |
| **Luxembourg** | General Public Prosecutor | |
| **Netherlands** | National Public Prosecutor's Office (1999) | |
| **Portugal** | Ministry of Justice, Public Prosecution Office | Antifraud coordination unit (UCLEFFA) (planned) |
| **Spain** | | |
| **Sweden** | Attorney General (RÅ) | Economic Crimes Authority (EBM) (1998) |
| **United Kingdom** | Home Office | Serious Fraud Office |

## 8.1 Organisational Convergence

The central expectation in our research project was a tendency towards convergence of organisational models of policing and public prosecution, owing to Europeanisation and a coordinated response to international organised crime. The findings may be summarised as follows:

- there are no indications of an integral or wholesale convergence of national law enforcement structures;
- there are some convergence tendencies concerning the creation of national structures for the control of organised crime, in particular the creation of a single central contact point for international police cooperation, which includes the Europol National Unit, and in most Member States (except the UK and Ireland) the SIRENE bureau;
- the way in which these national coordination structures are embedded is determined by pre-existing organisation structures and cultures (this is line with the neo-functional contingency thesis which emphasises the strength of national variables and contexts);
- there are a few instances of convergence due to "bilateral" cross-fertilisation (e.g. UK and Denmark, see below).

In summary, the comparison of the reforms throughout the different EU Member States reveals a markedly differentiated picture: national characteristics mainly determine the scope of organisational changes, but at the level of national coordination of international information flows seemingly similar organisational responses have been developed.

## 8.2 Centralisation Trends

First of all, it is worth mentioning the recent merger of the two Luxembourg police forces, the Police and the *Gendarmerie Grand-Ducale*, into one single force, as well as the merger of the three Belgian police forces, the Judicial Police, the Gendarmerie and the Municipal Police, into one integrated police force. Even if the aim and scope of these reforms are much broader than the necessity to better control organised crime, they will have an important impact on it, because it must be expected that, also in this specific field, resources will be pooled and a duplication of structures and work will be avoided.

More specifically, the control of organised crime demands special expertise, specific investigation tools and elaborate authorisation procedures, which are not always available at local or regional level. Moreover, the call for an internationally coordinated response often leads to central agencies, which is why "centralisation trends" have been at the heart of this research.[120] Several elements of the research findings indicate that the national criminal justice systems of the EU Member States are indeed experiencing a certain degree of centralisation.

In Denmark, the perceived need of national or interregional coordination has led to the creation of a forerunner of a National Criminal Intelligence Service (NEC), and the creation of a National Crime Squad is on its way. In the UK, where the 1997 Police Act makes the NCIS more independent and creates a National Crime Squad (NCS), both organisations are supposed to work very closely together. They may eventually merge. Similar centralisation tendencies at the level of law enforcement agencies have occurred in Austria, Belgium, France and Ireland, who have created national services for the central coordination of investigations. Austria also has some plans for the establishment of a Federal Office of Criminal Investigation on the model of the German *Bundeskriminalamt*.

At the level of the prosecution service, some Member States also made reforms towards more central coordination. Belgium recently established a Board of Prosecutor's General responsible for the national policies, and appointed national magistrates responsible for international cooperation. Finland also created a Prosecutor's General Office with national competence in 1997, while France set up a central office for the fight against organised crime at the Ministry of Justice.

In the Netherlands, centralisation is officially regarded as a complementary structure to that of regionalisation. Most significantly, the Public Prosecution Service has undergone a major process of centralisation, culminating in a Board of Procurators General. The dual responsibility for the police organisation has only recently been transferred to one single ministry, and the intelligence and operational arm of the National Police Agency were recently combined into one single organisation.

## 8.3 Enlargement of Scale Trends

On the basis of the current findings it is more difficult to establish whether this centralisation process is accompanied by (or inspired by) a significant enlargement of scale. But it is interesting to note that there is often a parallel centralisation at the level of intelligence processing. For example, in the UK it has been reported that the Greater Manchester Police have used data warehousing processes to integrate some 50 databases containing around 10 million records.[121] Meanwhile, in Denmark the establishment of the forerunner of NCIS led to a transfer from several special databases to the newly created organised crime database. In Greece, the Ministry of Public Order has

## Figure 7:
## Centralisation tendencies

| | Centralisation tendencies[122] |
|---|---|
| **Austria** | central coordination functions by:<br>– Ministry of Interior, Directorate General of Public Security, Division II/8 (1995)<br>– Ministry of Finance, Division III/8 (1995)<br>– Federal Office of Criminal Investigation (planned) |
| **Belgium** | – integration of the three police forces into one single police force (from 2001)<br>– central coordination functions by:<br>  - Board of Prosecutor's General; national magistrates (1997)<br>  - Federal Public Prosecutor's Office (planned)<br>  - Commissioner General's Office International Police Cooperation Policy |
| **Denmark** | centralisation of information by:<br>National Commissioner's Office, forerunner of NCIS (NEC) (1998) |
| **Finland** | – central coordination by: Prosecutor's General Office (1997)<br>– centralisation of information by: national intelligence database established at the National Bureau of Investigation (NBI) (1998) |
| **France** | – central coordination by:<br>  - Ministry of Justice, Central Office for the fight against organised crime (1995)<br>  - Anti-Mafia Investigation and Coordination Unit (UCRAM) (1993)<br>– central coordination and centralisation of information by:<br>  - Central Investigation and Organised Crime Section (SCICO) (1995) |
| **Germany** | |
| **Greece** | – central coordination by: Central Anti-Drug Coordination Unit (SODN) (1997)<br>– centralisation of information: National Criminological Archive (planned) |
| **Ireland** | central coordination by:<br>– Garda Siochana, National Bureau of Criminal Investigation (1990s)<br>– Garda Siochana, National Drugs Unit (1990s) |
| **Italy** | – central coordination by:<br>  - General Council for the Fight against Organised Crime (1991)<br>  - National Anti-Mafia Directorate (DNA) (1991)<br>– central operational powers:<br>  - Anti-Mafia Investigation Directorate (DIA) (1991)<br>  - central services of the National Police (SCI), the *Carabinieri* (ROS) and the Customs and Revenue Guard (SCICO) (1991) |
| **Luxembourg** | integration of the two police forces into one single police force (2000) |
| **Netherlands** | – central coordination by:<br>  - Board of Prosecutor's General and National Public Prosecutor's Office (1999)<br>  - National Police Agency (KLPD) (1993)<br>– centralisation of information and operational powers: the DCRI and the National Crime Squad (LRT) merged into the Criminal Investigation Division (2000) |
| **Portugal** | |
| **Spain** | |
| **Sweden** | centralisation of information: National Criminal Intelligence Service (KUT) (1995) |
| **United Kingdom** | – central coordination and centralisation of information by: National Criminal Intelligence Service (NCIS) (1992)<br>– central operational powers: National Crime Squad (NCS) (1998) |

initiated the creation of the National Criminological Archive, a central database with information on all kinds of offences; a similar database was set up in 1998 at the Finnish National Bureau of Investigation. The Swedish National Criminal Intelligence Service and the French Central Investigation and Organised Crime Section were both established in 1995 with the main purpose of gathering and analysing intelligence on a large scale. In the Netherlands, an enlargement of scale was one of the most explicit rationales for a new Police Bill (1993), which led to the abolition of municipal police forces and the national police force.

## 8.4 Decentralisation (Regionalisation) and Specialisation Trends

The question whether consolidation of the local/regional level (regionalisation process) and a fragmentation of tasks are taking place simultaneously can only be answered tentatively. From the literature, it appears that police services are undergoing a simultaneous process of decentralisation and centralisation, and that this is one of the most "striking paradoxes" of contemporary policing."[123] There are strong indications that the degree and intensity of regionalisation processes depend on the pre-existing character of the national system: in a traditionally centralised system, regionalisation is less likely to be introduced than in a decentralised system. In the Netherlands, the regionalisation of the police organisation was formally institutionalised by virtue of the 1993 Police Bill, whereas the Public Prosecution Service has traditionally been organised in districts. Both structures have been stable for a while and have not evolved from a strategy to improve the control of organised crime. In Greece, the law enforcement agencies now tend towards regionalisation: the Coast Guard plans to set up more regional groups for the control of drug trafficking, while the Greek Police has recently created "police cells" in each regional police division for the analysis of organised crime. A similar tendency can be recognised in Denmark with the creation of five regional police centres for special investigations and of seven Regional Criminal Intelligence Services.

However, the strengthening of regional bodies and units does not necessarily erode national competences, in some cases the regionalisation may have more the character of centralisation than decentralisation. In Finland, the 1996 administrative reform reduced the number of police districts, with the consequence that they are now better staffed and equipped to carry out more complex investigations. In Sweden, the parallel establishment of Regional Criminal Intelligence Units and the creation of the National Criminal Intelligence Service in 1995 seemed to express more the objective of ensuring the effective functioning of the latter than decentralising the task of intelligence gathering. The same principle may prevail in Austria for the planned setting up of the federal and several regional Criminal Investigation Offices (one in each *Land*). While in Italy most of the organisational reforms towards more centralisation were achieved in the early 1990s, the process nevertheless seems to continue with the planned reorganisation of the regional crime squads of the police.

At the same time, many EU Member States have considered in the past decade the creation of special law enforcement bodies at the national level with a view to control certain forms of organised/serious crime more efficiently. Specialisation may sometimes go hand in hand with a certain centralisation, in cases where new central agencies are created. A clear example are some of the bodies already mentioned in the previous chapter which have competence for the fight against economic and financial crime and cooperate with OLAF.

In Greece, a certain organisational fragmentation can be detected in the creation in 1998 of the Border Guards Corps, which bears the exclusive mission of preventing and combating illegal immigration and the criminal organisations which facilitate it. Other striking examples are the creation in 1996 of the Criminal Assets Bureau in Ireland and the Central Drug Enforcement Agency in Italy. However, generally, specialised units are just set up by internal reorganisation, as the services of the Spanish Police and Guardia Civil, which have competence for the fight against drug trafficking and organised crime. In the Netherlands, several crime-specific units have been created; examples are the Synthetic Drugs Unit and the Environmental Crime Unit. Nevertheless, if the tendency of specialisation of the law enforcement agencies seems to be present in many EU Member States, a great disparity has emerged regarding the size and powers of these services, which vary from small coordination units to sizeable agencies with operational powers at national level.

At the level of the prosecution service, specialisation seems to be less frequent, but has begun to take place in some Member States with the appointment of specialised magistrates as in Belgium and Sweden, or the creation of special multidisciplinary teams like in France.


## 8.5 Informal and Bottom-up Trends

The national reports remain rather silent about informal and bottom-up processes. Hence, it is impossible to draw general and reliable conclusions from the very thin amount of empirical material. There are, however, strong indications that "top-down" reforms are often accompanied by "bottom-up" movements, which often seem particularly inspired by alarmist perceptions of the threat of organised crime or of a major crisis in the national criminal

*Figure 8:*
*Regionalisation and specialisation tendencies*

| | Regionalisation tendencies | Specialisation tendencies |
|---|---|---|
| **Austria** | Regional Offices of Criminal Investigation in each *Land* (planned) | – Police task force for the fight against organised crime (EDOK) (1993)<br>– Special Police Unit for Surveillance (SEO) (1998) |
| **Belgium** | | – specialisation in the prosecution service (e.g. creation of supervising magistrates, assisting magistrates, confidential magistrates and magistrates for judicial cooperation) (1990s)<br>– several multidisciplinary units (hormone unit; meat fraud; trafficking in human beings) (1990s)<br>– Federal Anti-Corruption Service (planned) |
| **Denmark** | – 5 Regional Police Centres for Special Investigations (1993)<br>– 7 Regional Criminal Intelligence Services (planned) | |
| **Finland** | reduction of the number of police districts with the consequence of the pooling of resources (1996) | |
| **France** | | – Courts of appeals, Economic and Financial Units (1999)<br>– Central Police Office for the fight against illegal immigration (1996) |
| **Germany** | | |
| **Greece** | – "police cells" in each regional police division for the analysis of organised crime<br>– regional coast guard groups for drug control (planned) | – Financial and Economic Crimes Office (SDOE) (1995)<br>– Boarder Guards Corps (1998) |
| **Ireland** | | Criminal Assets Bureau (CAB) (1996) |
| **Italy** | interprovincial services of SCI, ROS and SCICO | Central Drug Enforcement Agency (1996) |
| **Luxembourg** | | Organised Crime Unit (1991) |
| **Netherlands** | – 7 Core Squads (interregional crime squads)<br>– organised crime branches in most regional police forces | – Synthetics Drug Unit (1996)<br>– Serious Environmental Crime Unit (1995) (integrated into the KLPD during 1999) |
| **Portugal** | | |
| **Spain** | | – Narcotics and Organised Crime Units of the Police (UDYCO) (1997)<br>– Organised Crime Investigation Units of the Guardia Civil (EDOA) (1998) |
| **Sweden** | Regional Criminal Intelligence Units (1995) | – Economic Crimes Authority (EBM) (1998)<br>– specialisation of two prosecutors of each local public prosecution office on organised crime (planned) |
| **United Kingdom** | | competence extension for the Security Service (MI5) to serious crime (1995) |

justice system.

In Italy, reforms were mainly called for in order to get to terms specifically with the Mafia problem, while the EU influence (top-down) seems to be limited to the establishment of the Europol National Unit and the SIRENE bureau, with the standardisation of the processing of data which accompanies it. In Greece, some of the reforms are obviously related to a "national crisis" (illegal immigration), while others respond to EU initiatives, but it seems difficult to determine to what extent many of these reforms would also have been achieved without EU influence. In Belgium, the well-known *"Dutroux"* case, which was a clear demonstration of the lack of coordination between the law enforcement agencies, is one of the main justifications for the recent reforms in its criminal justice organisations. In the Netherlands, reforms were predominantly fuelled by a national crisis in the criminal justice system (displayed by the findings of the Parliamentary Inquiry Committee), and by a rather critical report from the national court of auditors about the functioning of the national criminal intelligence service.[124] On the other hand, the creation of the SIS/SIRENE bureau and the Europol desk were unrelated to the assessment exercise. The reforms that have been proposed concerning the Northern Ireland police force (RUC) are clearly related to recent political developments.

## 8.6 Accountability Trends

The question about (reforms of) accountability structures was a subsidiary one in the questionnaire, which meant that many national reports did not include an in-depth analysis of this issue. The research findings regarding Austria, Germany, Greece, the Netherlands and Sweden nevertheless show that the adoption of new legislation on special investigation methods goes hand in hand with the strengthening of the authorisation procedures. In 1997, Greece created a National Data Protection Supervisory Board and an Ombudsman, as did most of the Member States at an earlier stage.

However, not all the reforms led to a strengthening of control. In Sweden, the police forces no longer always need the permission of the Data Protection Authority for the creation of police databases. A similar solution regarding the exchange of information was introduced in 1997 in Belgium, where the police forces no longer need to get the permission of the judicial authorities for all kinds of information.

## 8.7 Private Policing Trends

The question on private policing – and in particular forms of information-exchange between the regular law enforcement services and private agencies – was not at the heart of our research project. In the field of private policing, the Greek customs service and the coast guard signed a "Memorandum of Understanding" with some commercial associations for the information exchange on drug trafficking. In the Netherlands, which has around 300 private investigation bureaux, cooperation with police services is mostly welcome, especially when it concerns complex investigations. However, there is a certain degree of unease about the lack of transparency in the working methods of these bureaux.

## 8.8 Organisational Interaction Trends

The research project generated only a few clear examples of cross-fertilisation between law enforcement structures. One concerns the forerunner of the Danish National Criminal Intelligence Service, which is directly inspired by the UK model. But it seems that the Swedish National Criminal Intelligence Service, created in 1995, is also based on this model, while the Federal Criminal Investigation Office planned by Austria is inspired by the German *Bundeskriminalamt*. Both the creation of the National Crime Squad in the UK and the National Crime Squad (LRT) in the Netherlands have been remotely inspired by the American FBI model. Not covered by our research project, but interesting as a form of cross-fertilisation, is the 4 x 4-intelligence system,[125] which was first used in the UK, and which is now used in other countries like the Netherlands and Belgium as well.

## 8.9 Competition Trends

Organised crime can be seen as a market for law enforcement agencies, within which they compete for space. Our research project has generated rare indications of organisational rivalry, but we believe that this is based on our very piecemeal observations of this matter. Anticipating new developments and innovation strategies may be of crucial importance in this regard. Adaptations of organisational structures create new loci of power and dominance, which is why there may be resistance to innovative developments. In Greece, a certain rivalry occurred between the customs services and the coast guard on the one hand and the newly created SDOE on the other, as many competences and powers of the first two were transferred to the latter. With regard to the expected competition between police and private or state security services, we found differing evidence between the different countries. In the UK, the expansion of the state security service MI5 into the field of organised crime was perceived as a threat by police, while the police service in the Netherlands seems to have no problem with the fact that the BVD investigates selective elements of organised crime cases.

## 9. SUMMARY OF MAIN FINDINGS AND CONCLUDING REMARKS

The following chapter presents an inventory of the principal research findings, based on the hypotheses listed in chapter 6.

- Most of the EU Member States have designated or created one single central contact point for the exchange of information on organised crime; the implementation of the remaining recommendations of the 1997 Action Plan show a differentiated pattern across the Member States;
- Although there are no indications of an integral or wholesale convergence of national law enforcement structures, there is some convergence in the structure, mandate and function of national coordination and contact facilities;
- There is considerable variation between the EU Member States in the way these national coordination structures have been embedded within existing organisations;
- There are rare examples of cross-national copying or "mimesis", with a few exceptions like the NCIS model in Denmark;
- All national law enforcement systems of the EU Member States have centralised facilities for the control (i.e. investigation, information-exchange, repressive means) of international organised crime;
- Centralised facilities often flow from a perceived necessity to enlarge the scale of a range of facilities, such as expertise, equipment and strategic analysis; only in decentralised systems such as the UK and the Netherlands, has the enlargement of scale been an explicit motivation for centralisation;
- Decentralisation is a relatively rare occurrence, although there are clear indications that anti-organised crime facilities are accommodated at interregional level (interregional squads in the UK and the Netherlands, interregional fraud squads in the Netherlands, and interregional international contact centres, again in the Netherlands);
- Specialisation – the creation of a unit which is specifically designed to investigate a certain type of organised crime – is frequent at central level, but infrequent at lower levels; the Netherlands is rather exceptional with e.g. a Synthetic Drugs Unit at interregional level;
- Little headway has been made thus far with the formation of

multidisciplinary teams (except for a few countries like Belgium and the Netherlands);

- In some EU Member States, informal bottom-up processes have contributed to adaptations or reforms, which were mostly triggered by concerns about the quality and/or integrity of the criminal justice system;
- At first sight, accountability systems do not appear to be profoundly affected by Europeanisation and/or the creation of national facilities for the control of organised crime;
- Organisational interaction is neither systematic, nor structural; in the future, however, the further institutionalisation of police cooperation and judicial cooperation in criminal matters may contribute considerably to the exchange of best practices;
- Our research has generated some evidence of competition or rivalry between law enforcement agencies concerning the control of organised crime: some of these rivalries were historical (Belgium), in other countries they were related to the expansion of competencies from state security services or private agencies into traditional domains of regular law enforcement agencies (UK).

A general conclusion may be that at a very superficial level, processes of approximation may be perceived as an effect of Europeanisation. However, in some cases it is difficult to assess the effect EU instruments have had on the adaptation of domestic criminal justice systems, and to weigh their impact next to reforms that had already been initiated or next to "crises" in the national criminal justice systems (Dutroux, IRT). In the future, EU Presidencies will have the option to further infuse convergence between the organisational structures of the national law enforcement agencies, for instance by raising proposals for the establishment of common mechanisms for information exchange. The Justice and Home Affairs Directorate of the European Commission, may – as a co-initiator in this field – seize several opportunities to export its knowledge about the harmonisation of national policies (and about the resistances against it!) to the domain of Police and Justice Cooperation in Criminal Matters. One issue undeniably demonstrated by the underlying research project is that the establishment of a "European Judicial Area" cannot simply be superimposed by the EU on the Member States: its evolution is likely to follow the pattern of variable geometry and incremental logic.[126]

**NOTES**

1. Attached in the Appendix to this chapter.
2. Peter Clark, *Organisations in Action. Competition between contexts.*, London, Routledge, 2000, on p. 177.
3. Cyrille Fijnaut, "Observations concerning recent police service reorganisations in Western Europe", in G.J.N. Bruinsma and C.D. van der Vijver, *Public Safety in Europe*, International Police Institute Twente, University of Twente, 1999, pp. 129-135, on p. 135.
4. "Organizations in a field may be highly diverse on some dimensions, yet extremely homogeneous on others", in Paul J. DiMaggio and Walter W. Powell, "The Iron Cage Revisited: Institutional Isomorphism and Collective Rationality in Organizational Fields", in *American Sociological Review*, 1983, Vol. 48, April, p. 156.
5. Distinction made by the Helsinki Institute for Crime Prevention and Crime Control in a report entitled *Criminal Justice Systems in Europe*, Helsinki, Finland, 1985 (No. 5), on p. 14.
6. See e.g. for differences in legal definitions of drug offences: Nicholas Dorn (ed.), *Regulating European Drug Problems. Administrative Measures and Civil Law in the Control of Drug Trafficking, Nuisance and Use*, Kluwer Law International, The Hague, 1999.
7. Phill Fennell, Bert Swart, Nico Jörg and Christopher Harding, "Introduction", in *Criminal Justice in Europe. A Comparative Study*, Phill Fennell, Bert Swart, Nico Jörg and Christopher Harding (eds.), Oxford, Clarendon Press, 1995, pp. xv-xix, on p. xv.
8. Luciano Violante (ed.), *I soldi della mafia*, Laterza, Bari, 1998, p. 12; Phil Williams and Ernesto U. Savona, "Problems and Dangers Posed by Organized Transnational Crime in the Various Regions of the World", in *The United Nations and Transnational Organized Crime*, edited by Phil Williams and Ernesto U. Savona, Special Issue of *Transnational Organized Crime*, Vol. 1, autumn 1995, No. 3, p. 1.
9. Anderson *et al* (1995: 21f) describe this as the "adjacency of opportunities".
10. Ernesto Savona (1998), "Problemi e strumenti dell'azione internazionale di contrasto al riciclaggio", in Violante (ed.), *I soldi della mafia*, pp. 232-234.
11. Mario Centorrino (1998), "Il giro d'affari delle organizzazioni criminali", in Violante (ed.), *I soldi della mafia*, p. 11.
12. Didier Bigo, *Polices en réseaux*, Presses de Sciences Politiques, Paris, 1996.
13. B. de Ruyver *et al.*, *Kansarmoede, druggebruik, criminaliteit*, Ghent University Press, Ghent, 1992, p. 311; Monica den Boer, "The Quest for European Policing: Rhetoric and Justification in a Disorderly Debate", in Malcolm Anderson and Monica den Boer (eds.), *Policing Across National Boundaries*, Pinter, London, 1994, p. 188f; Henri Labayle, "L'application du titre VI du Traité de l'Union européenne et la matière pénale", in Mireille Delmas-Marty (ed.), *Vers un droit pénal communautaire? Actes de la journée d'études organisée le 28 novembre 1994 à Paris par l'Association de recherches pénales*

*européennes*, Dalloz, Paris, 1995, p. 48ff; Malcolm Anderson et al., *Policing the European Union. Theory, Law and Practice*, Clarendon Press, Oxford, 1995, p. 23.

14. Some Member States, such as Germany, have had a slightly longer experience with the codification of the use of proactive policing methods, whilst others, such as Belgium, issued secret, official guidelines. See e.g. Gropp (1993), Fijnaut and Marx (1995), Tak (1996), and Den Boer (1997).

15. Didier Bigo, *op. cit.*, p. 282.

16. Joint Action No. 98/733/JHA of 21 December 1998 adopted by the Council, on making it a criminal offence to participate in a criminal organisation in the Member States of the European Union (Official Journal No. L 351, 29 December 1998, pp. 1-3). The Joint Action follows Recommendation 17 of the 1997 EU Action Plan to combat organised crime.

17. The mechanism is described in the Council document No. 6204/2/97 ENFOPOL 35 rev 2 of 21 April 1997.

18. According to the mechanism, at least six of the characteristics must be present, four of which must be those numbered 1, 3, 5 and 11, for any crime or criminal group to be classified as organised crime.

19. The table is based on the information contained in the national reports. Therefore it does not have any official character and does not pretend to be complete. The information on Portugal contained in this and the following tables of the synthesis report is based on the data communicated by the Portuguese researcher, although the Portuguese national report could not be completed in time.

20. The Ministerial Agreement on EDU of 2 June 1993 covered unlawful drug trafficking and related money laundering activities. The Agreement was replaced by a Joint Action of 10 March 1995 (95/73/JHA, published in the Official Journal L 62/1 on 20 March 1995) which extended the competence of the EDU to illegal trafficking in nuclear and radioactive substances, illegal immigration smuggling and motor vehicle crime.

21. *Official Journal of the European Communities*, 95/C 316/01, p. 1-32.

22. See also Recommendation 2 of the Action Plan to Combat Organised Crime.

23. See Article 11 of the rules applicable to Analysis Files and the Confidentiality Rules.

24. The Schengen Implementing Agreement of 1990 (Article 114) imposes a similar requirement, namely that each Contracting Party shall designate a supervisory authority, responsible for exercising independent control in conformity with national law over the file of the national part of the Schengen Information System.

25. From: "Belgian Presidency – European Union; Priorities in the field of justice and home affairs", Brussels, 28 June 2001, Doc. 10415/01, JAI 67.

26. Speech by António Vitorino, 'Democratic Control for Europol', at Europol Conference organised by the Senate and House of Representatives of the Dutch States General, The Hague, 8 June 2001; http://europa.int/rapid/start/cgi/.

27. *Official Journal of the European Communities*, 97/C 251/01, p. 1-18.

28. Legislative decree 367/1991, transformed into legislative act 8/1992. See also Piero Luigi Vigna, "L'organizzazione della DNA per la risposta al riciclaggio", in Violante (ed.), *I soldi della mafia*, pp. 139-151.

29. Note from the General Secretariat of the Council to the Multidisciplinary Working Group on Organised Crime (MDG) on the evaluation of the implementation of Recommendations 1, 19 and 20 of the Action Plan to combat Organised Crime (6143/1/98 CRIMORG 24, 9 November 1998).

30. SIRENE = Supplementary Information Request at the National Entry.

31. See doc. 6143/1/98 CRIMORG 24.

32. Piero Luigi Vigna, *op.cit.*, p. 140.

33. See doc. 6143/1/98 CRIMORG 24.

34. *Official Journal of European Communities* L 191 of 7 July 1998, p. 4.

35. Heribert Ostendorf, "Europol – ohne Rechtskontrolle?", *Neue Juristische Wochenschrift* 1997, No. 51, pp. 3418-3420.

36. In general, these legal instruments were not referred to in the questionnaire.

37. *Official Journal of European Communities*, L 273 of 25 October 1996.

38. *Official Journal of European Communities*, L 342 of 31 December 1996.

39. *Official Journal of European Communities*, C 375 of 12 December 1996.

40. *Official Journal of European Communities*, L 342 of 31 December 1996.

41. *Official Journal of European Communities*, L 159 of 17 June 1997.

42. *Official Journal of European Communities*, L 191 of 7 July 1998, p. 1.

43. Directive 91/308/EEC, *Official Journal of European Communities*, L 166 of 28 June 1991, p. 77.

44. Monica den Boer, "The Incorporation of Schengen into the TEU: a Bridge Too Far?", in Jörg Monar and Wolfgang Wessels (eds.), *The Treaty of Amsterdam: Challenges and Opportunities for the European Union*, London, Pinter, 2001.

45. Committee of Independent Experts, First Report of 15 March 1999 on "Allegations Regarding Fraud, Mismanagement and Nepotism in the European Commission" (available on the web site of the European Parliament: www.europarl.eu.int).

46. Commission decision 1999/352/EC/ECSC/Euratom of 28 April 1999 establishing a European Anti-Fraud Office (*Official Journal* L 136 of 31 May 1999, p. 20-22); Regulation 1073/1999 of the European Parliament and of the Council of 25 May 1999 concerning investigations conducted by OLAF (*Official Journal* L 136 of 31 May 1999, pp. 1-7).

47. European Commission, *Schutz der finanziellen Interessen der Gemeinschaft, Betrugsbekämpfung, Jahresbericht 1996*, annual report published by Eur-Op in 1997, Luxembourg, p. 43.

48. European Commission, *op. cit.*, p. 43. The French special teams are respectively part of the police (*Direction Centrale de Police Judiciaire*) and the customs (*Direction Générale des Douanes et des Droits indirects*). According to the OLAF officer interviewed by us, ICLAF is much too small to cope with the amount of work and is therefore only useful for conceptual, but not for operational activities.

49. European Commission, *Protecting the Community's financial interests, The*

*fight against fraud, Annual Report 1997*, report published by Eur-Op in 1998, Luxembourg, p. 35. Denmark has one unit in the area of customs as part of the federal anti-fraud bureau (*Svigsbekæmpelsekontoret*) and one at the level of police (*Afd. for Særlig økonomisk Kriminalitet*). Greece set up SDOE, the economic and financial crime office as part of the Ministry of Finance. Portugal announced the creation of a coordination body called Ucleffa (*Unidade de Coordenaçao da Luta contra a Evasao e a Fraude Fiscal e Aduaneira*).

50. Committee of Independent Experts, *Second Report on Reform of the Commission – Analysis of current practice and proposals for tackling mismanagement, irregularities and fraud*, 10 September 1999, p. 164, point 5.9.13. (the report is available on the web site of the European Parliament: www.europarl.eu.int). At the date of the report, three more agreements were close to finalisation and nine other "on the table".

51. Presidency Conclusions, Tampere European Council, 15-16 October 1999, particularly the points 43-47 (available on the web site of the Council: www.ue.eu.int).

52. The scoreboard was issued by the Commission on 13 April 2000 (Communication from the Commission to the Council and the European Parliament). The last Biannual update of the Scoreboard (First half of 2001) shows that the ratification of Title VI instruments, such as the Extradition Convention and the Mutual Assistance Convention, has been delayed (COM (2001) 278 final, Brussels, 23 May 2001 which can be found at http://europa.eu.int/comm/dgs/justice_home/pdf/com2001-278-en.pdf).

53. Presidency Conclusions, Helsinki European Council, 10-11 December 1999, point 52.

54. Report on the finalisation and evaluation of the Action Plan on Organised Crime, Doc. No. 9917/3/99.

55. *Official Journal of the European Communities*, C 124 of 3 May 2000, p. 1-33.

56. See the press release of the JHA Council of 27 March 2000 on the web site of the Council of the EU (www.ue.eu.int).

57. Neil Walker, *Policing in a Changing Constitutional Order*, London, Sweet and Maxwell, 2000, on pp. 251-256.

58. Th.W.P.M. van der Krogt and C.W. Vroom, *Organisatie is beweging*, Utrecht, Lemma, 1991, p. 19.

59. Peter M. Blau and W. Richard Scott, *Formal organizations; a comparative approach*, London, Routledge and Kegan Paul, 1963.

60. Th.W.P.M. van der Krogt and C.W. Vroom, *Organisatie is beweging*, Utrecht, Lemma, 1991, p. 19.

61. Th.W.P.M. van der Krogt and C.W. Vroom, *Organisatie is beweging*, Utrecht, Lemma, 1991, p. 120.

62. David H. Bayley, "The Police and Political Development in Europe", in Charles Tilly (ed.), *The Formation of National States in Western Europe*, Princeton, Princeton University Press, 1975, pp. 328-379; Otwin Marenin, "Policing Change, Changing Police: Some Thematic Questions", in Otwin Marenin (ed.), *Policing Change, Changing Police*, New York and London, Garland Publishing,

1996, pp. 3-22, on p. 4; R. Reiner and S. Spencer, *Accountable Policing: Effectiveness, empowerment and equity*, London, IPPR, 1993.

63. C. Pollitt and G. Bouckaert, *Public Management Reform. A Comparative Analysis. Oxford, Oxford University Press*, 2000. According to the OECD, the New Public Management paradigm contains the following main trends: 1) devolving authority, providing flexibility; 2) ensuring performance, control, accountability; 3) developing competition and choice; 4) providing responsive service; 5) improving the management of human resources; 6) optimising information technology; 7) improving the quality of regulation; 8) strengthening steering functions at the centre; Walter Kickert, "Public Management in the United States and Europe", in Walter Kickert (ed.), *Public Management and Administrative Reform in Europe*, Edward Elgar, Cheltenham, 1997, pp. 15-38, on p. 18.

64. Trevor Jones and Tim Newburn, *Private Security and Public Policing*, Oxford, Clarendon Press, Clarendon Studies in Criminology, 1998.

65. Monica den Boer, " Internationalization: A Challenge to Police Organizations in Europe", in R. Mawby (ed.), *Policing Across the World: Issues for the Twenty-First Century*, London, UCL Press, 1999, pp. 59-74; Neil C. Walker, "Policing the European Union: the Politics of Transition", in Otwin Marenin (ed.), *Policing Change, Changing Police*, New York and London, Garland Publishing, 1996, pp. 251-283.

66. Paul Frissen, *Politics, Governance and Technology. A Postmodern Narrative in the Virtual State*, Cheltenham / Northampton, Edward Elgar, 1999.

67. For example the creation of joint management and information systems for the control of juvenile criminality.

68. Pollitt and Bouckaert, Public Management Reform, Oxford, Oxford University Press, 2000, p. 28 and 29; for an emphasis on globalisation as an interpretative schema in schools of business, see M. Albrow, *The Global Age*, Cambridge, Polity Press, 1996.

69. The overview is inspired by Pollitt and Bouckaert, Public Management Reform, Oxford, Oxford University Press, 2000.

70. See also Pollitt and Bouckaert, Public Management Reform, Oxford, Oxford University Press 2000, p. 165.

71. Paul J. DiMaggio and Walter W. Powell, "The Iron Cage Revisited: Institutional Isomorphism and Collective Rationality in Organizational Fields", in *American Sociological Review*, 1983, Vol. 48 (April: 147-160).

72. Paul J. DiMaggio and Walter W. Powell, *op. cit.*, p. 149.

73. Paul J. DiMaggio and Walter W. Powell, *op. cit.*, p. 150.

74. Paul J. DiMaggio and Walter W. Powell, *op. cit.*, p. 151.

75. Th.W.P.M. van der Krogt & C.W. Vroom, *Organisatie is beweging*, Utrecht, Lemma, 1991, p. 18.

76. Paul J. DiMaggio and Walter W. Powell, *op. cit.*, p. 154.

77. Phill Fennell, Bert Swart, Nico Jörg and Christopher Harding, "Introduction" in Phill Fennell, Bert Swart, Nico Jörg and Christopher Harding (eds.), *Criminal Justice in Europe. A Comparative Study*, Oxford, Clarendon Press, 1995, pp. xv-

xix, on p. xvii.

78. In this context, Giddens' concept of structuration may be instructive. See for example Anthony Giddens, *Central Problems in Social Theory; Action, Structure, and Contradiction in Social Analysis,* 1979, Berkeley: University of California Press.

79. Literature on (international) police networking: Bigo 1996; Sheptycki 1998; Nadelmann 1993; Johnston 2000b; Loader 2000.

80. Dietrich Rometsch and Wolfgang Wessels (eds.), *The European Union and Member States: Towards Institutional Fusion?*, Manchester University Press, 1996, p. 328.

81. Dietrich Rometsch and Wolfgang Wessels, *op. cit.*, p. 365.

82. Phill Fennell, Bert Swart, Nico Jörg and Christopher Harding, "Conclusion: Europeanization and Convergence: The Lessons of Comparative Study", in Phill Fennell, Bert Swart, Nico Jörg and Christopher Harding (eds.), *Criminal Justice in Europe. A Comparative Study*, Oxford, Clarendon Press, 1995, pp. 379-386, p. 386.

83. Robert Harmsen, "The Europeanization of National Administrations: A Comparative Study of France and the Netherlands", in *Governance: An international Journal of Policy and Administration*, Vol. 12, No. 1, January 1999, pp. 81-113, on p. 81.

84. Robert Harmsen, "The Europeanization of National Administrations: A Comparative Study of France and the Netherlands", in *Governance: An international Journal of Policy and Administration*, Vol. 12, No. 1, January 1999, pp. 81-113, on p. 82 and 83 respectively.

85. Pollitt and Bouckaert, *Public Management Reform*, Oxford, Oxford University Press, 2000, p. 36.

86. Tupman and Tupman (1999) argue that there is "considerably more uniformity in policing processes and structures in Europe" than generally assumed in the UK.

87. Here, we may require some reflection on the theoretical paradigm which we will use throughout the research project. Apart from Mawby's distinction between Anglo-Saxon and continental policing, we could think of Brodeur's distinction between "high" and "low policing" (Brodeur, 1983), or Tupman and Tupman's distinction between the "national model", the "German decentralised model", and the "county model" (Tupman and Tupman, 1999: 97). A concise overview of theoretical distinctions can be found in Marenin (1996) or Monet (1993).

88. R. Mawby, *Comparative Policing Issues. The British and American Experience in International Perspective*, London, Unwin Hyman, 1990, p. 32.

89. We have not specified the Scottish situation.

90. Monica den Boer, "Internationalisation: A Challenge to Police Organizations in Europe", in R. Mawby (ed.), *Policing Across the World: Issues for the Twenty-first Century*, London, UCL Press, 1999, pp. 59-74.

91. The term "national" also refers to " federal", which applies to federal states like Germany, Belgium and Austria.

92. A.F.A. Korsten and J.L.M.L. Soeters, "Parlementaire Enquête Opsporings-

methoden. Resultaten, beoordelingen en debatten", in *Bestuurskunde*, Jrg. 5, No. 2, 1996, p. 63.

93. See doc. 6143/1/98 CRIMORG 24 of 9 November 1998.
94. Justice Minister Sabine Leutheusser-Schnarrenberger. See e.g. http://www.zdfmsn.de/ratgeber/monalisa/starke_frauen/12317/content.html; Den Boer, 1997.
95. For a recent comparative study on this issue, see Peter Tak (ed.), 2000.
96. E.R. Muller, "Parlementaire Enquête Opsporingsmethoden. Organisatie en werkwijze", in *Bestuurskunde*, jrg. 5, No. 2, p. 74.
97. B. Hoogenboom, *De privatisering van de politiefunctie*, Den Haag, 1996; L. Johnston, *The Rebirth of Private Policing*, Routledge, London/New York, 1992; N. Walker, "Policing the European Union: The Politics of Transition", in O. Marenin (ed.), *Policing Change: Changing Police*, Garland Press, New Yrok, pp. 251-283.
98. Van Reenen, 1989.
99. Monica den Boer, "Internationalisation: A Challenge to Police Organizations in Europe", in R. Mawby (ed.), *op. cit.*, 1999.
100. Joint Action of 5 Dec. 1997, *Official Journal of European Communities*, L 344 of 15 Dec. 97, pp. 7-9.
101. The tables are based on the information contained in the national reports, if necessary complemented by other sources. Therefore they do not have any official character and do not pretend to be complete. In the event of a certain body having been created recently, the year of its creation is mentioned in brackets.
102. e.g. Finland, France, Greece, Ireland, Italy, Netherlands, Sweden, United Kingdom.
103. e.g. Austria, France.
104. e.g. Finland, Ireland, Italy, Luxembourg, Netherlands.
105. The General Council for the fight against organised crime, which operates at the political level, and the Anti-Mafia Investigation Directorate (DIA), which carries out the investigations, regroup the three law enforcement agencies (*Polizia di Stato*, *Carabinieri* and *Guardia di Finanza*).
106. In Greece, there are two Directorates at the Ministry of Public Order which have a coordinating role, one in the field of terrorism (State Security Directorate) and the other for general affairs (Public Security Directorate), while the fight against drug trafficking is coordinated by a special body, the Central Anti-Drug Coordination Unit (SODN).
107. In France, the Anti-Mafia Investigation and Coordination Unit (UCRAM) created in 1993 is responsible for policy coordination, while the Central Investigation and Organised Crime Section (SCICO), created in 1995, is responsible for national investigations.
108. The central contact points at the level of the prosecution service are listed below in Figure 6.
109. In England and Wales, where there is an adversarial system and relatively weak oversight of police investigations through the Crown Prosecution Service, the

national contact point is through the Home Office, the equivalent of the continental Ministry of Interior.

110. In this context, it is interesting to note how the national reports sometimes differ in their interpretation of this term.

111. In Greece, the Central Anti-Drug Coordination Unit (SODN) has representatives of the Ministry of Public Order, the Ministry of Mercantile Marine and the Ministry of Finance. In Ireland, the Criminal Assets Bureau (CAB) brings together the police (Garda Siochana), the Revenue Commissioners and the Social Welfare Authorities. In Italy, the Directorate of Anti-Mafia Investigations (DIA) regroups the State Police (*Polizia di Stato*), the Customs and Revenue Police (*Guardia di Finanza*) and the *Carabinieri*.

112. France, Netherlands.

113. Austria, Denmark, Finland, Luxembourg, Spain. *Ad hoc* usually refers to the temporary nature of the team, which is created for the investigation of one large and/or complex crime case.

114. In Austria, a local task force was set up in Vienna to combat organised crime.

115. Austria, Finland, Germany, Ireland, Italy, Sweden, United Kingdom.

116. Denmark, Luxembourg.

117. France, Netherlands. In the Netherlands, there is the so-called Unusual Transaction Unit (MOT), which is located at the level of the national police agency, but which is accountable to the Ministry of Justice.

118. Spain.

119. Greece.

120. Mintzberg's definition of centralisation is as follows: "When all the power for decision making rests at a single point in the organisation – ultimately in the hands of one person – we shall call the structure centralised…". From: Harry Mintzberg, *Structures in Fives: Designing Effective Organizations*, Prentice Hall, 1983, p. 95.

121. E. Neville, "The Public's Right to Know – The Individual's Right to Privacy", in J. Sheptycki (ed.) *Policing and Society*, Special Issue on Intelligence-Led Policing, 2000, Vol. 9 No. 4, pp. 416.ed more important.

122. Almost all services and units in this figure are also mentioned in the previous tables. The installation of the Europol National Units and the SIRENE bureaux, which contributes of course to the centralisation, is not mentioned in this table. As some services or units may at the same time show a centralisation and a specialisation tendency (described in figure 8), we had to choose the figure according to the tendency which we considered more important.

123. Les Johnston, *Policing Britain*, 2000a, on p. 90, and also on p. 29.

124. J. Sheptycki, "Political Culture and Structures of Social Control: Police-Related Scandal in the Low Countries in Comparative Perspective", *Policing and Society*, 2000, Vol. 9, No. 1, pp. 1-32.

125. The 4x4 intelligence system allows the classification of confidential information according to the reliability of the source and of the information itself.

126. De Kerchove and Weyembergh 2000; Walker 2000.

**BIBLIOGRAPHY**

Albrow, Martin (1996), *The Global Age*, Cambridge, Polity Press.

Anderson, Malcolm, Monica den Boer, Peter Cullen, William C. Gilmore, Charles D. Raab and Neil Walker (1995), *Policing the European Union. Theory, Law and Practice*, Oxford, Clarendon Press.

Bayley, David H. (1975), "The Police and Political Development in Europe", in Charles Tilly (ed.), *The Formation of National States in Western Europe*, Princeton, Princeton University Press, pp. 328-379.

Bigo, Didier (1996), *Polices en réseaux*, Paris, Presses de Sciences Politiques.

Blau, Peter M., and W. Richard Scott (1963), *Formal Organisations: a Comparative Approach*, London, Routledge and Kegan Paul.

Boer, Monica den (1994), "The Quest for European Policing: Rhetoric and Justification in a Disorderly Debate", in Malcolm Anderson and Monica den Boer (eds.), *Policing Across National Boundaries*, London, Pinter, pp. 174-196.

Boer, Monica den (1999), "Internationalization: A Challenge to Police Organizations in Europe", in R. Mawby (Ed.), *Policing Across the World: Issues for the Twenty-first Century*, London, UCL Press, pp. 59-74.

Boer, Monica den (ed.), (1997), *Undercover Policing and Accountability from an International Perspective*, Maastricht, European Institute of Public Administration.

Boer, Monica den (2001), "The Incorporation of Schengen into the TEU: a Bridge Too Far?", Jörg Monar and Wolfgang Wessels (eds.), *The Treaty of Amsterdam: Challenges and Opportunities for the European Union*, London, Pinter.

Brodeur, J.P. (1983), "High Policing and Low Policing: Remarks about the Policing of Political Activities", *Social Problems*, 3, 507-520.

Centorrino, Mario (1998), "Il giro d'affari delle organizzazioni criminali", in Violante, *I soldi della mafia*, pp. 7-21.

Clark, Peter (2000), *Organisations in Action. Competition between contexts*, London, Routledge.

DiMaggio, Paul J. and Walter W. Powell (1983), "The Iron Cage Revisited: Institutional Isomorphism and Collective Rationality in Organizational Fields", in *American Sociological Review*, Vol. 48, April, p. 156.

Dorn, Nicholas (ed.) (1999), *Regulating European Drug Problems. Administrative Measures and Civil Law in the Control of Drug Trafficking, Nuisance and Use*, Kluwer International, The Hague.

Fennell, Phill, Bert Swart, Nico Jörg and Christopher Harding (eds.) (1995), *Criminal Justice in Europe. A Comparative Study*, Oxford, Clarendon Press.

Fijnaut, Cyrille (1999), "Observations concerning recent police service reorganisations in Western Europe", in G.J.N. Bruinsma and C.D. van der Vijver, *Public Safety in Europe*, International Police Institute Twente, University of Twente, pp. 129-135.

Fijnaut, Cyrille, and Gary T. Marx (1995) (eds.), *Undercover. Police Surveillance in Comparative Perspective*, Kluwer, The Hague.

Frissen, Paul (1999), *Politics, Governance and Technology. A Postmodern Narrative in the Virtual State*, Cheltenham / Northampton, Edward Elgar.

Giddens, Anthony (1979), *Central Problems in Social Theory; Action, Structure and Contradiction in Social Analysis*, Berkeley, University of California Press.

Gropp, Walter (1993) (ed.), *Besondere Ermittlungsmaßnahmen zur Bekämpfung der Organisierten Kriminalität*. Beiträge und Materialien aus dem Max-Planck-Institut für ausländisches und internationales Strafrecht Freiburg i. Br., Freiburg, Band S 36.

Harmsen, Robert (1999), "The Europeanization of National Administrations: A Comparative Study of France and the Netherlands", in *Governance: An International Journal of Policy and Administration*, Vol. 12, No. 1, January 1999, pp. 81-113.

Hoogenboom, B. (1986), *De privatisering van de politiefunctie*, Den Haag.

Johnston, L. (1992), *The Rebirth of Private Policing*, London / New York, Routledge.

Johnston, L. (2000a), *Policing Britain. Risk, Security and Governance*, Pearson.

Johnston, L. (2000b), "Transnational Private Policing: The Impact of Commercial Security", in J. Sheptycki (ed.), *Issues in Transnational Policing*, London, Routledge.

Jones, Trevor, and Tim Newburn (1998), *Private Security and Public Policing*, Oxford, Clarendon Press, Clarendon Studies in Criminology.

Gilles de Kerchove and Anne Weyembergh (eds.) (2000), *Vers un espace judiciaire pénal européen (Towards a European Judicial Criminal Area)*, Institut d'Etudes Européennes, Editions de l'Université de Bruxelles, Bruxelles.

Kickert, Walter (1997), "Public Management in the United States and Europe", in Walter Kickert (ed.), *Public Management and Administrative Reform in Europe*, Edward Elgar, Cheltenham: 15-38.

Korsten, A.F.A., and J.L.M.L. Soeters, "Parlementaire Enquête Opsporingsmethoden. Resultaten, beoordelingen en debatten", *Bestuurskunde*, Jrg. 5, nr. 2, 1996: 50-65.

Krogt, Th.W.P.M. van der, and C.W. Vroom (1991), *Organisatie is beweging*, Utrecht, Lemma.

Labayle, Henri (1995), "L'application du titre VI du Traité de l'Union européenne et la matière pénale", in Mireille Delmas-Marty (ed.), *Vers un droit pénal communautaire? Actes de la journée d'études organisée le 28 novembre 1994 à Paris par l'Association de recherches pénales européennes*, Paris, Dalloz, pp. 35-64.

Loader, Ian (2000), "Plural Policing and Democratic Governance", *Social and Legal Studies*, 9/3: 323-345.

Marenin, Otwin (1996), "Policing Change, Changing Police: Some Thematic Questions", in Otwin Marenin (ed.), *Policing Change, Changing Police*, New York, Garland, pp. 3-22.

Mawby, R. (1990), *Comparative Policing Issues. The British and American Experience in International Perspective*, London, Unwin Hyman.

Mintzberg, Harry (1983), *Structures in Fives: Designing Effective Organizations*, Prentice Hall.

Monet, Jean-Claude (1993), *Polices et sociétés en Europe*, Paris, La Documentation française, pp. 71-94.

Muller, E.R. (1996), "Parlementaire Enquête Opsporingsmethoden. Organisatie en werkwijze", in *Bestuurskunde*, jrg. 5, nr. 2, pp. 66-76.

Nadelmann, Ethan (1993), *Cops Across Borders: The Internationalization of US Criminal Law Enforcement*, Philadelphia, Pennsylvania State University Press.

Neville, E. (2000), "The Public's Right to Know – The Individual's Right to Privacy", in J. Sheptycki (ed.), *Policing and Society*, Special Issue on Intelligence-Led Policing, Vol. 9 No. 4, pp. 413-429.

Ostendorf, Heribert, "Europol – ohne Rechtskontrolle?", *Neue Juristische Wochenschrift* 1997, n° 51, pp. 3418-3420.

Pollitt, C., and G. Bouckaert (2000), *Public Management Reform. A Comparative Analysis*, Oxford, Oxford University Press.

Reenen, P. van (1989), "Policing Europe after 1992: Cooperation and Competition", *European Affairs*, 2, pp. 45-53.

Reiner, R., and S. Spencer (1993), *Accountable Policing: Effectiveness, Empowerment and Equity*, London, IPPR.

Rometsch, Dietrich, and Wolfgang Wessels (eds.) (1996), *The European Union and Member States: Towards Institutional Fusion?*, Manchester University Press.

Ruyver, B. de (Promotor) (1992), and Onderzoeksgroep Drugbeleid, Strafrechtelijk Beleid en Internationale Criminaliteit, *Kansarmoede, druggebruik, criminaliteit*, Ghent, Ghent University Press.

Savona, E. (1998), "Problemi e strumenti dell'azione internazionale di contrasto al riciclaggio", in Violante (ed.), *I soldi della mafia*, pp. 215-241.

Sheptycki, James (1998), "The Global Cops Cometh: Reflections on Transnationalization, Knowledge Work and Policing Subculture", *British Journal of Sociology*, 49/1: 57-74.

Sheptycki, James (2000), "Political Culture and Structures of Social Control: Police-related Scandal in the Low Countries in Comparative Perspective", *Policing and Society*, Vol. 9, No. 1, pp. 1-32.

Tak, Peter J.P. *et al.* (1996), *Bijzondere opsporingsmethoden. De normering van bijzondere opsporingsmethoden in buitenlandse rechtsstelsels*. Den Haag, Ministerie van Justitie.

Tak, Peter J.P. (ed.) (2000), *Heimelijke opsporing in de Europese Unie*, Antwerpen-Groningen, Intersentia Rechtswetenschappen.

Tupman, Bill & Alison Tupman (1999), *Policing in Europe. Uniform in Diversity*, Intellect, Exeter.

Vigna, Piero Luigi, "L'organizzazione della DNA per la risposta al riciclaggio", in Violante, *I soldi della mafia*, pp. 139-151.

Violante, Luciano, Introduction to the Antimafia Report of 1998: *I soldi della mafia*, pp. VII-XV.

Violante, Luciano (ed.) (1998), *I soldi della mafia*, Bari, Laterza.

Walker, Neil (2000), *Policing in a Changing Constitutional Order*, London, Sweet and Maxwell.

Walker, Neil (1996), "Policing the European Union: The Politics of Transition", in O. Marenin (Ed.), *Policing Change: Changing Police*, Garland Press, New York, pp. 251-283.

Williams, Phil and Ernesto U. Savona (1995), "Problems and Dangers Posed by Organized Transnational Crime in the Various Regions of the World", in *The United Nations and Transnational Organized Crime*, edited by Phil Williams and Ernesto U. Savona, Special Issue of *Transnational Organized Crime*, Volume 1, Autumn 1995, Number 3, pp. 1-42.

# Appendix
# Questionnaire

**In the context of the Falcone Research Project (1998/TFJHA-FAL/145)**

## First Part: Essential questions

### 0. Preliminary questions

0.1  What are the main characteristics of the police system in your Member State (centralised/federal/community, military/civil statute, single/plural system)?

0.2  Could you provide a short and systematic description of the structure, tasks and competencies of the public prosecution service in your Member State?

0.3  Could you give a brief overview of the anti-organised crime units that existed in your Member State prior to 1990?

0.4  Does your Member State have an official definition of organised crime?

### 1. Organisational reforms foreseen or recommended by EU legal instruments

Please specify for each reform its legal basis (bill, administrative act, circulatory letter).

1.1  Reforms related to the Action Plan to Combat Organised Crime

Specify if a new service has been (will be) created or if an already existing service has been (will be) designated to carry out the new functions. Please provide an organigram.

1.1.1  **Body of coordination** (as foreseen by Recommendation No. 1 of the Action Plan)

    1.1.1.1 Is there (will there be) a body of coordination:

        – at the level of the prosecution service?

        – at the level of the law enforcement agencies?

    1.1.1.2 Please describe the competencies and powers of the body of coordination.

– Does it have operational competencies or only responsibilities in the field of policy coordination?

– Which services are under its coordination?

– Which are its powers on these services?

### 1.1.2 Central contact point

1.1.2.1 Is there (will there be) a central contact point for the exchange of information and the completion of application procedures for cooperation:

– at the level of judiciary (as foreseen by Recommendation No. 21)?

– at the level of law enforcement agencies (as foreseen by Rec. No. 19)?

1.1.2.2 Does (or will) this body include:

– the Europol National Unit;

– the SIRENE bureau (Schengen);

– the NCB (Interpol)?

If this is not the case, which services carry out these functions, and how are these services linked?

1.1.2.3 Please describe the competencies of the central contact point.

– Does it also function as a national centre that provides information to law enforcement agencies on national legislation, jurisdiction and procedures (as foreseen by Recommendation No. 19)?

– Which are its links with the body of coordination?

### 1.1.3 Multidisciplinary integrated teams

1.1.3.1 Are there (will there be) multidisciplinary integrated teams at the national level in the area of organised crime (Recommendation No. 20)?

1.1.3.2 Please describe the characteristics of these teams.

– Which law enforcement agencies take part in them?

–   Do these teams have a permanent or a temporary (ad hoc) status?

–   Which competencies and powers do they have?

–   Which are their links with the body of coordination and the central contact point (see Recommendation No. 20)?

1.2   Other EU legal instruments

1.2.1 Financial intelligence units*

–   Which authority does the financial intelligence unit (as foreseen by article 6 of the 1991 Money Laundering Directive) belong to, and which statute does it have?

–   What is the role and the position of the financial intelligence unit as regards the law enforcement agencies and the public prosecution service?

1.2.2 Did the police and customs services of your Member State establish formal agreements or other arrangements with the view to improving their cooperation (as foreseen by the Council Resolution 96/C 375/01 of 29 November 1996)?

## 2.  Other organisational reforms in the law enforcement agencies and public prosecution services

Please specify for each reform its legal basis.

2.1   Which general organisational reforms in the law enforcement agencies and public prosecution services have been carried out since 1990 or are planned, particularly in the context of efforts to combat organised crime?

2.2   Could you give a description of the organisational structure of specialised services which are responsible for the fight against organised crime (except those already mentioned under 1.1.1 to 1.1.3, e.g. units specialised in synthetic drugs or man smuggling)? Please provide an organigram.

2.3   What are the competencies and powers of these specialised services (e.g. operational, intelligence gathering, information-exchange, expertise, etc.)?

2.4   Are these specialised services subjected to a centralised structure or are they deconcentrated or delocated services with autonomous powers?

---

* In some Member States the financial intelligence unit may be known as the irregular transactions unit.

2.5  Have these reforms been accompanied by organisational changes at (inter-) regional or local level (such as, for instance, inter-regional crime squads)?

2.6  Could you mention instances of "Euregional" frameworks of cooperation that have been explicitly developed to control organised crime?

## 3. International cooperation

3.1  Which direct horizontal links (forms of cooperation, meetings, exchange of personnel, information exchange, etc.) exist with services, which are specialised in the fight against organised crime, in the other EU Member States?

3.2  What are the links (meetings, information exchange, joint investigations, etc.) between the specialised services in your Member State with the working structures of:
   – Europol?
   – Schengen (SIRENE)?
   – UCLAF?

3.3.  What are the links between the financial intelligence unit of your Member State and the financial intelligence units of the other EU Member States?

3.4  Have there been instances of practical cross-border cooperation that have given rise to reforms (bottom-up processes of reform and convergence)?

## 4. Information exchange with other bodies

4.1  Intelligence services

   – Are there any intelligence services which are not part of the law enforcement agencies (including military intelligence services), which have any competencies in the fight against organised crime?

   – Do the intelligence services have any form of cooperation with the law enforcement agencies and the public prosecution services?

   – Do they share intelligence regarding organised crime?

4.2  Private policing

   – With specific regard to organised crime, are there any formal arrangements (i.e.. legal provisions or covenants) for the exchange of information between public (i.e.. State) police bodies and private sector security providers?

– Are there informal arrangements between private and public sector security providers regarding matters to do with organised crime?

– Some multinational companies who operate in 'trouble spots' make use of 'risks assessors' and 'security consultants' in order to better protect their assets and personnel. These consultants may have information regarding organised crime activity, but it is not clear that such information is necessarily passed on to government authorities. Are there any formal or informal arrangements to facilitate such information flows?

– The Internet may be used to facilitate various forms of organised criminal activity. What arrangements are there with Internet providers to facilitate police investigations of this type?

## 5. External supervision, authorisation procedures and accountability of law enforcement agencies

5.1 Preliminary questions

– What are the main characteristics of the supervision of the law enforcement agencies in your Member State?

– What is the role of:

- the prosecution service?
- the *juge d'instruction* (if he forms part of the system?)
- the competent minister(s)?
- the national parliament?
- the national data protection supervisory board?
- the national ombudsman?

– Have there been any recent reforms in the supervision of the law enforcement agencies?

– Could you give an overview of the main authorisation procedures for the national law enforcement agencies for the use of proactive policing methods?

5.2 Supervision of the services specialised in the area of organised crime

– How are these special services, also those foreseen by the EU instruments (Europol National Unit; SIRENE bureau; body of coordination; central contact point; multidisciplinary integrated teams; etc.), supervised?

– Do these services have parallel/correspondent structures at the level of the prosecution service?

67

- Does the prosecution service (i.e. the national prosecutor or magistrate) exercise control on the activities of these services, particularly regarding international cooperation?

## Second part: Subsidiary questions

### 6. The rationale of the reforms

6.1 Which are the reasons of the organisational reforms that are mentioned under headings 1, 2 and 5?

6.2 The influence of the EU on the above-mentioned reforms

- Which EU instruments have had an influence on the organisational reforms in your Member State?

- Which one of these instruments is considered to be the most influential?

- What kind of influence (legal, organisational, epistemological, procedural) has each of the instruments had?

- To which extent did the different forms of international cooperation (Europol, Schengen and UCLAF) oblige the national services to adapt and conform their procedures regarding the processing of data, the preparation of statistics on organised crime, etc.?

- Do you expect in the medium or long term any organisational changes resulting from the Treaty of Amsterdam, or instruments that are currently being drafted (i.e. the draft Convention on Mutual Assistance in Criminal Matters)?

6.3 What is the extent of mutual influence or experience between your Member State and other Member States or third states (systemic interaction, cross-fertilisation by means of seminars, joint operations, practical experience in border areas, etc.)?

### 7. Acceptance of the reforms

7.1 What consultations (formal/informal, institution/police federation,....) have taken (will take) place before the adoption of each of the organisational reforms mentioned under heading 1, 2 and 5?

7.2 Could you provide a reconstruction of the opinions of the actors who were consulted and their impact on the reform process?

7.3　Are you aware of any resistance to the above-mentioned reforms?

## 8.　Anticipated effectiveness of the reforms

8.1　Which improvements in the effectiveness of controlling organised crime are expected to result from the organisational reforms?

8.2　Which effects in terms of rationalisation are expected to result from these reforms (e.g. resource management, enlargement of scale, etc.)?

8.3　Which improvements in the effectiveness of the supervision of the law enforcement agencies are expected to result from the organisational reforms?

## 9.　"Real" effectiveness of the reforms

9.1　Have there been (or will there be) official evaluations of the real effectiveness of the reforms? Which criteria are used for the evaluation?

9.2　Do the evaluations give the impression that the effectiveness of the fight against organised crime has become more effective as a result of the organisational reforms, especially regarding the coordination body, the central contact point and the multi-disciplinary integrated teams?

9.3　Do the evaluations give the impression that the management of the fight against organised crime has been rationalised as a result of the organisational reforms, especially regarding the coordination body, the central contact point and the multidisciplinary integrated teams?

9.4　Do the evaluations give the impression that the supervision of the law enforcement agencies has been improved as a result of the organisational reforms?

*End of Questionnaire*

# Austria*

## *Jörn Kessel and Kurt Schmoller*

### INTRODUCTION

Austria is a confederation consisting of nine federal states; one of these federal states is the town Vienna. All federal states – except Vienna – are divided into districts under the direction of a District Authority (*Bezirkshauptmannschaft*). Moreover the whole Federal territory is divided into autonomous communes and municipalities under elected mayors. Usually a district is larger than a commune or municipality.[1] Some large municipalities are also districts; they are called "town with its own charter" (*Stadt mit eigenem Statut*). A "town with its own charter" performs not only communal administrative duties but also those of a district.

In addition to their other competences, District Authorities and mayors (especially those of towns with their own charter, but within a limited field also those of other communes or municipalities) are also law enforcement agencies – or at least they can act as a security office in special cases. Within this function they have autonomous competence as well as duties on behalf of the public prosecution service and/or of the criminal courts.[2]

As far as the fight against criminality is concerned, one can differentiate crime prevention on the one hand and criminal investigation and prosecution on the other. In Austria, crime prevention is in most cases the responsibility of the law enforcement agencies.[3] Criminal investigations and prosecutions are principally the duty of the public prosecution service and the criminal courts. But the public prosecution service and the criminal courts are authorised to call on the law enforcement agencies for support and cooperation. Only

* This report mainly describes the situation in July 2000, at the time of the completion of the Falcone Project which gave rise to it. Developments which occurred afterwards could only be considered individually. Recent literature has been included as far as possible in the bibliography, but new editions of works quoted originally could not be referred to after this time.

exceptionally are the law enforcement agencies allowed to perform criminal investigations on their own authority.

Special tasks within the fight against crime are also given to the finance authorities (*Finanzbehörden*). In this respect they have – similar to the law enforcement agencies – autonomous competence as well as duties on behalf of the public prosecution service or of the criminal courts.[4]

## 1. THE LAW ENFORCEMENT AGENCIES AND FINANCE AUTHORITIES

### a) The law enforcement agencies

*aa)* The law enforcement agencies consist of security offices (*Sicherheits-behörden*) and executive bodies. Actions which the executive bodies perform are legally attributed to the security offices, which are therefore legally responsible, even if the executive bodies take action *ex officio* and on their own authority.[5]

The structure of the **security offices** is strictly hierarchical:[6] The top official within the security administration is the Federal Minister of the Interior. His office, the Federal Ministry of the Interior, is divided into four departments (*Sektion*). Department II, which is the most relevant department for crime prevention and criminal investigation, is called the Directorate General for Public Security (*Generaldirektion für die öffentliche Sicherheit*). It is led by the Director-General for Public Security and is split into six subdepartments (*Gruppe*). One of these subdepartments is Subdepartment II/D: Criminal Investigation – Interpol (*Gruppe II/D: Kriminalpolizei – Interpol*), where there are a number of units to fight crime, especially organised crime.

The top security office within each federal state is called Security Directorate (*Sicherheitsdirektion*), which is subordinated to the Minister of the Interior and led by a Director for Security (*Sicherheitsdirektor*).

At the level below, in some of the bigger towns (not in all towns with their own charter) there are Federal Police Directorates (*Bundespolizeidirektionen*) led by a Director of Police (*Polizeidirektor*). In the special case of Vienna, which is both town and federal state at the same time, the Federal Police Directorate is also Security Directorate; the president of the Federal Police Directorate in Vienna is at the same time Director for Security (he is called *Polizeipräsident*).[7] Outside of those towns where there is a Federal Police Directorate, the same competence lies with the District Authorities (*Bezirkshauptmannschaft*), which for towns with their own charter means the mayors (*Bürgermeister der Städte mit eigenem Statut*).

Moreover, in some special cases, the mayors of communes and municipalities that are *not* towns with their own charter can also act as a security office.[8]

Under the authority of the Federal Minister of the Interior there are, beside the security offices, also **three executive bodies**: The Federal Gendarmerie (*Bundesgendarmerie*), the Federal Security Guards (*Bundessicherheitswache*) and the Criminal Investigation Unit (*Institut der Kriminalbeamten*).[9] They are all so-called "guard units" (*Wachkörper*).

Outside the towns where a Federal Police Directorate is established, the executive duties of the law enforcement agencies are usually performed by the **Federal Gendarmerie**.[10] The Gendarmerie was originally part of the army. However, in 1876 it was separated from the army and received a civil statute, but remained an armed and uniformed guard unit.[11] It has its own hierarchical inner structure, which is organised in parallel to the structure of the security offices, although the Gendarmerie units – except at federal level – are organisationally separated from the security offices. At the top, the Central Gendarmerie Headquarters (*Gendarmeriezentralkommando*) are integrated within the Federal Ministry of the Interior.[12] At the highest level of each federal state – except Vienna – there is a Regional Gendarmerie Headquarters (*Landesgendarmeriekommando*), which carries out the executive duties on behalf of the Security Directorate. Subordinated to the Regional Gendarmerie Headquarters are the District Gendarmerie Headquarters (*Bezirksgendarmeriekommando*), which perform the executive duties on behalf of the District Authorities and mayors of towns with their own charter (except in towns where there is a Federal Police Directorate). At the local level there are Local Gendarmerie Units (*Gendarmeriepostenkommando*). Nowadays Austria has, besides the eight Regional Gendarmerie Headquarters (one for each federal state except Vienna), about 100 District Gendarmerie Headquarters and about 1.000 Local Gendarmerie Units.

In towns where there is a Federal Police Directorate, the Federal Security Guards and the Criminal Investigation Unit usually perform the executive duties instead of the Gendarmerie. The **Federal Security Guards** are an armed and uniformed guard unit with a civil statute. It is divided into separate guard corps (*Bundessicherheitswachekorps*). Each guard corps is attached to a Federal Police Directorate.[13] It usually performs all executive duties of the Federal Police Directorates except criminal investigations.[14] Therefore in towns where a Federal Police Directorate is established the Gendarmerie in general has no executive competence.

The **Criminal Investigation Unit** is an armed (but not uniformed) guard unit with a civil statute. It is – similar to the Federal Security Guards – divided into guard corps (*Korps der Kriminalbeamten*), which are attached to the Federal Police Directorates.[15] The guard corps of the Criminal Investigation

Unit in particular carry out those executive duties which the Federal Police Directorates are obliged to do on behalf of the public prosecution service or the criminal courts (criminal investigations).[16]

In some communes or municipalities there are, besides the Gendarmerie, communal police units (*Gemeindewachen*).[17] These are placed under the authority of the commune and carry out most of its executive duties. If such a communal police unit has the structure of a guard unit, which primarily means it consists of more than only a few officers, it partly takes over executive duties from the Gendarmerie on behalf of security offices.[18] In these (rare) cases the communal police units largely have the same competence as the Gendarmerie normally do.

*bb)* The law enforcement agencies have **two main tasks**. Both of them serve to combat crime, but they are strictly differentiated.[19] The first works in the field of general security police (*Sicherheitspolizei*),[20] and its tasks include crime prevention,[21] which means combating current and potential future crimes. The second works in the field of criminal investigation, within which the law enforcement agencies – mainly on behalf of the public prosecution service or the criminal courts – try to solve crimes that have already been perpetrated.

The competence of the law enforcement agencies in **crime prevention** is ruled within the SPG (= *Sicherheitspolizeigesetz*; Security Police Act). In the field of international police cooperation also the PolKG (= *Polizei-kooperationsgesetz*; Police Cooperation Act) is very much of importance.[22] According to the SPG, enforcement agencies have the duty to ward off the current and impending perpetration of a crime described in the Penal Code or in certain supplementary laws or even to ward off the preparation of such a crime, if there is an immediate temporal connection between that and the perpetration of the crime.[23] Furthermore, the law enforcement agencies are obliged to prevent crimes – especially organised crimes – by taking action against all so-called "criminal liaisons" (connections) of three or more people with the object of continuously carrying out crimes.[24] That task covers breaking up both less dangerous criminal gangs and organisations which stand behind organised crime.

The competence of the law enforcement agencies in relation to **criminal investigations** is laid down mainly within the StPO (= *Strafprozessordnung*; Code of Criminal Procedure).[25] According to the conception of the StPO the law enforcement agencies are in general not allowed to do investigations other than those they have been asked to do by the public prosecutor or the investigating judge. The only exception foreseen in the StPO concerns situations in which a further delay is likely to frustrate the aim of the investigation. In these situations the law enforcement agencies are authorised to perform those urgent investigations that cannot be postponed.[26]

Criminal investigations (by the law enforcement agencies) mainly take place during the preliminary proceedings (*Vorverfahren; Ermittlungs-verfahren*). According to the StPO the preliminary proceedings ideally are divided into two stages: the first stage is provisional inquiries (*Vorerhebungen*), led by the public prosecutor, who in an individual case also can decide that such inquiries are not necessary at all. The second stage – which is obligatory only in some special cases – are judicial investigations (*Voruntersuchung*) under the responsibility of an investigating judge.

In order to protect his objectivity, the public prosecutor is not allowed to investigate personally.[27] Therefore he instructs the law enforcement agencies – in some cases an investigating judge, a district court or a finance authority – to perform certain criminal investigations. Also the investigating judge can in special cases request the law enforcement agencies, a district court or a finance authority to carry out certain steps in a criminal investigation.

As with the StPO the concept for preliminary proceedings dates from 1873 and reflects the situation in the middle of the nineteenth century. At that time, as a result of experiences with absolutism, there was a deep mistrust of all state bodies which were subject to instructions by political leaders, particularly of the law enforcement agencies; only judges were trusted, which is the main reason why the investigating judge had to hold a dominant position in preliminary proceedings and the judicial investigation should be the regular form of preliminary proceedings.[28]

However, the concept of the StPO regarding preliminary proceedings, particularly the dominant position of judicial investigations conducted by the investigating judge, never really caught on in practice. Today the main part of investigative activities lies with the executive bodies of the law enforcement agencies, and they investigate independently. In this respect they rely on an increasingly broader interpretation of § 24 StPO,[29] but act to a large extent without a precise legal basis.[30] That is why in the near future the StPO will be reformed extensively, particularly the provisions on preliminary proceedings and consequently criminal investigations.[31]

### b) The finance authorities

*aa)* In Austria offences are not only punished by criminal courts; in lighter cases administrative authorities do this job. Only an offence which is punished by criminal courts is called a "crime" ("criminal offence"; *gerichtlich strafbare Handlung*). Furthermore, the term "organised crime" is restricted to such offences which are punished by criminal courts.[32] Offences which are punished by administrative authorities are called "administrative offences"

(*Verwaltungsstraftaten; Verwaltungsübertretungen*), e.g. cases of illegal prostitution.

Particularly **fiscal offences** (*Finanzvergehen*) involving less than a certain amount of damages are mere **administrative offences**,[33] even if they are offences displaying elements of fraud.[34] Although such cases do not constitute fiscal crimes (and therefore are not organised crimes either), but are only fiscal administrative offences, this is still an area relevant to the fight against organised crime, if only because punishment by the administrative finance authorities hits the sources of income of criminal organisations.

However, in cases involving above a certain amount of damages, fiscal offences will be tried by the criminal courts. Such cases concern real **fiscal crimes**, and sometimes organised crimes. In these cases the finance authorities (and the Customs Guards) are involved in the criminal proceedings, as – especially in the preliminary proceedings – they shall participate on behalf of the public prosecutor or of the criminal court (usually of the investigating judge).[35]

*bb)* The top **finance authority** is the Federal Ministry of Finance. It is divided into several departments, including a department for integration and customs (Department III) and a department for taxes (Department IV). Subordinated to the Ministry of Finance are the Regional Directorates of Finance (*Finanzlandesdirektion*) at the top of each federal state. The duties on the local level are performed by Finance Offices (*Finanzamt*)[36] and Customs Offices, that are divided into Main Customs Offices (*Hauptzollamt*) and other Customs Offices (*Zollamt*).[37]

Besides the finance authorities there is a special **executive body** placed under the authority of the Federal Ministry of Finance[38], the **Customs Guards** (*Zollwache*). It is (similar to the Gendarmerie and the Federal Security Guards) a uniformed and armed guard unit,[39] which is divided into stationary and mobile guards groups or guards divisions.

In so far as fiscal offences are punished by the finance authorities (fiscal administrative offences),[40] they fall under the jurisdiction of the Finance Offices (*Finanzamt*) and the Main Customs Offices (*Hauptzollamt*);[41] the Regional Directorates of Finance (*Finanzlandesdirektionen*) decide on the legal remedies. In this context the Finance Offices, Main Customs Offices and Regional Directorates of Finance act as **penal authorities for financial matters** (*Finanzstrafbehörde*),[42] partly without being subject to instructions.

*cc)* (1) With regard to **fiscal administrative offences** the proceedings as a whole lie within the competence of the finance authorities as penal authorities. The procedure is inquisitorial. The conduct of the preliminary investigations – the provisional inquiries (*Vorerhebungen*) as well as the main investigations

(*Untersuchungsverfahren*)[43] – is always the responsibility of an official who is bound by instructions.

As penal authorities for financial matters, the Finance Offices and Main Customs Offices in the first instance usually carry out all investigations and hearings of evidence, including the coercive measures, by themselves;[44] however, they may partly also ask other finance authorities to do this.[45]

Against acts of direct administrative power and compulsion (*Akt unmittelbarer verwaltungsbehördlicher Befehls- und Zwangsgewalt*) by the finance penal authority, e.g. if a house search goes beyond the terms of the search warrant,[46] an appeal may be lodged on which the Regional Directorate of Finance decides as a court of appeal without being subject to instructions.[47] This is in deviation from the rule applicable in other cases of an act of direct administrative power and compulsion,[48] according to which such acts should generally be disputed at the Independent Administrative Tribunals (*UVS*).[49]

The preliminary investigations are followed by a final oral hearing. If the accused so requests, this hearing will be conducted by a chamber instead of by just one official. Unlike the official, the chamber is not bound by instructions. In this way the accused can ensure that a body which is not subject to instructions will decide on his/her case. Also, in cases in which the accused has caused a certain amount of damage, the hearing is conducted by such a chamber.

(2) In the case of **fiscal crimes** (fiscal offences which are **punished by court**) special aspects apply in comparison with preliminary proceedings for other crimes. Above all, instead of calling in the help of the law enforcement agencies, the public prosecutor and the criminal courts[50] primarily have to employ the services of the finance authorities and the Customs Guards.[51] The public prosecutor and the criminal courts may only fall back on the general law enforcement agencies if the finance authorities and the Customs Guards cannot be reached in time or if the crime to be solved also constitutes a crime other than a fiscal one.[52]

In the criminal procedure the penal authority for financial matters (*Finanzstrafbehörde*) has, by operation of law, the position of a private party (*Privatbeteiligter*)[53] and can therefore bring the charge instead of the public prosecutor, if the public prosecutor unduly rejects or gives up the prosecution.[54]

If, during the investigations, acts of direct administrative power and compulsion are performed, an appeal may be lodged by those who believe that these acts have violated their rights.[55] Unlike in other criminal procedures, the Independent Administrative Tribunal (*UVS*)[56] will not decide on such matters[57] but rather – as in financial proceedings to solve administrative offences[58] – the Regional Directorate of Finance acts as a court of appeal; this even applies to any acts of direct administrative power and compulsion that, exceptionally,[59] are performed by the (general) law enforcement agencies.

## 2. THE PUBLIC PROSECUTION SERVICE AND THE INVESTIGATING JUDGE

### a) The public prosecution service

*aa)* The public prosecution service (*staatsanwaltschaftliche Behörden*) is not part of the criminal courts but a separate federal authority, established in the nineteenth century.[60] It is placed under the authority of the Federal Minister of Justice and has a hierarchical structure: the public prosecution service consists of offices which are installed at each criminal court,[61] except at the District Courts. At the Regional Courts there are Public Prosecutor's Offices (*Staatsanwaltschaften*), at the Courts of Appeal there are Senior Public Prosecutor's Offices (*Oberstaatsanwaltschaften*) and at the Supreme Court there is the Attorney-General's Office (*Generalprokuratur*). The Public Prosecutor's Offices are subordinated to the Senior Public Prosecutor's Offices; the Senior Public Prosecutor's Offices are directly responsible to the Federal Minister of Justice. The Attorney-General's Office is also answerable to the Federal Minister of Justice, but cannot give instructions to the Public Prosecutor's Offices or Senior Public Prosecutor's Offices.[62] There is now a general discussion on whether the duty of the Public Prosecutors and Senior Public Prosecutors to comply with instructions of the Federal Minister of Justice (as a political leader) should be maintained or abolished.

The public prosecution service performs its tasks using public prosecutors.[63] All public prosecutors are legal experts and have had the same training as judges. The business (tasks) of an office is distributed among sections (*Referat*). These sections are staffed with one or more public prosecutors.[64]

*bb)* As leader of the provisional inquiries (*Vorerhebungen*)[65] the public prosecutor at the competent Public Prosecutor's Office decides what investigations are necessary. However, as already mentioned above, the public prosecutor is not allowed to investigate personally.[66] Therefore the investigations are carried out by the law enforcement agencies (security offices, Gendarmerie, Criminal Investigation Unit), the finance authorities, the Customs Guards, the investigating judge or a District Court, as a rule in accordance with the instructions of the public prosecutor in charge.[67] The public prosecutor requests concrete criminal investigations, which he has to describe in detail.[68] The authority to which the request is made is only entitled to examine the legality of the requested investigations; the expediency can only be assessed by the public prosecutor.[69] The investigating judge, the District Courts, the law enforcement agencies, the finance authorities and the Customs Guards may in principle not do more than what they are specifically asked to do; only very urgent investigations or coercive measures may be carried out by them *ex officio* and on their own authority.[70]

According to the StPO the preliminary proceedings should regularly consist of brief provisional inquiries (*Vorerhebungen*) and a subsequent longer stage of judicial investigations (*Voruntersuchung*), led by the investigating judge;[71] but it is still up to the public prosecutor to request judicial investigations. Judicial investigations are only compulsory in special cases.[72] Even so, in such cases a judicial investigation may only be opened if the public prosecutor requests it.

Within the stage of judicial investigations the public prosecutor is only entitled to submit a request to the investigating judge if he thinks a concrete investigation is important.[73] The investigating judge may dismiss the request if he considers the investigation to be inexpedient. The public prosecutor may lodge an appeal with the Counsel Chamber (*Ratskammer*) against the dismissal of a request.[74]

After the preliminary proceedings the public prosecutor decides whether he will bring charges. Only if he brings charges may a main trial (final oral hearing; *Hauptverhandlung*) take place. The public prosecutor takes part in the main trial.

The public prosecutor is obliged to remain objective; he has to ensure that both incriminating and exonerating evidence is collected.[75] His objective should be to establish the material truth. If the public prosecutor considers a conviction to be unjustifiable, he should withdraw from the prosecution. Furthermore he has an obligation to dispute incorrect judicial decisions even when this means favouring the accused.[76]

As regards minor offences (petty crime), the public prosecutor has been obliged, since 1 January 2000, to examine whether a measure of *"Diversion"* (out of court solution) instead of a conviction can be considered.[77]

The concept of the StPO regarding preliminary proceedings never really caught on in practice[78] and in fact the main work is done by independently investigating law enforcement agencies (to a large extent without a precise legal basis). The role played by the public prosecution service within the preliminary proceedings is therefore not as important as it should be according to the *StPO*. As far as the fight against organised crime is concerned, the public prosecution service stays very much in the background.

## b) The investigating judge

All Regional Courts have investigating judges (= investigating magistrates; *Untersuchungsrichter*). The investigating judge works in the framework of preliminary proceedings. He may not also act as judge in the same case during the main trial (= final oral hearing). During the provisional inquiries led by the public prosecutor he only carries out those investigations which the public prosecutor requests.

With the launching of the judicial investigations (requested by the public prosecutor), the investigating judge takes charge of the procedure as *dominus litis*. The judicial investigations should complement the taking of evidence, the clarification of facts and the preparation of the main trial (= final oral hearing).[79] The investigating judge should carry out all investigations that serve to establish the truth. The public prosecutor and the accused can request concrete investigations.[80]

According to the StPO the investigating judge should carry out most investigations personally; however, the law gives him or her the possibility of having investigations carried out by District Courts or the law enforcement agencies (and – as far as fiscal crimes are concerned – by the fiscal authorities or the Customs Guards). Many coercive procedural measures which are important in the fight against organised crime can be ordered by the investigating judge himself; some, however, may only be ordered by the Counsel Chamber (*Ratskammer*), which consists of three judges.[81]

Since 1 January 2000, in the case of minor offences (petty crime) the investigating judge – as the public prosecutor before him – must also examine whether a measure of *"Diversion"* (out of court solution) instead of a conviction can be considered.[82]

If the investigating judge concludes that a prosecution is inadmissible, he will call the procedure to a halt. If not, he will close the judicial investigations upon completion of all investigations. It will then be up to the public prosecutor to decide whether or not to bring charges.[83]

### 3.  ORGANISED CRIME

### a)  Definitions

There is no (official) definition of organised crime in Austria.[84]

The SPG only contains a definition which covers both "gang crime" and "organised crime",[85] according to which one can speak of "gang or organised crime",

> "as soon as three or more persons jointly have the intention to commit crimes repeatedly".[86]

As this definition does not differentiate between mere gang crime and organised crime, it does not define the concept of organised crime.[87] Still, it may at any rate be gathered from the quoted provision that only offences which are punished by criminal courts (crimes; *gerichtlich strafbare Handlungen*), can constitute organised crime.[88]

Also the StGB (= *Strafgesetzbuch*; Penal Code) does not contain a definition of organised crime. However, since 1993 its § 278a includes a provision which makes the creation of a criminal organisation and membership of such an association punishable, and also defines the concept of "criminal organisation" in this context. According to this provision a criminal organisation is:

"an association similar to an enterprise, set up with a longer-term view and comprising a larger number of people
1.    which is orientated, even though not exclusively, towards the repeated and planned committing of serious criminal offences that endanger life, freedom from bodily harm, liberty or assets, or serious crimes in the field of the sexual exploitation of people, the smuggling of persons or the unauthorised trafficking of weapons, nuclear material or radioactive substances, hazardous waste, counterfeit money or drugs,
2.    which, as a result, aims at large-scale enrichment or considerable influence on political or economic life, and
3.    which aims to corrupt or intimidate others or to shield itself from prosecution measures in a special way".[89]

By inserting this penal provision the legislator aimed to make the fight against organised crime easier.[90] For instance, it is no longer necessary to wait with criminal investigations, especially with special investigation instruments (methods) available under criminal procedure law, until the members of the criminal organisation have committed a crime traditionally foreseen in the Criminal Code (e.g. murder). So a proactive fight against organised crime with special criminal investigation instruments can be launched instead of only using the less effective crime prevention measures available under security police law. Furthermore, it is no longer necessary to prove that an offender who is involved in organised crime has taken part in a conventional crime; instead, the proof that he is a member of the organisation behind it – proof which is often easier to produce – is already sufficient.[91]

From the fact that § 278a StGB should make it easier to fight organised crime, one may conclude that crimes (*criminal* offences) behind which there is a criminal organisation should be considered as organised crime.[92] It still needs to be clarified, however, what the nature and intensity of the connection should be between a criminal organisation and a specific crime in order for the respective crime to be classified as organised crime. In addition, it is an open question as to whether any type of crime[93] behind which there is a criminal organisation is organised crime or whether only the committing of crimes contained in the list of § 278a section 1 No. 1 StGB should be regarded as organised crime.

When in their daily work authorities have to distinguish between organised crime and other crimes, they use indicators and/or characteristics typical of organised crime.[94] These help them to recognise (probable) organised crimes, but do not constitute a definition of organised crime.[95]

In Austria organised crime takes place especially in the fields of the smuggling of persons, trafficking in persons, trafficking in addictive substances and money laundering; in addition, there is organised theft (in particular burglary and car theft) and various types of fraud.[96] This list is however not exhaustive and changes constantly, as organised crime continually adapts to new possibilities to make illegal profits.

In Austria it is controversial whether ideologically and politically motivated crime which is not primarily aimed at seeking profit – i.e. crimes based on extremism and terrorism – should be excluded from the concept of organised crime.[97] Finally it seems important to mention, that instead of the term "organised crime" sometimes the term "professional crime" is used in Austria.

### b) The postulated "danger of organised crime" – a catalyst for more organised prevention and more organised prosecution of crime in general

Although in Austria organised crime has existed for a longer time, it is only about 10 years ago that security authorities as well as the literature began to deal with the dangers and the ways to fight organised crime more intensively and publicly.[98] In this respect the discussion has been highly controversial. On the one hand, it was demanded that – with a view to the grave dangers posed by organised crime – special investigation methods to fight organised crime should be permitted, while, on the other hand, the resulting and inevitable conflicts with individual and civil rights were pointed out.[99] In the end new investigation methods (techniques) have been permitted, while at the same time special control mechanisms have been developed which should protect against abuse of these new possibilities and prevent unnecessary infringements of the rights of law-abiding citizens.[100]

It is interesting that those special investigation measures, which were demanded and finally permitted as a result of (mainly) arguments about the dangers of organised crime being put forward, can as a result be used not only in the fight against organised crime, but also in the fight against other crimes which were hardly mentioned (in the public debate) as reasons for introducing the new investigation methods.[101] So, it may be said that the emphasis on the "danger of organised crime" in Austria is acting as a catalyst and thus expediting innovations which in their turn – and perhaps even mainly – are being applied in other fields.[102]

In view of what can be seen in Austria, similar developments may occur there where legal acts of the EU recommend or call for measures to achieve better (organised) cooperation with the other Member States in the joint fight against organised crime. These measures also appear to be useful in the fight against non-organised crime and are also applied in such areas, e.g. to fight one single internationally active blackmailer or to prosecute a small but supra-regionally active group of swindlers (in the field of insurance or subsidies). However, they can also be used, for instance, to prosecute a murderer who after committing his crime disappeared from one Member State and went to another. The need for stronger Europe-wide cooperation in crime prevention and criminal prosecution in a common Europe as well as the creation of European central bureaux and coordination offices in this field is also clear, regardless of the threat posed by organised crime. Here too, the following applies: the debate on organised crime acts as a catalyst to the measures which are sensible irrespective of the phenomenon of organised crime.

## 4. SPECIAL UNITS TO FIGHT ORGANISED CRIME AND NATIONAL CONTACT POINTS

An interministerial coordination department for finance agencies, law enforcement agencies and perhaps also for the public prosecution service and the criminal courts[103] does not exist yet.

### a) At the level of the law enforcement agencies

The national law enforcement units to fight organised crime and the national central contact point at the level of the law enforcement agencies have been set up at the Federal Ministry of the Interior within Department II: Directorate General for Public Security (*Sektion II: Generaldirektion für die öffentliche Sicherheit*). They are concentrated within Subdepartment II/D: Criminal Investigation – Interpol (*Gruppe II/D: Kriminalpolizei – Interpol*), namely within the divisions (*Abteilung*) II/8, II/9 and II/10.[104] But also Subdepartment II/C: State Police (*Gruppe II/C: Staatspolizei*) accommodates some special units which among other tasks fight organised crime.[105]

### aa) Division II/8 – Central office for the fight against organised crime and drugs-related crimes

The central office for the fight against organised crime (*Zentralstelle zur Bekämpfung der organisierten Kriminalität*) is Division II/8.[106] Officially Division II/8 was set up as central office for the fight against organised crime in 1995.

This division is the central bureau of the law enforcement agencies not only for the fight against organised crime, but also for the fight against drugs-related crimes.

Division II/8 is particularly responsible for managing and coordinating the work of the Austrian law enforcement agencies in the fight against organised crime[107] and drugs-related crimes, it acts as a communications office for other agencies dealing with organised crime and drugs-related crimes, and is responsible for international police cooperation in these matters, especially within the framework of Interpol, Europol and as the central body pursuant to Art. 39, 40 and 46 Schengen Convention.[108]

Furthermore, some units for the specialised fight against organised crime have been placed in Division II/8, such as, in particular, the financial intelligence unit.[109]

### bb) Specialised central units for the fight against organised crime

By ordinance (the so-called *"Sondereinheiten-Verordnung"*), the Federal Minister of the Interior can form special units (*Sondereinheiten*) to fight criminal liaisons, hence also organisations which are supportive of organised crime, and put them in charge of the exclusive or selective performance of this task in the whole of Austria.[110] At the moment there are four such special units, namely:

- the Task Force for the Fight against Drugs-Related Crime (*Einsatzgruppe zur Bekämpfung der Suchtgiftkriminalität = EBS*), which dates back to 1981;
- the Task Force for the Fight against Terrorism (*Einsatzgruppe zur Bekämpfung des Terrorismus = EBT*), which was established in 1987;
- the Task Force for the Fight against Organised Crime (*Einsatzgruppe der Gruppe D zur Bekämpfung der organisierten Kriminalität = EDOK*), which was founded in 1993; and
- the Special Unit for Surveillance (*Sondereinheit für Observation = SEO*), which was established in 1998.[111]

However, the special units *EBS*, *EBT* and *SEO* are not only active in fighting organised crime, but also have other special tasks in the fields of drugs-related crime, terrorism and special observation.[112]

**EBS**   The task of the *EBS* is to fight supraregional or organised drugs-related crime; it is part of Department II: Directorate General for Public Security. An important condition for the efficient functioning of the *EBS* is close international cooperation. This cooperation takes place especially in the framework of the International Criminal Police Organisation ICPO/Interpol and through contact with foreign liaison officers. Especially useful in the field of the fight against organised drugs-related crime is the cooperation with the Austrian liaison officers of the European Drugs Unit – EDU/Europol.[113]

**EBT**   Besides fighting organised crime in the fields of arms trade, industrial espionage, technology transfer and smuggling persons, the *EBT* also fights ideologically motivated or political crime and gang violence. Because of these special tasks the *EBT* is part of Subdepartment II/C: State Police (not of Subdepartment II/D: Criminal Investigation – Interpol).

**EDOK**  The *EDOK* has also been set up within Department II: Directorate General for Public Security. Its task is to fight organised crime in fields where the *EBS* or the *EBT* do not have competence. An important objective of this special unit is to extract, collect, analyse and pass on information about organised crime. For this purpose, information is exchanged quickly through direct contacts with similar special units abroad.[114]

**SEO**   The task of the *SEO*, which is directly subordinated to the Directorate-General for Public Security[115], is to carry out all hidden (visual and audio) surveillance of non-public occurrences with the help of technical instruments in accordance with § 149d section 1 No. 3 StPO (so-called *"schwerer Lausch- und/oder Spähangriff"*). It is also responsible for the protection against interception of secret information, in so far as this interception involves a "dangerous attack" carried out with technical means in the framework of organised crime and the use of advanced technology is required for this protection.[116]

#### cc) Financial intelligence unit

Since 1994 Division II/8 also contains the Austrian financial intelligence unit[117] (*Meldestelle nach § 41 Bankwesengesetz für verdächtige Bank-transaktionen = Meldestelle für Geldwäscherei*) as provided for by Art. 6 of the Money Laundering Directive.[118]

#### dd) ENU

The Europol National Unit – ENU (*Nationale Europol-Einheit*), as provided for in Art. 4 of the Europol Convention[119] has also been placed within Division

II/8, but in a separate subdivision (Subdivision II/8/a; *Referat II/8/a*) and has been in existence since 1998.

### ee) SIRENE bureau
The Austrian SIRENE bureau was set up in 1997 in the framework of Subdepartment II/D: Criminal Investigation – Interpol within Division II/10 as a separate subdivision (Subdivision II/10/a: SIRENE Austria, *Referat II/ 10/a: SIRENE Österreich*).[120]

### ff) NCB (Interpol)
Subdepartment II/D: Criminal Investigation – Interpol[121] forms, as a whole, the Austrian NCB (*Nationales Zentralbüro = NZB*) of the International Criminal Police Organisation;[122] the management tasks and coordination tasks of the NCB is the responsibility of Division II/9[123] (while especially Division II/8 and Division II/10 are in charge of providing and using official assistance in Interpol matters[124]).

### gg) Other central units
Division II/10 acts additionally, and in particular, as the central office for the fight against crime involving counterfeit money, pornography, trafficking in persons or international trafficking in stolen motor vehicles, and since 1997 it has also included a reporting office for child pornography.

There also is a reporting office for right-wing extremism in Subdepartment II/C: State Police.

### hh) Local units
Besides the special units within the Federal Ministry of the Interior, the subordinate law enforcement agencies also have special units for the fight against organised crime (*OK Gruppen*).[125] In addition, in order to fight specific associations (e.g. of special organised, internationally active gangs of burglars), ad hoc special task commissions (*Sonderkommissionen*) with representatives from the foreign law enforcement agencies concerned are used.[126]

### ii) National contact point
As far as organised crime is concerned the international contact point at the level of the law enforcement agencies is Subdepartment II/D: Criminal Investigation – Interpol, especially Division II/8.

## b) At the Federal Ministry of Finance

In the fight against organised fiscal crimes (and organised fiscal administrative offences)[127] the Federal Ministry of Finance is becoming increasingly important as the central contact point for foreign authorities and as the national coordination office.

In 1995, when Austria acceded to the EU, Division III/8[128] of the Federal Ministry of Finance was set up as the central anti-fraud and anti-drugs unit in the field of customs and excise.[129] One of its areas of responsibility is the prevention and detection of organised fiscal offences partially with the aim of launching criminal proceedings.[130] In this context, operations of the participating units of the customs administration are coordinated centrally.

Another task of Division III/8 of the Federal Ministry of Finance is coordinating with the Federal Ministry of the Interior and the Federal Ministry of Justice in the fight against organised crime in the field of customs and excise.

Division III/8 is also the central authority for national, bilateral and Community assistance and cooperation in customs and excise affairs.[131]

Furthermore, it can carry out all assistance operations in customs matters (except for penal procedures relating to fiscal offences) and decide on requests coming from abroad regarding surveillance, controlled deliveries or the sending of investigation officers.

Altogether Division III/8 functions as the international contact point for organised crime in the area of customs (e.g. smuggling) and excise.[132] It has regular contact with all the central customs offices dealing with fraud prevention in the neighbouring states. Furthermore, it is the Austrian contact point for OLAF (formerly UCLAF) as far as customs matters and import/export matters are concerned.

## c) At the level of the public prosecution service

Organisational changes in the public prosecution service with a view to fighting organised crime have so far hardly been made. Only the Public Prosecutor's Office in Vienna has had a special section for organised crime since 1994/95.

The function of a central coordinating body at the level of the public prosecution service (*zentrale Koordinationsstelle für den Bereich aller staatsanwaltschaftlichen Behörden*) is traditionally performed by the Federal Ministry of Justice.

The international contact point for the public prosecution service has always been at the Federal Ministry of Justice, within Department IV:

Departrment for Penal Matters and Clemency Cases (*Sektion IV: Sektion Straf- und Gnadensachen*).

In addition, the Federal Ministry of Justice traditionally also acts as a central contact point for dealing with foreign requests for information on Austrian legislation, jurisdiction and legal proceedings.

### d) EJN

The Action Plan to Combat Organised Crime foresees the creation of a network for judicial cooperation at European level.[133] This includes the establishment of contact points in all EU Member States which communicate with each other and exchange service material under the direction of a central contact point at the Council of the European Union in Brussels. The network made from the contact points of all Member States will be known as the European Judicial Network (*Europäisches Justitielles Netzwerk – EJN*). In Austria, five contact points were established in 1998, one at the Federal Ministry of Justice (in the framework of Division IV/1), the other four at various Regional Courts.[134] It is notable that Austria is the only state where contact point directors are for the most part judges, namely in the Regional Courts.[135]

### 5.   MULTIDISCIPLINARY INTEGRATED TEAMS

Multidisciplinary integrated teams at the national level[136] have so far only been established in a very few cases and as temporary teams. Their job has always been to deal with a particular case of severe crime, for example a series of letter bombs.[137]

In 1991, a local task force was set up for Vienna, namely the working group to combat organised crime (*Arbeitsgruppe zur Bekämpfung des organisierten Verbrechens – ARBOV*). This working group consisted of members of the law enforcement agencies, finance authorities and the Public Prosecutor's Office in Vienna as well as judges from the criminal courts and administrative officers from the municipality of Vienna (especially of the *Gewerbebehörde*). The aim of this working group was to improve cooperation in practice, thereby enabling more efficient measures to be taken against organised crime. It was quite effective and therefore a further strengthening of this working group was planned.[138] But today there is no need for this working group any longer, because of the abovementioned national Task Force for the Fight against Organised Crime (*Einsatzgruppe der Gruppe D zur Bekämpfung der organisierten Kriminalität = EDOK*).[139]

## 6. SUPERVISION AND CONTROL

### a) General structure

*aa)* In principle all **administrative bodies** (the law enforcement agencies, the public prosecution service and the finance authorities) come under the direction of the superior administrative bodies; at the top of the hierarchy, within the area of federal administration,[140] is the appropriate federal minister. The power to direct the administration also gives the right of supervision over subordinated bodies, as direction without a right of supervision is inconceivable.[141] Internal supervision and direction are exercised mainly through instructions, as well as through annulment or amendment of decisions.[142] The highest authority, the competent federal minister, has final responsibility for the entire administration.[143]

As the highest authority in the federal administration, federal ministers are subject to a (usually *a posteriori*) parliamentary review.[144]

Decisions of first instance as well as acts of direct administrative power and compulsion can be contested:[145] against decisions there is in principle an appeal stage to the superior authority.[146] However, decisions in proceedings concerning administrative offences (*Verwaltungsstrafverfahren*), as well as acts of direct administrative power and compulsion, are contested to the responsible (quasi-judicial) Independent Administrative Tribunal (*UVS*).[147] After these possibilities to appeal have been exhausted, a complaint (*Beschwerde*) can usually be made before the Administrative Court (*Verwaltungsgerichtshof*) or the Constitutional Court (*Verfassungsgerichtshof*).[148]

Finally the entire federal administration undergoes the – usually *a posteriori* – review by the People's Advocates' Office (*Volksanwaltschaft*).[149] This Office is an institution offering action to remedy those grievances in the administration which cannot be addressed through specific legal remedies. Though an institution specific to Austria, it has similarities to the Scandinavian Ombudsman.[150]

*bb)* Unlike the administrative bodies, the **judges in the criminal courts** (in exercising their *judicial office*) are autonomous;[151] legal protection is provided above all through the possibility of appealing against judicial decisions and delays. This is also the case for the investigating judge, against whom there are particularly extensive possibilities for complaints.[152]

*cc)* According to the Austrian DSG 2000 (= *Datenschutzgesetz 2000*; Data Protection Act 2000) each individual has a "Constitutional Right to Data Protection" (*Grundrecht auf Datenschutz*), i.e. especially to the observance of the secrecy of personal data as far as that individual has an interest which merits its protection.[153] The monitoring institutions set up to safeguard data protection are the autonomous Data Protection Board (*Datenschutz-kommission*) and the Data Protection Committee (*Datenschutzrat*). Alongside other tasks,[154] the Data Protection Board has, in particular, the function of an instance of appeal.[155]

### b) Particularities of preliminary proceedings

Complaints about decisions of the public prosecutor (at the Public Prosecutor's Office) can be addressed to the chief of the Public Prosecutor's Office, to the Senior Public Prosecutor's Office or to the Federal Minister of Justice (*Aufsichtsbeschwerde*).[156] Complaints (*Beschwerden*) about a decision, an action or a delay of the investigating judge can be addressed to the Counsel Chamber (*Ratskammer*),[157] or in certain cases to the Court of Appeal.[158] As far as the law enforcement agencies perform criminal investigations according to the instruction of a public prosecutor within provisional inquiries (*Vorerhebungen*) or of an investigating judge within the judicial investigations (*Voruntersuchung*), the public prosecutor and the investigating judge, respectively, are responsible. As such, in these cases appeals are only possible against the decision of the public prosecutor or the investigating judge.

Certain serious procedural enforcement by means of coercion must be ordered in advance by the Counsel Chamber; in urgent cases, when a further delay is likely to frustrate the aim of the individual criminal investigation, the investigating judge can order the measures, but this order must normally be subsequently approved by the Counsel Chamber.

If the executive bodies (within the law enforcement agencies) exceed the instructions of the public prosecutor or the criminal court (investigating judge, Counsel Chamber), the security offices are responsible. Such an act of direct administrative power and compulsion[159] can be contested before the Independent Administrative Tribunal (*UVS*).[160]

As far as the security offices act within their autonomous competence, because a further delay is likely to frustrate the aim of the individual criminal investigation,[161] they are subject to the supervision of the superior bodies within the security offices.[162]

### c) Supervision and Controls of special investigation techniques

In 1997/98 new kinds of investigation techniques were introduced in the StPO: in particular, different forms of hidden electronic (audio and visual) surveillance of non-public activities/events with the help of technical instruments (so-called *"Lausch- und/oder Spähangriff"*) provided for in § 149d section 1 StPO and the search for unknown offenders by screening devices (so-called *"Rasterfahndung"*) provided for in § 149i StPO. In a *"Lausch- und/oder Spähangriff"* the non-public activity/event is filmed or the sound is recorded, or the occurrence is listened to or observed. In a *"Rasterfahndung"* usually files which presumably contain special personal data of the unknown offender are linked and compared by computer, so as to tighten the circle of suspects.[163]

The most far-reaching forms of both *"Lausch- und/oder Spähangriff"* and *"Rasterfahndung"* (§ 149d section 1 No. 3[164] and § 149i section 2 StPO respectively) were introduced to tackle organised crime in particular.[165] Both may only be ordered by the court (usually by the Counsel Chamber) at the request of the public prosecutor. In order to reduce democratic objections to these two far-reaching special powers of intervention, the following provisions for control were introduced at the same time:[166]

- Where there is an intention to request one of the two abovementioned special measures, the Public Prosecutor's Office must notify the locally responsible Senior Public Prosecutor's Office.[167]
- An independent and autonomous Commissioner for Legal Protection (*Rechtsschutzbeauftragter*) was established, an institution which is new in Europe.[168] The Commissioner's office is located at the Supreme Court. Among other things he has the task of controlling the implementation of both of the previously mentioned most far-reaching investigation techniques, and the possibility to lodge a complaint against it.[169]
- The decision by the Court ordering the *"Rasterfahndung"* must be immediately presented to the Data Protection Board (*Datenschutz-kommission*), which can lodge complaints against the decision with the Court of Appeal.
- The execution of a *"Lauschangriff"* provided for in § 149d section 1 No. 3 StPO should only be done by the special unit *SEO*.[170] Thereby the execution of this serious investigative measure should only be carried out by a few officers, through which the strict protection of professional secrecy can be better secured.[171]

It is interesting to note that the introduction of these measures was initially only made for four years; the relevant regulations expire on 31 December 2001. The legislator firstly wants to collect experience on these measures before it takes a definitive decision on a lasting adoption.

## 7. SIGNS AND DRAFTS OF FUNDAMENTAL CHANGES IN FUTURE

### a) Reform of the criminal preliminary proceedings

As already mentioned, the concept in the StPO for preliminary proceedings – particularly in mostly having an investigating judge direct the investigations (*"judicial* investigations") – in practice never really established itself.[172] Therefore nobody nowadays doubts the necessity of reform. In April 1998, a draft for discussion (*Diskussionsentwurf*) was produced by the Federal Ministry of Justice (JMZ 578.017/2-II.3/1998). As this draft produced generally positive reactions,[173] it will most probably serve as the basis for a reform of the law.[174]

According to the draft for discussion, judicial investigations (*Voruntersuchung*) in particular, as well as the investigating judge, should be abolished. In future, instead of provisional inquiries (*Vorerhebungen*) and judicial investigations there should only be a single kind of continuous preliminary proceedings. The structure of this investigative procedure should be compatible with most rules of procedure of the Member States and thereby able to provide a guarantee for "maximally effective cross-border cooperation".[175]

The draft for discussion envisages investigations being to a large extent left to the law enforcement agencies. As soon as there is suspicion of an offence, they should immediately take action and carry out the investigative procedure, without having to wait for an order of the public prosecutor or a criminal court. As the law enforcement agencies have most experience in criminal investigations, they are best able to carry them out and it makes sense that the law enforcement agencies in principle choose the most suitable investigative measures in specific cases and decide about the time and nature of their actions as well as about coordination with other investigative activities. So one can proceed on the assumption that *in principle* the investigative activity will be as a whole in the hands of the law enforcement agencies.[176]

At the same time, however, according to the draft for discussion the public prosecutor remains at the head of the investigative procedure.[177] That is expedient! It will continue to be a central task of the public prosecutor to decide whether due to the results of the investigation a charge will be made. The prosecutor must also formulate the charge and, in further procedures, judge whether instead of the charge a *"Diversion"* (diversional measure; out of court solution according to §§ 90a et seq. StPO) should be worked for. It is therefore logical and economical to give the public prosecutor the opportunity to set the course for the investigations from the beginning, to assign special investigations or to personally conduct specific investigations (particularly the questioning of the accused or a witness),[178] to ensure that the facts which the prosecutor needs to make his/her decisions and – if necessary – to bring a charge and which are important in the final oral hearing (= main trial) are actually collected.[179] To aid the public prosecutor better fulfil his/her role as director of the proceedings, it is planned that the security offices will regularly report to the prosecutor on the investigations and their results.[180]

Making the public prosecutor the director of the investigative process does not however mean that he/she has an obligation to provide *permanent* supervision or control for the *entire* criminal investigation.[181]

Procedural means of coercion and similar serious special investigative methods and techniques (e.g. observation[182]) may also in principle not be carried out by the law enforcement agencies without a priori supervision: with less serious measures, the approval of the public prosecutor is necessary, in the case of serious measures, additional supervision by the court is necessary.

Instead of the investigating judge, there will be a so-called "judge of the preliminary proceedings" (*Richter des Ermittlungsverfahrens*), who will be involved solely as a result of a specific request and is never to be the director of the proceedings. He/she should mainly offer legal protection and besides that only carry out certain special hearings of evidence, particularly hearings involving the active participation of all parties (*Tatrekonstruktion und kontradiktorische Einvernahme von Zeugen und Beschuldigten*).[183]

According to the draft for discussion where there is no investigating judge, who by the Austrian people is seen as a special guarantor of the rule of law in the framework of criminal investigations, this omission is compensated by other control mechanisms. The law enforcement agencies, which for the most part carry out criminal investigations independently, are subject to the internal supervision of both the superior authorities and the public prosecutor, who can intervene in the investigations at any time.[184]

The public prosecutor is subject to internal supervision by his superior authorities, and in the draft for discussion the point is made that the internal control mechanisms of the superior authorities should be strengthened.[185] On the other hand, the issue of limiting the right to give instructions to the public prosecutor (particularly the right of the Federal Minister of Justice), so as to avoid politically motivated intervention in criminal investigations has arisen in public debate.

In addition the draft for discussion aims to introduce a new, comprehensive legal remedy: a person who feels that any of his/her rights have been violated by the procedure of the public prosecution service or the law enforcement agencies should be able to raise an objection (*Einspruch*) in the court, which will be adjudicated by the "judge of the preliminary proceedings".[186] In this way a stage of appeal against the decisions of administrative bodies (law enforcement agencies, public prosecution service) will be opened up in the courts, which up to now does not exist in this form.

For some cases, particularly against decisions of the "judge of the preliminary proceedings", a complaint (*Beschwerde*) to the court of appeal is envisaged.[187]

## b) Changes within the public prosecution service

The strengthened inclusion and responsibility of the public prosecution service in the new investigative procedures implies a need for internal organisational changes.[188] In particular the establishment of teams of public prosecutors who have received special technical training is being considered (who could be responsible for the whole federal territory) in order to ensure more efficient investigation in dealing with complex criminal matters, e.g. such as organised crime.[189]

## c) Changes within the law enforcement agencies

In the area of law enforcement agencies there are also plans for fundamental innovations in the organisation – at least in the long term. As such, account must be taken of the demands posed by the fight against organised crime as well as the reform of the preliminary proceedings.[190]

A fundamental change in the organisation is urgently required;[191] as the existence of three different types of security offices at the same level (Federal Police Directorates, District Authorities and mayors of the towns with their own charter), the coexistence of three – sometimes competing – guard units (Gendarmerie, Federal Security Guards and Criminal Investigation Unit)[192] and the sometimes outdated and often impractical splitting up of tasks, legal powers and responsibilities between the security offices and their executive bodies[193] repeatedly lead to problems of coordination (e.g. parallel investigations of the same matter) or to considerable delays in the common completion of tasks or in the transfer of tasks to other agencies.

The first innovation that is planned is the creation of a Federal Office of Criminal Investigation (*Bundeskriminalbehörde, Bundeskriminalamt*) comparable to the German Bundeskriminalamt in Wiesbaden. This Federal Office of Criminal Investigation will either be an integral part of the Federal Ministry of the Interior or be directly subordinate to it.[194] The new authority should be the higher authority of all criminal investigation units at the Security Directorates. It will to a large extent replace the Subdepartment II/D: Criminal Investigation – Interpol (*Gruppe II/D: Kriminalpolizei* – Interpol) of the Federal Ministry of the Interior and primarily deal with coordination and analysis. However, it will not take part in operations.[195]

As a following step, reforms at the lower levels of the law enforcement agencies are to be expected.[196] One suggestion is that all competences of the law enforcement agencies in connection with severe crimes should be concentrated directly at the Security Directorates and not remain at the different subordinated law enforcement agencies. For that purpose Regional Offices of Criminal Investigation (*Landeskriminalämter*) should be installed at the Security Directorates in all federal states. As a consequence, the subordinated departments of criminal investigation (*Kriminalabteilung; kriminalpolizeiliche Abteilung*), e.g. those within the Federal Police Directorates, would only be responsible for dealing with less severe crimes. To realise these organisational changes many officers now working at the subordinated departments of criminal investigation would have to move to the new Regional Offices of Criminal Investigation.[197]

In the long run a fusion of the Gendarmerie with the other guard units is to be expected; however, the details as to which structures should be created have not yet been fully discussed. Pooling all guard units would make the organisational structures more transparent and also reduce costs, which are now incurred through the repeated acquisition of specialised equipment.[198]

**NOTES**

1.  Therefore the territory of a district usually includes the territory of more than one commune or municipality.
2.  Criminal courts are either District Courts (*Bezirksgericht*), Regional Courts (*Gerichtshof erster Instanz = Landesgericht*) or Jury Courts installed at the Regional Courts (*Geschworenengericht*). Regional Courts are located in most big towns. For the purposes of second instance decisions there are four Courts of Appeal (*Gerichtshof zweiter Instanz = Oberlandesgericht*), located in Vienna, Graz, Linz and Innsbruck, and one Supreme Court (*Oberster Gerichtshof*), which is located in Vienna.

    At each Regional Court there is a Counsel Chamber (*chambre du conseil*; *Ratskammer*), which is a panel of three judges dealing especially with complaints against decisions of the investigating judge (for the investigating judge see infra 2. b) and 6. b)) and deciding on certain procedural means of coercion; for more details see *Kessel*, Die Ratskammer nach dem StPÄG 1993, JBl 1995, pp. 291 et seq. and pp. 364 et seq.
3.  In special cases also the Austrian Military can be involved in the fight against crime, primarily in crime prevention. The new MBG (= *Militärbefugnisgesetz*; Military Authority Act) which entered into force on 1 July 2001 authorizes military persons and agencies to special actions and provisions that serve to protect military interests and goods (e.g. life and health of soldiers, military objects or secrets) against criminal attacks, for example a looting of an ordnance depot.

    For the duties of the finance authorities within the fight against criminality see infra before note 4 and under 1. b) as well as under 4. b).
4.  See infra under 1. b).
5.  *Giese*, Sicherheitspolizeirecht, in: *Bachmann* et al (eds.), Besonderes Verwaltungsrecht, 2$^{nd}$ edition., 1998, p. 24; compare also *Bundesministerium für Inneres. Gendarmeriezentralkommando* (ed.), Die Bundesgendarmerie im 3. Jahrtausend – Grundsatzpapier, 1999, p. II (*"ausnahmslos die Behörden auch für ein selbständiges Exekutivhandeln des Wachkörpers Bundesgendarmerie verantwortlich"*) and p. 9. – But for the special case in which law enforcement agencies perform criminal investigations according to the instruction of a public prosecutor or of an investigating judge see below under 6. b).
6.  Art. 78a et seq. B-VG (= *Bundes-Verfassungsgesetz*; Confederal Constitution); §§ 6 et seq. SPG (= *Sicherheitspolizeigesetz*; Security Police Act).
7.  *Wiederin*, Einführung in das Sicherheitspolizeirecht, 1998, marginal notes 171, 177.
8.  § 4 section 3 SPG, § 24 StPO (= *Strafprozessordnung*; Code of Criminal Procedure). For details see *Hauer/Keplinger*, Handbuch zum Sicherheitspolizeigesetz, 1993, comment No. 13 on § 4 SPG; *idem*, StPO. Erläuterungen zur Strafprozeßordnung für Exekutivorgane, 1997, comment No. I. a. on § 24 StPO; *Wiederin* (note 7) marginal note 188.
9.  The Federal Security Guards and the Criminal Investigation Unit *together* are

often called the Federal Police (*Bundespolizei*); cf. Art. 10 section 1 No. 14 B-VG; *R. Faber*, Die Wachkörper und das Erste Bundesrechtsbereinigungsgesetz, JRP 2000, p. 36 (there note 14).

10. For the tasks and the legal status of the Gendarmerie see *Bundesministerium für Inneres. Gendarmeriezentralkommando* (note 5) pp. 3-9, especially chapter 2.3. and 2.4.

11. § 1 Gendarmeriegesetz 1918. See *Moos*, Menschenrechte und Polizei in geschichtlicher Entwicklung, in: *Fehérváry/Stangl* (eds.), Menschenrechte und Staatsgewalt, 2000, pp. 36 et seq. See further to the Gendarmerie nowadays and to its history the numerous reports in: *Hörmann/Hesztera* (eds.), Zwischen Gefahr und Berufung. Gendarmerie in Österreich, 1999.

12. As subdepartment B of the Directorate General for Public Security (*Gruppe B der Generaldirektion für die öffentliche Sicherheit = Gruppe II/B*).

13. The members of the guard corps are employees of that Federal Police Directorate to which they are attached; see *Hauer/Keplinger,* Handbuch (note 8) comment No. 14 on § 5 SPG; *Wiederin* (note 7) marginal note 195.

14. Compare *Bundesministerium für Inneres. Gendarmeriezentralkommando* (note 5) p. 3; *Wiederin* (note 7) marginal note 196.

15. Like the members of the Federal Security Guards, the members of the guard corps of the Criminal Investigation Unit are also employees of the Federal Police Directorate to which they are attached. See *Adamovich/Funk*, Allgemeines Verwaltungsrecht, 3rd edition, 1987, p. 174; *Wiederin* (note 7) marginal note 197.

16. *Wiederin* (note 7) marginal note 197. – Outside the towns where there is a Federal Police Directorate the criminal investigations are in general performed by the Gendarmerie with its special Departments of Criminal Investigation (*Kriminalabteilung*).

17. *Wiederin* (note 7) marginal note 198.

18. § 5 section 1 and section 2 No. 4 SPG: *"Gemeindewachkörper"* (communal police guard unit). Particularly relevant are the executive duties of the District Authorities (§ 9 section 3 and section 4 SPG; on this regulation see *Dearing* [ed.], Sicherheitspolizeigesetz, 1999, comment on § 9 SPG). – Whether communal police units (*Gemeindewachen*) that are not guard units are authorised to carry out criminal investigations on behalf of mayors acting as a security office as provided for in § 24 StPO is not clear; apparently for such a competence *Hauer/Keplinger*, StPO (note 8) comment No. I. a. on § 24 StPO; apparently against it *Wiederin* (note 7) marginal note 198.

On the communal police guard units in general see: *R. Faber*, Die Neuordnung der Gemeindewachkörper durch die B-VG–Novelle 1999, ZfV 1999, pp. 828 et seq; *Keplinger*, Die verfassungsrechtlichen Neuerungen für Gemeindewachkörper, ÖGZ 1999 No. 9, pp. 25 et seq.

19. Compare *Dearing*, Sicherheitspolizei und Strafrechtspflege. Versuch einer Bestimmung des Verhältnisses zweier benachbarter Rechtsgebiete, in: *Fuchs/Brandstetter* (eds.), Festschrift für Winfried Platzgummer, 1995, pp. 225 et seq.

20. § 2 section 2 and § 3 SPG.

21. Especially § 21 section 1 in connection with § 16 section 1 SPG; with respect to organised crime *Fuchs*, Sicherheitspolizei und Gefahrbegriff, in: *Huber/ Jesionek/Miklau* (eds.), Festschrift für Reinhard Moos, 1997, pp. 193 et seq. – On special duties of the Austrian Military in the field of crime prevention see note 3.

22. The PolKG determines the scope of duties of the security offices and of the national central bodies in the field of international police cooperation (especially in the case of security police and criminal investigation) as well as with which authority a complaint can be launched against actions of Austrian law enforcement agencies in foreign countries or of foreign law enforcement agencies within the Austrian Federal territory; for more details see *Schwaighofer/Ebensperger*, Internationale Rechtshilfe in strafrechtlichen Angelegenheiten, 2001, pp. 79 et seq.

23. § 21 section 1 and section 2 in connection with § 16 section 1 No. 1, section 2 and section 3 SPG.

24. § 21 section 1 in connection with § 16 section 1 No. 2 SPG.

25. Especially §§ 26, 36, 88 StPO; see also Art. V EGVG (= *Einführungsgesetz zu den Verwaltungsverfahrensgesetzen*); see further PolKG (for the PolKG see note 22). The following explanations are only valid for the proceedings at the Regional Courts. The diverging proceedings at the District Courts are not relevant in the context of this report because District Courts hardly deal with organised crime.

26. § 24: "*wenn das unverzügliche Einschreiten des Untersuchungsrichters nicht erwirkt werden kann, die keinen Aufschub gestattenden vorbereitenden Anordnungen*", § 141 and § 177 StPO; cf. *Moos* (note 11) pp. 35 et seq; compare also *Bertel/Venier*, Grundriß des österreichischen Strafprozeßrechts, 6th edition, 2000, marginal note 551; *Hauer/Keplinger*, StPO (note 8) comment No. I. d. on § 24 StPO. On § 24 StPO see moreover note 29.

27. § 97 section 2 StPO. An exception is solely foreseen by § 90k StPO, which does not concern the criminal procedure in the strict sense, but cases of an out of court solution according to §§ 90a et seq. StPO (*diversionelle Erledigung; Diversion*).

28. Compare infra under 2. a) bb) and under 2. b). For historical background see also *Moos* (note 11) pp. 35 et seq.

29. § 24 StPO only authorises the law enforcement agencies to make the very first inquiries into a criminal case ("*nachforschen*") and beyond that to perform those urgent criminal investigations that cannot be postponed (see note 26); *Foregger/ Kodek*, Die österreichische Strafprozeßordnung. Kurzkommentar, 7th edition, 1997, comment No. II. on § 24 StPO; *Hauer/Keplinger*, StPO (note 8) comment No. I. c.-f. on § 24 StPO; *Kranewitter*, Die Sicherheitsbehörden im Dienst der Strafjustiz, 1990, pp. 22 et seq.; *Platzgummer*, Grundzüge des österreichischen Strafverfahrens, 8th edition, 1997, p. 134.
    On the broadening interpretation of this regulation see *Foregger/Kodek* loc. cit.; *Kranewitter* loc. cit. pp. 29 et seq.

30. Compare *Moos* (note 11) p. 36; see also *Kranewitter* (note 29) pp. 29 et seq.

31. See infra under 7. a).

32. Compare *Ellinger*, Organisierte Kriminalität, Der Kriminalbeamte, November 1991, p. 113; see also infra under 3.a).

33. § 53 FinStrG (= *Finanzstrafgesetz*; Financial Penal Code).

34. § 22 section 2 FinStrG.

35. § 197 FinStrG.

36. For further details about the various Finance Offices see §§ 3 et seq. AVOG (= *Abgabenverwaltungsorganisationsgesetz*).

37. See for further details also §§ 14 et seq. AVOG. – For more information on the organisation of the finance authorities see §§ 1 et seq. AVOG.

38. But for the field of international police cooperation see also § 15 section 1 sentence 1 PolKG (note 22): *"Das Handeln von Zollorganen [im Ausland] ist der Sicherheitsdirektion jenes [Bundes-]Landes zuzurechnen, von dem aus die Zollorgane die Grenze überschritten haben."*

39. § 15 section 1 ZollR-DG (= *Zollrechts-Durchführungsgesetz*).

40. Cf. above under aa).

41. As regards the competence of other Customs Offices (*Zollämter*) in the simplified procedure see § 58 section 1 lit. g. FinStrG.

42. Whenever fiscal offences fall under the courts' jurisdiction due to their severity, which means they are fiscal crimes, the finance authorities may participate in the preliminary investigations on behalf of the public prosecution service or the criminal courts (cf. above under aa)). In this respect, the public prosecutor and the criminal courts can involve nearly all finance authorities as well as the Customs Guards.

43. § 82 section 1 FinStrG; §§ 115 et seq. FinStrG; see also *Leitner*, Grundzüge des österreichischen Finanzstrafrechts, 1996, pp. 305 et seq.

44. But for some coercive procedural measures, especially for a liberty-restricting coercive measure against the accused in accordance with §§ 85 et seq. FinStrG a ruling (decision) issued by an organ not bound to instructions is needed. Compare, however, § 117 section 2 FinStrG; in this context, *Fellner*, Kommentar zum Finanzstrafgesetz, 5th edition (loose-leaf edition, including the supplementary instalment H from September 1998), §§ 116-118 marginal note 5.

45. For instance, a Customs Office, as finance penal authority, can ask a (general) Finance Office to question a witness who lives in the area of that Finance Office. Each request for assistance should indicate the precise investigation or hearing of evidence that is requested; see for further details *Sommergruber/Reger*, Das Finanzstrafgesetz mit Kommentar, 1990, comment on § 119 FinStrG. – § 119 FinStrG only offers this possibility within the organisation of the federal finance administration; *Sommergruber/Reger* loc. cit. As regards other possibilities of assistance see Art. 22 B-VG and, in addition, § 120 FinStrG.

46. *Dorazil/Harbich*, Finanzstrafgesetz (loose-leaf edition, including the 18th supplementary instalment from March 2000), comment No. 8 on section 2 of § 93.

47. §§ 152, 153 section 3 FinStrG; § 62 section 1 and 3 FinStrG.

48. Art. 129a section 1 No. 2 B-VG.

49. See infra under 6. a).

50. This will never concern a procedure at a District Court; § 196a FinStrG.
51. § 197 FinStrG; for the Customs Guards see above under bb). – In this context the criminal court and the public prosecution service may only ask the finance authorities as well as the Customs Guards to carry out specific concrete investigation measures; the investigation cannot be transferred as a whole; *Dorazil/Harbich* (note 46) comment No. 9 on § 197 FinStrG.
52. § 197 section 1 FinStrG.
53. § 200 section 1 FinStrG; for the term *"Finanzstrafbehörde"* see above under bb).
54. § 48 StPO.
55. Appeals against decisions and decrees of the competent bodies can only be lodged if the StPO provides for such an appeal procedure, *Leitner* (note 43) p. 280, with examples.
56. See infra under 6. a).
57. Art. 129a section 1 No. 2 B-VG.
58. See above under (1).
59. See above in notes 51 and 52.
60. Compare *Bundesministerium für Justiz* (ed.), 150 Jahre Staatsanwaltschaft. 80 Jahre Vereinigung österreichischer Staatsanwälte, 1999.
61. As regards the criminal courts see note 2.
62. For more details see §§ 1 et seq. StAG (= *Staatsanwaltschaftsgesetz*; Public Prosecution Service Act).
63. § 3 section 1 StAG. – The titles of the public prosecutors are: Public Prosecutor (at the Public Prosecutor's Office); Senior Public Prosecutor (*Oberstaatsanwalt*) (at the Senior Public Prosecutor's Office), Deputy Assistant Attorney-General (*Generalanwalt*) and Attorney-General (*Generalprokurator*) (at the Attorney-General's Office); for further details see § 13 section 1 StAG.
64. § 5 section 1 StAG. – In larger prosecution offices the sections have been put together in section-groups, whereby each section can only be in one section-group; § 5 section 3 StAG.
65. Compare above under 1. a) bb).
66. Cf. note 27.
67. § 88 StPO; § 9 DV-StAG; § 197 FinStrG.
68. See § 9 section 2 DV-StAG; compare also § 197 section 2 FinStrG.
69. *Foregger/Kodek* (note 29) comment No. II. on § 88 StPO; *St. Seiler*, Strafprozeßrecht, 3rd edition, 1999, marginal note 521.
70. § 24, § 89 section 1 and section 2, § 141, § 177 StPO; compare also § 197 section 2 FinStrG.
71. Cf. *Moos* (note 11) p. 35: *"Die Voruntersuchung, die nach dem Gesetz die Regelform des Vorverfahrens ist"* ("The judicial investigation, which according to the law is the normal form of preliminary proceedings"). – Compare above under 1. a) bb).
72. For instance, whenever pre-trial detention (*Untersuchungshaft*) must be imposed or in the case of a criminal offence (= crime) which has to be tried by jury (*Geschworenengericht*).

73. § 97 section 1 StPO.
74. § 113 StPO; cf. note 157. – On the Counsel Chamber (*Ratskammer*) see note 2.
75. §§ 3, 34 section 3 StPO.
76. *Bertel/Venier* (note 26) marginal note 236.
77. §§ 90a, 90c et seq. StPO.
78. See above under 1. a) bb) and below under 7. a).
79. §§ 91 section 2, 111 StPO.
80. §§ 97 section 1, 199 section 2 StPO. Compare above under a) bb). – As regards the possibility for appeal under § 113 StPO, which especially exists if the investigating judge has dismissed the request see note 157.
81. For further details on the Counsel Chamber (*Ratskammer*) see note 2.
82. § 90b StPO.
83. §§ 111 et seq. StPO. – If the investigation judge decides to stop the procedure the public prosecutor can lodge an appeal with the Court of Appeal against this decision; § 109 section 2 StPO. .
84. *Aichinger*, Neue Fahndungsmethoden zur Bekämpfung organisierter Kriminalität, 1997, p. 4; *Frotz/Konwitschka*, Vom organisierten Vergehen zum organisierten Verbrechen – Submissionskartelle als organisierte Kriminalität im Bereich des Kartell-, Vergabe- und Strafrechtes, in: *Landesgruppe Österreich der Internationalen Strafrechtsgesellschaft (AIDP)* (ed.), Organisierte Kriminalität und Wirtschaftsrecht, 1998, p. 99; *Kathrein*, Internationale Zusammenarbeit und Rechtshilfe, in: *Landesgruppe Österreich der Internationalen Strafrechtsgesellschaft (AIDP)* (ed.), Die organisierte Kriminalität als Prüfstein des Strafrechtssystems, 1999, p. 395. – Die *Arbeitsgruppe StPO-Reform des Bundesministeriums für Inneres* (ed.), Kriminalpolizei und Strafprozeßreform (1995, pp. 61 et seq.) describes essential aspects but in the end does not give a definition. – The law enforcement agencies orientate themselves by the definition (working term) used in Germany; compare *Edelbacher*, Organisierte Kriminalität in Österreich und Europa, in: *Edelbacher* (ed.), Organisierte Kriminalität in Europa, 1998, p. 31.
85. § 16 section 1 No. 2.
86. *"sobald sich drei oder mehr Menschen mit dem Vorsatz verbinden, fortgesetzt gerichtlich strafbare Handlungen zu begehen"*. – This definition today (since BGBl I 2000 Nr 85, which entered into force 1 October 2000) describes the term "criminal liaison" (*"kriminelle Verbindung"*) but originally it explicitly covered "gang and organised crime"; *Hauer/Keplinger*, Handbuch (note 8) § 16 SPG.
87. *Hauer/Keplinger,* Handbuch (note 8) comment No. 16 on § 16 SPG.
88. Cf. also *Ellinger* (note 32). – The wording of § 16 SPG leaves open whether the creation of the liaison or only premeditated (future) criminal offences constitute gang crime or organised crime. However, since the mere creation of the liaison – without there being additional circumstances – does not carry a (legal or administrative) penalty anywhere, it would not be correct to subsume it under the concept of "crime".
89. *"eine auf längere Zeit angelegte unternehmensähnliche Verbindung einer größeren Zahl von Personen [...]*

1. *die, wenn auch nicht ausschließlich, auf die wiederkehrende und geplante Begehung schwerwiegender strafbarer Handlungen, die das Leben, die körperliche Unversehrtheit, die Freiheit oder das Vermögen bedrohen, oder schwerwiegender strafbarer Handlungen im Bereich der sexuellen Ausbeutung von Menschen, der Schlepperei oder des unerlaubten Verkehrs mit Kampfmitteln, Kernmaterial und radioaktiven Stoffen, gefährlichen Abfällen, Falschgeld oder Suchtmitteln ausgerichtet ist,*
2. *die dadurch eine Bereicherung in großem Umfang oder erheblichen Einfluß auf Politik oder Wirtschaft anstrebt und*
3. *die andere zu korrumpieren oder einzuschüchtern oder sich auf besondere Weise gegen Strafverfolgungsmaßnahmen abzuschirmen sucht". –*

As regards this provision see, for example, *Frotz/Konwitschka* (note 84) pp. 99 et seq.; *Löschnig-Gspandl,* Fight against Organized Crime: Recent Changes to the Catalogue of Statutory Offences and the Confiscation System in Austrian Criminal Law, European Journal of Crime, Criminal Law and Criminal Justice 1997 (volume 5, issue 3), pp. 214 et seq.; *Mayerhofer,* Spezifische Straftatbestände der Organisierten Kriminalität, in: *Landesgruppe Österreich der Internationalen Strafrechtsgesellschaft (AIDP)* (ed.), Die organisierte Kriminalität als Prüfstein des Strafrechtssystems, 1999, pp. 255 et seq.; for further observations and literature references see *Hinterhofer,* Strafrecht Besonderer Teil II, 1999, pp. 188 et seq.

90. Compare JAB Strafgesetznovelle 1993, 1160 BlgNR 18.GP, p. 2.
91. Cf. *Kienapfel,* Bildung einer kriminellen Organisation (§ 278a Abs 1 StGB), JBl 1995, pp. 615 et seq.
92. Compare also EB RV Besondere Ermittlungsmaßnahmen, 49 BlgNR 20.GP, pp. 8, 10.
93. The above considerations about § 16 section 1 No. 2 SPG show that organised crime must always involve a "crime" (offence which has to be punished by a criminal court; "*gerichtlich strafbare Handlung*").
94. *Aichinger* (note 84) pp. 12 et seq.; *Edelbacher,* Das Tor zum Osten, Der Kriminalbeamte, October 1993, pp. 10 et seq.
95. For such lists of indicators see *Edelbacher* (note 84) pp. 35 et seq.; *idem,* Der Kriminalbeamte, October 1993, p. 10; *Hauer/Keplinger,* Handbuch (note 8) comment No. 16 on § 16 SPG.
96. For further details see the report of the federal government about internal security in Austria in 1998 = Sicherheitsbericht 1998, pp. 183 et seq.; see also, *Ebert,* Österreich, in: *Gropp* (ed.), Besondere Ermittlungsmaßnahmen zur Bekämpfung der Organisierten Kriminalität, 1993, p. 572, pp. 574 et seq.; *Edelbacher* (note 84) p. 32, pp. 37 et seq.; EB RV Besondere Ermittlungsmaßnahmen, 49 BlgNR 20.GP, p. 10.
97. See for this view *Arbeitsgruppe StPO-Reform des Bundesministeriums für Inneres* (ed.), (note 84) p. 62; a broader definition of the concept of "organised crime" seems to be supported by *Ellinger,* Der Kriminalbeamte, November 1991, p. 113; EB RV Besondere Ermittlungsmaßnahmen, 49 BlgNR 20.GP, p. 10.

98. The first publications on the subject of organised crime include *Császár*, Die Bekämpfung der organisierten Kriminalität als gesamtgesellschafliche Aufgabe, ÖS 1991 No. 5, pp. 3 et seq.; *Edelbacher*, Der Kriminalbeamte, October 1993, pp. 8 et seq.; *Ellinger*, Der Kriminalbeamte, November 1991, p. 113 et seq.; *Kienapfel*, JBl 1995, pp. 613 et seq. See also *Bundesminsiterium für Justiz* (ed.), Organisierte Kriminalität – Professionelle Ermittlungsarbeit – Neue Herausforderungen, Schriftenreihe des BMJ Band 77, 1995. – As regards the situation in the early nineties see *Ebert* (note 96) p. 572.

99. See, for instance, *Császár*, ÖS 1991 No. 5, pp. 5 et seq.; for references to the discussion see *Schmoller*, Geändertes Erscheinungsbild staatlicher Verbrechensbekämpfung? Zur Diskussion über Lauschangriff, Rasterfahndung, verdeckte Ermittler, Kronzeugen uä, ÖJZ 1996, p. 21.

100. Compare 6. c).

101. For instance, the possibilities, provided for in the StPO, for hidden electronic surveillance (so-called *"Lausch- und/oder Spähangriff"*) or a search for unknown offenders by screening devices (so-called *"Rasterfahndung"*) (compare below under 6. c)) were called for particularly in the light of the dangers posed by organised crime (see e.g. *Császár*, ÖS 1991 No. 5, pp. 7 et seq.; compare also *Bundesministerium für Justiz* [ed.], [note 98]) and finally introduced by a law on the introduction of special investigation methods (techniques) *to fight organised crime* ("*Bundesgesetz, mit dem zur Bekämpfung organisierter Kriminalität besondere Ermittlungsmaßnahmen in die Strafprozessordnung eingeführt [..] werden*", BGBl I 1997 No. 105); cf. also EB RV Besondere Ermittlungsmaß-nahmen, 49 BlgNR 20.GP, p. 8 (Vorblatt), pp. 10 et seq. – In fact, however, even the most far-reaching forms of both "*Lausch- und/oder Spähangriff*" and "*Rasterfahndung*" (§ 149d section 1 No. 3 respectively § 149i section 2 StPO) can now be used not only to fight organised crime, but also to solve any criminal act that is punishable by more than 10 years of imprisonment, in so far as solving such a crime would otherwise be hopeless or far more difficult. Therefore the title of a former draft on the mentioned special investigation methods (JMZ 578.016/1-II.3/95) is more appropriate, namely "Draft-law on special investigation measures in order *to fight serious and organised crime*" (the emphasis has been added).

102. For instance, it was intended to use the new possibility of a "*Rasterfahndung*" (for this term see note 101) to solve a serious crime involving letter bombs in Austria, which were suspected to be the work of a criminal or terrorist organisation (compare EB RV Besondere Ermittlungsmaßnahmen, 49 BlgNR 20.GP, p. 10: „*innerösterreichischer, politisch motivierter Terrorismus*"); however, as has become clear now that the case has been solved, the crime was committed by just one person.

103. As stated in recommendation No. 1 Action Plan to Combat Organised Crime, OJ-EC (*Abl-EG*) 97/C 251/01.

104. Subdepartment II/D: Criminal Investigation – Interpol (*Gruppe II/D: Kriminalpolizei* – Interpol) consists of 6 divisions (II/8 – 12, II/16), 4 subdivisions (*Referat*) and a number of special units.

105. For the organisation of the Directorate-General for Public Security see also above under 1. a) aa).
106. But as far as the fight against crime involving counterfeit money or the fight against pornography, trafficking in persons or international trafficking in stolen motor vehicles is concerned, Division II/8 is not the central office but another division within the same subdepartment, namely Division II/10.
107. So Division II/8 is the central body of coordination as far as the fight against organised crime *at the level of the law enforcement agencies* is concerned. A central national body of coordination for *all* agencies that deal with the fight against organised crime does not yet exist; cf. above around note 103.
108. Schengen Convention = Convention applying the Schengen Agreement of 14 June 1985 between the Governments of the States of The Benelux Economic Union, The Federal Republic of Germany and The French Republic, on the Gradual Abolition of Checks at Common Borders of 19 June 1999. For more information on this convention see *Schomburg/Lagodny*, Internationale Rechtshilfe in Strafsachen – International Cooperation in Criminal Matters, 3rd edition, 1998, p. 913 et seq.
    Division II/8 is also responsible for the participation in international committees dealing with the fight against organised crime and drugs-related crime. – For more and at the time up to date information on the main tasks of Division II/8 see the annual Austrian "Amtskalender" (Österreichischer Amtskalender; see Abbreviations) of the current year.
109. For this special unit see the following body text.
110. § 6 section 3 SPG. Latest ordinance: *Sondereinheiten-Verordnung 1998*, BGBl II 1998 No. 207. However, the special units *EBS* and *EBT* were already in existence before the first ordinance as provided for in § 6 SPG was enacted in 1993.
111. See for more details *Hauer/Keplinger,* Handbuch (note 8) comment No. 16 on § 6 SPG; *Hübner*, Das neue Instrumentarium gegen "OK", RZ 1999, p. 86.
112. Under § 6 section 3 SPG, the Federal Minister of the Interior can also set up special branches "to end dangerous attacks"; such a special unit is the *Gendarmerieeinsatzkommando* (= *GEK*) also known as *Cobra*. *Cobra* does not especially deal with organised crime. See *Sondereinheiten-Verordnung 1998* (note 110).
113. See for further details: The report of the federal government about internal security in Austria in 1997: Sicherheitsbericht 1997, pp. 178 et seq. and additionally Sicherheitsbericht 1998, pp. 179 et seq.
114. *Hauer/Keplinger,* Handbuch (note 8) comment No. 16 on § 6 SPG; *Brenner*, EDOK gegen die Mafia, ÖS 1993 No. 1-2, p. 22; *Hübner*, RZ 1999, p. 86.
115. For the Director-General for Public Security see above under 1. a) aa).
116. See for further details below under 6. c).
117. Also known as the "Irregular Transactions Unit".
118. Council Directive 91/308/EEC of 10 June 1991 on prevention of the use of the financial system for the purpose of money laundering; OJ-EC (*Abl-EG*) L 166, 28 June 1991, p. 77; cf. the mention of this Directive as a reason for the creation

of the Austrian financial intelligence unit in *EB RV Finanzmarktanpassungsgesetz 1993*, 1130 BlgNR 18.GP, p. 143.

119. Europol Convention, OJ-EC (*Abl-EG*) 95/C 316/01; for Austria see also BGBl III 1998 No. 123.

120. See for further details Sicherheitsbericht 1998, p. 220; *Oberleitner*, Schengen und Europol, 1998, p. 84; see also the article "SIRENE Österreich – Das Schengener Informationssystem und seine Auswirkungen auf den Exekutivdienst", in: ÖS 1996 No. 6, pp. 19 et seq., and the article "SIRENE Österreich", in: ÖS 1997 No. 6, pp. 11 et seq.

121. See above note 104 as well as the body text under 1. a) aa).

122. Compare Sicherheitsbericht 1998, p. 215; *Hauer/Keplinger*, Handbuch (note 8) p. 640; see also the article "Gegenseitige Unterstützung", in: Der Kriminalbeamte 1999 No. 11, p. 40.

123. Österreichischer Amtskalender 1999/2000, p. 193.

124. Österreichischer Amtskalender 1999/2000, p. 193; Edict of the Federal Ministry of the Interior, 7.4.1998, Zl 8181/112-II/D/a/98.

125. *Hauer/Keplinger*, Handbuch (note 8) comment No. 16 on § 6 SPG; *Hübner*, RZ 1999, pp. 86, 88 (there note 42).

126. *Hübner*, RZ 1999, p. 86 with further references.

127. For the terms "fiscal crime" and "fiscal administrative offence" see above under 1. b).

128. Division III/8 = Division (*Abteilung*) 8 within Subdepartment III: Subdepartment for Integration and Customs (*Sektion III: Integrations- und Zollsektion*).

129. The creation of this central unit was also a response to Art. 280 of the Treaty establishing the European Community (= TEC; *Vertrag zur Gründung der Europäischen Gemeinschaft = EGV*); for more details about this provision (ex Art. 209a) see *H. Schneider*, in: Landesgruppe Österreich der Internationalen Strafrechtsgesellschaft (AIDP) (ed.), *Organisierte Kriminalität und Wirtschaftsrecht*, 1998, pp. 23 et seq. and pp. 34 et seq. – In the field of *taxes* (VAT matters) a central anti-fraud unit will be set up in the year 2001, also within the Federal Ministry of Finance.

130. An example is the fight against the smuggling of cigarettes, i.e. a crime which costs the EU a great deal of revenue and in which the involvement of organised crime is considerable. As regards the scale of cigarettes smuggling see *Fischler*, Der Schutz der finanziellen Interessen der Europäischen Gemeinschaften – eine gemeinsame Aufgabe von Mitgliedstaaten und Europäischer Kommission, ÖJZ 1997, p. 523.

131. This division also collects, analyses and evaluates data in the framework of a customs information and analysis centre (identification of risk areas, control methods, trends in the field of fraud, smuggling routes, etc.); cf. Österreichischer Amtskalender 1999/2000, p. 177.

132. It is however not responsible for official assistance in the framework of penal procedures relating to fiscal offences (fiscal administrative offences and fiscal crimes) ("*Rechts- und Amtshilfeverkehr und Nachrichtenaustausch in Angelegenheiten des Finanzstrafrechts*"); in this area Division IV/16 at the

same Ministry is responsible.

133. Recommendation No. 21 Action Plan to Combat Organised Crime (note 103).
134. Namely in Vienna, Graz, Linz und Innsbruck, that is to say, at the seat of each Court of Appeal; compare note 2.
135. On the network as a whole and particularly in Austria, see *Bittmann*, Das Europäische Justitielle Netzwerk (EJN), RZ 2000, pp. 13 et seq.
136. As foreseen by recommendation No. 20 Action Plan to Combat Organised Crime (note 103).
137. On special task commissions with foreign participation (as a kind of *local units*) see above under 4. a).
138. More detailed *Edelbacher* (note 84) p. 48; *Hübner*, RZ 1999, p. 88.
139. For this task force see above under 4. a).
140. This report only deals with areas of the *federal* administration.
141. *Mayer*, Das österreichische Bundes-Verfassungsrecht, Kurzkommentar, 2$^{nd}$ edition, 1997, comment No. I.2. on Art. 20 B-VG.
142. *Adamovich/Funk* (note 15) p. 428; compare also *Mayer* (note 141) comment No. I.2. on Art. 20 B-VG. – Usually the exercise of supervision can be prompted (but not required) by a supervisory complaint. On supervision and instruction in the area of the public prosecution service see §§ 29 et seq., §§ 36 et seq. StAG.
143. For more details see *Mayer* (note 141) comment No. I.2. on Art. 20 B-VG.
144. The possibility for an *a posteriori* parliamentary review of its legality (*Kontrolle der Rechtmäßigkeit*) is provided for in Art. 142 section 1 and section 2 lit. b) B-VG. On this rule and various possibilities for *political control* see *Adamovich/ Funk* (note 15) pp. 428 et seq. (especially pp. 429 et seq.); *Antoniolli/Koja*, Allgemeines Verwaltungsrecht, 3$^{rd}$ edition, 1996, pp. 751 et seq., p. 754.
145. *Koja*, Einführung in das öffentliche Recht, 1998, pp. 14 et seq.; *Stolzlechner*, Einführung in das öffentliche Recht, 1999, marginal notes 500, 521 et seq., 542; for the proceedings concerning fiscal administrative offences see *Leitner* (note 43) pp. 368 et seq., further p. 277.
146. *Koja* (note 145) pp. 14, 127 et seq.; *Stolzlechner* (note 145) marginal notes 521 et seq.
147. Especially Art. 129a section 1 No. 1 and 2 B-VG; § 51 VStG (= *Verwaltungsstrafgesetz*); § 67a section 1 No. 2 AVG (= *Allgemeines Verwaltungsverfahrensgesetz*); § 88 section 1 SPG; see also § 17 PolKG (on the PolKG see above note 22); *Koja* (note 145) pp. 15, 134 et seq.; *Stolzlechner* (note 145) marginal notes 500, 542. There are exceptions in proceedings concerning fiscal offences; see (§§ 150 et seq. in connection with) § 62 FinStrG and above under 1. b) cc) (1) and (2); here a penal authority at the Regional Directorate of Finance is the court of appeal, that is not bound to instructions.
    In accordance with § 88 section 2 SPG the Independent Administrative Tribunals (*UVS*) are also responsible for judging complaints by persons who claim that their rights have been violated by the security administration in other ways than through rulings or acts of direct administrative power and compulsion; with that all (simple) national administrative activities in the area of the security administration are included; for more details see *Grabenwarter/Wiederin*, Das

neue Polizeirecht, JAP 1992/93, pp. 146 et seq.; *Hauer/Keplinger,* Handbuch (note 8) comment No. 14 on § 88 SPG; *Wiederin* (note 7) marginal notes 733 et seq.

148. Compare art. 130 et seq., 144 B-VG; § 169 FinStrG; *Koja* (note 145) pp. 14 et seq., 136 et seq.; *Stolzlechner* (note 145) marginal notes 500, 524, 542; for the proceedings concerning fiscal administrative offences see *Leitner* (note 43) p. 277.

149. Art. 148a et seq. B-VG.

150. *Adamovich/Funk* (note 15) pp. 434 et seq.; *Antoniolli/Koja* (note 144) pp. 755 et seq.; *Hausmaninger,* The Austrian Legal System, 1998, pp. 52 et seq.

151. Art. 87 section 1 B-VG.

152. See infra under b).

153. § 1 DSG 2000 (= *Datenschutzgesetz 2000*; Data Protection Act 2000); *Berka,* Lehrbuch Grundrechte, 2000, pp. 104 et seq.; *Jahnel,* Datenschutzrecht, in: *Jahnel/Schramm/Staudegger* (eds.), Informatikrecht, 2000, pp. 166 et seq.

154. See e.g. infra under c) third bullet.

155. See e.g. §§ 30 et seq. DSG 2000 and § 90 SPG.

156. § 37 StAG.

157. § 113 StPO: "Any person who feels aggrieved due to a decision or delay on the part of the investigating judge during the provisional inquiries, the judicial investigation or in the procedure following the introduction of the bill of indictment, has the right, as far as the law does not provide otherwise, to demand a decision of the Counsel Chamber" ("*Alle, die sich während der Vorerhebungen, der Voruntersuchung oder in dem der Einbringung der Anklageschrift nachfolgenden Verfahren durch eine Verfügung oder Verzögerung des Untersuchungsrichters beschwert erachten, haben das Recht, darüber, soweit das Gesetz nichts anderes bestimmt, eine Entscheidung der Ratskammer zu verlangen*"). – Since 1993 there is no longer a general official control of the investigating judge through the Counsel Chamber. On the Counsel Chamber see note 2.

158. Especially in the case of § 179 section 5 or § 182 section 4 StPO.

159. Compare *Giese* (note 5), p. 22.

160. See above under a) aa). – In the case of a fiscal crime the Regional Directorate of Finance (*Finanzlandesdirektion*) is competent instead of the Independent Administrative Tribunal (*UVS*); see above under 1. b) cc) (2).

161. §§ 24, 141, 177 StPO; see above under 1. a) bb).

162. Applies in so far as the abovementioned under a) aa).

163. Compare *Bertel/Venier* (note 26) marginal notes 539 and 543 respectively.

164. § 149d section 1 No. 3 entered into force 1 July 1998.

165. Compare however above under 3. b).

166. For further details see *Machacek,* Die Bekämpfung der organisierten Kriminalität in Österreich, ÖJZ 1998, pp. 559 et seq., pp. 563 et seq.

167. § 10a section 1 StAG.

168. *Machacek* (note 166) pp. 556 et seq. and p. 561.

169. §§ 149n, 149o StPO; *Machacek* (note 166) pp. 560 et seq.; see also *Aichinger*

(note 84) pp. 80 et seq. and *Miklau/Pilnacek*, Optische und akustische Überwachungsmaßnahmen zur Bekämpfung schwerer und organisierter Kriminalität ("Lauschangriff") – Paradigmenwechsel im Verfahrensrecht? JRP 1997, pp. 299 et seq.

170. § 6 Sondereinheiten-Verordnung 1998, BGBl II 1998 No. 207; for the spezial unit *SEO* see above under 4. a).
171. JAB Besondere Ermittlungsmaßnahmen, 812 BlgNR 20.GP, p. 16.
172. See above under 1. a) bb).
173. Recently, *Lagodny*, Staatsanwaltschaft oder/und Kriminalpolizei? – Zur Ermittlungsmacht im österreichischen strafprozessualen Vorverfahren bei Abschaffung des Untersuchungsrichters, ÖJZ 2000, p. 325; *Moos*, Polizei und Strafprozeß. Gutachten zum ÖJT 2000, in: Verhandlungen des Vierzehnten Österreichischen Juristentages Wien 2000, Band IV/1, 2000; *Schmoller*, Grundstrukturen eines künftigen strafprozessualen Vorverfahrens, in: *Österreichische Juristenkommission* (ed.), Kritik und Fortschritt im Rechtsstaat. Rechtsstaat – Freiheit und Sicherheit. Tagung der Österreichischen Juristen-kommission 1999, 2000, p. 73, containing further literature.
174. And indeed recently a further elaborated draft bill on a reform of the criminal procedure, mainly of the preliminary proceedings, has been presented by the Federal Ministry of Justice (*Entwurf eines Strafprozessreformgesetzes*, JMZ 578.017/10-II.3/2001) which in its contents to a very large extent coincides with the draft for discussion.
175. Preliminary remarks to the draft for discussion, p. V 10.
176. § E 5 draft for discussion; for further details *Schmoller* (note 173) pp. 92 et seq.
177. § E 3 section 1 draft for discussion.
178. § E 7 draft for discussion.
179. See *Schmoller* (note 173) pp. 86 et seq.; further arguments for the public prosecutor as *dominus litis* in *Moos* (note 11) p. 36.
180. Critical of (overly comprehensive) reporting requirements however *Lagodny* (note 173) pp. 330 et seq. as well as *Schmoller* (note 173) pp. 95 et seq.
181. Compare *Schmoller* (note 173) p. 91.
182. § Z 15 draft for discussion.
183. §§ G 1 et seq. draft for discussion; *Schmoller* (note 173) pp. 96 et seq.
184. See the body text above.
185. Preliminary remarks to the draft of discussion, p. V 15.
186. §§ G 5 et seq. draft for discussion.
187. § G 8 draft for discussion.
188. Compare the article "Neue Kriminalbehörde geplant", in: SN 7.1.2000, p. 6.
189. For demands made in this area see *W. Hauptmann*, Unkonventionelle Gedanken zu einem Strafrechtsänderungsgesetz 2000, StPdG No. 22, 1995, pp. 136 et seq.; *Hübner*, RZ 1999, p. 88; *Moos*, Grundsatzfragen der Reform des Vorverfahrens, ÖJZ 1996, pp. 895, 897.
190. Compare SN 7.1.2000 (note 188); see also *Bundesministerium für Inneres. Gendarmeriezentralkommando* (note 5) p. III and pp. 16 et seq.
191. In this connection the detailed considerations of the Gendarmerie on an

appropriate form of the cooperation between security offices and executive bodies are to be considered; see *Bundesministerium für Inneres. Gendarmeriezentralkommando* (note 5).

192. For these guard units see above under 1. a).
193. On organisational deficiencies and their effects from the point of view of the Gendarmerie see *Bundesministerium für Inneres. Gendarmeriezentralkommando* (note 5) pp. 12 et seq.
194. Compare SN 7.1.2000 (note 188); additional the article "*Die Kripo im Umbruch*", in: SN 24.3.2000, p. 4. See also *Wiederin*, Verfassungsfragen der Errichtung eines Bundeskriminalamtes, JBl 2001, p. 273.
195. Compare SN 7.1.2000 (note 188).
196. Compare SN 7.1.2000 (note 188); SN 24.3.2000 (note 194).
197. Compare SN 24.3.2000 (note 194).
198. Compare SN 7.1.2000 (note 188).

## BIBLIOGRAPHY

*Aichinger*, Neue Fahndungsmethoden zur Bekämpfung organisierter Kriminalität, 1997.

*Aichinger*, Bundesgesetz zur Einführung besonderer Ermittlungsmaßnahmen in die StPO, JAP 1997/98, p. 56.

*Arbeitsgruppe StPO-Reform des Bundesministeriums für Inneres* (ed.), Kriminalpolizei und Strafprozeßreform, 1995.

*Bertel/Venier*, Grundriß des österreichischen Strafprozeßrechts, 6th edition, 2000.

*Bittmann*, Das Europäische Justitielle Netzwerk (EJN), RZ 2000, p. 13.

*Brenner*, EDOK gegen die Mafia, ÖS 1993 No. 1-2, p. 22.

*Bundesministerium für Inneres. Gendarmeriezentralkommando* (ed.), Die Bundesgendarmerie im 3. Jahrtausend – Grundsatzpapier, 1999.

*Bundesministerium für Justiz* (ed.), Organisierte Kriminalität – Professionelle Ermittlungsarbeit – Neue Herausforderungen. Enquete des BMJ und des BMI Oktober 1995, Schriftenreihe des BMJ Volume 77, 1995.

*Bundesministerium für Justiz* (ed.), Entwicklungslinien im Straf- und Strafprozeßrecht. Richterwoche 1996, Schriftenreihe des BMJ Volume 82, 1996.

*Bundesministerium für Justiz* (ed.), 150 Jahre Staatsanwaltschaft. 80 Jahre Vereinigung österreichischer Staatsanwälte, 1999.

*Burgstaller*, Entwicklung des Strafrechts in Österreich seit 1975, in: *Gössel/ Triffterer* (eds.), Gedächtnisschrift für Heinz Zipf, 1999, p. 3.

*Császár*, Die Bekämpfung der organisierten Kriminalität als gesamtgesellschafliche Aufgabe, ÖS 1991 No. 5, p. 3.

*Dearing*, Die Abwehr organisierter Kriminalität. Bestandsaufnahme und Zukunftsperspektiven, in: *Österreichische Juristenkommission* (ed.), Kritik und Fortschritt im Rechtsstaat. Tagung der ÖJK 1994, 1995, p. 33.

*Dearing*, Sicherheitspolizei und Strafrechtspflege. Versuch einer Bestimmung des Verhältnisses zweier benachbarter Rechtsgebiete, in: *Fuchs/ Brandstetter* (eds.), Festschrift für Winfried Platzgummer zum 65. Geburtstag, 1995, p. 225.

*Ebert*, Österreich, in: *Gropp* (ed.), Besondere Ermittlungsmaßnahmen zur Bekämpfung der Organisierten Kriminalität, 1993, p. 567.

*Edelbacher*, Das Tor zum Osten, Der Kriminalbeamte, part October 1993, p. 8.

*Edelbacher*, Organisierte Kriminalität in Österreich und Europa, in: *Edelbacher* (ed.) Organisierte Kriminalität in Europa. Die Bekämpfung der Korruption und der organisierten Kriminalität, 1998, p. 15.

*Edelbacher/Seyrl*, Geschichte und Gegenwart des österreichischen Polizeiwesens, Polizei Juristische Rundschau 1998 No. 1, p. 1.

*Ellinger*, Organisierte Kriminalität, Der Kriminalbeamte, part November 1991, p. 113.

*Faber R.*, Die Wachkörper und das Erste Bundesrechtsbereinigungsgesetz. Ein Nachruf auf die "Organisationsstatute der Bundessicherheitswache und Kriminalbeamtenkorps", JRP 2000, p. 35.

*Faber R.*, Die Neuordnung der Gemeindewachkörper durch die B-VG–Novelle 1999, ZfV 1999, p. 828.

*Fischler*, Der Schutz der finanziellen Interessen der Europäischen Gemeinschaften – eine gemeinsame Aufgabe von Mitgliedstaaten und Europäischer Kommission, ÖJZ 1997, p. 521.

*Fuchs*, Sicherheitspolizei und Gefahrbegriff, in: *Huber/Jesionek/Miklau* (eds.) Festschrift für Reinhard Moos zum 65. Geburtstag, 1997, p. 181.

*Fuchs*, Zum Entwurf eines Bundesgesetzes über besondere Ermittlungsmaßnahmen zur Bekämpfung organisierter Kriminalität, in: StPdG 24, Schriftenreihe des BMJ Volume 85, 1997, p. 263.

*Funk*, Sicherheitspolizeiliche Maßnahmen zur Bekämpfung organisierter Kriminalität, JRP 1996, p. 26.

*Gegenseitige Unterstützung*, Der Kriminalbeamte 1999 No. 11, p. 40.

*Grabenwarter/Wiederin*, Das neue Polizeirecht, JAP 1992/93, pp. 50, 70, 144.

*Giese*, Sicherheitspolizeirecht, in: *Bachmann* et al (eds.), Besonderes Verwaltungsrecht, 2nd edition, 1998, p. 1.

*Haas*, Die Schengener Abkommen und ihre strafprozessualen Implikationen, 2001.

*Harnischmacher*, Organisierte Kriminalität, Österreichische Polizei-Zeitung 2000 No. 11, p. 5.

*Hausmaninger*, The Austrian Legal System, 1998.

*Hauer/Keplinger*, Handbuch zum Sicherheitspolizeigesetz, 1993.

*Hauer/Keplinger*, StPO. Erläuterungen zur Strafprozeßordnung für Exekutivorgane, 1997.

*Hauer*, Ruhe Ordnung Sicherheit. Eine Studie zu den Aufgaben der Polizei in Österreich, 2000.

*Hauptmann W.*, Unkonventionelle Gedanken zu einem Strafrechtsänderungsgesetz 2000, in: StPdG 22, Schriftenreihe des BMJ Volume 72, 1995, p. 105.

*Hörmann/Hesztera* (eds.) Zwischen Gefahr und Berufung. Gendarmerie in Österreich, 1999.

*Hübner*, Das neue Instrumentarium gegen "OK", RZ 1999, p. 85.

*Hummer* (ed.), Rechtsfragen in der Anwendung des Amsterdamer Vertrages, 2001.

*Keplinger*, Zwei grundlegende Fragen zu den Gemeindewachen, ÖGZ 1992 No. 10, p. 27.

*Keplinger*, Die verfassungsrechtlichen Neuerungen für Gemeindewachkörper, ÖGZ 1999 No. 9, p. 25.

*Kessel*, Die Ratskammer nach dem StPÄG 1993, JBl 1995, pp. 291, 364.

*Kienapfel*, Bildung einer kriminellen Organisation (§ 278a Abs 1 StGB), JBl 1995, p. 613.

*Kranewitter*, Die Sicherheitsbehörden im Dienst der Strafjustiz, 1990.

*Landesgruppe Österreich der Internationalen Strafrechtsgesellschaft (AIDP)* (ed.), Strafrecht und organisierte Kriminalität. Grundsatzfragen und Lösungsansätz, 1996.

*Landesgruppe Österreich der Internationalen Strafrechtsgesellschaft (AIDP)* (ed.), Organisierte Kriminalität und internationales Strafrecht, 1997.

*Landesgruppe Österreich der Internationalen Strafrechtsgesellschaft (AIDP)* (ed.), Organisierte Kriminalität und Wirtschaftsrecht, 1998.

*Landesgruppe Österreich der internationalen Strafrechtsgesellschaft (AIDP)* (ed.), Die organisierte Kriminalität als Prüfstein des Strafrechtssystems. Vorbereitung des XVI. Internationalen Strafrechtskongresses Budapest 1999, 1999.

*Lagodny*, Staatsanwaltschaft oder/und Kriminalpolizei, ÖJZ 2000, p. 325.

*Lepuschitz*, Lauschangriff, 2000.

*Löschnig-Gspandl*, Fight against Organized Crime: Recent Changes to the Catalogue of Statutory Offences and the Confiscation System in Austrian Criminal Law, European Journal of Crime, Criminal Law and Criminal Justice 1997 (volume 5, issue 3), p. 210.

*Löschnig-Gspandl*, Österreich, in: *Gropp/Huber* (eds.), Rechtliche Initiativen gegen organisierte Kriminalität, 2001, p. 549.

*Machacek*, Die Bekämpfung der organisierten Kriminalität in Österreich, ÖJZ 1998, p. 553.

*Matousek*, Die Staatsanwaltschaft im Wandel, WR 1997 No. 35, p. 9.

*Mayer*, Das österreichische Bundes-Verfassungsrecht, Kurzkommentar, 2nd edition, 1997.

*Miklau*, Die neue Rolle der Staatsanwaltschaft im strafprozessualen Vorverfahren, in: *Schmoller* (ed.), Festschrift für Otto Triffterer zum 65. Geburtstag, 1996 (Nachdruck 1998), p. 493.

*Miklau/Pilnacek*, Optische und akustische Überwachungsmaßnahmen zur Bekämpfung schwerer und organisierter Kriminalität ("Lauschangriff") – Paradigmenwechsel im Verfahrensrecht? JRP 1997, p. 286.

*Miklau*, Zur Rollenverteilung im Strafprozeß, in: *Huber/Jesionek/Miklau* (eds.), Festschrift für Reinhard Moos zum 65. Geburtstag, 1997, p. 283.

*Moos*, Grundsatzfragen der Reform des Vorverfahrens, ÖJZ 1996, p. 886.

*Moos*, Menschenrechte und Polizei in geschichtlicher Entwicklung, in: *Fehérváry/Stangl* (eds.), Menschenrechte und Staatsgewalt, 2000, p. 21.

*Moos*, Polizei und Strafprozeß. Gutachten zum ÖJT 2000, in: Verhandlungen des Vierzehnten Österreichischen Juristentages Wien 2000, Volume IV/1, 2000.

*Müller*, Antrags- und Ermittlungsrecht des Staatsanwaltes als Ausfluß des Anklagegrundsatzes. Einige Bemerkungen zur Reform des Vorverfahrens, in: *Huber/Jesionek/Miklau* (eds.), Festschrift für Reinhard Moos zum 65. Geburtstag, 1997, p. 293.

*Novak*, Organisierte Kriminalität im Bereich der Europäischen Union und ihrer Mitgliedstaaten unter besonderer Berücksichtigung der Wirtschaftskriminalität – neueste Entwicklungen – Bekämpfungsstrategien (Bericht über ein Seminar), RZ 2001, p. 71.

*Oberleitner*, Schengen und Europol, 1998.

Projekt VISION – Die Umsetzung des Schengener Durchführungsübereinkommens (SDÜ) in Österreich in fremdenpolizeilicher Hinsicht sowie für Visaangelegenheiten, ÖS 1997 No. 7-8, p.16.

*Pretzner*, Das organisierte Verbrechen, 2001.

*Schauer*, Schengen – Maastricht – Amsterdam, 2000.

*Schmoller*, Geändertes Erscheinungsbild staatlicher Verbrechensbekämpfung? Zur Diskussion über Lauschangriff, Rasterfahndung, verdeckte Ermittler, Kronzeugen uä, ÖJZ 1996, p. 21.

*Schmoller*, Grundstrukturen eines künftigen strafprozessualen Vorverfahrens, in: *Österreichische Juristenkommission* (ed.), Kritik und Fortschritt im Rechtsstaat. Rechtsstaat – Freiheit und Sicherheit. Tagung der Österreichischen Juristenkommission 1999, 2000, p. 73.

*Schomburg/Lagodny*, Internationale Rechtshilfe in Strafsachen – International Cooperation in Criminal Matters, 3rd edition, 1998.

*Schwaighofer/Ebensperger*, Internationale Rechtshilfe in strafrechtlichen Angelegenheiten. Einführung – Texte – Materialien, 2001.

SIRENE Österreich – Das Schengener Informationssystem und seine Auswirkungen auf den Exekutivdienst, ÖS 1996 No. 6, p. 19.

SIRENE Österreich, ÖS 1997 No. 6, p. 11.

*Thienel*, Die Aufgaben der Bundesgendarmerie, 1986.

*Weber/Schlag*, Sicherheitspolizei und Föderalismus, 1995.

*Wessely*, Die Rasterfahndung – viel Lärm um nichts?, ÖJZ 1998, p. 291.

*Wiederin*, Einführung in das Sicherheitspolizeirecht, 1998.

*Wiederin*, Verfassungsfragen der Errichtung eines Bundeskriminalamtes, JBl 2001, p. 273.

## NAMES AND FUNCTIONS OF RESPONDENTS.

- For answering the questionnaire, on which this report largely is based, many thanks to:
  - *Dearing Albin* Dr. iur., Chief of Subdepartment III/K: Law and legislation at the Federal Ministry of the Interior.
  - *Heller Herwig* Dr. iur., Chief of Division III/8 at the Federal Ministry of Finance.
  - *Miklau Roland* Dr. iur., Chief of Department II: Department for legislation concerning criminal law at the Federal Ministry of Justice.

- For further valuable information thanks are due to.
  - *Dick Josef* Mag. iur., Chief of Subdepartment II/D: Criminal Investigation – Interpol at the Federal Ministry of the Interior.
  - *Kneidinger Christian* Dr. iur., Chief of the Division for criminal matters at the Finance Office in Linz.
  - *Leimüller Karl-René*, Division III/1 at the Federal Ministry of Finance.
  - *Sperlhofer Thomas* Mag. iur., Main Audit Division (*Groß-betriebsprüfung*) Linz.
  - *Strondl Robert*, Subdepartment II/B: Central Gendarmerie Headquarter at the Federal Ministry of the Interior.
  - *Vogl Mathias* Mag. iur., Division III/2 at the Federal Ministry of the Interior.

## ABBREVIATIONS.

| | | |
|---|---|---|
| ABl-EG | Amtsblatt der Europäischen Gemeinschaften | Official Journal of the European Communities |
| Amtskalender | see: Österreichischer Amtskalender | |
| AVG | Allg. Verwaltungsverver-fahrensgesetz 1991 BGBl 1991 Nr 51 | |
| AVOG | Abgabenverwaltungs-organisationsgesetz BGBl 1975 Nr 18 | |
| BGBl | Bundesgesetzblatt | Federal law gazette |
| BlgNR | Beilage(n) zu den steno-graphischen Protokollen des Nationalrats | Appendix to the stenographic protocols of the sessions of the Nationalrat (National Council) |
| BMF | Bundesministerium für Finanzen | Federal Ministry of Finance |
| BMI | Bundesministerium für Inneres | Federal Ministry of the Interior |
| BMJ | Bundesministerium für Justiz | Federal Ministry of Justice |
| B-VG | Bundes-Verfassungsgesetz | Confederal Constitution |
| DSG | Datenschutzgesetz 2000 BGBl 1999 Nr 165 | Data Protection Act |
| DV-StAG | Verordnung des Bundes-ministers für Justiz vom 16. Juni 1986 zur Durchführung des Staatsanwaltschafts-gesetzes BGBl 1986 Nr 338 | |
| Der Kriminalbeamte | Der Kriminalbeamte | Professional journal |
| EB | Erläuternde Bemerkungen | Explanatory annotations |
| EBS | Einsatzgruppe zur Bekämpfung der Suchtgiftkriminalität | Task force to fight drug crimes |
| EBT | Einsatzgruppe zur Bekämpfung des Terrorismus | Task force to fight terrorism |

| | | |
|---|---|---|
| EDOK | Einsatzgruppe der Gruppe D [des BMI] zur Bekämpfung der organisierten Kriminalität | Task force of "Gruppe D" [at the federal Ministry of the Interior] to fight organised crime |
| EGV | Vertrag zur Gründung der Europäischen Gemeinschaft BGBl III 1999 Nr 86 | Treaty establishing the European Community |
| EGVG | Einführungsgesetz zu den erwaltungsverfahrensgesetzen BGBl 1991 Nr 50 | |
| FinStrG | Finanzstrafgesetz 1958 BGBl 1958 Nr 129 | Financial Penal Code |
| Fremdengesetz 1997 | Fremdengesetz 1997 BGBl I 1997 Nr 75 | Foreigner Act 1997 |
| Gendarmerie-gesetz 1918 | Gendarmeriegesetz 1918 StGBl 1918 Nr 75 | Gendarmerie Act 1918 |
| GP | Gesetzgebungsperiode | Legislative period |
| JAB | Bericht des Justizausschusses des Nationalrats | Report of the parliamentary judicial committee on a government bill |
| JAP | Juristische Ausbildung und Praxisvorbereitung | a legal journal |
| JRP | Journal für Rechtspolitik | a legal journal |
| JBl | Juristische Blätter | a legal journal |
| MBG. | Militärbefugnisgesetz BGBl I 2000 Nr 86 | Military Authority Act |
| ÖGZ | Österreichische Gemeinde-Zeitung | a journal |
| ÖJK | Österr. Juristenkommission | Professional Austrian Committee of Lawyers |
| ÖJT | Österr. Juristentag | |
| ÖS | Öffentliche Sicherheit. Illustrierte Monats-Rundschau | a journal |
| Österreichischer Amtskalender | Österreichischer Amtska-lender – Das Lexikon der Behörden und Amtskalender Institutionen | The annual Austrian "Amts-kalender" contains a survey of most national, regional and local authorities and offices |

| | | |
|---|---|---|
| PolKG | Polizeikooperationsgesetz BGBl I 104/1997 | Police Cooperation Act |
| RV | Regierungsvorlage | government bill |
| RZ | Österreichische Richterzeitung | a legal journal |
| SEO | Sondereinheit für Observation | special unit for observation |
| Sicherheitsbericht | Bericht der Bundesregierung über die innere Sicherheit in Österreich | Official annual report of the federal government about internal security in Austria |
| SN | Salzburger Nachrichten | a newspaper |
| SPG | Sicherheitspolizeigesetz 1991 BGBl 1991 Nr 566 | Security police act 1991 |
| StAG | Staatsanwaltschaftsgesetz BGBl 1986 Nr 164 | Public prosecution service act |
| StGB | Strafgesetzbuch BGBl 1974 Nr 60 | Penal Code |
| StPdG | Strafrechtliche Probleme der Gegenwart. (Erscheint als Band der Schriftenreihe des BMJ) | (Title of) an annual omnibus volume |
| StPO | Strafprozeßordnung 1975 BGBl 1975 Nr 631 | Code of Criminal Procedure |
| UVS | Unabhängiger Verwaltungssenat | (Regional) Independent Administrative Tribunal |
| VStG | Verwaltungsstrafgesetz 1991, BGBl 1991 Nr 52 | |
| Vorbem | Vorbemerkungen | Preliminary remarks |
| WR | Der Wiener Richter | a journal |
| ZfV | Zeitschrift für Verwaltung | a legal journal |
| ZollR-DG | Zollrechts-Durchführungsgesetz BGBl 1994 Nr 659 | |

# Belgium

## Gert Vermeulen

### I. THE LAW ENFORCEMENT AGENCIES

The Belgian police structure has recently been reformed. Previously, there were three distinct general police forces in Belgium that carried out investigative tasks: the Gendarmerie (a), the Judicial Police (b) and the Municipal Police (c). In 1994, a General Police Support Service (d) was created, charged with improving cooperation between and within these three police forces.[1]

The tragic events in the summer of 1996 (the *Dutroux* case), as well as the numerous difficulties that have arisen in the context of previous investigations in cases of serious crime, have driven the federal government to question the former police organisation and in particular to do away with the system within which two police forces have competing jurisdiction in judicial matters concerning the entire Belgian territory (Gendarmerie and Judicial Police) (*see below*). Rivalry between the two forces has persisted over the past decades and has been proven to cause high levels of inefficiency in numerous investigations.

Several parliamentary inquiry committees, *inter alia* those installed for identifying dysfunctions in the cooperation between the police forces (and the judicial authorities) in the investigations into a series of armed robberies in department stores, committed in the mid-1980s by the so-called "gang of Nivelles" (*Bende van Nijvel*),[2] and the *Dutroux* case[3] had also come to comparable conclusions. Therefore, the federal government decided in December 1996 to establish a so-called "Committee for a more efficient police structure" (*Commissie voor een efficiëntere politiestructuur*), which had to produce its final report by mid-1997.[4] On the basis of this report and the recommendations of the abovementioned parliamentary inquiry committees,[5] and in order to prevent the country ending up in an even deeper political and moral crisis, the parties of the then coalition – together with the main opposition parties – concluded a so-called "*Octopus*" agreement, setting the framework for a far-reaching reform of the police and judicial structure.

The police reform, which envisaged the establishment of one single integrated police force, structured on two levels (federal and local), has come into effect as of 1 April 2001.[6] As the changes concerned have primarily been propelled by repeated incidences of national crises and scandals, and not specifically by the idea that they could lead to a more effective fight against organised crime nor by the EU integration process, they will not be discussed in detail hereafter. Before the reform was operational and a final agreement on all details of the future police structure had been achieved, the government already decided that the cooperation and coordination between the existing police forces with national jurisdiction regarding judicial policing had to be maximized.

To this end, a circular letter was issued in February 1997 by the Minister of Justice[7] following consultation with the board of prosecutors-general (*college van procureurs-generaal*), which, together with the Minister of Justice, is responsible for defining the general lines of criminal policy throughout the country (*see below*). This ministerial circular, which must be read in conjunction with another circular letter issued by the Minister of Justice in December 1996, with regard to proactive investigation,[8] as well as with the federal action plan for combating organised crime, adopted by the cabinet council in June 1996,[9] introduced a sort of specialisation between the Gendarmerie and the Judicial Police in the field of judicial policing. The judicial authorities in charge of criminal investigations – either His Majesty's prosecutor, as regards preliminary investigations (*opsporingsonderzoeke*n), or the investigating judge (*onderzoeksrechter*), as regards judicial investigations (*gerechtelijke onderzoeken*) – were urged to take the (non-binding) assignment of duties between both forces into account when allocating cases to either of them. For the forces concerned, specialisation implied that they each had to give priority to dealing with certain types of crime in the context of judicial investigations, including the carrying out of strategic crime analysis[10] as well as proactive policing, tactical crime analysis and project-oriented (multidisciplinary) investigation under the supervision of the competent judicial authority.

According to the ministerial circular, both the Gendarmerie and the Judicial Police had to take responsibility in the fight against organised crime, as the different types of crime within their respective specific expertise might show an "organised"[11] character. Within the consultation platforms for investigations into (organised) crime cases, the so-called confidential magistrate (*vertrouwensmagistraat*), who – as (a deputy of) His Majesty's prosecutor in the court's district – is the locally competent magistrate in cases where special, covert investigative techniques need to be applied, or the national magistrate, as the corresponding competent judicial authority at the federal level (*see below*), was responsible for assigning investigations into organised crime to either the Gendarmerie or the Judicial Police, according to their "specialisation", or to jointly involve them in a particular case requiring the specific input and expertise of both forces.[12]

No specific types of crime were allocated to the Municipal Police, acting on local level only. In large cities in particular, however, the urban police forces of the Municipal Police also investigated organised crime, e.g. in the field of drug trafficking or trafficking in human beings.

## A.  Gendarmerie

The Gendarmerie (*Rijkswacht*) fell under the responsibility of the Ministry of the Interior. The Gendarmerie had jurisdiction in the whole of the Belgian territory and it was responsible for performing police tasks of an administrative nature (maintenance of public order) as well as of a judicial nature (investigation of criminal offences).

At a local level, the Gendarmerie was organised in squads, each serving a municipality or small group of municipalities. Districts, which covered a larger group of municipalities, also had a Security and Investigation Squad (*Bewakings- en Opsporingsbrigade*) at their disposal, which was a specialised squad for investigating (organised) crime. The general management and directing responsibilities of the force lay with the general *(generaal)* of the Gendarmerie, who also had a General Staff *(Generale Staf)* at his disposal. Before the establishment of the Federal Police, the Central Bureau of Investigations *(Centraal Bureau der Opsporingen)* – as a part of the General Staff, really used to be the driving force in investigations into (organised) crime requiring coordinated action throughout the country or between several districts.

According to the ministerial circular of February 1997, the Gendarmerie had to specialise in the fight against: terrorism, hold-ups, acts of violence against people, (networks of) trafficking in human beings and vice, sexual exploitation (including procuring), paedophilia, disappearances and kidnapping, capturing and holding hostages, trafficking in organs and human tissue, hormones, drugs, labour exploitation and social fraud, racketeering, sects, car-jacking, illegal immigration and trafficking in stolen vehicles, weapons, nuclear materials, protected fauna and flora, imitations and counterfeiting (of both bank-notes and coins).

## B.  Judicial Police

The Judicial Police (*Gerechtelijke Politie*)[13] was established in order to compensate for a shortcoming of other police forces in the area of criminal investigations and to place officers and agents directly at the disposal of the magistracy.

Unlike the other two general police forces (the Gendarmerie and the Municipal Police), which also carried out duties of a preventive nature and tasks of administrative policing, the Judicial Police – as indicated by their name – had an exclusively judicial competence. They only acted after crimes or offences had been committed in order to investigate them, collect evidence, inform the proper authorities, with a view to arresting the perpetrators and to bringing them before the judicial authorities. Their investigators had national jurisdiction.

Due to its special duties, the judicial police fell exclusively under the Ministry of Justice, which determined the terms and rules for its organisation and functioning. The five prosecutors-general (*procureurs-generaal*), being in charge of the public prosecutor's office in the respective jurisdiction of the courts of appeal, had authority over and supervised the judicial police, whereas His Majesty's prosecutors, being in charge of the public prosecutor's office in the 27 court's districts, exercised legal supervision.

The Judicial Police was organised in 23 squads, i.e. 22 squads linked to the public prosecutor's office in the court's districts and one National Squad (*Nationale Brigade*), also called the 23rd Squad. All of the 22 local squads were supervised by a chief commissioner (*hoofdcommissaris*), without prejudice to the duties of the commissioner-general (*commissaris-generaal*), chief of the entire force and responsible for coordination, logistic support and defining the general policies of the force in collaboration with the prosecutors-general. The commissioner-general was the head of the **General Commissariat** (*Commissariaat-generaal*), which encompassed three divisions: an administration and logistics division (*afdeling administratie en logistiek*), a technical support division (*afdeling technische ondersteuning*) and the operational support and detection division (*afdeling operationale ondersteuning en opsporing*). The latter in its turn comprised three central units of particular relevance in the fight against organised crime:[14] the abovementioned **National Squad**, the principal task of which was the investigation and repression of serious banditry that could, by its size or its impact, take national or international proportions (such as terrorism-related crime or internationally organised crime);[15] the **Central Unit for Combating Economic and Financial Delinquency** (*Centrale Dienst ter Bestrijding van de Economische en Financiële Delinquentie*); and the **Central Unit for Combating Corruption** (*Centrale Dienst voor de Bestrijding van de Corruptie*). The General Commissariat and the three central units it comprises were of particular relevance in the context of combating organised crime.

The scientific and technical police also fell within the domain of responsibility of the Judicial Police. Each local squad was equipped with a laboratory which worked closely with a national laboratory, the National Institute for Criminalistics and Criminology (*Nationaal Instituut voor Criminalistiek en Criminologie*),[16] which has been entrusted inter alia with the task of maintaining a central DNA database for the purpose of investigations into crime (see below).

Apart from that, according to the ministerial circular of February 1997, the Judicial Police had to specialise in the fight against: all kinds of financial and economic delinquency, IT crimes, arson, parental kidnapping, gambling, antiques and art fraud, misfeasance and abuse of power by officials, money laundering, corruption and homicide.

## C. Municipal Police

Before the police reform each Belgian municipality had its own police force. Depending on the size of the municipality, it was either called an urban police force or a rural police force. Small rural police forces (sometimes composed of a single officer) usually formed a squad with other neighbouring small forces. In principle, the jurisdiction of the Municipal Police (*Gemeentepolitie*) was restricted to the territory of their own municipality or, in rural forces, to the territory of their squad. However, in certain cases the provincial governor could extend their jurisdiction outside these territorial limits. This resulted in some provincial governors extending the territorial competence of municipal police officers in their province to all municipalities in the province.

Like the gendarmerie, the municipal police could perform administrative as well as judicial tasks. The judicial tasks of the municipal police were carried out (or directed) by police officers with the capacity of officer of judicial police, assisting His Majesty's prosecutor (*procureur des Konings*), who was in charge of the public prosecutor's office in the relevant court's district. Only these officers were competent for the drawing-up of police reports of their findings. Other officers could only draw up ordinary reports that had to be submitted to the officer assisting His Majesty's prosecutor.

The Municipal Police also had a Standing Committee for the Municipal Police (*Vaste Commissie van de Gemeentepolitie*) at its disposal, which could discuss policy issues and represent the interests of the force at federal level, e.g. in the context of the present police reform.

Since the police services have been reformed into an integrated police service structured on two levels, i.e. the local and the federal level, the local level is divided in 196 police zones, each corresponding with one police force having one police post per municipality within the zone. Each local police force is under the guidance of a local force chief (*lokale korpschef)* and guarantees the community policing (*basispolitiezorg)* on the administrative and judicial level. While carrying out their tasks, the local police forces have to take into account the local security plan (*lokaal veiligheidsplan*) which has been prepared by the zonal security board (*zonale veiligheidsraad*) and approved of by the Ministry of the Interior. In order to create an effective, functional bond between the local and the federal level, the local security plans have to be in accordance with the national security plan (*national veiligheidsplan*). The latter has been elaborated in mutual consultation between the Minister of Justice and the Minister of the Interior.[17]

### D. General Police Support Service

As indicated above, the **General Police Support Service** (*Algemene Politiesteundienst*) was created in 1994[18] with a view to improving cooperation between and coordination of three general police forces. It was also entrusted with the support and coordination of the police policies of the ministries involved. The General Police Support Service originally consisted of four divisions: one responsible for operational support (*afdeling operationele ondersteuning*), one for telematics (*afdeling telematica*), one for police policy support (*afdeling politiebeleidsondersteuning*) and one for international police cooperation (*afdeling internationale politiesamenwerking*), the latter playing a central role in the international exchange of police information, *inter alia* in the field of combating organised crime.

Since the police reform, the four divisions of the General Police Support Service have been integrated in several directorates of the federal police. The operational tasks of the former division international police cooperation (SIS, contacts with liaison officers abroad, the support of operational contacts with foreign police services...) are now being carried out by the **Directorate operational police cooperation** (*Directie operationele politiesamenwerking*) of the General Directorate Operational Support of the federal police (*Algemene Directie Operationele ondersteuning*). The management of the international police cooperation, has been entrusted to the **Commissioner General's Office International Police Cooperation Policy** (*Directie van het beleid inzake Internationale Politiesamenwerking, also referred to as CGI*).[19]

### II. THE PUBLIC PROSECUTION SERVICE

The public prosecutor's office is also currently undergoing reform.[20] The part of the *Octopus* reform (*see above*) that concerns the judiciary introduces *inter alia* a federal public prosecutor's office (*federaal parket*) (f) and a board of His Majesty's prosecutors (*raad van procureurs des Konings*) (g).[21]

## A. General

The public prosecutor's office is a hierarchical body with a pyramidal structure. It also holds the monopoly of prosecution: only members of this body are entitled to exercise the right to prosecute. Police officers have to draw up reports of all their findings and send them to the public prosecutor's office. The public prosecutor then decides whether or not to prosecute.

At the level of the 27 Magistrates Courts, the public prosecutor's office consists of His Majesty's prosecutor, assisted by his deputies. Their territorial competence is restricted to the district of the Magistrates Court they are attached to, although they can perform investigative activities outside their district once they have initiated an inquiry in a specific case. His Majesty's prosecutor – and likewise his deputies – has discretion in whether or not to proceed with a case (expediency), taking into account, however, the general lines of criminal policy as identified by the Minister of Justice in consultation with the **board of prosecutors-general** *(see below)*. The majority of offences reported to the public prosecutor's office are actually dismissed. Dismissal needs to be justified and the victim needs to be notified, but the dismissal is not binding. The prosecutor's office reserves the right to reconsider such a decision and may reopen the case at any time, provided, of course, the right to prosecute has not expired. His Majesty's prosecutor and his deputies are in charge of so-called preliminary investigations, including proactive policing *(see below)*, while the investigating judge is in charge of so-called judicial investigations *(see below)*. In principle, the members of the public prosecutor's office have a general mandate, i.e. for all types of offences. In practice, however, the internal organisation of the work flow within the public prosecutor's office generally results in specialised magistrates or units dealing with specific types of crime (e.g. drug or fiscal offences). In the context of the fight against organised crime, reference must (once again) be made to the existence of a so-called **confidential magistrate** *(see above)* within the public prosecutor's office in the court's district, who is the locally competent magistrate as regards the application of special, covert investigative techniques by the police. In the same context – organised crime often having an international dimension – the so-called **magistrates for judicial cooperation** *(rechtshulpmagistraten)* must be mentioned. In a number of districts, they have been entrusted, as deputies of His Majesty's prosecutor, with specific responsibilities in the field of judicial cooperation. Hence, a growing fragmentation of tasks within the public prosecutor's office in the court's districts can be observed.

At the level of the courts of appeal (5), the public prosecutor's office consists of the prosecutor-general with the court of appeal, assisted by solicitors-general *(advocaten-generaal)* and by deputy prosecutors-general (*substituten-procureur-generaal*). The prosecutor-general is in charge of all the magistrates of the public prosecutor's office within the territorial jurisdiction (realm) of the court of appeal concerned.

## B. Board of prosecutors-general

In the mid-1990s, the five prosecutors-general started to meet on a regular basis as the so-called board of prosecutors-general, in order to allow a better coordination of the activities of the public prosecutor's office throughout the country and with a view – under the supervision of the Minister of Justice – to delineating the criminal policy covering the prosecution of offences, the punishment of offenders and the position of the victim.

As announced in the 1996 federal action plan for combating organised crime (*see above*),[22] the board of prosecutors-general was legally established in 1997.[23] The board has national competence and its decisions are binding upon the prosecutors-general at the level of the courts of appeal and all members of the public prosecutor's office within the territorial jurisdiction of the respective courts of appeal. The main *rationale* for establishing the board, having national competence and binding authority, was to promote a coherent and uniform criminal policy for the entire Belgian territory.[24] The board of prosecutors-general is in charge of implementing the criminal policy guidelines it draws up in cooperation with and under the authority of the Minister of Justice, who retains the overall responsibility for the country's criminal policy.

Midway through 1997, and following consultation with the board of prosecutors-general, the government decided to entrust each of the board's members with the task of preparing and defining the general lines of criminal policy for a number of specific crimes or offences.[25] The prosecutor-general at the level of the court of appeal of Ghent[26] was also assigned a number of (more operational) tasks, with particular relevance in the context of combating (international) organised crime. *Inter alia*,[27] his portfolio includes terrorism and serious banditry, international cooperation in criminal matters, the relationship with the intelligence and security services and the operational supervision of the national magistrates (*see below*).

The board of prosecutors-general is assisted by the **national magistrates** (c), who have national jurisdiction. In the execution of its (policy) tasks, it can also call on the support of members of the public prosecutor's office with the courts of appeal, referred to then as **assisting magistrates** (*bijstands-magistraten*) (d).

## C. National magistrates

The second half of the 1980s was in part characterised by a number of terrorist bombings, committed by the so-called *Cellules Communistes Combattantes* and the "Gang of Nivelles". In this context, two national magistrates were appointed by the Minister of Justice in May 1990, on the basis of a circular letter of 24 April 1990.[28] Their task was to act as privileged interlocutors on behalf of Belgium in its relationship with foreign judicial authorities in cases where prompt judicial intervention was needed. They were also to take care of the coordination of investigations into crime having a (potential) nation-wide or even international impact.

In line with the 1996 federal action plan for combating organised crime[29] – and as with the board of prosecutors-general *(see above)* – the function of national magistrate was formally established in 1997.[30] Since then, the national magistrates have been entrusted, under the supervision and direction of a member of the board of prosecutors-general, with the task of facilitating international cooperation, *inter alia* by coordinating or facilitating the execution of letters rogatory. Thus, the national magistrates can be looked upon as an operational extension of the board of prosecutors-general.

Further, according also to the 1997 act, the national magistrates coordinate connected cases that are dealt with by the office of His Majesty's prosecutor in several districts, and they facilitate international cooperation in criminal cases. If required, they can even give binding instructions to the local prosecutors concerned. They have competence for the entire Belgian territory. In addition, they are charged with taking all the necessary measures for exercising the right to prosecute, as long as the competent public prosecutor has not been identified or has not yet exercised his legal competence. In case of disagreement between the national magistrate and the competent local prosecutor in one of the court's districts, the final decision is taken by the prosecutor-general whose jurisdiction spans the relevant district.

Until now, there has been no formal assignment of duties among the national magistrates. In practice, however, the acting national magistrates each specialize in specific areas of crime, though each is in a position to take over the tasks of the other. The appointment of a specific national magistrate is envisaged, to be in charge of the coordination of the international execution of confiscation orders.[31]

The current national magistrates will eventually be replaced by the federal magistrates *(federale magistraten)* once the Federal public prosecutor's office has become operational. The federal magistrates are expected to take up their tasks as of 21 May 2002.[32]

## D. Assisting magistrates

As has already been mentioned above, the board of prosecutors-general can call on the support of members of the public prosecutor's office with the courts of appeal, referred to then as **assisting magistrates**. These magistrates (with the rank of solicitor-general or deputy prosecutor-general) are to support and assist the board of prosecutors-general in developing and implementing criminal policy with regard to a specific type of crime in cooperation with the Minister of Justice. Accordingly, their main tasks include: to continually evaluate the current policy status; to look into the necessity and feasibility of an integrated, multidisciplinary approach towards the type of crime concerned; to contribute to the development of specific expertise with the members of the public prosecutor's office in charge of prosecution of the offences concerned; to promote cooperation between the different services involved in combating the phenomenon, if required; and to improve coordination and detection in the area concerned.

Today, magistrates at the level of the court of appeal assist the board of prosecutors-general in the areas of hormone-related crime, financial, economic and fiscal crime and drug-related crime. The appointment of an additional assisting magistrate in the area of organised crime is envisaged.[33]

## E. Supervising magistrates

Prior to the police reform, the authority and supervision over the division operational support and detection of the General Commissariat of the Judicial Police was entrusted to one or more members of the public prosecutor's office, referred to as supervising magistrates (*toezichtsmagistraten*), who were to be appointed by the Minister of Justice on the recommendation of the board of prosecutors-general.[34]

In addition to one supervising magistrate with general competence for the division concerned, a magistrate had also been appointed specifically to exercise supervision over the former Central Unit for Combating Corruption.

## F. Federal public prosecutor's office

As already stated above, the part of the *Octopus* reform concerning the judiciary introduces *inter alia* a federal public prosecutor's office, directed by a federal prosecutor (*federaal procureur*) and consisting of federal magistrates (*federale magistraten*), who eventually will replace the current national magistrates. Unlike the present national magistrates, however, the federal public prosecutor's office will have the right to remove cases from the local prosecutors. The federal prosecutor is not a member of the board of prosecutors-general; he is allowed, however, to take part in its meetings. The board of prosecutors-general has to evaluate *both* the way in which the federal prosecutor applies the criminal policy directives it has issued *and* the functioning of the federal public prosecutor's office.

The federal prosecutor has the same competences as His Majesty's prosecutors, albeit at federal level, having federal jurisdiction. His competences thus include the right to prosecute, the coordination of prosecutions, the facilitation of international cooperation and the supervision of the general and specific functioning of the future federal police. This implies that specific federal magistrates will be entrusted with the task of supervising *inter alia* the General Directorate Judicial Police of the federal police, the Directorate fight against economic and financial delinquency of the General Directorate Judicial Police of the federal police as far as the fight against corruption is concerned, and the Directorate national database (*Directie nationale gegevensbank*) of the General Directorate Operational Support of the federal police, in which all data from the police (both local and federal) will be stored.

## G. Board of His Majesty's prosecutors

As part of the *Octopus* reform, a board of His Majesty's prosecutors will also be established, which is meant to be an advisory body to the board of prosecutors-general.[35] Thus, a sort of vertical consultation will be realised between the board of prosecutors-general and the local prosecutors, who themselves can benefit from horizontal interaction with their colleagues, in the new board of His Majesty's prosecutors. The latter can also advise the Minister of Justice directly. According to a Royal Decree of 10 July 2001, the Board of His Majesty's prosecutors will come into force on 21 May 2002.[36]

## III. ORGANISED CRIME

## A. Definition

It was decided in 1992, at the suggestion of the then national magistrates and with the agreement of the board of prosecutors-general and the government, to use the definition of organised crime as developed by the *Bundeskriminalamt* (BKA) in Germany as the "official" Belgian definition for operational purposes. This definition never gained legal status, but was endorsed both in the 1996 federal action plan for combating organised crime and 1997 ministerial circular on specialisation between the Gendarmerie and the Judicial Police. According to the definition, the following criteria define organised crime (translation):

The commission,[37] in a methodical manner, of offences:

(1) that, on their own or together, have a considerable importance;
(2) by pursuit of gain or power;
(3) by more than two persons acting together;
(4) during a long or indefinite period of time;
(5) relying on an assignment of duties:
    a) misusing commercial structures and/or;
    b) having recourse to violence or other intimidation techniques and/or;
    c) exercising influence on political life, the media, the public administration, the justice system or economic life.

In January 1999, a legal definition of "criminal organisation" (*not* organised crime) was introduced in the Penal Code,[38] fully meeting the requirements contained in the EU Joint Action of 21 December 1998 on making it a criminal offence to participate in a criminal organisation in the EU Member States.[39] The term "criminal organisation" has been defined as follows: any structured association consisting of more than two persons, established over a period of time with a view to committing offences which are punishable with imprisonment of three years or more, with a view to gaining direct or indirect profits, and having recourse to intimidation, threats, violence, fraudulent manipulation or corruption, or using commercial or other structures to cover up or facilitate the perpetration of offences. However, organisations the goal of which is merely political, trade unionist, philanthropic, philosophical, ideological or religious or that exclusively pursue any other lawful objective, cannot be regarded as criminal organisations as defined above.

## B. Policy

Since the mid-1990s, substantial political attention has been given to the phenomenon of organised crime. In 1996, the government came up with a federal action plan for combating organised crime, and in 1997 it issued a federal action plan for combating economic and financial delinquency. These action plans, both of which preceded the 1997 EU's "Action Plan to Combat Organised Crime", have been the main points of reference in policy making for the past few years. Both legal and organisational reforms or changes have been propelled by the need to fight organised crime more effectively. **Although a number of legal and/or organisational reforms that have been**

**implemented in recent years may have been provided for or recommended by EU legal instruments, they never resulted directly from EU (decision-making) processes. Essentially, the impetus for change has always stemmed from the national level.**

As a result of the 1996 action plan, a multidisciplinary "central working group on organised crime" *(centrale werkgroep georganiseerde misdaad)* was established within the Ministry of Justice. The group, consisting of officials from the cabinet and the Department of Justice as well as of policemen, public prosecutors and academics, is responsible for mapping organised crime officially, especially in the annual situation reports on organised crime that must be produced for both the Belgian Parliament and the EU.

Chiefly as a result of the two action plans, a number of important legal changes have been made or announced in recent years.

As mentioned above, the concept of "criminal organisation" was introduced in the Penal Code in 1999. It was thereby made a punishable offence to deliberately form part of a criminal organisation, to be in control of such an organisation and to participate in (the preparation of) unlawful activities of a criminal organisation or in the making of any decisions in the context of the activities of the criminal organisation, knowing that, by participating, a contribution is made to the goals of the organisation.

As corruption often shows clear links with organised crime, allowing the criminal entrepreneur to expand his power and impact in the "upper world", it was proposed to change the existing legislation. In February 1999, a new bill was adopted,[40] making private corruption and attempted passive corruption criminal offences, raising the penalties for the different forms of corruption and introducing the possibility of prosecuting foreign and international officials in Belgium. The change in the law has clearly been propelled as much by OECD[41] and CoE developments as by EU developments.[42]

In May 1999, the concept of criminal liability of legal persons was officially recognised in penal law.[43]

Draft legislation – drawn up in 1998-1999 by university specialists, but clearly needing revision – regarding the use of special investigative techniques and proactive investigation and policing as well as regarding the use of anonymous testimony and the introduction of a settlement for so-called *pentiti* (collaborators). In line with the Federal Security and Detention Plan of 31 May 2000, the draft texts have in the meantime been revised, partly within the Ministry of Justice and partly by additional university specialists *(see below)*.[44]

The 2000 Federal Security and Detention Plan referred to above reflects the vision, position and response of the new government – formed following the federal elections of June 1999 – with regard to security and detention problems and challenges. The plan had already been announced in the coalition agreement of the new government of July 1999,[45] with this in mind that it would focus on mapping and combating organised crime, improving detection of and reducing white collar crime and combating trafficking in human beings, *inter alia* by combating corruption, corrupt behaviour and the decay of moral standards (by establishing a reinforced anti-corruption unit within the new federal police), by international cooperation in the fight against organised and white collar crime and by the efficient freezing and seizure of criminal assets.

## IV. LAW ENFORCEMENT UNITS TO COMBAT ORGANISED CRIME

### A. Regular law enforcement units before the police reform

At the level of the law enforcement agencies, the coordinating bodies with operational competences in the fight against organised crime at national level were the **Central Bureau of Investigations** (of the Gendarmerie) and the **General Commissariat** (of the Judicial Police). In the context of the use of special investigative techniques, which of course are of particular importance in the fight against organised crime, these bodies were also entrusted with the operational task of processing information collected with the assistance of informers; these bodies were then referred to as "national information services" *(nationale informatiediensten)*, working under the overall responsibility of the national magistrates.

Also in this context of special investigative techniques, specialised units within both the Gendarmerie and the Judicial Police were also created for the purpose of specialised observations. Mention must be made of the Special Intervention Squadron *(Speciaal Interventie-Eskadron – SIE)* and the Observation, Support and Arrest Platoon *(Peloton Observatie, Steun en Arrestatie – POSA)* within the Gendarmerie. As for the Judicial Police, the unit concerned was the Surveillance and Observation Group *(Groep Schaduwing en Observatie)* within the National (23rd) Squad of the Judicial Police.

In the context of proactive policing, the Gendarmerie's Central Bureau of Investigations and the General Commissariat of the Judicial Police were in charge of setting up and conducting national proactive investigations, under the obligation to inform the national magistrates thereof.

## 1. Gendarmerie

The Gendarmerie's Central Bureau of Investigations developed a project-oriented approach in combating (organised) crime. This approach was reflected in the organisation of the Bureau's work flow, the Bureau being organised in different units.

A number of the units were set up as a result of internal Gendarmerie decisions. This was the case for the following units:

- drugs;
- trafficking in human beings (this unit encompassed the official unit for combating trafficking in human beings, installed by decision of the cabinet council – see below);
- offences against persons, violence and hold-ups (this unit comprised the official multidisciplinary hormone unit[46] and the official unit for disappearances, both installed by a decision of the cabinet council – see below);
- terrorism;
- environmental crime;
- property offences (trafficking in stolen vehicles and/or weapons, theft);
- organised crime and assets (this unit was created as a support unit for the other units, which all might have to deal with *organised forms* of the crime for which they had been designed).

Three units had been set up as a result of decisions of the cabinet council. This was the case for:

- the (official) unit for combating trafficking in human beings;
- the unit for disappearances, which, amongst other things, was intended to deal with cases where the disappearance of a minor causes considerable anxiety;
- the multidisciplinary hormone unit (see below).

Within the Central Bureau of Investigations, the Directorate of Operations (*Directie Operaties*) also took a central position. This directorate coordinated and maintained an overview – in management terms – of the whole of operational activities by all units mentioned above. Amongst other things, this involved the taking of decisions on the capacity (e.g. in terms of number of undercover agents, duration of undercover actions, etc.) which was or could be put at the disposal of the various units, which themselves, however, remained in charge of the practical application of special investigative techniques.

## 2. Judicial Police

As indicated above, the General Commissariat of the Judicial Police comprised three central units: the National Squad, the Central Unit for Combating Economic and Financial Delinquency and the Central Unit for Combating Corruption.

Following the terrorist bombings by the so-called "*Cellules Communistes Combattantes*" and the "gang of Nivelles" in the second half of the 1980s, the Minister of Justice decided that the Judicial Police needed some reorganisation. He therefore set up the National Squad, entrusted specifically with the repression of serious banditry that could, due to its extent or impact, take national or international proportions (such as terrorism-related crime or internationally organised crime) (see above).

The Central Unit for Combating Economic and Financial Delinquency was initially set up within the General Commissariat of the Judicial Police. The unit was later transferred to the General Police Support Service (for a short period of time) and later (in December 1996) reintegrated into the General Commissariat of the Judicial Police by a government decision.

The unit was *exclusively* active in the area of *organised* economic and financial delinquency, economic and financial crimes which had particular potential to disrupt certain economic sectors if they were of an *organised* nature. Its range of action comprised combating money laundering, serious fiscal offences, insider trading and fraud against the EC/EU budget. It was part of the unit's official mission, moreover, to maintain contacts in this area with the EC (in practice: OLAF) and to provide support whenever requested.

The range of action of the Central Unit for Combating Corruption included (supporting) the detection of serious and complex offences against the material or moral interests of the public service, (supporting) the detection of serious and complex offences in the preparation, allocation and execution of public tenders, in the preparation, granting and use of public subsidies and in the conferring of authorisation, permission, approval and recognition, as well as the dynamic management and exploitation of specialised documentation for the police services.

The unit, having jurisdiction for the entire Belgian territory, had its seat in Brussels and had local bureaux at its disposal in the country's most important cities. In general, the unit acted on the basis of guidelines issued by the Minister of Justice or by the board of prosecutors-general, or upon the instructions of the Commissioner-General of the Judicial Police. In individual cases, the unit also acted upon the request of the (local) judicial authorities, on the advice of its supervising magistrate.

Lastly, the unit had an important task in coordinating complex investigations as well as investigations exceeding the territorial definition of a given court's districts or having an international dimension, in cooperation with the national magistrates.[47]

According to the 2000 Federal Security and Detention Plan, the unit will be merged into a new federal anti-corruption service.

With organised crime increasingly showing links with the internet and the virtual society (online illegal gambling, child pornographic industry, etc.), the central notification point for illegal or harmful content on the internet *(centraal gerechtelijk meldpunt)*, lodged within the national computer crime unit of the Judicial Police,[48] must also be mentioned here. The unit was established as a result of a "memorandum of understanding" concluded in May 1999 between the Minister for Telecommunications, the Minister of Justice and the Belgian association of internet service providers (ISPA Belgium), intended to improve the fight against illegal material on the internet. As a result of this memorandum, the former notification point for child-pornographic material, which had been set up within the Judicial Police in the mid-1990s, was also merged into the central notification point.

## B. Regular law enforcement units since the police reform

Since the police reform, both the Gendarmerie, the Judicial Police and the Municipal Police have ceased to exist. A new and integrated police service structured on two levels, i.e. the federal and the local level, have been installed. The federal level consists of five general directorates which are all under the authority of the Commissioner General of the federal police: the **General Directorate Administrative Police** *(Algemene Directie Bestuurlijke Politie)*, the **General Directorate Judicial Police** *(Algemene Directie Gerechtelijke Politie)*, the **General Directorate Operational Support** *(Algemene Directie Operationele Ondersteuning)*, the **General Directorate Human Resources** *(Algemene Directie Personeel)* and the **General Directorate Logistics** *(Algemene Directie Materiële Middelen)*.

The General Directorate Judicial Police and the General Directorate Operational Support are of particular relevance in the fight against organised crime on the federal level.

The **General Directorate Judicial Police** is composed of seven directorates, five of which have an important role to play in the fight against organised crime: the Directorate of the operations and information of judicial, police nature *(Directie van de operaties en inlichtingen van gerechtelijke politionele aard)*, the Directorate fight against crime concerning persons *(Directie strijd tegen criminaliteit inzake personen)*, the Directorate fight against organised crime *(Directie strijd tegen georganiseerde criminaliteit)*, the Directorate fight against crime concerning goods *(Directie strijd tegen criminaliteit inzake goederen)*, and the Directorate fight against economic and financial delinquency (*Directie strijd tegen economische en financiële delinquentie*).

The **Directorate fight against crime concerning persons** deals with trafficking and smuggling in human beings, aggression (crime against persons and disappearances), terrorism, sects and psychotropic substances, and replaces the units drugs, trafficking in human beings, offences against persons, violence and hold-ups (including the official unit for disappearances) and terrorism of the former Gendarmerie's Central Bureau of Investigations.

The **Directorate fight against crime concerning goods** is responsible for the fight against hold-ups (which used to be a task of the former unit offences against persons, violence and hold-ups of the CBO that integrated in the Directorate fight against crime concerning persons), hormones, environmental offences, serious and organised property crime, escapes or FAST (Fugitives Active Search Team), trafficking in stolen vehicles, art and antiques theft and weapons. It substitutes the previously existing units which carried mandates concerning environmental crime, property offences, organised crime and assets and the official multidisciplinary hormone unit (which used to go with the former unit offences against persons, violence and hold-ups that integrated in the Directorate fight against crime concerning persons) of the former Central Bureau of Investigations of the Gendarmerie.

The **Directorate fight against organised crime** in its turn is engaged in projects relating to the fight against organised crime, witness protection (comprising the witness protection service, *see below*) and patrimonium [check English] research.

In the same manner, **the Directorate of the operations and information of judicial, police nature** replaces the Directorate of Operations of the former Central Bureau of Investigations of the Gendarmerie, which played an important role in the coordination of all operational activities executed by all units of the former Central Bureau of investigations; it deals with, *inter alia,* the national management of informants, operational crime analysis, telephone interception and special techniques.

Finally, the **Directorate fight against economic and financial delinquency** is exclusively active in the area of corruption, economic and financial delinquency (acting as a central service), computer crime (comprising the Federal Computer Crime Unit of the former Judicial Police and its central judicial notification point) and forgeries. It assumes the tasks of the Central Unit for combating Economic and Financial Delinquency and the Central Unit for Combating Corruption of the former Judicial Police.

The **General Directorate Operational Support** consists of a Directorate management, policy and development (*Directie beheer, beleid en ontwikkeling*), a Directorate special units (*Directie speciale eenheden*), a

Directorate national database (*Directie nationale gegevensbank*), a Directorate telematics (*Directie telematica*), a Directorate operational police cooperation (*Directie operationale politiesamenwerking*) and external services. The **Directorate special units** is considered of special importance in the fight against organised crime, as it deals with specialised security, specialised surveillance, specialised interventions and special techniques; it assumes the tasks of the former Special Intervention Squadron, the Observation, Support and Arrest Platoon within the former Gendarmerie, and the Observation Unit within the National Squad of the former Judicial Police.[49]

## C. Other relevant national units

### 1. The Financial Information Processing Unit

The EC Council Directive 91/308/EC of 1991 was implemented in the Belgian legal system at the beginning of 1993.[50] The 1993 Act combats money laundering by imposing an obligation on financial institutions and individuals to report transactions or situations that are suspected to be connected with or may indicate money-laundering activities to the so-called Financial Information Processing Unit (*Cel voor Financiële Informatieverwerking – CFI*).

According to the same Act, one may be convicted of committing the offence of money laundering if the following elements can be proven:

(1) the exchange or transfer of money or assets with the intention to conceal or cover up the illegal origin thereof, or to help a person who is involved in a crime, from which this money or these assets are the proceeds, to escape from the legal consequences of his deeds;

(2) the concealment or covering up of the nature, origin, place of discovery, relocation or (change of) ownership of money or assets of which the illegal origin is known;

(3) the acquisition, possession or use of money and assets of which the illegal origin is known;

(4) participation in, complicity in, the attempt to carry out, assistance with, the incitement to carry out, the facilitation of, or the giving of advice regarding one of the activities referred to above.

As indicated above, the 1993 Act relates to money and assets with an illegal origin. Money and assets, according to the law, are illegal when they proceed from a crime connected with terrorism, organised crime, drug trafficking, illegal trade in weapons, goods or merchandise, trade in clandestine workers, slave trade, exploitation of prostitution, forbidden use of or trade in hormones, illegal trade in human organs or tissues, fraud adversely affecting the financial interests of the EC, serious and organised tax fraud (i.e. where very complex procedures of an international scope are being used), bribery of public servants, stock exchange crimes, capital investment fraud, or fraudulent bankruptcy. In other words, any and all violations of a provision of criminal law are sufficient to define the money or the assets that proceed therefrom as having an illegal origin as referred to in the 1993 Act, provided that there is a connection of some kind between the violation and one of the criminal activities listed above. As such, the scope of Belgian legislation *ratione materiae* is much broader than required by EC Directive 91/308/EC, which, strictly interpreted, exclusively relates to the proceeds of crime in the area of drug trafficking (albeit that the EU Member States have been given the possibility, in view of the implementation of the EC Directive, to bring other criminal activities under its field of application as well).

The Financial Information Processing Unit is an independent incorporated administrative body, working under the authority of the Ministers of Justice and Finance and consisting of financial experts. The daily supervision of the unit is the responsibility of a magistrate of the public prosecutor's office, who has been seconded to the unit.

As regards its relationship with the public prosecutor's office, the unit may, once it has received a report of suspicious transactions or activities, notify His Majesty's Prosecutor thereof. Such notification has the same effect as reporting a crime to the legal authorities for the purpose of instituting criminal prosecution. Thus, bank information or financial information that in itself has a confidential nature is brought into the preliminary investigation or the judicial investigation.

In the meantime, the scope *ratione personae* of the obligation to report suspicious transactions and situations to the Unit, as contained in the 1993 Act, has been extended from financial institutions only to *inter alia* process servers, public notaries, accountants and real estate agencies. The 1996 federal action plan for combating organised crime had called for this extension, announcing an initiative by the Minister of Justice on the matter, long before the European Commission came up with a similar proposal in 1999.[51]

Together with the American financial intelligence unit, the Financial Information Processing Unit has promoted the setting up of the so-called Egmont Group, comprising all financial intelligence units worldwide.[52] Further, the unit has established bilateral contacts as well as international contacts with the Financial Action Task Force (FATF), the European Commission, the EU's new anti-corruption unit (OLAF), the PHARE programme, the Money Laundering Experts Group (which the EU's Multidisciplinary Group on Organised Crime has entrusted with an analysis of the strong and weak points in the fight against money laundering in the EU), Europol, the Council of Europe and the UN.

### 2. Meat fraud notification point

In 1997, the cabinet council decided to install a permanent meat fraud notification point within the Institute for Veterinary Inspection (see below: multidisciplinary integrated teams).

### 3. Economic Inspectorate

The Economic Inspectorate *(Bestuur Economische Inspectie)* is a separate department within the Ministry of Economic Affairs, consisting of central and regional directions (see below), in charge of both administrative and penal control on the enforcement of economic regulations. The inspectorate's task is to act as the federal law enforcement unit for economic crimes in all possible sectors, to deal with complaints and to cooperate with the public prosecutor's office.

### 4. Customs and excise department

The customs and excise department, being a fiscal administration lodged within the Ministry of Finance, also has a role to play in the fight against organised crime, as its primary mission[53] is to control the import, export and transit of goods. To this end, the department cooperates with the police services under the supervision of the public prosecutor's office.

The department consists of a central directorate and outside services, which in their turn encompass general services (regional directorate) and special services. Among the latter, the national investigations directorate *(nationale opsporingsdirectie)* has a special position, having been entrusted with the national coordination of investigations conducted by the regional directorates as well as with the mutual (administrative) assistance of foreign customs and excise authorities. All customs and excise officials have the competence to establish that a criminal (customs and excise) offence has been committed.[54]

### 5. Special Tax Inspectorate

The Special Tax Inspectorate *(Bijzondere BelastingInspectie – BBI)*, which also falls under the Ministry of Finance, consists of a central administration and outside services, like the customs and excise department. The outside services encompass four regional directorates, which in principle are all competent to trace fiscal fraud within the entire Belgian territory. In practice, however, the regional directorates only exercise their jurisdiction within the linguistic area where they have been established. In its turn, the central administration comprises several branches with specific competences, the 7th branch having national jurisdiction for all linguistic areas.

### 6. Central DNA and other forensic databases

As indicated above, DNA identification was officially introduced in March 1999 as an investigative technique for investigations into crime.[55] The new law provided for a central DNA database, of which the task of maintaining has been entrusted to the National Institute for Criminalistics and Criminology, which will also be in charge of maintaining central databases on ballistics, drugs, weapons, fingerprints, paints and textiles.

## V. PUBLIC PROSECUTION UNITS TO FIGHT ORGANISED CRIME

### A. National level

At the level of the public prosecutor's office, the coordinating bodies or agents in the domain of anti-organised crime initiatives (both from an operational and policy perspective) are the board of prosecutors-general (or its individual members, depending on the types of crime covered by their respective portfolios), the national magistrates – who, as a result of the Octopus reform, will be replaced by federal magistrates (from the federal public prosecutor's office) as of 21 May 2002, the supervising magistrates, and the assisting magistrates. Their respective tasks and roles are commented on extensively elsewhere in this chapter.

### B. Local level

The same applies for the functions of the confidential magistrate and the magistrates for judicial cooperation who are the most relevant members of the public prosecutor's office in the context of combating organised crime (see above).

## VI. MULTIDISCIPLINARY INTEGRATED TEAMS

A number of multidisciplinary integrated (interdepartmental) teams have been established in recent years or are about to be set up with a view to adopting a more integrated approach towards specific forms of (organised) crime. The impetus for this development was not given by the 1997 EU Action Plan to Combat Organised Crime, though this plan encouraged the Member States to set up multidisciplinary teams in the fight against organised crime (Recommendation 20).

## A. Interdepartmental (hormone) residue unit

Since the mid-1990s in particular, meat fraud and hormone-related crime have taken very serious proportions in Belgium, culminating in the murder by the so-called "meat mafia" of a veterinary surgeon who acted as an official inspector on behalf of the government (*Van Noppen*) in the field of hormone detection.

However, an interdepartmental (hormone) residue unit (*interdepartementale cel residuen*) had been established even before this, in 1994. The unit, presided by the assisting magistrate for hormone-related crime and representatives from all relevant departments (Justice, Agriculture, Public Health and Finance), is a non-operational unit, intended to facilitate administrative and policy coordination, consultation and, if necessary, the resolution of conflicts between the departments involved.[56] The importance of this unit has ceased since the multidisciplinary hormone unit (see below) was established in 1997.

## B. Multidisciplinary hormone unit

Until 1997, the operational counterpart of the interdepartmental (hormone) residue unit was the national hormone unit (*nationale hormonencel*), established within the former Central Bureau of Investigations of the Gendarmerie. It was then transformed into the multidisciplinary hormone unit (*multidisciplinaire hormonencel*), still lodged within the Central Bureau of Investigations, to which officials from the different departments involved were posted on a full-time basis. Apart from officers from the Gendarmerie, the unit comprises representatives from the Ministries of Agriculture (veterinary medical inspectorate (*diergeneeskundige inspectie*), inspectorate for raw materials (*grondstoffeninspectie*)), Public Health (Institute for Veterinary Inspection (*Instituut voor Veterinaire Keuring* – IVK*), pharmaceutical inspectorate (*farmaceutische inspectie*)) and Finance (customs and excise department, tax department, VAT department).

## C. Interdepartmental prevention unit

In 1996, an interdepartmental prevention unit (*interdepartementale preventiecel*) was established within the Ministry of Agriculture. The unit organises the cooperation between the Department of Agriculture, the institute for veterinary inspection (which falls under the Public Health department) and the Department of Economic Affairs. Its mission is to coordinate preventive action against fraud with regard to expenditures chargeable to the European Agriculture Orientation and Guarantee Fund (*Europees Oriëntatie- en Garantiefonds voor de Landbouw*). The guarantee division of this European Fund finances restitutions in the case of exports to third countries as well as financial interventions to regulate the markets. The largest part of those financial contributions is paid directly by the Member States, which act as an intermediary between the European Fund and the beneficiary. The Belgian intermediary body is the "Belgian intervention and restitution bureau/BIRB" (*Belgisch interventie- en restitutiebureau*).

## D. Multidisciplinary unit for combating meat fraud

Another integrated unit is the multidisciplinary unit for combating meat fraud (*multidisciplinaire vleesfraudebestrijdingscel*), which is an operational unit and, in this way, comparable to the multidisciplinary hormone unit. The unit meets on a monthly basis and brings together the assisting magistrate in the area of financial, economic and fiscal crime, the national magistrate if necessary, the assisting magistrate in the area of hormone-related crime or the magistrate dealing with (a) particular case(s), a federal police officer from the multidisciplinary hormone unit, as well as representatives from the BIRB, customs, the VAT department, the social inspectorate, the economic inspectorate, the Directorate fight against economic and financial delinquency of the General Directorate Judicial Police of the federal police and other relevant services, depending on the case(s) concerned.

## E. Interdepartmental coordination unit for combating international trafficking in human beings

Following a parliamentary inquiry committee on the matter,[57] the fight against trafficking in human beings was substantially reinforced in Belgium. Apart from entrusting the centre for equal opportunities and combating racism (*centrum voor gelijkheid van kansen en voor racisme*) with the coordination and follow-up of the policy to fight trafficking in human beings, the government also established a permanent structure for policy coordination and implementation, intended to guarantee that the social and criminal law approaches towards this activity would coincide.

The Minister of Justice is the president of this unit, which is referred to as the interdepartmental coordination unit for combating international trafficking in human beings (*interdepartementale coördinatiecel ter bestrijding van de mensenhandel*); the centre for equal opportunities and combating racism has been entrusted with the secretariat and coordination of the unit's activities. Further, the unit comprises representatives from all departments and federal agencies involved in the fight against trafficking in human beings, both from a social viewpoint and a criminal law viewpoint. Other persons or bodies not belonging to public administration or not enjoying a federal status may also be involved in the work of the unit.

The interdepartmental unit's principal task is to facilitate information exchange between all relevant partners, with a view to ensuring the proper coordination of both operational actions and policy. At the same time, the unit is intended to facilitate critical evaluation of results and developments in the field and to formulate proposals and recommendations with a view to improving the efficiency of the fight against trafficking in human beings. Finally, if required, the unit can also take the initiative to set up coordination structures at the level of the court's districts.

## F. Interdepartmental unit for combating financial, economic and fiscal delinquency

Whereas the 1997 federal action plan for combating economic and financial delinquency only called for a feasibility study to set up an interdepartmental unit for combating financial, economic and fiscal crime – as was also the case with the interdepartmental (hormone) residue unit – the 2000 Federal Security and Detention Plan envisaged the establishment of such a unit at short notice. Preparations, including the drafting of a protocol that should serve as a starting point for the elaboration of the organisational structure and functioning of the unit, were made by the assisting magistrate in the area of financial, economic and fiscal crime, under the auspices of the board of prosecutors-general (in particular of the prosecutor-general, with financial, economic and fiscal crime falling within his portfolio). In this preparatory stage, close contacts have been established with the departments involved which will eventually be represented in the unit, i.e. the Ministry of Justice, the Ministry of Finance and the special tax inspectorate (*bijzondere belastinginspectie – BBI*), the Ministry of Economics and the economics inspectorate, the Directorate fight against economic and financial delinquency of the General Directorate of the Judicial Police (before the police reform, the Central Unit for Combating Economic and Financial Delinquency of the Judicial Police), and the Financial Information Processing Unit. Representatives of the private sector will also be involved in the unit's current activities. One of the central aims of setting up the unit is to identify structural measures in the fight against various forms of serious fiscal fraud, such as VAT *carrousels.*

## G. National consultation platform on telecommunications

As criminal organisations commonly rely on modern and highly sophisticated information and communication technology, the 2000 Federal Security and Detention Plan considers improved consultation and coordination between all relevant bodies and agencies (both private and public) to be a top priority in the fight against forms of crime of which the use/misuse of telecommunications means is a constituent element or specific *modus operandi*. Therefore, a **national consultation platform on telecommunication** (*nationaal overlegplatform telecommunicatie – NOT*) was established at the end of the year 2000. It will continue to meet on a regular basis in future. One of the primary goals of the platform is to implement the extended (legal) obligation for telecommunication operators and providers of telecommunication services to cooperate with the judicial authorities in tracing, identifying and intercepting "targets" making use of telecommunications.

The members of the platform include the Minister of Justice, the Minister for Telecommunications, the operators of telecommunication networks and services, and the Belgian association of internet service providers (ISPA Belgium). In addition to the platform, there also exist an **internal working group** composed of the Minister of Justice, the Minister for Telecommunications and the central notification point for illegal content of the internet (*centraal gerechtelijk meldpunt*), lodged within the Federal Computer Crime Unit of the Directorate fight against economic and financial delinquency of the federal police.

## H. Commission for the protection of witnesses and persons collaborating with the judicial system

The 2000 Federal Security and Detention Plan envisaged the establishment of a commission for the protection of witnesses and persons collaborating with the judicial system, bringing together all relevant partners (the various ministries and departments involved, the police, the judiciary etc.). The commission's task would be to ensure an objective and uniform approach and follow-up of protection cases and dossiers. In the framework of this Federal Security and Detention Plan, a research project has been conducted with a view to preparing adequate legislation in the field of protecting and collaborating with (crown) witnesses and other persons collaborating with the judicial system in the fight against (organised) crime.[58] The project was completed by the end of September 2000, allowing the Minister of Justice to introduce a (number of) bill(s) on the matter soon thereafter. In this context, the cabinet council approved of a preliminary draft of law concerning the arrangement of the protection of threatened witnesses (*Voorontwerp van wet betreffende een regeling voor de bescherming van bedreigde getuigen*).[59]

With regard to the persons collaborating with the judicial system, internal political disagreement within the cabinet council has prevented the adoption of the draft of law concerning the introduction of an arrangement with regard to persons collaborating with the judicial system (*Voorontwerp van wet betreffende de invoering van een regeling inzake medewerkers met het gerecht*). The preliminary draft of law concerning the arrangement of the protection of threatened witnesses, which has recently been submitted to the Council of State (*Raad van State)* for advice, and which will be submitted to the Parliament by the end of this year, envisages the establishment of a **witness protection commission** (*getuigenbeschermingscommissie*) and a **witness protection service** (*getuigenbeschermingsdienst*). The witness protection commission will be competent for the adjudication, modification, withdrawal and execution of protective measures and financial assistance. The commission will be composed of the federal prosecutor, acting as its chairman, a representative of the Board of His Majesty's Prosecutors, the Prosecutor-general responsible for the international relations, the Director-general Judicial Police of the federal police, the Director-general Operational Support, a representative of the Ministry of Justice and a representative of the Ministry of the Interior. The coordination of the protection will be ensured by the witness protection service which will reside under the authority of the Directorate fight against organised crime of the General Directorate Judicial Police of the federal police.

## VII. INTERNATIONAL CONTACT POINTS

### A. At national level

The EU Action Plan provides for the establishment of a central international contact point (for the exchange of information and the completion of application procedures for cooperation) within each Member State, both for judicial (in recommendation 21) and law enforcement agencies (recommendation 19).

In Belgium, the national magistrates and the service in charge of processing individual requests for judicial assistance within the Ministry of Justice[60] *(Dienst Individuele Strafrechtshulp)* were officially appointed as national *judicial* points of contact for the functioning of the European Judicial Network, as provided for in the Joint Action of 29 June 1998. Both the national magistrates and the relevant ministerial service, however, had been functioning as national contact points before this. Taking into account that the idea of establishing a European Judicial Network was aimed more specifically at EU level by the *Belgian* Ministry of Justice, it may very well be the case that Belgian good practice (having excellent national contact points for judicial cooperation, both within and outside the ministry) has actually influenced EU decision making on the matter. **Thus, the decision to set up a European judicial network would have been inspired by national developments rather than the other way around.**

With regards to the *law enforcement* agencies, the new Directorate operational police cooperation of the General Directorate Operational Support of the federal police (which carries out the operational tasks of the international police cooperation division of the former General Police Support Service) now plays a central role in the international exchange of police information, *inter alia* in the field of combating organised crime.

The need to establish a general support service for the various police services with general competence (the Gendarmerie and the Judicial Police in particular) had already been stressed in the late 1980s by the first parliamentary inquiry committee into the offences committed by the so-called "gang of Nivelles". One of the main objectives of the support service was to contribute to better coordination and cooperation between the different police services, *inter alia* in the field of information exchange with foreign police services (by establishing a single contact point that could be relied upon both by Belgian policemen in their contacts with foreign colleagues, and by foreign policemen in their contacts with Belgian colleagues) and to develop specific expertise in the field of international police cooperation, amongst other things with a view to (assisting in) the conclusion of international (bilateral) agreements with regard to police cooperation.

These tasks were entrusted to the international police cooperation division, which thus became responsible for managing the international information flow in the field of policing. Since 10 April 1996, the division has centralised the processing of messages and notices on behalf of the three police forces, encompassing the Interpol National Central Bureau (NCB), the national part of Europol, the service desk for Belgian liaison officers abroad, the national part of the Schengen Information System (NSIS) as well as the SIRENE[61] Bureau. As such, recommendation 19 of the EU Action Plan to Combat Organised Crime was implemented even before the Action Plan had been drawn up.

The international police cooperation division of the General Police Support Service was organised in "pillars". The organigram comprised support services, operational services and expert services as distinct pillars. The "support" pillar encompassed a legal affairs division and an information brokerage division, which had the task of ensuring smooth internal information management.

Within the "operational" pillar, the division dealing with international messages and notices took a central position. Since 10 March 1997, all messages and notices have been routed through a single technical operations room, irrespective of the channel of information exchange being used (Interpol, SIS, Europol-liaisons, Belgian liaisons abroad). The actual *routing of enquiries* from police and judicial authorities contacting the division was done by the division itself, in order to avoid the need for field officers and individual magistrates to work their way into the complex field of national and international regulations regarding international police information exchange. In addition, the "operational" pillar consisted of a 24-hour service, intended to guarantee continuity in processing information requests; a follow-up division, the task of which was to check the quality of the content both of Belgian requests and answers to foreign requests, and a record office, keeping archives and logs of all data processed, mainly in order to allow *a posteriori* data protection control.

Lastly, the "expert" pillar consisted of a number of centres or units of expertise, in charge of studying (developments within) the different police structures from a policy point of view. There used to be an Interpol unit, a unit that supported non-Europol-related EU police activities, and a unit which coordinated the Europol liaison officers, the Belgian liaison officers abroad, and the foreign liaison officers in Belgium, and a SIRENE-NSIS unit. An "operational support – confidential files" division had been established alongside the pillar-structure, with a specific mandate in the area of organised crime. Its task was to provide for support at the international level – both to judicial and police authorities – in the context of the exchange of information regarding organised crime.

Lastly, it must be mentioned that the international police cooperation division of the General Police Support Service maintained direct and permanent contacts with the national magistrates in a number of areas. This was the case *inter alia* with regards to judicial control of police information exchange and juridical validation of notices in the SIS (in complex or sensitive cases).

## B.  At regional level

Through the agreement of 4 July 1994, the Belgian Ministers of Justice and Home Affairs introduced so-called operational points of contact in the border areas *(Operationele Invalspunten in de Grensgebieden – OIPG's)*. These points of contact have been entrusted with providing operational and information-related assistance regarding international cooperation in the border areas, both to Belgian and foreign police services in the areas concerned. As such, they act as regional central points of contact for the international exchange of "border related" information. In addition, "non-border related" information may also be exchanged through the operational points of contact in the border areas in urgent[62] cases, as the police are then allowed to contact foreign colleagues directly on the basis of Article 39 (3) of the Schengen Implementing Convention. Naturally, in non-urgent cases, however, the Directorate operational police cooperation of the General Directorate Operational Support of the federal police remains the mandatory transmission centre for "non-border related" information exchange.

## VIII.   SUPERVISION AND CONTROL

According to the law and to doctrine, Belgian police officers are obliged to keep written records of their findings and must report offences to the public prosecutor's office His Majesty's prosecutor or his deputies immediately. In principle, they have no discretionary powers concerning any further action to be taken, and failing to record or report an offence is a breach of duty, for which they can be reprimanded by the disciplinary authority or even face criminal prosecution. Beyond their initial reporting of the offence, which they are obliged to make *ex officio*, they have no investigative powers of their own. Once they have reported the crime, they must wait for further instructions from the public prosecutor.

If the public prosecutor's office decides to prosecute, two kinds of investigation must be distinguished: either a "preliminary investigation" is carried out by the police under the authority of His Majesty's prosecutor ("information"), or the investigation is conducted by the investigating judge ("instruction"), in which case the investigation is referred to as a "judicial investigation" (see above). If a case is particularly complicated or requires the use of special means of coercion, the public prosecutor's office can request an "instruction" to be carried out by the investigating judge. In addition, the victim can ask the investigating judge to carry out such an investigation. The investigating judge is only competent for the investigation of the offence referred to him. Hence, he cannot start an investigation *ex officio*, nor can he expand the scope of the investigation at his own discretion.

As far as the use of special investigative techniques and proactive investigations are concerned, the appropriate judicial authorities – His Majesty's prosecutor (and, in cases of judicial investigations, the investigating judge), the confidential magistrate and/or the national magistrate – must either be informed or even asked for their written permission prior to the employment of certain techniques.

The same rules apply regarding the international exchange of information or intelligence. In principle, this means that the police are not allowed to exchange any data with foreign colleagues, not even "for police use only", unless the judicial authorities have given explicit permission to do so. A circular letter, issued by the board of prosecutors-general in 1997,[63] has brought a *modus vivendi*, however, allowing the police to autonomously exchange *certain categories* of information and intelligence of a "judicial nature"[64] with their colleagues abroad. In the meantime, this circular letter has been further developed and "fine-tuned" in a new circular letter, issued jointly in mid-February 2000 by the Minister of Justice and the board of prosecutors-general,[65] and applicable since 1 May 2000. A regulatory initiative in this matter will be taken following the delivery of a scientific report[66] to the Minister of Justice by the end of 2001.

In addition to judicial control, the police is also under the control of the Ministers of the Interior and of Justice, depending on the purpose of their work. In the context of administrative policing and public order maintenance, they are under the supervision of the Minister of the Interior, whereas for judicial police work, they are under the supervision of the Minister of Justice. In addition, the police is also accountable to Parliament. To this end, an independent standing committee for the supervision of the police services (*vast comité van toezicht op de politiediensten, also referred to as Comité P*), which reports to Parliament, has been established as a means of external control.

## NOTES

1.  Koninklijk Besluit over de algemene politiesteundienst, *B.S.* 30 juli 1994.
2.  See: *Gedrukte Stukken*, Belgische Kamer van Volksvertegenwoordigers, 1989-1990, No. 59/8-1988 (first parliamentary inquiry committee); Landuyt, R. and Viseur, J.-P., "Parlementair onderzoek naar de noodzakelijke aanpassingen van de organisatie en de werking van het politie- en justitiewezen op basis van de moeilijkheden die gerezen zijn bij het onderzoek naar de 'Bende van Nijvel'", *Gedrukte Stukken*, Belgische Kamer van Volksvertegenwoordigers, 1997-1998, No.s 573/10 – 95/96 (second parliamentary inquiry committee).
3.  See: Landuyt, R. and de T'Serclaes, N. "Parlementair onderzoek naar de wijze waarop het onderzoek door politie en gerecht werd gevoerd in de zaak 'Dutroux-Nihoul en consorten'", *Gedrukte Stukken*, Belgische Kamer van Volksvertegenwoordigers, 1996-1997, No. 713-6, 14 April 1997.
4.  Commissie voor een efficiëntere politiestructuur, *Eenheid in verscheidenheid – vrijheid in gebondenheid*, Brussels, 1997, 116 pp.
5.  Other proposals for the reorganisation of the police forces can also be mentioned. See for example: Caluwé, L. and Happart, J., "Evaluatie van de politiediensten. Verslag namens de Commissie voor de Binnenlandse en de Administratieve Aangelegenheden", *Gedrukte Stukken*, Belgische Senaat, 1996-1997, No. 1-700/1-3; Commissie voor een efficiëntere politiestructuur, *Eenheid in verscheidenheid – vrijheid in gebondenheid*, Brussels, 1997, 116 pp.
6.  See: *De brug naar de eenentwingste eeuw – regeerakkoord – 7 juli 1999*, URL: http://www.belgium.fgov.be/pb/pbb/nlbb13.htm, 27-7-99, p. 6.
7.  Richtlijn van de minister van Justitie van 21 februari 1997 tot regeling van de samenwerking en coördinatie inzake opdrachten van gerechtelijke politie tussen de politiediensten (Col. 1/97).
8.  *Omzendbrief proactieve recherche*, Brussels, December 1996, 6 pp. + annexes.
9.  Actieplan van de regering tegen de georganiseerde criminaliteit, *Gedrukte Stukken*, Belgische Senaat, 1995-96, No. 1-326/5 (annex).
10. Of the crime sort (impact, type and extent), the sectors at risk and the effectiveness of the criminal policy towards the phenomenon.
11. See below for the operational definition of the concept of "organised crime" as applied in Belgium.
12. For example in a money laundering or corruption case (types of crime within the specific field of expertise of the Judicial Police) that shows links to a trafficking case (type of crime within the specific field of expertise of the Gendarmerie).
13. In full: Judicial Police of the Bench (*Gerechtelijke Politie bij de Parketten*).
14. Next to the central operational documentation for the squads linked to the public prosecutor's office in the court's districts and the central services.
15. The unit has important technical means at its disposal for supporting the local brigades.
16. Which in the near future will be transformed into the National Institute for Criminalistics *(Nationaal Instituut voor Criminalistiek)* (see below).
17. See: X., *De Gerechtelijke pijler, Functioneel-organisatorische afstemming*,

URL: premier.fgov.be/topics/reports/report8/gerechtelijke-pijler_N.doc, 18-09-01, 35 pp.

18. See: Koninklijk Besluit van 11 juli 1994, *B.S.* 30 juli 1994.
19. See: Koninklijk Besluit met betrekking tot de Commissaris-generaal en de algemene directies van de federale politie, *B.S.* 23 september 2000; *Algemene Directie Operationele Ondersteuning,* URL: http://www.rijkswacht.be/fedpol/orga/org-op-ond.htm, 18-09-01, p. 1.
20. See *inter alia* Themanummer "Octopus – de justitiehervorming", *Orde van de dag,* Kluwer Editorial, 1999, No. 7, 63 pp.; Huybrechts, L., "De tentakels van de octopus", *Panopticon,* 1999, pp. 1-2.
21. A bill on the subject has already been passed, but has not yet entered into force. See: Wet 22 december 1998 betreffende de verticale integratie van het openbaar ministerie, het federaal parket en de raad van de procureurs des Konings, *B.S.* 10 februari 1999; Koninklijk Besluit 12 augustus 2000 tot vaststelling van de datum van inwerkingtreding van sommige bepalingen van de wet van 22 december 1998 betreffende de verticale integratie van het openbaar ministerie, het federaal parket en de raad van de procureurs des Konings, *B.S.* 24 augustus 2000; Koninklijk Besluit 10 juli 2001 tot vaststelling van de datum van inwerkingtreding van sommige bepalingen van de wet van 22 december 1998 betreffende de verticale integratie van het openbaar ministerie, het federaal parket en de raad van de procureurs des Konings, *B.S.* 20 juli 2001. The provisions with regard to the federal public prosecutor's office (*federaal parket*) in the original bill of 22 December 1998 have already been revised. See: Wet 21 juni 2001 tot wijziging van verscheidene bepalingen inzake het federaal parket, *B.S.* 20 juli 2001; Koninklijk Besluit 4 juli 2001 tot vaststelling van de datum van inwerkingtreding van de bepalingen van de wet van 21 juni 2001 tot wijziging van verscheidene bepalingen inzake het federaal parket, *B.S.* 20 juli 2001.
22. Under 4.3.4.
23. See: Wet 4 maart 1997 tot instelling van het college van procureurs-generaal en tot instelling van het ambt van nationaal magistraat, *B.S.* 30 april 1994.
24. S. De Clerck, *Het bos en de bomen: justitie hervormen,* Tielt, Lannoo, 1997, p. 90.
25. See: Koninklijk Besluit 6 mei 1997 betreffende de specifieke taken van de leden van het college van procureurs-generaal, *B.S.* 14 mei 1997.
26. The portfolios of the other prosecutors-general include: for *Antwerp*: criminal policy in general, including detection and prosecution policy; follow-up of the execution of sentences; organisation of the courts; relations with the Ministry of Justice and its Criminal Policy Department; for *Brussels*: financial, economic and commercial law; financial, fiscal and economic crime; environmental crime; protection of minors; victim-related policy and, in as far the Communities and regions are competent in this area, cooperation between the latter and the federal level; corruption; for *Mons*: relations with the police services, in particular with regard to the "inter police zones" and the "pentagonal consultation"; citizen safety, in particular in the context of road traffic and crime in the cities; relations with the general commissariat of the Judicial Police, the

General Staff of the Gendarmerie, the Standing Committee for the Municipal Police, the General Police Support Service and the National Institute for Criminalistics and Criminology; civil and procedural law, provided the organisation of the court is not concerned, and for *Liège*: offences against persons, in particular trafficking in human beings, paedophilia and child abuse; sects; bio-ethics; drug-related crime; non-accountability for criminal behaviour and recidivism; social law, in particular with regard to social criminality and social fraud; gambling etc.

27. Apart from hormone-related crimes.
28. See: Ministeriële Omzendbrief 24 april 1990 betreffende de bijzondere opsporingstechnieken om de zware of georganiseerde criminaliteit te bestrijden.
29. Under 4.3.4.
30. See: Wet 4 maart 1997 tot instelling van het college van procureurs-generaal en tot instelling van het ambt van nationaal magistraat, *B.S.* 30 april 1997.
31. See: *Federaal Veiligheids- en Detentieplan van de Minister van Justitie*, Brussels, Ministerie van Justitie, January 2000, p. 9.
32. Koninklijk Besluit 10 juli 2001 tot vaststelling van de datum van inwerkingtreding van sommige bepalingen van de wet van 22 december 1998 betreffende de verticale integratie van het openbaar ministerie, het federaal parket en de raad van de procureurs des Konings, *B.S.* 20 juli 2001; Koninklijk Besluit 4 juli 2001 tot vaststelling van de datum van inwerkingtreding van de bepalingen van de wet van 21 juni 2001 tot wijziging van verscheidene bepalingen inzake het federaal parket, *B.S.* 20 juli 2001.
33. See: *Federaal Veiligheids- en Detentieplan van de Minister van Justitie*, Brussels, Ministerie van Justitie, January 2000, p. 73.
34. Koninklijk Besluit 17 februari 1998 betreffende het commissariaat-generaal, de raad van bestuur en de raad van overleg van de gerechtelijke politie bij de parketten, *B.S.* 19 februari 1998.
35. See: Wet 22 december 1998 betreffende de verticale integratie van het openbaar ministerie, het federaal parket en de raad van de procureurs des Konings, *B.S.* 10 februari 1999.
36. See: Koninklijk Besluit tot vaststelling van de datum van inwerkingtreding van sommige bepalingen van de wet van 22 december 1998 betreffende de verticale integratie van het openbaar ministerie, het federaal parket en de raad van procureurs des Konings, *B.S.* 20 juli 2001.
37. It must be stressed that the definition also covers forms of so-called organisational crime, i.e. when members of a legal person or organisation commit offences without the legal person or organisation committing offences itself.
38. See Article 324*bis* Penal Code, introduced by: Wet 10 januari 1999 betreffende de criminele organisaties, *B.S.* 26 februari 1999.
39. It is worth mentioning that the adoption of the EU draft joint action on the matter had been postponed for a number of months due to a parliamentary reservation in Belgium, a parliamentary inquiry committee on organised crime looking into the question of the definition of "criminal organisation" to be inserted in the Belgian Penal Code.

40. Wet 10 februari 1999 betreffende de bestraffing van corruptie, *B.S.* 23 februari 1999.
41. See: OECD Convention of 17 December 1997 on Combating Bribery of Foreign Public Officials in International Business Transactions; CoE Criminal Law Convention of 27 January 1999 on Corruption. See also: Common Position of 6 October 1997 defined by the Council on the basis of Article K.3 of the Treaty on European Union on negotiations in the Council of Europe and the OECD relating to corruption; Second Joint Position of 13 November 1997 defined by the Council on the basis of Article K.3 of the Treaty on European Union on negotiations held in the Council of Europe and the OECD on the fight against corruption.
42. See for example: Protocol of 27 September 1996 drawn up on the basis of Article K.3 of the Treaty on European Union to the Convention on the protection of the European Communities' financial interests; Convention of 26 May 1997 drawn up on the basis of Article K.3 (2) (c) of the Treaty on European Union on the fight against corruption involving officials of the European Communities or officials of Member States of the European Union.
43. See: Wet 4 mei 1999 tot invoering van de strafrechtelijke aansprakelijkheid van rechtspersonen, *B.S.* 22 juni 1999.
44. See: *Federaal Veiligheids- en Detentieplan van de Minister van Justitie*, Brussels, Ministerie van Justitie, January 2000, p. 74 and pp. 76-77.
45. *De brug naar de eenentwingste eeuw – regeerakkoord – 7 juli 1999*, http://www.belgium.fgov.be/pb/pbb/nlbb13.htm, 27-7-99, p. 7.
46. This may seem illogical, the fight against hormone-related crime having no obvious links with offences against persons. However, as meat fraud and hormone-related crime have taken very serious proportions in Belgium, especially since the mid-1990s, ranging from alleged attempts on the life of a Belgian member of European parliament who was very active in the fight against these forms of crime and culminating even in the murder by the so-called meat mafia of a veterinary surgeon who acted as an official inspector on behalf of the government in the field of hormone detection (see below), the multidisciplinary hormone unit was lodged within the unit for offences against persons, violence and hold-ups.
47. Centrale Dienst voor de Bestrijding van de Corruptie, *Een nieuwe lente, een nieuw geluid*, Brussels, 1999, pp. 6-7.
48. URL: http://www.gpj.be/nl/gpj_n_mk.html.
49. URL: http://www.rijkswacht.be/fedpol/orga/organogram.htm, 18-09-01, 2 pp.
50. Act of 11 January 1993, purporting to prevent the use of the financial system for the purposes of money laundering, as amended by Royal Decrees of 22 April 1994, 24 March 1995, 6 May 1999, 28 December 1999 and 15 February 2000 as well as by Acts of 11 July 1994, 7 April 1995, 10 August 1998, 22 April 1999 and 4 May 1999.
51. See: COM (1999) 352 final.
52. So far, 48 notification points for suspicious financial transactions have been recognised by the Egmont Group as financial intelligence units. See: Cel voor

Financiële Informatieverwerking, *6e Activiteitenverslag. 1998/1999*, Brussels, 1999, p. 77.

53. In addition, the department fulfils a large number of tasks on behalf of other fiscal administrations and departments.

54. The taking of certain investigative measures, however, is only allowed for officials of the required rank.

55. See: Wet 22 maart 1999 betreffende de identificatieprocedure via DNA-analyse in strafzaken, *B.S.* 20 mei 1999.

56. Keysers, P., *Moord op een veearts. Het testament van Karel Van Noppen*, Antwerpen, Icarus, 1996, p. 86.

57. Parlementair onderzoek naar een structureel beleid met het oog op de bestraffing en de uitroeiing van de mensenhandel. Verslag namens de Onderzoekscommissie, *Gedrukte Stukken*, Belgische Kamer van Volksvertegenwoordigers, 1993-1994, No. 637/7-91/92.

58. N. Siron, G. Vermeulen, B. De Ruyver, P. Traest en A. Van Cauwenberge, *Bescherming en samenwerking met getuigen*, Antwerpen, Maklu, 2000, 188 pp.

59. Persbericht Bedreigde Getuigen, 9 March 2001, URL: www.faits.fgov.be, 21 September 2001, 2 pp.

60. Within the general directorate for Penal Legislation and Human Rights *(directoraat-generaal Strafwetgeving en Rechten van de Mens)*.

61. Supplementary Information Request at the National Entry.

62. Cases are considered to be urgent "[...] when the prolongation of the delay of transfer to the local service [...] because of the impossibility to have immediate contact with it, threatens to entail the failure of the prevention or tracing action".

63. *Omzendbrief 22 september 1997 inzake de internationale uitwisseling van gegevens met gerechtelijke finaliteit door Belgische politiediensten aan het buitenland*, College van Procureurs-generaal, COL. 7/97, 9 pp.

64. The circular letter does not apply to the international exchange of intelligence with regard to tasks of administrative policing or public order maintenance.

65. See: *Omzenbrief nr. COL 2/2000 van het College van Procureurs-generaal bij de Hoven van Beroep*, Brussels, 18 February 2000, 15 pp.

66. The Minister asked the Universities of Ghent, Antwerp and Liège to develop a coherent and transparent body of legislation with regard to judicial cooperation in criminal matters, including the relationship with the police services in the field of information exchange. The deadline for delivery of the report was 30 November 2001, after which the Minister was able to introduce a bill on the matter.

**BIBLIOGRAPHY**

*Actieplan tegen de economische, financiële en fiscale delinquentie*, Brussels, 18 July 1997, 34 pp.

Actieplan van de regering tegen de georganiseerde criminaliteit, *Gedrukte Stukken*, Belgische Senaat, 1995-96, No. 1-326/5 (annex).

Berkmoes, H., Vandale, R. and De Bie, B., *Misdaad loont niet (meer)?*, Brussels, Politeia, 1994, pp. 19-20 and 96-136.

Berkmoes, H., "De wettelijke regeling van bijzondere opsporingsmethoden en hun toepassing binnen het nieuwe politiewezen", in *De reorganisatie van het politiewezen*, Fijnaut, C., De Ruyver, B. and Goossens, F. (ed.), Louvain, Universitaire Pers Leuven, 1999, pp. 239-253.

Caluwé, L. and Happart, J., "Evaluatie van de politiediensten. Verslag namens de Commissie voor de Binnenlandse en de Administratieve Aangelegenheden", *Gedrukte Stukken*, Belgische Senaat, 1996–1997, No. 1–700/1–3.

Cel voor Financiële Informatieverwerking, *6e Activiteitenverslag. 1998/ 1999*, Brussels, 1999, pp. 75-82 and annex 2.

Centrale Dienst voor de Bestrijding van de Corruptie, *Een nieuwe lente, een nieuw geluid*, Brussels, 1999, 8 pp.

Commissie voor een efficiëntere politiestructuur, *Eenheid in verscheidenheid – vrijheid in gebondenheid*, Brussels, 1997, 116 pp.

Cornelis, L., "Voorkoming van het gebruik van financiële stelsel voor het witwassen van geld", *Revue de la Banque*, 1994, No. 2, pp. 90-108.

Coveliers, H. and Desmedt, C., "Parlementaire commissie van onderzoek naar de georganiseerde criminaliteit in België. Eindverslag", *Gedrukte Stukken*, Belgische Senaat, 1998–1999, No. 1-326/9, 8 December 1998.

*De brug naar de eenentwingste eeuw – regeerakkoord – 7 juli 1999*, URL: http://www.belgium.fgov.be/pb/pbb/nlbb13.htm, 27-7-99, 26 pp.

De Clerck, S., *Het bos en de bomen: justitie hervormen*, Tielt, Lannoo, 1997, 194 p.

De Nauw, A., "De strafrechtelijke aspecten van de Wet van 11 januari 1993 tot voorkoming van het gebruik van het financiële stelsel voor het witwassen van geld" in *Om deze redenen. Liber Amicorum Armand Vandeplas*, Arnou, P. et al. (ed.), Ghent, Mys & Breesch, 1994, pp. 127-143.

De Ruyver, B., Bullens, F., Vander Beken, T. and Siron, N., *Anticorruptiestrategieën*, Antwerp – Apeldoorn, Maklu, 1999, 309 pp.

*Federaal Veiligheids- en Detentieplan van de Minister van Justitie*, Brussel, Ministerie van Justitie, januari 2000, 254 pp. + annexes.

Fijnaut, C., De Ruyver, B. and Goossens, F. (ed.), *De reorganisatie van het politiewezen*, Louvain, Universitaire Pers Leuven, 1999, 277 pp.

Huybrechts, L., "De tentakels van de octopus", *Panopticon*, 1999, pp. 1-2.

Landuyt, R. and de T'Serclaes, N. "Parlementair onderzoek naar de wijze waarop het onderzoek door politie en gerecht werd gevoerd in de zaak 'Dutroux_Nihoul en consorten'", *Gedrukte Stukken*, Belgische Kamer van Volksvertegenwoordigers, 1996–1997, No. 713–6, 14 April 1997.

Landuyt, R. and Viseur, J.-P., "Parlementair onderzoek naar de noodzakelijke aanpassingen van de organisatie en de werking van het politie- en justitiewezen op basis van de moeilijkheden die gerezen zijn bij het onderzoek naar de 'Bende van Nijvel'", *Gedrukte Stukken*, Belgische Kamer van Volksvertegenwoordigers, 1997–1998, No.s 573/10 – 95/96.

*Ministeriële Omzendbrief 24 april 1990, zoals aangepast op 5 maart 1992, betreffende de bijzondere opsporingstechnieken om de zware of georganiseerde criminaliteit te bestrijden*, 7/SDP/690/MN/NIX/RB6/6, 30 pp.

*Omzenbrief nr. COL 2/2000 van het College van Procureurs-generaal bij de Hoven van Beroep*, Brussels, 18 February 2000, 15 pp.

*Omzendbrief 22 september 1997 inzake de internationale uitwisseling van gegevens met gerechtelijke finaliteit door Belgische politiediensten aan het buitenland*, College van Procureurs-generaal, COL. 7/97, 9 pp. + annexes, also published in: Vanderborght, J., *De grenzen verlegd. Internationale informatieve samenwerking in de praktijk*, Kessel-Lo, Centrum voor Politiestudies, 1998, p. 132-140.

*Omzendbrief proactieve recherche*, Brussels, December 1996, 6 pp. + annexes.

Siron, N., Vermeulen, G., De Ruyver, B., Traest, P. en Van Cauwenberge, A., *Bescherming en samenwerking met getuigen*, Antwerpen, Maklu, 2000, 188 p.

Stessens, G., "De nationale en internationale bestrijding van het witwassen", Antwerp – Groningen, *Intersentia*, 1997, pp. 165-251.

Themanummer "Octopus – de justitiehervorming", *Orde van de dag*, Kluwer Editorial, 1999, No. 7, 63 pp.

Traest, P. "The putting into perspective of the exclusionary rule: some general remarks and the Belgian perspective", paper presented at the Second World Conference on New Trends in Criminal Investigation and Evidence, held in Amsterdam, 10-15 December 1999.

Van Roosbroeck, A., *Voorkoming en bestraffing van witwassen van geld en illegale vermogensbestanddelen.Witwassen*, Antwerp, ETL, 1995, pp. 29-106.

Vander Beken, T., Carion, T. and De Ruyver, B., *Een geïntegreerd anti-corruptiebeleid voor België*, Antwerp – Apeldoorn, Maklu, 1999, 131 pp.

Vander Beken, T., Vermeulen, G. and De Ruyver, B., "Belgium", in *International Tracing of Assets*, Volume 1, Ashe, M. and Rider, B. (ed.), London, FT Law & Tax, N5, loose-leaf, 1997.

Verstraeten, R., Van Daele, D. and Dewandeleer, D., "Het federaal parket", *Panopticon*, 1999, pp. 56-85.

# Denmark

*Peter Kruize*[1]

## 1. ORGANISED CRIME IN DENMARK

Denmark has no legal definition of organised crime. For a long time the term of organised crime has been linked to what is called serious economic crime. In 1973, the Regional Public Prosecution Service for Serious Economic Crime was founded as "a natural result of the debate about the so-called *"Bagmandsrapport"*.[2] The type of cases investigated and prosecuted by this special unit are those in which "there is reason to assume that the offence is of significant dimension, is associated with organised crime, is conducted in a particular fashion, or in another way has a special qualifying character."[3]

Even though the Ministry of Justice was using the term of organised crime already in 1973, the concept of organised crime is still recent in the Danish context. The Danish criminologist Joi Bay provided a historical sketch of the introduction of the concept of organised crime to Denmark.[4] According to Bay this introduction is closely related to "rocker crime" (crime committed by motor-cycle gangs). In 1991 the concept of organised crime was introduced officially by a report[5] of the Ministry of Justice about rocker crime. That report suggested creating a special database of organised crime for the purposes of police investigations. In 1992 the National Commissioner was authorised to establish such a database.

In 1995, a committee under the Ministry of Justice presented an action plan to combat organised and rocker crime. In this action plan, new initiatives were suggested, such as improved witness protection and investigation methods. Initially, left-wing politicians were sceptical about widening police powers, but as a result of the *Nordic Biker War*[6] a compromise was reached. The result – the so-called "rocker package" – extends for instance the ability of the police to intercept telephones and to confiscate property on the basis of an inverse burden of proof.

According to guidelines of the European Union, Denmark has produced situation reports about organised crime since 1996. The EU criteria are used to define organised crime. In the conclusions of the last report (Organised Crime 1998) the level of organised crime in Denmark was still considered to be moderate. There is no reason to assume that internationally known criminal organisations have penetrated Danish society. Even though Denmark is a target country of the Russian Mafia, the impact is relatively modest compared to Denmark's eastern and southern neighbours. Organised crime in Denmark – according to the above-mentioned report – focuses on illegal markets (narcotics), the smuggling of cigarettes and alcohol and illegal immigration (smuggling humans).

Motor-cycle gangs (Hells Angels and Bandidos) are considered to be criminal organisations, even though legal evidence is lacking.[7] In Denmark 116 "stable members"[8] of the Hells Angels are organised into eight Chapters. The Bandidos have 107 members, and 11 Chapters.[9]

The Danish police did not use the concept of organised crime prior to 1991. It is, however, a question of labelling and defining. By focusing on narcotics and fraud – which are the most frequent forms of what was later to be called organised crime – a picture of the organisation of the police and the public prosecution services in the fight against organised crime, prior to 1991, may be drawn.

At the end of 1999, a steering group "Organised Crime" was established. This group prioritises investigation and prosecution of organised crime in Denmark. The steering group consists of the National Commissioner (as chairman), the Director of Public Prosecutions, a representative of the Union of Chief Constables and a representative of the Union of Police Personnel.

## 2. THE LAW ENFORCEMENT AGENCIES IN DENMARK

The Constitutional Act of 1849 distinguishes legislative, executive and judiciary powers. The executive authority is vested in the Queen as Head of State. She exercises this authority through the Minister of Justice.[10] Judicial authority is vested in the courts of justice, while legislative powers belong to the competences of parliament (*Folketinget*). Until 1911 Denmark had municipal police forces. The Chief of Police was appointed by the Crown, and often functioned as judge and mayor as well. In the years from 1911 to 1938 the municipal police were gradually transformed into a national force. The rationale behind this transformation was that it was deemed more effective. In 1919 special judges were appointed and an elected mayor took over most of the municipal tasks.[11]

Today Denmark[12] has a national police force and the country is divided in 54 police districts. The Danish police consisted of 12,360 employees as at 1 January 1998, of which 9,962 were trained police officers, 402 lawyers and

1,996 were employees who had not had legal or police-related training (administrative personnel). If one compares the number of trained police officers to the number of inhabitants, the outcome is 188 police officers per 100,000 inhabitants.[13] In Denmark only the police have the competence to investigate criminal activities. The tax and customs services do not have these powers. The National Security Service is incorporated within the police organisation (National Commissioner's Office).

In 1973 the number of police districts was reduced from 72 to 54. The rationale of the reform was to provide every district with a 24-hour service. Originally 48 police districts were recommended, but the politicians decided to support the view of a minority of the "Structure Commission" (*strukturudvalg*) to maintain six more police districts. The commission was doubtful about the feasibility to establish a 24-hour service in all police districts. To compensate the negative side effects of the centralisation, "community police stations" (*nærpolitistationer*) were established in 1985, after a pilot in nine police districts.[14]

The duties of the police are laid down in the Administration of Justice Act (*retsplejeloven*). These duties are 1) the maintenance of security, peace and order, 2) ensuring that laws and regulations are complied with, 3) taking the necessary steps to prevent crime, and 4) carrying out necessary investigation of crime and prosecuting offenders.[15]

The head of a police district is a Chief Constable[16] (*politimester*). A Danish Chief Constable is a lawyer by training, because s/he is not only head of the (district) police, but also head of the local prosecution service (see next section).

The responsibilities and powers of the National Commissioner (*rigspolitichefen*) are defined in the Administration of Justice Act. This act gives the National Commissioner two major areas of responsibility – the administration of personnel and finances. The National Commissioner's Office was established in 1938. The Chief Constables were anxious that the function of the National Commissioner would jeopardise their independence. However, in the 1950s, a proposal of a working group under the authority of the Ministry of Finance to eliminate the function of the National Commissioner was not put into effect. Instead of eliminating the function of the National Commissioner, more tasks of the Ministry of Justice were delegated to this function.

Nowadays the National Commissioner's Office consists of eight departments (A to H), each responsible for special fields of duties.[17] The National Commissioner is not only responsible for the eight departments, but is also empowered to supervise and establish guidelines for the general organisation, administration and performance of duties. The National Commissioner may not, however, interfere with concrete law enforcement activities in the districts. The Chief Constables are responsible for the management and discharge of police duties.

As mentioned above Denmark is divided in 54 police districts. To ensure assistance across district boundaries, the country is divided in seven police regions. The Chief Constable of one of the districts in the region – usually the largest – is head of the region as well. The heads of the regions are Chief Constables in the following police districts: Aalborg, Aarhus, Haderslev, Odense, Slagelse, Copenhagen and Bornholm.

## 3.   THE PUBLIC PROSECUTION SERVICE IN DENMARK

The public prosecution service comes, as do the police, under the authority of the Minister of Justice. The Minister of Justice is, formally, the highest public prosecutor, and has the power to interfere in individual criminal cases. In reality the Minister does not exercise this right.[18] The public prosecution service is organised as a parallel system to that of the court. A Chief Constable – or one of their lawyers – is prosecutor at the District Courts (*Byret*). As mentioned before, Chief Constables and his lawyers are part of the Danish police organisation, but they are – like all other public prosecutors – employed by the Ministry of Justice. Police officers in contrast are employed by the National Commissioner. District courts handle two kinds of cases; those in which the suspect plead guilty and so-called "police cases". Police cases do not carry penalties exceeding four years imprisonment. In reality nearly all criminal cases start in a District Court. Over the years an increasing number of criminal cases have been transferred to Chief Constables as the prosecution authority. Since 1984 the vast majority of proceedings have been initiated by Chief Constables under the superintendence of the regional public prosecutor.

The high courts (*Landsret*) can be found on the next layer in the hierarchical order of courts. A regional public prosecutor (*Statsadvokat*) is prosecutor at this court. There are six regional public prosecutors responsible for a given geographical area. The boundaries of the police regions (7) and the prosecutors' regions (6) do not correspond. The police regions are based on civil defence (Ministry of Defence) areas. A regional public prosecutor's office consists of 10 to 15 lawyers and clerical support. As stated before, regional public prosecutors are less occupied with criminal proceedings than Chief Constables.

The seventh regional public prosecutor is responsible on a national basis for serious economic crime (*særlig økonomisk kriminalitet*). The regional public prosecution service for Serious Economic Crime will be discussed in detail in Section 5.1.

The Director of Public Prosecutions (*Rigsadvokat*) conducts proceedings before the Supreme Court (*Højesteret*) and represents the Prosecution Service in the Court of Special Appeals.[19] The Director of Public Prosecutions is the highest authority of all public prosecutors and superintends the discharge of their duties. In practice it is, however, the task of the regional public prosecutors to supervise the prosecution activities of police lawyers (prosecutors under the authority of the Chief Constable). This is done in two ways, by inspection and by appeal. The Director of Public Prosecutions' Office consists of 15 lawyers and clerical support. The office is organised in three units, each responsible for certain kinds of cases.

In the beginning of the 1990s, the Director of Public Prosecutions' Office was extended considerably because of an increasing workload. Not only domestic businesses, but also international obligations demand more and more of the office's capacity (see also Section 6.3).

## 4. LAW ENFORCEMENT UNITS TO FIGHT ORGANISED CRIME

### 4.1 National Level

The fight against organised crime at the national level is concentrated in Department A of the National Commissioner's Office. This department has the task of acting as the international contact point concerning police matters (see Section 8), providing police districts with knowledge and manpower, and the collection and analysis of intelligence. Department A also houses the Serious Economic Crime Squad (*afdeling for særlig økonomisk kriminalitet* (SØK)). This squad will be discussed in Section 5.

The Serious Crime Squad (*Rejseafdeling*) has 80 employees and assists local police districts in serious crime investigations. The squad offers specialisation and resources. Police officers of the squad work under the authority of the local Chief Constable. In Greater Copenhagen[20] the situation is different. The Copenhagen police accomplish this task in Greater Copenhagen due to the size and the level of specialism in the force. The squad also assists in cases which may be labelled as organised crime.

The forerunner of a National Criminal Intelligence Service (*Nationalt Efterforsknings-støttecenter*; (NEC)) was founded in June 1998 and has 62 employees. The service was established following the British example. The creation of a NCIS had already been a point of discussion for some time,[21] but the Nordic Biker War accelerated the process.[22] The NEC was established as a forerunner in the way the EDU was a forerunner of Europol. In establishing it the National Commissioner bypassed the regular bureaucratic procedures. The NEC is supposed to analyse crime on the basis of intelligence, in cases

163

where crime can be qualified as of an international and/or organised nature. According to the National Commissioner's Annual Report,[23] the following types of crime belong to the competence of the NEC:
- rocker crime
- street gang crime
- sexual abuse of children
- environmental crime
- organised car theft
- hooliganism
- theft and smuggling of arms and art.

In practice the NEC focuses on rocker, street gang and narcotic crime. Lately child pornography was added to the competences of the NEC. In 1999, a special database with information about narcotics (*Narkotikainformationen*) was erased and relevant information transferred to the organised crime database. The organised crime database is under the competence of the NEC. It is confidential what kind of information the database contains, but the information may be categorised as hard or soft as well. Since 1997, soft information has been evaluated by the 4x4 system.[24] The narcotics database was established in 1984 and the organised crime database in 1992.

Information was also in the past coordinated by the National Commissioner's Office Department A. The added value of the NEC is that it provides analysis as an operational and strategic tool. This is where the influence of Europol becomes visible. Crime analysis was an unknown phenomenon in Denmark for many years, but its value has been confirmed by Europol.

Another department of the National Commissioner's Office of interest for this inventory is Department E. This department is responsible for all national police businesses concerning legal and illegal immigration to Denmark. Refugees who wish to demand asylum in Denmark are accommodated in *Sandholm*. Employees of the Department of Immigrants (since July 1993, under the competence of the Ministry of Interior[25]) decide whether a person is granted residence in Denmark. They cooperate with police officers of Department E of the National Commissioner's Office. Department E is responsible for a special database with information about illegal immigration. This database was established in 1997 and contains hard and soft information. The reason for establishing this database was the (perceived) growing problem of illegal immigration in Denmark.

The final department of the National Commissioner's Office with relevance to this project is Department G, which hosts the National Security Service

(*Politiets Efterretnings Tjeneste*). In organisational terms, the Security Service resides under the National Commissioner, but the Chief of the Service refers to the Minister of Justice directly. The Service has about 380 employees – lawyers, police officers and clerical support. The Service concentrates on espionage and terrorism. If an investigation by the Security Service leads to charges, arrests or other steps in the criminal procedure, the responsibility for the case is transferred to the local Chief Constable.[26]

## 4.2  Local and Regional Level

Police districts do not have special departments to fight organised crime, or at least they are not labelled as such. There is, however, a narcotics department (Department N) in the Copenhagen police force where drug cases at the level of the "*bagmand*" (see Section 3) are investigated and prosecuted. Sales at street level are policed by the Special Patrol Unit. Department N has existed for decades and has built up an expertise in drug cases which extends beyond that of any other unit in Denmark. Department n employs 57 persons.

Other special departments of the Copenhagen police which may be linked to the fight of organised crime are Department B (Fraud) and Department S (Customs and Environment). Both departments have existed for many years. VAT Fraud is handled by Department B, for instance alcohol and cigarette smuggling inside the European Union. In the case of smuggling from outside the EU it belongs to the competence of Department S. Money laundering is dealt with by Department B (see Section 5.2). A relatively new working area of Department Bs is IT crime. Two police officers have been active in this area for 3-4 years, for instance in the field of child pornography on the Internet. 48 persons ARE employed in Department B and 13 in Department S.

As mentioned in Section 1 Denmark is divided into 7 police regions. Regional police Centres for Special Investigations (PSE) are, however, concentrated into 5 regions: Aarhus, Aalborg, Kolding, Odense and Copenhagen. The regional centres are coordinated by Department D of the National Commissioner's Office. The regional centres have been active since 1993. Cases handled by the regional centres are for instance murder, robbery and complicated theft. The centres are responsible for a special database containing information about an individual's criminal record and information about unsolved cases. When investigations have an inter-territorial character, the investigation is led and coordinated by one police district. In general it will be the district with the most expertise and/or the best information position.

### 4.3 Cooperation between Police and Customs

The police and customs service are involved in a permanent cooperation arrangement. The border control function – e.g. checking passports – is carried out by police officers, while baggage checks are performed by customs officers. As stated in Section 1 the police are the only organisation in Denmark with investigative powers. Customs officers may, however, check someone's baggage without having suspicion of an offence, which the police are not allowed to do. Respondents reported that together they establish a strong team. At the borders there is a close cooperation between both services.

### *Outside Borders*
Over land Denmark is only accessible through another EU country (Germany). The external border crossing points of Denmark are airports and seaports. Control at the main airport (*Kaastrup*) is undertaken by the Copenhagen police. There is informal cooperation between the Copenhagen police and the regional customs services in the form of information exchange, joint risk analyses and joint control actions. Control of the second largest airport of Denmark (*Billund*, situated in Jutland) is part of the competences of the local police districts and together with the customs officers and the Drugs Intelligence Unit (*Narkotikainformation*) it carries out joint actions.

The control of containers coming into Denmark by sea is exercised by the local authorities, but supported by information from the National Commissioner and the Central Customs service (in Copenhagen and Århus the regional customs services produce analyses as well).

The Baltic Sea has received special attention after the change of systems in Eastern Europe. "Project Bornholm"[27] was started in 1994. The main purpose of this project is to strengthen control in the areas of the smuggling of narcotics, tobacco, alcohol, weapons, radioactive material and human beings. In Project Bornholm the police and customs are cooperating with other authorities and private partners. Project Bornholm is part of the international Baltic Sea cooperation (see Section 6.1.).

### *Inside Borders*
Since 1987, two police-customs groups (shortened to PT groups) have been operational on *Lolland-Falster* and in *Sønderjylland*.[28] At the start each PT group consisted of about ten officers (police as well customs). At the Drugs Intelligence Unit[29] of the National Commissioner's Office a special police-customs-border group (shortened to PTG group) was founded. The PTG group supported the two PT groups with expertise and exchanges of information at an international level.

Since the Schengen Agreement entered into force in Denmark, two operational flying squads have been established. One in the *Lolland-Falster* area and one in *Sønderjylland*. These two squads operate under the authority of the local Chief Constable and may be assisted by the National Task Force on organised smuggling of human beings.

## 4.4 Current Developments

It has not been decided when the NEC will lose its forerunner status. Neither has it been decided to what extent the competences of the NEC will be enlarged. It is for instance conceivable that all special databases related to (aspects of) organised crime will be concentrated in the NEC. In that case the financial intelligence and the illegal immigration databases will be transferred. This will most likely be decided after the Police Commission (*Politikommissionen*) has delivered its report.[30] The Ministry of Justice established this Police Commission in July 1998. The commission's task is to develop a well-argued proposal for a new police structure. The need for a new police structure is rooted in several considerations:[31]

- **Effectiveness**. The importance of effectiveness has increased in the last years because of a financial arrangement between the police and the Ministry of Finance. It is assumed that small police districts are not able to use police resources effectively. The discussion about the effectiveness of small police districts has been intensified by the current process of decentralising budgets.
- **Crime pattern**. Technological and societal developments demand more specialists, for instance in the field of environmental, computer and economic crime. Small police districts may face difficulties in carrying out specialist tasks.
- **Borderless crime**. In the international and national context police tasks are not restricted to one police district. Nowadays interregional cooperation exists through Task Forces,[32] coordinated by one police district.

The commission will evaluate to what extent the current distribution of competences is adequate. Another point of discussion will be whether there is a need for a national crime squad with operational competences. Presumably regional criminal intelligence services (RECs) will be established. The idea is to create 7 RECs, one in each police region. The question is under whose competence the REC will be. Under the competence of the NEC (the National Commissioner) or the Regional Chief Constable? The answer will probably be provided by the Police Commission.

## 5. PUBLIC PROSECUTION UNITS TO FIGHT ORGANISED CRIME

### 5.1 National Level

There is no body of coordination at the level of public prosecution as foreseen by Recommendation 1 of the EU Action Plan to Combat Organised Crime for all organised crime, only for (EU) fraud and money laundering.

The regional public prosecutions' office responsible for Serious Economic Crime (SØK) was founded in 1973. The SØK consists of three investigation teams and an information and analysis section. The information and analysis section collects, registers, analyses and exchanges information on economic crimes. Economic crimes are limited to several sections in the Criminal Code.[33] The SØK investigates and prosecutes for instance VAT crimes, crimes related to the stock market and cases of EU fraud. Since April 1998, the SØK has taken care of all EU fraud cases which involve UCLAF, several police districts, or if they are of a principal character.[34] The lawyers of the SØK conduct proceeding at the District Court in Copenhagen, in contrast to the lawyers of the geographically orientated regional public prosecutions' offices, who are linked to the High Courts (see Section 3).

It is not always clear whether the investigation and prosecution of a case belongs to the competences of the SØK or to a local police district. In general the SØK investigates and prosecutes the more complex cases. Another criterion is to which authority the case should be reported. If for instance the case is reported to the Copenhagen police it is more or less up to them whether they communicate it to the SØK.[35]

The Financial Intelligence Unit, as foreseen by Article 6 of the 1991 Money Laundering Directive, is situated at the information and analytical section and acts more like a contact point.[36] The contact point was created in 1993 as a result of the "Law of Preventive Measures Against Money Laundering" (*Lov om forebyggende foranstaltninger mod hvidvaskning af penge*). According to that law financial institutions have to inform the police in cases where a transaction is suspected of being carried out for purposes of money laundering. Later on casinos also came under the legal obligation to report suspicion of money laundering.

When a case is reported to the contact point the persons and/or companies involved are checked in several databases and the case is usually sent to one of the police districts. If they decide to intervene,[37] the case is investigated by police officers of the district and the contact point is informed about the results. In the case of criminal charges being brought the financial institute which reported the case is informed. The contact point is also responsible for international contacts with foreign financial intelligence units, FATF, and Interpol (see also Section 6.3).

The SØK consists of lawyers (around 25 persons) and clerical staff who work under the competence of the regional public prosecutor. The police officers (around 60 persons) work under the competence of a Chief Superintendent. From an organisational point of view, the police officers are a unit of the National Commissioner's Department A, while the lawyers are under the regional public prosecution service. The SØK is unique in the Danish context for more than one reason: the National Commissioner is responsible for police officers with operational powers; and the Regional Public Prosecution Service works directly with police officers.

The SØK may be labelled as a permanent multidisciplinary integrated team as described in Recommendation 20 of the EU Action Plan to Combat Organised Crime. When necessary the SØK hires financial experts from private firms to support an investigation. Its policy is to not employ financial experts itself. It is assumed that external experts have better and more up-to-date knowledge of several financial constructions.

## 5.2 Local and Regional Level

For the public prosecution service, the organisation at the local and regional level is more or less the same as for the police. There are no special units, but the working field of some special departments may be related to organised crime. As shown in Appendix 2 specialist criminal investigation departments of the Copenhagen police are directly linked to specialist public prosecutors. There is not only a police Department N (Narcotics) in Copenhagen – see Section 4.2. – but a public prosecutor's Department N as well.

At the regional level there are the six regional public prosecutor's offices. There are no special organisational arrangements at this level as a consequence of the fight against organised crime.

## 5.3 The (near) Future

There have not been recent organisational changes at the level of Public Prosecution Service as a consequence of the fight against organised crime. It is not likely either that the organisation will change as a result of the Police Commission (see Section 4.3.), since the Commission has been told that the double position of the Chief Constable (Head of the Police and public prosecutor) is out of the question. Maybe – but it is no more than speculation – when the NEC has lost its forerunner status, the public prosecution service will create a unit like the SØK linked to the NEC. Another thinkable scenario is an integration of the SØK (police officers as well as lawyers) and the NEC.

## 6. INTERNATIONAL COOPERATION AND CONTACT POINTS

### 6.1 Cooperation with Scandinavian and Baltic Countries

Denmark is not only a European country, it is first and foremost a Scandinavian country. Police cooperation between Scandinavian countries is based on the Nordic Police Agreement (1968). Danish police officers and prosecutors are allowed to contact their colleagues in another Scandinavian country without any formal barriers and procedures. In the context of organised crime the police and Customs Cooperation in Scandinavia (*Politi-og Toldsamarbejde i Norden*, shortened to PTN) is important to mention. In 1984 the PTN cooperation was established and consisted of two basic elements:

- A corps of Scandinavian liaison officers with the competence to act on behalf of all Scandinavian countries in cases of drug crimes. Nowadays there are about 34 liaison officers all over the world.
- The strategic analysis of drug crimes.

In 1996 the Scandinavian Ministers of Justice decided that PTN cooperation should not be limited to drug crimes, but should be enlarged to all forms of international and cross-border crime. Since 1998 the new, enlarged concept of PTN cooperation has been formalised. PTN cooperation exists not only at the national level, but also at the level of police districts. Some major districts (in Denmark: Copenhagen) are part of a local PTN-network.

Denmark is also participating in the police cooperation in the Baltic Sea Region.[38] In 1996 the Task Force on Organised Crime in the Baltic Sea Region was founded and has resulted in information exchange centres in all countries since 1998. As a result joint control activities are taking place in connection with the smuggling of human beings, narcotics, cigarettes and stolen cars.

In 1997, a joint Scandinavian steering group as part of the fight against "Rocker crime" was established as a consequence of the Nordic Biker War. In the European context Denmark was the forerunner in Rocker crime. In the context of the Baltic Sea cooperation, Denmark hosted a conference on Rocker crime in 1998.

In July 2000 the bridge between Denmark and Sweden (*Øresundsbro*) was opened. Danish and Swedish police officers may pursue and stop persons for every offence according to Danish and Swedish law. On the Danish side of the bridge an arrest can only be performed by Danish police officers. Swedish police officers are allowed to pursue persons up to 25 km. on the Danish territory, but only for crimes mentioned in the Schengen Convention Article 41.4.b (crimes which may lead to extradition). Danish police officers are not limited in their pursuit of offenders on the Swedish territory.

## 6.2  Contact Points

The international office of the Ministry of Justice functions as the central contact point for foreign countries. Requests for extradition and mutual legal assistance – like the controlled delivery of narcotics – is handled by the Ministry. The Director of Public Prosecutions' Office functions as the contact point for requests and questions about prosecution. The contact point is not consulted frequently. The International Relations Unit (Department A of the National Commissioner's Office) carries out this task at the level of law enforcement. For serious economic crime the SØK is the contact point. The formal relationship between the contact points and the central contact point of the Ministry of Justice is hierarchical, but not in practice.

Denmark is represented in committees, working groups, etc. of the European Union or the Council of Europe by employees of the Ministry of Justice (international office), the Director of the Public Prosecutions' Office, the SØK and/or the National Commissioner's Office. It is not only a question of […] who represents Denmark, but also a question of resources. Since Denmark is a relatively small country and officials are familiar with one another, cooperation is rather informal. In general the representatives of the Ministry have political responsibility, while the other participants have substantive competences.

## 6.3  Europol, SIRENE, FATF and Interpol

The International Relations Unit includes the Europol National Unit and the NCB (Interpol). Since the entry into force of Schengen on 25 March 2001, it also includes the SIRENE bureau. The International Relations Unit is also the contact point for PTN cooperation and police cooperation in the Baltic Sea region. The International Relations Unit has 37 employees. The Danish SIRENE bureau became active in October 2000. Information (intelligence) about money laundering is coordinated by the regional public prosecutor's office for serious fraud (SØK). This unit is the contact point for foreign counterparts, FATF, Interpol, and several institutions inside Denmark.

## 7.  ACCOUNTABILITY

Officially a prosecutor is responsible for an investigation. The prosecutor works under the authority of a Chief Constable. The Chief Constables (police prosecutors) are supervised by the Regional Public Prosecutor, who is hierarchically under the Director of Public Prosecution. Finally the Minister of Justice is the highest prosecution authority (see Section 3). The parliament does not have direct control over the police or the public prosecution services but, since the Minister needs the support of the majority of parliament, its impact is substantial.

For the use of non-traditional investigation methods, like police infiltration[39] or telephone tapping, the approval of the court is needed *in advance*. Only in a case of *"periculum-in-mora"*, which means that the circumstances demand immediate action, approval may be given afterwards.[40]

The National Register Committee (*Registerrådet*) controls whether databases are in conflict with the law. In general the committee announces inspections in advance, but they have the legal possibility to inspect without warning. The members of the Committee are appointed on the basis of their specialist knowledge and not as the representative of a particular organisation. The personnel and finances of the Committee are part of the Ministry of Justice, but the Committee works independently from the Ministry. All special databases of the police and the money laundering database are under the supervision of the Committee. This also applies to Danish information to be added to the Schengen Information System (SIS).

The National Ombudsman's Office controls the police and the public prosecution services among other public services. The Ombudsman has access to all relevant reports and cases, but does not have the formal powers to impose changes or procedures. In practice, however, the authorities are in general cooperative to accept the recommendations of the National Ombudsman.

**NOTES**

1. This part of the project is financially supported by the Danish Ministry of Justice.
2. The term *bagmand* may be translated to backer or financier.
3. *Justitsministeriets bekendtgørelse,* No. 648, 20. December 1973.
4. Joi Bay, 1998.
5. Justitsministeriets redegørelse (November 18th, 1991) vedrørende "*Rockerkriminalitet*".
6. During the Biker War (1996-1997) two rival motor-cycle clubs – Hells Angels and Bandidos – fought each other with heavy weaponry, potentially endangering other civilians. In total five killings were incurred and a few dozen attempted murders.
7. An integrated team created on the initiative of the public prosecution service had to find an answer to the question posed by the Minister of Justice as to whether MC clubs could be forbidden by law on the basis of their violent nature. The team – under supervision of the Director of Public Prosecutions – came to the conclusion that the answer is they could not.
8. Often a distinction is made between full-colour members, prospective members and hangers on.
9. Numbers are given in *Årsrapport om Organiseret kriminalitet 1998.*
10. This contrasts with most other countries, where the police forces reside under the authority of the Ministry of Interior.
11. Henricson (1996) *Politiret,* p. 13.
12. Denmark in this text means Denmark without Greenland and the Faroe Islands.
13. Source: Rigspolitichefen (1999) *Årsberetning 1998,* København, p. 136-137.
14. Henricson (1996) *Politiret,* p. 19.
15. *The Police in Denmark,* 1998, p. 14.
16. In the district of Copenhagen the head of the police is called Commissioner (*politidirektør*) to underscore the "special status" of the Copenhagen police. Due to the fact that the Copenhagen police force covers far the largest district in the country. According to the pamphlet *The Police in Denmark* "the Copenhagen police have a special position because of the size of population and all the other features of a metropolitan structure, and are organisationally quite different from the other police districts in Denmark." (*The Police in Denmark, 1998,* p.12-13 ).
17. Department A is the most important in relation to the theme of this volume and will be discussed in detail in Section 4, as well as Departments E and G. An overview of all departments is given in Appendix 1 to this chapter.
18. There are, however, exceptions to the rule. The regional public prosecutor withdrew the charges against three police officers in connection with them using their firearms during riots after the EU referendum of 18 May 1993. The Director of Public Prosecutions had overruled the decision of the regional public prosecutor. The police union complained about this decision to the National Ombudsman. Because the former Director of Public Prosecutions recommended charging the police officers, the incumbent Director was considered

"incompetent" (in Danish: *inhabil*). Even though the Ministry of Justice agreed with the national Ombudsman about the question of incompetence, the decision of the regional public prosecutor was overruled [...] (Henricson, 1996, p. 15).

19. In the Court of Special Appeals closed criminal cases are re-opened because of for instance new evidence.

20. Greater Copenhagen includes the city of Copenhagen and its suburbs. Greater Copenhagen consists of eight police districts.

21. For example in the discussion paper of the National Commissioner of 1996 about the future of the Danish police (*Fremtidens politi*).

22. *National Commissioner's Annual Report 1998*, p. 15.

23. Ibid, p. 16.

24. The 4x4 evaluation of information was introduced in Denmark by a police-officer who had attended an international course on crime analysis in Zutphen, the Netherlands in 1994.

25. Before July 1993, the Department of Immigrants was part of the Ministry of Justice.

26. *Politiets Efterretnings Tjeneste* (1997), København, p. 15.

27. *Bornholm* is a Danish Island in the Baltic Sea, off the coast of Sweden.

28. *Lolland-Falster* are two small islands connecting Copenhagen (on the island of Zealand) to Germany (via Rødby). *Sønderjylland* is the southern part of Jutland and borders directly onto *Sleswig-Holstein* (Germany).

29. Since 1999, the Drug Intelligence Unit has been part of the NEC.

30. It was originally planned that the Commission would deliver its report at the end of 2001; now 2002 is more likely.

31. Not all considerations are mentioned in this context. Source of the statements is the official installation letter by the Ministry of Justice (3 July 1998).

32. Today there is a Task Force on Rocker Crime and a Task Force on Illegal Immigration.

33. Chapter 28 (§§278-284, §289) – paragraphs of the law related to acquisitive offences; Chapter 29 – other offences against property. A translation of the Danish Criminal Code is published by Gitte Høyer, Martin Spencer and Vagn Greve (1997).

34. Directive of the Director of Public Prosecutions, No. 4/ 1998. Principal means cases in which suspects have used new methods of fraud.

35. A recent example of a case which was investigated and prosecuted by the Copenhagen police is the so-called "PFA case". According to the guidelines it would be more natural for such a case to be handled by the SØK.

36. In Danish this unit is called *hvidvasksekretariat*.

37. It is up to a police district whether they want to investigate the case.

38. The cooperation includes the following countries: Estonia, Latvia, Lithuania and the Scandinavian countries bordering the Baltic Sea.

39. Civil infiltration is forbidden by law in Denmark.

40. In such a case the police have to be quite sure of their case, because if in the opinion of the court the method used was not allowed in the given situation, a disciplinary or criminal case may be the result. Ib Henricson (1996) *Politiret*, København, p. 244.

**BIBLIOGRAPHY**

Bay, Joi, Da organiseret kriminalitet blev indført til Danmark (When Organised Crime was Imported to Denmark) in: *Nordisk Tidsskrift for Kriminalvidenskab*, 1998, Vol. 85, No. 3-4, p. 175-201.

*Det fremtidige samarbejde mellem politiet og Told-Skat* (Cooperation between Police and Tax-Customs Services in the Future), København, 1996.

Henricson, Ib, *Politiret* (Police Law), Jurist- Økonomforbundets Forlag, Randers, 1996.

Høyer, Gitte, Martin Spencer and Vagn Greve, *The Danish Criminal Code* (3rd. edition), Københavns Universitet, København, 1997.

Justitsministeriet (Ministry of Justice), Politikommissionen, København, July 1998 (Installation Letter).

Politiets Efterretningstjeneste (National Security Service), Pamphlet, København, 1997.

Rigspolitichefen (National Commissioner), *Politiets årsberetning* (Annual Report of the Police), København (several editions).

Rigspolitichefen (National Commissioner), *The Police in Denmark, in the Faroe Islands and in Greenland*, København, 1992-edition and 1998-edition.

Rigspolitichefen (National Commissioner), *Årsrapport om organiseret kriminalitet 1998* (Organised Crime 1998), København, 1999.

Statsadvokaten for særlig økonomisk kriminalitet (SØK), *Årsrapport 1998* (Annual report), København, 1999.

**LIST OF RESPONDENTS**

Mr. Ole Andersen, National Commissioner's Office, Department A

Mrs. Dorrit Kjær Christiansen, Regional Prosecutor for Serious Economic Crime

Mr. Jesper Hjortenberg, Director of Public Prosecutions' Office

Mr. Erik Langhoff, National Commissioner's Office, Department A

Mr. Jacob Scharf, Ministry of Justice, International Office

Mr. Arne Stevns, Police of Copenhagen

**LIST OF ABBREVIATIONS**

NEC:    Forerunner of National Criminal Intelligence Service

PSE:    Regional Police Centres for Special Investigations

PT:     Police-Customs Cooperation at the borders

PTG:   Police-Customs-Border group as part of the Drug Intelligence Unit
PTN:   Police and Customs Cooperation in Scandinavia
REC:   Regional Criminal Intelligence Service
SØK:   Regional Public Prosecutor's Office for Serious Economic Crime

# Appendix 1:
## Organisational Structure of the National Commissioner's Office

**Department A**
- Secretariat and International Section
- Uniform Branch Bureau
  - Tactical Support Unit
  - Traffic Patrols (National)
  - Large Scale Action Unit
  - Police Dogs Unit
  - Missing and Wanted Persons Search Squad
- Serious Crime Squad
- National Identification Bureau
- International Contacts/Interpol
- Special Economic Crime Squad
- The Crime Prevention Council
- Forerunner of the National Criminal Intelligence Service

**Department B**
- Personnel and Recruitment

**Department C**
- Administration Section
- Section of Budgets and Accounts
- Radio/Motor Section
- Uniform and Equipment
- Audit Screen
- Travel Agency
- Office Supplies
- Ministry of Justice Department of Forensic Psychiatry
- Museum of Police History

**Department D**
- Data Section
- National Register of Stolen Vehicles
- Central Motor Vehicle Register
- I.D.-Papers Registration Office
- Central Register of Parking Fines
- Central Criminal Register
- Local Motor Vehicle Registration Office

**Department E**
- Aliens Division
- Information and Documentation Services

**Department F**
- Police College
- Police Studies and Research

**Department G**
- National Security Service

**Department H**
- Building Surveying Section
- Maintenance Section

# Appendix 2:
# Organisational Structure of Police Districts

---

Regular Police Districts:

Chief Constable

Prosecutors

Uniform Branch           CID           Police Office Section

(possible)
Joint Reception

---

The Copenhagen Police:

Commissioner

| Uniform Branch | CID and Prosecution | | Administrative Services |
|---|---|---|---|
| 6 precincts | | Public Prosecutions (Dept. O) | Secretary |
| Civil Defence & Regional Office | | Public Prosecutions (Dept. K) | Administration Dept. − secretary − planning |
| Tactical Support Unit (homicide) | Dept. A Dept. A | Public Prosecutions | − personnel − computer support - statistics and policy analysis |
| Special Patrol Unit | Dept. B (Fraud) | Public Prosecutions Dept. B | − cartage and stolen goods |
| Dog Section | Dept. C (Robbery) | Public Prosecutions Dept. C | Road-safety Division |
| Radio Communications | | | |
| | | | Civil Staff |
| Missing Persons Search Squad | Dept. N (Narcotics) | Public Prosecutions Dept. N | − book-keeping − accountancy − driver-license office |
| Traffic Police Dept. | Dept. E (Security) | | − lost property − telephone exchange |
| | Dept. S (Customs) | Public Prosecutions Dept. S | |
| | Crime Prevention | | |

# Finland

## Tuija Hietaniemi

### I.   ORGANISATION OF THE FINNISH LAW ENFORCEMENT AND PROSECUTION SERVICES

The Finnish police forces maintain public order and security, prevent and investigate crimes and forward investigated cases to prosecutors for them to consider whether charges should be brought. The police forces also issue various licences to the public.

The competences of the police authorities are based on the Police Act (493/1995), which lays down the general provisions concerning the police, their powers and acquisition of information, as well as police investigation. In addition, police operations are guided by international agreements. The police forces work in close cooperation with several other organisations, among them the frontier guard, customs, as well as education and social and health care authorities.

The police organisation acts under the auspices of the Ministry for the Interior (*Sisäasiainministeriö – Inrikesministeriet*). The Police Department (*poliisiosasto – polisavdelning*) of the Ministry for the Interior acts as the Supreme Police Command of Finland. The Supreme Police Command (*poliisin ylijohto – polisens högsta ledning*) is in charge of planning, developing and supervising police operations in the whole country. It decides on national strategies and priorities as well as on guidelines for international police cooperation. According to the Act on Police Administration (110/1992), the Supreme Police Command has the duty to plan, develop and manage police functions in the whole country, to develop legislation, and is responsible for the management, training and research in the police field, and to see to all other duties established in law or assigned to it. There are five Provincial Police Command Units (*poliisin lääninjohto – polisens länsledning*) situated in their respective State Provincial Offices (*lääninhallitus – länsstyrelsen*). These command units report to the Supreme Police Command in the Ministry and their duties are to plan, develop and manage police functions in a province, to ensure the cooperation of the local police, National Bureau of Investigation (NBI) and National Traffic Police in the province as well as to see to all other duties enacted in law or assigned to it. In addition to planning, leading and developing policing, the Provincial Police Command Units are also in charge of joint operations with the National Bureau of Investigation and National Traffic Police as well as the local police forces. The joint actions between the provincial police commands and the NBI in the field of criminal investigation are based on joint cooperation agreements.

The 90 local police departments operate under their respective Provincial Police Command Units. The operational police activities are taken care by National and Local Police Units.

The national police units operating directly under the Supreme Police Command comprise the National Bureau of Investigation (*keskusrikospoliisi – centralkriminalpolisen*), the Security Police (*suojelupoliisi – skyddspolisen*), the National Traffic Police (*liikkuva poliisi – rörliga polisen*), the Police School (*poliisikoulu – polisskolan*), the Police College (*poliisiammattikorkeakoulu – polisyrkeshögskolan*) and the Police Technical Centre (*poliisin tekniikkakeskus – polisens teknikcentral*). The national information technology services of the police administration have been reorganised during the first part of 2000 into a Police Data Management Agency (*poliisin tietohallintokeskus – centralen för polisens informationsteknologi*) which has been part of the NBI organisation for two years. The Agency is preparing to take its position as one of the national police units directly under the Supreme Police Command. Unlike other local police forces, the Helsinki Police Department also answers directly to the Ministry for the Interior as it is in charge of certain specific functions at national level (e.g. security operations during official state visits and meetings).

According to the Act on Police Administration, the duty of the National Bureau of Investigation is to prevent and investigate international, organised, professional, economic and other serious crime, and to develop methods of criminal investigation as well as police data systems. The NBI also monitors the development of criminal phenomena, carries out forensic services requested by law enforcement and judicial authorities and functions as the central contact point for international police cooperation and exchange of information. The cooperation between the NBI and the local police forces is based on mutual agreements on cooperation between the Provincial Police Command Units. The Supreme Police Command may, in individual cases, also give orders concerning the arrangement of investigations between the NBI and local police units.

According to the present strategy, the NBI concentrates on the prevention, detection and investigation of organised, professionally planned and serious crime requiring international cooperation between authorities. The NBI also prevents and investigates new kinds of crimes as well as complicated crimes, crimes that may set a precedent and crimes infiltrating the structures of the society. The NBI is also the leading actor in the national initiative against professional and organised crime by cooperating with other police units and other law enforcement authorities in detecting and investigating the criminal activities of professional criminals and criminal groups. The choice of targets is based on the amount of harm and danger caused by the criminal activities. The detection of the targets is based on the joint efforts of the intelligence and tactical investigation. Special training for law enforcement staff is also an integral part of the duties of the NBI, particularly in the field of criminal investigations concerning new criminal phenomena such as economic and corporate crime, particularly evident from the 1970s onwards, and information technology-related crime today.

The Security Police are another national police unit worth considering in connection with countering international organised crime. They are responsible for preventing schemes and crimes likely to endanger the established governmental order and the internal and external security of the state. They also investigate these kinds of crimes.

The number of Finnish police officers in relation to population is the smallest in Europe: there is one police officer per 650 inhabitants. The total number of persons employed by the police administration in Finland is circa 10,700, of whom about 7,900 are police officers, approximately 7% of them women.[1]

Historically, the Finnish police organisation is a hybrid of national, regional and local interests.

The police forces form a government organisation, even if there are local advisory boards, and various authorities cooperate in matters concerning security, law and order at all levels. Since the sixteenth century, the local sheriffs, until then representatives of local interests, have been "crown servants". These officials – as well as the local police constables in the countryside – have maintained their role as a kind of local trustees and aids in judicial affairs. The cities were also involved in the local police administration until 1903, and after that the cities still paid a share of the police costs. The traditional strength of the Provincial Governors (*maaherra – landshövding*; these were also representatives of the state administration) and their energy to defend local and provincial interests has counterbalanced the aims of the central government including in the field of police administration. The creation of a centralised national unit for criminal investigations and criminal information management succeeded only after a lengthy development process in 1955. The political police, i.e. the predecessor of the present Security

Police, was established in 1919 against a background of left-wing radicalism and the bitter political division of the Finnish people of the time. A Bureau for Criminal Investigation (*rikostutkimuskeskus – kriminalunderrättelsecentralen*) – which comprises a forensic laboratory and a national fingerprint collection – was established in 1926, and later on, the Bureau developed its information services to improve satisfaction of criminal investigation requirements.[2]

The Finnish provincial administration was renewed in 1997 and the number of provinces was cut from eleven to five. Also the number of local police departments has been noticeably reduced. These reforms are a result of long discussions about the status and effectiveness of the administration at the intermediate level. From a wider perspective, these administrative changes are a result of long-term developments in the structure of economic activity and mobility of people and capital in the country. The traditional division of the country into provinces no longer served the interests of the new centres of economic activity and their spheres of influence. Another reason for the reform has been the aim to decrease the heavy bureaucracy and simplify the administrative machinery to reduce state expenditure. It is appropriate to mention that the National Bureau of Investigation, responsible for the investigation of serious criminal cases with a national, trans-provincial or international character, updated its organisation to anticipate the reform of provincial administration back in 1922.

The role of the police forces in criminal investigations is unique in Finland compared to several other European countries, as the investigation of a criminal case is led by a police official of officer rank who is entitled to decide about the detention of a suspected person. The role of the prosecutor is a complementary one. The police authorities have to inform the prosecutor about suspects who have been uncovered without delay so that the prosecutor has the opportunity to observe the preliminary investigation and also have an influence on it. The prosecutor may order the investigation to be dropped or stopped in cases where it is evident that he will not prosecute. If the prosecutor demands the continuation of the investigations or supplementary investigations to a court case, the police have to follow his orders. Nevertheless, the prosecutor does not lead criminal investigations in Finland. Historically, the status of the prosecution authorities in Finland has been fairly weak: until the recent reform, the prosecution of crime was partly a duty of local and provincial police chiefs and full-time prosecutors were employed only in the largest towns.

In addition to the police authorities, the Customs (*tulli – tull*) and the Frontier Guard (*rajavartiolaitos – gränsbevakningsväsendet*) also belong to the security authorities in the framework of the Finnish law enforcement organisation. The Customs are a national organisation for the taxation, control and services in the field of foreign trade and have the responsibility to encourage legal foreign trade as well as to prevent illegal activities in the field. The Customs act under the auspices of the Ministry of Finance; the Customs Districts and the Customs Laboratory are run by the Board of Customs (*tullihallitus – tullstyrelsen*). The crime investigators in the Customs organisation have an important role in countering international crime, such as smuggling – in the field of drugs, alcohol, tobacco and counterfeit products, in particular – and economic crime. The Frontier Guard maintains peaceful and safe conditions in the border areas and its most important tasks are border control and maritime search and rescue services. The Frontier Guard also handles customs control in the areas where the Customs Administration cannot perform the task. The Frontier Guard operates under the Ministry for the Interior but it also has a role in national defence, in cooperation with the Defence Forces.[3] The Finnish military intelligence service has no specific duties concerning organised crime.

The highest prosecuting authority in Finland is the Prosecutor-General (*valtakunnansyyttäjä – riksåklagaren*). Administratively, the public prosecution service acts under the control of the Ministry of Justice (*oikeusministeriö – justitieministeriet*). The Prosecutor-General manages and supervises the prosecution service as its director. The State Prosecutors (*valtionsyyttäjät – statsåklagare*), stationed in the Prosecutor-General's Office (*valtakunnansyyttäjänvirasto – riksåklagarämbetet*), appraise the evidence and decide on prosecution in cases with wide national significance. They also have the right to operate throughout the country. The local prosecution authorities in Finland are the District Prosecutors (*kihlakunnansyyttäjät – häradsåklagare*) who are appointed by the Prosecutor-General.

In connection with the reform of the Finnish prosecution service, the Prosecutor-General's Office was established in 1997 to manage and supervise the prosecution services in the country. Prior to this, the Chancellor of Justice (*oikeuskansleri – justitiekanslern*) acted as the head of the local and provincial prosecutors. Now, the Chancellor of Justice concentrates on work in connection with the Council of State (*valtioneuvosto – statsrådet*) – i.e. the government – and along with the Parliamentary Ombudsman as the supreme guardian of the law in Finland. The Chancellor of Justice supervises the legality of actions of the Cabinet Ministers and public officials as well as the observance of civil and human rights. The State Prosecutors stationed in the Prosecutor General's Office concentrate on cases with special national importance. The Prosecutor-General and the State Prosecutors have independent powers in the whole country and the Prosecutor-General's Office acts as the central administrative body for the prosecution services. The Prosecutor-General's Office also has a central role in the training of prosecutors and other law enforcement personnel.

The prosecutors make their decisions to bring charges on the basis of preliminary investigations carried out by the police and have the right to influence the course of police investigations.

## II.   PROFESSIONAL AND ORGANISED CRIME AND EFFORTS OF LAW ENFORCEMENT AGENCIES

Prior to 1990, and prior to the fall of the Soviet Union in particular, Finland was a backwater as far as organised crime was concerned. From the 1970s onwards, there were some indications of the development of organised structures in the Finnish crime scene, but the number of uncovered cases was very low. One of the first milestones of the Finnish mission against organised crime was an ad hoc police working group[4] which analysed the nature and scope of professional crime in Finland in 1979 and made recommendations how to make intelligence on crimes and investigation more effective. The group expressed concern about the small amount of effectively usable information about professional and organised crime, because there were indications that professional crime in Finland was also developing into organised structures with connections to legal economic and administrative action. In the analysis, special emphasis was laid on the large and complicated economic crime cases uncovered in the 1970s. The group called for more effective use of information concerning professional and organised crime, more coordination in criminal intelligence activities as well as more centralisation in the investigation of professional and organised crime. Apart from some minor improvements, the report did not lead to any organisational rearrangements. The introduction of information technology in the collection and use of police data from the 1980s onwards, also called for by the working group, decentralised the input and processing of the data. However, this was done without changing traditional working cultures and resources in an appropriate manner, and proceeded to weaken the generation of timely overall information on the current situation.

The last decade of the twentieth century brought about a profound change in the working environment of the Finnish law enforcement authorities. The roots of the change bifurcate in two different directions. The fall of the Soviet Union in the beginning of the 1990s opened the frontiers from east and south to new kinds of economic activity, and significantly increased the number of border crossing points as well as the transit traffic to and from the areas of the former Soviet Union via Finland. When it comes to crime during the 1990s, according to Finnish crime statistics, the Russians and Estonians (see below) have had the most noticeable impact on crime statistics (petty theft, illegal selling of spirits, and traffic offences). On the other hand, Finland's accession to the European Union and the Schengen Agreement has opened the borders to the west. This brings along new kinds of criminal threats, but above all, a new international administrative and law enforcement environment which is profoundly different from the former conditions.

During the first half of the 1990s, the threat of Russian organised crime, in the form of corruption and prostitution spreading rapidly as well as large-scale economic crime, was a popular mantra in the Finnish media. These misgivings did not materialise as expected in scale and scope but the impact of post-Soviet economic and social cultures has become a permanent factor of importance in Finnish economic and administrative practice, including law enforcement activities. Little by little, the role of Finland as a gateway for illegal economic transactions relative to post-Soviet crime took shape, and during the last years of the 1990s, Estonia and Russia also took their positions as the main routes for hard drugs intended for the Finnish market.[5]

The vicinity of part of the former Soviet Union gives a particular character to the problem of organised crime in Finland. It should be kept in mind that most of the organised crime with Post-Soviet connections is international crime in the very sense of the word. Accordingly, the impact of European integration cannot be clearly distinguished from the impact of the post-Soviet sphere as regards the development of the instruments against organised crime in Finland. It is also worth mentioning that post-Soviet organised crime often takes the shape of organised business crime instead of traditional organised crime, taking advantage of symbiotic relationships between representatives of corporate and organised crime as well as of legal functions of the society.

Towards the end of the 1990s, drug abuse increased in Finland and also considerably more hard drugs started to flow into the country via Russia and particularly via Estonia. Finland is also used as a route for drug smuggling to other parts of Europe, particularly to Sweden and other Nordic Countries. According to the Russian authorities, the city of St. Petersburg is the most important drug centre in Russia. Drug smuggling from the Central Asian republics and also from elsewhere in the world is controlled by tightly organised criminal groups famous for their ability of cooperation and discipline. Post-Soviet organised crime became fully international, even global, in the 1990s. Along with drug-trafficking, during the year 2000, particularly Estonian and Estonian-Russian criminal groups gained strong foothold in Finland for the first time in history. At the moment, Estonian-Russian and Russian criminal leaders have a stronger position in the Finnish drug market than ever before, because the smuggling and distribution of drugs used to be in the hands of our domestic criminals. The role of young émigrés from the St. Petersburg area – particularly the ingrians (an ethnic minority with Finnish origin) – has been important in this transformation. Their integration into the Finnish society has failed due to language difficulties for instance, and hundreds of young immigrants have been recruited to take care of the street-level dealing of heroin and synthetic drugs which are smuggled into the country mostly by Estonian-Russian criminal groups. These developments clearly demonstrate the necessity of both proper risk analysis and preventive work including multi-agency efforts and cooperation to develop feasible legal subsistence strategies for risk groups.

These developments have led to joint efforts to strengthen the cooperation between the Finnish and Estonian police organisations as well as the tripartite Baltic Sea Area police cooperation including also the Swedish police authorities. A good example of the efforts is the FINESTO project, a framework for the cooperation of the most important Finnish and Estonian criminal intelligence and investigative services to fight organised drug crime. In June, 2000, the National Police Commissioners of Finland, Estonia, Latvia and Lithuania signed a joint communiqué on mutual cooperation particularly in matters concerning the prevention and investigation of transnational drug crime.

It is also interesting to consider the opinion of the advisory Crime Prevention Board (*rikoksentorjuntaneuvosto – rådet för brottsförebyggande* – under the Ministry of Justice) on the criminal threat in Finland. This was expressed in the National Programme on crime prevention published and approved by the Finnish government in 1998. The report of the Board is an extensive paper aimed at mobilising all authorities, enterprises, interest groups and citizens into preventive action against it. The work was based on a considerable amount of research as well as expert opinions, and the role of local communities as well as the role of the school was underlined, in particular.[6]

In its assessment of the present level and quality of crime in Finland, the Board underlined that by far the most criminal activities taking place in Finland are of a local character and only a small part of crime is organised. No particular attention was paid in the paper to the action against or prevention of international organised crime. This does not mean, however, that dangerous international organised crime was an unknown phenomenon in Finland.

At the moment, several proposals concerning the development of criminal justice and law enforcement instruments which have an effect on countering organised crime are being drafted or are being considered by parliament (*eduskunta – riksdagen*). The ongoing reform of the legislation giving more extensive powers to the police authorities in the investigation of serious crime aims at providing new and more effective means to the police authorities in the investigation of professional and organised crime. As a consequence of the internationalisation of crime and the more and more complicated *modi operandi*, conventional investigation methods are not sufficient to clear up crimes. The need for secret and unconventional investigative methods has increased. **The aim of the reforms is also to harmonise the Finnish legislation with the legislation of other EU Member States and to improve reciprocity.**

The most important legislative measures against professional and organised crime include the extension of undercover intelligence instruments to cover pseudo purchase and infiltration as well as the extension of the scope of application of identification of call-associated data and technical surveillance under certain relatively tight preconditions. The legislation entered into force in the beginning of March 2001. The Government has to submit an annual report on the use of pseudo purchase and infiltration to the Parliamentary Ombudsman.[7] Telecommunication tapping was made possible in Finland only in 1995 and it has been carried out mostly in serious drugs cases.

A bill on the criminalisation of participation into the activities of a criminal organisation has been given recently to the Finnish parliament in order to implement the Joint Action of the Council of the European Union on criminalising the participation into the activities of a criminal organisation. The preparation of the bill began in 1996 as the activities of outlaw motorcycle gangs had reached Finland and aroused anxiety and public attention.[8] According to the current Finnish criminal code, the penalty for a crime may be increased in cases where the accused has committed the crime as a member of an organised criminal group.

In the bill, the organised character of a crime is defined and identified on the basis of the stability, and collaborative nature of the relationships between offenders and of their hierarchically organised structure. The requirement for there to be an organisation is also present in the current Finnish criminal code but the bill clarifies the contents of the concept. The preparatory documents of the current legislation also provide a list of components of the definition of organised crime, including hierarchically subordinate relationships and a division of labour.

## III. COORDINATION OF INTERNATIONAL LAW ENFORCEMENT AND JUDICIAL ACTIVITIES: EVOLUTIONARY PERSPECTIVES

In the field of countering organised and international crime, the essential bodies from the point of view of coordinating international judicial and law enforcement cooperation in Finland are the Ministry of Justice, the Prosecutor-General's Office, the Ministry for the Interior and the National Bureau of

Investigation.

The Ministry of Justice acts as the central contact point for international judicial assistance in Finland. The Unit for International Affairs (*kansainväliset asiat – internationella enheten*), acting directly under the Secretary General of the Ministry, follows the development of international treaties on judicial assistance and takes care of the commitments indicated by the treaties to the national central authority. The unit for European law of the law drafting department (*lainvalmisteluosasto – lagberedningsavdelningen*) of the Ministry of Justice acts as an expert body in matters concerning the rule of law in the European Union.[9]

Compared to the role of law enforcement authorities in most of the European countries, the role of the Finnish law enforcement authorities carrying out preliminary criminal investigations is unique in the sphere of international judicial assistance. In 1994, Finland modified its declaration to the European Convention on Mutual Assistance in Criminal Matters, ratified by Finland in 1981, by extending the role of judicial authorities also to the police, customs and frontier guard authorities. In 1994, the new Act on International Assistance in Criminal Matters came into force in Finland, defining, among other things, authorities performing preliminary criminal investigations capable of requesting and providing judicial assistance. For the purposes of the Convention, the Ministry of Justice, the courts of first instance (*käräjäoikeus – tingsrätt*), the courts of appeal (*hovioikeus/hovrätt*), the Supreme Court (*Korkein Oikeus – Högsta Domstolen*), the prosecutors as well as the police authorities, the customs authorities and the frontier guard officers in their capacity of preliminary criminal investigation authorities are deemed to be judicial authorities in Finland.[10]

The criminal intelligence division (*rikostietopalvelu – kriminal-underrättelsetjänsten*) of the NBI acts as the central contact point for the international exchange of information concerning criminal matters and for judicial assistance in cases where assistance is requested or is to be given by police authorities. According to the Act on Police Administration, the criminal intelligence division of the NBI performs the duties of the National Central Bureau in the international law enforcement cooperation and also other international duties assigned to the NBI. In addition to various registered data usually exchanged in international police cooperation, the Finnish police authorities also have the competence to carry out seizures, house searches, confiscations of the proceeds of crime, technical surveillance as well as get information about bank accounts and also in several cases carry out interrogations. That being the case, the competences of judicial and law enforcement authorities in Finland differ from the competences of judicial and law enforcement authorities presumed by the Schengen *acquis*.

The Finnish legislation on international judicial assistance in criminal matters allows direct contact between authorities including those not in the Nordic countries, although this is not usually allowed in international legal practice.

Closer directions for law enforcement authorities for requesting and providing judicial and executive assistance are given in an order of the Ministry for the Interior. The NBI is tasked to give supplementary directions and recommendations concerning the matter.

From an operational and intelligence point of view, it is the task of the NBI to act as a coordinating body for uncovering criminal networks of national and international scale and organising the investigations in cooperation with other police units. In 1998, a new national relational database containing intelligence data was established in order to provide better facilities to detect and analyse relationships and networks between criminals.

The criminal intelligence division of the NBI acts also as the Finnish Europol National Unit and as the national *Bureau de Liaison* (BdL) unit. Even if the majority of the Finnish police liaison officers are formally administered from the Ministry of Foreign Affairs, they work within the authority of the NBI, with the exception of the two police specialists working in Brussels directly under the Ministry for the Interior. During the 1990s, the number of Finnish police liaison officers increased noticeably and grew into an established framework for international police cooperation. The liaison activities cover the law enforcement cooperation related to Interpol, Europol and other law enforcement activities in the framework of the European Union, the Nordic PTN (*Polisen och tullen mot narkotika i Norden* – Nordic Police and customs authorities against drugs) cooperation, and presence in the neighbouring areas in Russia and Estonia. The SIRENE Bureau, which became operational in 2000, is also part of the NBI criminal intelligence division. The Division also performs the duties of the Finnish Interpol National Central Bureau (NCB). The NBI also is the central authority referred to in bilateral agreements of Finland with Russia (1993), the Baltic States (Estonia 1995, Latvia 1997, Lithuania 1997) and Poland (1999) on cooperation against crime. An agreement on the principles of cooperation against crime at the local and regional level was made between Finland and Russia in August 1996. A part of criminal matters related to the cooperation with Russian law enforcement authorities is handled in the operative divisions of the NBI.[11]

In 2000, a new section was established in the criminal intelligence division of the NBI to take charge of all international law enforcement communication channels. The criminal intelligence division also comprises sections in charge of technical intelligence, data exchange and follow-up concerning various criminal phenomena, language services as well as intelligence analysis and strategic research.

The Finnish Money Laundering Clearing House (*rahanpesun selvittelykeskus – utredningcentralen för penningtvätt*) was established in 1998, and it is a part of the organisation of the NBI. Finland is a member of the Financial Action Task Force on Money Laundering. The clearing house joined the international Egmont Group in June 1998, and is directly involved in an international exchange of financial intelligence via the Egmont Secure Web System. As a unit of the NBI, the clearing house is an integral part of the Finnish police organisation and has the opportunity to use the international communication systems of the police administration. The clearing house is authorised to exchange information also in cases where the prerequisites are insufficient for staging a criminal investigation.

In 1998, the legislation concerning money laundering was renewed and the obligation to submit information about suspicious transactions was extended to also cover betting, casinos and real estate businesses in addition to financial institutions such as banks and insurance companies. The clearing house also investigates cases uncovered on the basis of received information and intelligence. **The aim of the reform was to meet the requirements of the Council Directive on Money Laundering which became applicable in domestic law upon Finland's accession to the European Union in 1995.**

## IV. COMPETENCES OF ESSENTIAL AUTHORITIES IN INTERNATIONAL CRIMINAL MATTERS

International cooperation in criminal matters is regulated in Finland by several national instruments, such as the Act and Decree on International Assistance in Criminal Matters (4/1994 and 13/1994), and several international multilateral and bilateral agreements.

The directions and orders to be followed by the law enforcement authorities in the implementation of these legal instruments are given by the Supreme Police Command of the Ministry for the Interior. Directions and orders concerning the duties of the NBI or other national police units are usually prepared in close cooperation with these units and most often on their initiative. Both the Supreme Police Command and the NBI as well as other police units acting directly under the Supreme Police Command provide, when appropriate, information to law enforcement agencies on legislation, jurisdiction and procedures through internal information channels. Information can also be obtained from the Ministry of Justice, if appropriate.

In the practice of Finnish investigations, if international judicial or executive assistance is needed in relation to a criminal investigation, it is the police officer acting as the leader of the investigation who compiles the request for assistance. Despite the opportunity for the prosecutor to influence the course of the investigation, the leader of the investigation usually exercises exclusive discretion concerning coercive measures, interrogations and other investigative measures. In problematic cases, the leader of the investigation negotiates with the prosecutor about the appropriate procedures. The prosecutor is informed about requests of international judicial or executive assistance, but the request is authorised by the leader of the investigation. Occasionally also the prosecutor is requested to sign the request to avoid potential difficulties flowing from the differences of competence between the authorities of various countries.

When a request for international assistance arrives at the criminal intelligence division of the NBI, it is examined as to its quality and contents and forwarded to the Ministry of Justice or directly to the contact point or the executive authority in the country concerned, if appropriate according to the existing practice in the receiving country. Between Nordic countries, the requests may also be forwarded directly from the requesting authorities to the executive authorities.

Accordingly, requests coming from other countries directly through law enforcement communication systems or via the Ministry of Justice are delivered by the criminal intelligence division of the NBI to the appropriate law enforcement authorities in Finland. Negotiations and guidance from the criminal intelligence division are often necessary to complete the outgoing requests as well as to define the most suitable authority to perform tasks required by the incoming requests. Requests concerning extradition are always passed via the Ministry of Justice. There are certain pressures to reconsider the organisation of international cooperation in criminal matters in Finland, but no general agreement on possible rearrangements has emerged.

In the Prosecutor-General's Office, a State Prosecutor is in charge of duties concerning international judicial assistance. If it is necessary to request judicial assistance from abroad when the preliminary criminal investigation has ended and the prosecutor is considering charges, the prosecutor compiles the request for judicial assistance, and consults the Prosecutor-General's Office. The prosecutor forwards the request himself to the Ministry of Justice. Between the Nordic prosecution authorities, requests for judicial assistance are forwarded directly to the relevant authorities. In practice, the need for judicial or executive assistance usually becomes apparent during preliminary criminal investigations, and in by far the most cases, the request is compiled by the leader of the investigation in appropriate consultation with the prosecutor.

In large international criminal cases, it is important that the prosecutor is well informed about the course of the criminal investigation process because he has the final responsibility for pursuing a successful case in court. The prosecutors also participate actively in the preliminary investigations of such cases. In addition, the Prosecutor-General's Office is concentrating resources on the improvement of the cooperation between law enforcement and prosecution authorities. The role of the Prosecutor-General's Office is essential in training the prosecutors. In addition, law enforcement staff often participate in these training courses.

The duty of the Ministry of Justice as the central contact point for international judicial assistance is to receive the requests for judicial assistance and see that the requests are fulfilled. This is usually done by another competent authority. The Ministry of Justice has also the duty to forward the requests of Finnish authorities for international judicial assistance to the authorities concerned and see to the translation of documents, as well as other duties assigned to the central authority in international judicial affairs. Usually, the criminal intelligence division of the NBI sees to the translation of documents concerning law enforcement authorities. The Ministry of Justice also organises training and guidance in the field of international judicial cooperation and represents the judicial expertise in the EU Third-Pillar working groups.

In February 2000, a comprehensive report on the current international cooperation practices also containing proposed measures to strengthen the coordination of international judicial and executive assistance in criminal matters was published by a multi-agency working group appointed by the Ministry of Justice in November 1998.[12] As regards the coordination of international judicial and executive assistance in criminal matters in Finland, the essential authorities to be considered are the Ministry of Justice, the Prosecutor-General's Office and the National Bureau of Investigation.

The opinion of the working group is that the national regulation and the international agreements concerning international cooperation in criminal matters as well as the organisational and functional structures satisfy present requirements. The basic goal set by the working group is the creation of joint strategies and cooperation models for the essential authorities, if necessary, on a high political level, in order to steer the course of the Finnish judicial and law enforcement administration in international criminal justice cooperation. The group underlines the horizontal character of the future developments and calls for practical models for cooperation.

An imminent need for a cooperation model arises e.g. between the Ministry of Justice and the NBI in connection of the implementation of the new extradition instruments and the Schengen Information System.

In order to strengthen the judicial and law enforcement cooperation with the neighbouring areas, the Ministry of Justice sent a liaison magistrate at the beginning of 2001 to Estonia in order to support the Estonian judicial authorities in the preparation of international criminal justice matters. The experiences of the police liaison officer activities in Russia and Estonia have proved to be very positive and the liaison activities have matured into a basic structure for international police cooperation.

The cooperation in criminal matters with Russia has been based on the bilateral agreement on judicial assistance (1987) and the bilateral agreement on law enforcement cooperation against crime (1993 and 1996). Unlike the field of criminal investigations, diplomatic channels are used in the cooperation between Finland and Russia in judicial matters. The ratification by Russia, in December 1999, of the European Convention on Extradition and the European Convention on Mutual Assistance in Criminal Matters is changing the existing conditions and the bilateral agreement on judicial assistance will remain in a secondary role. The central authority for judicial cooperation in Finland will be the Ministry of Justice, and Russia, for its part, has defined five different authorities as competent bodies for international judicial cooperation.

In particular, the national cooperation arrangements of the Finnish law enforcement and prosecution authorities have to be coordinated with the arrangements required for the participation of Finland in the European Judicial Network and the Eurojust cooperation. Moreover, the increasing joint activities in the framework of Europol require the settling of questions concerning the competences of the Finnish law enforcement and prosecution authorities. The cooperation between the essential authorities in the field of operation in particular has to be strengthened.

Until now, joint operational activities by the essential authorities have been based on the personal contacts between a few officials. This kind of cooperation has been successful and flexible due to the low number of cases. During recent years however, the total number of criminal cases of international character has increased and also the amount of extensive and particularly complicated cases is on the increase. This requires coordinated efforts and the effective use of the joint expertise of both prosecution and law enforcement authorities.

The working group proposes the establishment of an expert board comprising the representatives of all essential authorities to support the authorities in international criminal matters as well as to develop and maintain the strategic coordination of the activities in the field of international criminal justice matters. The board would also have the duty to supervise the documentation of problems and solutions in order to use them as a basis for the establishment of good practices and feasible normative regulation. All the essential authorities also have to reconsider the internal organisational and functional arrangements.

The implementation of both the Schengen Agreement and the European Convention on Mutual Assistance in Criminal Matters has increased the amount of direct contact between competent authorities. Direct contact between the Nordic judicial and law enforcement authorities was already an established tradition. Direct contacts between authorities require the development of existing information management solutions in order to make the appropriate contacts accessible. Better coordination of information management concerning international criminal matters is also necessary in order to facilitate the follow-up of developments in the field, planning and implementation of appropriate improvements.

The working group also strongly underlined the importance of special training for judicial and law enforcement personnel in matters concerning international judicial and executive assistance in criminal matters.

## V. COOPERATION BETWEEN FINNISH AUTHORITIES AGAINST PROFESSIONAL AND ORGANISED CRIME

The close cooperation between law enforcement and tax and debt collection authorities has produced established practices in uncovering and investigating financial and economic crime since the beginning of the 1990s, in particular. This extensive cooperation also has a great importance for uncovering and investigating organised crime. The cooperation between the tax authorities and the law enforcement authorities is based on close working relationships and negotiations between the tax crime investigators and the police officers particularly the NBI and the criminal investigation units of the largest police departments.

The joint permanent cooperation steering group of the police and the tax authorities dates from 1981, when it was established on the basis of the need provoked by several large-scale economic crime investigations. The activity of the tax authorities to organise inspections and investigations was essential to this development.

For the investigation of economic and computer crime, as well as drug crime, there are specialist investigation squads within the crime investigation divisions of the largest local police forces and the NBI. The economic crime unit of the NBI was incorporated into the NBI main investigative division in 1999. In the NBI, there are also expert teams for the intelligence and investigation of illegal immigration and illegal activities of environmental activists as well as specialist personnel for several other types of criminal activities often connected to organised crime. The forensic services are provided by the NBI laboratory; the district forensic units provide routine services for several local police forces each.

In October 1998, the second action plan against economic crime and "grey economy" was approved by the Finnish government. This programme for

1999-2001 requires, as did its predecessor for 1996-1998, extensive cooperation and the engagement of various authorities and interest groups in order to prevent and uncover illegal activities in the field of economic activity. Legislative reforms and various research activities to support the action are an integral part of the programme. The main idea of the programme is the strengthening of close cooperation between various authorities and other partners. The implementation of the programme is coordinated by a multi-sectoral executive board, taking into account the projects prepared in the Third-Pillar working groups of the European Union, such as the Action Plan for prevention and control of organised crime. The participating authorities in the programme represent the administrative sectors of the Ministry of Justice, the Ministry for the Interior, the Ministry of Finance, the Ministry of Trade and Industry, the Ministry of Social Affairs and Health and the Ministry of Agriculture and Forestry.[13]

One of the main objectives of the police administration has been to increase the number of prosecutors who have expertise in complicated economic crime cases to increase the number of successful prosecutions. This aspect should be regarded as crucial given the fact that the reform of the criminal justice proceedings which was carried out in 1998 introduced oral proceedings and abolished the possibility to postpone a criminal court case. The prosecutor has the leading role in the court proceedings of a criminal case.

The main objective of the National Programme on crime prevention of 1998 has been to create a joint national strategy in order to decrease crime and to increase security by considering and taking into account the effects of crime on all decision-making levels in public administration. Partners in this cooperation include law enforcement, judicial, education, employment, social and health care as well as urban planning authorities at all administrative levels, the private business sector, churches and voluntary organisations. The activities included in the programme and their implementation are coordinated by the Crime Prevention Board which is to pay special attention also to the European Union Action Plan against organised crime. The Crime Prevention Board is an expert body in which the above-mentioned authorities and organisations, and appropriate research expertise, are represented. It acts under the Ministry of Justice. An evaluation report on the programme will be prepared by the end of 2002.

The cooperation of the Finnish police, customs and frontier guard authorities dates from the late 1970s, and the decree on the cooperation was passed in 1978. As a result of the challenges caused by the opening of the frontiers of the Baltic states and the fall of the Soviet Union, the development of the cooperation arrangements gained new momentum. But it was only the accession of Finland to the Schengen Agreement that necessitated a reconsideration of the legislation, regulations and practices concerning the cooperation. In 1999, an act on the frontier guard authorities was passed by the parliament which also required the authorities concerned to consider whether the legislation concerning the cooperation between the police, customs and frontier guard authorities should be renewed and included into a new act. In their joint negotiations, the authorities agreed on new administrative orders concerning the cooperation during the years 2000-04 and concluded that until the entry into force of the Schengen Agreement, the cooperation could be maintained and developed on the basis of the principles of the 1978 decree. It was also decided that the preparation of a new decree-level document on the cooperation arrangements would be started during 2000. The 1978 decree provides for joint negotiation arenas for cooperation on national, provincial and local level, and the regulation of cooperation at the level of administrative orders.

The division of tasks and the exchange of information between the NBI and the Security Police, who are both agents in gathering intelligence on phenomena concerning organised crime, is based on a joint agreement made in 1997. In the field of international crime, the duty of the NBI is to observe and act against international crime as well as act as the Finnish national central contact point in matters concerning international crime. The Security Police has the duty to observe, from the point of view of national security, the infiltration of crime into the administrative structures of neighbouring countries, and into the Finnish enterprises active in these countries. The Security Police also has the duty to acquire and gather information about the possible infiltration of international criminal organisations through legal economic or other activities into the Finnish society.

The cooperation of the NBI and the National Traffic Police is also regulated by a joint agreement, made in 1998.

In 1996, the local police administration was renewed as a part of the regional administration reform. The local police forces became a part of the State Local District Offices, also comprising the local prosecutor's office, the local debt collection office and the local register services. The State Local Districts/local state offices (*kihlakunta – härad*) are subordinate to the provincial administration. Administratively, the State Local Districts, and the local police as a part of them, are separate from the municipal administration. To tackle local problems, local joint consultative security boards serving as arenas for discussions and negotiations concerning the maintenance of law and order have been established, but these boards do not exist everywhere and are mostly passive. The number of police districts decreased remarkably, and this made it possible for local police forces to also carry out reasonably large and difficult criminal investigations requiring expertise previously available only in fairly large and well-equipped police units. On the other hand, problems arose as the availability of police services weakened in minor and scattered municipalities and sparsely populated areas.

In connection with the reform of provincial administration in 1996, the security division of the committee preparing the reform proposed reorganising the national operative police units according to a regional model by transferring most of their operative personnel under the provincial police command units. The reform plan was justified by the large degree of acceptance both in Finland and in the European Union of the efforts to move the power of decision from the central government to regional or local authorities. The positive effect of this kind of reform on the services provided by the police authorities to the citizens was underlined, in particular. The reform was designed to promote the action of local police forces and their cooperation partners, and the effectiveness thus attained at the regional level was considered essential also from the point of view of the implementation of the international agreements such as the Schengen Agreement, which Finland then anticipated becoming party to. The proposal raised a lot of discussion but was not carried out as it was evident that intelligence and investigation activities at the national level needed to be preserved and even strengthened to achieve the necessary coordination in an environment of increasing international police duties and the increasingly extensive and complicated criminal investigation cases.[14]

This discussion took place as a long series of struggles between the regional interests represented by the provincial administration and the national interests represented by efforts to create centralised national authorities to improve the investigation of extensive criminal cases with contact points in several parts of the country, and even abroad. The creation of the national crime investigation unit, the NBI, took more than 30 years of discussions, and since the establishment of the Bureau in 1955, proposals to disperse the operative personnel of the bureau into the provincial police units have been raised on several occasions. **It is interesting to see how the strong internationalisation of action against crime, starting also in Finland from the beginning of the 1990s, has redefined the scope of the discussions concerning the organisation of crime investigation and intelligence in Finland.** The reorganisation of the Finnish provincial administration in 1997 was also a considerable step towards larger police units and more effective cooperation between police authorities as well as towards more coordinated planning and management of police activities. The reform was made necessary by the increasingly international and rapidly changing environment where mobility of people, goods and information is increasingly high and where the use of communication technology may even obscure the place and time of a crime.

The NBI and also other Finnish law enforcement authorities participate in several international intelligence and investigative operations. Cooperation concerning neighbouring countries, some of which are applicant countries, is particularly active and particularly important from the viewpoint of the European Union. The Nordic police cooperation, well known from the direct contacts between the police authorities and the network of Nordic police liaison officers, is an integral part of the international cooperation of the Finnish police administration.

Law enforcement cooperation with Europol is an integral part of the daily routine of the criminal intelligence division of the NBI. There is no particular unit which concentrates on Europol affairs only. Instead, the processing of documents and other matters related to Europol is integrated into the normal process of criminal intelligence data exchange in the NBI. Since Europol took up its full activities in 1999, two responsible cooperation coordinators have been nominated. These coordinators receive the messages and distribute the related tasks to the appropriate expert desks.

Finland has two liaison officers in the Europol headquarters, one from the police administration, the other from the Customs. In the European Commission's anti-fraud unit, OLAF, a Customs representative is in charge of the Finnish liaison desk.

The administration of Interpol affairs, as well as of other international operative contacts, happens in a similar way. Particular effort has been dedicated to the reforms required by the implementation in the Nordic countries of the Schengen *acquis* during 2001. Meanwhile, the SIRENE unit has become part of a communications section of the criminal intelligence division which integrates all international communications activities related to international police cooperation. In addition to the preparations of the central contact point for Schengen affairs, several projects to adapt the national police activities into the Schengen environment have been started. Special emphasis has been laid on the development of criminal intelligence activities and the capabilities of local police authorities to deal with matters of international character such as illegal immigration.

The Nordic law enforcement cooperation is firmly rooted in the increasing mobility of people between the Nordic countries. The basic milestones of the cooperation were set up in the early 1950s when the first steps towards a single Nordic passport zone were taken. In 1954, a common Nordic labour market was established followed by a joint convention on social security of Nordic citizens in 1955. The Helsinki Treaty of 1962 set the general principles for cooperation between the Nordic countries and encouraged the investigation and prosecution of a crime committed in a Nordic country anywhere in the Nordic area. The principle of direct contacts is based on a joint agreement between Nordic National Police Commissioners, made in 1968. In 1970, the Nordic prosecutors also agreed on the framework of their cooperation. The efficient Nordic liaison officer network dates from 1977. Cooperation between the Nordic police and customs authorities was organised on a systematic basis in 1984.

Direct contacts between authorities also at the local level are a generally accepted principle in Nordic law enforcement cooperation. However, Nordic 24-hour alerts, warrants as well as requests for the confirmation of identity are always issued through the NBI, which acts as the principal intermediary. Requests for extradition addressed to Nordic authorities are also made with the NBI as an intermediary.

## VI. NEW SECURITY AGENTS

In Finland, the law enforcement authorities, the police forces in particular, are highly esteemed by the citizens. According to opinion polls, the police authorities are considered to be one of the most trustworthy authorities in the government organisation. However, growing business activities and the related increase in business premises and other forms of property have strengthened the demand for private security services and therefore the private security business sector is gradually increasing in Finland. In a rapidly changing and in many cases even global business environment, confidence in the service quality and untarnished background of an entrepreneur is no longer based on his good reputation but also requires formal checks and certification. The growing risk of improper business activities and the protection of the consumer against this are therefore the main focus of the updating of the legislation and regulations concerning the private security business in Finland, now under preparation. The main aims of the reform are to strengthen the legal protection of citizens' rights and to offer protection for consumers, to clarify the distinction and relationship between the security services provided by the state administration and the services provided by the private sector, to define the services subject to licences, and to renew the legislation concerning training for private security service jobs.

It is proposed that the training of private security staff should be developed and increased. The content and scope of the training should be defined by a decree issued by the Ministry of the Interior. The trainees should be accepted by the local police authority. The powers of detention of a private security agent should be the same as those of an ordinary citizen, with the exception of the right to make security checks which should be granted to security staff for safety reasons as many of those they detain are armed. The right to carry firearms or other weapons or use a dog should presuppose working under the threat of violence.

Furthermore, the control and guidance of the private security sector should be strengthened by establishing a unit for the control of private security services in the Ministry for the Interior. This unit would have national coordination tasks and provide for the authorisation of the private security companies and persons in charge of them. The companies and their staff should also be registered.

According to the draft bill recently prepared by the Ministry of the Interior, private sector security agents would be able to take the responsibility for private security only. The government approved the draft in May 2001 but it has not been given to the Parliament for consideration yet.

The cooperation between private and public security sectors would be strengthened by establishing a security services board, in which the producers and consumers of private security services as well as the public security authorities should be represented. The board would have the duty to make initiatives concerning the equipment and quality standards for security services to encourage and support the self-control of the private security sector instead of tight supervision and control of the field by government authorities.

So far, the exchange of experiences and in some cases also information between the private security providers and the public sector security providers has taken place on an informal basis. Cooperation between the police and the insurance business – the risk management, in particular – is an informal, established tradition and concerns several sectors of security work, usually crime prevention or intelligence at a general level, such as the exchange of information concerning new criminal phenomena. On the basis of the Police Act, the police authorities may warn businesses about the risks caused by criminal activities. Another cooperation partner of the police is the document security business, the cooperation between them mainly concentrates on the exchange of forensic expertise and information concerning risks.

## VII. ACCOUNTABILITY OF LAW ENFORCEMENT AGENCIES

The accountability of the Finnish law enforcement activities is mainly based on the strong institution of the ombudsman and political regulation as shown partly in the preliminary expert discussions concerning matters under preparation, partly in the arenas for political discussion such as the parliament and the media. The relationship between the justice and law enforcement administrations is particularly interesting.

The Parliamentary Ombudsman (*eduskunnan oikeusasiamies – riksdagens justitieombudsman*) is an independent authority who oversees the observance of laws as well as the implementation of constitutional rights and international human rights in the exercise of official and public functions. These competences are exercised by the Parliamentary Ombudsman and two Deputy Parliamentary Ombudsmen, each overseeing certain branches of public administration. The Ombudsmen also investigate complaints submitted to them, intervene in matters of concern on their own initiative and conduct on-site inspections of public offices and institutions. The Parliamentary Ombudsman focuses particularly on prisons, military units, and institutions in the social welfare and health sector in order to provide prisoners, conscripts and persons confined in closed institutions with an opportunity to have confidential discussions with an Ombudsman.

The Parliamentary Ombudsman oversees, e.g., public authorities, including courts of law and government offices and institutions, such as law enforcement authorities, and public servants, including police officers and other law enforcement staff. Anyone may complain to the Parliamentary Ombudsman, regardless of age, citizenship or other similar factors.

A complaint will be investigated if the Parliamentary Ombudsman finds there is a reason to suspect unlawful or improper action subject to the Ombudsman's jurisdiction. The authorities in question are requested to provide reports and give statements concerning the matter to the Ombudsman and the person complained against will be heard. Additional information will be obtained through questioning by the police authorities or the Parliamentary Ombudsman's own investigating officers. The decision of the Ombudsman will be delivered to both the complainant and the person complained against, and in addition to that, will often be released to the media as well.

The complaint may lead to a criminal charge against a public servant, or the Ombudsman may reprimand a public authority or a public servant for improper conduct or faulty proceedings. The Ombudsman may also express critical views concerning the interpretation of law by public authorities or public servants or call the authority's attention to principles of good administration. The Parliamentary Ombudsman may also recommend law reforms with regard to statutory provisions he or she finds ambiguous, defective or inconsistent.

According to the Act on Police Administration, a warning to a member of the police staff may be given by the appointing authority (usually the chief of the police unit concerned), with the exception of the chiefs of the NBI and the Security Police who are appointed by the President of the Republic. Warnings to them may be given by the Ministry for the Interior. A reform of legislation concerning misconduct in office was drafted recently in a working group of the Ministry of Justice.

The main aim of the project is to define the legal responsibility of an official for his/her actions as clearly as possible in the criminal code and clarify this responsibility from the point of view of the use of public authority. The working group is also to draft the amendments required by the Criminal Law Convention on Corruption established by the Council of Europe on 27 January 1999. In the case of Finland this requires the establishment of penal responsibility of the Members of Parliament in cases of corruption, in particular.

The legislation and regulations concerning criminal investigations in cases where the suspect is a policeman were reformed in 1997-98.

Normally, the criminal investigation is led by a police officer, but in cases where a police officer is suspected of crime, the investigation is led by a prosecutor. This also concerns crimes committed by officers when not on duty. The Prosecutor General's Office has named the prosecutors whose duty it is to take the lead in criminal investigations concerning police officers. A crime suspected to have been committed by a police officer is not investigated by the State Local District Office where the relevant police officer is employed. If the policeman belongs to the staff of the national police units, the performer of the investigation is determined by the location of the unit concerned. The Provincial Police Command makes the decision about the local police units responsible for these kinds of investigations. In cases where the suspect is a member of the staff of the Supreme Police Command or a Provincial Police Command, the case is investigated by the NBI.

If a complaint made against a member of the police staff requires preliminary investigation, the matter is transferred to the competent police authority who transfers it to relevant prosecutor.

The Office of the Data Protection Ombudsman (*tietosuojavaltuutetun toimisto – dataombudsmannens byrå*) was established in 1987 and acts under the auspices of the Ministry of Justice.[15]

The Office of the Data Protection Ombudsman supervises, gives guidance and inspects the activities of file-keepers as well as gives them orders. The dissemination of information to both file-keepers and the "data subjects" has a central role in the work of the office, but the Data Protection Ombudsman (*tietosuojavaltuutettu – dataombudsmannen*) also has wide powers, having the right to request information regarding file-keepers' activities and the right to inspect personal data files regardless of confidentiality. The Data Protection Ombudsman may also give specific advice to file-keepers in cases where there has been a violation of law, or may inform the Public Prosecutor.

The Data Protection Ombudsman has powers to make his/her own legislative initiatives and his/her authoritative view is often asked for when making legislative decisions.

The Data Protection Board is the most important governing body in the area of personal file keeping. The Board makes decisions on e.g. applications submitted by the Data Protection Ombudsman regarding the imposition of an obligation upon a file-keeper to proceed in accordance with the Personal Data Act (523/1999). The Board also issues exceptions to the provisions of the Personal Data Act and the Personal Data File Decree (476/1987).

The regulations concerning the particular practices related to law enforcement data files are in the Police Personal Data File Act and the related Decree from 1995 ( 509/1995 and 1116/1995). The recently renewed Act on the Publicity of Government Activities (621/1999) and the related provisions have been implemented from the beginning of December 1999. The exceptions to the general principle of openness of official documents are defined in the Publicity Act, and these exceptions define, *inter alia*, the prerequisites for the secrecy of law enforcement documents.

The scope of application of the updated Finnish transparency legislation is more extensive than that of the former publicity legislation dating from 1951, as various provisions concerning documents and official secrecy have now been collected under one heading and the law also applies to private bodies and persons when performing tasks of public authority on the basis of law (i.e. pension insurance companies). The new legislation strengthens and enlarges the implementation of the principle of publicity in public administration, increases the publicity of matters under preparation and strengthens good information management practices as well as the opportunities of the citizen to obtain information. Also the criteria of secrecy were clarified by the new legislation, and a basis for a uniform regulation for the exchange of information between various authorities was established. At the present moment, it is too early to estimate the real impact of the reform on the transparency of the exercise of public functions.

According to the Police Personal Data File Act, the delivery of law enforcement data abroad is possible, for the purposes of police duties, i.e. to the Interpol organisation or to a national police or other law enforcement authority of an Interpol member state. The delivery of data to non-Interpol states is possible only on certain conditions mentioned in the Act. The delivery of data is also subject to particular regulations and binding international agreements.

The delivery of data always happens after a careful consideration of each particular case. With the prerequisite that crime investigations related to the subject matter have been started or that the subject matter is related to preventive law enforcement measures, executive assistance is usually given and also the use of coercive measures is possible. The international exchange of information is an integral part of the established and daily routine of the Finnish law enforcement administration.

In Finland, traditionally, the role of the competent minister, i.e. the

Minister of the Interior, has been to back up and promote urgent reforms in the police administration that need political support and require legislative measures. Many a time, these kinds of reforms have been politically controversial and several Ministers of the Interior in Finnish history have been chosen and nominated to perform duties connected to carrying out of certain politically precarious reforms. The political importance and the attractiveness for professional politicians of being the Minister of the Interior lie in the activities possible in the field of the police administration. At present, the role of the Minister of the Interior in carrying out reforms such as the legislation concerning more extensive powers to the police authorities in the investigation of serious crime is crucial. The Minister himself has to ensure that the preparations proceed without critical delays and that the necessary political support will be acquired to the proposals.

Depending of the personal opinions of the ministers, the Minister of Justice may also be particularly important to the police administration. Sometimes, the close cooperation between the Minister of Justice and the police authorities has been essential in carrying out legislative reforms of importance to crime investigation. Hence, the Minister of Justice may occasionally assume the task performed by the Minister of the Interior in relation to parliament and the public in passing critical legislation.

On the other hand, the authorities which draft Finnish law and which belong to the administrative branch of the Ministry of Justice, represent a traditional counterweight to the aspirations which emerge from time to time in the police administration to strengthen the powers and means available to the police authorities in the field of criminal intelligence and investigation. During the history of independent Finland, the debates concerning police powers have been vehement and particularly fascinating from political point of view. Populist conceptions of the more threatening types of crime and the necessity to extend police powers justified by such crime are easily visible in the Finnish media. However, during the latest two decades, legislative regulation and control over the means and powers available to the law enforcement authorities in criminal investigation has tightened remarkably.

In matters concerning law enforcement authorities and their action, the national parliament is an arena for legislative decisions and political debate. As such, it has a remarkable impact on the resources directed annually into the law enforcement sector as well as on the legislation concerning both the general criminal policy and the working methods and organisation of the law enforcement authorities.

## VIII. CONCLUDING REMARKS

During the first years of the 1990s ideas concerning the internationalisation of law enforcement and the judicial environment were presented now and then in professional fora. These ideas did not seem readily approachable then even if they were not at all far-fetched. The fall of the Soviet Union and the European integration process bringing with it Finland's membership of the European Union and the Schengen Convention accelerated a fundamental change of existing conditions for law enforcement activities. Once and for all, Finland ceased to be a backwater in terms of the threat of international crime. Instead, as the country developed into a gateway for economic activities between the east and west, opportunities in Finland for illegal activities became increasingly apparent. The changes can currently be observed in international matters, which have become an integral part of daily law enforcement action in the field of professional and organised crime.

Statistics concerning the number of international contacts in law enforcement matters do not indicate any dramatic changes. However, there are numerous indications that the complexity and scope of criminal investigations are on the increase. The most impressive change concerning the law enforcement administration has happened in the field of the development and maintenance of administrative readiness for international action required as a consequence of international integration in the law enforcement environment.

Several organisational reforms have been implemented, and the development towards an internationalised environment of law enforcement work has had its distinct effect on the character of the reforms. However, the reforms implemented during the last decade of the twentieth century in Finland cannot be reduced to the impact of international instruments only. The basic structures of the reforms have grown out of the traditional national organisations and their views and ways of action. These reforms also often have a long history of preparations and their original aim has been to remedy the defects in the organisation and actions of authorities from a purely national point of view. Arrangements that would significantly change the duties or competences of various authorities have not been made. Instead, strengthening cooperation and coordination between various authorities as well as the training and recruitment of expertise are envisaged as a solution that should ensure that international obligations are performed more effectively.

International cooperation requires a remarkable amount of additional resources, and this is not always fully understood in the field of traditional law enforcement activities. Changes in the essential conditions of law enforcement work also require adjustments in arrangements and peoples' ways of action. The traditional thinking in local terms is in a process of adapting itself to the requirements of increased mobility of people, property and information.

In 1995, professor Markku Temmes envisaged a shift towards a formal-legalistic approach from the then strengthening managerial trend in the Finnish administration as a consequence of the country's joining the European Union.[16] Still, this managerial control is also new in the Finnish administrative system. The managerial trend has led in practice to a decentralisation of national regulatory systems. As regards the strengthening of formalism, it is evident that the increasing amount and complexity of law enforcement tasks, brought about by internationalisation, underline the importance of legal and other experts, careful regulation and good organisation. The need for regulation is increasing, e.g. cooperation between authorities as well as the actual regulation itself. Also the need of expertise and special training for international activities are high on the agenda for developing the organisation and staff to perform new duties of related to the increasing international character of their work.

On the other hand, several reforms, particularly the renewed transparency legislation, contribute to the legal protection of citizens and the right of citizens to obtain information concerning administrative activities. In the international environment of today, finding a feasible model for the balancing of political control and regulation of administrative activities is a particular challenge. Until now, the public debate concerning these questions has remained fragmented and also the experiences of the renewed publicity norms are but a few.

Throughout this chapter, we also observed the impact of the internationalisation of crime-fighting initiatives, which in Finland commenced at the beginning of the 1990s. Internationalisation as such has redefined the scope of the discussions concerning the organisation of crime investigation and intelligence in Finland. Moreover, the reorganisation of the Finnish provincial administration may be regarded as an enlargement of scale and as the introduction of a more effective cooperation between police authorities, more coordinated planning and management of police activities. The reform was triggered by the increasingly international and rapidly changing environment where mobility of people, goods and information is increasingly high and where the use of communication technology may even obscure the place and time of a crime.

## NOTES

1. For general information about the Finnish police organisation, see www.intermin.poliisi.fi/. When not specifically mentioned, the data concerning various authorities, activities and projects presented in this article are based on public and internal bulletins, directions and reports as well as discussions with several expert officials.

2. For the history of the Finnish police administration, see Tuija Hietaniemi, *Lain vartiossa. Poliisi Suomen politiikassa* 1917-1948 (Police in the Finnish Politics, 1917-1948, Vammala 1992) and Tuija Hietaniemi, *Totuuden jäljillä. Suomalaisen rikospoliisin taival* (Criminal Investigation in the History of the Finnish Police Organisation, Helsinki 1995).

3. General information about the Finnish customs authorities is available in www.tulli.fi/, and about the frontier guard authorities in www.intermin.fi/raja

4. Ammattimaisen rikollisuuden kartoittamista ja tutkinnan järjestelyjä selvittänyt työryhmä. Documents KDSM 1802/403/1979, Archives of the Ministry of the Interior, Helsinki.

5. On the phenomena and reactions related to the criminal threats in Finland from the areas of the former Soviet Union, see e.g. eastern crime. A Selection of Reports on Crime in the St. Petersburg Region and the Baltic Countries, 1993-1999. National Research Institute of Legal Policy Publication 168 (Helsinki 1999).

6. The Action Plan is published in Finnish as Turvallisuustalkoot – kansallinen rikoksentorjuntaohjelma. Oikeusministeriön Yleisen osaston julkaisu 2/1999 (Helsinki 1999).

7. Proposal HE 34/1999, www.eduskunta.fi/triphome/, Acts 21/2001 and 22/2001, Suomen Säädöskokoelma.

8. Proposal HE 183/1999, www.eduskunta.fi/triphome/.

9. Data concerning the administrative branch of the Ministry of Justice are available in www.om.fi.

10. The Finnish Declaration is available in www.coe.fr/tablconv/30t.htm/.

11. About the role of the NBI, see e.g. *Kansainvälisten rikosoikeusapuasioiden koordinointi*. Työryhmän mietintö. Oikeusministeriö, yleisen osaston julkaisuja 1/2000, p.125-143.

12. The extensive report of the working group is available in Finnish: *Kansainvälisten rikosoikeusapuasioiden koordinointi*. Työryhmän mietintö. Oikeusministeriö, Yleisen osaston julkaisuja 1/2000.

13. Talousrikollisuuden ja harmaan talouden torjuntastrategia 1999-2001, www.vn.fi/vn/suomi/vnyleis/vn981022.htm.

14. The reform plan is available in Finnish as *Koottuun poliisin aluehallintoon*, Aluehallinto 2000 turvallisuusjaoston mietintö 14.5.1996.

15. Information concerning data protection in Finland is available on www.tietosuoja.fi/.

16. Markku Temmes: *The EU and Finnish Administration*, Hallinnon tutkimus 4/1995, p. 258-263, and *Optimal mix between managerism and the legal-administrative regulatory system*, Hallinnon tutkimus 1/1997, p. 70-79.

## BIBLIOGRAPHY

Eastern crime. A Selection of Reports on Crime in the St. Petersburg Region and the Baltic Countries, 1993-1999. National Research Institute of Legal Policy Publication 168, Helsinki 1999.

Hietaniemi, Tuija: Lain vartiossa. Poliisi Suomen politiikassa 1917-1948 (Police forces in Finnish Politics, 1917-1948), Vammala 1992.

Hietaniemi, Tuija: Totuuden jäljillä. Suomalaisen rikospoliisin taival (Criminal Investigation in the History of the Finnish Police Organisation), Helsinki 1995.

Kansainvälisten rikosoikeusapuasioiden koordinointi. Työryhmän mietintö. Oikeusministeriö, yleisen osaston julkaisuja 1/2000, Helsinki 2000.

Temmes, Markku: The EU and Finnish Administration, Hallinnon tutkimus 4/1995, p. 258-263.

Temmes, Markku: Optimal mix between managerism and the legal-administrative regulatory system, Hallinnon tutkimus 1/1997, p. 70-79.

Turvallisuustalkoot – kansallinen rikoksentorjuntaohjelma. Oikeusministeriön Yleisen osaston julkaisu 2/1999, Helsinki 1999.

## ABBREVIATIONS

NBI     National Bureau of Investigation (Finland)
PTN     *Polisen och tullen mot narkotika i Norden* – Nordic Police and customs authorities against drugs

## RESPONDENTS

The author expresses her gratitude to a great number of colleagues who have knowingly and unknowingly shared their most valuable expertise for the purpose of this project.

# France

## Franziska Hagedorn and Didier Bigo

## 1. ORGANISED CRIME IN FRANCE

### 1.1 Legal definition

There is no official definition of organised crime in France. The legislator has not defined the term but has instead used a variety of expressions and definitions to refer to collective behaviour aimed at committing serious offences with the help of an organised structure:

*   *"groupement" or "entente"* (a grouping or alliance), for instance in relation to a *"bande organisée"* (an organised gang) or *"association of malfaiteurs"* (criminal conspiracy);
*   *"doté d'une organisation hierarchisée"* (endowed with a hierarchical organisation) concerning, for example, a violent gang;
*   *"groupement"*, in the area of trafficking, especially drugs;
*   *"entreprise"* for terrorism; *"plan concerté"* (organised plan) for genocide and other crimes against humanity;
*   *"manière concertée"* (in a concerted manner) for endangering public liberties; and *"organisation criminelle"* (criminal organisation) for money laundering and crimes concerning financial matters abroad.[1]

The law of 1993 on the prevention of corruption and the 1996 law against money laundering both refrain from defining the term although they use it as a central concept.[2] After an investigation into the use of the term in contemporary legislation, Jean Cédras finds that the legislator has not come to any more precise definition than that of 1810, of an *association de malfaiteurs,* or criminal conspiracy.[3]

This situation has led both the justice system and the police to finding interpretations and definitions of the term which are useful for their day-to-day work.

Lacking an autonomous legal definition of the term, legal practice defines it therefore by means of an offence committed with the aggravating circumstance of the involvement of an organised gang and incrimination provided by participation in a conspiracy with a view to committing a crime or a serious offence. This practice is similar to the one used for terrorism.[4]

In terms of the use of the term in police practice, an article written by a *commissaire* of the DCPJ in a journal read mostly by police professionals is indicative;[5] he identifies five elements that can be extracted from various definitions such as those of Interpol, legal theorists or the EU group "Drugs and Organised Crime". They are:

* an organised structure used as a framework for committing an offence;
* serious offences, such as those covered by the seven central offices of the DCPJ (see below);
* the pre-eminence of profit as the motive for the crime;
* an international dimension as a result of searching for profitable markets and the intention to avoid prosecution;
* use of modern methods of management.

Furthermore, the DCPJ mentions in its information material several types of offences that the expression "organised crime" can refer to:

* an *individual act* committed with premeditation and malicious intent;
* a *"professional crime"*, prepared and executed by several people, often organised as a gang, who live on the fringes of society and on the profits gained from their crimes;
* the *"criminal syndicate"*, a permanent association of criminals which has reached such a degree of organisation that it holds a monopoly in its sector of crime in a given area.

## 1.2 Data collection on organised crime

It is the *Centrale du renseignement et de l'analyse du crime organisé* (CRACO), which is responsible for collecting the data on organised crime and analysing it. More generally speaking, the DST and the department of *Renseignements généraux* of the PN have a central role in collecting data.

As regards the collection of data, it has been mentioned in several interviews that this was problematic due to a number of obstacles which relate to the lack of a precise definition: the difficulty of determining the line between organised and other crime and the question of when in the enquiry to determine the nature of the offence.

It was also mentioned that these problems are often regarded as largely academic by practising police officers. They are viewed as important questions but there is little time in the day-to-day work to overcome such obstacles. There are therefore no overall statistics for organised crime in France.

For the observer, it seems that the lack of a legal definition for organised crime leads to a number of problems:

- Practitioners encounter difficulties in classifying the offence and therefore the legal rights they have in the enquiry.
- The process of the preliminary investigation in France encourages the police to classify crimes as organised crime, giving them more rights of enquiry (for example the right to search houses outside the legally provided hours – 6 am to 9 pm – when the preliminary enquiry is concerned with offences of drug trafficking, pimping or terrorism).

## 1.3 The fight against organised crime: the context of organisational changes

Organised crime in France has received growing attention in the media, and from the general public and the political class in the last decade. The fight against organised crime in France is not new: most units were founded well before the 1990s. Organisational changes have taken place and can be linked to a number of reasons:

### 1.3.1 Rationale put forward by professionals

The reason most cited by the professionals for the reforms which took place in France is the greater risk of organised crime today compared to 20 years ago. The opening of borders, ease of communication, use of high technology, etc. are all cited as augmenting the danger of the rise of organised crime. "We know that there is a higher risk in general and that the growing wealth of the criminal organisations can pose serious problems to democracies and for the stability of certain countries. After the end of the Cold War, a new type of threat is emerging, particularly the organised crime which is developing in central and eastern Europe. Given the means of communication today, there is a need to find common answers to these problems together with a number of countries."[6]

The rationale that emerges from this quote shows a typical line of thought: the development of high communication technology coinciding with the end of the Cold War has led to a new type of danger which the law enforcement services have to counter with increased means and reinforced international cooperation.

At the same time, practitioners admit that it is hard to assess exact numbers of offences committed in the framework of organised crime. It has been mentioned that it is difficult to quantify organised crime, especially in the area of money laundering and the financial aspects of organised crime. One has to take into account institutional logic in this argumentation: the suggestion of high numbers of undetected organised crimes can serve as a justification of funding. However, the police and public prosecution services are also careful not to give the impression of inefficiency in the fight against organised crime. In their information material and representations in the media, they emphasise the structures put in place to fight organised crime and their efficiency.

Similarly, we have seen in our contacts with officials, that the effectiveness of the reforms in the fight against organised crime is very hard to assess. As one interlocutor put it: "This is very difficult to quantify. This is not to be equalled to a free-market system where a company will restructure in order to improve sales. Statistics can show nearly everything. I also think that the fight against organised crime becomes more efficient when accompanied by means other than organisational and legal instruments: educational means and a certain ethical sanity of a country need to be encouraged, as we have done for example with the work regarding professions susceptible to the influence of organised crime."

There is an awareness, therefore, that although structures to fight organised crime have been put in place, they achieve the best results only in combination with other instruments in a wider social context – and in coordination with other countries.

### 1.3.2 *Importance of the context of European and internal political events*

The rationale for organisational changes in the fight against organised crime has to be seen in the framework of European and internal political events in France.

There was certainly a European dimension to the changes, but rarely can a direct link to EU measures or recommendations be found.[7] As will be spelled out below, **most institutions in the fight against organised crime were established before the EU made any recommendations.**

Events at a European level have nevertheless to be taken into account in order to sketch out the general climate in which the debate on organised crime was taking place. It could be validly argued that they acted as a facilitator for the changes in the services engaged in the fight against such crime. The end of the cold war and the fall of the Iron Curtain with its strictly policed borders increasingly led to a security-focused discourse in western European countries. The east was portrayed as a latent threat, harbouring potential immigrants, criminals and asylum seekers likely to flood the wealthy western European countries.[8]

At the same time, the Schengen Agreement (1985) and even more so the Schengen Implementation Agreement (1990) provided for the suppression of border controls at the "internal borders" of the EU. The professional and public discussion quickly concentrated on compensatory measures to ensure the internal security of all countries concerned. In this context, the fear of the infiltration of organised crime originating from outside the EU was often voiced. This line of argument was often present in the media and contributed to a general concern about organised crime.

The European dimension becomes most visible in relation to the impact of European events on France. The deaths of the Italian judges Borsellino and Falcone in the early 1990s has led to a heightened general awareness of the danger of organised crime for public life. It became a problem of public policy, much discussed in the media, especially with respect to the possibility of the spread of criminal organisations to France.

Internal political events were linked to that debate. In the 1970s, a lot of national and international attention was focused on Marseille as the first city for drugs in the world. The expression "French Connection" dates from that time. The activities of the *Office central pour la répression du trafic illicite de stupéfiants* (OCRCTIS) were reinforced during this period.

In 1993, a report by a member of parliament, the *rapport d'Aubert* (the Aubert report), on the infiltration of the Mafia into France raised a lot of interest.[9] This report found that the definition of offences related to organised crime was not coherent enough for an efficient fight against infiltration. At the same time, it emphasised the need to give the law enforcement authorities and services supplementary and specific means to fight this form of transborder crime.

Another internal event which played a role in the organisational development of the fight against organised crime was the scandal around the murder of the member of parliament Yanne Piat in 1994. The public discussion in that case concentrated on links between the death of Piat and revelations about corruption. The affair sparked an investigation into the links between criminals in southern France and the political class.

Such events put pressure on the services for results in the area of organised crime. At the same time, the Thatcherite revolution and Anglo-Saxon reforms also had an effect in France with increased expectations of efficiency. However, politicians feared any implicit connections made between corruption, political parties and organised crime – as were sometimes made in speeches advocating the reinforcement of the fight against organised crime.

The *Institut des Hautes Etudes de la Sécurité Intérieure* (IHESI) also played an implicit role in deliberations about the reinforcement of this fight. It brought together delegates from all the relevant services for a research seminar during which they had the space and time to deliberate over appropriate strategies.

These events all pushed in a direction of reinforcing and diversifying the existing structure of the fight against organised crime, if only to satisfy the public demand for action. Therefore, the UCRAM (*Unité de Coordination et de Recherche Anti-Mafia*) came to life in 1993. It was set up as a response to political pressures, it is modelled on the existing anti-terrorist unit UCLAT, and is also dependent on the latter in terms of personnel and structures: the head of UCRAM is the Director-general of UCLAT, and the anti-Mafia unit uses UCLAT's network abroad for all cooperation.

Furthermore, the *Section Centrale d'Investigations sur le crime organisé* (SCICO) was formed within the DCJP in 1995 as a unit charged with centralising all information on organised crime and analysing the data. Also in 1995, the Ministry of Justice established a central office for the fight against organised crime which manages and coordinates all judicial aspects of the treatment of organised crime.

**Organisational reforms in the fight against organised crime in the 1990s were a response to public policy concerns where the agenda was set by a mixture of internal events, European political developments and the perception of events in other European countries.**

## 2. THE LAW ENFORCEMENT AGENCIES IN FRANCE

### 2.1 Centralisation and plurality of services

The French policing system is a centralised and plural law enforcement system, where several forces are charged with parallel tasks and where all of these forces are largely centralised in their administrative set-up. However, the extent of centralisation in the organisation of the services has been a subject of debate for some time and has to be viewed with some caution.[10] The French policing system is most often characterised as centralised when it is compared with the English one. Therefore, some authors have voiced a warning not to neglect the complexity of the situations and to avoid over-simplification and exaggerating the differences between the systems.[11]

First of all, there is not a single police force in France but rather the police service is constituted by at least two national institutions which have largely similar competences but rely on different statutes: the *Police nationale* (PN) has a civil statute and is placed under the authority of the Ministry of the Interior (*ministère de l'Intérieur*), whereas the *Gendarmerie nationale* (GN) has a military statute and is therefore part of the Ministry of Defence (*ministère de la Défense*). The two forces both have general national competence, but there is a rough division where the PN police the urban areas whereas the gendarmerie have responsibility for suburban and rural areas. Another force is the municipal police which employs around 10,000 officers and retains strictly local competence.[12]

The media have repeatedly reported on a *"guerre des polices"*, a war of the police forces, and alleged inefficiencies due to lack of cooperation. Every five to ten years, there are plans to unify the services in France. However, this is met by resistance both in the services and from politicians.

Secondly, the extent of centralisation must not be exaggerated. Even originally the police system could have been deemed as being partly de-centralised and centralisation and nationalisation of police forces has historically been a slow process. The revolution gave the power and responsibility for the police entirely to the local mayor and only subsequently the *préfectures* in all the *départements* were granted increased power during the nineteenth century. A national police service was only created in 1941 and kept after the liberation. Not until the late 1960s was the national police service truly unified; subsequent laws providing for decentralisation of public services did not concern the police. Therefore, the co-existence of the services, the diversity of structures at the national, regional and departmental level as well as the division between officers and other policemen have escaped the effect of strong centralisation tendencies. Furthermore, Journès speaks of a "discovery of local interests" in the police services in general. It was hoped that the effectiveness of crime prevention would be increased by the way it was organised territorially and through the involvement of the mayors. Urban, political and air police have increasingly worked together locally in joint departments since 1990 (this is not the case for the criminal police which are the main actors in fighting organised crime). Furthermore, a rise in the numbers of municipal police has been noted.[13]

It has to be said, however, that despite these factors impeding the complete unification of the police service and despite tendencies encouraging decentralisation, the police system in France is largely centralised and has a national focus. The following account of the organisation of the various services will illustrate this.

## 2.2 The Organisation of the Police

The *Police nationale* had around 147,731 agents in 1999, of which 113,088 were police officers on active duty.[14] Its task is mainly to police the urban and suburban areas of the country. Attached to the Ministry of the Interior, the police come under the *Direction générale de la police nationale* (DGPN), (the headquarters of the *Police nationale*) which directs the administrative and operational departments, the central services and the *inspection generale*, the body policing the police.

Since 1995, the police personnel on active duty have been divided into three corps with the following duties:

- conception and direction (2,001 *commissaires* (superintendents); charged with the structural and operational management of all services);
- command and managerial staff (16,776 police officers; assist or replace the *commissaires* in their functions; command the officers in the supervision and application corps);
- supervision and application (95,121 uniformed or plainclothes officers in active units)

The DGPN consists of a cabinet and several units:
- *la Mission sur la police dans la ville* (the commission for the policy in the city)
- *la Mission de la lutte anti-drogue* (MILAD) (drug enforcement commission)
- *l'Unité de coordination de la lutte anti-terroriste* (UCLAT) (anti-terrorist coordination unit)
- *l'Unité de coordination et de recherches anti-mafia* (UCRAM) (anti-Mafia investigation and coordination unit)
- *le Service de sécurité du ministère de l'Intérieur* (SSMI) (the Ministry of the Interior internal security service)
- *le Service central automobile* (SCA) (central automobile service)
- *l'Unité de recherche, assistance, intervention et de dissuasion* (RAID) (rapid deployment special task unit)
- *la Mission emplois-jeunes* (commission for "job opportunities for the youth")

A number of administrative departments deal with the management and the training of the police force: *l'Inspection générale de la police nationale* (IGPN) (Inspectorate-general of the National Police): *Direction de l'administration de la police nationale* (DAPN) (National Police Administrative Directorate): *Direction de la formation de police nationale* (DFPN) (Directorate for Training).

The active departments are organised according to tasks:
- *Direction centrale de la police judiciaire* (DCPJ) (Criminal Investigation Central Directorate)
- *Direction centrale de la sécurité publique* (DCSP) (Public Security Central Directorate)
- *Direction de la surveillance du territoire* (DST) (territorial intelligence service)
- *Direction centrale de la police aux frontières* (DCPAF) (Central Directorate for Air and Border Policing)
- *Direction centrale des renseignements généraux* (DCRG) (Community Intelligence Central Directorate)

- *le Service central des compagnies républicaines de sécurité* (SCCRS) (Central Service of Republican Security Companies)
- *le Service de coopération technique internationale de police* (SCTIP) (International Technical Police Cooperation Service)
- *le Service de protection des hautes personnalités* (SPHP) (VIP Protection Department)

The *police judiciaire* (PJ) (criminal investigation service) conducts all criminal investigations and is the main service charged with the fight against organised crime.

The *Direction centrale de la police judiciaire* has the following subdivisions:

- *Sous-direction des affaires criminelles* (Sub-Directorate of Criminal Investigation)
- *Sous-direction de la police technique et scientifique* (Sub-Directorate of Forensic Science)
- *Sous-direction des affaires économiques et financières* (Sub-Directorate of Economic and Financial Crime)
- *Sous-direction des liaisons extérieures* (Sub-Directorate of External Liaisons)

The PJ consists of the centralised departments at the Ministry of the Interior and of 19 decentralised departments. These departments together employ nearly 7,800 officers. Most of the 6,475 central investigative personnel are qualified criminal investigation officers (OPJ) who, when requested or delegated, work under the supervision of investigating judges (*juges d'instruction*) or the magistrates of the public prosecution service (*ministères publics*). The officers are entitled to organise themselves in trade unions.

The *Gendarmerie nationale* (GN) with its military statute and organisation also has a general competence, but is mainly responsible for rural and suburban zones. About 90,000 officers work for the GN. The GN participates in military defence, but also has the task to ensure public safety and to maintain order. About 90% of its work is in the area of administrative or criminal police services, the remaining 10% is military in nature.

The GN is organised in a *Direction générale de la gendarmerie nationale et de l'inspection générale de la Gendarmerie*. The Directorate-general includes:

- *le Centre technique de la gendarmerie nationale* – technical centre[15]
- *le Centre administratif de la gendarmerie nationale* – administrative centre
- *le Commandant des écoles* – the Commander of Schools

- *le Commandant de la gendarmerie d'outre-mer* – the Commander of the Overseas Gendarmerie
- *les Formations spécialisées* – specialised units

Amongst these last ones, one can distinguish:
- *la Garde républicaine* – the Republican Guard
- *la Gendarmerie maritime* – the maritime service
- *la Gendarmerie de l'air* – air service
- *la Gendarmerie des transports aériens* – air transport service
- *la Gendarmerie des forces françaises en Allemagne* – French gendarmerie service in Germany
- *le Groupement spécial de sécurité* – nuclear safety
- *le Groupement spécial de sécurité et d'intervention de la gendarmerie* – the special security and operations service

The gendarmerie is organised according to military principles, in *brigades* (squads), *compagnies* (companies), *groupements départementaux* (departments). It is the *brigades* which provide a presence close to the citizens all over the territory. They fulfil the typical tasks of criminal investigation. In their work, they are supported by research *équipes, brigades* and *sections* (teams, squads and sections). Since they are organised more in terms of territory than service specialisation, officers of the GN can exercise a number of police tasks in parallel and are polyvalent. For example they have tasks related to public security as well as criminal investigations. The hierarchy of the organisation is that of the military, to which it belongs, and the officers have therefore no right of trade union association.

The central *Direction des relations internationales* of the g*endarmerie* is responsible – amongst other things – for cooperation abroad. Within this division, there are one or two people especially responsible for dealing with organised crime.

Another force which some see to be establishing itself as the third national police is the customs service – *Douanes et droits indirects*. The customs service is attached to the Ministry of Economics and Finances, operates with about 20,000 officers and has a level of organisation, the material means and extensive powers to match those of the police forces. The *Douanes* are organised as the *Direction générale des douanes et des droits indirects,* with three units directly attached to the Director-general's department (cabinet, information and the communication and coordination of European affairs), and six sub-directorates.
- *Sous-direction A: Personnel et budget* – personnel and budget[16]
- *Sous-direction B: Organisation, surveillance et moyens* – organisation

and surveillance
- *Sous-direction C: Informatique, statistiques et études économiques* – information technology, statistics and economic studies
- *Sous-direction D: Affaires juridiques, contentieuses et lutte contre la fraude* – juridical and legal affairs, and the fight against fraud
- *Sous-direction E: Union douanière et coopération internationale* – customs union and international cooperation
- *Sous-direction F: Droits indirects* – indirect taxes

The **customs service** possesses wide powers of investigation and arrest. Its powers are limited, however, to customs offences. Should any offences it investigates also be potential subject of prosecution under the ordinary penal code, they have to be transferred to the police services. The law of 23 June 1999 reinforcing the efficiency of the penal procedure has given the *Douanes* a number of competences in the field of criminal investigation, mostly concerning the areas of economic and financial crime. Since the abolition of border controls, the customs service aims to justify its existence. Therefore the fight against drugs and organised crime is nowadays a central argument in the rhetoric of the customs service. A transfer of resources and personnel to *Sous-direction B* has occurred since 1990 (mainly originating from *Sous-direction F*, due to the completion of the internal market).

## 2.3 Structural multiplicity of services

The efficiency of such reforms is nearly impossible to assess. What has to be mentioned, however, is the fragmentation which can be observed in the system. There is a multiplicity of units and services dealing with aspects of organised crime. The police, *gendarmerie,* customs, and public prosecution all have their own units to fight various areas of this area of crime. On the other hand, their officers collaborate in a number of units, mostly located within the DCPJ.

Furthermore, one needs to be aware of the competition between different law enforcement services in France, and more importantly, the different professional culture which prevails in these services. Competition between services occurs partly for budgetary reasons, but the different internal practices and culture also sometimes impede an effective exchange of communication.[17] The civil and military statutes of the *Police nationale* and *gendarmerie* have led to very different internal structures of command and control, administration, and the conception of their values and role in society. The developments in the European field have certainly had a very different impact on the services depending on traditional ties abroad, ties with the ministries concerned, the perceived necessity to cooperate... no detailed study of this has yet been conducted however.

## 3. THE PUBLIC PROSECUTION SERVICE IN FRANCE

The public prosecution service in France, the *ministère public*, has the general task of representing society in legal proceedings in court.

### 3.1 Structure

Public prosecution is organised in the following way: The basis of division of the national territory is a so-called "jurisdiction"; the 181 *parquets* (prosecution service) are located at the *tribunaux de grande instance* (similar to a district court); the 33 *parquets généraux* (Principal State Counsels' Offices) are attached to the 33 *cours d'appel* (court of appeals); and one *parquet général* is at the *Cour de cassation* (Supreme Court of Appeal). Each of these parquets consists of the *Procureur de la République* (State Counsel) who, as the *chef de parquet*, is seconded by a team of *magistrats* (magistrates) called *substituts,* and is supported by a secretariat composed of civil servants belonging to the judiciary services.

The *Garde des Sceaux*, the Minister of Justice, has the final authority over the magistrates of the *ministère public* (magistrates of the prosecution service). As a minister, he/she both defines a coherent national judicial policy and is responsible for its execution. He/she is also accountable to parliament.

### 3.2 Tasks and competences

The tasks of the public prosecution service can be grouped in three areas: pursuing criminal offences, representing the interests of a civil party or group of society and exercising control over the administration.

More concretely these tasks can be enumerated as:
- In the criminal field:
    - managing of the work of the criminal investigation service (Article 12, 40, 41 of the *Code de procedure pénale*);
    - deciding to start investigations;
    - conducting of legal proceedings, acting as the state's counsel i.e. defines the legal framework of prosecution, calls the witnesses, translators and experts, authorises the use of exhibits, etc.;
    - executing verdicts.

- In civil litigations:
  - as a main party: it acts as one of the litigants in order to defend public interests (protection of the law, of minors, of mentally handicapped, etc.);
  - as a secondary party: it gives its opinion on an affair, although it rarely intervenes in the proceedings and does so only in a limited fashion;
  - it represents a person or administration (i.e. it acts to defend a particular interest)
  - it executes verdicts in civil cases when the private parties refuse to comply with the verdict

- In the administrative field:
  - it controls juridical and legal activities and exercises disciplinary measures on *avocats, officiers publics and ministériels, experts judiciaries* (i.e. barristers, public (legal) officers, legal officials and experts appointed by the court);
  - it controls of the following institutions: penitentiaries, psychiatric institutions, educational institutions, establishments selling alcoholic beverages;
  - with regard to external relations: it represents the interface between its own competences and the state administration, civil society and foreign authorities
  - it intervenes in the administration of areas of public order where basic rights or liberties are at stake.

## 3.3 The Criminal Investigation Process

The penal procedure in France is regulated by the *Code de procédure pénale* (Code of Criminal Procedure). This set of rules governs police action in France and details which actions can be taken under which circumstances. This code prescribes a close link between the magistrates of the prosecution service and the criminal investigation service during investigations.[18]

The code distinguishes between two legal situations, namely one before the opening of an inquiry by the *juge d'instruction* (investigating judge), which includes the expedited police investigation ad the preliminary investigation. All these tasks are exercised under the supervision of the *Procureur de la République* or one of his or her substitutes. The work of the police falls under the public prosecutor and there are a number of legal provisions and obligations which regulate the inquiries by the police. For example, the police have to inform the *Procureur* without delay of all notifiable offences and flagrant misdemeanours.

The second stage is the opening of a judicial enquiry by the *Procureur de la République* (*ouverture d'une information judiciaire*) if an offence constitutes a notifiable offence or a serious misdemeanour, which is then entrusted to a judge, the *juge d'instruction*.

In French criminal law, this investigating judge has a central role in conducting the investigation. He/she has all the powers necessary to direct the investigations. His/her task is to uncover all necessary evidence, to interview witnesses, collect statements and reports in order to prepare further evidence in order to prosecute or release the suspect. He/she can place a suspect on remand if he/she deems it necessary for the preservation of evidence or public order.

In the case of the opening of an investigation, all legal acts are executed by the police on the orders of the abovementioned judge. The instrument of *commission rogatoire* (letters rogatory) allows for a police officer to exercise a number of functions in the name of the judge. In general, the autonomy of the police in such investigations depends on the powers which are given to it by the judge.

## 4.  LAW ENFORCEMENT UNITS TO FIGHT ORGANISED CRIME

The most important structures for the fight against organised crime in France have been established at the national level. They have national responsibility and usually rely on regional structures which support them in their work.

### 4.1 Established Structures

There is no effective overall body of coordination uniting services in the fight against organised crime, as foreseen in the Recommendation 1 of the 1997 Action Plan. However, there are a number of centralised structures which coordinate the work done in specific areas of crime. Generally speaking, the centralisation of investigation is achieved by each ministry via a coordinating body, the *Cellule de coordination*. There is little cooperation between the services and the ministries. Overall inter-ministerial coordination is achieved within the General Secretariat of the Inter-Ministerial Committee for Economic Cooperation Issues (*Secrétariat général du comité interministériel pour les questions de coopération économique européenne* (SGCI)).

The police services established a number of units to deal with organised crime rather early on, although different names were given to phenomena which are now often subsumed under the category of organised crime. Seven (since 1996, eight) inter-ministerial specialised offices in the fight against organised crime have been set up within the *Direction centrale de la police judiciaire* (DCPJ), more precisely the *Sous-direction des affaires criminelles* and the *Sous-direction des affaires économiques et financières*, some of them dating from as early as 1929. They are mentioned as central instruments of the fight against organised crime today in an article by Michel Quillé, *Commissaire divisionnaire* (Chief Superintendant) of the DCPJ:[19]

- *Office Central pour la Répression du Faux Monnayage* (OCRFM) – central office for the fight against counterfeiting,[20] founded in 1929
- *Office Central pour la Répression du Trafic Illicite des Stupéfiants* (OCRTIS) – central office for the fight against illegal drug trafficking, dating from 1953
- *Office Central pour la Répression de la Traite des Êtres Humains* (OCRTEH) – central office for the fight against the trade in human beings, 1958
- *Office Central pour la Répression du Banditisme* (OCRB) – central office for the repression of organised crime by gangs, 1973
- *Office Central de Lutte contre le Trafic des Biens Culturels* (OCBC) – central office for the fight against the trafficking of cultural goods, 1975; current name since 1996
- *Office Central pour la Répression du Trafic des Armes, Explosifs et Matières Sensibles* (OCRTAEMS) – central office for the fight against trade of arms, explosives and other sensitive material, 1982
- *Office Central pour la Répression de la Grande Délinquance Financière* (OCRGDF) – central office for the fight of serious financial crime, 1990
- An eighth office was created in 1996: *Office Central pour la Répression de l'Immigration Irrégulière et de l'Emploi d'Étrangers sans Titre* (OCRIEST) – the central office for the fight against illegal immigration and the employment of strangers without permits; this office is located in another Directorate, the DCPAF.

These offices were created by inter-ministerial decree, which means that officers from at least two ministries are present in each office. Notably, each office has liaison officers from the GN as part of its staff. The offices have national competence both for coordination of investigations and enquiries.

Their main tasks are: centralisation of information and documentation in their fields of their competency, participation in the elaboration of preventive policies, establishment of international relations with their peers abroad and operational competences. Amongst these offices, the OCRB and OCRGDF are most particularly concerned with the fight against organised international crime, but in all other fields of work they are also strongly associated with this type of crime.

The seven offices can rely on the 19 regional services of the PJ, the *service régional de la police judiciaire* (SRPJ), which can act as operational extensions of the divisions and offices of the DCPJ.

By nature, the customs service is involved in the fight against organised crime. Therefore, all parts of the service are potentially involved in this fight. The fight against fraud and against money laundering are the areas of concentration in the work of the service (see also TRACFIN).

Our interlocutor at the service confirmed that an awareness of the problems of organised crime has defined the work of the service since as far back as the 1960s. The fight against fraud as a typical offence dealt with by the customs service has necessitated a practice of cooperation with European counterparts. Liaison officers, so-called *"attachés douaniers"*, have been established in six European capitals – London, The Hague, Berlin, Rome, Madrid and Vienna – with responsibility also for adjacent countries.

## 4.2  Changes since the 1990s

The one unit which may formally be termed the national body of coordination is the national Unit of Anti-Mafia Coordination and Research – *Unité de coordination et de Recherche Anti-Mafia* (UCRAM). This body was created in 1993 – therefore not in direct relation with the EU Action Plan on Organised Crime – with two objectives: to coordinate the fight against Mafia structures and to centralise information gathering. This office may be seen as a direct result of the *rapport d'Aubert* (Aubert Report) in 1992 on the penetration of the Mafia into France. It is located in the PN, directly attached to the *Direction générale de la police nationale*. The unit analyses the evolution of the Mafia in France and ensures cooperation in this field, mainly through the (bilateral) exchange of liaison officers with Italy and other countries. Although the explicit task of the unit concerns the Mafia, in daily practice this has meant dealing with a wide range of organised crime. The UCRAM was set up on the model of the UCLAT, which has similar tasks in its area of competence.

The unit was set up as a loose structure with hardly any hierarchy; it brings together all the heads of services who in the course of their work might acquire knowledge in the area of organised crime in regular monthly meetings – whether on the purely criminal or the financial aspect. These services include: all services in the DCPJ which deal with organised crime (CRACO, OCRDF), the corresponding services at the *Préfecture de la Police* in Paris, the DST, the SCTIP, the DCPAF, the *gendarmerie*, the *Direction Générale de Sécurité Extérieure* (DGSE), and the customs and fiscal services. In practice, the PN can be assumed to be the dominant party. Due to this, the unit may be seen as a coordinating body within the police services, but not as an overall coordinating body.

The system works like a market place for the exchange of information. The people present information their services are in possession of, and on the basis of this information UCRAM – either the person directly responsible but mostly in partnership of all people concerned – decides which service is best placed to conduct the enquiry.

In order to complement this loose structure with a more permanent unit, the police established the *Section centrale d'investigations sur le crime organisé* (SCICO) within the *Sous-direction des affaires criminelles* of the DCPJ in 1995. The unit has a double mission:

- Firstly, it has the task of centralising crime information and its analysis. This is done in the *Centrale du renseignement et de l'analyse du crime organisé* (CRACO), which brings together agents of the DCPJ and liaison officers of the DST (*Direction de la surveillance du territoire*), the DCRG (*Direction centrale des renseignements généraux*) and of the *gendarmerie*. The liaison officers from the two PN departments DST and DCRG are present in the CRACO to provide a background to the information which came from their departments, which themselves invest a lot of effort in the area of organised crime. The pooling of efforts is considered necessary in order not to lose important work already done. A close link is therefore ensured between operational and analytical units. The CRACO has very recently been moved into the OCRB in order to make up for its earlier lack of operational power. Different from UCRAM, CRACO has at its disposal databases, work files and operational documentation which allow it to analyse the information received and to aim at the most exhaustive overview possible of organised crime activities in France. CRACO also concentrates mainly on aspects of the Mafia in four areas: organised crime originating from Italy, eastern and Asian countries and motorcycle gangs.
- Secondly, it has a mission to elaborate a doctrine and more importantly new instruments for the fight against organised crime. In this function, it is responsible also for many links abroad with the aim of improving the way in which organised crime is dealt with in operational and analytical respects. It is the DCPJ which is traditionally charged with international operational cooperation. Therefore the CRACO has been in a position to fulfil this role in the area of organised crime, rather than UCRAM.

Furthermore, the knowledge and expertise that the SCICO acquires through the collection of data and its analysis as well as through its position in the DCPJ have led to it being charged with representing (alone or in conjunction with other services) the Ministry of Interior in the institutions where new instruments in the fight against organised crime are developed. On 9 May 1997, an interministerial instruction created a *Cellule interministérielle de liaison sur la délinquance itinérante* (CILDI) in the Directorate-general of the gendarmerie. It is charged with analysing the actions of itinerant criminals, proposing measures to reduce such crime and coordinating investigations.

### Financial Intelligence Units
In 1990, two units to fight financial crime were also set up (by decree of 9 May):
* a unit specialised in the fight against money laundering, the TRACFIN (*Traitement du renseignement et action contre les circuits financiers clandestins*), an administrative service which is directly attached to the Ministry of Economics and Finances; and
* the *Office central pour la répression de la grande délinquance financière* (OCRGDF), attached to the *Direction centrale* of the PJ (see above).

TRACFIN was established on the recommendation of the G8 in order to receive the "declarations of suspicion" by financial organisations which are obliged to transmit information on any sums or operations which could result from narcotics trafficking or organised crime. It is up to the individual financial organisation to judge whether such a declaration is necessary. TRACFIN analyses these declarations and transmits them to judicial authorities. It has special powers such as the right to block a suspicious transaction. The secrecy obligation of banks is lifted for TRACFIN, but the unit is obliged to keep strict confidentiality. The Director-general of the *Douanes et droits indirects* is the Secretary-general of TRACFIN – he/she therefore has at his/her disposal customs service investigators for enquiries.

The OCRGDF is usually charged with investigations into the information transmitted by TRACFIN, but it also has the right to initiate investigations. The office has a national competence for all criminal offences of an economic or financial character. Apart from investigative missions, the unit also centralises all information in this matter and coordinates the activities of French and foreign police in the area of economic crime.

### 4.3 Links with abroad and European structures

The *Sous-direction des liaisons extérieures* (SDLE) of the DCPJ (with its *Division des relations internationals*) directs the international operational cooperation with Interpol, Schengen and Europol. The French national unit of Europol, the national SIRENE office and the National Central Bureau of Interpol are all located there.

Of central importance is SCTIP, the *Service de coopération technique internationale de police.* This is a department within the *Police nationale* and is concerned with most aspects of European police cooperation: The *Sous-direction des affaires Européennes et de la coopération institutionnelle* coordinates and if necessary initiates work with regard to questions of security in the framework of the European Union and also Schengen. International cooperation includes regular exchanges of information in a number of areas, including organised crime.

The SCTIP also represents the single entry point of the *ministère de l'Intérieur* for all the Title VI working documents, which flow from the EU Working Groups that are active in the domain of police and judicial cooperation in criminal matters. The SCTIP directs the *Bureau de Liaison France* (BDL), the operational messenger service linking all police services of the 15 Member States. Furthermore, the SCTIP is responsible for all bilateral cooperation with western and central European countries and relies on a network of police attachés in all major capitals. The French liaison officers in the fields of drugs and terrorism depend on the SCTIP. The SCTIP therefore works in close cooperation with all directorates of the *ministère de l'Intérieur* and also with the administrations of *gendarmerie, douanes* and *justice.*

For the police services in general, liaison officers in the European and non-European context have become an important means of exchange of knowledge and information between the services concerned with the fight against organised crime. The DCPJ started this process in 1970, sending officers from OCRTIS to New York and Bangkok. This has now been widened to practically all western European states. The objective of those missions is to assure information and communication, but also to start up common projects or enquiries. Analyses have shown that the scheme has been successful for a number of reasons: the direct contact between operational services assures the transmission of pertinent information, the states concerned do not have to give up sovereignty if they consent to receiving a foreign officer, and the "human factor" has led to much more information being transmitted than through the traditional channels.[21]

The customs services also has liaison officers in Europe and internationally. The *attachés douaniers* are mainly responsible for the exchange of information. Operational cooperation takes place through centralised structures. Transborder cooperation mainly concerns the exchange of information.

In the area of organised crime specifically, as mentioned above, it is the CRACO which is responsible for most international links. The DCPJ and CRACO are for example involved in operational cooperation with the German Federal Criminal Police Office (*Bundeskriminalamt*) in Wiesbaden and the anti-Mafia investigation unit in Italy, with Spanish officers, the FBI and the Swiss service against organised crime. CRACO also participates in various multilateral European Working groups on organised crime. The main objective of CRACO's work is to establish links with corresponding services for operational, analytical and strategic objectives.

Furthermore, UCRAM has liaison officers installed in the European cities of Rome, Wiesbaden, London and Madrid. Part of their work is to participate in the coordination of operational work and to assist in the exchange of information.

## 5. PUBLIC PROSECUTION UNITS TO FIGHT ORGANISED CRIME:

The public prosecution service has made a number of changes in the last few years in order to be better equipped for the fight against organised crime. A number of specialised units in relation to this objective have been created. It is in this service – if at all – that one can identify the direct influence of European-level recommendations in France.

### 5.1 New units in the 1990s

In 1995, the public prosecution service created an organised crime office (*Bureau de la criminalité organisée*) within the *Direction des affaires criminelles et des grâces* in the *ministère de la Justice*. The *Bureau de la criminalité organisée* is the central unit dealing with all aspects of organised crime. Despite the fact that it was established in 1995, the office can be considered a national body of coordination on the level of public prosecution as recommended in the 1997 EU Action Plan on Organised Crime.

It manages and coordinates the implementation of the actions taken by the public prosecutor's offices with regard to economic, financial, fiscal and labour law violations involving corruption, drug trafficking and organised crime in general. The unit is therefore charged with the analysis and the coordination of judicial treatment of all procedures linked to organised crime. Given the central role of public prosecution in investigation procedures in France, this office has an important coordinating function. The unit also participates in the elaboration of crime policy in subject matters linked to its competence and in work conducted at international and European levels.

There are some teams specialised in the fight against organised crime at the regional level of the *cours d'appel*, of the magistrates working in the units of the European Judicial Network (see below) and in other places. There are not many such officers, but efforts are made to increase their number. Such specialised units have legislative as well as operational aspects in their competences. Information gathering, however, is centralised at the Ministry of the Interior.

The judiciary also has established a Bureau of Legal Assistance and Crime Conventions (*Bureau de l'entraide judiciaire et des conventions pénales*) in the Criminal Affairs Directorate (*Direction des affaires criminelles*) of the Ministry of Justice. There is also – located in the same Directorate – a *Bureau* specialised in anti-terrorist measures.

In the framework of the European Judicial Network (EJN), two contact points have been set up within the Ministry of Justice (see below under international contact points).

## 5.2 *Pôles Économiques et Financiers*

*Pôles économiques et financiers* were established in 1999. The creation of these units was announced by the Minister of Finance in December 1997, and the law of 2 July 1998 provided for the recruitment of *assistants spécialisés* who form a central part of these multidisciplinary units. They are placed under the authority of the magistrates in the *cours d'appel*.

It is hoped that these units will permit the prosecution service to rely on specialised knowledge in very technical and complex matters with the help of permanent, interdisciplinary groups. The groups have modern logistical means and multidisciplinary personnel. They comprise the *magistrats de parquet* and the *magistrats de l'instruction* (both members of the prosecution service), civil servants of the judiciary services, *assistants de justice* and the new so-called "specialised assistants". The specialised assistants are either civil servants or experts in financial matters with a proven record of experience in the field. They are, for example, employees of the *Banque de France* and civil servants in the Ministry of Economics, Finances and Industry. It is envisaged that by the end of 2000, 45 special assistants will be working in France.

## 5.3 Links with Foreign Countries and European Structures

In the public prosecution service, it is mainly the *Service des affaires européennes et internationales* of the *ministère de la Justice* which is responsible for the liaison with European and other national working structures.

Furthermore, an active policy of placing liaison officers (*magistrats*) who also deal with the issue of organised crime has been established. French liaison officers have been seconded to Italy, Germany, the UK, Spain, the United States, the Netherlands and the Czech Republic. Foreign liaison officers from the US, the Netherlands, Italy and Germany are stationed in France in the *Service des affaires européennes et internationales*. This is a fairly recent system to have been put in place. The first liaison officer was sent to Italy in 1993, the last to be sent were those to the US and the Czech Republic in 1999. These liaison officers are described as successful, enormously facilitating judicial cooperation, especially in the case of the execution of rogatory commissions and applications for extradition.[22]

Two trends were mentioned as a result of international cooperation:

- On the one hand, there is the trend of encouraging direct contact between the magistrates of the countries concerned in order to improve the speed and flow of the work.
- On the other hand, there is a trend to centralise information-gathering and organisational structures in the fight against organised crime in order to be able to respond centrally to enquiries from abroad. It will be necessary to find ways to reconcile these trends.

## 6. MULTIDISCIPLINARY INTEGRATED TEAMS

Most of the teams mentioned above may be classified as multidisciplinary as recommended by the Action Plan since they unite officers from either several directorates of the *Police nationale* or officers from different services.

The seven offices specialised in areas of organised crime at the DCPJ all have representatives from other directorates of the PN and of the GN and work as multidisciplinary teams. However, they have not been set up as a result of the recommendations of the 1997 EU Action Plan on Organised Crime: most of them date from before 1990.

The *Centrale du renseignement et de l'analyse de crime organisé* (CRACO) is one of the newest and most operational of the units engaged in the fight against organised crime. Founded in 1995 within the *Sous-direction des affaires criminelles* of the DCPJ, it was first located within the *Section centrale d'investigations sur le crime organisé* (SCICO) and has recently been transferred to the OCRB. It unites OPJs, agents of the DCPJ, and liaison officers of the DST (*Direction de la surveillance du territoire*), the DCRG (*Direction centrale des renseignements généraux*) and of the gendarmerie. Again, although no reference was made to the team being set up in reference to the Action Plan, in its set-up it resembles a multidisciplinary unit recommended by the plan.

The UCRAM, which was set up in 1993, can be considered a multidisciplinary team since its meetings are attended by all French security services which could have knowledge about organised crime. These are: all directorates of the PN, the GN and the *Direction générale de la sécurité extérieure* of the Ministry of Defence, as well as representatives from the Ministry of Finance (Customs and Taxation)

## 7. INTERNATIONAL CONTACT POINTS

### 7.1 Law enforcement services

There is not one central contact point in the law enforcement services as intended in the Action Plan. The closest unit to such a function is the SCTIP – the *Service de coopération technique internationale de police*. However, this unit does not deal exclusively with organised crime, but with the whole range of internationally oriented police activity.

The national French unit of Europol, the national SIRENE office (founded in 1993) and the French national office of Interpol are all located within the *Division de relations internationales* in the *Sous-direction des liaisons extérieures* of the DCPJ.

### 7.2 Public prosecution

**With a view to translating Recommendation 21 in the Action Plan, the Minister of Justice has named a special magistrate to supervise the setting up of the European Judicial Network.** Two national central contact points were established in 1999 by decree as part of the European Judicial Network. They are the *Directeur des affaires criminelles et des grâces* and the *Chef du service des affaires européennes et internationales*. An objective of these central contact points is to assure better cooperation and better transmission of information, to facilitate the work of rogatory commissions and to give information on legislative developments.

There are also regional contact points in each of the *parquets généraux* in France. They act as relays between the national French contact points and those of other Member States and are alerted if the national contact point intervenes to set up an investigation in the jurisdiction of their competence.

## 8. ACCOUNTABILITY

It is interesting to note that the word "accountability" translates into French only with difficulty despite the fact that the etymological source of *"compte"* – account – can easily be traced to Latin and Roman roots. The words used in French are those of *contrôle* and *surveillance*.

Despite the fact that the police are strictly subordinate to the magistrates of the prosecution service, that the *Code de procedure pénale* gives detailed information on the competence of police in various legal situations and that the powers of the police are distinguished according to rank, the efficiency of control and accountability of the criminal investigation service is limited.

The control of the public services is a constitutional right in France. The French Constitution includes in its preamble the Declaration of Human and Citizen Rights of 1789, which states in Article 12 that the guarantee of human and citizen rights necessitates a public force which is set up for the advantage of all and not for the particular use of those to whom it is entrusted. Article 15 continues that society has the right to demand accountability from each public servant in its administration. The control of the police force is exercised through its own hierarchy, the judiciary and political power.

The ministers responsible, with the help of their services, especially the *Inspections générales*, (Inspectorate-general) have authority over their respective agents and can impose disciplinary sanctions. The Inspectorate-general of the PN has national jurisdiction over all PN operational departments and training establishments. It is charged with ensuring that the PN respects the laws and regulations of the PN deontological code and investigates complaints when requested by administrative or judicial authorities. The *gendarmerie* has a parallel system.

The parliament also has at its disposal various means of censure, the most important of which is the vote on the budget.

The judiciary exercises its control in the framework activities related to administrative and judiciary enquiries (see above). The control by the judiciary is carried out as follows: the prosecution departments (*parquet*) – The *Procureur de la République* directs them, the *procureur général* oversees them and the *chambre d'accusation* (Indictment Division) controls them in the strict sense of the word. The law of 1978 holds that the control extends to both types of servants: the agents (APJ) and the officers (OPJ) of the criminal investigation service. The Code of Criminal Procedure of 1966 provides mainly for a control of the OPJ, who have to be authorised by the *Procureur de la République* and receive specialised training in order to be able to exercise their powers (these are *commissaires*, *officiers*, *gendarmes* but also mayors and directors of the PN). All police activity which necessitates or leads to an engagement of the judiciary has to pass through the prosecution department.

In practice, this system does not work well. The central responsibility of control lies with the judiciary. However, the judiciary is in a weakened position since it has neither the knowledge of actual proceedings nor independent access to documentation. In fact, it is the police service itself which gives the necessary information to the judiciary and which thus exercises self-selection. The two services therefore act interdependently. In the Fifth Republic, the parliament has little power with regard to control of the executive. The control through the police's own hierarchy is hampered by the fact that the institution does not wish to obstruct its capacity to act. This system of control in France is unique in Europe and implies significant deficits in the area of accountability.

The units engaged in the fight against organised crime are controlled in the same way as all police services through the double control of internal hierarchy and the magistrates. There are no special controls for these units. The interviewees maintained that there had been no problems so far since all enquiries by the police have to pass through the regular legal framework including a magistrate. All information that is stored has to be presented to a magistrate if it is to be used in an enquiry.

As regards the judiciary, the control of the national contact points in the framework of the European Judiciary Network is done purely internally by the judiciary with the help of a central contact person in the SAEI and designated magistrates in the *cours d'appel*. The *Bureau de la criminalité organisée* is supervised by the Ministry of Justice.


## 9. CONCLUSION

Most structures in the fight against organised crime in France were established before the Action Plan of the EU was envisaged. In the police services, the structures are centralised with each unit specialising in the fight against a particular area of organised crime. None of the existing units was created as a direct reaction to the Action Plan, mostly due to the fact that the structures already existed.

The public prosecution service has set up a national central office for the fight against organised crime and also has established central contact points in the framework of the European Judicial Network as recommended in the Action Plan.

Changes during the 1990s in France were related to a number of reasons: a rising perception within the services and the public of the threat from organised crime, European level developments and events, and internal political events.

**NOTES**

1.  cf. Maynaud, Y. (1994). *Le nouveau Code pénal, enjeux et perspectives*. Paris: Dalloz, p. 61-68 and Cédras, Jean (1998). "France" in *International Review of Penal Law. The Criminal Justice System Facing the Challenge of Organised Crime*. 69, pp. 341-367.
2.  Loi du 29 janvier 1993 relative à la prévention de la corruption et à la transparence de la vie économique et des procédures; Loi du 13 mai 1996 relative à la lutte contre le blanchiment et le trafic des stupéfiants et à la coopération internationale en matière de saisie et de confiscation des produits du crime.
3.  Cf. Jean Cédras (1998), op. cit., p. 366.
4.  Fiche technique française. *La lutte contre la criminalité organisée*.
5.  Quillé, Michel (1999), "Les démocraties sont-elles désarmées face au crime organisé?". *La Tribune du commissaire de police,* No. 73, April 1999, pp. 13-19.
6.  Some of our interviewees have expressed a wish to remain unnamed. All quotes will therefore remain anonymous in order not to render them identifiable.
7.  The coordination of European officials in common working groups such as the Trevi group in the fight against organised crime has certainly influenced the thinking about such structures in the country. No concrete changes have taken place in reference to such coordination, however.
8.  Cf. Bigo, Didier (1992), *L'Europe des polices et de la sécurité intérieure*. Paris: Editions Complexe.
9.  Assemblée Nationale (1993), *Rapport de la commission d'enquête sur les moyens de lutter contre les tentatives de pénétration de la mafia en France*. No. 3251, O.J, 28 January 1993.
10. Cf. Bayley, D. (1975). The Police and Political Development in Europe. In Tilly, C. (ed.) *The Formation of National States in Western Europe*. Princeton: Princeton University Press; Gleizal, J.J., Gatti-Domenach, J., Journès, C. (1993). *La Police, le cas des démocraties occidentales*. Paris, Presses Universitaires de France; Journès, Claude (1993). "The Structure of the French Police System: Is the French Police a National Force?". *International Journal of the Sociology of Law*, 21, pp. 281-287.
11. Cf. Gleizal et al. (1993), op. cit.
12. Within these three services, this report concentrates on the police nationale and its units in the fight against organised crime. Through its task of policing the urban areas, it is well placed for the fight against organised crime. At the same time, collaboration between the services takes place in a number of units established within the central directorate of the *police judiciaire* (PN).
13. cf. Journès (1993), op. cit. p. 286.
14. Numbers quoted from Ministère de l'Intérieur (1999). *Direction Générale de la Police Nationale*. Information Brochure. Translation of names of services and units of the PN are taken from this multi-lingual booklet, unless otherwise stated.
15. Authors's translations.

16. Author's translations.
17. Cf. Monjardet, Dominique (1996), *Ce que fait la police. Sociologie de la force publique*. Paris: Éditions la Découverte.
18. In principle, this relationship is also maintained for the work of the *gendarmerie*.
19. Quillé (1999), op. cit.
20. Author's translations
21. Quillé (1999), op. cit.
22. De Baynast de Septfontaines. "La cooperation judiciaire européenne". *http://www.defense.gouv.fr/.../dossiers*

## BIBLIOGRAPHY

Bayley, D. (1975). The Police and Political Development in Europe. In Tilly, C. ed. *The Formation of National States in Western Europe*. Princeton: Princeton University Press.

De Baynast de Septfontaines. "La coopération judiciaire européenne". *http://www.defense.gouv.fr/.../dossiers*

Cédras, Jean. "Les Systèmes Pénaux à l'épreuve du crime organisé", *Revue Internationale de Droit Pénal*. Vol. 69, 1998, pp. 341-367.

Frydman, Nathalie and Martineau, Hélène. *La Drogue: Où en sommes-nous? Bilan des connaissances en France en matière de drogues et de toxicomanies*. Paris: La Documentation Française, 1998.

Gleizal, Jean-Jacques. *La Police en France*. Paris: Presses Universitaires de France, 1993.

Gleizal, Jean-Jacques et al. *La Police. Le cas des démocraties occidentales*. Paris: Presses Universitaires de France, 1993.

*L'Évolution de la Criminalité Organisée. Actes du XVIIIe Cours International de Haute Spécialisation pour les Forces de Police, Paris 17-24 septembre 1996*. La Documentation Française, 1996.

Journès, Claude. "The Structure of the French Police System: Is the French Police a National Force?". Discussion Paper. *International Journal of the Sociology of Law*, No. 21, 1993.

"Les Pôles économiques et financiers". *Les Notes de la Chancellerie*, No. 7 – March 1999.

Monjardet, Dominique. *Ce que fait la police. Sociologie de la force publique*. Paris: Éditions la Découverte, 1996.

Quillé, Michel. "Les démocraties sont-elles désarmées face au crime organisé?". *La Tribune du commissaire de police,* No. 73, April 1999.

Salomon, Jean-Claude (1998). *Lexique des termes de police*. Paris: Institut des Hautes Etudes de la Sécurité Intérieure.

Volff, Jean. *Le Ministère Public*. Paris: Presses Universitaires de France, 1998.

## OTHER MATERIAL

• La lutte contre la criminalité organisée. Fiche technique française.
• Service de l'Information et des Relations Publiques. *L'Intérieur aujourd'hui*. Paris, n.n.
• Service de l'Information et des Relations Publiques. *La Direction Générale de la Police Nationale*. Paris, 1999.
• Web Site of the ministère de l'Intérieur http://www.interieur.gouv.fr

- Web Site of the ministère de la Défense http://www.defense.gouv.fr
- Web Site of the ministère de la Justice http://www.justice.gouv.fr
- Web Site of the ministère des Finances http://www.alize.finances.gouv.fr

*Franziska Hagedorn and Didier Bigo*

**GLOSSARY***

CILDI          *Cellule Interministérielle de Liaison sur la Délinquance Itinérante* (CILDI); established in the Directorate-general of the *gendarmerie* in 1997; interministerial unit charged with analysing the actions of itinerant criminals, with proposing measures to reduce such crime and with coordinating investigations.

CRACO        *Centrale du Renseignement et de l'Analyse du Crime Organisé*; situated within the SCICO in the DCPJ; recently moved into the OCRB; centralises crime information and its analysis; brings together agents of the DCPJ and liaison officers of the DST (*Direction de la Surveillance du Territoire*), the DCRG (*Direction Centrale des Renseignements Généraux*) and of the gendarmerie

DCPAF        *Direction centrale de la police aux frontières* – Central Directorate for Air and Border Policing

DCPJ         *Direction centrale de la police judiciaire* –Crime Investigation Central Directorate
Has four subdivisions:
*Sous-direction des affaires criminelles*
*Sous-direction de la police technique et scientifique*
*Sous-direction des affaires économiques et financières*
*Sous-direction des liaisons extérieurs*

DCRG         *Direction centrale des renseignements généraux* – Community Intelligence Central Directorate

DGPN         *Direction générale de la police nationale*

DGSE         *Direction générale de sécurité extérieure*

---

\* For the translation of terms, reference has been made to Salomon, Jean-Claude (1998). *Lexique des termes de police*. Paris: Institut des Hautes Etudes de la Sécurité Intérieure.

238

DST

*Direction de la surveillance du territoire –* Territorial Intelligence Service. A unit in charge of counter espionage in France. Its organisation and work is classified.

GN

*Gendarmerie nationale*

IHESI

*Institut des Hautes Études de la Sécurité Intérieure*

OCBC

*Office Central de lutte contre le Trafic des Biens Culturels –* central office for the fight against the trafficking of cultural goods, 1975; current name since 1996; located in *Sous-direction des affaires criminelles* of the DCPJ

OCRB

*Office Central pour la Répression du Banditisme –* central office for the repression of organised crime by gangs, 1973; located in the *Sous-direction des affaires criminelles* of the DCPJ.

OCRFM

*Office Central pour la Répression du Faux Monnayage* (OCRFM) – central office for the fight against counterfeiting* founded in 1929; located in the *Sous-direction des affaires économiques et financiers* of the DCPJ.

OCRGDF

*Office Central pour la Répression de la Grande Délinquance Financière –* central office for the fight against serious financial crime, 1990; located in the *Sous-direction des affaires économiques et financières* of the DCPJ.

OCRIEST

*Office Central pour la Répression de l'Immigration Irrégulière et de l'Emploi d'Étrangers sans Titre* (OCRIEST) – the central office for the fight against illegal immigration and the employment of aliens without permit; 1996; this office is located in the DCPAF.

---

* Author's translations

OCRTAEMS

*Office Central pour la Répression du Trafic des Armes, Explosifs et Matières Sensibles* – central office for the fight against trade of arms, explosives and other sensitive material, 1982; located in the *Sous-direction des affaires criminelles* of the DCPJ.

OCRTEH

*Office Central pour la Répression de la Traite des Êtres Humains* – central office for the fight against the trade in human beings, 1958; located in the *Sous-direction des affaires criminelles* of the DCPJ.

OCRTIS

*Office Central pour la Répression de Trafic Illicite des Stupéfiants,* – central office for the fight against illegal drug trafficking, dating from 1953; located in the *Sous-direction des affaires criminelles* of the DCPJ.

PJ

*Police judiciaire* (PJ)

PN

*Police nationale*

PP

*Préfecture de Police de Paris.* Part of the PN since 1966, it remains very autonomous and unites all of the activities of the rest of the PN.

UCLAT

*l'Unité de coordination de la lutte anti-terroriste* (anti-terrorist coordination unit)

UCRAM

*l'Unité de coordination et de recherches anti-Mafia* (anti-Mafia investigation and coordination unit)

SCICO

*Section Centrale d'Investigations sur le Crime Organisé;* founded in 1995 within the *Sous-direction des Affaires Criminelles* of the DCPJ includes the CRACO; and assists in elaborating new instruments for the fight against organised crime

SCTIP

*Service de coopération technique internationale de police*, International Technical Police Cooperation Service is a department within the Police Nationale and concerned with most aspects of European police cooperation

SGCI

*Secrétariat Général du Comité Interministériel pour les questions de coopération économique européenne*

SRPJ

*Service régional de la police judiciaire*

TRACFIN

*Traitement du renseignement et action contre les circuits financiers clandestins*, an administrative service which is directly attached to the Ministry of Economics and Finances; receives declarations of suspicion from financial institutions

*Bureau de la Criminalitée Organisée*

Central office for the fight against organised crime in the prosecution service; established within the *Direction des Affaires Criminelles et des Grâces* in the *ministère de la Justice* in 1995.

*Bureau de l'Entraide Judiciaire et des Convention Pénales*

Office for Mutual Assistance and Penal Conventions, set up by the Ministry of Justice in the *Direction des Affaires Criminelles*

*Cour de cassation*

Highest court of the judiciary order

*Douanes*

Customs and Excise

*Magistrat*

Magistrate, judge

*Ministère public*

All magistrates involved with prosecution who are part of the *Parquet*

*Parquet*

The prosecution service;
The prosecution service is organised the following way: The lowest level of the public prosecution service are the *procureur de la République*, working at the *tribunal de grande instance*. The

second level of prosecutors work at the *cour d'appel*, are called the *parquet général* and directed by the *procureur général*. In the *Cour de cassation* a *procureur général* represents the prosecution service.

The *procureur de la République* and the *procureur général* are on each level supported by *substituts* or *avocats*.

| | |
|---|---|
| *~ général* | See *parquet* |
| *Pôles Économiques et Financiers* | Financial intelligence units; established in 1999; multidisciplinary units which support the work of the public prosecution with the help of expert assistants. |
| *Procureur* | See *parquet* |
| *~ de la République* | See *parquet* |
| *Rapport d'Aubert* | Parliamentary report on the infiltration of the Mafia into France. Advocated more efficiency in the fight against organised crime and more means for the repressive services. |
| *Service des Affaires Européennes et Internationale* | Located in the *ministère de la Justice*; responsible for the liaison with European and other national working structures. |

**RESPONDENTS**

- Service des Affaires Européennes et Internationales, Ministère de la Justice
- Christine Dubois, Politique des contrôles et lutte contre la fraude, Douanes et Droits Indirects
- Jérôme Ferret, Chargé de Recherche, Institut des Hautes Études de la Sécurité Intérieure (IHESI)
- Joël Mansuy, Inspecteur Principal des Douanes, Chargé de mission, Institut des Hautes Études de la Sécurité Intérieure (IHESI)
- Michel Quillé, Commissaire Divisionnaire, Chef de la Section Central d'Investigation sur le Crime Organisé (SCICO), Ministère de l'Intérieur

# Germany

## *Hans-Heine Kühne*

**THE OFFICIAL DEFINITION OF ORGANISED CRIME**

The term 'organised crime' is contained neither in substantive criminal law nor in criminal procedure law. Hence, there is no legally fixed definition. For police use, however, one definition has been agreed on for informal use as a working term, although, extensive as it is, it is inaccurate. This definition compiled under the aegis of the BKA (*Bundeskriminalamt* – Federal Criminal Investigation Agency) has been quoted in the parliamentary discussion leading to the Law Against Organised Crime and reads as follows:

The term 'organised crime' is to be understood as

"a planned perpetration of serious offences committed by several accomplices who cooperate functionally for a longer period of time or an unlimited duration, using business or business-like structures and are aiming at power or financial gain, acting through
- violence or means of intimidation
- influencing politics, the media, public administration, the judicial system or the business communities".[1]

The informal definition – the German Parliament did not transfer this into any part of the law – has met considerable criticism.[2] It is being argued *inter alia* that
- terrorism should be exempted from the definition
- the style of administration (extremely strict and entailing absolute informational barriers between the different levels of organisation) should be part of the definition
- organised crime is notorious for combining illegal and legal business as an instrument for laundering money, obscuring crime and maximizing profit.

This working definition makes efforts to combat organised crime rather opaque. On the political and on the journalistic level the term is used relatively freely and inaccurately, partly with the clear intention of reinforcing public anxiety. Due to the absence of a legally fixed definition and the uncertainty of the description it is sometimes hard to determine whether in the course of a discussion on this topic one actually converses about identical matters. To that extent, critical concerns that the definition is more of a slogan than an objective description do not appear unfounded. As a result, an objective and professional debate about this topic has become difficult.

Yet the BKA has registered data on organised crime. Previously handled as classified secret information, now the BKA is publicly displaying the data.[3] According to this, organised crime in Germany approached around 800 cases per year in the last five years.

This apparent stagnation is most probably due to limits of police capacities and does not give an accurate impression of the reality of organised crime in Germany. Nor do such numbers display information on the extent and seriousness of the crime concerned.

If we rely on assessments of police specialists,[4] we can identify four sectors of priority for organised crime in Germany:

- Red light district criminal activities, including gambling, prostitution, drugs, and trafficking in human beings, which have mostly come under the rigid and extremely brutal control of groups from countries from the former socialist systems including the former Jugoslavia and Albania.
- Car theft – though in recent years dramatically on the decrease – is mostly organised by groups from the above-mentioned countries.
- Racketeering is mostly a hidden phenomenon, but is on the increase due to the internationalisation of German society.
- Environmental criminality has become a serious issue with laws drastically controlling production and disposal of dangerous waste throughout the European Union.
- Corruption – possibly, but surely not exclusively, due to the endeavours of organised criminals – is on the rise in Germany. As the focus of attention has only recently been directed to the phenomenon of corruption, rising numbers are mostly due to improved control strategies.

## II. THE POLICE

### 1. The organisation of the police

In the Federal Republic of Germany the police are basically organised at state (*Land*) level. To that extent there are 16 independent police forces. Therefore statutory authority concerning police regulations is vested with the states (*Länder*), which issue their own statutory police regulations. Structurally, the organisation of the police is to a large extent identical in the individual states of the Federal Republic. The individual organisational units in each state are the *Polizeipräsidium* and the *Polizeidirektion*. The *Polizeipräsidium* are the headquarters found mostly in cities, whereas the *Polizeidirektion* are those which occur in rural areas at the district level. Both the *Polizeipräsidium* as well as the *Polizeidirektion* are directly subordinate to the Ministry of the Interior of the respective state.

This decentralized organisation was chosen for Germany after the end of the Second World War by the allied forces, in order to avoid a concentration of powers with the attendant possibilities of abuse, as had very much been the case during the Third Reich.

Due to a carefully worded understanding, the *Bundeskriminalamt* located in Wiesbaden functions as the only police authority at the federal level. The competences of the *Bundeskriminalamt* and its officials are described in the *Bundeskriminalamtsgesetz (BKAG)* of 07.07.1997. The main and essential function of the *Bundeskriminalamt* is to scientifically support crime detection in the states. Recently, the competences of the BKA have been increased within the area of criminal prosecution. In cases of internationally organised criminal offences, in particular, the BKA according to § 4 I 1 BKAG has a primary competence for investigation.

Beyond that, the BKA has a discretionary competence to investigate if:
* the authority responsible in an individual state asks for cooperation;
* the Federal Minister of the Interior after being informed by the competent authority of a state, has significant reasons to order such cooperation;
* or the Chief Federal Prosecutor asks for it or issues an order for it (§ 4 II BKAG).

Furthermore, the BKA is the national central office responsible for the International Criminal Police Organisation (ICPO-Interpol) and for the handling of the official service contacts between the national police offices and their counterparts abroad (§ 3 I, II BKAG). In relation to the European Union Member States, this remains the authority of the regional police of each state as far as criminality of regional importance in the border areas is concerned. To that extent the police force authorities may arbitrarily make contact with neighbouring police authorities of other EU states (§ 3 III BKAG).

Within the scope of its own investigative competence the BKA is also justified and obliged to conduct activities in relation to witness protection. There are no further statutory provisions for witness protection in Germany, which is considered to be a deficiency.

In the broader sense the *Bundesgrenzschutz* (BGS, Federal Border Police) are also federal police and these are subordinate to the Federal Minister of the Interior just like the BKA. The *Bundesgrenzschutz* performs police functions in terms of border protection. To that extent it deals with certain areas of criminality such as trafficking in human beings, illegal immigration and particularly drug smuggling, and is therefore a cooperative partner of the states' police forces and the *Bundeskriminalamt*. However, the transfer of data between the BGS and the police authorities is limited to areas where competences overlap.

The *Zoll* (customs office) is another federal police authority in the broader sense. This is subordinate to the Federal Department of Finance and protects the financial interests of the *Federation* and the states in connection with border crossings.

In the Federal Republic of Germany there are three secret services exclusively organised at the federal level: the *Bundesnachrichtendienst* (BND, Federal Information Service), the *Militärischer Abschirmdienst* (MAD, Military Counter-Intelligence Service) and the *Bundesverfassungsschutz* (Federal Office for the Protection of the Constitution). The *Bundesnachrichtendienst* is the classical secret service which fights internal espionage and pursues external information policies for the protection of the country. The *Militärische Abschirmdienst* ensures appropriate protection within the area of the German federal armed forces. The *Bundesverfassungsschutz* investigates activities at home and abroad, which are directed against the German constitution. All secret services have a privileged ability to act and interfere with civil rights which is superior to that of the police. They are not subject to judicial control, but only to political observation and control, as far as this is meant to be exercised.

According to the present legal opinion – which is, however, not laid down in law – there is a so-called need for separation *(Trennungsgebot)*. This means that the secret services cannot intervene in police competences and are also not allowed to communicate with the police authorities. The latter rule has been introduced because otherwise the various judicial checks on police activities could be unhinged by the police diverting their activity through the secret services. Recently, however, there has been discussion on a political level about whether or not the secret services should be authorized to cooperate with the police in a few cases which would be explicitly described by legislation, especially in connection with the fight against organised crime. But presently there is apparently no support from a parliamentary majority for such a project, and the judiciary seems to be unwilling to give permission by way of legal interpretation.

At the level of the general administration we also find authorities with powers which are, in the sense of administrative law, police powers. Thus, for instance concerning food and trade control or the supervision of industrial plants within the environmental sector, the administration offices assume controlling functions, which can also be enforced by means of coercion. But this scope of responsibility usually lies outside the criminal law. Therefore, as far as criminal prosecution is concerned, these administrative authorities have to depend upon the police.

## 2. Competences of the police

At the regional level a distinction may be drawn between the uniformed police, who are responsible for crime prevention and investigating minor crimes, and the criminal police, who are responsible for tackling serious and most serious crimes and do not wear uniforms. In spite of being organised within the Ministry of the Interior, the police, when prosecuting criminal offences, act as auxiliary officials of the public prosecutor's office, and are therefore in that context subordinate to the Ministry of Justice. Individual regulations of the states determine which ranks of the uniformed and non-uniformed police are auxiliary officials of the public prosecutor's office. The higher echelons of the police remain, however, outside such a bipartition and stay exclusively under the authority of the Ministry of the Interior. This leads to a peculiar situation.

Officers up to the *Polizeioberrat* (about superintendent) are usually simultaneously auxiliary officials of the public prosecutor's office, whereas the police director (about chief superintendent) and the president of the police are not. Thus police officers in such double positions are placed in extremely difficult and stressful positions since they are dependent both on the instructions of their police director, or the president of the police, and their respective public prosecutors. If these two instructions are contradictory, the resulting conflicts are almost impossible to resolve. This is in particular the case if the decision is whether a criminal activity should be observed further or whether an arrest should be made directly. Hence, a conflict may arise between the interests of the police in investigating and the prosecutorial needs of the public prosecutor's office. In the case of illegal behaviour during mass-demonstrations this conflict has become notorious. While the police, for preventive reasons, mostly prefer to tolerate the hooligan activities of a few to keep the demonstration as a whole under control, the prosecutors' attitude is rather to arrest and identify the small group of perpetrators.

This double position of the police also means that officers are subject to different rules of law depending on the functional area in which they are active. Within the area of their preventive activity they are subordinate to the law of the state governing the police force. If they are active as auxiliary officials of the public prosecutor's office in terms of crime prosecution, then they are subject to the rules of the *Strafprozeßordnung* (Federal Criminal Procedure Code), which has been adopted in the form of a federal law.

The classical distinction between preventive and repressive police action used to be quite clear. In the area of prevention the term "police danger" enables the police to employ coercive means and to encroach on citizens' rights. From the middle of the nineteenth century onwards, with the jurisdiction of the Prussian Higher Administrative Court up to today's jurisdiction of the administrative courts, this term has undergone significant reification.

The police have the competence to become active in terms of repression on the basis of suspicion. Different procedural measures of a coercive nature are used depending on the level of suspicion. The police are authorized to use these partially on the basis of their original competence, partially on the basis of the public prosecutor's office, and – in cases of interventions which significantly infringe on citizens' rights – only when authorized by the examining judge (*Ermittlungsrichter*) granting them an exemption.

Today, this separation of preventive and repressive police activity is no longer clearly visible. The reason for this lies in the police regulations which have been passed since the beginning of the 1990s in the German states – with the exception of Bremen.

*Vorfeldermittlungen* (investigations in advance of a crime being committed, which can also be described as pro-active investigations) caused the fusion of police law and criminal procedure law. In all the states' statutory regulations relating to the police (with the exception of Bremen), the latter are requested and authorized to become active in advance of a crime being committed. This was justified on the basis of criminal policy by the fact that it is not meaningful to wait for a real police danger or for a criminal offence to have taken place in situations where a criminal activity is likely to occur. Rather it is better to prevent offences or, if a crime does occur, to be able to catch the perpetrators immediately. It was argued that especially with the subtle nature of organised crime structures one could hardly proceed successfully in another way.

But from a doctrinal point of view *Vorfeldermittlungen* are not easy to define. At their very core they are repressive, because they represent investigative actions in relation to criminal offences that have not yet been committed. This implies that the police either have an exact knowledge of the persons who want to commit criminal offences or that the police basically regard every citizen as a potential criminal and can therefore initiate investigations as a consequence. While the first assumption may be wishful thinking, the second one is quite disturbing, because a citizen – even without falling under the suspicion of being involved in crime – is seen to be basically suspicious and may consequently become the subject of police investigations at random.

In addition, features of prevention also correspond to *Vorfeldermittlungen*. These aspects are better expressed semantically by the term 'pro-active activities'. The police are to become active before the emergence of a police danger, which can naturally also be due to a criminal offence. This concept corresponds to classical police prevention work as carried out through patrolling for instance. If, however, the statutory police regulations of the states allow undercover investigators to probe into the lives of those suspected of planning a crime only in order to access their personal data, then this type of prevention encroaches on the right of individuals to know what data is held on them and why. As the Federal Constitutional Court of Germany has held that any individual is constitutionally protected with regard to his/her personal data (*Recht auf informationelle Selbstbestimmung*) – including access, storage, transfer and use – such pro-active police investigation against non-suspects amounts to a violation of constitutional rights. The problem in Germany is still under discussion, and the Federal Constitutional Court has not yet decided in this concrete context.

The police function to become active within the area of *Vorfeldermittlungen* has thus led to a doctrinal change in German law, which dilutes the former separation between preventive and repressive police actions and the respective allocations of competence, and also weakens the protection of civil rights.

## 3. Private police

Although private security has a large market in the Federal Republic of Germany, it is not officially acknowledged as police activity. All private security providers or policing agencies are active in the private sector and are without any privileges. They do not have any official authority, and like any other private citizen they have to request a gun license if they want to carry a weapon. This permission is given only after an intensive check of the individual's personal reliability and technical competence in handling the weapon concerned. There is an absolute requirement to document the individual's need to carry a weapon, but being active in the security field is not yet generally considered a convincing reason to justify a license. At the state level the policy concerning the distribution of gun licenses is extremely restrictive.

For all of these reasons there is no official communication between private security operators and the national police.

The establishment of a recognized private police organisation with limited privileges in terms of intervention is presently under discussion in Germany. Under the current situation, however, it is not expected that there will be a parliamentary majority in favour which could free the way for such a private police. Both the police and the judiciary are clearly against such an institution and want to keep the monopoly of power under state control.


### III. THE PUBLIC PROSECUTOR'S OFFICE

### 1. Structure and competences

The public prosecutor's office is in charge of preliminary investigations and to that extent directs the work of the police. It is organised at a regional level, but is still subject to the Federal Criminal Procedure Code (*Strafprozeß-ordnung*). The public prosecutor's office, which is hierarchically structured, is led by a prosecutor general at the level of the higher regional court (*Oberlandesgericht*) and by a "leading senior public prosecutor" at the level of the regional court (*Landgericht*). There is a hierarchical dependency, so the prosecutor general can give directions and instructions to any individual public prosecutor.

At the federal level there is the Federal Prosecutor's Office, competent mainly for cases concerning subversive activities and placed under the authority of the Federal Ministry of Justice.[5]

The prosecutor's duties are to investigate crime and, in doing so, to look for both incriminating and exonerating circumstances. Empirical data demonstrate, however, that prosecutors usually do not obey this legal rule and predominantly look for incriminating evidence. If sufficient evidence is available, the prosecutor is obliged to bring the charge before the court. Without this formal act initiating arraignment the court is unable to proceed with the case.

Due to his limited discretionary power, it is only with respect to minor crimes that the prosecutor may drop the case in spite of sufficient evidence.

The prosecutor must be present at the court proceedings. He acts as a representative of the state and has the responsibility for discharging the burden of proof.

In some cases where intensive measures which encroach on the rights of individuals are used, such as pre-trial detention and the interception of communication or the search of private premises, the prosecutor requires a judicial decision.

Until the procedural reform of 1974, pre-trial investigations were directed by an investigating judge (*Untersuchungsrichter*). Ever since the creation of the first common code of criminal procedure in Germany in 1877, there has been a controversy with respect to the concept of the investigating judge. The legislator decided to install these judges because distrust in the neutrality of the prosecutor had arisen – at that time this was also a fairly new position in the procedural system. By 1975 it appeared that this distrust was unjustified and the system was changed. Since then, the prosecutor has directed investigations under his own responsibility, while the position of the judge under the Basic Law (the Constitution) has made it necessary to keep him out of any activity which was not of a purely judicial nature.

## 2. Special public prosecutor's offices

In order to fight against special forms of criminality in a more concentrated manner, the state judicial authorities (*Landesjustizbehörden*) have created special public prosecutor's offices, which – in addition to being allocated to regional court districts – are able to become active at the complete state level. This has been the case concerning criminal offences which presuppose special legal authority in the course of an investigation, like white-collar crime for example. In addition, the same steps have been taken in order to pursue all crime, not merely local crime, more efficiently.

At the level of international organised crime, the *Bundeskriminalamt* has competence. This agency can then become active at a federal as well as on an international level under the aegis of the Federal Prosecutor's Office.

The establishment of a special public prosecutor's office at state level is solely subject to the discretionary decision of the Minister of Justice of the respective state. He is also responsible for the budgetary control, which directly limits the number of such special public prosecutor's offices. In this context co-financing with the *Bund* is not possible for legal reasons.

The composition of special investigation groups at the federal level is limited by the narrow description of competence. It is up to the discretion of the Federal Minister of the Interior which special investigation groups apply to which cases. Since he carries the budgetary responsibility for this decision a certain restraint on his part is only natural.

## IV. INNOVATIONS IN THE FIGHT AGAINST ORGANISED CRIME AND OTHER FORMS OF SERIOUS INTERNATIONAL CRIMES

### 1. Police law

In the course of (re-)discovering organised crime since the end of the 1980s, the German states have amended and clearly strengthened their statutory police regulations. As already mentioned above under II, with the exception of Bremen all the other states incorporated the *Vorfeldermittlungen* as a police function into their respective police regulations. In addition, new concrete coercive measures were integrated into these regulations. For example, it is permitted in practically all states to conduct, without judicial control, the interception of the telephone service and also the interception of any other communication. According to these police regulations the employment of undercover agents is also possible. These relatively new investigative techniques have been inserted with deliberate reference to the threat of organised crime and the corresponding necessity to designate special measures to control it.[6]

As far as **international police cooperation** is concerned, the German police administration has coped with the needs without establishing new forms of organisation specially designed for fighting international crime. So far contact points for international cooperation form part of the given administrative structures of the German police forces.

Interpol has been integrated for a long time in the German police system. There are no new developments in relation to Interpol. On the contrary, it seems that with increasing intensity of EU-cooperation, notably Schengen, the importance of Interpol has been slightly reduced.

Concerning Europol, which at the moment is directed by a German officer, the BKA is responsible for any contacts to German police authorities, § 3 BKAG. In fact, however, there is quite a bit of direct contact between the state criminal investigation bureaus (*Landeskriminalämter*, LKA) and Europol, as Germany has seconded liaison officers to Europol, quite a few of whom are members of LKA's, who use their old contacts. A similar situation applies to the SIRENE Bureau.

As long as these European police institutions have no operational powers of their own, German police work will remain a national problem which is being solved with the help of the international institutions which can give some support relative to information and coordination.

Although leading politicians have started to address the necessity of an operational European police force (see lately Chancellor Schröder), it is doubtful whether the European Union is ready for this. When the Schengen

Agreement was completed by the Schengen Implementation Convention, the numerous additional national protocols – most of which concerned the principle of border-crossing police activities – demonstrated that the EU Member States are still guarding their national police autonomy.

In any event a European Police Force would require a special Convention on the principles ruling their repressive as well as their preventive work. This means that a respective European police law and an EU-wide penal procedure would have to be created. Whereas the Corpus Juris has prepared certain standards for the procedural sides, no preparatory work has yet been accomplished for the establishment of a common European police law.

## 2. The level of criminal procedure law

For the purpose of being able to fight organised crime more effectively, the catalogue of the procedural coercive measures has also been extended at the federal level, by modifications to the Criminal Procedure Code (*StPO*). Already existing possibilities like those of telephone tapping were extended to other areas of crime. Other coercive measures were newly introduced, as for instance the large and the small bugging-operation (*Lauschangriff*) according to § 100c StPO. Common to both interceptive operations are the monitoring and registration of communication by means of surveillance instruments (e.g. microphones, tracking devices). The difference between a small and large bugging operation is that the latter also allows for the listening and recording of communication within the constitutionally protected area of the private dwelling. For this purpose, article 13 of the *German Grundgesetz* had to be specially modified.

Also the use of undercover agents and informants was expressly regulated in the criminal procedure code. In this context, there had been a special necessity for regulation, because these techniques had been used as part of investigation without a legal basis. Now these instruments are acquiring legality and belong to the coercive measures whose application is foreseen in the Criminal Procedure Code.

On both issues, prior to the introduction of the wire-tapping as well as in relation to the legalization of the use of undercover agents and informants, there was a very vigorous political debate. Basically, it was questioned whether such substantial interventions into the privacy of citizens – who according to the presumption of innocence are to be treated as innocent even in suspicious situations – is justifiable in a state in which the rule of law prevails. Beyond that, the benefit of these instruments for increasing the success of investigation as part of criminal procedures has been questioned.

With reference to violent terrorists, in 1989 the so-called "statute concerning king's evidence" (*Kronzeugengesetz*) was passed by the German *Bundestag*. According to this statute it is now also officially possible to grant a mitigation of punishment to accomplices or to release them from punishment for serious, even the most serious, criminal offences if they had made themselves available as witnesses for the prosecution against their former accomplices. But also in this context, the suitability of such a regulation was seriously doubted during the course of the political discussion. The danger that these witnesses might rescue themselves by furnishing evidence against the other accomplices which was not quite truthful, in order to satisfy the expectations of the court and the public prosecutor's office, is easy to see. The legislator obviously considered these doubts in so far as it adopted the statute concerning king's evidence on a limited three-year basis. After two further extensions of three years, the legislator in 1999 abolished this king's evidence regulation because it could not ascertain a positive impact on the prosecution in cases of serious and very serious criminal offences. This is particularly remarkable with regard to the EU resolution of 20 December 1996 on cooperation by former members of criminal organisations. To that extent the German legislator dissociated itself clearly from this resolution.

## 3. The level of the substantive criminal law

Recently the German legislator has passed four new laws focusing on prevention and repression of organised crime:
* Law to fight illegal drug trafficking and other appearances of organised crime of 15 July 1992
* Money laundering law of 25 October 1993
* Anti-corruption law of 28 October 1994
* Law to improve the fight against organised crime of 9 May 1998

Here, above all § 261 of the *Strafgesetzbuch* (StGB = Criminal Procedure Code), the new law concerning money laundering which has been subject to various extensions, needs to be mentioned. At the same time, in this context the regulations concerning the seizure of assets (*Vermögensgegenstände*) were facilitated and the *Vermögensstrafe* (property penalty) was introduced as a new type of punishment. The purpose of these regulations is to undermine the prime objective of organised crime, which is the acquisition of financial assets. The new regulations concerning the fight against corruption served similar purposes. Here, the existing regulations relating to office-holders were extended and new regulations were introduced regarding private businesses (§§ 299, 300 StGB). Since, besides drugs, the slave trade/prostitution and child pornography also belong to the substantial sources of income of organised crime, the German legislator has also intensified the existing regulations in the context of § 180b and § 184 3 III StGB.

## V. FINAL REMARKS

In Germany there are no special structures for the fight against organised crime. Rather it is fought on the grounds of existing structures, described above, and by concentrating the efforts of individual departments on special points of interest (which, however, as mentioned, are subject to budgetary restrictions).

Still, it should be pointed out that the general measures which serve to improve cooperation – particularly among the European Union Member States – also have positive effects concerning the fight against organised crime at the level of the police and of the judiciary. At the level of the judiciary the European Judicial Network should be emphasized. This assists in establishing contact offices in the EU Member States, which deal with foreign requests for concrete judicial cooperation in individual cases or point out the correct form of cooperation.

## NOTES

1. See Bundestags-Drucksache v. 15.07.1992, 12/989, 24.
2. See Wittkämper/Krevert/Kohl, *Europa und die innere Sicherheit*, Wiesbaden 1996, p. 52.
3. The details on methodology and contact, see Meywirth, Kriminalistik 1999, 447; Ullmann, *Kriminalistik* 1996, 328, if only apart from their annual compendium "Politische Kriminalstatistik" (police crime statistics).
4. See e.g. Schwind, Kriminologie, 11.ed. 2001, p 591-599.
5. See §§ 142a, 120 GVG – Court Organisation Law.
6. For the doctrinal and policy problems of this change in law, see *infra*.

## BIBLIOGRAPHY

*Albrecht, Hans-Jörg* (Ed.), Kriminalität und Kriminalitätskontrolle, 1999 (ISBN 3-866113-026-2).

*Aulehner, Josef*, Polizeiliche Gefahren- und Informationsvorsorge: Grundlagen, Rechts- und Vollzugsstrukturen, dargestellt auch im Hinblick auf die deutsche Beteiligung an einem Europäischen Polizeiamt (Europol), Schriften zum Recht des Informationsverkehrs und der Informationstechnik / Bd. 16, Berlin 1998 (ISBN 3-428-09058-6).

*Borchert, Heiko*, Europäische Sicherheitsinstitutionen: Arbeitsteilung und Kooperation, 2. Auflage, Eidgenössische Technische Hochschule, Forschungsstelle für Internationale Beziehungen / Nr. 13, Zürich 1998 (ISBN 3-905648-12-1).

*Bundeskriminalamt* (Hrsg.), Moderne Sicherheitsstrategien gegen das Verbrechen: Vorträge und Diskussionen der Arbeitstagung des Bundeskriminalamtes vom 17. bis 19. November 1998, BKA-Forschungsreihe / Bd. 49, Wiesbaden 1999.

*Bundeskriminalamt* (Hrsg.), Kersten, Klaus Ulrich (Red.), Neue Freiheiten, neue Risiken, neue Chancen: aktuelle Kriminalitätsformen und Bekämpfungsansätze, Vorträge und Diskussionen der Arbeitstagung des Bundeskriminalamtes vom 18. bis 21. November 1997, BKA-Forschungsreihe / Bd. 48, Wiesbaden 1998.

*Bundeskriminalamt* (Hrsg.), Mischkowitz, Robert (Red.), Organisierte Kriminalität: Vorträge und Diskussionen bei der Arbeitstagung des Bundeskriminalamtes vom 19. bis 22. November 1996, BKA-Forschungsreihe / Bd. 43, Wiesbaden 1997.

*Gropp/Huber* (Hrsg.), Rechtliche Initiativen gegen Organisierte Kriminalität, 2001 (ISBN 3-86113-919-7).

*Harings, Lothar*, Grenzüberschreitende Zusammenarbeit der Polizei- und Zollverwaltungen und Rechtsschutz in Deutschland, Schriften zum öffentlichen Recht / Bd. 763, Berlin 1998 (ISBN 3-428-09438-7).

*Huppertz, Martina / Theobald, Volkmar* (Hrsg.), Kriminalitätsimport, Schriftenreihe zur neuen Sicherheitspolitik, Berlin 1998 (ISBN 3-87061-791-8).

*Kühne, Hans-Heiner*, Strafprozeßrecht: Ein Lehrbuch zum deutschen und europäischen Strafverfahrensrecht, 5. Auflage, Heidelberg 1999 (ISBN 3-8114-9935-19).

*Kühne, Hans-Heiner*, Das Paradigma der inneren Sicherheit: polizeiliche Möglichkeiten – rechtsstaatliche Grenzen, Leipziger juristische Vorträge / H. 26, Leipzig 1998 (ISBN 3-931922-56-1).

*Kühne, Hans-Heiner* (Hrsg.), Internal security in modern industrialized societies: a comparative perspective, 1. Auflage, Baden-Baden 1998

(ISBN 3-7890-5585-9).

*Lange, Hans-Jürgen*, Innere Sicherheit im politischen System der Bundesrepublik Deutschland, Reihe: Studien zur inneren Sicherheit / 2, Opladen 1999 (ISBN 3-8100-2214-4).

*Mayerhofer, Christoph / Jehle, Jörg-Martin* (Hrsg.), Organisierte Kriminalität: Lagebilder und Erscheinungsformen; Bekämpfung und rechtliche Bewältigung, Neue kriminologische Schriftenreihe der Neuen Kriminologischen Gesellschaft e.V. / Bd. 103, Heidelberg 1996 (ISBN 3-7832-0596-4).

*Meier-Walser, Reinhard C. / Hirscher, Gerhard / Lange, Klaus / Palumbo, Enrico* (Hrsg.), Organisierte Kriminalität: Bestandsaufnahme, transnationale Dimension, Wege der Bekämpfung, Akademie für Politik und Zeitgeschehen, München 1999 (ISBN 3-88795-178-6).

*Pitschas, Rainer*, „Neues" Polizeirecht, Deutsche Hochschule für Verwaltungswissenschaften Speyer, Speyerer Arbeitshefte / 121, Speyer 1999.

*Pütter, Norbert*, Der OK-Komplex: organisierte Kriminalität und ihre Folgen für die Polizei in Deutschland, 1. Auflage, Münster 1998 (ISBN 3-89691-439-1).

*Theobald, Volkmar* (Hrsg.), Von der Europäischen Union zur „Europäischen Sicherheitsunion"?: Die gemeinsame Politik der inneren Sicherheit in der EU, Schriftenreihe zur neuen Sicherheitspolitik, Berlin 1997 (ISBN 3-87061-624-5).

*Tipke, Klaus*, Innere Sicherheit und Gewaltkriminalität: die Sicherheitsdefizite unseres Rechtsstaats, München 1998 (ISBN 3-7766-7055-X).

*Wielsch, Torsten*, Die europäische Gefahrenabwehr: Stand und Perspektiven europäischer Polizeiarbeit nach dem Maastrichter Vertrag, Leipziger juristische Studien: Öffentlich-rechtliche Abteilung / Bd. 3, Leipzig 1998 (ISBN 3-933240-28-X).

*Winter, Martin*, Politikum Polizei : Macht und Funktion der Polizei in der Bundesrepublik Deutschland, Politische Soziologie / 10, Münster 1998 (ISBN 3-8258-3494-8).

*Wittkämper/Krevert/Kohl*, Europa und die innere Sicherheit, 1996 (ISSN: 0174-5433).

*Zoller, Manfred*, Auswärtige Sicherheit als nachrichtendienstliche Aufgabe: Herausforderungen in veränderter Globallage, Fachhochschule des Bundes für Öffentliche Verwaltung, Fachbereich Öffentliche Sicherheit (Hrsg.), Beiträge zur inneren Sicherheit / 9, Brühl/Rheinland 1999 (ISBN 3-930732-45-9).

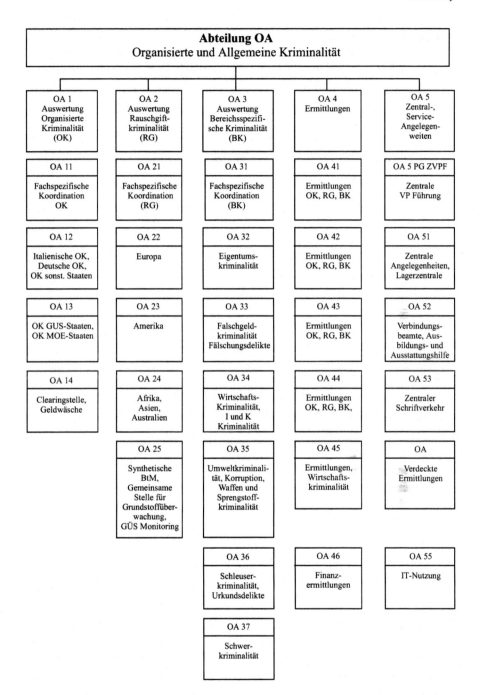

**Abteilung OA**
Organisierte und Allgemeine Kriminalität

| OA 1 Auswertung Organisierte Kriminalität (OK) | OA 2 Auswertung Rauschgift-kriminalität (RG) | OA 3 Auswertung Bereichsspezifi-sche Kriminalität (BK) | OA 4 Ermittlungen | OA 5 Zentral-, Service-Angelegen-weiten |
|---|---|---|---|---|
| OA 11 Fachspezifische Koordination OK | OA 21 Fachspezifische Koordination (RG) | OA 31 Fachspezifische Koordination (BK) | OA 41 Ermittlungen OK, RG, BK | OA 5 PG ZVPF Zentrale VP Führung |
| OA 12 Italienische OK, Deutsche OK, OK sonst. Staaten | OA 22 Europa | OA 32 Eigentums-kriminalität | OA 42 Ermittlungen OK, RG, BK | OA 51 Zentrale Angelegenheiten, Lagerzentrale |
| OA 13 OK GUS-Staaten, OK MOE-Staaten | OA 23 Amerika | OA 33 Falschgeld-kriminalität Fälschungsdelikte | OA 43 Ermittlungen OK, RG, BK | OA 52 Verbindungs-beamte, Aus-bildungs- und Ausstattungshilfe |
| OA 14 Clearingstelle, Geldwäsche | OA 24 Afrika, Asien, Australien | OA 34 Wirtschafts-Kriminalität, I und K Kriminalität | OA 44 Ermittlungen OK, RG, BK, | OA 53 Zentraler Schriftverkehr |
| | OA 25 Synthetische BtM, Gemeinsame Stelle für Grundstoffüber-wachung, GÜS Monitoring | OA 35 Umweltkriminali-tät, Korruption, Waffen und Sprengstoff-kriminalität | OA 45 Ermittlungen, Wirtschafts-kriminalität | OA Verdeckte Ermittlungen |
| | | OA 36 Schleuser-kriminalität, Urkundsdelikte | OA 46 Finanz-ermittlungen | OA 55 IT-Nutzung |
| | | OA 37 Schwer-kriminalität | | |

# Greece[1]

## *Effi Lambropoulou*

## 1. INTRODUCTION

The study that was undertaken in Greece is based mainly on interviews with officials of law enforcement agencies, and on analysis of relevant documents written for foreign authorities, such as the Council of the European Union, the *Bundeskriminalamt* or the US Coastguard, as well as of legal provisions concerning the competences of these agencies, their organisation, and the regulations for issues relating to organised crime. Moreover, some information was generated from the annual reports of the crime prevention services.

A number of articles published recently on the subject of the control of organised crime, although being restricted to normative issues,[2] have also been taken into account, as well as literature and information from the press.

Overall, with few exceptions, cooperation with the agencies was constructive and effective.

In conclusion, the information was not simply registered, but the data or the arguments were subject to crosschecking on points for which the interpretation was insufficient. However, the responsibility for the contents of this chapter rests solely with the author.

## 2. OFFICIAL DEFINITION OF ORGANISED CRIME

Until recently the special term "organised crime" had not been used in Greek penal law. However, the elements of organised crime were generally provided for under the Penal Code, which contained a provision, Article 187, making the constitution of, as well as membership and participation in criminal gangs punishable. Criminal intent, which consists in the will of two or more persons for the perpetration of felonies[3] or misdemeanours,[4] was punished irrespective of the commission of a criminal act or its attempt. Articles 45-48, regulating, in general, issues concerning complicity, accessory before the fact and cooperation were also applied to these activities.

For the classification of behaviour in the category of "organised transnational crime", and the composition of Annual Reports on organised crime, the Greek police used the relevant guidelines of the European Union until 2001.[5]

In June 2001, the Greek Parliament, not without problems, passed new provisions (Law 2928/2001) for the fight against organised crime and terrorism based on international and European conventions, namely the *United Nations Convention against transnational organised crime* signed in Palermo, Italy, in December 2000 by the member states of the European Union, and the *Action Plan to combat Organised Crime* of the Council of the EU of April 1997 (JAI 14), as well as the *European Union Strategy for the beginning of the new Millennium*[6] of the Council.

The articles set the definition of criminal organisation as a group of three or more persons who collaborate for a prolonged time or constitute a gang having a structure for the commitment of serious criminal offences, using violence or threat of force against the judicature, witnesses, experts, interpreters etc. and exerting influence by corruption. The articles describe the offences and foresee high penalties, where only judges constitute the juries for these crimes and the participation of citizens in them is abolished. The examination of DNA is introduced, and according to the article, the court can ask the examination, which is obligatory for the accused but not coercive, in cases where there are strong indications of guilt. The participation of undercover agents in the dismantling of criminal organisations is also regulated, but their role is a passive and not an active one, namely they cannot participate in the commitment or the attempt of the commitment of a crime. Electronic surveillance is introduced but not in the home or at the work of the suspect. Anonymous testimonies are permitted, however, these are not taken into consideration for the conviction of the accused. Witness protection programs are also included. Those showing remorse are foreseen to be treated with leniency or clemency, which means that their sentence can be suspended for three to ten years or they can be acquitted if they contribute to the disruption or breaking up of the criminal organisation.

It is interesting that, according to the Report of the Ministry of Public Order for 1995 and 1996,[7] organised criminal groups in Greece do not yet play an important role in general criminality. Mostly persons who work independently, and are not organised on a long-term basis undertake criminal activities which concerned the police. The existing criminal groups in Greece do not meet the criteria of the record of ENFOPOL 161 (Annex A), namely they do not have the structure, cohesion and organisation which would allow their activities to continue after the arrest of some of their members, and mainly of their leaders.

However, the Report for the next year emphasises on a "qualitative" differentiation of criminality and concludes that "organised crime emerged in Greece; although the groups do not have a compact structure and strategy, they act rather in ambiguity and obscurity and are not part of a network".[8] The Reports for the following years, 1998 and 1999, give a very extensive account of "organised criminal activities and groups".[9] This is why we have considerable reservations over the validity of the evaluating or rather the issue of categorising, because the variance from one year to another is remarkable. It seems that many forms of serious crime are categorised as "organised" criminality. This is asserted by the Report for 1998 itself, where it is stated that "*Several* (emphasis, EL) cases met the criteria of organised crime",[10] indicating that the Report referred to criminality *in general*, as well as by the Report for 1999, where it is stated that "the groups have a rather opportunistic character (emphasis, EL) and are not organised on a long-term basis".[11] It is remarkable that the Report also refers to the "occasional activities of juvenile gangs", namely to a few cases of robberies committed by juveniles groups (2-3) against people of the same age, without there existing systematic research on the issue.[12]

This typifies also the general problem of defining "organised" crime. Namely, while in the Report for 1995 and 1996, it seems that the degree of organised crime in the country was "under-estimated", since it was emphasised that criminal activities are not organised, the Reports of the next years were over inclusive. This happens perhaps because of pressure for the Report to fulfil the requirements of the ENFOPOL document 35, 2nd revision, on which its compilation is based. It is worth mentioning that the conclusions of the latter Report are almost the same as those of the previous, which seems inconsistent with the presented situation, since it states that the organised criminal groups do not have stable structures and in most cases they give up their operations after the arrest of their members.[13]

According to Greek police officers, they realised the rising problem of organised criminal groups from the study of reports of regional police and from the analysis of information from several other sources. The reports refer to criminal groups engaged in drug trafficking, trafficking in human beings for sexual exploitation, steeling cars and the illicit traffic in antiquities, etc. These groups are not numerous, and inferences related to the existence of permanent and stable structures are risky.

In general, the Greek Reports specify that the dismantled organised criminal *groups* were relatively small (2-10 persons), structured on a personal basis, with an ambiguous hierarchy, pursuing economic profits. The national make-up of the groups varies, while sometimes operating within a different ethnic-constitution. The use of violence or the exercise of influence to achieve their goals is rare.[14]

Since systematic research concerning organised crime has not been carried out in Greece, except in separate cases referred to by journalists based mainly on police information and on other investigation authorities, it is quite difficult to come to a conclusion. The development of criminality in Greece, the way it is conducted and with an intensity not known some years ago, such as armed robberies, as well as the inflow of foreign criminal groups, demand reflection. So, it would be useful to regard Greece as a country where transnational criminal activities are developing.

## 3. LAW ENFORCEMENT AGENCIES

The authorities responsible for the fight against organised crime in Greece are the law enforcement agencies. These comprise the police, coastguard, customs services and the Financial and Economic Crimes Office.

The Greek **police** are an organised, special, armed military force with their own organic regulations.

In Ancient Greece and Byzantium as well as during the Turkish occupation, eminent citizens exercised police authority. The institution of the police in Greece took a new form during the first National Assembly in Epidaurus, on 9 January 1822, when the Greek state was constituted after its liberation from the Turks.

After many changes made to the previous dual system of policing (state and municipal) and the 60-year division of the police into judicial and administrative, the gendarmerie took over complete authority for policing the country in 1906. In 1921, a new corps, the Metropolitan Police, was established in the four major cities of the country (Athens, Piraeus, Patras and Corfu) in line with the British system.[15]

In 1984, the Metropolitan Police force was unified with the gendarmerie to form the Greek police (ELAS).[16]

The Greek police are under the authority of the Ministry of Public Order, which also includes the Agrarian Service, responsible for the enforcement of the law in agrarian regions in relation to the security of farmlands, the Fire Brigade and the Directorate for Extraordinary Situations (natural catastrophes, such as earthquakes, floods, etc.).[17]

The police have authority for policing the whole country, and this may overlap with the competence of the coastguard for the sea, ports and vessels. Their administrative duties are the maintenance of order in the country, and their judicial duties are the investigation of criminal offences. As regards their judicial duties, the police are supervised and guided by the public prosecutor.

In April 1999, the Greek police force was staffed by 41,324 agents, of which 2,800 (6.7%) were women. This corresponds to 393 policemen per 100,000 inhabitants for a total population of 10,521,669. In March 2000 their number was increased to 44,898 agents, of which 3,729 (8,3%) were women, corresponding to 425 policemen per 100,000 inhabitants for a total population of 10,557,900.

Special police services are: 1) criminological research services, 2) the drug units, 3) the police operations units, 4) the special anti-terrorist units, 5) the special anti-violent crime units, 5) the bomb disposal units, 7) the Juvenile Service, 8) the Unit for the Control of Air Transport, 9) police forces for the state airports, 10) the Border Guards Corps, 11) the Service of Internal Affairs, and 11) the Market Inspection and Municipal Veterinary Inspection Police (for the control of the quality of food in restaurants, meat supplied to the market etc.).[18]

After a long discussion about the necessity of the creation of a police headquarters, in February 2000 (Law 2800/2000) the Greek Parliament passed the relevant bill introducing three major reforms: the establishment of the police headquarters as an independent authority; the appointment of the Chief of Police for a specific period of at least two years with a possible renewal for one more year, similar to the armed forces; and finally the composition of a Council for Operational Planning and Crisis Management.

Besides, there are some moves to transform the Ministry of Public Order into a Ministry of Internal Affairs. However, it is not possible to evaluate whether this corresponds to a real need and whether it will ultimately be carried out, or whether it is just an effort by Greece to conform with other countries, since it is the only EU member state with a Ministry of Public Order. Still, it must be taken into account that the Minister of Police has existed since the constitution of the Greek state.

Furthermore, before the unification of the two forces in 1984, both the gendarmerie and the metropolitan police had their own headquarters. It was argued that the creation of the abovementioned headquarters would speed up decision making, because the Minister would cooperate with only one person, the Chief, and not with the Directors of the two Branches (of Security and Order, and of Administrative Support), and with the several Directorates (Public Security Directorate, State Security Directorate, International Police Cooperation Directorate, etc.) as happens now.[19] However, this may not be the main reason, but perhaps the change will diminish political intervention in the police force, and so contribute to improving the self-esteem of the police and sense of independence.

Another law enforcement unit is the **coastguard**[20] which has police authority over the sea. The coastguard is an armed military corps belonging to the Ministry of Mercantile Marine. The Coastguard Corps was instituted in 1919

(Law 1753) similar to the coastguard of the USA and France. It is staffed by 4,459 agents.

Mainly the Security Directorate of the Coastguard, which includes the Department of International Police Cooperation, the Department of State Security and the Department for the Control of Drug Trafficking, exercises police authority. The Department of International Police Cooperation is responsible for all criminal offences under the Penal Code and the special penal laws except those related to drugs, and the country's international cooperation with foreign law enforcement agencies. This department is also responsible for the implementation of the Schengen Agreement, cooperation with the Greek police, Interpol and the police forces of other countries. The Department of State Security deals with the law enforcement concerning state security as well as the collection, processing and the analysis of relevant data.

The powers of the Department for Drugs Control have recently been enhanced, as it is not only responsible for the coordination and operational activities in the field of drugs, but also of contraband cigarettes, fuels, weapons and the illegal trafficking of human beings, etc. At the same time, it collects and analyses information not only for itself, but also for the whole Coastguard Corps, so it can also be regarded as the intelligence service of the services. It holds a local database for the Security Directorate, under which it comes; however, this is not accessible to other services. The National Data Protection Supervisory Board has approved the operation of this database (Law 2472/1997). The Security Directorate of the Coastguard is also connected on-line with the police for information registered in the criminological archive. All port authorities access the coastguard's information services.

The Security Directorate belongs to the second of the four Branches ("branch of port police and operational means") of the coastguard (Presidential Decree 242/1999 -hereinafter referred to as: PD). To the same branch belong also the port police authorities (Port Police Directorate), which are responsible for policing, order, cleanliness, hygiene, and protection of the coast and the sea, as well as the development of marine tourism, etc. The Air Transport Service belongs to the Directorate of Operational Means and Special Units of the Coastguard, and is responsible for the supervision of Greek waters and assisting with their better policing along with the Submarine Unit (scuba teams), while in some regions special squads to confront illegal acts and terrorist actions have been established.

Coastguards are authorised to undertake full preliminary investigations like the police. Each port authority in the 71 districts of the Ministry has an office or a security department. The port authorities also include 103 coastguard stations.

The **customs services,** which belong to the Ministry of Finance, have similar responsibility for criminal offences related to illegal imports into or export from Greece (control of tax evasion and the smuggling of goods).[21]

The **Financial and Economic Crimes Office** (hereinafter referred to as: SDOE),[22] which is also under the Ministry of Finance, is responsible for the prevention and fight against economic crime as related to the economic interests of the Greek state and the European Union and started its operations in April 1997.

## 4. PUBLIC PROSECUTION SERVICE

The Public Prosecution Service is independent of the judicial authority and the executive (Article 24, Law 1756/1988, Article 6 par. 3, Law 1868/1989). The legal framework for the operation of the prosecution service is prescribed in the Greek Constitution (Articles 86 ff.), under the Code for the Status of Judicial Personnel (Articles 1-25, Law 1756/1988) and the Code of Penal Procedure (especially Articles 13, 27, 31, 43, 44, 45).

The public prosecutor is responsible for indicting a suspect, but, if he is convinced that the charged person is innocent, also for proposing his acquittal.

The Public Prosecution Service acts in a unified and indivisible way. This means that the actions of a Prosecutor are not his own, but of the whole authority. The Public Prosecution Service is hierarchically structured. The head of the service is the general public prosecutor (public prosecutor of the Supreme Court).

A public prosecutor has to carry out the instructions of his superior. However, for the performance of his duties and the expression of his opinion he is free and under no obligation, but follows only "the law and his conscience" (Article 24, Law 1756/1988).

The Public Prosecution Service has authority for the investigation of criminal offences,[23] and the guidance and supervision of the police in the fulfilment of their judicial duties.

The hierarchy of the Public Prosecution Office is as follows: general public prosecutor (public prosecutor of the Supreme Court), deputy public prosecutor of the Supreme Court, public prosecutor of second instance, deputy public prosecutor of second instance, public prosecutor of first instance, deputy public prosecutor of first instance, deputy public prosecutor.

Special laws regulate the number of public prosecutors on the basis of demand. In 1999 their number rose to 467 and in 2000 to 512. Admission to the public prosecution service is achieved through examinations and graduation from the National School of Judges.

The supervisors, who are the Judges of the Supreme Court of Appeal as well as the public prosecutor of the same court, perform control of public prosecutors in the exercise of their duties and behaviour. Infractions by prosecutors are controlled by the plenary session of the Council of State, the plenary session of the Supreme Court and the plenary session of the State Audit Council, as well as the relevant disciplinary councils (Articles 84 ff., Law 1756/1988).

Organisational reforms have not taken place in the public prosecution service in relation to the control of transnational crime. However, it is worth mentioning that the role of prosecutors has been upgraded because of the increased requirements imposed on them by the creation of new mechanisms, such as the SDOE (addendum to par. 17 in the Article 4 of Law 2343/1995), the Service of Internal Affairs of the Police (Article 3, Law 2713/1999), the National Board for the Protection of Communication Privacy (Article 3, Law 2225/1994), the Money Laundering Committee (Articles 7 par. 5, Law 2331/1995), and their participation in the SIRENE Bureau.

In this respect, it is noteworthy that the public prosecutors, who were interviewed, emphasised the lack of education and training for undertaking duties to confront organised crime.

## 5. LAW ENFORCEMENT AGENCIES AND INTERNATIONAL EFFORTS TO CONTROL ORGANISED CRIME

### 5.1 Law enforcement units to control organised crime[24]

#### 5.1.1 Ministry of Public Order

Before 1990, several **special services** in the Greek police force had already been working on organised crime, such as the Sub-division for the Control of Drug Trafficking, Drug-Control Units, Anti-terrorist Units, Anti-violent Crime Units, and the Bomb Disposal Units.

For the control of illicit drug trafficking, an inter-ministerial body, the **Central Anti-Drug Coordination Unit** (hereinafter referred to as: SODN) in the Ministry of Public Order was established under Article 20 of Law 1729/1987.[25] Representatives of the Ministry of Public Order (police), the Ministry of Mercantile Marine (coastguard) and of the Ministry of Finance (Customs Services, SDOE) participate in this unit. Its general task is the processing of information, the examination of the legality of foreign requests for controlled deliveries and the coordination of their operations (Article 38, Law 2145/1993, amended by the Article 15, Law 2331/1995). The Chief of the Public Security Directorate leads the central anti-drug coordination unit.

Although the Unit (SODN) has been operating since 1987, a coordinated effort for the control of organised crime started in 1995 with the creation of the Committee Responsible for the Prevention of Money Laundering,[26] of the SDOE (Financial and Economics Crime Office, FECO),[27] and with some other specialised groups and services against organised crime such as in the Security Directorate of Attica, the Border Guards Corps, etc.

Another service relevant to the control of serious crimes is the **Department for the Prosecution of Economic Crimes**, which belongs to the Directorate of Public Security of the MPO, cooperating closely with other competent services or organisations in Greece as well as abroad.[28] In Athens and Thessaloniki, special departments exercise authority at an operational level in the control of economic crime and money laundering. For the rest of Greece, the security departments operating in the capital of the prefectures have this responsibility, while the police stations serve the smaller cities.

In 1998, following a decision of the Chief of Police, an **operational group** for the fight against organised crime – having special responsibilities for Russian organised crime – was created at the Security Directorate of Attica, in the sub-division responsible for homicides and crimes against property.[29] Recently the group has been upgraded to an autonomous sub-division at the same directorate. In addition, in each regional police directorate, police officers ("police cells") have been assigned responsibility for the collection and processing of information on organised crime on the basis of specific guidelines, while in DDA, the 4th Department for Analysis of Criminality has been established.

Furthermore, with Law 2622/1998, a **Border Guards Corps** was formed within the police. This has the exclusive mission of preventing the illegal entry of foreigners into the country, establishing their location, arresting them, arranging their committal for trial or their deportation, as well as the arrest of those who facilitate the illegal entry of foreigners into the country (Article 1 par. 1). In 1999, 1,000 border guards were serving, while in 2000 their number rose to 3,230.

### 5.1.2  Ministry of Mercantile Marine

Furthermore, in the coastguard, the **Drugs Control Office**, being under the Port Police Directorate, had authority for investigations and prosecutions in the area of illegal drug trafficking. In 1993, the office was upgraded to a department and became part of the Security Directorate. As mentioned above, it has a coordinating as well as an operational role not only for controlling drug trafficking but also for other forms of organised crime, namely, the illegal trafficking of human beings, illicit arms trafficking, contraband, etc.

Other special units of the coastguard, with exclusive operational activities in the field of combating organised crime, are the Service of Air Transport, the Unit of Submarine Missions and the Special Squads. Such Squads exist in many port offices (i.e. Corfu, Igoumenitsa and Patras) and intervene wherever needed to control illegal acts and terrorist activity. In general, the main responsibility to control organised crime within the coastguard belongs to the Security Directorate.

Organisational changes related to the fight against organised crime by the coastguard have not been signalled, except those mentioned above. The creation of more **regional groups for the control of drug trafficking** is also planned, with emphasis being placed on educating staff on the issue. This is due to the expansion of illicit drug trade, committed mainly – according to the official reports – by Albanian and Nigerian groups in the Aegean, as well as to the increase of cocaine shipments from Colombia.

### 5.1.3 Ministry of Finance

Until 1995, the Special Services of Custom Investigations (EYTE) of **the customs services** had investigative powers in relation to organised crime, mainly to the smuggling of goods and illegal drug trafficking; they were abolished in 1995 and the new body, the SDOE, assumed their authority. This did not affect the power of the Directorate for the Supervision and Control of Cars/Vehicles of the customs services, the Department for Prosecution for Arms and Drug Trafficking and contraband offences.

The **33rd Directorate of Customs Control** is responsible for investigating organised crime in the area of customs, also operating as a receiver for information from all the national customs services and from abroad. Its role consists mainly in the management and collection of information on contraband. SODN sends the information to the customs service concerning drugs. Information is also exchanged with many services, such as the SDOE, NCB Interpol, etc. The **customs services' "investigation squads"** are activated by decrees of the Ministry of Finance (1228/351/A0034/19-4-1997), as are "**control groups**" (1088/345/7-598), which are activated for the prevention and control of contraband and other customs infractions.

Law 2343/1995 founded a special body for the prevention of and fight against economic crime, the SDOE or **Financial and Economic Crimes Office**,[30] while Presidential Decree 218/1996 laid down its organisation and Presidential Decree 154/1997 regulated its operations. Its task includes the prevention and control of economic crime, namely, tax evasion related to the production, transportation and trade of goods, as well as the supply of services and contraband plus illegal trafficking in narcotics and psychotropic substances, arms, explosives and antiquities, illegal acts against national currency and public property, as well as fraud and any other offences against the economic interest of the Greek state, the public sector, the national economy and the European Union (Article 1 par. 4, Law 2343/1995). The main target in the creation of this body seems to be more the control of tax evasion than the fight against organised crime.

The SDOE is an independently controlled service supervised by the Minister of Finance. Its authority extends throughout Greece (Article 4 par. 6, Law 2343/1995). An executive secretary is in charge of the SDOE, who is directly answerable to the Minister of Finance.

Seconded tax and customs officials staff it. With the institution of the SDOE, as mentioned above, four investigation services of the Ministry of Finance were abolished, among them the Special Services for Customs Investigations (EYTE), well known for its operations against contraband and drug trafficking. The Central Service of SDOE's brief is to plan the prevention and investigation mechanisms of economic crime, to supply guidelines, to coordinate operations and to supervise its 13 regional services.

Under the Directorate of Special Economic Investigations of the SDOE is the *Department of Special Economic Affairs*, which is also responsible for the prevention and control of money laundering (Article 1, PD 152/1997), while in the two big regional services, in Athens and Thessaloniki, special departments for the fight against money laundering are planned – the first service covering all Greece. Under the Directorate of Planning and Coordination of Audits and Control of the SDOE is the *Department of Operational Planning and Prosecution of Drug and Arms trafficking* with two subdivisions in Athens and Thessaloniki. In each regional service a drugs and arms department is planned to be also responsible for offshore controls, together with the coastguard and customs services.

The SDOE participates in the inter-ministerial body, the SODN, in relation to the control of drug trafficking. Its contacts and cooperation with foreign authorities concerning issues of police cooperation, mainly concerning the European Union, as well as the Schengen Agreement are fulfilled through the Directorate of International Police Cooperation (hereinafter referred to as DDAS). Its contact with relevant bodies abroad is carried out directly or through the customs services, as happens with OLAF (*Office de lutte anti-fraude*). Contact and cooperation with OLAF occur mainly through the 33rd Directorate for Customs Controls.

According to the SDOE's published annual report for 1998, 130,268 inspections were carried out and 631,361 infractions were registered; 61.5% of them required further investigation and concerned economic infringements, mainly tax evasion of local or national interest. Only 513 (0.08%) were violations of the Penal Law and, after investigation, 369 (0.05%) were forwarded to the public prosecutor. In 1999, 162,030 inspections were carried out and 518,764 infractions – mainly tax evasions – were registered, while in 2000, the inspections rose to 174,910 and the infractions detected were 234,485, which included 720 (0.3%) violations of the Penal Law.

271

The SDOE has been assigned many responsibilities by law, since it has replaced the majority of prosecution services of the Ministry of Finance. The SDOE's Central Service provides for a 24-hour public prosecutor (Article 20, Law 2459/1997, addendum of par. 17 in the Article 4 of Law 2343/1995).

In the legal framework of the SDOE, the *Department for Data Evaluation, Documentation and Analysis* operates within its Central Service and is responsible for collecting, processing, and analysing information concerning economic crimes. Moreover, in its regional directorates, departments for data administration have become operational. Each regional directorate of the SDOE has its own information department, cooperating with the police and the SODN.

### 5.1.4 Other units

For the enforcement of Article 6 of the 1991 Money Laundering Directive of the EU, Law 2145/1993 was passed and then amended two years later, with Law 2331/1995. In Article 7, the Law foresees the constitution of an *"authorised/competent committee"* for the collection of information, evaluation and investigation of irregular transactions and **money laundering**. The committee is composed of eight members with their deputies. Participation includes a representative of the Ministries of National Economy, Finance, Commerce and Public Order, as well as representatives of the Bank of Greece, the Stock Exchange, and the Association of Greek Banks. The chairperson of the committee is a high-ranking judge or prosecutor.

The members of the committee are authorised to undertake preliminary investigations for crimes relating to money laundering (Law 2331/1995), held under the supervision and direction of the competent public prosecutor (Article 31 par. 1 Code of Penal Procedure, hereinafter referred to as: CPP, Article 7 par. 7, Law 2331/1995).

When the committee suspects a certain transaction or contract, etc. to be illegal and related to money laundering, namely when the probative evidence is well founded, it sends the file of the case to the relevant public prosecutor who can start prosecution (Articles 32, 33, 36 CPP), order regular interrogation (Article 246 CPP) or, if required, ask the committee to complete its proceedings (see also Articles 35, 243 CPP). If the evidence is inadequate, the committee puts the case "on file". However, the committee can draw on the file whenever information relevant to this case or other illegal or suspect transactions associated with it come up (Article 7 par. 5, Law 2331/1995). The committee has to finish its investigation within five days at maximum and is responsible for informing the person or the organisation, who supplied the information on illegal transactions, of its findings. The members of the committee are bound by confidentiality (Article 7 par. 6, Law 2331/1995). Three liaison officers from the police assist the committee's investigations.[31]

Furthermore, the committee evaluates and investigates all the relevant information on money laundering received by the Greek law enforcement agencies from foreign services, to which it also supplies possible assistance (Article 7 par. 9, Law 2331/1995, Article 7 par. 1, PD 401/1996). Thus, the necessary international cooperation for the fight against money laundering is ensured.[32]

According to our information, in 1997, the authorised committee forwarded to the prosecutor for further investigation 12 (15.4%) of the 78 cases referred to it, and in 1998, 22 (9.8%) of the 224 cases. The cases reported to the committee rose to 373 in October 1999, 23 (6.2%) of them forwarded to the public prosecutor; no other information was given beyond this. From relevant publications in the press, there is the suspicion that, in some cases, bank employees are also involved.

It is of interest that, while the number of cases had increased fivefold in a three-year period, the number of cases forwarded to the prosecutor corresponded to two-thirds of that of the previous year. This may be because while information of the public opinion about the operation of the committee has led to an increase in the number of charges made by public officers or citizens, many of those were unsubstantiated. Moreover, the committee itself investigates on its own initiative, for example, from information obtained from the press, while the SDOE also forwards cases.

### 5.1.5 Evaluation
#### Coordination versus operation
As regards the coordinating or operational role of the services, the specialised departments of the Ministries' central services have a coordinating role, while in the regions they have operational tasks. Inter-ministerial bodies, such as the SODN, have coordination competencies. Independent bodies, such as the SDOE, have coordination competencies at the central level, and operational duties at the regional one.

The Department for the Drug-Control Trafficking of the Hellenic Coastguard, as already mentioned, has a coordinating and operational role in the prevention of drug-related crimes but in other forms of organised crime as well, such as illegal immigration, illegal arms trafficking, contraband, etc. The Unit of Submarine Missions and the special squads have an operational role only, such as in confronting terrorist and other illegal activities (i.e. by the seizure of ships, arrests, searching for drugs in the ship's hull, etc.), while the Departments for the Security Offices of the port authorities have a dual role.

The structure of the specialised services depends on the kind of service provided. The Money Laundering Committee (Article 7, Law 2331/1995), as an autonomous administrative authority, and the inter-ministerial body SODN are de-centralised. The SDOE operates "in parallel with and

273

independently of" other relevant services of the Ministry of Finance (Article 4 par. 6, Law 2343/1995). While its structure is centralised, regular meetings of all head officers from the regional services are held every six months. At these meetings decisions are taken and the office programme is planned.

The abovementioned "investigation squads" and "groups of control" of the customs services are de-centralised, operating in the regional customs services and restricted to the local area of the service to which they belong. The competent division of the General Customs Service Directorate defines the guidelines of the operations performed by these investigation squads.

*Decentralisation*
The special police groups or squads belonging to the Security Directorate of Athens and Thessaloniki are de-centralised at an operational level and autonomous, but they are obliged to report their activities to the authority in charge. For example, the several sub-divisions and departments of the Security Directorate of Attica, such as the sub-division for *homicides* and *crimes against property,* the sub-division for the *control of drug trafficking* and six relevant departments/units (1987),[33] the sub-division for *economic crimes, illegal trafficking in antiquities* and *crimes against morality,* the latter two having their own separate departments (department for illicit trade in antiquities and a vice department), the sub-division for the *protection of juveniles* etc., are independent dealing with particular crimes and they are not obliged to seek approval for an operation. They themselves organise their work according to their needs and their information. However, they do have to announce their activities to the authority in charge, namely either to the Directorate or to the Sub-Division. The same applies with the coastguard and its special squads. Their activities are guided and supervised by the directorate in charge, even though, in the area of their responsibility, they maintain autonomy and coordinate their activities with other forces, whenever this is needed.

*Multidisciplinary Integrated Teams*
Cooperation and information exchange for controlling organised crime have been attained in the multi-disciplinary integrated teams, as defined in Recommendation 20 of the Action Plan (1997). However, apart from the SODN and the Money Laundering Committee, no other multi-disciplinary teams have been created. Other forms of such groups operating are not permanent, but are constituted on an ad hoc basis whenever there is a need to face problems from a multi-disciplinary point of view. For example, for the control of illicit drug trafficking or illegal immigration, meetings are held of all the authorities involved, namely: the Ministries of Public Order, of Health and Social Welfare, of Justice, of Foreign Affairs, as well as of other

governmental (i.e. Organisation against Narcotics, OKANA) or non-governmental organisations (i.e. for refugees).

The work group established in the MPO to combat economic crime has a rather stable character, following the suggestion of the General Secretariat of Interpol to all national police forces and credit financing organisations. The police assemble this group, as soon as an increase in counterfeit bank notes in the market has been noticed.

A group was established in the MPO for the creation of a database for the control of fraud involving false identification papers, such as passports, driving licenses, or even consular visas, as well as credit card fraud, etc. because of the special interest of many ministries on the issue. Changes in the hierarchy of ELAS last year (2000) however affected its operations. Representatives of the relevant ministries – of the Interior, of Transport and Communications, of Justice, of Foreign Affairs, of Health and Social Welfare, of Finance, of Industry and Development –, and interested institutions, such as the Association of Greek Banks, the Association of Insurance Companies, of Notaries and car rental companies participate. Stolen identification certificates and other lost official personal documents would be registered in the databank.

The MPO has also initiated the creation of the National Criminological Archive, specifically, a central databank which will include information concerning criminal acts and the personal data of offenders, providing on-line information to all linked regional directorates and stations. The databank will operate using specified regulations concerning the access and the evaluation of information. *The initiative stems mainly from the need to meet the requirements of Europol and other international organisations for a quick and reliable registration of information.* In September 2001 the Archive was operating experimentally, with "fictitious" data, as it was referred to. In any case, the databank will be fully functional, using specified regulations concerning the access and the evaluation of information until the Olympic games in 2004, unless problems are detected in the system.

Some small databases for money laundering, stolen cars, identification documents, etc. are currently operating in the Ministry, but the anticipated database is expected to fill the gaps. The delay and hesitation in the creation of such a database may be rooted in recent political history, when, following the civil war of 1945-50, information on the political convictions and personal data of a great number of citizens were kept for decades.

There are direct links between these multi-disciplinary groups, the coordination body and the central contact point for planing the relevant policy. If the case is of international interest, such as with the creation of a national databank of criminological information, the DDAS with its bureaux, NCB Interpol,

Europol or SIRENE, participate in supporting the system. If the case is of purely national interest, such as the creation of a local database, then the Directorate of Public or State Security is authorised.

## 5.2 Inter-regional, Euregional, EU and International cooperation

### 5.2.1 Inter-regional, Euregional cooperation

Although significant organisational changes have not been carried out in the law enforcement agencies, a growth in intensive inter-regional cooperation has been observed, not only among similar services but among diverse ones as well. For example, since the creation of "police cells" at the end of the 1990s in each regional police directorate for the analysis of organised crime, the efforts of inter-regional cooperation seem to have reached beyond the operational level. In addition, the leadership of the MPO has advised that there should be close cooperation between the police and the other law enforcement agencies, namely the coastguard and the customs service, and there are several examples of success because of this cooperation. Moreover, new bodies such as the Financial and Economic Crime Office (SDOE) or the Anti-Drug Coordination Unit (SODN) require and facilitate interregional cooperation.

Euregional programmes for cooperation with EU Member States have not been developed, since Greece has no common landborders with them, except Italy. Besides, the cooperation with third countries – although necessary – is difficult, because of the special conditions which apply to these cooperative agreements (i.e. the degree of corruption present in these countries). In addition, despite the signing of cooperation protocols with some, such as Albania, it is noted that they do not supply assistance on an "extended time basis". The coastguard states that even in the "controlled deliveries", the role of those countries is not clear. Satisfactory cooperation exists only with Cyprus. So, it can be said that reforms resulting from practical cross-border cooperation, especially from the bottom up, have not taken place.

However, some Euregional programmes for cooperation between law enforcement agencies to control organised crime have been developed, such as the "Southeast Cooperative Initiative". This is a programme for the creation of a database, which supports the interchange of information between the countries of southeastern Europe concerning organised crime. Another case of regional cooperation is that with the "Organisation for Cooperation with the Black Sea Countries", which foresees mutual technical assistance for training in the prevention of money laundering, as well as exchange of experience.

Furthermore, except for the control of drug trafficking, Greek law enforcement agencies support cooperation with the relevant agencies in adjacent countries in fighting several other forms of transnational crime, such as car thefts, trafficking in stolen cars, alcohol/contraband, etc. Since 1999, regular meetings of the Greek and Albanian police have been convened, during which there has mainly been an exchange of information on problems and issues concerning organised crime; some cases were solved on the spot. According to officials, in order to confront organised crime, the Greek police try to cooperate as closely as they can with countries with which they have signed bilateral agreements mainly for the prevention of money laundering and drug trafficking, such as with the USA, Italy, Tunisia, Bulgaria, Romania, Albania, Hungary, Russia, Poland, Cyprus, Slovenia, Croatia, China, Israel, Latvia and Armenia.[34]

The customs services cooperate with neighbouring countries on the basis of bilateral agreements, while some separate forms of cooperation at a regional level are also carried out. The same applies to the SDOE and coastguard. So, there is a form of cooperation and exchange of experience with other adjacent Balkan countries, however, not at a central level and only in an ad hoc way.

### 5.2.2   EU and International cooperation

Since Greece, as already mentioned, does not have common borders with other EU countries, the most important forms of cooperation between its law enforcement agencies and services specialised in the fight against organised crime and the other EU Member States are horizontal, consisting of meetings, exchanges of personnel, experience and information, as well as ad hoc cooperation. This is also the case with the working structures of Europol and Interpol. Information exchange is carried out through SIS, and through the Information Systems of Europol and Interpol. Bilateral information networks between Greece and other countries of the EU do not exist.

Although the Mediterranean countries do not have identical bodies, the coastguard has developed contacts and cooperation with similar corps such as those in Spain, but mainly with the *Guardia di Finanza* in Italy. In general, it cooperates mostly with the customs services and the police of foreign countries and of EU member states (i.e. inspection of the cargoes of ships sailing in Greek waters for stolen cars, drug trafficking, etc., in association with the inspection of freight trains and air transport).

The customs services cooperate with the customs services of the EU member countries and with third countries when there is a bipartite agreement. They have signed the Naples II Agreement, regulating the mutual assistance between the customs authorities of EU member states, as well as other special forms of cooperation, such as, "hot pursuit" and "continuous surveillance".[35] They are also connected with CIS, SCENT, and information systems of the customs services of the EU member states for contraband and fraud. Responsibility for the management of the system on the part of Greece goes to the 33rd Directorate for Customs Controls. The customs services also participate in MARINFO, a programme of the European Union for the Mediterranean countries concerning cargo inspections for drugs and goods contraband (alcohol, cigarettes, etc.). After all, the necessity for operational programmes in the Mediterranean Sea and for the strengthening of the role of the Hellenic Coastguard needs to be pointed out, since opportunities for criminal groups at sea are much easier to exploit than in the air or on land.

The customs services and the coastguard have jointly appointed representatives to the SIRENE Bureau, and participate in the Schengen work group for drug trafficking, as well as in the common operations which have been organised in the context of the Agreement. The customs services have created special investigation teams for the fight against organised crime. In addition, they participate in all operations of the European Union for the control of transnational crime and the strengthening of cross-border controls. Such is the case with common operations of the Member States for overland transport controls, as well as sea and air, whether regular (four per year) or extraordinary. The majority of bilateral agreements of customs services also include the SDOE, which as a new body has not had time to liaise with other respective EU bodies.

The SDOE, for its part, participates in European Union operations, as well as in the context of Europol and the Schengen Agreements; it participates also in the Naples II Agreement (see above). Furthermore, the Bureau of Mutual Administrative Assistance, the link between Member States of the EU, international organisations and third countries with the Central Service of SDOE and the regional divisions of the office, assists the better cooperation of the Financial and Economic Crime Office.[36] The SDOE participates in the Money Laundering Committee and in the SODN (Anti-Drug Coordination Unit), so cooperation with the financial units of other EU countries is achieved in this way, if not directly. As regards Europol, Schengen and Interpol issues, it cooperates with the Directorate of International Police Cooperation (the DDAS) and the customs services, as well as with the help of its liaison officers appointed to the bodies of the EU.

The SODN cooperates with other countries in "controlled deliveries" examining the legitimacy of their requests and coordinating their operations in the Greek territory.

The Greek police have not yet established any special contacts with OLAF, although the customs services and the SDOE do cooperate with them. Furthermore, the customs services have appointed a liaison officer to the headquarters of Europol in The Hague.

The Money Laundering Committee is in touch with and also exchanges information and cooperates with respective foreign institutions (Article 7 par. 1, PD 401/1996, Article 7 par. 9, Law 2331/1995). It is also planned that the committee will be able to authorise its members to participate in meetings with other foreign institutions for issues concerning its brief, in order to further improve its cooperation with other countries.

## 6. EU AND INTERNATIONAL CONTACT POINTS

A *new* **Coordination Body**, foreseen by Recommendation 1 of the Action Plan for the Fight Against Organised Crime, has not yet been created, and is unlikely to be established. However this role was fulfilled by two and from 2001 by three services: the Public Security Directorate (hereinafter referred to as DDA), the State Security Directorate (hereinafter referred to as DKA) and lately (2001) the Directorate for Aliens (hereinafter referred to as DA) of the Ministry of Public Order, whose responsibility includes illegal migration, relating also to criminal networks.[37] The Directorates are under the same "Branch of Security and Order Police", supervised by the Deputy-Chief and the General Inspector of the Greek police. According to high-ranking police officers, because organised crime has several appearances (crimes against the constitution: i.e. terrorism, involving the inter-state and international relations, such as illegal immigration), is better investigated and fought either by the DDA or the DKA, as well as the DA respectively; hence, no new coordination body has been created.

In summary, as stated, coordination to confront organised crime has been undertaken at a central level by the three directorates of the Ministry of Public Order, which have under their guidance and control all the police directorates of the country and the operational squads belonging to them (Order and Security Departments, the Department for the Control of Drug Trafficking, special units, etc.).

The coordination and the exchange of information about organised crime, and other issues, at an international level are in the hands of the DDAS, while especially for cases concerning Drugs, the Central Anti-Drug Coordination Unit (SODN) operates as the national contact point with Europol.

The DDAS is charged with the role of **central contact point**, since a new service with that function has not been created. Besides, it is operating as a national centre that provides information to foreign law enforcement agencies on national legislation, jurisdiction and procedures (as foreseen by Recommendation 19 of the EU Action Plan on Organised Crime). The DDAS has existed since 1984 and includes the Department of International Organisations which is the NCB Interpol, the Department of European

Union-Europol, the SIRENE Department, and lately (Article 9, PD 14/2001) the Department of International Relations, Missions and Delegations.

The Department of the European Union (Article 25, PD 582/1984, Article 9, PD 14/2001) deals with the EU on issues of justice and home affairs, such as illegal immigration, asylum, etc. Moreover, it prepares the participation of the Minister of Public Order in the Council of Ministers of Justice and Home Affairs, provides the information requested by the EU member states concerning national legislation, and coordinates the participation of law enforcement agencies in EU programmes (i.e. ODYSSEUS, SHERLOCK, OISIN, FALCONE, etc.). Although Greece ratified the Europol Convention with Law 2605/1998, only recently (2001) created the national Europol Unit due to a disagreement of law enforcement agencies that would assume the authority of the Unit.

The SIRENE Bureau has been operating since December 1997 and is supervised by the Head of the DDAS. 25 officers staff the Bureau, the majority of who are policemen, while the rest of them are customs civil servants and coastguard officers.

The NCB Interpol has been in operation since 1953, and is staffed by 50 police officers. Due to a lack of personnel, the coastguard is neither represented in the NCB Interpol nor in the Department of the European Union of the DDAS. However, it stays in direct contact with them through the requests to other countries.

According to Presidential Decree (14/31.1.2001) effecting the new Department of International Relations, Missions and Delegations this works towards police cooperation with other countries, the exchange of information, knowledge, the implementation of police conventions, as well as the support and evaluation of the police personnel working in Greek embassies, in international organisations operating in crisis situations etc. It must also be taken into account that the DDAS offers other services except for acting as the national contact point for cooperation with foreign law enforcement agencies, as it relates to the social function of the police such as in the search for the missing persons.

The DDAS is also the contact point for foreign law enforcement agencies *with the coordination body* and vice versa. When foreign law enforcement agencies have a request, they address it to the DDAS who then transmits it to the relevant Directorate (i.e. when it concerns terrorism to the State Security Directorate, when it concerns illegal immigration, to the Directorate of Aliens, when it refers to stolen cars, to the Public Security Directorate, and when it refers to drugs, to the SODN). These directorates then coordinate the activities by transmitting the request to the operational agencies.

Cooperation between the national contact point, i.e. the DDAS, and the other three Directorates of Public and State Security as well as the Foreigners

Directorate is close, since all are under the same security and order branch of the police, and their relationship is horizontal (Articles 14 and 23, PD 582/1984, Article 3 par. 5, PD 14/2001). The DDAS coordinates the exchange of information and its transmission to the central service in charge.

## 7. INFORMATION EXCHANGE OF LAW ENFORCEMENT AGENCIES WITH OTHER BODIES AND SERVICES

The **National Intelligence Service** (NIS; Legislative Decree 2421/1953, Law 1645/1986) is also involved in the control of organised crime but it mainly focuses on terrorism and cases concerning the relations between Greece and other countries. It is an independent civil service, the Governor of which is directly answerable to the Minister of Interior, Public Administration and Decentralisation. The service is responsible for collection and processing information concerning state security, and coordinating all the information services of the state. So it depends on the information and the evaluation of its significance as to whether it is shared with the police, which is the main body for communication with NIS. However, in general, it cooperates with the Greek police, transmitting information concerning crimes which come to its attention during the exercise of its duties to the Directorate of Public or State Security respectively.

With specific regard to organised crime, there are no formal or informal arrangements for the exchange of information between public police bodies and **private sector security providers.** A detail that should be mentioned is that, just in 1997, the law defined the formal requirements for satisfying operating permits for such companies, along with their obligations (2518/1997). The supervision and control of these companies belong to the competent law enforcement agencies (local cooperation). The owners of the security companies are obliged to comply with the instructions of the police and to assist, if they are asked, in cases.

The customs authorities do not have any cooperation arrangements with security companies. However, it is relevant to point out that the customs services have signed a "Memorandum of Understanding" with some commercial associations to exchange information and prevent illicit drug trafficking, such as with the Baltic and International Maritime Council (BIMCO) and the Association of Chemical Industries of Greece. The coast-guard too has signed the Memorandum with BIMCO; however, this is not the case with the SDOE.

No kind of agreement exists with **multinational companies** who operate in "trouble spots" and make use of "risks assessors" and "security consultants" in order to better protect their assets and personnel. However, it is worth mentioning the case of *protection and insurance clubs* (P & I Clubs). These are organisations which insure ships' cargoes when they have to make a hazardous voyage such as in hostile or dangerous regions (i.e. Persian Golf, Colombia, etc.) and when the carried goods are at risk of either being stolen or destroyed. The P & I Clubs sometimes permit the coastguard access to the Lloyds' list they maintain, which contains the identification of the ships, their activities, ownership, etc. There are also no relevant arrangements with **Internet providers**. However, the interviewed officers from the coastguard and the SDOE have emphasised the need for such cooperation.

## 8. ACCOUNTABILITY

### 8.1 Internal Control of law enforcement agencies

All law enforcement agencies are accountable to a dual system of control, internal and external. The Chief of the Police, the Vice-Commander and the General Inspector in the form of inspections, as well as the Service of Internal Affairs carries out internal control in the police. The inspections have to verify the legitimacy of the activities and operations of the agencies, the state of the relations between the heads of the services and personnel, as well as their degree of readiness and effectiveness. The inspections are performed by high-ranking police officers.[38]

The **Service of Internal Affairs** is a new agency created for the investigation and prosecution of crimes committed by policemen, referred to particularly in Law 2713/1999 (Article 1 par. 2). It is under the direct authority of the Chief of Greek police and it is staffed by police officers distinguished for their integrity, effectiveness and dedication. Article 10 of the law provides the Minister of Public Order with the right to demand, from the Minister of Justice, what information is held by the competent public prosecutor as regards any sworn data from a special administrative inquiry for the relevant offences.

Despite Public Order Ministry statements in its 1997 Annual Report on Organised Crime that there was no probative evidence of corruption and bribery of governmental civil servants, at central or local levels, nor of any undermining of the activities of businessmen,[39] in 1999, the Ministry set up the Service of Internal Affairs to combat corruption in the police along US lines (Law 2713/1999).[40] The arrests of police officers in November 1998, because of their involvement in prostitution rings, as well as in other cases revealed from time to time by the police and published by the media, have shown that the situation was more serious than had been admitted. It must be pointed out that although Greek penal law contains anti-corruption provisions, the creation of a new law befitting its symbolic function is preferred in order to stress its importance and the will of the police authorities to fight the problem.[41]

Apart from the creation of the Service of Internal Affairs, the policemen are obliged to submit, in addition to the usual annual income declaration, an extra declaration to the Chief Public Prosecutor (Article 7 par. 1, Law 2622/1998) just as the members of the parliament do. Furthermore, according to the "Disciplinary Law of Police Personnel" (PD 22/1996), penal offences relating to the fulfilment of the duties of the police officers result in their dismissal from the agency (Article 9 par. 1f and 1g). The Service of Internal Affairs, the declaration of additional income and the new regulation of the Disciplinary Law of Police Personnel, although internal mechanisms of control, comprise also elements of external control.

The **Marine Chief and the two Vice-Commanders supervise the coastguard**. Coastguard officers are not judged for disciplinary and criminal offences associated with their duties by the usual penal courts, as are policemen, but by Naval Courts. The role of the public prosecutor remains the same, specified by the Code of Penal Procedure, the Special Penal Laws and the Code for the Organisation of Courts (Law 1756/1988).

The relevant official or disciplinary council supervises the **customs services**, in issues concerning their official duties and infractions. Complaints or suspicions of corruption are investigated by Economic Inspectors. According to their findings, the suspect may be referred to the disciplinary council.

The same applies to the servants of the **SDOE**; they are supervised by the official or disciplinary council coming from either the customs service or the Taxation Office (Article 4 par. 11, Law 2343/1995) and by the Economic Inspectors. The Economic Inspection Service has similar competences to the Service of Internal Affairs of the Police (Article 2, Law 2343/1995).

All officials responsible for the investigation of crimes (policemen, coastguard officers, the Money Laundering Committee, customs services officials and the SDOE officials) are obliged to refer to the public prosecutor all information they receive on a criminal offence without delay, otherwise they are disciplined.

## 8.2 External Control of law enforcement agencies

External control is exercised by the *parliament* (through questions, reports, etc.), which is generally responsible for the supervision of activities and authorisations given by the ministers to the relevant *bodies* and *services*, and by the Parliamentary Inquiry Committee. From time to time the Greek parliament has been occupied by the police financing criminal informers – a functioning for which the parliament had neither access to information nor any control over – and with the activities of the National Intelligence Service, but on most occasions the issues have been quickly by-passed.[42]

The competent Minister of each law enforcement authority exerts political control, while the Chief of the Corps exerts a regular/permanent control. In any event, the Minister of Justice has the right to order prosecutions in respect to any particular offence (Article 30 par. 1 CPP).

Furthermore, as regards the privacy of communications and the danger of law enforcement agencies, as well as of private companies and third parties violating this, the *National Board for the Protection of Communication Privacy* was created on the basis of Law 2225/1994. The board is composed of representatives of the parliamentary parties, the Vice-President of the Parliament as head of the committee and a qualified scientist (Article 1 par. 3, Law 2225/1994).

It grants permission for the lifting of secrecy (Article 19 of the Greek Constitution) for reasons of national security (Article 3 par. 1, Law 2225/1994) and for the investigation of certain felonies (Article 4, Law 2225/1994) after gaining permission from either the public prosecutor or from the Judicial Committee of First or Second Instance, depending on the seriousness of the crime (Article 4 par. 5, 6, Law 2225/1994).

According to its recent report (1998), although the legal framework for the protection of privacy in communications is sufficient, this is not the case for technical measures. The system needs permanent technical assistance and to be constantly updated in respect of technological developments, while the legislators must always be aware of the risks.[43]

The *National Ombudsman* (Articles 1-5, Law 2477/1997) has competence, for the investigation of administrative oversights or operations of public services violating the rights or infringing upon the legal interests of persons or institutions, police officers included. However, he does not deal with cases concerning state security, national defence or pending lawsuits. The ombudsman investigates the submitted petition, composes a report, informs the competent minister and services relevant to the case, and mediates a solution to the problem. If it is found from investigations that the public servant violated the law, the ombudsman submits the report to the competent authority, requesting the disciplinary prosecution of the servant or he can resort to other measures if the public servant cannot be subjected to disciplinary control (Article 4 par. 9, Law 2477/1997). However, if sufficient evidence turns up, then he transmits the report to the competent public prosecutor (Article 4 par. 10).[44]

The Ombudsman was established on 1 October 1998. According to the

Annual Reports for 1998 and 1999, the cases that concerned the police mainly referred to violations of personal freedom (i.e. lengthy investigations by the Security Directorate of Police into the "morals and character" of a foreigner when processing applications for Greek citizenship and an identity card).[45] However, as already emphasised, the ombudsman as well as the Inspectors-Controllers Body for Public Administration – both instituted by the same Law (Articles 6-10) – whose objective is to improve the effectiveness of public administration and the quality of services provided by it (i.e. state insurance organisations, hospitals, police stations, etc.),[46] do not examine cases relating to foreign policy, national defence or state security.

The second form of external control for the law enforcement agencies is *judicial control*, since, especially for the police the investigation of criminal cases is carried out under judicial supervision and the administrative directorship of the Public Prosecution Service (Article 9, Law 1756/1988). In general, the activities of the police are under the control of the judicial authorities as regulated by the Constitution (Article 95) and Greek Law.

If disciplinary offences committed by policemen are associated with their judicial duties, the public prosecutor is responsible for starting prosecution. However, according to our information this has rarely been used. The relationship between the judicial and police authorities is regulated by Article 9 of Law 1756/1988, which states that the agencies which have general (police and coastguard) or special investigation duties (the Money Laundering Committee, customs services and the SDOE) are obliged, immediately and in a forthright manner, to carry out the instructions of the judicial authority, to provide assistance to it and to facilitate the enforcement of its public office. The Prosecutors, however, regard the general supervision of the police (cf. Article 9, Law 1756/1988) from their side as insufficient, because of the work pressure.

The *General Secretaries of the Districts* exercise a form of external control too. They are high-ranking governmental officials coordinating state policies in the 13 administrative districts of Greece. The other control body is the Prefecture-Police Committee, which operates in the 53 prefectures of the country. It consists of a judge, serving in the prefecture, representatives of the local authorities and the Police Director of the Prefecture.[47] The committee decides on the measures which have to be enforced in urgent cases (i.e. fires, earthquakes etc.).

285

### 8.3 Supervision and Control of Pro-active Investigation techniques

For the fight against organised crime, Greece has introduced pro-active investigation techniques. Several legal provisions concern authorisation procedures for national law enforcement agencies in the use of such methods. According to Article 38 of Law 2145/1993, as amended by Article 15 par. 1 of Law 2331/1995, the "controlled delivery" of drugs is permitted, on information from the competent public prosecutor. In this case, although the public prosecutor is obliged by Greek Law to bring a charge, as well as in any other case which constitutes a criminal offence, he refrains so that the offenders can be arrested (Articles 43 par. 1, 47 CPP, cf. indicatively Articles 44, 45 CPP).

Requests to Greek law enforcement agencies for controlled deliveries must be made to the SODN or to NCB Interpol, which transmits the request to the SODN, so as to examine the origin and the legitimacy of the demand. A prerequisite is that the applying state ensures the surveillance of the delivery and the possibility of arrest of the offenders; in addition, the identification of the foreign police escort is necessary.

According to Article 21 of Law 2161/1993 (amended Article 24 of Law 1729/1987), the prosecution of a drug-dealer, importer, producer or producer's assistant is suspended (Article 5, Law 1729/1987) if he has contributed, on his own initiative, to the detection or dislocation of the criminal drug trafficking group, and he fulfils certain criteria, namely, that he is not recidivist, a career criminal, or the crime(s) he committed is not associated with his profession, etc. (see Article 8 par. 1, Law 1729/1987, amended by Article 2 par. 15 b, Law 2479/1997, Article 6 par. 1, Law 1729/1987, amended by Article 11, Law 2161/1993).

**Undercover activities** were at first regulated for police officers, coastguard members, customs officers, and recently for the SDOE officers who, operating on the orders of their superiors, would present themselves as interested purchasers of drugs, so that the offenders could be detected and arrested (Article 25b, Law 1729/1987, added to by Article 22 of Law 2161/1993, and by Article 33 par. 3, Law 2648/1998).

The abovementioned article 25b has been widened with a recent regulation (Article 5, Law 2713/1999), which allows for the non-prosecution of a policeman, or "other persons", who, following the order of the Head of the Internal Affairs Service and with concurrence of the public prosecutor, acts as an accomplice to specific crimes (i.e. crimes against property, against life, concerning drugs, contraband, trafficking in human beings, illicit trade in antiquities, etc., Article 1 par. 2a and 2b) for the detection and dislocation of the engaged criminal group(s). Especially in relation to drugs, the undercover operations of the police officer are not restricted to acting as a purchaser, but also as an accomplice in these activities or facilitating them. This is also the case for other law enforcement agencies and third persons as far as drug trafficking is concerned. In any case, the cooperation of the public prosecutor must be obtained (Article 25b, Law 1729/1987, added to by Article 22 of Law 2161/1993, and by Article 33, par. 3, Law 2648/1998). The necessary protection is offered to policemen who operate under these orders. The same applies to "other persons" who have been ordered to carry out such duties, however, only if this order is requested by the public prosecutor. The law does not give more details on protection (Article 5 par. 5, Law 2713/1999).[48]

Although rarely, police or customs officers presenting themselves as an interested purchaser have been used for many years in cases of the illicit trade in antiquities (Laws 2674/1921, 5351/1932, 1103/1980, see also European Regulations 752/1993, 2469/1996, 3911/1999). Moreover, witness-protection measures have been introduced informally in a few cases before 2001 when the new provisions for the fight against organised crime were issued (2928/2001), with the agreement of the public prosecutor and under the responsibility of the police officer with competence for the person who facilitated the dislocation of an (organised) criminal network or the detection and arrest of an offender.

In general, the Code of Penal Procedure gives the law enforcement agencies the authority to use the most appropriate method for the processing of the crime during its investigation, on the approval of the public prosecutor. However, probative evidence that has been obtained illegally is not taken into consideration in the prosecution, sentencing or enforcement of coercive measures, except of a felony punishable by a life sentence. Only the competent court in the case of such a felony decides upon the admissibility of illegally obtained evidence (Article 177 par. 2 CPP).

Moreover, according to Article 6 par. 1 and 2 of Law 2713/1999, the privacy of every kind of communication, as well as of bank and other monetary transactions, can be overridden with the approval of the Judicial Committee of Second Instance, submitted by the public prosecutor, either on his own initiative or at the request of the Head of the Service of Internal Affairs. This article extends the lifting of privacy provided for in Law 2225/1994, as far as monetary transactions are concerned. Besides, unlike the previous regulation, the Judicial Committee of Second Instance is responsible for approving this action and not the Judicial Committee of First Instance. In the same way, the impounding of a suspect's property can be ordered (Article 6 par. 3).

With Article 6 par. 4, the use of electronic surveillance and the material gained through such activities as probative evidence is permissible in court and by any other public authority. Although physical surveillance is not regulated, it is obvious that it can be employed legally since electronic interception has become a legitimate means of surveillance.

In the past, there was a legal prohibition on all forms of surveillance, including physical surveillance, even in the period of the dictatorship. Now the public prosecutor can, on his own accord or on the request of the Head of the Service of Internal Affairs, ask permission of the Judicial Committee of Second Instance for the electronic surveillance of a suspect. In "extremely urgent" cases, he himself can order the surveillance (Article 6 par. 4, Law 2713/1999).

As concerns informers, it is worth mentioning that the only service with the legal provision to use informers is the customs services for contraband and drug trafficking, by old Ministerial Decrees (614/25-1-1968 and 2070/24-4-1985). However, the regulation of their use is very complicated, firstly, because the submission of the supplied information to the court cannot be anonymous, so the informer can be called to testify. Secondly, because the Minister of Finance must approve the granting of a reward after the operation, and, what is more, it is very low. To avoid these complications, the customs services ask the public prosecutor to give them the order to investigate information and evidence from an "anonymous source". In any event, informers are used occasionally in controlled deliveries, and after being screened for reliability. The coastguard makes use of the same decrees for informers as well. What must also be taken into consideration is that, according to the Greek Code of Penal Procedure (Article 224) the witness must reveal the source of her/his information, otherwise her/his testimony is not taken into account. Other special techniques used by the Hellenic Coastguard in its operations are controlled deliveries, surveillance and officers presenting themselves as purchasers for drugs, after the approval of the public prosecutor, and in "hot pursuit" of drugs.

As we have been informed, a system of electronic surveillance for controlling contraband and drug trafficking in cargoes, freight and another forms of transport has been designed in cooperation with OLAF. It remains to seen who will be entrusted with the management of the system.

The Greek police were not very forthcoming concerning the use of informers. Reference to them was made in an old regulation of the gendarmerie.

The SDOE participates in controlled deliveries, as do the other law enforcement agencies, and makes use of pro-active techniques as they relate to its duties (mainly in the detection of drug trafficking), on the approval of the public prosecutor (Article 25b, Law 2161/1993, Article 33 par. 3, Law 2648/1998).

The new Electronic Analysis Section in the Criminological Laboratory of the Ministry of Public Order is intended for the training of police in dealing with electronic criminality. Until now, investigations have been carried out concerning some types of electronic criminality, e.g. child pornography on the Internet, as well as offences related to faxed documents. The Section has the technical cooperation of other criminological services and private enterprises in the area, thus improving the skills of its personnel and meeting the demands of technological development.

In summary, all pro-active methods (controlled deliveries, under-cover activities, lifting restrictions to ensure the privacy of communication and the use of electronic surveillance) need the permission of the Judicial Committee of Second Instance or, in "extremely urgent" cases, that of the competent public prosecutor, otherwise probative evidence which has been obtained illegally is not taken into consideration in the prosecution or sentencing. The same control framework applies to the new provisions for the "protection of citizens from illegal activities of criminal organisations", namely Law (2928/2001) combating organised crime, referred to above.

## 8.4 Supervision of EU instruments

As far as the supervision of the services foreseen by the EU instruments is concerned, this is firstly, official, secondly, in relation to the exchange and the security of information, and thirdly, judicial.

a) SIRENE, NCB Interpol, the National Europol Unit are supervised by the Head of the Directorate of International Police Cooperation (the DDAS), by the Head of the Branch (of Security and Order Police), by the General Inspector and the deputy-Chief of the police. The Head of the Department to which they belong supervises the remaining instruments, operational groups and services.

b) The National Data Protection Supervisory Board (Law 2472/1997) exercises supervision, as regards the exchange and security of information, especially that used by the SIRENE Bureau and the SIS.

The National Data Protection Supervisory Board was established in 1997 with Law 2472 (Articles 15,16). It is the competent body for providing permission to the DDAS to use and exchange information concerning personal data with the law enforcement agencies of other states or for reasons associated with the exercise of public authority (Article 5 par. 2b). It is also competent to give permission, as already mentioned, to any public service or private enterprise for the creation of electronic bases with personal data. The granted permission is restricted to the processing of personal data. "Sensitive data" can only be made accessible for reasons of national security and criminal justice policy (Article 7 par. 2e). The permission is personal, for reasons of responsibility, and for a specific time-period. The applying service defines the goal for the creation of the database or for the processing of information, as well as the kind of personal data that will be processed, the final recipients of the information, the basic characteristics of the system used, the eventual destinations, as well as the reasons for transmission of the information to third countries (Article 6 par. 2).[49]

The authorised person faces disciplinary sanctions if he violates its terms as well as penal prosecution for operating a database without the permission of the Board, for linking files illegally (file-linking), for illegal intervention, for altering, removing, destroying personal data, or making them available to unauthorised persons. He is also responsible for monetary compensation in the case of causing damage to property (Article 23).[50]

For the special services of the other law enforcement agencies (coastguard, SDOE and customs services) the general rules already mentioned apply. Especially concerning the Unit of Submarine Missions and the special squads of the Hellenic Coastguard, the Department of Special Units of the Directorate of Operational Means and special units exercise their supervision.

c) Furthermore, although these special units and services do not have corresponding structures because of their different needs, all their judicial duties are supervised by public prosecutors, especially in cases of international cooperation (i.e. Article 436 CPP concerning extradition). Moreover, in the SIRENE Bureau, a public prosecutor is always available. The NCB Interpol is a "pure" police agency. In the SIRENE Bureau, customs officers, coastguard members, as well as policemen participate, and eventually, officers of the SDOE will do so also. The operations and competences of the bureaux sometimes coincide (such as in the case of the arrest and extradition of an offender). What is more, this is why they reside under the same Directorate of International Police Cooperation.

## 9. THE RATIONALE, THE ACCEPTANCE, AND THE EFFECTIVENESS OF THE REFORMS

Although not all, however many organisational reforms have been realised. For those that have been carried out the main reasons are, in my opinion, the influence of the European Union and the international commitments of the country. It is also worth mentioning that wherever this influence has been significant and cooperation close, such as with FATF, – although this is an international organisation – and the creation of the Money Laundering Committee, the reform is carried out and not avoided through the use of half-measures. However, the pressure of the facts at the time the measures were adopted cannot be underestimated. Such is the case with the illegal acquisition of Greek citizenship by people from the ex-Soviet Union, which resulted in the creation of a special group in the police to confront the problem, developed in a sub-division after a while upgrading its authority to the organised criminal activities in general. Members of criminal organisations operating in Russia and other republics took advantage of the opening of the borders. They presented false documents at the Greek Consulate and managed to obtain identity cards and ordinary passports, so as to facilitate the extension of their illegal activities to Greece. Moreover, the creation of the Border Guards Corps was due to the massive inflow of illegal immigrants mainly from Albania. According to the registered number of expulsions, between 1990 and 1996, 1,147,048 Albanians crossed the Greek borders, which correspond to an average of 191,175 per year, or 523 each day.

The officers interviewed reported that the majority of the reforms would be carried out even without urging from the European Union, since they are regarded as necessary for an improvement in the effectiveness of the police. The Recommendations of the EU Action Plan on organised crime are considered very useful concerning the coordination of European countries in the fight against organised crime, as well as the creation of specialised services and units.

Moreover, the spread of organised crime has motivated law enforcement agencies to realise the necessity for cooperation for its better prevention, by exchanging information, experience and knowledge, as well as common operations. This implies that Greece's obligations to the EU have made it more aware of the problem of transnational criminal activities and pressed it to take measures, as happened with the new Law 2928/2001.

According to our information, it seems that there were no objections or reservations in the police concerning the main aim of the reforms, except the creation of a coordination body. The case for the central contact point is rather different because of the unique existence of the Directorate of International Police Cooperation. On the contrary, the necessity for the re-organisation, modernisation and coordination of law enforcement agencies to confront organised crime in a timely way was endorsed. Although the pro-active measures issued in the Law that established the Service of Internal Affairs have rarely been criticised,[51] this is not the case for the same measures instituted by the recent regulations to combat organised crime.

Concerning the creation of specific new services to confront organised criminal activities, and especially in finance, reservations have been expressed over their real need, and their high cost, since their objectives were assumed to have been covered already by other existing services or units.

It is difficult to assess the effectiveness since no official evaluations are available and the undertaken measures are relative new. It has also been pointed out that the technical improvements in the organisation and equipment of the agencies (i.e. the creation of qualified databanks) may increase the possibilities in locating offenders, but it would be very difficult to affect the commitment of crimes (i.e. passport-thefts).

Because of Greece's geographical position, the best climate for reforms would be close cooperation with the other EU member states and for Greece to be entrusted with duties, in addition to close monitoring, evaluation and being responsible for deadlines for different tasks. For the future, it may be interesting and useful for the active involvement of Greece in the fight against transnational criminal activities that some agencies, like the customs officers, regard their "prestige" as having been upgraded because they operate as officers of the European Union.

Hence, we can conclude that international and European cooperation crucially influences Greek law enforcement agencies. This applies primarily at a legal and procedural level, secondly at an organisational one and, to a much lesser extent, at an epistemological level. Moreover, the influence of the European Union concerns training and expertise. It also includes financial support for the country in improving its technical equipment especially for the control of borders.

In the future, the most significant development for Greece will be the convergence of procedures and legislation in specific criminal matters (i.e. drugs). It may thus be expected that police cooperation will be improved, and that judicial cooperation will be promoted, since it is far behind the former. The European judicial network would be also helpful for the police, since the procedures would be simplified (i.e. extradition). However, because Greece tends to be slow not in issuing but in implementing new legislation, frequent control and a time-schedule for the enforcement of decisions has been proved until now effective and useful.

**NOTES**

1. The information in this chapter has been updated since the completion of the original report in January 2000, and includes information up to September 2001.
2. Vasilakopoulos, P., "Money Laundering (critical remarks to Law 2331/1995)", *Penal Annals* 46 (1996), pp. 1361-1373, Giannopoulos, T., "Money Laundering (Article 394 PC)", in: *Penal Annals* 43 (1993), pp. 1238-1249.
3. Crime punishable by a 5 to 20-year prison sentence or by a life sentence (Article 52 PC).
4. Crime punishable by a 10-day to 5-year prison sentence (Article 53 PC).
5. ENFOPOL documents 35, rev. II and 161 rev. I.
6. *The Prevention and Control of Organised Crime,* CRIMORG 80 REV 4, 4.2.2000.
7. Ministry of Public Order, *Annual Report on Organised Crime (1995,1996),* Athens, 10 September 1997, p. 2.
8. Ministry of Public Order, *Annual Report for Organised Crime in Greece (1997),* Athens, May 1998, pp. 1,16.
9. Ministry of Public Order, *Annual Report for Organised Crime in Greece (1998),* Athens, May 1999, pp. 3, 38 ff., and *Annual Report for Organised Crime in Greece (1999),* Athens, May 2000, pp. 2 ff. Cf. also Kourakis, N., "Organised crime: Phenomenology of the problem and possibilities of its confrontation", *Penal Justice 2* (1999), pp. 1017-1026.
10. *Annual Report,* May 1999, p. 39.
11. *Annual Report,* May 2000, p. 2.
12. *Annual Report,* May 2000, op.cit., p. 3.
13. *Annual Report,* May 1999, p. 3.
14. MPO, *Annual Report,* May 1999, pp. 3, 38 f.
15. See, Ktenadis, N.E., *The Greek Gendarmerie. Historical Pages,* 2nd ed., w.p.c., Athens 1960, Antoniou, K.E., *History of Greek Royal Gendarmerie,* vol. 4., w.p.c., Athens 1965-1967.
16. See, Zianikas, C., *Police Today,* Estia: Athens 1990; *The Invisible Side of the Police,* Gnosi: Athens 1992; *Police System,* A. N. Sakkoulas: Athens, Komotini 1995; see also, Lambropoulou, E., *Crime Control,* Papazissis: Athens 1994, pp. 203-221.
17. MPO, Studies Directorate 15 October 1999, *Doc. 1016/36/23-a',* p. 2.
18. See Organograms in Annex 1a and Annex 1b.
19. See Organogram in Annex 1a.
20. See Organogram in Annex 2.
21. See Organogram in Annex 3.
22. Law 2343/1995, PD 218/1996, PD 154/1997. See Organogram in Annex 4.
23. Article 27 par. 1, Article 43 CPP, Article 20, Law 663/1977.
24. It must be taken into account that some *International* Contact Points, such as the Money Laundering Committee, also operate as *national* units, or as national units which have a coordinating role at national level and an operational one at *local* level, so there are both, national and local "units". In this respect, it is not

easy to make a clear distinction between international/national and national/local services.

25. See also, PD 139/1989, PD 126/1990.
26. Article 7, Law 2331/1995.
27. Law 2343/1995, PD 218/1996, PD 154/1997.
28. MPO, Directorate of Public Security (DDA) 30.1.1998, *Doc. 4915/35/2-a*, p. 5 f.
29. See Organogram in Annex 1b.
30. See Organogram in Annex 4.
31. MPO, *DDA Doc. 1998*, op.cit., p. 6.
32. MPO, *DDA Doc. 1998*, op.cit., p. 5.
33. Article 80, PD 582/1984, MD 7001/2/22.5.1987.
34. MPO, *DDA Doc. 1998*, op.cit., p. 7.
35. In October 1999, the operational groups of customs services participated in a common operation with the name "PURPLE", controlling the container-trucks for narcotics precursors.
36. *Annual Report* of SDOE 1998, p. 20.
37. See updated Organogram in Annex 1a.
38. MPO, Studies Directorate 1999, *Doc. 1016/36/23-a'*, pp. 15 ff.
39. MPO, *Annual Report on Organised Crime*, Athens 1997, p. 3.
40. Cf. State Department, *Drug Report*, 1997, p. 2.
41. The attempt of the new service to legitimise its existence is apparent from its "successes" in clearing about four cases of corruption in the (roughly) first two months of its operation, which were made known by the mass media (November, December 1999).
42. The mass media has lately alluded to the allocations in the state budget for 2000 for "informers" (not specifying whether for crime or for the National Intelligence Service), which have risen to 7 billion drachmas (nearly US$ 18,5 million).
43. *Annual Report* 1998, p. 22.
44. The national Ombudsman is an independent administrative service, not responsible to any governmental body or administrative authority. It is staffed by 80 public officials and qualified scientists. The Cabinet appoints the chief after the approval of the Transparency Committee of the Parliament, while the Minister of the Interior appoints the four assistants of the Ombudsman. The remaining members of the institution are assigned after the successful completion of an examination. The term of the Ombudsman and his/her assistants is five years, and not renewable, though for the other numbers it is renewable.
45. See *Annual Report 1998*, p. 31, *Annual Report* 1999, pp. 66 ff, 72 ff.
46. SEEDD, *Annual Report 1998*, National Printing Office, Athens, March 1999, p. 11, see also *Annual Reports* 1999, 2000.
47. MPO, DDA 1999, p. 19, without special Protocol No., referring to questions of Council of European Union (6602.15/10/AS181, 21 April 1999, 6600/20/AS1450, 30 December 1998) to the MPO.
48. See Anagnostopoulos, I., "Police infiltration and fair trial", *Penal Annals* 51 (2001), pp. 193-200.

49. The transmission of information concerning personal data for the EU countries is permitted by Article 9 par. 1a of Law 2472/1997.

50. The national data protection supervisory board consists of seven members with their deputies; the President of the board is a high-ranking judge. Four members have a four-year term of office, while the remaining three have a three-year term. Their term can be renewed only once. The members of the board are bound by confidentiality. In case of the violation of their duties, they are subject to disciplinary sanctions. Disclosing data, which have been made available to them in their professional capacity, may lead to penal prosecution (Article 18, Law 2472/1997).

51. See, generally, Dimopoulos, P., "Cross-border crime prevention and cooperation of EU member states in the context of mutual legal aid", *Penal Annals* 48 (1998), p. 313, Livos, N., "Penal protection of linking data", *Penal Annals* 47 (1997), pp. 737-759, Lynderis, Ch., "The lifting of communication privacy as a means of crime policy", *Penal Annals* 45 (1995), pp. 119-127.

## ABBREVIATIONS/GLOSSARY

**Authorised or Competent Committee** is the committee responsible for the collection, evaluation and investigation of irregular transactions and money laundering. It is an independent service. It evaluates and investigates all the relevant information on money laundering received by the Greek law enforcement agencies from foreign services, to which it also supplies all possible assistance (Article 7, Law 2331/1995).

**CPP**, Code of Penal Procedure.

**33rd Directorate of Customs Control,** which is responsible for operations against organised crime in the area of customs, also operates as a receiver of information from all the customs services nationally and from abroad. Its role consists mainly in the management and collection of information on contraband and tax evasion. The sender of information to the customs service concerning drugs is the SODN. Information is also exchanged with many services, such as the SDOE, NCB Interpol, etc. Contact and cooperation with OLAF occurs mainly through this Directorate for Customs Controls.

**DA, Directorate of Aliens.** The newly established (2001) Directorate of MPO previously belonging to the DKA, State Security Directorate, and, along with the DDA, Public Security Directorate, now constitutes the Coordination Body. Among other matters, it deals with illegal migration.

**DDA, Public Security Directorate.** The Directorate of the MPO, which deals with the majority of crimes, and has official supremacy in the fight against organised crime. It resides under the Branch of Security and Order Police. Along with the DKA, the State Security Directorate, it constitutes the Coordination Body.

**DDAS, Directorate of International Police Cooperation.** The Directorate of the MPO is charged with cooperating with the police services of EU member states, as well as with other countries. It includes the Department of International Relations, which is the NCB Interpol, the Department of European Union and the SIRENE Bureau. It has the role of the "alternative" contact point and comes under the Branch of Security and Order Police.

**DKA, State Security Directorate.** The Directorate in the MPO, which is responsible mainly for crimes against the constitution and the inter-state and international relations. It comes under the Branch of Security and Order Police. Along with the DDA and the DA consist the Coordination Body.

**Drugs Control Department** is the Service of the **coastguard** (HCG) which comes under the Security Directorate of the Mercantile Marine and has a coordinating as well as an operational role not only for drug trafficking control, but also other forms of organised crime, such as the illegal trafficking of human beings, illicit arms trafficking, contraband. The department can be regarded as an intelligence service of the Coastguard Corps for collecting and analysing information on organised crime.

**Law 2225/1994** established the National Board for the Protection of Communication Privacy, the body responsible for the Protection of Communication Privacy. It grants the lifting of secrecy for reasons of national security and for the investigation of certain felonies, after gaining the permission either of the public prosecutor or of the Judicial Committee of first instance or of second instance, depending on the severity of crime.

**ELAS,** Hellenic Police.

**HCG,** Hellenic Coastguard.

**Law 2331/1995.** The Law for the Prevention of Money Laundering.

**Law 2472/1997** has instituted the National Data Protection Supervisory Board (Article 15). It is the competent body for providing permission to the DDAS to use and exchange information concerning personal data with the law enforcement agencies of other states or for reasons associated with the exercise of public authority. It is also competent to give permission to any public service or private enterprise for the creation of electronic bases with personal data.

**Law 2477/1997** established the National Ombudsman (Articles 1-5).

**Law 2713/1999** enacted the Service of Internal Affairs of the Police and instituted special investigative techniques (pro-active methods).

**Law 2800/2000** created the Headquarters of the Greek police.

**Law 2928/2001** reformed the provisions of Penal Code and Penal Procedure Code concerning organised criminal activities.

**MD,** Ministerial Decree.

**MPO,** Ministry of Public Order.

**NIS,** the Service responsible for collection and processing information concerning state security; for the time being answerable to the Minister of the Interior, Public Administration and Decentralisation (Legislative Decree 2421/1953, Law 1645/1986).

**PC,** Penal Code.

**PD,** Presidential Decree.

**SDOE, the Financial and Economics Crime Office.** Its task is the prevention and control of economic crime, namely, tax evasion as related to the production, transportation and trade of goods, as well as the supply of services, contraband and illegal trafficking in narcotics and psychotropic substances, arms, explosives and antiquities, illegal activities against national currency and public property, as well as fraud and any other offences against the economic interest of the Greek state, the public sector, the national economy and the European Union. The SDOE is an independently controlled service supervised by the Minister of Finance. In charge of the SDOE is an executive secretary, directly answerable to the Minister of Finance.

**SODN, Central Anti-Drug Coordination Unit.** An inter-ministerial independent body responsible for the control of illicit drug trafficking, which operates as a national contact point in cooperation with Europol for cases concerning drugs. It is charged with holding the "controlled deliveries" of drugs and psychotropic substances (Article 20, Law 1729/1987, PD 139/1989, 126/1990).

## LIST OF RESPONDENTS

### I. Ministry of Public Order

Mr Nikos **Tassiopoulos**, Police Brigadier-General, Director of the International Police Cooperation Directorate (DDAS).

Mr Vassilios **Konstantopoulos**, Police Captain, Public Security Directorate (DDA).

Mr Chrisanthos **Tsantrisos**, Police Lieutenant-Colonel, Head of the Department of Economic Crimes, Public Security Directorate (DDA).

Mrs Athanassia **Founda,** Police Captain, Public Security Directorate (DDA).

Mr George **Galanis**, Lieutenant, Studies Directorate, Branch of Administrative Support.

Mr Nikitas **Kalogiannakis**, Police Captain, SODN, Central Anti-Drug Coordination Unit.

### II. Ministry of Mercantile Marine (Hellenic Coastguard)

Mr Nikos **Vergadis**, Lieutenant, Head of the Department for the Control of Drug Trafficking, Hellenic Coastguard, Security Directorate.

Mr Emmanouil **Zimarianakis**, Ensign, Department for the Control of Drug Trafficking, Hellenic Coastguard, Security Directorate.

### III. Ministry of Finance (Customs Services, SDOE)

Mr Nikos **Pennas**, Head of the Section for Prosecution and Control of Drug and Arms Trafficking, 33rd Directorate for Customs Controls.

Mrs Angelica **Matsouka**, Senior Custom Officer, 33rd Directorate for Customs Controls.

Mr Nikos **Vasdekas**, Senior Custom Officer, 33rd Directorate for Customs Controls.

Mr Vangelis **Karamanos**, Head of the Department for Operational Planning and Prosecution of Drug and Arms trafficking, Directorate of Planning and Coordination of Audits and Control, SDOE.

Mrs Elisabeth **Georgiadou**, Head of the Department of Legal Support, Directorate of Administrative Support, SDOE.

Mr Kyriakos **Boundouris**, Department of Data Documentation and Analysis, Directorate of Planning and Coordination of Audits and Prosecutions, SDOE.

### IV. Public Prosecution Service

Mr John **Angelis**, Public Prosecutor of Second Instance.

Mr Efstratios **Papathanassopoulos**, Public Prosecutor of First Instance.

## SPECIAL UNITS IN LAW ENFORCEMENT AGENCIES TO CONTROL ORGANISED CRIME

### 1) Greek Police

Before 1990:

- Anti-terrorist Units, Anti-Violent Crime Units, Neutralisation of Explosive Mechanisms Units (NATIONAL/LOCAL)
- Department for the Prosecution of Economic Crimes (INTERNATIONAL/ NATIONAL/LOCAL)
- Sub-division for the Control of Drug Trafficking (NATIONAL)
- Six Departments for the Control of Drug Trafficking (LOCAL)

After 1990:

- Assignment of police officers in each police directorate for the collection and processing of information concerning OC (LOCAL)
- 4th Department for Analysis of Criminality (NATIONAL)
- Border Guards Corps (NATIONAL/LOCAL)
- Electronic Analysis Section (Criminological Laboratory) (NATIONAL)
- Operational Group for the Fight against OC, especially the Russian OC, upgraded to Sub-division (national)
- Police Cells (Intelligent Analysis of OC) (LOCAL)

## 2) Coastguard

Before 1990:

- Drugs Control Office (INTERNATIONAL/NATIONAL)

- Operational Groups (NATIONAL)

- Service of Air Transport: supervision and policing of the Greek waters, (NATIONAL)

- Special Squads: combat illegal acts and terrorist actions (i.e. seizure of ships, arrests, search for drugs about the ship's hull etc.) (NATIONAL/LOCAL)

- Unit of Submarine Missions (NATIONAL/LOCAL)

After 1990:

- Drugs Control Department (1993) (INTERNATIONAL/NATIONAL)


## 3) Customs Services

Before 1990:

- Five **Special Investigation Units of Customs Services** with prosecution powers in relation to the smuggling of goods and illegal drug trafficking; four abolished in 1995 and their authority was assumed by the new body, SDOE (INTERNATIONAL/NATIONAL)
  - Department for Prosecution of Arms and Drug Trafficking
  - Department for Contraband
  - Directorate for Supervision and Control of Vehicles

- Investigation Squads (NATIONAL)

- Information Department (NATIONAL)

- Operational groups for contraband and other customs infractions (NATIONAL/ LOCAL)

- Services of customs investigations concerning trafficking of stolen cars, and three departments for drugs, arms and contraband (NATIONAL)

- 33rd Directorate for Customs Controls (EU/INTERNATIONAL/NATIONAL)

After 1990:

- Investigation Squads (NATIONAL)

- Information Department (NATIONAL)

**4) SDOE**

- Department of Special Economic Affairs responsible for the prevention and control of money laundering (1997) (EU/INTERNATIONAL/NATIONAL/LOCAL)

- Department of Operational Planning and Prosecution of drug and arms trafficking (1997) (EU/INTERNATIONAL/NATIONAL/LOCAL)

**COORDINATION BODY (EU/INTERNATIONAL/NATIONAL)**

Ministry of Public Order

- Public Security Directorate (DDA)

- State Security Directorate (DKA)

- Directorate of Aliens (DA)

    Branch of Security and Order Police, supervised by the Deputy-Chief

    And the General Inspector of the Greek Police

**CENTRAL CONTACT POINT (EU/INTERNATIONAL/NATIONAL)**

Ministry of Public Order

- Directorate of International Police Cooperation (DDAS):

    (1) Department of International Organisations-NCB Interpol,

    (2) Department of European Union-Europol,

    (3) SIRENE Department,

    (4) Department of International Relations, Missions and Delegations

- National Contact Point for Drugs (SODN): Central Anti-Drug Coordination Unit

**OTHER (EU) LEGAL INSTRUMENTS, OFFICES**

- **Authorised/Competent Committee** responsible for the prevention of money laundering

    (Article 7, Law 2331/1995) (EU/INTERNATIONAL/NATIONAL)

- **SODN**, Central Anti-Drug Coordination Unit

  **Independent** inter-ministerial body responsible for the control of illicit drug trafficking, "controlled deliveries" of drugs and psychotropic substances (EU/INTERNATIONAL/NATIONAL)

## ORGANOGRAMS

1a. Hellenic Police/MINISTRY OF PUBLIC ORDER

1b. Security Directorate of Attica/MINISTRY OF PUBLIC ORDER (a complete update not possible)

2. MINISTRY OF MERCANTILE MARINE/Coastguard

3. MINISTRY OF FINANCE/Customs Services (and SDOE)

4. Financial and Economic Crimes Office (SDOE)/MINISTRY OF FINANCE

# Annex 1a: Hellenic Police (Law 2800/29.2.2000, PD 14/31.1.2001)/MINISTRY OF PUBLIC ORDER

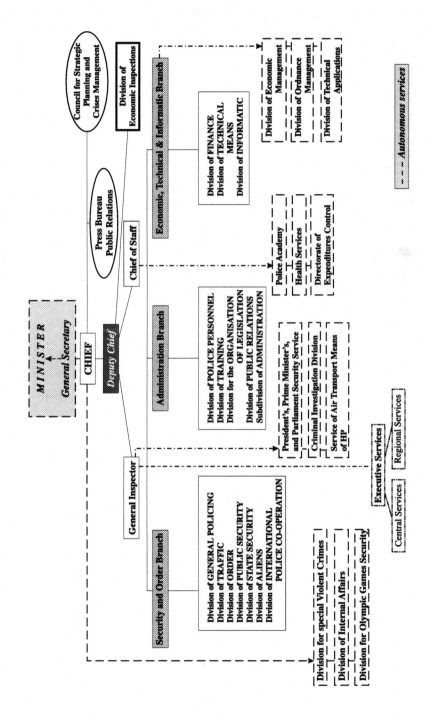

# Annex 1b: Security Division of Attica (PD 378/1995 [A-210])/MINISTRY OF PUBLIC ORDER

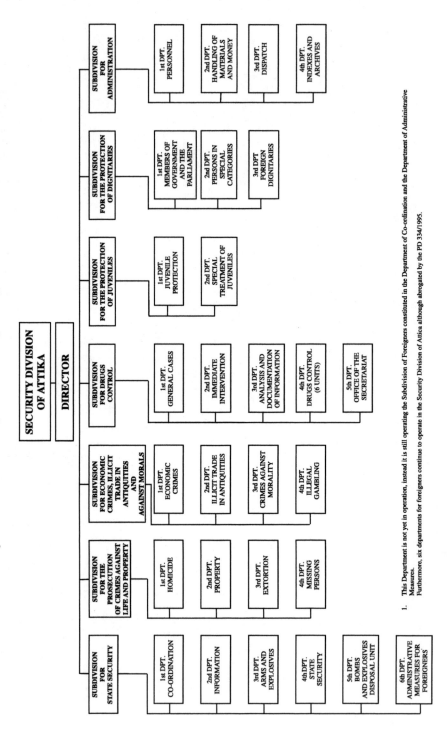

1. This Department is not yet in operation, instead it is still operating the Subdivision of Foreigners constituted in the Department of Co-ordination and the Department of Administrative Measures.
   Furthermore, six departments for foreigners continue to operate in the Security Division of Attica although abrogated by the PD 334/1995.

# Annex 2: MINISTRY OF MERCANTILE MARINE/Coastguard

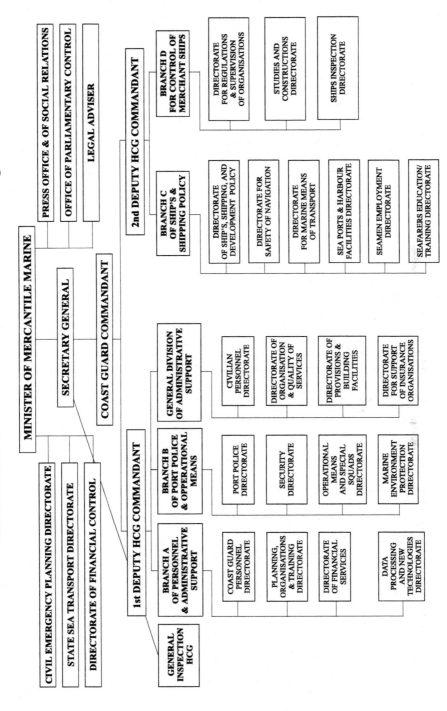

## Annex 3: MINISTRY OF FINANCE/Customs Services (and SDOE)

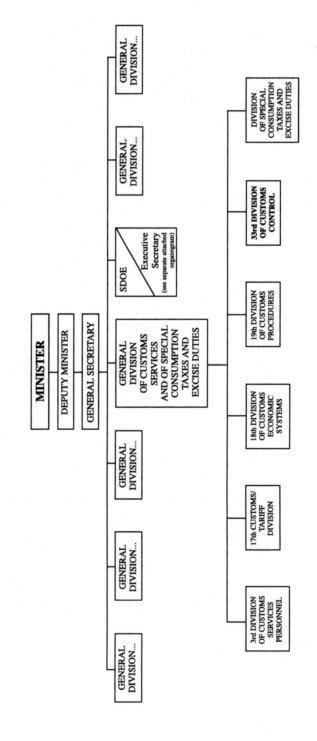

# Annex 4: Financial and Economic Crimes Office (SDOE)/MINISTRY OF FINANCE

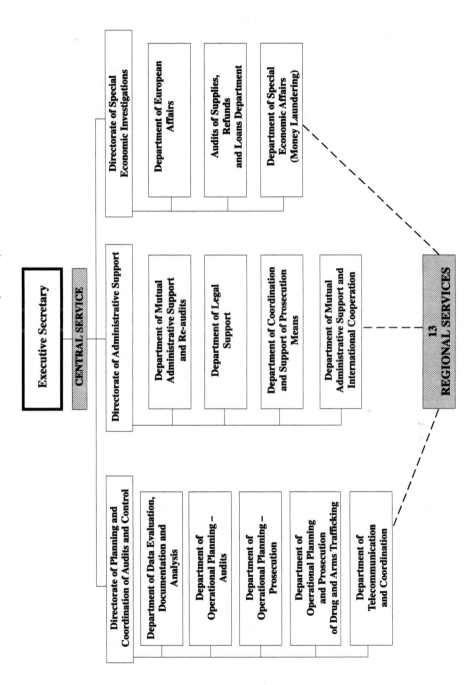

**Executive Secretary**

**CENTRAL SERVICE**

**Directorate of Planning and Coordination of Audits and Control**

- Department of Data Evaluation, Documentation and Analysis
- Department of Operational Planning – Audits
- Department of Operational Planning – Prosecution
- Department of Operational Planning and Prosecution of Drug and Arms Trafficking
- Department of Telecommunication and Coordination

**Directorate of Administrative Support**

- Department of Mutual Administrative Support and Re-audits
- Department of Legal Support
- Department of Coordination and Support of Prosecution Means
- Department of Mutual Administrative Support and International Cooperation

**Directorate of Special Economic Investigations**

- Department of European Affairs
- Audits of Supplies, Refunds and Loans Department
- Department of Special Economic Affairs (Money Laundering)

**13 REGIONAL SERVICES**

# Ireland

## *Dermot Walsh*

### COMBATING ORGANISED CRIME IN IRELAND

Up until the 1990s in Ireland terrorism associated with the armed conflict in Northern Ireland was considered a much more potent threat than organised crime. The Offences against the State Act, 1939 (as amended) makes provision for special police powers, special criminal courts and special rules of criminal procedure to combat the threat of organised terrorism. Since 1972 all of these measures have been in full force in response to the situation in Northern Ireland. Equally, within the *Garda Síochána* there are special units which deal almost exclusively with terrorism associated with Northern Ireland. The military intelligence section of the Defence Forces has also been active in these matters.

Organised crime, as distinct from terrorism, did not attract serious public attention in Ireland until the mid-1990s when organised criminal gangs involved in drug trafficking resorted increasingly to "gangland murders" to protect their trade. At the same time the volume of robberies, burglaries, larcenies and muggings committed by addicts to feed their habit increased as the number of addicts increased. Public alarm at the apparent rise in serious crime reached fever pitch in the wake of the high profile and shocking murders of journalist Veronica Guerin and Detective Garda Gerry McCabe only three weeks apart in 1996. The former was shot dead by members of a crime gang who wished to silence her investigative reporting on their activities, while the latter was shot dead by terrorists in the course of a robbery.

As the threat posed by terrorism diminished throughout the 1990s and the public profile of organised crime rose, so the authorities began to focus more on the latter. Increasingly, the state began to use the anti-terrorist measures against organised crime, virtually all of which was based in Ireland. These measures were complemented by new powers and structures aimed more specifically at organised crime. The Criminal Justice Act, 1994, for example, was enacted in order to give effect to Ireland's obligations under EC Council

309

Directive 91/308 on money laundering. It also includes important confiscation and forfeiture provisions for the assets of persons charged with or convicted of drug trafficking or other serious crimes, as well as provisions facilitating cooperation with law enforcement and judicial authorities abroad.

In 1996 an important package of measures was introduced for the specific purpose of tackling the assets of those suspected of involvement in organised crime. The measures in questions are: the Criminal Assets Bureau Act 1996, the Proceeds of Crime Act 1996 and the Disclosure of Certain Information for Taxation and Other Purposes Act 1996. Unlike the Criminal Justice Act 1994, these measures were not enacted directly in response to Ireland's European and international obligations. They have been devised purely as a domestic and innovative response to the problem of organised crime and have very quickly become established as the most important provisions in this context.

The latest statutory measure to be introduced relevant to combating organised is the Europol Act 1997. It has been enacted in order to fulfil Ireland's obligations under the Europol Convention. To that end it makes provision for the establishment of Ireland's Europol National Unit. Ireland is not yet fully bound by the Schengen Agreements, although it has recently applied to opt in to certain parts of them. Full compliance with the Schengen Agreements will require legislation to confer the necessary powers on the Garda Siochana and relevant executive and judicial bodies.

Account must be taken of the specialist units within the *Garda Síochána* and the Revenue Commissioners which have a particular relevance to combating organised crime. Apart from the CAB and the Europol National Unit, these specialist units have not been established on a statutory basis. They have been established through internal administrative decision making. Like all other specialist units in the two services, their remit, structure, composition and *modus operandi* are determined as a matter of internal management. They can be disbanded or reformed from time to time as seen fit by the Garda Commissioner or the Revenue Commissioners, as the case may be. In so far as these units have been established or reformed during the 1990s, the motivation almost invariably has been the demands for internal organisational efficiency, as distinct from compliance with EU obligations.

Before outlining the primary units within the *Garda Síochána* and the Revenue Commissioners which deal with organised crime, it is important to point out that Irish law does not recognise organised crime as a distinct offence. There are, of course, some offences which are often committed by members of organised criminal gangs or their associates. In Ireland the most frequent are: drug trafficking, money-laundering, robbery and murder. Individuals who participate in the activities of organised criminal gangs can be charged only with such offences or some other appropriate offence known to the criminal law. They cannot be charged with "organised crime". Indeed, there is no distinct offence of membership of a criminal organisation. The closest is membership of an unlawful organisation which has been declared by Government Order to be an unlawful organisation.[1] This offence, however, was introduced to deal with terrorism and, in practice has only ever been used against terrorist organisations. Another possibility is the common law offence of conspiracy, but it must be charged with reference to a specific crime such as a conspiracy to murder. From this, we can draw the conclusion that EU provisions on membership of a criminal organization have not had any influence on Irish law: the official view is that EU requirements are fully covered by the existing offence of membership coupled with the common law inchoate offences and degrees of secondary participation.

## The *Garda Síochána* and Organised Crime

There is no single unit within the *Garda Síochána* which deals exclusively with organised crime. All members of the force have a duty to combat crime, including organised crime. In practice, of course, some units are much more heavily involved than others in the monitoring, investigation and detection of organised crime.

The central body in this context is the National Bureau of Criminal Investigation (NBCI). Previously it was known as the central detective unit. In the mid-1990s, however, there was a major internal reorganisation of crime investigation structures within the force and this resulted in the establishment of the NBCI. It is a centralised body which handles investigations into serious crimes throughout the country. For this purpose it incorporates a range of specialist units. Those most relevant to organised crime include: the murder squad, the anti-racketeering squad, the arts and antiques unit, the stolen computer parts unit and the stolen cars unit.

Separate from the NBCI is the National Drugs Unit. It was established in the mid-1990s as part of the drive to strengthen the Garda's capacity to combat the threats posed by the rapidly growing trade in drug trafficking. Like the NBCI it is a centralised service which concentrates on major drug trafficking throughout the country. Serious fraud and money-laundering investigations are handled by the Garda Bureau of Fraud Investigation (GBFI) which is also a centralised service. It fulfils the role of the financial intelligence unit envisaged by the 1991 EU Money Laundering Directive.[2]

All of these national Garda units have been established through internal administrative decision making. They all come within the remit of the Assistant Commissioner with responsibility for Crime and Security. They lack a statutory basis and statutory powers and duties separate and distinct from their individual members. They are composed of members of the *Garda*

*Síochána* in the same manner as any other unit of the force. They can be reformed and abolished from time to time as the Commissioner considers necessary. Equally their internal procedures and working practices are a matter for the Commissioner. With the possible exception of the GBFI, the establishment (or reform) of these units has been unaffected by obligations flowing from the EU. Currently, their management is being reviewed as part of a wider review of centralised management structures within the force. That review, however, has not been initiated in response to the EU Action Plan on organised crime. It is part of a strategic management initiative aimed at enhancing efficiency throughout the force.

The CAB plays a critical role in combating organised crime. It, however, is more properly classified as a multidisciplinary body as distinct from an internal Garda unit. Accordingly, it is dealt with separately below under the heading of multidisciplinary integrated teams. Similarly, the Europol National Unit is dealt with separately below under international cooperation.

There are also some centralised units which concentrate primarily or exclusively on terrorism, namely the Special Detective Unit (Special Branch), the National Surveillance Unit and the Intelligence Section. The members of the Special Detective Unit are plain-clothed detectives who engage in the investigation and detection of subversive crime. They are normally armed. The National Surveillance Unit specialises in surveillance operations against persons suspected of involvement in terrorism and other serious organised crime. It relies heavily on proactive methods of surveillance, involving authorised postal and telecommunications intercepts. The employment of proactive investigation techniques is largely unregulated, although a major exception is postal and telecommunications. The Intelligence Section is closely allied with the National Surveillance Unit. Unlike the latter, however, it is non-operational. Its members who are drawn from the ranks of the *Garda Síochána* specialise in the assessment of intelligence gathered by other sources such as the National Surveillance Unit. In effect it is the state's Secret Service.

All three of these units have been created purely on the basis of internal administrative decision making. They all come within the remit of the Assistant Commissioner, Crime and Security. The establishment and maintenance of these units are driven primarily by the threat of terrorism flowing from the conflict over Northern Ireland. Their remit, however, is not confined to domestic Irish terrorism.

**Customs and Excise and Organised Crime**

As with the *Garda Síochána* the customs and excise do not target organised crime as a distinct category of offending. Their primary concern is detecting the unlawful importation of goods into the state, irrespective of whether such activities are carried on by individuals or organised conspiracies. Major enforcement priorities are drug trafficking and the smuggling of alcohol and cigarettes. In practice, these feature prominently in the activities of organised criminal gangs in Ireland.

Major enforcement priorities are drug trafficking and the smuggling of alcohol and cigarettes. These are reflected in the existence of the Customs National Drugs Team (CNDT) and the Anti-Smuggling Units which are attached to the Revenue Mobile Service. There is also a Central Investigation Bureau, a National Coordination Centre for Intelligence, a Maritime Unit, Dog Units and Liaison Officers with the chemical industry. These units do not have a statutory basis or security of tenure. Their remit, structure, composition and *modus operandi* can be varied from to time as the occasion requires. Equally they can be disbanded or reformed from time to time through internal administrative decision making.

The structural efficiency of the enforcement teams have been reviewed recently. It is anticipated that this will result in more streamlined enforcement structures with more efficient use of resources. Enforcement teams will be formed with an input from existing CNDT and Mobile Service Units. These will be intelligence driven and it is envisaged that they will result in investigative operations which are leaner and more focused.

The enforcement structures and practices of the customs and excise are based on internal administrative rules. The proposed reforms have been devised purely in response to domestic pressures to become more efficient. They are not a response to developments at EU level, nor have they been designed to satisfy EU objectives. They will be implemented purely through the medium of internal administrative rules. Neither these rules nor the document which advocates the reform are publicly accessible.

**The Prosecution Service and Organised Crime**

There is no distinct unit within the DPP's office for dealing specifically with organised crime or indeed any specific type of crime and as such there is no central coordination unit for international cooperation. The distribution of work within the office is not affected by crime classification. Difficult or sensitive prosecutions are normally handled by senior staff, or even sent up to the DPP himself on occasions. However, the basic principles applied in deciding whether to prosecute, who to prosecute, what charges to prefer, mode of trial, etc. do not differ from those applied generally to other cases.

## Inter-agency Cooperation against Organised Crime

Apart from the CAB, which is dealt with below, there are no formal structures for inter-agency cooperation in tackling organised crime or, indeed, any type of crime in Ireland. It does not follow that the agencies do not cooperate. Drug trafficking or smuggling operations, for example, often require inter-agency cooperation. Technically, the customs and excise service have primary responsibility in such operations at the point of importation while the *Garda Síochána* have responsibility inland. Where drug trafficking is undertaken by uncanalised maritime means, the Naval Service and Air Corps also form part of a task force.

Where the need for such inter-agency cooperation arises it is normally secured through the establishment of an operational task force on an ad hoc basis. The task force includes representatives from all of the appropriate services. It is formed purely for the purposes of the individual operation. Once that operation is complete the task force is disbanded. Such task forces have no statutory basis. They are formed from time to time as a matter of internal management decision making as the occasion demands. An individual member of a task force does not enjoy any powers beyond those invested in him or her as a result of his or her status as a member of the *Garda Síochána*, customs and excise service, naval service or the DPP's office as the case may be.

Cooperation between the *Garda Síochána* and the customs and excise service is governed by a Memorandum of Understanding (MOU) designed to facilitate information exchange between the two agencies. This MOU provides also for the appointment of liaison officers at both headquarters and local level to facilitate the exchange of information. It is purely an administrative document with no statutory authority whatsoever. The customs and excise service also liaises with the Criminal Assets Bureau (see below) and other Garda units on the seizure of drug-related cash at the point of import to or export from the state.

Both the *Garda Síochána* and the customs and excise service exchange intelligence with the military intelligence branch of the Defence Forces. The customs and excise service operate the exchange on a case by case basis concerning the importation of firearms primarily by terrorist organisations. The *Garda Síochána* maintain a more regular liaison, again largely on the subject of firearms and terrorist organisations.

Technically, there is a body of coordination at the level of law enforcement.

It consists of representatives of the Department of Justice, Equality and Law Reform, the *Garda Síochána*, the Revenue (International Customs Branch) and the Customs and Excise Enforcement Division. It has no operational capacity and, in practice, is little more than a "talking shop". It meets on a regular basis primarily to develop a coordinated Irish position on matters to be discussed at the meetings of the EU Multi-Disciplinary Group on Organised Crime (MDG). This body has no statutory basis. It is located in the Department of Justice, Equality and Law Reform and was established in conjunction with the meetings of the EU multidisciplinary group on organised crime.

Both the *Garda Síochána* and the customs and excise service liaise with private sector bodies. The former is regularly in contact with the insurance industry, the private security industry and the chemical industry. As part of this contact there is a mutually beneficial exchange of information. The Garda Bureau of Fraud Investigation also keeps in close contact with the financial services sector. These contacts are useful in keeping the former informed of suspicious transactions and new developments in the fraud and money-laundering practices. Such interactions and exchanges of information between the *Garda Síochána* and the private sector are conducted purely as an internal administrative matter. There are no formal structures or public rules governing the exchange.

The customs and excise service has a more structured approach to the exchange of information between it and private sector interests. Since the completion of the single market in 1992 the customs and excise service has been attaching increasing importance to cooperation with the trading community as part of their enforcement strategy. To this end they are parties to memoranda of understanding with shipping lines, airlines, road hauliers, door-to-door couriers and other commercial and industrial undertakings engaged in the manufacture, processing or distribution of drugs and fiscal goods. These agreements are designed to improve the information flow between the customs and excise service and the undertakings concerned. This permits the faster movement of legitimate traffic and enables the customs and excise to focus attention on the illicit traffic in drugs and other contraband.

The memoranda of agreement have no statutory basis. They are entered into and operated voluntarily by the parties concerned. By 1998 there were over 40 such agreements in existence. Currently the customs and excise is reviewing their operation with a view to improving their effectiveness.

*Dermot Walsh*

## POLICE ORGANISATION

### History

From 1836 to 1922 Ireland, outside Dublin, was policed by the Royal Irish Constabulary (RIC). Dublin was policed by the Dublin Metropolitan Police (DMP). Both police forces were centrally organised and controlled from the British administration in Dublin. The members of each were structured hierarchically on the basis of ranks defined by statute. Generally, these ranks reflected seniority as opposed to functional specialisations. The top rank was occupied by a chief officer who was statutorily entrusted with the direction and control of the force. Below him the ranks fanned out in a pyramidal structure from senior management ranks down to the lowest rank of constable. Surprisingly, the legislation did not attempt to define the remit of either force. Instead each individual member was invested with all of the common law and statutory powers, duties and privileges enjoyed by the constable. In effect this meant that each member was under a common law duty to enforce the law, keep the peace and maintain public order.[3] To assist him in this task he was endowed with a very large body of common law and statutory powers to act coercively in a manner which curtailed the rights and freedoms of the individual in defined situations.

One of the most distinctive features of the police organisation in Ireland before 1922 was its unitary and centralised nature. Within their respective territorial jurisdictions, each police force was responsible for all aspects of law enforcement. Generally, there was no functional specialisation in the form of separate police forces for distinct tasks. Within each force, of course, there were specialist units. These, however, were established purely on the basis of administrative decision making by the chief officer. They functioned as integral parts of the police force in question and their members did not enjoy any powers or status different in kind from other members of the force. The only serious police functions discharged by bodies outside of the two police forces concerned the enforcement of the customs and excise and tax laws. These were the responsibility of the Commissioners of Customs and Excise and the Commissioners of Inland Revenue. Although their law enforcement functions could sometimes overlap with those of the two police forces, they were entirely separate organisations. They were established on their own statutory basis, with their own personnel and management structures and their statutory law enforcement powers and duties. Unlike the two police forces their law enforcement powers were confined solely to tax and customs and excise matters.

316

## The *Garda Síochána*

After Ireland had secured its independence from Britain in 1922 the new government set about reorganising the police system. The RIC was disbanded and replaced by a new police force, the *Garda Síochána* (Guardians of the Peace).[4] In 1925 the DMP was merged with the *Garda Síochána* to create a single, unitary force for the whole country. The new police arrangements, however, do not represent a fundamental departure from the pre-1922 system.

The *Garda Síochána*, unlike most other Irish public authorities, has not been established with its own legal personality, separate and distinct from that of its individual members.[5] Instead the legislation stipulates that it is to consist of "such officers and men" as the government shall from time to time determine. The legislation also makes provision for the members to be organised into a hierarchical structure based on rank with a single officer, the Garda Commissioner, at the apex. The Garda Commissioner is statutorily invested with the power of general direction and control over the force. Accordingly, he is the closest that the legislation comes to designating a legal personality for the force. Below the Commissioner the ranks are (in descending order): Deputy Commissioner, Assistant Commissioner, Surgeon, Chief Superintendent, Superintendent, Inspector, Station Sergeant, Sergeant and Garda.

Since the *Garda Síochána* lacks its own separate legal personality it follows that it cannot exercise police powers or discharge police duties as a corporate entity. Nor can it delegate these to the individual members of the force. Instead, each individual member, irrespective of rank, enjoys the full complement of police powers and duties known to the law in exactly the same manner as their predecessors in the RIC and DMP. These powers and duties are invested in each individual by law, by virtue of the office which he or she holds. The decision to exercise these powers in any individual case is a matter for the discretion of the individual member, as opposed to the direction of his or her senior officers or the force as a whole.

It does not follow, of course, that the *Garda Síochána* cannot function as a collective entity. In reality it has always been a highly centralised force. The legislation which prescribes the structures of executive government, the Ministers and Secretaries Act, 1924, allocates police to the Department of Justice, Equality and Law Reform. As such the *Garda Síochána* comes under the general administration of the Minister for Justice, Equality and Law Reform. Accordingly, the Minister controls the budget for the force and, by implication, key factors such as the size of the force and the material resources available to the force. He also has the power to make regulations governing all aspects of the internal management of the force, including: admissions, appointments, promotions, retirement and discipline.[6] If the members of the force require additional powers then it falls to the Minister for Justice, Equality and Law Reform to steer the necessary legislation through Parliament. The Minister also answers to Parliament for the police and accepts responsibility for major shortcomings which can be attributed to a lack of resources or supervisory mechanisms. The combined effect of these measures ensures that the Minister is in a position to ensure that the *Garda Síochána* functions as a disciplined, coherent and accountable police organisation.

The Minister's administrative, budgetary and regulatory powers over policing do not enable him to exercise direct control over the operational aspects of policing. The general direction and control over the force is entrusted to the Garda Commissioner who is constitutionally independent in his exercise of this power.[7] It follows that it is for the Commissioner alone to determine the operational policies and priorities of the force, including the establishment, disbandment and operation of specialist units within the force. The Commissioner's management decisions obviously play a vital role in shaping the collective police response to organised crime and all other forms of criminal activity.

Although the Commissioner is operationally independent of the Minister, it is important to note that the Minister is in a position to influence the Commissioner's operational decisions.[8] The Minister's control over the budget, in particular, can have a decisive impact on the establishment and maintenance of specialist units and the conduct of major operations. Ultimately, of course, the Commissioner and all officers down to and including the rank of Superintendent are appointed and can be removed at will by the government. It follows that the Commissioner's scope to act in defiance of government wishes, while constitutionally protected, is limited in practice.

## Specialist Units

The legislation establishing the *Garda Síochána* does not make specific provision for specialist units. While the Minister for Justice, Equality and Law Reform could exercise his general regulatory power to establish specialist units he has never used it for that purpose. The Commissioner, however, has exercised his general power of direction and control over the force to establish, maintain and disband specialist units and services from time to time. Some of these units are very large and have been in existence for as long as the force itself. The primary example is the detective branch. More specialised units include the national drugs unit, the murder squad, the bureau of fraud investigation, the fingerprint section, the ballistics section and the sub-aqua unit. Others are created on an *ad hoc* basis and last for only a short period before being disbanded or reformed.

These specialist units share one feature in common. They have all been created and maintained as a matter of internal management by the Commissioner exercising his general power of direction and control. In other words they lack a statutory base and security of tenure. The Commissioner can disband them or reform them from time to time as he sees fit. Equally, he determines their remit, size, composition, structure and *modus operandi*. While the members of these units specialise in a particular area of policing they do not normally possess any specialist powers over and above those invested in every other member of the force. Indeed, their legal status is no different from that of any other member of the force holding similar rank. They are subject generally to the normal rank structure, internal management regulations, pay and conditions as all other members.[9] It is also worth noting that members of these specialist units do not necessarily enjoy a monopoly in their functional specialisation. They can be deployed from time to time on other duties. Equally, other members of the force could find themselves from time to time engaged in functions which overlap with those of the specialist units.

There is one specialist unit within the *Garda Síochána* whose establishment is mandated by specific statutory provision. The Europol Act 1997 obliges the Minister for Justice, Equality and Law Reform to designate by order a National Unit within the *Garda Síochána* pursuant to Ireland's obligations under the Europol Convention. This National Unit is the only example of a specialist unit within the *Garda Síochána* being established on its own legislative basis as distinct from internal standing orders issued by the Commissioner. The existence, structure, composition, management, remit and powers of the Unit have their own separate statutory basis, despite the fact that the Unit has been established as an integral part of the *Garda Síochána*.[10] The only other body which compares is the Criminal Assets Bureau (CAB). This, however, has not been established as a unit of the *Garda Síochána* despite the fact that its chief officer must be a senior officer in the *Garda Síochána*. This chief officer is appointed, and can be removed by the Garda Commissioner to whom he or she is accountable. Both the Europol National Unit and the CAB are dealt with in more detail later.

## THE REVENUE COMMISSIONERS

Shortly after Ireland was established as an independent state in 1922, all of the jurisdictions, powers and duties conferred by law on the British Commissioners of Customs and Excise and the Commissioners of Inland Revenue were transferred to the Board of Revenue Commissioners.[11] The legislative basis for the Board is the Revenue Commissioners Order 1923. Each annual

319

Finance Act enacted since 1923 has included a provision to the effect that all taxes imposed or continued by the Act are placed under the care and management of the Revenue Commissioners. Inevitably, this involves the Commissioners in the investigation, detection and prosecution of crime associated with tax evasion and smuggling. The *Garda Síochána* are also competent to act in these matters and often work with the Commissioners in such matters. The Commissioners, however, do not have any official policing competence outside the enforcement of the tax and customs laws.

There are three Revenue Commissioners all of whom are appointed by and hold office at the pleasure of the *Taoiseach* (the Irish Prime Minister). Although the 1923 Order stipulates that they are subject to the control of the Minister for Finance and must obey all orders and instructions which might be issued to them by the Minister, the convention is that the Commissioners are independent in the exercise of their statutory powers and duties in any individual case. In other words there is a close similarity between the independence of the Revenue Commissioners from political direction and the independence of the Garda Commissioner.

The three officers of the Revenue Commissioners rely on the services of a large body of tax officials and customs and excise officers to discharge their functions. Their role in combating organised crime falls largely, although not exclusively, to the customs and excise officers of whom there are about 1,400. Unlike members of the *Garda Síochána* these officers are not appointed to a specific office and rank defined by law and peculiar to the Revenue Commissioners. They are civil servants and are structured in accordance with the normal civil service grades. Equally, they do not acquire a range of statutory or common law powers and duties automatically on appointment. Individual officers, however, can be given a commission. The effect is to confer on the officers concerned the full range of relevant powers provided by statute. These include powers to stop and search vehicles and individuals in certain circumstances, powers of arrest and powers of entry, search and seizure for the purposes of enforcing the customs and excise laws. Only officers who have been duly commissioned are competent to exercise these powers. Moreover, they are competent only for the period of time they actually hold a commission. Commissions can be issued to individual officers by the Revenue Commissioners who can also revoke them. A commission is revoked when the officer in question is no longer engaged in an enforcement function; as, for example, where he or she is transferred to another division of the Revenue Commissioners.

As with the *Garda Síochána* the internal organisation of the customs and excise service is based on administrative decision making as distinct from statutory structures. The primary administrative divisions with any relevance to organised crime are: the Customs and Excise Enforcement Division, the

Customs and Residence Division, the Customs and Excise Collections Division and the Information Communications Technology Division. Each of these are headed up by an officer holding the civil service grade of Assistant Secretary.

The customs and excise service is organised on a regional structure based on the collection areas. The state is divided into five collection areas: Dublin, Cork, Limerick, Galway and Dundalk. Each area has a collector (Principal Officer) in charge of all customs and excise business in the area concerned. Each area has its own enforcement team comprising units from the Customs National Drugs Team (CNDT) and the Revenue Mobile Service. The CNDT is structured on the basis of intelligence and operational units dedicated to the detection of drug trafficking, while the Mobile Service in addition to its anti-smuggling functions plays an active role in combating the "black economy" through intelligence gathering and the identification of traders operating outside of the tax system. The capacity of the regional enforcement teams is also enhanced by inputs from the CNDT, the National Freight Intelligence Unit and the Investigation Bureau.

## THE PROSECUTOR

Most prosecutions on indictment in Ireland today are taken by the Director of Public Prosecutions (DPP), although the Attorney General still retains a prosecutorial competence in some matters. Summary prosecutions can be taken by the DPP, individuals acting in their capacity as common informers and public bodies exercising a limited authority conferred upon them by statute. Many summary prosecutions are taken by members of the *Garda Síochána* acting in their capacity as common informers.

### Attorney General

Although the office of Attorney General in Ireland originates in common law,[12] it now enjoys a constitutional status.[13] The incumbent is a practising lawyer by profession and is a member of the government. He or she advises the government in matters of law and legal opinion and represents the public interest, where appropriate, in litigation. Prior to the establishment of the office of DPP the Attorney General had a monopoly in the prosecution of criminal offences on indictment.[14] He or she was also competent to prosecute crimes in courts of summary jurisdiction in any case in which another competent authority had not already taken a decision on prosecution.[15]

## Director of Public Prosecutions

The Office of Director of Public Prosecutions (DPP) was established by the Prosecution of Offences Act, 1974.[16] Although it did not form part of the official explanation, there can be little doubt that the establishment of the office of DPP was at least partly motivated by the need to secure the appearance of independence in prosecutions.[17] Given that the Attorney General was effectively a political appointee and functioned as legal adviser to the government, there was always the danger that the appearance of independence would be compromised in prosecutions which had domestic political implications. The integrity of prosecutions and the judicial process in criminal matters required not only that prosecutions were handled impartially, but that they also had the appearance of being handled impartially. Accordingly, the 1974 Act specifically provides that "[t]he Director shall be independent in the performance of his functions".[18] He is not answerable either to the government or to the Attorney General for the performance of his functions. Admittedly, he is appointed by the government,[19] he can be removed by the government[20] and his office comes under the general remit of the Department of Justice, Equality and Law Reform. There is no suggestion, however, that any of these can be used as an improper means of influencing his prosecutorial policies or decisions in individual cases. The qualifications for appointment to the office are laid down by statute[21] as are the procedures for his appointment[22] and removal.[23] These procedures severely limit the scope for any political interference in the independence of the office. Similarly, the Minister for Justice, Equality and Law Reform is not answerable to the *Dáil* for the actual prosecutorial policies or decisions applied or taken by the DPP.

The 1974 Act transfers to the DPP all of the functions of the Attorney General in relation to the initiation and conduct of criminal prosecutions.[24] In practice this means that most prosecutions upon indictment can be brought only by the DPP. The Attorney General is no longer competent to prosecute on indictment in these matters. The transfer is absolute. Appropriate legislation would be required before the Attorney General could initiate a prosecution on indictment in any of the transferred matters.[25] Furthermore, the independence of the office of DPP precludes the Attorney General from exercising any control over the decisions he takes with respect to prosecutions. Although there is provision for them to consult from time to time,[26] this does not mean that the DPP is under any obligation to seek or to act upon the advice of the Attorney General.[27]

The 1974 Act also extends to prosecutions in courts of summary jurisdiction. The DPP can prosecute in courts of summary jurisdiction where "a Minister, Department of State, or person (official or unofficial) authorised in that behalf by the law for the time being in force" has declined to prosecute.[28] He has replaced the Attorney General in these matters. If, however, another person or body is authorised to prosecute in an individual case before a court of summary jurisdiction, the DPP can prosecute in that case only if the "duly authorised person or body" has declined to prosecute. Moreover, where a person has exercised the right to prosecute as a common informer, the DPP cannot intervene to have the prosecution withdrawn.[29]

It would be a mistake to conclude that the 1974 Act has completely divested the Attorney General of his prosecutorial authority. In fact, the Act specifically retains some functions for the Attorney General. For example, the functions of the Attorney General in relation to the question of the constitutional validity of any law are unaffected.[30] More particularly, the Act preserves the requirement for his consent before prosecutions can be taken for certain offences.[31] In addition, he retains his power (also enjoyed by the DPP) to certify cases to the Supreme Court under the Courts of Justice Act, 1924 and the Criminal Procedure Act, 1967.[32] The government has also retained a limited power to transfer back to the Attorney General any of the powers over criminal matters which the 1974 Act purports to transfer to the DPP. This power can be exercised where the government is of the opinion that it is expedient to do so in the interests of national security.

It is also worth noting that legislation enacted since 1974 has vested the power to prosecute certain offences on indictment exclusively on the Attorney General. All of these offences have an extra-territorial element. Examples include offences created by section 11(1) of the Dumping at Sea Act, 1996, the Sea Pollution Act, 1991 and the Fisheries (Amendment) Act, 1978. This action has been explained on the basis that the offences in question may involve sensitive political and diplomatic considerations which are more suitable for the Attorney General than the DPP.[33]

The DPP's office is staffed by a team of practising lawyers working full time as professional officers of the DPP. The 1974 Act permits the DPP to delegate any of his functions to any of these professional officers.[34] This delegation can relate to a particular case, category of cases or cases generally.[35] The delegatee acts on behalf of the DPP and subject to his instructions. The sort of matters that might be delegated under this provision include the making of decisions, issuing of specific directions to lawyers acting on behalf of the DPP and the issuing of certificates of decisions or consents of the DPP where such are statutorily required by statute in individual prosecutions.[36] The fact that a function of the DPP has been performed, whether by him personally or by his delegatee, may be established by a statement of that fact in writing and signed by the DPP, or orally to the court concerned by a person appearing on behalf of, or prosecuting in the name of, the DPP.[37]

The DPP does not conduct the actual prosecution in any case. Nor does he have a staff of prosecutors to conduct prosecutions along the lines of the

Crown Prosecution Service in England and Wales. Instead he relies primarily on lawyers in private practice to proceed with cases on indictment. In summary cases he also relies on members of the *Garda Síochána* and other persons authorised by law to do likewise in summary cases.

When the DPP engages lawyers in private practice to conduct a prosecution he normally relies on the services of the State Solicitors. These consist of a Chief State Solicitor whose responsibility is confined to criminal cases in Dublin, and local State Solicitors who deal with criminal cases within their localities outside of Dublin. In practice they are appointed primarily on a county basis. For the most part they are lawyers in private practice who carry on their responsibilities as State Solicitors on a part-time basis. Although technically servants of the state when discharging their functions as State Solicitors, they do not form part of the staff of the DPP.[38] Nevertheless, the DPP must rely on them for the implementation of his prosecutorial decisions.[39] It is also worth noting that the DPP is not obliged to rely on the services of a State Solicitor in order to conduct a prosecution. He is free to engage any practising solicitor.[40]

The standard practice is for the *Garda Síochána* to send the files on persons charged with indictable offences to the State Solicitor of the relevant county. His or her primary function is to prepare the book of evidence, undertake other preparatory work necessary to prepare the case for trial and conduct the preliminary proceedings. In serious cases counsel might be engaged to assist in the preparation of the book of evidence and/or in the conduct of the preliminary proceedings. In the event of a committal for trial, the State Solicitor transmits the files to the DPP for further directions. Where the DPP directs a prosecution on indictment, the file normally goes back down to the State Solicitor to advance it accordingly. The trial itself is normally conducted by counsel briefed by the State Solicitor.[41] If the matter is to be disposed of summarily, the State Solicitor might handle it himself or herself. Summary charges are normally left to the *Garda Síochána* and other persons duly authorised by law to prosecute. Occasionally, members of the Garda Siochana will seek directions or advice from the State Solicitor in individual cases.

Prosecutions in the Special Criminal Court are in a class of their own. They arise either where the offence in question is scheduled under the Offences Against the State Act or where it is considered that an ordinary offence, even one triable summarily, might come within the remit of the Special Criminal Court. The DPP has complete control over all of these cases. The practice is for the *Garda Síochána* to refer them to the Chief State Solicitor who, in turn, seeks the directions of the DPP.

## The Common Informer

A common informer is the technical name given at common law to an individual who is capable of giving information about the commission of an offence. He or she is most likely to be the victim of the offence, a witness to the offence or someone who has received reliable information about the offence.[42] It follows that a common informer in any individual case is often a member of the *Garda Síochána*.

The common law has always recognised the right of a common informer to prosecute in courts of summary jurisdiction and on indictment.[43] This right was abolished in the case of charges prosecuted on indictment by section 9(1) of the Criminal Justice (Administration) Act, 1924. Its survival in the case of summary charges has been confirmed in a number of cases.[44] Today, most summary prosecutions are brought by individual members of the *Garda Síochána* acting in their capacity as common informers.

Although the common informer is not competent to prosecute on indictment, he or she can initiate a prosecution in respect of a criminal offence which will not be tried summarily.[45] The DPP has no power to intervene in order to effect the withdrawal of such a prosecution.[46] However, once the accused is returned for trial on indictment the common informer must give way to the DPP who can either elect to proceed with the prosecution or to withdraw it at that stage.

## The *Garda Síochána*

Although the office of DPP has been established in Ireland now for about a quarter of a century, it is still the case that most prosecutions are taken by members of the *Garda Síochána*. This practice has its roots in the centuries old office of constable, the common law attributes of which have been inherited by each member of the *Garda Síochána*.[47] Just as it was the normal practice for the constable to prosecute as a common informer in respect of criminal offences which came to his notice, so also have members of the *Garda Síochána* brought such prosecutions since the establishment of the state. Their competence to do so has been upheld by the courts.[48] A member of the *Garda Síochána* who brings a prosecution in his or her capacity as a common informer is quite independent of the DPP in the manner in which he or she handles the prosecution. The DPP has no authority to intervene in such matters. However, it would not be unusual for a member of the *Garda Síochána* to consult with or seek the advice of the DPP on any aspect of a prosecution or legal issue associated with a criminal investigation.[49]

## Other Prosecutors

It is quite common for specific statutory bodies or government Ministers to be given a statutory power to prosecute for specified criminal offences. Typically, this occurs where the body or Minister in question has been given enforcement responsibilities in the context of a regulatory scheme. Where enforcement includes resort to the criminal law it normally involves conferring the body or Minister with a power to prosecute for statutory offences which have been created as part of the scheme. It is worth repeating that conferral of such power on a specific body is normally in addition to, instead of in substitution for, that inherent in the common informer. Moreover, the DPP still retains his residual power to prosecute for any of these offences where a competent prosecutor has declined to prosecute.[50]

A feature common to all of these statutory powers is that they relate to prosecutions in a court of summary jurisdiction. Where the offence is triable either summarily or on indictment, the legislation almost invariably confines the body's power of prosecution to summary proceedings.[51]

## Prosecutorial Discretion

As a general rule the DPP will initiate a prosecution in any case where the evidence is credible and reliable and is sufficient to establish a *prima facie* case against the defendant. A *prima facie* case in this context is one in which a jury, properly instructed on the relevant law, could conclude beyond a reasonable doubt that the defendant was guilty of the offence charged. It does not follow, however, that the DPP is obliged to prosecute in every such case. It is generally accepted that he has a discretion to prosecute in any individual case.[52] Surprisingly, perhaps there is no legal provision in Ireland specifically governing when the discretion to prosecute comes into play. Equally, there is no statutory provision in Ireland compelling the DPP (or any other public prosecutor) to publish a code giving guidance on the policy.[53] However, basic principles of legality require that there should actually be a policy and that the prosecutor should normally apply that policy in order to ensure that like cases are treated alike. Nevertheless, it has never been the practice in Ireland to spell out precisely the terms of prosecutorial policy. The most that the DPP has done so far is identify the sort of issues which necessitate the availability of discretion. These include: personal responsibility, youth, age, health, special mitigating circumstances, the public interest (particularly the likelihood that the suspect will never re-offend) and "a wide range of other factors which can properly influence prosecutorial decisions but to which no legal measuring tape can readily be applied."[54] Unlike his counterparts in England and Wales and Northern Ireland, he does not apply a 51% percent rule; i.e. prosecute only in those cases where it was more likely than not that a conviction would be obtained. Despite this attempt to exclude the prospects of a conviction from the discretionary aspect of the decision to prosecute, the DPP acknowledges that he rarely prosecutes if there are no prospects of securing a conviction. To prosecute in such a case would constitute an irresponsible waste of public money and scarce resources. In some cases, however, he has considered a prosecution to be in the public interest even though there was a substantial likelihood of an acquittal. It is clear, therefore, that the prospects of a conviction is a factor which, at least occasionally, impinges upon the prosecutorial discretion. Even if the evidence is sufficient to establish a *prima facie* case there is always the possibility that the courts will intervene to prevent a prosecution going ahead in the interests of fairness to the accused.[55]

It is possible, of course, that some light might be shed on prosecutorial policy through the medium of judicial review. In practice, the courts have always displayed a marked reluctance to interfere with the exercise of the DPP's discretion to prosecute in any individual case. While they accept that the DPP's decision on prosecution in any individual case is open to review, the grounds upon which it may be reviewed are very limited.[56] The courts will interfere only if the decision has been taken in *mala fides* (in bad faith) or if it has been influenced by an improper motive or policy, the expressions "improper motive or improper policy" to be given a very narrow interpretation in the prosecutorial context. It would be a rare and most exceptional case in which the courts would find that the DPP's decision on prosecution in any individual case was *mala fides*. In effect it would amount to a finding that the DPP's decision was motivated by personal interest or malice. It is also likely that "improper motive or improper policy" would be given a very narrow interpretation in this context. Before interfering with the DPP's decision under this heading, the court would have to be satisfied that it bordered on the perverse.[57]

Closely related to the question of the judicial review of the DPP's discretion is the issue of whether he is obliged to give reasons for a decision not to prosecute in any individual case. The DPP follows a clear policy of not giving reasons.[58] He justifies this reticence on the basis of natural justice to the parties affected. Moreover, he feels that if he gives reasons in one case he will have to give reasons in all cases, with consequent unfairness to the individuals concerned in many such cases. His position has been upheld by the Supreme Court.[59] However, the DPP has issued a standing instruction to the effect that the State Solicitor and the *Garda Síochána* should be informed of the reasons why a decision is taken not to proceed with a prosecution in any case submitted by them.[60]

327

## Consent to Prosecute

Although persons other than the DPP can prosecute criminal offences in courts of summary jurisdiction, some prosecutions can proceed only with the consent of the DPP (or the Attorney General in some cases). For the most part the offences concerned were created statutorily in the nineteenth century when the private prosecutor was much more active than he or she is today.[61] It was useful therefore to have some device whereby the state could exercise some control in individual cases where a decision to prosecute might raise issues of public policy. Examples of such offences which are still in force and which require the prior consent of the DPP before a prosecution can proceed include: offences under the Explosives Substances Act, 1883. There are also a number of offences for which the consent of the Attorney General only will suffice. For the most part, these have been created by legislation which has been enacted during the second half of the twentieth century. Not surprisingly, they concern matters affecting either the security of the state or the state's international obligations. Examples include offences under: Official Secrets Act, 1963, s.14(1); the Geneva Conventions Act, 1962, s.3(3); the Genocide Act, 1973, s.2(3); and the Criminal Law (Jurisdiction) Act, 1976, s.20(2).

## Prosecutions in the Special Criminal Court

Article 38.3 of the Constitution permits the establishment of special criminal courts for the trial of offences in cases where the ordinary courts are deemed inadequate to secure the administration of justice and the preservation of public peace and order. The inadequacy of the ordinary courts in this context must be determined in accordance with law. Similarly, where special criminal courts are established pursuant to Article 38.3 they must be established by law and their constitution, powers, jurisdiction and procedure must be prescribed by law. The primary difference between them and the ordinary courts is that trials on indictment in the former are heard by three judges sitting without a jury.

The Offences against the State Act, 1939 makes provision for the government to establish one or more of these Special Criminal Courts by issuing a proclamation to the effect that it is satisfied that the ordinary courts are inadequate to secure the effective administration of justice and the preservation of public peace and accordingly that it is necessary for the legislation establishing the Special Criminal Court to come into effect. The government has issued such a proclamation on several occasions since 1939. The most recent was in 1972 when the current Special Criminal Court was established. On each occasion the Court was established to deal with cases arising out of the conflict over Northern Ireland. In recent years, however, the workload of the Court has been dominated by cases associated with organised crime.

When the relevant provisions of the Offences against the State Act have been brought into effect by government proclamation, the government may proceed to declare any offence to be a scheduled offence if it is satisfied that the ordinary courts are inadequate to ensure the effective administration of justice and the preservation of public peace and order in relation to that offence.[62] Where a person is charged with a scheduled offence which is to be tried on indictment he or she must be tried in the Special Criminal Court unless the DPP directs otherwise. If it is a scheduled offence which can be tried summarily the accused is tried in the Special Criminal Court only if the DPP makes a positive direction to that effect. The offences currently scheduled are: any offence under the Explosive Substances Act, 1883; any offence under the Firearms Acts, 1925-71; and any offence under the Offences against the State Acts, 1939-1998.

If an accused is charged with any other offence (i.e. a non-scheduled offence) he or she will normally be tried in the ordinary courts. However, the DPP has a discretion to send any person charged with a non-scheduled offence for trial in the Special Criminal Court. The DPP can issue such a direction in any case where in his opinion the ordinary courts are inadequate to ensure the effective administration of justice and the preservation of public peace and order in relation to the trial of such person on such charge.

It is apparent that the DPP plays a major role in determining whether an accused will be tried in the Special Criminal Court. Of particular significance here are the consequences of his certification that the ordinary courts are inadequate to ensure the effective administration of justice and the preservation of public peace and order in relation to an individual offence. Naturally, the question arises whether the DPP's decision in this matter in any individual case is subject to judicial review. So far the courts have declined all invitations to interfere with the DPP's decisions in such cases by way of judicial review.[63]


**MULTIDISCIPLINARY INTEGRATED TEAMS**

**Introduction**

Combating organised crime traditionally has been the preserve of the *Garda Síochána*. With the exception of terrorist crime there has never been an organised crime unit within the *Garda Síochána*. While the work of some specialist units, such as the Garda Bureau of Fraud Investigation or the

National Drugs Unit, tends to be more concerned with organised crime than others, they can hardly be described as organised crime units. Up until the establishment of the Criminal Assets Bureau there has never been a multidisciplinary integrated criminal law enforcement team involving the *Garda Síochána*. Even in the area of drug trafficking, where the Revenue Commissioners have a substantial detection and prevention role, there has never been a joint *Garda Síochána* and Revenue Commissioners drug trafficking squad before the establishment of the Criminal Assets Bureau.

## Criminal Assets Bureau (CAB)

### Introduction
A serious upsurge in the volume and degree of organised criminal activity in Ireland spurred the government into action in 1996. A package of three legislative measures was introduced: the Criminal Assets Bureau Act, 1996; the Proceeds of Crime Act, 1996 and the Disclosure of Certain Information for Taxation and Other Purposes Act, 1996. The primary objective of these measures was to confiscate the wealth of criminals by combining the expertise and resources of the *Garda Síochána*, the Revenue Commissioners and the Social Welfare authorities. To this end the legislation made provision for the establishment of a CAB composed of officers drawn from the three independent bodies. The Bureau is equipped with the necessary powers and resources to track down and quantify the assets of individuals suspected of being engaged in criminal activity and to pursue the seizure and confiscation of those assets through the High Court.

The most distinguishing feature of the CAB is its multidisciplinary and integrated character. It is the first statutory body to bring together the resources and expertise of the *Garda Síochána*, the Revenue Commissioners and the Social Welfare authorities in order to tackle crime. Its remit, however, is criminal activity generally. While that clearly covers organised crime it is by no means confined to it. In practice, however, the Bureau concentrates on organised crime and corruption.

### Composition
The Criminal Assets Bureau (CAB) was established as a body corporate on 15th October 1996.[64] The composition of the Bureau is not formally prescribed in statute. However, the Criminal Assets Bureau Act, 1996 makes provision for the appointment of a Chief Bureau Officer, Bureau Officers and Bureau staff.

The Act obliges the Garda Commissioner to appoint a Chief Bureau Officer from time to time.[65] The Commissioner is also given the power to remove the Chief Bureau Officer from his or her appointment occasionally. The Chief Bureau Officer must be appointed from the members of the *Garda Síochána* of the rank of Garda Chief Superintendent.[66] He or she manages and generally controls the administration and business of the Bureau.[67] Despite the fact that the Bureau is a multidisciplinary team the Chief Bureau Officer is responsible to the Garda Commissioner for the performance of the functions of the Bureau.[68] This together with the Commissioner's powers of appointment and removal suggests that the Bureau is very closely associated with the *Garda Síochána*. Indeed, its offices are located in *Garda Síochána* premises.

The multidisciplinary character of the CAB is reflected in the composition of the Bureau officers. The Minister for Justice, Equality and Law Reform may appoint, with the consent of the Minister for Finance, Bureau officers from members of the *Garda Síochána*, officers of the Revenue Commissioners and officers of the Minister for Social, Community and Family Affairs.[69] In each case the appointments can be made only from members and officers nominated for the purpose by their respective authorities. The power to remove a Bureau Officer from his or her appointment to the Bureau is vested in the Chief Bureau Officer, acting judicially with the consent of the Garda Commissioner.[70] The 1996 Act stipulates that the Chief Officer may, at his or her absolute discretion, at any time, with the consent of the Commissioner, remove any Bureau officer from his or her appointment as a Bureau Officer.

The Minister for Justice, Equality and Law Reform is not statutorily obliged to appoint Bureau officers from all three services. The Bureau, however, was specifically designed to bring together the resources and expertise of all three services into a single functional unit. It follows, therefore, that the Minister appoints officers from all three services as a matter of course. The officers from the Revenue Commissioners and the Minister for Social, Community and Family Affairs are given special protection in the Act to conceal their identities.[71] Accordingly, it is not always possible to specify the number or status of such officers in the Bureau.[72]

### Powers and Status of Bureau Officers
The Bureau officers do not automatically acquire any additional powers on their appointment to the Bureau. However, they do retain the powers vested in them by virtue of their status as members of the *Garda Síochána*, officers of the Revenue Commissioners or officers of the Minister for Social, Community and Family Affairs, as the case may be.[73] It is expected that they will use these powers in the service of the Bureau. Indeed, the 1996 Act specifically states that their exercise or performance of any power or duty for the purposes of the Act is to be exercised or performed in the name of the Bureau. Moreover, a Bureau officer is under the direction and control of the Chief Bureau Officer when exercising or performing any powers or duties for

the purposes of the Act.[74] The Chief Bureau Officer also acquires those powers of direction and control to which Bureau officers were subject prior to their appointment as Bureau officer. So, for example, if it was lawful for the officer (prior to his or her appointment to the Bureau) to exercise any power or perform any duty on the direction of any other person, then it is lawful for the officer to exercise that power or perform that duty at the direction of the Chief Bureau Officer.[75]

It is also worth noting that a Bureau officer may be accompanied or assisted in the exercise or performance of his or her powers or duties by such other persons as he or she considers necessary.[76] Where this other person is also a Bureau officer he or she has the powers and duties of the Bureau officer whom he or she is assisting.[77] These additional powers are available for the purposes of that assistance only. It follows, for example, that a Bureau officer from the Revenue Commissioners who is assisting a Bureau officer from the *Garda Síochána* under these provisions will acquire the powers of a member of the *Garda Síochána* for the purposes of the assistance. The same, of course, applies in reverse if it is the officer from the *Garda Síochána* who is assisting the officer from the Revenue Commissioners. In practice the most likely situation is that officers of the Revenue Commissioners and/or the Minister for Social, Community and Family Affairs would assist an officer from the *Garda Síochána*.

Most police powers in Ireland can be exercised only on the basis of a reasonable suspicion that certain specified circumstances are present. A police officer who entertains a relevant suspicion on reasonable grounds can use his own discretion to decide lawfully to exercise power in that individual case. It would not normally be lawful, however, for a police officer to exercise the power in any individual case simply because he or she was directed to do so by another police officer who entertained the relevant suspicion on reasonable grounds. In order to exercise his or her powers lawfully on the basis of instructions from another police officer, the instructions in question would have to be sufficient to raise the relevant reasonable suspicion in the mind of the officer under instruction. The 1996 Criminal Assets Bureau Act makes it clear that a Bureau officer is permitted to exercise the powers or duties vested in him or her on the basis of information received by him or her from another Bureau officer in the exercise or performance of that other Officer's powers or duties.[78] Equally a Bureau officer may exercise his or her powers or duties on the basis of any action taken by another Bureau officer in the exercise or performance of that other officer's powers or duties. Any information, documents or other material lawfully obtained by Bureau officers pursuant to these provisions is admissible in evidence in any subsequent proceedings.[79]

The combined effect of these measures suggests that the Bureau is meant to function as a collective body under the direction and control of the Chief Bureau Officer. This compares with the situation in the *Garda Síochána* where each individual member of the force exercises his or her powers in any individual case on the basis of his or her own discretion.

### Bureau Staff

In addition to the Chief Bureau Officer and the Bureau Officers there is provision for Bureau staff. The 1996 Act empowers the Minister for Justice, Equality and Law Reform, with the consent of the Minister for Finance, and after such consultation with the Garda Commissioner as may be appropriate, to appoint persons to be professional or technical members of the staff of the Bureau.[80] Apart from specific provision for a Bureau Legal Officer, the legislation does not elaborate further upon what is meant by professional or technical staff in this context. It is certainly wide enough to include accountants, computer technicians and experts in any field relevant to the work of the Bureau. Each member of the staff assists the Bureau officers in the exercise and performance of their powers and duties. He or she performs his or her functions at the direction of the Chief Bureau Officer.[81] It is the Garda Commissioner, however, who is invested with the power to remove a member of the Bureau staff from his or her position as a member of the staff.[82]

### Protection for Staff and Officers

Bureau officers and staff also benefit from certain statutory measures aimed at protecting them from violence or intimidation from the individuals targeted by the Bureau. The Act states that all reasonable care must be taken to ensure that the identity of a Bureau officer who is an officer of the Revenue Commissioners or an officer of the Minister for Social, Community and Family Affairs is not revealed.[83] The same applies to a member of the Bureau staff. Even where one of the Bureau officers is exercising his or her powers or duties in the company of a Bureau officer who is a member of the *Garda Síochána*, the former is not required to identify himself or herself. When exercising any power or duty in writing, he or she does so in the name of the Bureau.

The anonymity of non-Garda Officers of the Bureau and Bureau staff also extends to court proceedings. Where the officer or staff member is required to give evidence in any such proceedings, whether by affidavit, certificate or orally, the judge or person in charge of the proceedings may, on the application of the Chief Bureau Officer, if satisfied that there are reasonable grounds in the public interest to do so, give such directions for the preservation of the anonymity of the officer or staff member as he or she thinks fit.

The 1996 Act makes it a criminal offence to identify non-Garda Bureau officers, Bureau staff and their families.[84] It is equally an offence to publish their addresses. The Act also introduces specific offences of assault, obstruction and intimidation with respect to officers, their staff and families.[85]

### Bureau Objectives

The 1996 Act spells out the objectives and functions of the Bureau. There are three objectives. The first is to identify the assets of persons which derive or which are suspected to derive, directly or indirectly, from criminal activity.[86] It does not matter where the assets are situated. They could, for example, be located outside the jurisdiction. The emphasis is very much on the status of the assets as distinct from the person who owns or possesses them. So long as the assets derive or are suspected of deriving, directly or indirectly, from criminal activity, their identification is one of the objectives of the Bureau. It does not matter that the owner of the assets has not been, or is not suspected of having been engaged in criminal activity. The *Garda Síochána*, by comparison, focus on the identification of persons engaged in criminal activity. Assets are not defined in the legislation. Undoubtedly, it covers real property and chattels. Presumably, it also covers intangible assets such as debts, copyrights and patents.

The second objective of the Bureau is to take appropriate action under the law in order to deprive or deny those persons of the assets, or of the benefit of the assets, either wholly or in part, whichever is appropriate.[87] Once again the focus is on the assets as distinct from the person who owns the assets. The objective is to deprive the person of the assets rather than to secure a conviction against the person who owns the assets.

The third objective is ancillary to the first two. It is the pursuit of any investigation or in carrying out any other preparatory work in relation to any proceedings arising from the first and/or second objectives.[88] This could, of course, embrace the investigation and/or prosecution of persons who own the assets which the Bureau is seeking to identify and confiscate.

### Bureau Functions

Although the legislation sets out four distinct functions of the Bureau, they really reflect the functions of the three constituencies of the Bureau, namely the *Garda Síochána*, the Revenue Commissioners and the Minister for Social, Community and Family Affairs in connection with the proceeds of crime or suspected criminal activity. The four functions comprise the taking of all necessary actions

(1) in accordance with police functions, for the purposes of the confiscation, restraint of use, freezing, preservation or seizure of assets deriving or suspected of deriving, directly or indirectly, from criminal activity.[89]

(2) under revenue legislation to ensure that the proceeds of crime or suspected criminal activity are subject to tax and that the revenue legislation is fully

applied to such proceeds or activities.[90]

(3) under the social welfare legislation for the investigation and determination of any claim for social welfare benefit by any person engaged in criminal activity.[91]

(4) the request of the Minister for Social, Community and Family Affairs, to investigate and determine any claim in respect of welfare benefit where the Minister certifies that there are reasonable grounds for believing that, in the case of a particular investigation, officers of the Minister may be subject to threats or other forms of intimidation.[92]

The Bureau's actions pursuant to these specific functions can include cooperation with any other police force, tax authority or social welfare authority of a territory or state other than Ireland.

The Minister for Justice, Equality and Law Reform may, after consultation with the Minister for Finance, confer additional functions by order on the Bureau or Bureau officers.[93] These must be connected with the statutory objectives and functions of the Bureau. Functions in this context are defined as including "powers and duties".[94] The Minister may also make provision in relation to ancillary matters arising out of the conferral of any such additional functions.

The combination of the Bureau's objectives and the functions confirm that it is designed to employ an inter-agency approach to tackling organised crime. The *Garda Síochána*, the Revenue Commissioners and the Minister for Social, Community and Family Affairs pool their expertise, resources and competencies in targeting the assets of those suspected of being engaged in organised crime and those enjoying the benefits of such assets.

The traditional police approach of securing convictions against the offenders has been complemented by a strategy which focuses on the wealth which is believed to derive, directly or indirectly, from organised crime. The wealth, as distinct from the offender, is the primary target. The objective is to deprive criminals of the proceeds of their crime and thereby take away the incentive of engaging in such activity. By combining the knowledge and skills of the revenue commissioners and the social welfare officers with those of the *Garda Síochána*, it will be easier to identify suspects who appear to be enjoying a life-style which grossly exceeds their publicly declared income and capital. The resources and competencies of all three services can then be used to ensure that the individuals in question are denied social welfare benefits to which they are not entitled, are taxed on their undeclared income and capital and, where appropriate, are deprived of wealth which is suspected of deriving directly or indirectly from criminal activity.

## Civil Process

One of the most striking features of the CAB is that it relies heavily on the civil, as distinct from the criminal, process to confiscate the proceeds of crime. Prior to the establishment of the CAB, Irish criminal law already made provision for the forfeiture of criminal assets in certain circumstances.[95] These provisions are applicable only in the context of a criminal conviction against one or more individuals associated with the assets in question.[96] The package of legislative measures which established the CAB, however, has taken the bold step of providing for the confiscation of criminal assets through standard civil procedures. The precondition of a criminal conviction is not required. The key provisions are to be found in the Proceeds of Crime Act, 1996.

## Interim Orders

The Proceeds of Crime Act 1996 empowers the High Court to issue interim, interlocutory and disposal orders in certain circumstances. An interim order can be issued prohibiting the respondent, or any specified person having notice of the order, from disposing of or otherwise dealing with specified property or diminishing its value during the period of 21 days from the date of the order.[97] The application is heard *ex parte* and in private. The court may issue an order under these provisions where it is shown to its satisfaction that a person is in possession of the property concerned and that it constitutes, directly or indirectly, the proceeds of crime or was acquired, in whole or in part, with or in connection with property that, directly or indirectly, constitutes the proceeds of crime and the value of the property is not less than £10,000. In the course of the application, or while an interim order is in force, the court may grant an application compelling the respondent to file information on his assets and income (see below). Equally, once an interim order has been issued the court may appoint a receiver to manage or deal with the property (see below).

The net effect of the order is to ensure that the property in question is available for confiscation at a later date should that prove necessary. Its singular nature is emphasised by the ease with which it can be obtained, the potentially far-reaching scope of the order and the extent to which it encroaches on the property rights of the individual. There is provision for the respondent (or any person claiming an interest in the property) to challenge an order after the event. However, the onus is on the individual to satisfy the court that the property, or any part of it, is not the proceeds of crime or that its value is less than £10,000. If the applicant succeeds the court may vary or discharge the order.

### Interlocutory Orders

An interim order lapses automatically after 21 days unless an application for an interlocutory order is brought within that period. An interlocutory can be issued where the applicant tenders admissible evidence to the effect that a person is in possession or control of property which constitutes the proceeds of crime and which has a value of not less than £10,000.[98] Notice of the application must be given to the person or persons concerned unless the court is satisfied that it is not reasonably possible to ascertain their whereabouts.

A striking feature of this provision is that the case for an order can be made out simply by a member of the *Garda Síochána* not below the rank of Chief Superintendent or an authorised officer of the CAB stating, either in an affidavit or in oral evidence, his or her belief that: (i) the respondent is in possession or control of specified property and that the property constitutes directly or indirectly the proceeds of crime; or (ii) that the respondent is in possession or control of specified property and that the property was acquired in whole or in part with or in connection with property that directly or indirectly constitutes the proceeds of crime; and (iii) that the value of the property is not less than £10,000. Where such evidence is placed before the court it must grant the order unless the respondent introduces evidence to the contrary or the court is satisfied that there would be a serious risk of injustice.

As with the procedure for an interim order, an application can be made to the court for an order compelling the respondent to file an affidavit in the Central Office of the High Court specifying the property in his possession or control or his income or sources of income during such period as the Court may specify. The period may not exceed ten years ending on the date of the application. This is a particularly draconian provision when it is considered that the respondent need not have been charged with, let alone convicted of, a criminal offence. When this provision is combined with the provision on the acceptability of opinion evidence it is clear that the 1996 Act places the state in a very strong position to deprive suspected criminals of the proceeds of their crime. Astute use of these provisions can place such persons in a position where they effectively have to establish that their assets have been acquired legitimately.

The interlocutory order has much the same effect on the property as an interim order, subject to the critical difference that it can last much longer. Unless a person concerned establishes at some point that the property does not satisfy the criteria for an interlocutory order, the order remains in force until the determination of an application for a disposal order.

### Disposal Orders

After an interlocutory order has been in force in respect of specified property for a period of at least seven years an application can be made for a disposal order in relation to that property.[99] The application is made to the High Court, with due notice to the respondent and other such persons as the Court should order. The Court must grant the disposal order unless it is shown to its satisfaction that the property is not the proceeds of crime. The Court cannot make the order if it is satisfied that there would be a serious risk of injustice. Any person claiming ownership of any of the property must be given an opportunity to show cause why a disposal order should not be made.

Once granted the order deprives the respondent of his or her rights in the property which automatically transfers to the Minister for Justice, Equality and Law Reform or such other person to whom the order relates. Where property vests in the Minister pursuant to these provisions he can sell or otherwise dispose of it and the proceeds of any such disposition (or moneys transferred to him) are for the benefit of the Exchequer.

There are provisions for the payment of compensation to persons who suffer loss as a result of orders being issued under these provisions in respect of property which does not constitute directly or indirectly the proceeds of crime or which was not acquired in whole or in part with or in connection with such property.[100] Compensation can be awarded where the applicant shows to the satisfaction of the court that he or she is the owner of the property in question and that the order has been discharged or varied or has lapsed. Where compensation is awarded it is paid by the Minister for Justice, Equality and Law Reform.

### Gathering the Evidence for an Order

Although the CAB is not the only authority which may seek interim, interlocutory and disposal orders under the 1996 Act, in practice it is the source of virtually all applications.[101]

For the purpose of gathering the evidence necessary to sustain an application for any of the court orders Bureau Officers can exercise the powers vested in them by virtue of their status as members of the *Garda Síochána* or as officers of the Revenue Commissioners. In practice, Garda powers such as the powers of arrest and entry, search and seizure, as well as powers to access financial records are of particular importance in this context.

### Charging Criminal Assets to Tax

The CAB's activities are not confined to a confiscation of assets deriving or which are suspected of deriving from criminal activity. It also tackles such assets by ensuring that they are subject to tax. To this end the Revenue Officers in the Bureau are empowered and obliged to charge to tax, profits or gains from an unlawful or unknown source and to deal with the assessment and collection of any tax following an investigation by the Bureau. The necessary additional powers are provided primarily by the Disclosure of Certain

Information for Taxation and other Purposes Act, 1996. This Act permits the exchange of information between the Revenue Commissioners and the *Garda Síochána* in certain circumstances.

## Results

The CAB's application of the Revenue Acts has been extremely effective in depriving persons of the benefit of suspected criminal activity. Revenue officers in the CAB have benefited from the investigations, enquiries and information of the other two agencies represented in the Bureau. On the basis of this information they have been able to raise substantial assessments on persons in possession of money or property who are suspected of having obtained the money or property from drug trafficking or other criminal activity. Of particular importance in this context is the fact that such assessments become final and conclusive unless the persons concerned can establish that the money or property came from a lawful source. If they fail or decline to do so then the enforcement procedures available are used by the CAB to give effect to the assessments. Once again it would appear that the onus moves from the authorities to the person in possession of income or capital to establish that the CAB's demands are not warranted.

The general consensus is that the CAB and the package of statutory measures introduced in 1996 have been very effective in combating the growth of organised crime gangs in Ireland. Apart from one or two high profile convictions this success has not been measured in terms of the number of convictions secured against crime bosses or their associates. Rather it is measured in terms of a significant decrease in the number of major crimes attributed to organised gangs, the value of assets subjected to interim and interlocutory orders, the number and amount of tax assessments levied and recovered against the assets and income of individuals suspected of involvement in organised crime and the number of high profile crime bosses who have fled the country. It must be said, however, that there has been some evidence in recent months of renewed activity among organised crime gangs. It is also worth noting that the use of the civil process to confiscate assets which are suspected to derive from criminal activity has attracted, and is continuing to attract, a number of legal and constitutional challenges

*Dermot Walsh*

## INTERNATIONAL COOPERATION IN COMBATING ORGANISED CRIME

### Introduction

Cooperation and the exchange of information between law enforcement agencies in Ireland and their counterparts in other Member States is substantial. For the most part, however, it is conducted on a non-statutory basis and separately by the *Garda Síochána* and the customs and excise service. The Criminal Justice Act 1994 makes detailed statutory provisions for judicial cooperation, but it is considered that these are outside the scope of this paper. The only statutory provisions governing cooperation or information exchange between the law enforcement agencies is the Europol Act 1997, which establishes the Europol National Unit. Since the Schengen Agreements have not been fully implemented in Ireland there is no SIRENE Bureau.

The Europol National Unit is considered in some detail below. Before that it is worth outlining the current practices of cooperation and information exchange between the Irish law enforcement agencies and their counterparts in other Member States.

### *Garda Síochána*

Requests to the *Garda Síochána* for mutual assistance from foreign law enforcement agencies are normally processed through the National Criminal Intelligence Unit. The same applies to Garda requests for mutual assistance from other police forces. The unit is an integral part of the *Garda Síochána*. It is quite separate from the Europol National Unit and the Interpol unit. These last two units are located within the Liaison and Protection Service of the *Garda Síochána*. Apart from the Europol National Unit none of these units have a statutory basis. Their establishment, remit and procedures are determined by administrative decision making within the *Garda Síochána*.

In addition to these centralised points of contact, there are substantial contacts between units within the force and their counterparts in other Member States. The Garda Bureau of Fraud Investigation, for example, is part of a network of such agencies throughout Europe and beyond. It has also concluded individual Protocols of cooperation with other such agencies abroad. Equally, specific units within the NBCI are in regular contact with their counterparts in other Member States on a person to person basis. The same applies to personnel in the National Drugs Unit. The *Garda Síochána* also has a liaison officer based in the Irish Embassy of some European capitals. The role of these liaison officers is to promote and facilitate direct cooperation between the *Garda Síochána* and the law enforcement authorities of the state in question.

## The Customs and Excise Service

Cooperation and information exchange between the customs and excise service and their counterparts in other Member States is channelled through designated individuals as distinct from units. One individual is designated the central contact point for fiscal matters and another individual is designated for drugs. These contact points are entirely separate from the Europol National Unit or the Interpol unit which are located within the Liaison and Protection Service of the *Garda Síochána*. The individuals in question process requests from other EU countries for information exchange and intelligence assistance. They also provide information on national legislation, jurisdiction and procedures in so far as they feel able. It must be remembered, however, that their competence is confined to revenue and drug smuggling matters. Reciprocal requests from Ireland to law enforcement authorities in other EU countries are also routed through these same individuals. These two contact points do not have a statutory basis. Their establishment, remit and *modus operandi* depend purely on administrative decision making within the customs and excise service.

There are personnel exchanges between the customs and excise service and their counterparts in other Member States. These exchanges are vocational in nature and are organised under various European programmes. It is expected that they will result in the mutual exchange of ideas and experience.

## Other Central Contact Points

There is a unit within the Department of Justice, Equality and Law Reform which coordinates contact with the appropriate authorities in other Member States in the context of mutual assistance. It deals primarily with requests for cooperation in the gathering of evidence. The Attorney General's office advises whether an individual request should be dealt with formally through judicial procedure or whether it can be dealt with informally through police action. The central authority within the Department of Justice, Equality and Law Reform does not have a statutory basis. It is established pursuant to internal administrative decision making.

## The Europol National Unit

### Introduction
In accordance with the Europol Convention liaison between the *Garda Síochána* and the customs and excise service in Ireland and Europol is conducted through the Europol National Unit.[102]

### Statutory Base
The Europol Act, 1997 Act makes provision for the Minister for Justice, Equality and Law Reform to establish a National Unit within the *Garda Síochána* pursuant to Ireland's obligations under the Europol Convention.[103] Following consultation with the Garda Commissioner the Minister must by order designate a unit within the *Garda Síochána* to be known as the "National Unit" for the purposes of the Act and the Convention. In several respects this constitutes a unique provision in Garda legislation. In effect it confers statutory authority for the creation of an embryonic police force within the *Garda Síochána* to serve the needs of a European police organisation based outside the state. This is the first occasion on which a distinct unit within the force has been created by a ministerial order. Unlike other distinct units within the *Garda Síochána* the existence, structure, composition, management, remit and powers of this National Unit have their own separate statutory basis, despite the fact that the Unit also appears to have been established as an integral part of the *Garda Síochána*. Other peculiarities are evident in the composition, management and control of the Unit.

### Composition and Appointments
Although the National Unit is created "within the *Garda Síochána*", its membership is not confined to members of the force. Indeed, there is no strict delimitation or definition of membership. The clear implication, however, is that the Unit includes members of the *Garda Síochána*. The Act specifically empowers the Garda Commissioner to "assign such and so many members of the *Garda Síochána* to be members" as he thinks fit from time to time.[104] In addition to Garda members, the Act also envisages that the Unit will include individuals who are not members of the *Garda Síochána*. Surprisingly, perhaps, it does not even attempt to identify the qualifications or status of possible non-Garda members, apart from an implication that they are likely to include officers of customs and excise. It is also apparent, however, that membership can be drawn from any source or background. This vagueness extends to the fact that nowhere is there an obligation to appoint non-Garda members, nor is there a statutory limitation on the maximum number of such members. Indeed, it is theoretically possible that the whole Unit, apart from its head, could be composed of non-Garda personnel.

Another peculiarity is that the non-Garda members are not appointed by the Garda Commissioner, despite the fact that the National Unit is statutorily designated as a unit within the *Garda Síochána* and is clearly designed to function as part of the *Garda Síochána*. The power of appointment over all non-Garda members lies with the Minister for Justice, Equality and Law Reform.

Currently all of the individuals appointed to the National Unit are members of the *Garda Síochána*. However, the appointment of two officers from the customs and excise service is imminent.

### Powers and Status of Members

Where the Commissioner appoints members of the *Garda Síochána* to the National Unit, the members continue to possess their full powers and duties as members of the *Garda Síochána*, and they may exercise these powers and discharge these duties for the purposes of the Act and for purposes unconnected with the Act.[105] This suggests that Garda members of the national unit can be deployed for ordinary police purposes totally unconnected with the functions of the Unit even while they are members of the Unit. In practice, of course, the real significance of this provision is that the Garda members can exercise the full range of their powers of arrest, detention, entry, search and seizure, etc. in the service of the Unit.

Just like the Garda members, customs and excise officers appointed to the Unit retain their powers and duties as customs and excise officers, and they may exercise these powers and discharge these duties both for the benefit of the Unit and for other purposes. Once again the significance of this provision is that the customs and excise officers can exercise their full range of powers in their role as members of the Unit.

### Governance of the Unit

The uniqueness of the National Unit in terms of police organisation in this state is reflected by the fact that it is considered necessary to make distinct provision for its governance. While the 1997 Act specifically place the Unit "under the control and general superintendence of the Commissioner",[106] it also obliges the Commissioner to assign the management of the Unit to a member of the *Garda Síochána* not below the rank of Chief Superintendent.[107] The member so assigned is known as the "Head of the national unit." This provision is unique in terms of Garda organisation. There is no other statutory provision which obliges the Commissioner to assign the management of a unit in the force to a senior officer. Indeed, the concept of "management" of a unit within the *Garda Síochána*, as distinct from the direction and control of the force as a whole, is not recognised anywhere else in the legislation governing the force prior to this Act. That is not to say that senior members of the force, in addition to the Commissioner, are not allocated distinct management responsibilities within the force. Indeed, major management responsibilities are delegated quite widely among the senior ranks and personnel. For the most part, however, these responsibilities are delegated. They derive from the Commissioner's power of general direction and control. In the case of the National Unit, however, the Commissioner is statutorily obliged to assign the management to a member. The implication is that the management of the Unit derives from a source independent of the Commissioner's power of general direction and control. Nevertheless, it is unlikely that this affects what is meant in practice by management of the Unit in this context. Presumably, the intention is to confer on the Head of the Unit direct responsibility for formulating the policies and strategies and implementing the procedures necessary to ensure that the Unit discharges its functions under the Europol Convention efficiently and satisfactorily, as well as directing the day-to-day operations of the Unit.

### Liaison Officers

One or more members of the Unit must be sent as the liaison officer or officers to Europol.[108] Each National Unit must send at least one officer and the maximum number that may be sent by any one unit is fixed by a unanimous decision of the Management Board of Europol.[109] Subject to these provisions it is generally a matter for the Commissioner to determine how many liaison officers should be sent from the National Unit. There are no stipulations concerning the status of those sent, apart from the fact that they must be members of the Unit. A non-Garda member, however, can be sent only after consultation with the Minister for Justice, Equality and Law Reform.[110] Moreover, a customs and excise officer can be sent only on the nomination of the Revenue Commissioners.[111] A member of the Unit who is neither a member of the *Garda Síochána* nor a customs and excise officer can be sent only on the nomination of such other Minister of the Government (if any) as the Minister for Justice, Equality and Law Reform considers appropriate in the circumstances.[112] Surprisingly, the legislation is vague on the matter of who determines the identity of the individuals to be sent and who actually takes the decision to send them. The legislation is also vague on their accountability, or privileges and immunities. Presumably the responsibility rests on the Commissioner. The legislation, however, would appear merely to confer a power on him to determine how many members of the Unit should be sent as liaison officers. While it also imposes a clear obligation to send one or more liaison officers it does not specifically impose this obligation on the Commissioner or on anyone else.

## ACCOUNTABILITY

## Introduction

The accountability of the *Garda Síochána*, the customs and excise service and the DPP can be considered from legal, managerial and democratic perspectives. None of them, however, have special rules or procedures governing their accountability with respect to their role or activities in combating organised crime. Equally, the EU Action Plan on Organised Crime has had no influence on the accountability rules, structures or processes.

## *Garda Síochána*

### *Accountability to the Law*

Each member of the *Garda Síochána* is answerable to the law for the exercise of his or her powers and the discharge of his or her duties in exactly the same manner as any other citizen. There are no special exemptions or concessions for the member who acts beyond the law in apprehending an offender or investigating an offence. Accordingly, if he or she uses more force than is necessary when effecting an arrest, or unlawfully breaks into a dwelling when searching for contraband goods, he or she is liable to be prosecuted for an appropriate offence against the person or property, as the case may be. In practice, however, it can be very difficult to secure a conviction against a member of the *Garda Síochána* for an alleged offence committed in the course of his or her functions as a member of the *Garda Síochána*.

Where a criminal complaint is made against a member of the force it is investigated by another member of the force. If the Garda Commissioner considers that the investigation report may disclose a possible criminal offence he refers the matter to the DPP who decides whether a criminal charge should be preferred.[113] The DPP has no power of direction or control over the *Garda Síochána*. Accordingly, he cannot direct or supervise the investigation of the complaint. Since 1987, however, such investigations can be carried out under the supervision of the independent Garda Siochana Complaints Board where the complaint has been made by a citizen (see later). The DPP rarely prefers criminal charges on the basis of a citizen's complaint against a member of the *Garda Síochána*.[114] In those cases where he does prefer charges convictions rarely result. Indeed, since the Garda Complaints Act was enacted in 1986 not one single criminal conviction has resulted from a citizen's complaint under the Act against a member of the force. It is also worth noting that no member of the *Garda Síochána* has been convicted in the past decade of a criminal charge arising out of his or her actions in combating organised

345

crime.

Individual members of the *Garda Síochána* can be called to account by the private citizen through a civil claim for damages. This can provide a remedy where a member of the *Garda Síochána* has intentionally used unlawful force against the person or property of the citizen and where the member has been negligent in circumstances where his actions or inaction have caused loss or injury to the citizen. The remedy through the civil action is personal to the complainant in contrast to the criminal prosecution which is conducted on behalf of the state. In that sense it offers a more direct and individual form of police accountability than the criminal prosecution.

As in criminal matters, members of the *Garda Síochána* are subject to the civil law and process in exactly the same manner and to the same extent as ordinary citizens. Apart from the fact that damages awarded against a member will normally be paid by the state, an individual's status as a member of the *Garda Síochána* does not afford him or her any special treatment or protection even in respect of wrongs committed in the course of his or her duties.

The attractions of the civil action as a police accountability mechanism are being realised in practice. The number of actions and the amounts being paid out in damages are increasing annually. This, of course, could simply be the result of a sustained deterioration in police standards. A more likely explanation, however, is an increased willingness among members of the public to call individual members of the force to account through an action for damages. A similar trend is evident in Northern Ireland and in police forces throughout Great Britain.

Since the *Garda Síochána* does not have a legal status separate and distinct from its individual members the force itself cannot be prosecuted or sued. Technically, however, it is possible to seek a judicial review of the legality of specific force policies or practices, or administrative decisions taken by the Garda Commissioner in the exercise of his power of general direction and control over the force. In practice, the courts are notoriously reluctant to interfere with the Commissioner's operational discretion in law enforcement matters. As yet there has been no case in which an operational decision taken by the Commissioner, or any other senior member of the force, has been struck down by the courts as an abuse of power.

The exclusionary rule in criminal trials can operate to call members of the *Garda Síochána* to account indirectly. If a member resorts to unconstitutional or unlawful methods to gather evidence against an individual who is subsequently charged with a criminal offence, the tainted evidence is normally excluded at the trial of the accused. Equally an admission of guilt which has been secured from a suspect by the use of improper methods by the police is usually excluded at the subsequent trial. Although the purpose of excluding the evidence in such circumstances is to ensure a fair trial for the accused in the Irish accusatorial and adversarial process, it also has the effect of punishing members of the force for resorting to improper methods. This can be particularly important in the context of the investigation, detection and prosecution of organised crime where the police may be tempted to stretch the rules in order to combat the tactics of experienced criminals.

### Managerial Accountability

The accountability of each member of the *Garda Síochána* to the law is complemented by his or her accountability within the managerial structures of the force. As a general rule each member is answerable for his or her performance to his or her immediate superior in the hierarchy of the force. This chain of accountability leads all the way to the Commissioner at the top. Members of a distinct unit are answerable to the head of that unit who in turn is answerable to the appropriate Assistant Commissioner. For most of the units relevant to organised crime the latter is the Assistant Commissioner, Crime and Security who, in turn, is answerable to the Commissioner. The Heads of the CAB and the Europol National Unit are answerable directly to the Garda Commissioner. This chain of management accountability is essential to the operation of democratic accountability (see below). When the Commissioner receives a request from the Minister for Justice, Equality and Law Reform for information about a particular Garda operation the Commissioner relies on the chain of management accountability to provide the information necessary to respond to the Minister.

Managerial accountability within the force is backed up by a formal disciplinary procedure. If a member of the force is suspected of having breached any provision of the Garda code of discipline he or she will normally be the subject of an internal investigation which may result in a disciplinary inquiry. If the inquiry finds that the member has breached the code then a disciplinary punishment is imposed, subject to the member's right of appeal. The whole procedure from investigation through to punishment and appeal is highly formal and wholly internal to the *Garda Síochána*.[115] It is essentially an internal, administrative, disciplinary procedure aimed at enforcing high standards of discipline within the force.

Up until 1986, citizen complaints against members of the *Garda Síochána* were handled through the internal disciplinary procedure, unless they involved a criminal matter. In 1986, however, legislation was enacted to introduce an independent element into the handling of citizen complaints against members of the force.[116] This independent element takes the form of a multi-member complaints board composed almost exclusively of non-police personnel. The actual investigation of complaints is still carried out by Garda personnel. However, the investigation report in any individual case goes to the complaints board, which can establish a tribunal to hear specific charges against the

347

member concerned. This tribunal is composed of two members of the board and a member of the *Garda Síochána*. If it finds the member to be guilty of a breach of discipline it can impose a punishment, subject to a right of appeal for the member concerned. In practice this complaints procedure has proved highly ineffective in enhancing public confidence in the manner in which citizen complaints against the police are handled.[117]

Both the Commissioner and the Minister for Justice, Equality and Law Reform have powers to establish an inquiry into any policing operation or incident which has given rise to public concern. The Commissioner, in particular, has exercised this power from time to time. In practice, however, such an inquiry and its report are kept confidential. Accordingly, the important public accountability potential of this power is rarely realised.

### Democratic Accountability

The democratic accountability of the *Garda Síochána* is achieved through the Minister for Justice, Equality and Law Reform in parliament. The Minister presents the budget for the force to Parliament, proposes legislation on policing matters, defends the government's record on policing in parliament and generally answers questions from members of parliament in policing matters. In order to discharge these functions the Minister relies heavily on information supplied by the Commissioner. Indeed, the Minister's capacity to deliver effective democratic accountability for policing is limited. Because he has no powers to issue directions to the Commissioner on operational policing matters he refuses to accept responsibility for operational policing policies, practices or incidents which have given rise to public concern. The most he will do in such matters is pass on whatever information he has been supplied by the Garda Commissioner.[118]

The Commissioner, and other senior officers, can be called to account more directly through the parliamentary committee system. The remit of the Parliamentary Select Committee on Justice, Equality, Defence and Women's Rights includes policing within its remit. However, its remit is so broad that the Committee rarely gets the opportunity to address policing. Nevertheless, there have been occasions where the Commissioner and other senior officers have appeared before the Committee and for questioning on police priorities. The capacity of this Committee to inquire into controversial policing incidents is currently the subject of a major legal challenge in the High Court arising out of the refusal of members of the Garda Emergency Response Unit to give evidence to the Committee about their role in the shooting of an armed and mentally-ill person outside his home.

## Customs and Excise

### *Accountability to the Law*
Officers of the customs and excise service are answerable to the law in exactly the same manner as members of the *Garda Síochána*. As with the latter, however, successful prosecutions of members of the customs and excise for acts or omissions in the course of the exercise of their official functions are very rare. While a civil action for damages is equally applicable to customs and excise officers as to members of the *Garda Síochána*, the former do not appear to have attracted the sort of increase which has been experienced by the latter. The policies and administrative decisions of the Revenue Commissioners are subject to judicial review in the same manner as any other public authority. It can be expected, however, that the courts will be just as reluctant to interfere with the discretion of the Revenue Commissioners in the enforcement of the revenue laws as they are with respect to the Garda Commissioner and the enforcement of the law generally.

### *Managerial Accountability*
The officers of customs and excise are subject to the standard internal accountability processes applicable within the civil service. This is similar to that applicable to the *Garda Síochána*, except that it is the Revenue Commissioners, rather than the Garda Commissioner, who are at the top of the managerial chain of accountability. Unlike the *Garda Síochána*, however, the customs and excise service does not have its own internal disciplinary procedure.

### *Democratic Accountability*
The Minister for Finance answers in parliament for the Revenue Commissioners (including the customs and excise service) in much the same manner as the Minister for Justice, Equality and Law Reform answers for the *Garda Síochána*. Since the Revenue Commissioners enjoy a similar constitutional independence to that of the Garda Commissioner, the Minister refuses to accept responsibility for operational matters. His role in response to parliamentary questions on such matters is confined to communicating information supplied by the Revenue Commissioners.

One significant difference between the democratic accountability of the Revenue Commissioners and the *Garda Síochána* arises from the fact that the Chairman of the Revenue Board is a designated accounting officer. Accordingly, the activities of the Revenue Commissioners, including the customs and excise service, is subject to annual scrutiny by the powerful Public Accounts Committee of Parliament. In the case of the *Garda Síochána* the accounting officer is the principal secretary in the Department of Justice,

349

Equality and Law Reform. Accordingly it is he rather than the Garda Commissioner who must appear before the Committee to answer for police expenditure. It is also worth noting that the Revenue Commissioners are subject to the Ombudsman and the Freedom of Information Act.

## The Director of Public Prosecutions

### Accountability to the Law
Although the decision whether or not to prosecute in any individual case is not often taken by the DPP personally, he is answerable in law for all prosecutorial decisions taken by his staff. In practice, of course, he is unlikely to be the subject of a criminal prosecution or civil claim for damages in respect of such decisions. Occasionally, however, his decisions are the subject of challenge by way of judicial review. While the courts have accepted that his decision whether or not to prosecute in an individual case is amenable to judicial review, they have also demonstrated an extreme reluctance to interfere with his exercise of discretion in such matters.

### Managerial Accountability
All of the staff working in the office of the DPP work under the direction of, and are answerable to, the DPP. Because it is not a large disciplined organisation such as the *Garda Síochána* there is no requirement for a distinct code of discipline and formal disciplinary procedure.

### Democratic Accountability
The DPP is accountable to parliament through the Attorney General. In practice, however, the DPP does not normally give reasons for his prosecutorial decision in any individual case. It follows that democratic accountability is confined to general policy matters. The Deputy DPP is the Accounting Officer for the Office and as such he appears before the Parliamentary Public Accounts Committee to answer questions on the expenditure, general administration and effectiveness of the Office.

## CONCLUSION

There is no clear definition of "organised crime" in Ireland. While the law enforcement and prosecutorial authorities regularly deal with organised crime on a case by case basis they do not have distinct branches or units which deal exclusively with organised crime. The most high profile body in combating organised crime is undoubtedly the CAB. Its most distinctive characteristics are its statutory basis, its multidisciplinary team and the fact that it can use a special civil process to target the assets of those suspected of involvement in serious crime. While it is not confined to organised crime it is credited with having broken up some of the main organised crime gangs in Ireland in the period of only a few years.

With the exception of the CAB and the Europol National Unit, none of the law enforcement units which deal most with organised crime have been established on a statutory footing. Their establishment, composition, remit and methods are determined by internal administrative decision making. Their accountability is delivered through a combination of law, regulation and internal management in much the same manner as all other units and branches of the law enforcement services.

**It would appear that the EU Action Plan on Organised Crime has had only a negligible effect on the design and operation of law enforcement and prosecutorial structures in Ireland. The primary components of those structures and methods were in place before the Plan was adopted.** In so far as any of them have been reviewed or reformed since the adoption of the Plan, the motivation almost invariably would appear to have been internal efficiency objectives rather than compliance with the Plan. The Irish authorities consider that their existing structures, processes and methods have always satisfied the requirements of the plan and go well beyond them in some respects.

## NOTES

1.  See Offences against the State Act, 1939, ss.18-25.
2.  Pursuant to the Criminal Justice Act 1994, the customs and excise service is also competent to seize drug-related cash which is being imported to or exported from the state.
3.  See D.P.J. Walsh, *The Irish Police* (Dublin: Round Hall Sweet & Maxwell, 1998) at ch.3.
4.  *Ibid.* at pp.7-12. See also C, Brady, *The Guardians of the Peace* (Dublin: Gill and Macmillan, 1974); L. McNiffe, *A History of the Garda Síochána* (Dublin: Wolfhound Press, 1997).
5.  Walsh *op. cit.* Ch.2.
6.  *Ibid.* Ch.5.
7.  *Ibid.* Ch.4.
8.  *Ibid.* Ch.5.
9.  *Ibid.* Ch.2.
10. *Ibid.* Ch.13.
11. See S. Reamonn, *History of the Revenue Commissioners* (Dublin: Institute of Public Administration, 1981).
12. See J. Casey, *The Office of the Attorney General in Ireland* (Dublin: Institute of Public Administration, 1980) at chs 1 and 2.
13. Irish Constitution 1937, Art.30.1.
14. Irish Constitution 1937, Art.30.3 and Criminal Justice (Administration) Act, 1924, s.9(1).
15. Criminal Justice (Administration) Act, 1924, s.9(2).
16. Prosecution of Offences Act, 1974, s.2(1).
17. The office of DPP for Northern Ireland was established in 1972 to subsume the Attorney General for Northern Ireland's prosecutorial functions (see Prosecution of Offences Act (Northern Ireland) Act 1972). Interestingly, the explanation given for this development in Northern Ireland was to remove prosecutions from any hint of political influence.
18. Prosecution of Offences Act, 1974, s.2(5).
19. Prosecution of Offences Act, 1974, s.2(2).
20. Prosecution of Offences Act, 1974, s.2(9).
21. To be eligible a person must, at the date of appointment, be a practising barrister or a practising solicitor and have practised as a barrister or a solicitor for at least ten years; Prosecution of Offences Act, 1974, s.2(3)(a). Service in the Civil Service in a position for which practice as a solicitor or barrister was a prerequisite qualifies as practice; s.2(9)(b). The current DPP, Eamonn Barnes, is a barrister and the first holder of the office.
22. When making an appointment the government must choose from a list of candidates selected by a committee composed of: the Chief Justice, the Chairman of the Bar Council, the President of the Law Society, the Secretary to the Government and the Senior Legal Assistant in the Office of the Attorney General; Prosecution of Offences Act, 1974, s.2(7).

23. Before removing the DPP the government must request a committee composed of the Chief Justice, a Judge of the High Court and the Attorney General to investigate the health of the Director or inquire into his conduct either generally or in an individual case. Armed with all the powers, rights and privileges vested in a judge of the High Court this committee must carry out the investigation or inquiry into the matters mentioned in the request and report to the government. The government may remove the DPP after consideration of the report. Prosecution of Offences Act, 1974, s.2(9).

24. This includes the power to enter a *nolle prosequi*; see *The State (O'Callaghan) v O'hUadaigh* [1977] IR 42. However, it does not affect the functions of the Attorney general in relation to any question as to the Constitutional validity of any law. Prosecution of Offences Act, 1974, s.3(3). Moreover, the DPP has not stepped into the shoes of the Attorney General for the purposes of the requirement that the consent of the Attorney General must be forthcoming before prosecutions can proceed for offences under section 3 of the Geneva Conventions Act, 1962, the Official Secrets Act, 1963 and the Genocide Act, 1973.

25. Section 5(1) of the Prosecution of Offences Act, 1974 permits the Government, in certain limited circumstances to clawback for the benefit of the Attorney General any of the functions in criminal matters transferred to the DPP. Furthermore, legislation has been enacted to confer on the Attorney General exclusive powers of prosecution on indictment in relation to certain criminal offences. See Later.

26. Prosecution of Offences Act, 1974, s.2(6) reads:
    "The Attorney General and the Director shall consult together from time to time in relation to matters pertaining to the functions of the Director."

27. Paragraph 4 of the Explanatory Memorandum issued by the Taoiseach's Department states: "The provision (for consultation) would not confer on the Attorney General any right to give directions to the Director as to how he will perform his functions in relation either to particular cases or generally." Quoted in Casey op. cit, p.227 footnote 12.

28. Criminal Justice (Administration) Act, 1924, s.9(2) and *Attorney General v Healy* [1928] IR 460.

29. *State (DPP) v District Justice Ruane* [1985] ILRM 349.

30. Prosecution of Offences Act, 1974, s.3(3).

31. Prosecution of Offences Act, 1974, s.3(5). The offences in question arise under the Geneva Conventions Act, 1962, the Official Secrets Act, 1963 and the Genocide Act, 1973.

32. Prosecution of Offences Act, 1974, s.3(4).

33. 461 Dail Debates col.377. See also, Casey op. cit at pp.117-118.

34. Prosecution of Offences Act, 1974, s.4(1). The terms of section 4 also apply to the Attorney General. However, solicitors or a barrister appointed by the DPP or the Attorney General to conduct the prosecution in a case are not considered "professional officers" for the purposes of this provision; *Flynn v DPP* [1986] ILRM 290.

35. The delegation can also be revoked; Prosecution of Offences Act, 1974, s.4(2).

36. *Flynn v DPP* [1986] ILRM 290 at 294.
37. Prosecution of Offences Act, 1974, s.4(3).
38. *McLoughlin v Minister for Social Welfare* [1958] IR 1.
39. The DPP is of the opinion that the State Solicitors are not answerable to him nor subject to his day-to-day control for the implementation of his prosecutorial decisions; see E. Barnes, "The Role of the Office of the Director of Public Prosecutions" *Communique (September, 1995) 3 at 10*. In *Flynn v DPP* [1986] ILRM 290, however, the Supreme Court proceeded on the basis that a solicitor appointed by the DPP to conduct a prosecution would remain entirely within the control and subject to the detailed instructions of the DPP; at p.295.
40. *Flynn v DPP* [1986] ILRM 290.
41. The DPP is under a duty to ensure that such briefs are distributed on the basis of inclination and ability; Prosecution of Offences Act, 1974, s.7(2). In practice, the counsel for any individual case are chosen from a panel drawn up by the DPP. They are paid fees only for each case they undertake.
42. See *McCormack v Carroll* 45 ILTR 7; and *R (Wilbond) v Armagh JJ* [1918] 2 IR 347 for authority for the proposition that a common informer does not need to be an eye witness of the offence which he prosecutes.
43. *People (DPP) v Roddy* [1977] IR 177; *Attorney General v Thompson* 7- ILTR 161; *Murphy v Cryan* [1952] IR 225; *Kenealy v O'Keeffe* [1901] 2 IR 39; *Lawler v Egan* [1901] 2 IR 589.
44. The point is now regarded as settled by the Supreme Court in *The State (Ennis) v District Justice Farrell* [1966] IR 107.
45. *The State (Ennis) v District Justice Farrell* [1966] IR 107.
46. *State (DPP) v District Justice Ruane* [1985] ILRM 349.
47. See D. P. J. Walsh, "The Legal Status of a Member of the *Garda Síochána*: New Clothes for the Ancient Office of Constable", *Anglo-American Law Review* 23, 1 (1994) 63-99.
48. *The State (Cronin) v The Circuit Court Judge of the Western Circuit* [1937] IR 34; *The State (DPP) v District Justice Ruane* [1985] ILRM 349.
49. See, for example, *The State (McCormack) v Curran* [1987] ILRM 225.
50. *Attorney General v Healy* [1928] IR 460.
51. Ryan and Magee cite the example of the Restrictive Practices Act, 1972, s.24(1).
52. In *The State (McCormack) v Curran* [1987] ILRM 225 at 237 the Supreme Court, per Finlay CJ, acknowledged that the discretion to prosecute is not related solely to the sufficiency of evidence. It indicated that there are many other factors which can appropriately and properly be taken into account. However, it considered that it would not be wise or helpful to seek to list them in any exclusive way.
53. The UK's Prosecution of Offences Act, 1985, s.10 obliges the DPP in the UK to issue a code of practice for Crown Prosecutors giving guidance on, *inter alia*, when a prosecution should be discontinued and charging policy in general.
54. E. Barnes, "The Role of the Director of Public Prosecutions", *Communique September 1995*, 3 at 8.
55. In *The State (O'Callaghan) v O'hUadhaigh* [1977] IR 42 it was held that any

act carried out by the DPP in the course of a criminal prosecution which contributed to or was likely to contribute to an unfair or unjust proceeding is restrainable by the courts on those grounds alone. See also, *Murphy v DPP* [1989] ILRM 71; *Rogers v DPP* [1992] ILRM 695.

56. *The State (McCormack) v Curran* [1987] ILRM 225.
57. *H v DPP* [1994] 2 ILRM 285; *Norris v Attorney General* [1984] IR 36 at 81.
58. Barnes op. cit, at p.9.
59. *H v DPP* [1994] 2 ILRM 285.
60. Barnes op. cit, at p.9.
61. Notable exceptions are the offences created by the Criminal Assets Bureau Act, 1996, s.13 (intimidation of bureau personnel) and s.15 (assault on bureau personnel). Where a person is charged with any of these offences, no further proceedings can be taken in the matter (other than for them to be remanded in custody or on bail) except by or with the consent of the DPP; s.17.
62. Offences against the State Act, 1939, s.36.
63. *The State (Littlejohn) v Governor of Mountjoy Prison* (Supreme Court, 18.3.76); *Savage & McOwen v DPP* [1982] ILRM 284; *O'Reilly v Judge* [1984] ILRM 224; *Kavanagh v Ireland* [1997] 1 ILRM 321.
64. Criminal Assets Bureau Act, 1996, s.3 and Criminal Assets Bureau Act, 1996 (Establishment Day) Order, 1996.
65. Criminal Assets Bureau Act, 1996, s.7(1) & (2). There is provision for the appointment of an Acting Chief Bureau Officer in the event of the incapacity through illness, or absence otherwise, of the Chief Bureau Officer; s.7(5).
66. Criminal Assets Bureau Act, 1996, s.7(6).
67. *Ibid.* s.7(3).
68. *Ibid.* s.7(4).
69. *Ibid.* s.8(1)(a).
70. *Ibid.* s.8(9).
71. Criminal Assets Bureau Act, 1996, ss.10 and 11.
72. Currently, two customs and excise officers are assigned to the CAB.
73. *Ibid.* s.8(2).
74. *Ibid.* s.8(3).
75. *Ibid.* s.8(4).
76. *Ibid.* s.8(6)(a). There is also a suggestion that a Bureau Officer may be equipped with firearms to assist him or her in the exercise or performance of his or her duties; see s.8(6)(b).
77. *Ibid.* s.8(6)(c).
78. *Ibid.* s.8(5).
79. *Ibid.* s.8(6)(d).
80. *Ibid.* s.9(1)(b).
81. *Ibid.* s.9(2).
82. *Ibid.* s.9(4).
83. *Ibid.* s.10.
84. *Ibid.* s.11.
85. *Ibid.* ss.12, 13 and 15.

86. *Ibid.* s.4(a).
87. *Ibid.* s.4(b).
88. *Ibid.* s.4(c).
89. *Ibid.* s.5(1)(a).
90. *Ibid.* s.5(1)(b).
91. *Ibid.* s.5(1)(c).
92. *Ibid.* s.5(1)(d).
93. *Ibid.* s.6(1).
94. *Ibid.* s.6(4). It is submitted that a ministerial power to confer powers by order on the *Garda Síochána*, revenue officers or officers of the Minister for Social, Community and Family Affairs which constrict the personal rights of the individual is constitutionally suspect.
95. See F. Murphy and B. Galvin, " Targeting the Financial Wealth of Criminals in Ireland" and P McCutcheon and D Walsh "Confiscation of Criminal Assets: An Overview" in P. McCutcheon and D. Walsh (eds), *The Confiscation of Criminal Assets: Law and Procedure* (Dublin: Round Hall, 1999) at pp. 5 and 17-18.
96. The provisions in the Criminal Justice Act 1994 permitting the confiscation of the proceeds of drug trafficking were applied for the first time recently to confiscate a total of £223,000 from members of the Felloni family who had been convicted of drug trafficking offences. See *Irish Times* 5 April 2000.
97. Proceeds of Crime Act, 1996, s.2.
98. *Ibid.* s.3.
99. *Ibid.* s.4.
100. *Ibid.* s.16.
101. The applicant must either be an authorised officer of the CAB or a member of the *Garda Síochána* not below the rank of Chief Superintendent.
102. See Walsh *op. cit.* Ch.13.
103. Europol Act, 1997, s.3(1).
104. Ibid. s.3(3).
105. Ibid. s.3(7).
106. Europol Act, 1997, s.3(2).
107. Ibid. s.3(4).
108. Europol Act, 1997, s.4(1).
109. Europol Convention, Art.5(1).
110. Europol Act, 1997, s.4(2).
111. Ibid. s.4(2)(a).
112. Ibid. s.4(2)(b).
113. If the criminal complaint is made by a citizen the investigation report will be submitted to the independent *Garda Síochána* Complaints Board which will then refer it to the DPP.
114. In 1997, out of 169 Garda complaints referred to the DPP, 3 prosecutions resulted (with no convictions).
115. See D Walsh *op. cit.* Chs.7 and 8.
116. See D Walsh *op. cit.* Ch.9.
117. See D Walsh "Who Guards the Guards?" *Studies* .
118. See D Walsh *The Irish Police* op. cit. Ch.12.

## SELECT BIBLIOGRAPHY

*Annual Report of the Criminal Assets Bureau* (Dublin, 1998).

*Annual Report of the Director of Public Prosecutions* (Dublin, 1998).

*Annual Reports of the Garda Siochana* (Dublin).

Ashe, M. and Reid, P. *Money Laundering* (Dublin: Round Hall, 2000).

Barnes, E., "The Role of the Office of the Director of Public Prosecutions" *Communique* (September, 1995) 3.

Barrett, G. (editor), *Justice and Cooperation in the European Union* (Dublin: Institute of European Affairs, 1997).

Brady, C., *The Guardians of the Peace* (Dublin: Gill & Macmillan, 1974)

Casey, J., *The Office of the Attorney General in Ireland* (Dublin: Institute of Public Administration, 1980).

Casey, J., *The Irish Law Officers: Roles and Responsibilities of the Attorney General and Director of Public Prosecutions* (Dublin: Round Hall, 1996).

Law Reform Commission, *Report on the Confiscation of the Proceeds of Crime* (Dublin, 1991).

McNiffe, L., *A History of the Garda Siochana* (Dublin: Wolfhound Press, 1997).

Owen, N. and Regan, E., *The New Third Pillar: Cooperation against Crime in the European Union* (Dublin: Institute of European Affairs).

Reamonn, S., *History of the Revenue Commissioners* (Dublin: Institute of Public Administration, 1981).

Ryan, E. and Magee P., *The Irish Criminal Process* (Dublin: Mercier Press, 1983)

Walsh, D.P.J., *The Irish Police: a Legal and Constitutional Perspective* (Dublin: Round Hall Sweet & Maxwell, 1998).

Walsh, D.P.J., "The Legal Status of a Member of the Garda Siochana: New Clothes for the Ancient Office of Constable" *Anglo-American Law Review* 23, 1 (1994) 63.

Walsh, D.P.J., "Who Guards the Guards?" *Studies* 88, 350 (1999) 154.

Walsh, D.P.J., "Europol Act, 1997, *Irish Statutes Annotated* (Dublin: Round Hall Sweet & Maxwell, 1998).

Walsh, D.P.J. and McCutcheon, P. (editors), *The Confiscation of Criminal Assets: Law and Procedure* (Dublin: Round Hall Sweet & Maxwell, 1999).

Walsh, D.P.J. and McCutcheon, P., "Ierland" in *Heimelijke Opsporing in de Europese Unie* edited by P. Tak (Groningen: Intersentia Rechtsweten-sschappen, 2000).

**ABBREVIATIONS**

| | |
|---|---|
| CAB | Criminal Assets Bureau |
| CNDT | Customs National Drug Team |
| DMP | Dublin Metropolitan Police |
| DPP | Director of Public Prosecutions |
| GBFI | Garda Bureau of Fraud Investigation |
| MDG | EU Multi-Disciplinary Group on Organised Crime |
| MOU | Memorandum of Understanding |
| NBCI | National Bureau of Criminal Investigation |
| RIC | Royal Irish Constabulary |

# Italy

## Francesca Longo

### INTRODUCTION: ORGANISED CRIME AND THE ITALIAN POLITICAL AND LEGISLATIVE AGENDA IN THE 1990S

The political and theoretical debate on the need to reform the Italian penal legislation in order to improve the effectiveness of the repression activity of stable criminal groups arose at the middle of the seventies. Since then special acts against terrorist groups and drug traffickers and organised criminal groups has been approved. At the middle of eighties the activity of a pool of magistrates, directed by Giovanni Falcone – who was working in the *Procura* in Palermo and who aimed not only to investigate specific Mafia offences, but also to understand the real nature of the Mafia – had brought to light a new perception of the Mafia as a stable organisation, named *"Cosa Nostra"*, which had a formal and secret internal organisation with a hierarchical structure, continuous illicit links with several sectors of civil society and aimed to acquire economic power and political influence. The effect of this new perception suggested the potential the Mafia had to destabilise the political system.

In 1992, the Mafia massacres in Capaci and in Palermo[1] were the culmination of a process of increased Mafia violence aimed at showing the organisation's power.

The consequence of new knowledge about the Mafia organisation and the extreme violence of the Mafia strategy was that at the beginning of the 1990s organised crime, in its territorial branches – *Mafia, Camorra, Ndrangheta, Sacra Corona Unita*[2] – was widely perceived as a threat to state security in Italy. Criminal behaviour was discovered to no longer be the domain of individuals, but that of organised groups aiming to control the economic and political centres and to pervade the structures of civil society. Organised crime was singled out as a menace facing the democratic structure of the nation. In the early 1990s, the term "Mafia terrorism" emerged, describing not only the use of extreme violence against the population as the new Mafia strategy of fighting, but also the serious potential organised crime has for destabilising the social and political system.

The political and legislative reaction of the Italian institutions has been based on the adoption of a specific model for the judicial and policing system in the fight against organised crime.

The Italian government stepped up anti-Mafia activities at the beginning of the 1990s, starting from a new anti-Mafia policy paradigm stemming from the above-mentioned new perception of Mafia phenomena. The new strategy was based on the idea that an organic and coordinated anti-Mafia system was needed in order to face the challenge deriving from a structured criminal system, as the Mafia had been discovered to be. The "Anti-Mafia System" was established during the first half of the 1990s and was based on three main concerns: reform of the criminal and criminal procedure codes in order to establish a special legislation against organised crime, establishment of specialised law enforcement agencies and public prosecution services dealing with organised crime offences only, improvement in the coordination activity either at judicial and police level and at political level. This represented the main points of a criminal policy characterised by a differentiated strategy for organised crime, and by two main features of organisation: centralisation and high specialisation.

Even if we cannot assume that the Italian judiciary, police and prosecutorial system are fully centralised, a centralisation process has nevertheless been taking place since 1990 in the sense of an ongoing process of transferring authority from local authorities to national bodies. Such a process has occurred at the level of both the prosecution service and the law enforcement agencies as well as at the political level, as demonstrated by the establishment of the *Consiglio Generale per la lotta alla criminalità organizzata* (General Council for the fight against organised crime) in 1991.[3] It consists in a political body responsible for the coordination of anti-Mafia activities. It is composed of the Minister of Interior, who is also its president, the national chiefs of the three national law enforcement agencies, and the directors of the two national agencies for the secret services.[4] The director of the *Direzione Investigativa Antimafia* (DIA[5]) takes part in the meeting of the General Council with the specific task of informing it about the functioning and the activities of the DIA.

The General Council acts at the political level. It has the legal competence for direction, control and coordination of the criminal policy in the field of fighting organised crime. It elaborates the national strategies for fighting organised crime both in terms of prevention and repression, determines the specific areas of activities for each law enforcement agency, rationalises the economic and structural resources and instruments of the anti-Mafia policing activities, verifies the achievement of targets in relation to the proposed strategies and, if necessary, controls potential ineffectiveness or inefficiency and verifies the responsibilities. It can also issue directives which the DIA and the police forces have to implement.[6]

Specialisation is the feature of the Italian policy for fighting organised crime. Since the early 1990s, a dual criminal investigation and prosecution system has been created: one for ordinary organised crime and one for Mafia-organised crime. The police system and public prosecution system are divided in two levels with different organisations, different legislation and different rules. The Italian penal law has a formal, normative system for fighting the Mafia, which was established in early 1990 as emergency legislation and consolidated throughout the 1990s. Such a system permits different treatment for people suspected of being Mafiosi.[7]

There is also specialisation as regards the institutions: at judicial level, there are both national prosecutors for Mafia crime and district public prosecutors, who are specialised magistrates, dealing with Mafia-related offences only. At the law enforcement level, the Anti-Mafia Investigation Directorate is the specialised body with the specific task of carrying out proactive investigation activities and judiciary police investigations in the field of Mafia-related crime.

This dual model system causes problems of coordination between the two levels, above all in the investigative stage. In some situations, it is very difficult to clearly identify the border between Mafia and ordinary crime. As stressed below, the difficulties involved in defining *a priori* an offence as Mafia related could mean that there is a risk of overlapping actions and the wasting of resources. But if we evaluate the double system for efficiency it is possible to say that it has worked. During the 1990s the more important Mafia bosses were captured.[8]

## 1. ORGANISED CRIME IN ITALY: DEFINITION AND LEGAL PROVISIONS

Even if the notion of organised crime began to be used in Italy around the middle of the seventies, in correspondence with the increase in some offences requiring the involvement of an organised group of people for being carrying out (kidnappings, terrorist attacks, the spread of drugs), the Italian penal code defines neither the terms *criminalità organizzata* (organised crime) nor a definitive list of organised-crime related offences. Art. 416 of the criminal code defines the *associazione per delinquere*[9] (criminal organisation) as the association of three or more people for the purpose of committing illegal activities. It is a very vague definition that causes continual problems in the practice of policing and judicial activity. In fact even if the criminal code does not define this category of crime, several acts refer to organised criminal offences in establishing different procedural rules, both at investigation and judicial procedure levels if the suspect is charged with an organised criminal offence.[10]

In 1982, an official definition of the *associazione di tipo mafioso*[11] (Mafia-organised crime) was introduced in the criminal code: The *associazione di tipo mafioso*[12] is defined as those criminal organisations which use intimidation, a conspiracy of silence or the subjection to an organisation in order to commit crime, to acquire control of or to manage economic activities, public contracts and licences, to realise illicit profits, to impede the freedom of voting, or to influence political votes during the elections. The main variable defining Mafia-organised crime is the use of intimidation deriving from the senior levels of an organisation characterised by hierarchy, extreme violence and strict ties, comparable to the family ties. The official definition of Mafia organised crime is valid for all criminal organisations having the same characteristics and the same criminal purposes of the Mafia, as they result from the Art. 416 bis.

Moreover, while the notion of organised crime organisation is univocally accepted,[13] the list of organised crime offences is subject of an ongoing debate.

To date debates about the definition of organised crime offences have produced two different approaches to this. The first approach identifies organised criminal offences those offences listed in the act establishing the *Direzione Nazionale Anti-Mafia* and the *Direzione Investigativa Anti-Mafia* and those offences considered in the article 416 bis and 630 of the penal code. The second approach adopts a broader definition of organised crime offences, including not only the offences referred to in Art. 416 bis and 630, but also a long list of other offences quoted in Art. 372.1 *bis* of the criminal procedure code[14] for which it is foreseen that the national public prosecutor at the court of appeal could assume responsibility for enquiries, for reasons of coordination. Such a broader conception arises from some rulings of the *Corte di Cassazione* (the Italian Supreme Court) stating that the concept of organised crime offences includes all offences in which an organisation is prominent in the action in question.[15] That definition underlies a teleological interpretation of the complex norms in the fight against organised crime. In this perspective, the counter organised crime legislation is considered to be a means of fulfilling the specific purpose of defeating this particular form of crime. Nevertheless, practitioners and academics would like to see an official definition of the term.

## 2. THE LAW ENFORCEMENT AGENCIES IN ITALY

The Italian policing system can probably best be characterised as a centralised and plural system with both military and civilian statutes. In fact, it is based on the traditional division into three law enforcement agencies: the *"Polizia di Stato"*, the *"Carabinieri"* and the *"Guardia di Finanza"*,[16] which are centralised in their organisation, but rely on different statutes.

The *"Carabinieri Corps"* is the oldest Italian police institution. It was established in 1814 by the King as the *"Corpo dei Carabinieri Reali"* (Royal *Carabinieri* Corps), on the basis of the statute of the *"Gendarmerie Française"*. Since its establishment, it has had the tasks of both military defence and policing activity. In 1861 it was the first military division to be included in the new national army of the united Italy. Its strong involvement in Italian history created the perception of the *Carabinieri* as the symbol not only of the Italian policing system, but ALSO of the Italian state.[17] In 1864 the parliament gave the *"Carabinieri"* the formal appellation of *"Benemerita"* (the Meritorious Corps). It had around 111,000 officers in 1999.

It has a two-fold task: participation in the military defence of the country, as the 4th corps of the Italian Army, and responsibility for public order, public safety and judiciary police activity. It also had the sole role of military police at national level and, in cooperation with the allied forces, in the NATO military bases located in Italy. The *Carabinieri Corps* comes under the Ministry of the Defence in relation to its military activity and the Ministry of the Interior in relation to its public security and judiciary police duties.

The *Carabinieri Corps* is organised within a *Comando Generale* (General Command) directed by a *Comandante Generale* (General Commander) and in the following territorial units:
- *Stazione,* at the urban area level;
- *Compagnie,* comprising several *Stazioni*;
- *Comando Provinciale* (Provincial Command) constituted by several *Compagnie*;
- *Comando Regionale* (Regional Command), which groups the *Comandi Provinciali* of one region;
- *Divisione,* a grouping of more regional commands standing directly under of the General Command. The territorial units have a hierarchical organisation.

The *Carabinieri Corps* has specialised units, with the task of safeguarding specific public interests:
- *Nucleo Anti Sofisticazioni* ((NAS) anti-adulteration unit located at the Ministry of Public Health. This has the task of dealing with cases involving the adulteration of foodstuffs and is also involved in controlling

the production and sale pharmaceutical produce.

- *Nucleo Operativo Ecologico* ((NOE) environmental operations unit), with a "special radioactive materials squad" having the task of investigating on the illegal traffic of radioactive materials and nuclear waste.
- *Comando Tutela patrimonio artistico* (TPA) – investigating on the illegal traffic of works of art.
- *Comando Ispettorato del Lavoro* – involved in the protection of the workers' safety.
- *Comando Tutela Norme Comunitarie* – having the special task of controlling the application of the European Union law in the field of the food production and distribution.

The *Carabinieri Corps* also has a number of units with highly specialised personnel:

- *Raggruppamento Operativo Speciale* ((ROS) special operational group), which has specific competences in the field of national and international terrorism and offences related to organised crime.
- *Gruppo Intervento Speciale* ((GIS) special intervention group) specialised in high-risk operations (rescue of hostages, counter-terrorist operations, and protection of public personalities).
- *Centro Carabinieri Investigazioni Scientifiche* ((CCIS) Central Forensic Service) specialised in high technology applied to investigation activities.

The *Polizia di Stato* (state police) dates back to 1922, when the *Corpo degli Agenti di pubblica sicurezza* (Corps of Public Security Officers) was established. During the Badoglio government, in 1943, the Corps was militarised. During the first post-liberation government the *Corpo delle guardie di pubblica sicurezza* (Corps of Public Security Guards) was established with the task of guaranteeing public order, the safety of persons and the protection of property as well as policing.

In 1981, the Public Security Reform Act[18] reformed the *Polizia di Stato*: the demilitarisation, the possibility to organise trade-unions, equal career opportunities for women and men and a new name for the Corps of the Public Security Guards – *Polizia di Stato* (state police) – were the main innovations.

In 1999, the *Polizia di Stato* had about 100,000 officers. It is placed under the authority of the Ministry of the Interior and its tasks are mainly to police the urban and suburban areas. It is directed by a *Capo Nazionale* (National Head) and comprises several units:

- The *Polizia Stradale* (Automobile Service).
- The *Polizia di Frontiera* (Border Service), including a specialised unit for the illegal immigration.
- The *Polizia Ferroviaria-Polfer* (Railway Service).

- The *Polizia Postale* (Postal and Communication Service), including a specialised unit on high technology crime.
- The *Polizia Marittima – PolMare –* (Maritime Service).
- The *Servizio Aereo* (Air Service).
- The *Reparti Mobili* (the Rapid [Auto]mobile Intervention Service).
- The *Polizia Scientifica* (Forensic Service), including a specialised service: the *Unità per l'analisi del crimine violento* ((UACV) the violent crime analysis unit).

Moreover, the *Polizia di Stato* includes two highly specialised squads:
- The *Nucleo Centrale Operativo di Sicurezza* ((NOCS) Central Security Operational Unit), a highly specialised squad, set up in 1978. The NOCS is the police squad responsible for high-risk operations (rescuing hostages, arresting dangerous fugitives, carrying out counter-terrorism operations). The NOCS squad is endowed with special equipment and its personnel are trained for working daily with sophisticated intervention techniques.
- the *Servizio Centrale Operativo* ((SCO) National Operational Service) is specialised in the fight against all serious forms of crime, also in relation with the financial, economic and high-tech crimes.

The territorial organisation of the state police is based on the *"Questura"*, the office of the state police and the Department of Public Security in each provincial district.[19] The *Questura*'s basic organisation consists of two divisions – judiciary police and social-administrative police – and six main offices: the secretariat, the personnel office, the general investigations and special operations office, the accounting-administrative office, the health office and the juvenile office.

The *"Questore"* is the chief of the *Questura* and he has the responsibility for the provincial management and coordination of all the police services. The coordination and the uniformity of the activities of each *Questura* are guaranteed by the centralised system controlled by the Department of Public Security under the Ministry of Interior.

The *Guardia di Finanza* ((GdF) customs and revenue police) is also known by the popular name of *Fiamme Gialle* (yellow flames). Its activity is related to the protection of the financial and economic interest of the Italian state and it is attached to the Ministry of the Finance. Its traditional task is related to the fight against fiscal fraud. Nevertheless, the increase in the amount of financial crime, such as fraud, usury,[20] plus increased smuggling activities by criminal organisations, are transforming the *Guardia di Finanza* into an important pillar of the policing and public safety services. The service is currently involved, together with the other law enforcement agencies, in policing activity as well, above all in the field of the fight against smuggling, fraud, and usury. It participates in the public safety service, having at its disposal for this task the rapid intervention units. In 1992 the Ministry of Interior recognised the *Guardia di Finanza* as the specialised corps in the investigation activities in the field of money laundering and related crime.

The GdF is organised in a *Comando Generale* (General Command) directed by a *Comandante Generale* (General Commander), and in the following territorial units: the *Comandi Interregionali*, with the competence of supervising large areas, the *Comandi Regionali* and the *Comandi Provinciali*.

The GdF central command is organised into several central *nuclei* (units):

- The *Nucleo Speciale di Polizia Valutaria*, specialised in fiscal enquiries.
- The Servizio *centrale investigativo sulla Criminalità Organizzata* ((SCICO) National Investigative Service on Organised Crime).
- The *Nucleo Speciale Repressione Frodi Comunitarie* (Special Units anti-EU fraud)
- The *Nucleo Investigativo* – the Investigative Unit.

A special central command for economic and financial investigations will be established soon and it will be under the central units.[21]

Up to now the Department of Public Security, directed by the head of the state police who is also the General Director of the Public Safety, has had the responsibility to direct and coordinate the national policing and public safety service of the three police forces – through the *Direzione Centrale della Polizia Criminale* (Central Directorate of Criminal Police), established in 1984 in order to coordinate the judiciary police investigations – the general crime prevention activity and territorial policing at national level. The *Direzione Centrale della Polizia Criminale* is the main directorate of the Department of Public Security in relation to criminal activity. Its main task is to ensure the coordination at the national level of judiciary police investigation and the collection and analysis of data for all forms of serious crime, but it also delivers several services regarding the national coordination of policing activity.

Several services[22] are included: *Servizio Anticrimine* (Crime Service): provides an updated analysis of the national situation of the public security; *Servizio Interpol* (Interpol Service): it is responsible for the international operational cooperation with the International Criminal Police Organisation; *Servizio Polizia Scientifica* (Forensic Science Service): it is a highly multidisciplinary, specialised service, providing high-tech policing to investigations; *Servizio Contrasto Grande Criminalità* (Serious Crime Service): provides analyses of information and data on serious crime; *Servizio Centrale Operativo* – ((SCO) National Operative Service): it is the national unit responsible for the coordination of the investigative and operational services of the state police in the field of organised crime. It is directly responsible for 26 organised crime sections which are specialised squads investigating activity related to organised crime at district level – at the level of *Questura*; *Servizio Centrale di Protezione* (Central Witness Protection Service) responsible for the protection services for the "pentiti"; *Servizio Controllo del Territorio* (Territorial Control Service); Servizio Economico e Finanziario (Budgetary Service); *Divisione SIRENE* (SIRENE Division); *Unità Nazionale Europol* (Europol National Unit).

On 30 March 2000, a reform of the police forces was established by virtue of an act of parliament.[23] This gave the government the main directives for the reorganisation of the law enforcement system. The main aspect of the reform is the transformation of the *Carabinieri Corps* from a military division of the Army into the 4th Army Corps directly under the Ministry of Defence. In attending to its public order tasks, the *Carabinieri Corps* functionally remains under the Ministry of Interior. The structure of the coordination and direction of the police forces has not been changed: it is supervised by the Ministry of Interior, who is responsible for public security through the Department of Public Security. The first draft of the reform project stated that the Ministry of Interior, who is responsible for coordination and direction, should provide the central command of each police force with directives for the public security activity. But this version was strongly contested by the state police, because it was supposed to transform the *Carabinieri Corps* into an independent corps acting in the fields of military service, military policing and public security, with a strong concentration of power. This first draft version of the Reform act was criticized as allowing *Carabinieri Corps* to conduct its public security activity without the control of the Department of Public Security, which is a civilian institution. Such a situation was considered very dangerous for the democratic stability of the country because the *Carabinieri Corps*, as a division of the Army, has a military status. The first draft of the reform was considered also as a threat to the effectiveness of the national public security activity, because it deprived the Department of Public Security of its power to coordinate the national public security activity of the three police forces. A vigorous debate arose on the text, and the parliament preferred to change the text of the reform project and to maintain the current structure of coordination. As result, the Carabinieri Corps has obtained the status of military corps, but it remains under the coordination of the civilian authority, the department of Public Security, in carrying out its public order activity.

## 3. THE PUBLIC PROSECUTION SERVICE

The *Pubblico Ministero* (Public Prosecutor) could be considered from a two-fold perspective. The first perspective regards its task as controlling the application of the law and the administration of justice, under the surveillance of the Minister of Justice.[24] From this perspective, the *Pubblico Ministero* might appear to be a representative of the executive power at judiciary proceedings.[25] At the same time the *Pubblico Ministero* belongs to the judiciary which is autonomous and independent from every other political institution.[26] This has caused a theoretical debate on the real nature of the Public Prosecution Service in Italy. The *Pubblico Ministero* is a judge with the same professional education as the magistrates of the courts, but he or she does not have the power of *jus dicere*.[27] His primary task is to represent society in the legal proceedings (the public accuser role).

Since 1989, following the reform of the penal procedural code that substituted the inquisitor model of trial with the adversarial one, public prosecutor researches the "notizia criminis", starts and coordinates the enquires, decides the legal category under which the offence should be subsumed, decides whether to charge a person with an offence and, if he has enough evidence, makes a request for proceedings to the *Giudice di Udienza preliminare* (the judge of the preliminary hearing).[28] According to Art. 109 of the Italian Constitution, the Public Prosecutor, in conducting enquiries, has at his disposal the criminal police, which include personnel from the three police forces.

The public prosecution offices are organised according the different level of the jurisdiction. The first level is the *Procuratore della Repubblica* at the *Tribunale* (the court of first instance). The second level is the *Procuratore Generale della Repubblica* at the *Corte di Appello* (court of appeal), the criminal court having second instance jurisdiction. The system also has specialised public prosecutors for juvenile and military crimes.

Furthermore, the Public Prosecution service is organised in territorial units. The district offices of the *Procure della Repubblica* are located in each district court to whom they belong. Each *Procura* is headed by a magistrate called the *Procuratore della Repubblica* and consists of a pool of magistrates with the role of *Sostituto Procuratore della Repubblica* (substitute prosecutor).

The peripheral offices of public prosecution service of the Court of Appeal are the *Procura Generale di Corte d'Appello*. Each Court of Appeal groups several district courts of first instance. A *Procura Generale* (National Prosecution Bureau), headed by a *Procuratore Generale* (National Prosecutor) having national competence, is located at the "*Corte di Cassazione*", the third level criminal court, which has the competence to control the activities of the first two courts only on procedural points.

The structure of the public prosecution service is not completely hierarchical. Each bureau is autonomous, but since 1988[29] the heads of the *Procure* have been entrusted with the power of overseeing the magistrates forming the team. Moreover, the general public prosecutor at the Court of Appeal can take over an enquiry from a lower public prosecution office, even if only on specific conditions.

## 4. THE ANTI-MAFIA[30] SPECIALISED INSTITUTIONS

### 4.1. Law enforcement units to fight organised crime

On 6 September 1982, the General Commander of the *Carabinieri Corps*, Carlo Alberto Dalla Chiesa, was murdered in Palermo by the Mafia. The same day the government established the *"Alto Commissario per il coordinamento della lotta contro la delinquenza mafiosa"*[31] (High Commissioner for the Coordination of the Fight against the Mafia) with the power to coordinate the administrative offices and the police forces both at national and local level in the field of the Mafia, a post which came directly under the Ministry of Interior. The High Commissioner also had the task of gathering information on the Mafia phenomena, including by pro-actively intercepting communication. The High Commissioner did not have at his disposal his own personnel but rather worked with the ordinary police forces. Specialised services charged with collecting information and elaborating an evaluation on the Mafia were established at local level, under the authority of the local public security authorities.

Although the establishment of a specialised anti-Mafia institution was considered as an innovation in the policing system, the results of its action were not satisfactory. The lack of specialised staff, capabilities and sufficient power over the local police authorities are the main reasons for the partial failure of the Commissioner's activities before 1988, when the government provided him with a wider range of powers and responsibilities in order to improve his capability.[32] Nevertheless, the reform of the High Commissioner failed in not including operational tasks among the list of his/her powers.[33]

Moreover, a Central Directorate of Criminal Police was established in 1984 within the Public Security Department of the Ministry of Interior. It is charged with the responsibility for coordinating criminal police investigations at national level in the field of organised crime,[34] for collecting data and coordinating the national analysis of data, and for coordinating the crime prevention activities and territorial policing at national level.

At the beginning of nineties, as result of the new above mentioned approach to the Mafia phenomena, the law enforcement agencies were provided with specialised organised crime squads. In 1991 the *Reparto Operativo Speciale* (ROS) within the *Carabinieri Corps,* the *Servizio Centrale Operativo* (SCO) within the state police and the *Servizio centrale investigativo sulla Criminalità Organizzata* (SCICO) within the customs and revenue police were instituted.

These special squads have been located both at national level, with the establishment of central services, and at the peripheral level with the establishment of inter-provincial services.[35] The act establishing these special services entrusted them with the responsibility to conduct investigative activities in the field of organised crime, in conjunction with the judiciary police services. In particular, the SCO is specialised in the fight against all serious forms of crime, including in relation to financial, economic and high-tech crimes. The ROS is specialised in serious crime in the field of dangerous fugitives, kidnapping and in the field of Mafia-organised crime. The SCICO is specialised in financial investigations, with particular regard to money laundering and the fight against usury. These special squads can carry out undercover activities if they act as judiciary police. In this case they are obliged to inform the judicial authority.

In 1998, the Ministry of Interior, by virtue of an administrative act, modified the role of the central services of ROS, SCO and SCICO, denying them the possibility to conduct investigations and giving them tasks in the field of information and data analysis and providing logistic support to the interprovincial services[36] that retained their responsibility for conducting enquiries at the request of the national or district anti-Mafia public prosecutor. In March 2000, the new Ministry of Interior also re-established the investigative power for the central services of the special corps. In this new directive the peripheral branches could ask the district anti-Mafia public prosecutor for assistance from the national service if they are conducting enquiries relating to organised criminal groups acting at the national level or in connection with transnational criminal groups.

Since 1991, the establishment of the *Direzione Investigativa Anti-Mafia*[37] ((DIA) Anti-Mafia Investigation Directorate) has modified the organisation of the anti-Mafia law enforcement system. The perception of the need for a permanent national anti-Mafia police service has concerned three main processes: to enhance the gathering and coordination of anti-Mafia intelligence, to improve the effectiveness of anti-Mafia investigations and to provide the DNA with a specialist policing service. The *Direzione Investigativa Anti-Mafia* represents a new element in the Italian policing model. It has been set up with the two-fold task of a specialist anti-Mafia police service, with both intelligence and operative powers, and a national central body for the coordination and direction of the anti-Mafia policing activity with the specific task of carrying out proactive investigation activities and judicial police investigation only in the field of national and international Mafia-related crime. It is included in the Public Security Department of the Ministry of Interior and is defined as an 'inter-force' agency, with 1,500 officers coming from the three police forces: state police, *Carabinieri* and customs and revenue police. It has a rotating leadership: it is headed by a commander of one of the three police forces.

It is possible to define three areas of the DIA's tasks: the coordination of policing anti-Mafia activity, the establishment of a permanent specialised anti-Mafia intelligence unit and operational anti-Mafia activity.

It is divided in three sections:

- **The proactive investigations section** is the anti-Mafia central intelligence bureau and has the task of collecting and analysing information on Mafia-organised crime in order to elaborate the general strategy of the proactive investigation activity against Italian and foreign Mafia-type organisations; this section is sub-divided into four divisions. The first division has the task of gathering and analysing information only on the Sicilian Mafia. The second has the competence to gather and analyse information on the other Italian Mafia-type organisations and on foreign criminal organisations that are supposed to act throughout the Italian territory or to have a link with Italian Mafia-type organisations. The third division is entrusted with the responsibility for proposing restrictive measures in relation to personal freedom that must be adopted for those suspected of belonging to a Mafia organisation and the treatment of their assets. The fourth division is specialised in the analysis of Mafia assets. It gathers economic information on suspected persons and is involved in the analysis of the suspected financial flows with the particular task of identifying money laundering activities.
- **The judicial investigations section** has the task of planning the investigation activities of the DIA and of verifying the results. It is also involved in the analysis of the information received from the intelligence services. This section represents the anti-Mafia judiciary police at the disposal of the DNA and DDA.
- **The international cooperation section** has the task of promoting and developing cooperation and the sharing of information with foreign intelligence and policing organisations, in order to study the international interconnection of the various organised crime groups.

The DIA was created with the specific task of "nationalising" the fight against the Mafia and, for that reason, it has not been organised in peripheral sections. It has competence throughout the entire national territory. However, twelve functional "operational services" have been set up at the peripheral level in order to monitor the Mafia phenomenon at local level.

In implementing its tasks the DIA and special organised crime squads of the police forces can carry out proactive investigations and undercover activities. In fact, Art. 266 of the procedural penal code allows proactive policing methods, with particular regard to the interception of communications. According to the law, "communication" means all the possible forms of exchanging ideas and information between two or more people. In this sense, the law permits "tapping", the interception of electronic forms of communication (e-mail, fax and videos), including the use of "bugs" (microphones, cameras) in private houses and offices. Such instruments of proactive policing are allowed under some conditions that are different for investigations in the field of "ordinary" crime than in the field of "Mafia-type" crime. The public prosecutor must ask authorisation from the judge for the preliminary enquiry (*giudice per le indagini*). For ordinary crime, authorisation is allowed if **significant** evidence of an offence exists; for Mafia-type crime the existence of **sufficient** evidence is enough to allow interception.

In 1996, the *Servizio Centrale Antidroga* (central drug enforcement agency) was established under the authority of the national chief of the state police. It consists of an interforce-agency, formed by personnel from the three law enforcement agencies, and has the task of coordinating international and national drug–related enquiries. It is also the national contact point for the drugs squads of foreign police forces. It is the only institution allowed to conduct controlled delivery and simulations of drug trafficking.

It also has an intelligence-gathering task. This information is used by the police forces, especially the police and customs service.

A special integrated team is the *Servizio Centrale Protezione Testimoni* (Central witnesses protection service), which is a multi-agency team involving the three law enforcement agencies (Carabinieri, state police and customs and revenue police), who work in order to implement the special protection and assistance measures, including the social re-integration of cooperating witnesses and other individuals admitted to the protection programme. It has been developed by the Central Commission under Art. 10 of Decree-Law No. 8 of 15 January 1991. To this end, it maintains contact with national and foreign judicial and police authorities, as well as with the relevant prison administration bodies and any other central and local authorities concerned. Through its fourteen operational units with regional or inter-regional jurisdiction, the service directly implements the financial assistance measures included in the programme and ensures the necessary support.

Some problems arise in the relationship between the DIA and the anti-organised crime squads. In fact the legislation does not describe a clear division of competences. The analysis of the full legislation on the anti-Mafia seems to indicate an integrated system operating at different levels.[38] The national level is centred on the DIA, the specialised central point with both national coordination and intelligence tasks. At the peripheral level the special inter-provincial anti-organised crime squads have territorial competence and they are compelled by law to cooperate with the DIA's personnel. The relationships between the central cervices of the SCICO, ROS and SCO are more problematic. Even if it is impossible to deny the pre-eminent role of the DIA in the anti-Mafia policing activity, it is not clear how this priority should be translated into practical criteria for the division of tasks and power in relation to the central anti-organised crime services of the police forces. Risks of overlap and inter-agency rivalries arise in everyday activities.

### 4.2. Public prosecution units to fight organised crime

In 1991, the *Direzione Nazionale Anti-Mafia* (DNA) was established.[39] It consists of a national public prosecution bureau which has responsibility for the public prosecution activity related to Mafia-related offences only. The DNA is located at the national prosecution bureau of the *Corte di Cassazione*, is headed by the *Procuratore Nazionale Anti-Mafia* (the national public prosecutor for Mafia cases) and is under the supervision of the National Prosecutor of the *"Corte di Cassazione"*. *Procure Distrettuali Anti-Mafia* (district public prosecution offices for Mafia cases) have been established at each district court of appeal. Each district public prosecution office for Mafia cases is directed by the *Procuratore Distrettuale Anti-Mafia* (district public prosecutor for Mafia cases) and is composed of judges having specific skills and experience in anti-Mafia activity, appointed by the *Procuratore Distrettuale Anti-Mafia*, after the consent of the *Procuratore Nazionale Anti-Mafia*.

The DNA[40] and the DDA are special public prosecution offices which only have competence in the field of Mafia offences, kidnapping and drug offences.[41]

The DDA are the peripheral anti-Mafia public prosecution offices located at each district *Procura* office and directed by a district anti-Mafia public prosecutor. Each DDA is competent in conducting specific enquiries for Mafia-related offences only. The DNA is the national anti-Mafia public prosecution office and has the task of boosting the district's anti-Mafia activity, coordinating the district's investigative enquiries and optimising the work of the judiciary police and the use of investigation means and structures.

In light of the above tasks, the role of the *Direzione Nazionale Anti-Mafia* seems to be the elaboration of anti-Mafia judicial policy to be implemented by the anti-Mafia public prosecution services at district level. In order to attain this target the DNA and its director have been provided with powers and competences both at the coordination and operative level. The anti-Mafia national public prosecutor has at his disposal the police squads of the DIA, the anti-Mafia squads of the three police forces (ROS, SCO, SCICO) and the peripheral judiciary police forces. Nevertheless, the legislation does not provide the DNA the direct power to start and conduct judicial enquiries: it has the task of coordinating the enquiry activity of the district anti-Mafia public prosecutors. Some academics have spoken about the possibility of the DNA carrying out investigative activity under the form of "potential or preliminary enquiries",[42] such that it can maximise its role of investigative coordinator and such that it can identify the focus points of the national anti-Mafia policy.

The national anti-Mafia public prosecutor also has at his disposal the following operational instruments: the possibility to give directives to the peripheral public prosecutors on some judicial issues (coordination of specific enquiries, use of police forces, indications of judicial competencies in specific cases); the possibility to decide on the appointment of the magistrates forming the Anti-Mafia National Direction team and district anti-Mafia public prosecution offices; the possibility to take over specific enquiries on Mafia offences from the peripheral public prosecution offices, if the latter have not been effective or coordinated in their activities. Similar to the ordinary public prosecution services, the relationship between the national and district anti-Mafia public prosecution offices is not fully hierarchical. Each DDA is obliged to follow the coordination directives, but is not subjected to the direct hierarchical power of the DNA in conducting each judicial enquiry. It is possible to say that the DNA's coordination power and the possibility for the national anti-Mafia public prosecutor to instigate enquiries by the peripheral offices provide the DNA with a wide range of directional tools.

The general prosecutor of the "*Corte di Cassazione*" supervises the activity of the national anti-Mafia public prosecution service and the national anti-Mafia public prosecutor.

## 5.  INTELLIGENCE SERVICES AND THE FIGHT AGAINST ORGANISED CRIME

The extension of responsibility for organised crime to the secret services is an additional result of the anti-Mafia system of the early 1990s. The Italian national secret service agencies are the *Servizio Informazioni sulla sicurezza militare* ((SISMI) information agency on the military security), and the *Servizio Informazioni sulla sicurezza democratica* ((SISDE) Information Agency on Democratic Security). The first has the responsibility for the control of the international activities menacing the state security. The second is responsible for the preservation of democratic order and is entrusted with the responsibility to control the internal threats facing the State and its institutional apparatus. They are under the control of the premier and of a interministry department formed by the Ministries of the Defence, Interior and Foreign Affairs.

In 1991, legislation[43] entrusted both the Italian security agencies with responsibility in the field of organised crime. Since then SISMI and SISDE were to work in this area with the specific task of collecting sensitive national and transnational information in the field of Mafia organisations and of following the complete evolution of every national and transnational criminal organisation that could represent a threat to the democratic institutions and civil society. The secret services' role in the anti-Mafia system is very different from the role of the police forces. SISMI and SISDE are entrusted with the responsibility for gathering covert information by means of undercover methods of investigation and pass it to the DIA. SISMI and SISDI have no operational role, but their task is to obtain information that other institutions are not able to obtain. Information that SISMI and SISDI pass to the DIA is analysed and verified on the basis of the formal anti-Mafia investigative procedures or is utilised by the intelligence office of the DIA. The secret services' role in the area of anti-Mafia policing is configured as a large range activity aimed at informing political and police institutions on the potential or actual dangers facing the country. The director of the DIA is the direct interlocutor of the secret services in the area of the anti-Mafia, and a parliamentary committee on the security services is charged with the responsibility of ensuring the accountability of their work.

## 6. INTERNATIONAL CONTACT POINTS

The establishment of international contact points, both at the level of police and judicial activity, is a new phenomenon in Italian legislation. If endogenous variables could be considered as the sources of the anti-Mafia reform process set up in the early 1990s, some exogenous variables have certainly also contributed to the establishment of international contact points. The latter are furnished with the specific task of managing the relationship with foreign judicial and police authorities and of exchanging international information on the Mafia and the organised-crime phenomena. Even if all actors involved in the control of organised crime were already practising international cooperation in the face of growing transnational crime, Italian participation in Schengen and Europol has led to the creation of new official bodies, which have been entrusted with international police cooperation and international judicial matters.

The **National Central Bureau of ICPO-Interpol** is the standing body and the contact office for international cooperation matters within the framework of Interpol. It is formed by personnel from the three law enforcement agencies and acts as a liaison between Italy, the central Interpol institutions and the contact points of the other Interpol member states. At national level, it also represents the contact point for the other institutions involved in international cooperation activities (e.g. Ministry of Justice, Ministry of Foreign Affairs, etc.). To this end, it provides judicial assistance to the magistrates involved in proceedings having some links with foreign countries: international letters rogatory, international searches for wanted persons and judiciary police enquiries; it exchanges information with Member States' law enforcement agencies and also deals with the tracing of minors. The director of the national central bureau of Interpol has the task to coordinate the activities of the SIRENE Division and Europol National Unit.

The **SIRENE Division** was established in 1993 within the Central Directorate of the Criminal Police. It ensures liaison with the SIRENE offices of the Schengen area. The SIRENE division is a multi-agency office formed by personnel from the state police, the *Carabinieri Corps* and the customs and revenue police with the task of facilitating information-exchange between the schengen member countries' law enforcement agencies. The official tasks and the operational activities carried out by the SIRENE division are regulated by the Schengen Convention and are related to the following activities: cooperation among law enforcement agencies, provisional arrest of foreign wanted persons with a view to extradition, dealing with aliens inadmissible to the Schengen territory, notifying individuals of judgements, and keeping data on persons and vehicles to be placed under surveillance or subject to specific checks, or procedures (stolen, misappropriated or lost firearms, vehicles, documents and registered banknotes). In 1998, with a national act (act No. 93), a **Europol National Unit** was established within the Office of the Deputy Director General of Public Security – Director General of Criminal Police. The unit provides the liaison service with the Europol headquarters.

Within the Europol body it is the only liaison service between the Italian law enforcement agencies and those in the other EU Member States; it mainly handles two-way information flows concerning the current areas of international cooperation against organised crime (the illegal trafficking in drugs, radioactive and nuclear substances, stolen cars, illegal immigration networks, money laundering, terrorism, trade in human beings, forgery of money and other means of payment). A new *ad hoc* liaison office has been established in Montenegro, in the framework of a bilateral cooperation agreement between Italy and the Montenegro Republic in the area of the fight against organised crime, illegal immigration and smuggling.

## 7.  ACCOUNTABILITY

The differences between the policing and judicial procedures for the ordinary crime and organised crime has created a sort of double system in which the anti-Mafia special legislation provides for a body of more restrictive criminal procedures, different from the procedures provided for the ordinary crime. The special procedures are mainly in relation to the rules for remanding suspects in custody, the treatment of personal assets and the procedures of the prosecution. All these rules are related to the personal freedom and the guarantee of personal rights. The accountability of the anti-Mafia system, both at judicial and at policing level, is the focal point of a debate between two opposing positions: the first is more interested in the defence of personal guarantees while the second supports the need to have a special and stronger anti-Mafia system.

Regarding the control of the policing and judiciary system, no difference exists between the ordinary system and the anti-Mafia system: the formal control of all the investigation activities carried out by the police forces is exercised by the judge for the preliminary enquiry who has the responsibility to authorise the judiciary police to employ proactive policing methods, for the interception of communications, and for remanding those charged in custody. The judge is responsible to the law, but the Ministry of Justice can carry out inspections of the "*procure*" in order to verify that the law has been respected. The difference between Mafia crime and ordinary crime is that proactive interception of personal communication is only allowed only in the field of organised crime. In cases of organised crime the competent "*Procuratore della Repubblica*" gives the legal authorisation for the proactive interception of personal communication.

The parliamentary control of the policing activity is carried out by means of the parliamentary committees. The parliamentary committee on the security services is entrusted with verifying that the activity of the secret services is carried out with the respect to the law, including in relation to the anti-Mafia activity of the secret services. However, the limited power of this committee makes effective democratic control of the secret services activity very difficult. This committee is formed by eight deputies of the parliament and has the faculty to ask the government for information on the activity of the SISME and SISDI, but it is not able to conduct enquiries or inspections.

In 1993, a parliamentary committee on the Schengen Agreement was established in order to control the implementation of the Schengen system in Italy and to ensure its consistency with Italian legislation. In 1998, this Committee was entrusted with the responsibility to control the activity of the Europol National Unit.

## 8. CONCLUSION

Since the 1980s the Italian criminal policy developed in a double pathway. A stable set of separate measures for the organised crime was provided for by the "anti-Mafia" system, constituted by two pillars: specialised institutions dealing with organised crime offences and special legislation on enquires and trials related with organised crime. It will be noticed that the special legislation on the "pentiti" – people belonging to a criminal organisation who decide to turn evidences and useful information on his/her organisation – is considered as a strategic tool in breaking the wall of the conspiracy of silence and, in this perspective, one of the most important instrument for combating organised crime. The legislation on "pentiti" is based on two kind of measures. The first provided for alternatives to the imprisonment and reduction of the penalty, the second provided for a protection system assuring the safety of the "pentito". Legislation against money laundering and on confiscation of the proceeds from organised crime are further elements of the Italian anti-Mafia system.

The most frequent political discourses and debate affecting the development of the anti-Mafia legislation is the idea that the organised crime is a great social and political menace "which represent a danger to public order".[44] Moreover, the Mafia-type organisation envisaged in article 416-bis of the criminal code, is characterised not only by the permanence of associative among the participants, but also by "the use of intimidation…, subjugation and conspiracy of the silence".[45]

In this perspective the anti-Mafia system seems to be assumed not only as a part of criminal policy, but as a constitutive element of guaranteeing state security, the latter menaced by a form of crime defined by an organisational structure and the use of the strategic violence.

The establishment of a special pathway for the managing of the criminal issues dealing with organised crime and related offences could be seen as the result of a process that has securitising the issue of organised crime. The concept of securitisation is defined by Ole Weaver as the process by which an issue is "presented as an existential threat….(and) the actor has claimed a right to handle it with extraordinary means, to break the normal political rules".[46] The special legislation on organised crime, affecting either the criminal code and the procedures for conducting enquires, "breaks" the normal criminal rules dealing with ordinary crime and allows to use extraordinary means to handle the issue.

**NOTES**

1. The Capaci massacre caused the death of the Judge Giovanni Falcone and the Palermo massacre caused the death of the Judge Borsellino.
2. For an overview of the different groups see Nanula: Nanula, *La Lotta alla Mafia: strumenti giuridici, strutture di coordinamento, legislazione vigente*, Milano, Giuffrè, 1999.
3. Act 410, 30 December 1991.
4. The Italian national secret service agencies are the *Servizio Informazioni sulla sicurezza militare* ((SISMI) information agency on the military security) and the *Servizio Informazioni sulla sicurezza democratica* ((SISDE) Information Agency on Democratic Security). The first has the responsibility for the control of the international (*spionaggio*) and the military security of the nation. The second is responsible for the preservation of democratic order. They are both under the control of the premier and of an interministerial department formed by the Ministries of the Defence, Interior and Foreign Affairs.
5. On DIA see point 4.1 of the chapter.
6. For an overview of the main directives and activities of the General Council see: Iannielli F and Rocchegiano M.: *La Direzione Investigativa Anti-Mafia*, Milano Giuffrè (ed.) 1995, p. 90/91.
7. Several procedural rules of the penal prosecution are different in cases of Mafia-related offences. The most famous: the so-called " Maxi prosecution", where there is a combined single prosecution for several offences if they are related and regarded as part of the same criminal Mafia plan. There is also the possibility of accepting interrogations and examinations at a distance, by means of the video-conference in order to safeguard the life of the witnesses or in order to avoid contact between the Mafia bosses and their people. In fact the police discovered that some bosses gave orders and messages to their families with little movements of their eyes or hands during prosecutions.
8. In this paper the legislation on the "pentiti" (informers) is not considered because it is not part of the research objectives, but it is important to consider that this legislation has been one of the main elements permitting the capture and the incrimination of *Mafiosi*.
9. Art. 416 of penal code.
10. On this issue see: Maddalena M., "I Problemi pratici delle inchieste di criminalità organizzata nel nuovo processo penale", in Grevi V. (ed.), *Processo penale e criminalità organizzata*, Laterza, 1993. (ed.) 1993.
11. Art. 416 bis of the penal code was introduced by the Act No. 646 in 1982, in the wake of the murder of Prefetto Dalla Chiesa.
12. The category of Mafia-organised crime is valid also for the "Camorra" and all the other criminal organisations which have the same characteristics as the Mafia.
13. The list of the Mafia-related offences is deduced from the act establishing the *Direzione Nazionale Anti-Mafia*, which entrusted the anti-Mafia national and district public prosecution offices with the responsibility for conducting judicial

enquires referring to offences foreseen by Arts 416 bis and 630 of the criminal code plus drug-related offences. Article 416 bis refers to the offences of participation in Mafia organisations and Art. 630 refers to the offences of kidnapping.

14. The article includes the following types of crime: terrorism, massacre, political conspiracy, kidnapping, and membership of illicit organisations.

15. See, for example, Cassazione penale, section VI, 7 January, 1997 and Cassazione penale, Sez VI, 16 May, 1997. On the problems of trying to deduce the definition of organised crime from the literal interpretation of the Acts, see: Maddalena M.. *I problemi pratici delle inchieste di criminalità organizzata nel nuovo processo penale*, in Grevi V. (ed.), Processo penale e criminalità organizzata, Laterza, 1993.

16. It is possible to translate *Polizia di stato* as state police and *Guardia di Finanza* as the Custom and Revenue Police. The *"Carabinieri Corps"* is used only in Italian as it is impossible to translate.

17. *"Faithful Throughout the Centuries"* is not only the Carabinieri's "motto" but also the household name of the corps.

18. Act No. 121, 1 April 1981.

19. Italy has 103 *Questure*.

20. Usury means the fact or practice of lending money at interest, especially the practice of charging, or taking, excessive or illegal rates of interest for money on loan.

21. See: Press release of the General Commander of the GdF, on the GdF web site: http://www.gdf.it/informa/comunicati/ds151299.htm

22. See the annexes organisational Chart.

23. Act No. 6249, March 2000.

24. Act number 12, January 1941 and Art. 73 of the Judiciary Act.

25. See: Siracusano D., Galati A. and others: *Diritto Processuale Penale*, Giuffrè (ed.), 1996, p.133.

26. Art. 104 of the Italian Constitution.

27. See: Siracusano et al., op. cit.

28. In the Italian Penal system, the Judge d' Instruction is defined as *Giudice per le indagini preliminari* if he acts during the preliminary enquires and *Giudice dell'Udienza preliminare* if he decides whether to proceed with a prosecution.

29. Act No. 499, 1988.

30. Even if, as stressed above, a legal definition of organised crime does not exist, organised crime is quoted as a specific category of crime in several acts. Sometimes it seems to be used as synonymous with the Mafia. In this report the terms "Mafia" and "organised crime" are utilised on the basis of the terminology of the Acts.

31. Act No. 629, 1982.

32. For the list of power see Act 486, 1988.

33. See: De Gennaro G., *Le tecniche anti-Mafia di una polizia speciale*, in "Micromega", No. 3, 1993, p.72. The position of High Commissioner was dismantled in 1993 and its powers and functions passed to *Prefetti*, to the chief

of state police and to the Director of the DIA.

34. Note that such an institution is charged with activity in the field of organised crime, but it acts also in the field of anti-Mafia activity.

35. The interprovincial services have the following names: *sezione criminalità organizzata* (organised crime section) for the SCO, *sezione anticrimine* (criminal section) for the ROS, and *Gruppi investigativi sulla criminalità organizzata – GICO*, (investigative service on organised crime) for the SCICO.

36. For a critical examination of this administrative act see: Vigna, *Non smantelliamo le Superpolizie*, in "Micromega", No. 1,2000.

37. Act No. 345, 1991.

38. See: Iannielli, F. and Rocchegiano, M.: *La Direzione Investigativa Anti-Mafia*, Milano Giuffrè (ed.) 1995, pp. 292-297.

39. Act No. 367, 1991.

40. The DNA is also known by the name of "superprocura".

41. Kidnapping and drug offences have been considered as Mafia type offences on the basis of the consideration of Giovanni Falcone that the main element for recognising a Mafia type offence is a large movement of money. Kidnapping and drug traffic cause such movements and for this reason Falcone defined them as "first level offences". See Falcone, G. and Turone, G., "Tecniche di indagine in materia di Mafia", in *Riflessioni ed esperienze sul fenomeno mafioso, Quaderni del Consiglio superiore della magistratura*, Rome, 1983, quoted in Turone G.: "Indagini collegate, Procure distrettuali e Procura Nazionale Anti-Mafia", in Grevi, G. (ed): *Processo penale e Criminalità Organizzata*, Laterza, 1993.

42. On this point see: Iannielli, F. and Rocchegiano, M.: *La Direzione Investigativa Anti-Mafia*, Milano Giuffrè Ed. 1995, pp. 274-277.

43. Art. 2 of the act 410/1991.

44. Ruling of the Italian Supreme Court,11/10/1991.

45. Ruling of the Italian Supreme Court,15/4/1994.

46. Weaver (1998), p. 80.

## LIST OF ABBREVIATIONS

| | |
|---|---|
| DIA | Direzione Investigativa Antimafia |
| DDA | Direzione Distrettuale Antimafia |
| DNA | Direzione Nazionale Antimafia |
| ROS | Raggruppamento Operativo Speciale |
| GIS | Gruppo Intervento Speciale |
| CCIS | Centro Carabinieri Investigazioni Scientifiche |
| NOCS | Nucleo Centrale Operativo di Sicurezza |
| SCO | Servizio Centrale Operativo |
| GdF | Guardia di Finanza |
| SCICO | Servizio Centrale Investigativo sulla Criminalità Organizzata |
| NAS | Nucleo Anti Sofisticazioni |
| NOE | Nucleo Operativo Ecologico |
| TPA | (Comando) Tutela Patrimonio Artistico |
| SISMi | Servizio Informazioni Sicurezza Militare |
| SISDe | Servizio Informazioni Sicurezza Democratica |
| UNE | Unità Nazionale Europol |

## BIBLIOGRAPHY

De Gennaro, G., *Le tecniche anti-Mafia di una polizia speciale, in "Micromega", n. 3, 1993.*

Grevi, V. (ed.), *Processo penale e criminalità organizzata*, Laterza, 1993.

Iannielli, F. and Rocchegiano, M.: *La Direzione Investigativa Anti-Mafia*, Milano Giuffrè Ed. 1995.

Nanula, *La Lotta alla Mafia: strumenti giuridici, strutture di coordinamento, legislazione vigente*, Milano, Giuffrè, 1999.

Siracusano, D., Galati, A. and others, *Diritto Processuale Penale*, Giuffrè Ed. 1996.

Violante, L. (ed.): *Mafia e anti-Mafia: rapporto 96*, Bari, Laterza, 1997.

Violante, L. (ed.): *Mafia e società italiana*, Bari, Laterza, 1996.

Weaver, O., "Insecurity, Security and Asecurity in the West European non-war Community", in Adler E. and Barnet M., *Security Communities*, Cambridge University Press, 1998, pp. 69-118.

**WEB SITES**

| | |
|---|---|
| Carabinieri corps: | http://www.carabinieri.it |
| State Police: | www.poliziastato.it |
| Ministry of Justice: | http://www.giustizia.it |
| Ministry of Interior: | http://www.mininterno.it |
| Department of Public Security: | http://www.mininterno.it/dip_ps/index.htm |
| DIA: | http://www.mininterno.it/dip_ps/dia/home.htm |
| Parliamentary Committee on Schengen: | http://www.parlamento.it/parlam/bicam/schengen/home.htm |

**Hierarchy in the Coordination of the Policing Service**

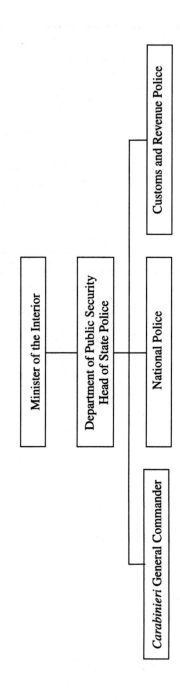

***Central Directorate of Criminal Police***

**ORGANISATIONAL CHART**

## Organisation Chart

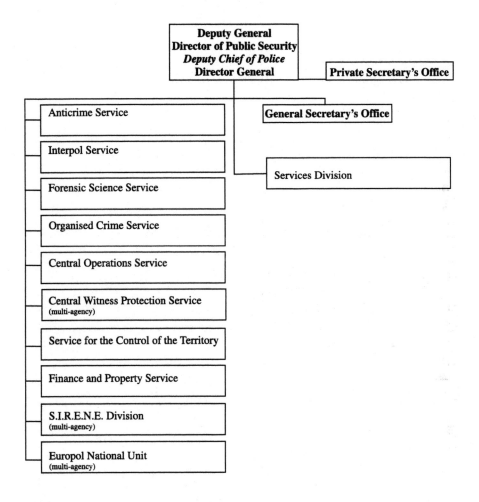

Deputy General
Director of Public Security
*Deputy Chief of Police*
Director General

Private Secretary's Office

General Secretary's Office

Services Division

- Anticrime Service
- Interpol Service
- Forensic Science Service
- Organised Crime Service
- Central Operations Service
- Central Witness Protection Service
  (multi-agency)
- Service for the Control of the Territory
- Finance and Property Service
- S.I.R.E.N.E. Division
  (multi-agency)
- Europol National Unit
  (multi-agency)

# Luxembourg

## *Armand Schockweiler*

### 1. ORGANISED CRIME

In 1998, a definition of the term "criminal organisation" was introduced in the Luxembourg Criminal Code. The text of this definition is largely inspired by the definition proposed in the Joint Action adopted on 21 December 1998 by the Council of the European Union, which relates specifically to Recommendation 17 of the Action Plan to Combat Organised Crime adopted by the Council on the 28th of April 1997.

Participating in activities of a so-called "criminal organisation" has become illegal. A criminal organisation is a structured association of more than two people established on a long-term basis in order to commit crimes punishable by at least four years of imprisonment and aiming to obtain, in some way, financial or economic profit. Besides this general definition, the text describes some illegal activities in relation with this criminal organisation. For example it is punishable:

- to participate actively in a criminal organisation,
- to take part in preparing activities of such a criminal organisation,
- to participate in taking decisions within such an organisation,
- to play a leading role in a criminal organisation.

### 2. THE LAW ENFORCEMENT AGENCIES IN LUXEMBOURG

Luxembourg is a country of about 2,600 square kilometres. Its administrative organisation is rather centralised and there is a national central administration with 119 municipalities. Mayors only have a few competences in policing matters. Since 1952, the influence of mayors has been substantially reduced, as municipalities lost their own police forces and the management over these forces since this date.

On 1 January 2000, the Luxembourg police forces, the *Gendarmerie*

*Grand-Ducale* and the Police, were merged into one single police force, the *Police Grand-Ducale*. In fact, for the last 70 years the two separate police administrations were organised in order to bring together more and more units and to have equal competences in administrative and judicial matters. It is important to mention that since 1930 the two police forces have organised a lot of common services and units in order to avoid double competences, loss of information and a lack of cooperation. Some of the common institutions were for example the common police school, the common information centre for the gathering, organising, evaluating and transmitting information, and one single criminal investigation department, which is the service responsible for major criminal investigations. There was also a very close cooperation at the level of the direction and execution of important operational issues.

The police force has been organised as a national state police department. The new law gives the police the status of national police, with a military statute (different from the state employees), and competent for general matters. The police are organised in six regions, which implies that to some extent, some competences and general services have been decentralised. However, there is only one commanding structure for the whole police service.

At this moment, the police have about 1,200 policemen at this time. In the next decade, the staff will be increased to 1,600 police officers.

The Minister of Interior is responsible for the police, except for the matters relating to the judicial police, where the Minister of Justice, for general matters, and the judicial authorities, for specific investigations, direct and control police activities.

Police and customs work on the basis of different laws. However, customs officers have certain competences in the field of criminal proceedings, mainly in the field of drugs.

## 3. THE PUBLIC PROSECUTION SERVICE IN LUXEMBOURG

Luxembourg is divided into two judicial districts, in both of which a public prosecutor is responsible for the prosecution office. Each office is composed of one or two deputy prosecutors and substitutes for the prosecutor. At the national level, one general public prosecutor is responsible for the general policy in judicial areas and the execution of sentences. He also deals with several matters relating to coordination activities. He is assisted by a deputy general prosecutor and several advocates general. The general public prosecutor is also the head of the national bureau of coordination of the ICPO-Interpol.

In each judicial district, one or several investigating judges are responsible for the instruction in criminal matters; their involvement is optional in other cases. The investigating magistrate is for example responsible for the pre-trial detention and several coercive measures during investigations.

The prosecution is usually, but not necessarily, initiated by the public prosecutor. The system follows the principle of opportunity.[1] The public prosecutor decides whether to take legal action or not and also decides how to qualify the offence.

In fact, each public prosecutor is in charge of the prosecutions in his district. But for money laundering and for international cooperation in this field, the public prosecutor of the Luxembourg district is in charge at national level.

## 4. THE LAW ENFORCEMENT UNITS TO FIGHT ORGANISED CRIME

At the central level of the new police organisation, there is a criminal investigation department dealing mainly with complex and highly criminal investigations. This department is actually divided into several units dealing for example with:
- general criminal matters,
- organised crime,
- drugs,
- youth protection,
- economic and financial investigations,
- illegal immigration,
- criminal scene investigations and forensic science.

Prior to 1990 no specific unit for fighting organised crime existed. Investigations in relation to organised crime, if there were any, were dealt with by the drugs squad or the squad which had a mandate for general investigations. In 1990 the establishment of a specific unit for combating organised crime began and it was completed in 1991. The reasons for setting up this unit were as follows. There was:
- a need to collect information related to organised crime more systematically;
- a need to have criminal investigators with specialised knowledge about organised crime;
- a need to have the best possible structure to organise cooperation with similar units in neighbouring countries (Germany for example) where these units have just been set up.

Today this unit is composed of 10 members out of a total of 92 members of the criminal investigation department. Nevertheless, other units also contribute to the investigation of organised crime, for example in drugs cases, matters are dealt with either by the drugs squad or by a team composed of officers of several units; the same holds for investigations in economic and financial crime. A team of specialist investigators deals with money laundering.

**No service has been created as a consequence of the recommendations of the Action Plan to combat organised crime.** The reasons are mainly due to the geographic dimension of the country, the simple organisation of the police forces and judicial authorities. Furthermore, in contrast to most other EU member states, there seemed no need to refurnish the criminal justice organisation in response to phenomena which were initially not considered as critical.

## 5. THE PUBLIC PROSECUTION UNITS TO FIGHT ORGANISED CRIME

The judicial organisation has been described in Section 3. One general public prosecutor is responsible on a national basis and there are two public prosecutors' offices.

These two public prosecutors' offices are organised in a way that only one prosecutor is nationally responsible for each field, e.g. there is only one for money laundering. This situation largely facilitates the coordination of matters related to organised crime.

The public prosecution service has been organised according to specialisation, particularly in the field of economic and financial crime. The last ten years were marked by improved specialisation among the substitutes of the public prosecutor. Moreover, the role of some of these members in the area of money laundering has become more defined.

No specific body of coordination has been set up. On the level of the prosecution service, the general public prosecutor has assumed this task because he is responsible in general for the implementation of the criminal policy under the supervision of the Minister of Justice.

The public prosecutor of the judicial district of Luxembourg acts as the **financial intelligence unit**. He receives information from banks on irregular transactions. He has a mandate to take the necessary measures at the judicial level. He transmits cases to the money laundering section of the Crime Investigation Department for further investigation. Hence, the Luxembourg financial intelligence unit is in the position to decide whether or not investigations are necessary, and to direct these investigations.

## 6. MULTIDISCIPLINARY INTEGRATED TEAMS

Until today it has not been necessary to create permanent, integrated, multidisciplinary teams. The main investigations are dealt with by the national criminal investigation department. If there is a need to work together with customs or other organisations, the decision to set up a temporary team, bringing together people from different administrations for that specific issue, is taken case by case.

Teams with temporary status have for example been set up in investigations related to drugs matters in which different agencies took part. The same model was used for a recent team organised to cope with illegal immigration where the police, the customs office and the immigration bureau worked together on an *ad hoc* basis.

In these teams links to their respective authorities are not changed, each service remains dependent of its normal authority.

The cooperation between police and customs is also improved by the fact there is close cooperation in the gathering of information. In respect to this some personnel of the customs office work in the information department of the police.

The Luxembourg intelligence service has no competence in the fight against organised crime. This service is not a part of the law enforcement agencies. If necessary, some forms of cooperation exist, for instance when the intelligence service and law enforcement agencies share intelligence regarding organised crime.

## 7. INTERNATIONAL COORDINATION AND CONTACT POINTS

Due to its geographical situation, Luxembourg is very keen on international cooperation, which implies that the country is actively represented in all forms of collaboration organised at the EU or another level. It has actively cooperated in the exchange of information organised via the Interpol channel, and on the basis of Schengen or Europol. Some bilateral conventions with neighbouring countries have been signed or are under discussion at the moment. These forms of cooperation are however not limited to organised crime.

During a considerable period, the police organisation has been organised in such a way as to facilitate coordination at the national level, and of course to act as one national partner in international cooperation.

As far as the coordination body of the law enforcement agencies is concerned, a unit of the police is in charge of collecting, evaluating and disseminating information at the national and international level. This unit is called the "Bureau of International Police Cooperation", and has only executive power, but no operational function. This unit is located in the city of Luxembourg. It is part of the national units of the police; it existed prior to the recent police reform and the international obligations formulated in the area of international police cooperation. The international coordination function has just been added to the coordination function at the national level. The Director General of the police is responsible for the main decisions on policy concerning this unit.

The "Bureau of International Police Cooperation" also has the function of the central contact point. Since the beginning of international cooperation, this body has been working as a central contact point for the exchange of Europol, Schengen/SIRENE and Interpol information. Since the creation of these channels of information, Luxembourg has always participated in these different means of cooperation.

Luxembourg authorities participate in direct horizontal links with the European structures of Europol, OLAF and Schengen. For cooperation with OLAF in the field of penal fraud, besides the exchange of information, certain specific resources were put at the disposal of Luxembourg police to increase the efficiency of investigations.

As far as the prosecution service is concerned, the personnel of the general public prosecutor's office act as the central contact point for the exchange of information and completion of procedures in international cooperation. At the judicial level, they participate in the European Judicial Network. Being part of the national general prosecutor's office, the function of centralising information and making links to other coordination bodies is obvious. The public prosecutor of Luxembourg is the only one who is in charge of organising international exchanges of information in the field of money laundering.

Between financial intelligence units there is collaboration specially concerning the development of legal instruments, as some internationally based investigations are executed in close cooperation. Recently, and due to the new legislation about criminal organisations and the way to transmit information on irregular transactions, conventions have been signed with the corresponding French and Belgium authorities in order to implement information exchanges. This is vital for Luxembourg, because in most of the cases dealt with the persons involved are foreigners.[2]

## 8. ACCOUNTABILITY

Police and other law enforcement agencies work under the direct control of the Minister responsible for the respective agency. The work of agencies is under the supervision of the parliament and of course under direct hierarchical control. In the field of investigations, control is organised under the authority of the general public prosecutor and the investigating judge of the specific investigation. Recent measures have been introduced for sanctioning judicial investigators, in the event of personal activities against the law and against the direction of the investigation.

The single police force which was established on 1 January 2000 is controlled by a newly created general inspectorate. This service works under the direct authority of the Minister of Interior. Its functions are:

- to guarantee the respect of the law in police procedures,
- to study special areas of proceedings in order to improve police work,
- to investigate policemen who are charged with illegal procedures or activities in general.

The creation of specific supplementary control was asked for in order to counterbalance power of the police force. Furthermore, police work is controlled by some agencies, for example the data protection supervisory board, the general inspectorate of public finance, and national administration for personnel.

National law enforcement agencies may use proactive policing methods. Depending on the different measures, a special authorisation procedure is organised either by the code for criminal investigation or by other legislative texts. Other measures are under the control of the public prosecutor or the investigating judge.

No special supervision of the units responsible to fight organised crime has been institutionalised, except those already mentioned.

## 9. CONCLUSION

We have to conclude that the challenge to control organised crime itself did not constitute the most significant impact on the new structures, but the fact that Luxembourg wanted to be able to collaborate in a more efficient way with neighbouring countries or on a European or international level.

No organisational reforms have until now directly resulted from the impact of EU legal instruments.

The main reasons for reforming the police organisation were:

- to increase efficiency and effectiveness

- a national will to reform the public administration
- cost-benefit analysis

As a result some recommendations of an external audit were put into practice.

The influence of the European Union on reforms:

### • *on organisation reforms*
Police reform must be explained by the need to have an efficient police organisation, to be prepared to cope with international crime connections and to participate actively in international cooperation.

No aspect of the reform was directly caused by EU recommendations, but indirectly reforms involved the organisation of services and the adaptation of existing procedures to various demands in the field of international cooperation. Reforms at the level of public prosecution were directly due to the EC Money Laundering Directive.

### • *on legal instruments*
The European Union instruments have contributed to the introduction of a definition of criminal organisations, and to the introduction of some procedural elements on international law enforcement cooperation. At the time of writing, a draft legislative text about corruption is was under discussion in parliament. This text is largely inspired by a draft text worked out in the European forum.

### • *other influences*
Most of the European Union instruments demanded the national organisation to adapt its procedures of collecting, processing and exchanging information. Mutual assistance in criminal matters was organised more systematically, taking into account the needs formulated on international level.

**RESPONDENTS**

- Mr Guy Schleder, First Government Counsellor, Ministry of Justice
- Mr Robert Biever, Public Prosecutor, Luxembourg
- Mr Marcel Reiter, Commander Gendarmerie grand-ducale, Inspector General of Police
- Ms Claudine Konsbruck, Attachée de Gouvernement, 1ère en rang, Ministry of Justice
- Mr Roland Genson, JHA Counsellor at the Permanent Representation
- Mr Jeff Neuens, Principal Commissioner, CID

**NOTES**

1.   This deviates from the principle of legality which is used in Germany, and which means that prosecution may not be waived. It is unclear to what extent these procedural differences make cross-border law enforcement cooperation between the Luxembourg and the German authorities more difficult (note from the editor).
2.   See e.g. Police Grand-Ducale, *Rapport d'activité 2000*, "Evolution de la délinquance", 33 pp, at p. 20 and 22.

# The Netherlands

## Monica den Boer

### 0. INTRODUCTION

During the last decade, the organisation of the Dutch police and prosecution system has undergone several changes, which were due to large-scale reorganisation processes, but also to a fair amount of reflexive reasoning following a major crisis in the criminal investigation system. Moreover, the police and prosecution services increasingly apply managerial concepts to their organisations, which implies a series of continued reorganisation processes (re-clustering, revision of functions and tasks, changes of name, etc.).

It has been very difficult to establish straightforward causal relationships between organised crime and national reorganisation tendencies on the one hand, and European instruments in the area of justice and home affairs cooperation and national reorganisation tendencies on the other. However, reading through this chapter one may be able to trace the undeniable impact that organised crime and Europeanisation have had on the inner architecture of the Dutch police and prosecution services.

The first section of this chapter contains a general introduction on the organised crime situation in the Netherlands, the public debate on this issue, and the legal definitions that are applicable in this domain. Section II describes the general features of the Dutch law enforcement agencies, and devotes attention to the balance between regionalisation and centralisation. Likewise for the Public Prosecution Service, which will be discussed in section III. Section IV provides an overview of organised crime units. Section V contains a brief introduction of the special public prosecution units for the control of organised crime. Section VI gives an overview of multidisciplinary integrated teams, including the Financial Intelligence Units. In the analysis of organisational responses to the phenomenon of organised crime, international coordination and contact points are pivotal; they are introduced in section VII. Section VIII reviews informal and formal processes of information exchange between police and prosecution services and bodies like the national secret service and the private sphere.

Special attention to reform processes, their rationales, and their acceptance is given in section IX, which discusses recent or upcoming reforms in the law enforcement agencies and the public prosecution service: this section bifurcates in a retrospective look at the police reform which took place after 1993, and into a perspective which describes the recommendations of the Parliamentary Inquiry Committee and its successor. Accountability structures (supervision and control) shall be outlined in section X, which looks at the role of internal accountability structures, administrative accountability structures, the prosecution service, the *juge d'instruction*, the competent Ministries, the Parliament, the national Data Protection Supervisory Board, the national Ombudsman, and recent changes in the system of supervision and control. The chapter concludes with final observations, a list of interviewees and correspondents, an additional bibliography, and an explanatory listing of abbreviations and Dutch terminology.[1]

## I.    ORGANISED CRIME IN THE NETHERLANDS

No one single definition of organised crime seems to be generally accepted. However, as the realisation that organised crime represented a serious threat to Dutch society took hold, discussion about how organised crime should be defined gained momentum.

A first formal attempt to tackle organised crime was laid down in a general action plan (*Plan van Aanpak Georganiseerde Criminaliteit*) in 1992, which comprised a proposal to create five or six large interregional crime squads. Moreover, criteria were established which were used as indicators to determine periodic crime analyses and national priorities.[2] Criteria are however regarded as supportive means only, and a need for a general framework has been recognised.

The Research and Documentation Centre of the Ministry of Justice (WODC) was charged with the development of a method to present and evaluate crime situations.[3] The research was undertaken together with the National Criminal Intelligence Service (*Directie Recherche*) and the Serious Crime Committee (Cczwacri).[4] The serious crime committee is chaired by the Procurator General who carries the portfolio on serious and organised crime. The Serious Crime Committee (CcZwaCri) advises the Board of Procurators General on priorities in criminal investigations concerning organised crime that manifests itself nationally and internationally.

One of the main findings of a working conference at the criminal investigation school at Zutphen was that a national framework for criteria to tackle organised crime was lacking. The former Coordinating Policy Forum

(CBO) studied the definition brought forward by the "Fijnaut Group", which conducted the investigation into character, size and threat of organised crime in the Netherlands in the context of the Parliamentary Inquiry into proactive investigation methods.[5] Although the CBO recognised the workability of the definition, it queried the interest which might be served by it.

In the end, CBO (which is now the Serious Crime Coordination Committee – CcZwaCri) distilled the characteristics, which apply both to organised crime and white-collar crime (*organisatiecriminaliteit*), to the following five:
(1) Infringement of physical and material goods or of personal or business life
(2) Financial profit
(3) Effect on public administration
(4) Effect on legal markets
(5) Counter strategies.

This has resulted in the establishment of a rating system. Further research on organised crime has demonstrated that this type of criminality is generally not undertaken by individual, self-supporting criminal organisations, but is carried out by national and international networks. Ideally, the strategy against organised crime should be focused on identifying and tackling crucial "nodes" inside these networks, by professional teams, resulting in effective penal or other type of responses. It is formally accepted that these priorities are determined on a national level.[6]

Concrete proposals to undertake criminal investigations into organised crime are "weighed" by a central group, which is under the responsibility of the National Public Prosecutor's Office (*Landelijk Parket*), with the participation of the National Criminal Intelligence Service. The group is responsible for the critical adjudication of the proposals, the factual material (reliability of the information and the sources), the feasibility of the investigation, and the time span within which the investigation is supposed to lead to concrete results. This approach is supposed to prevent an isolated and segmented position of the core squads. On the basis of this weighing exercise, investigations are delegated to the various core squads.[7]

A recent recommendation concerning the criminal investigation of man smuggling is that investigations which are considered to be suitable for the supra-regional police squads are put on the agenda of the Serious Crime Committee so that – if the investigation is chosen by this committee – the Board of Procurators General may decide to charge one of the supra-regional (core) squads or the National Crime Squad (LRT) with the investigation.[8]

## II.   LAW ENFORCEMENT AGENCIES IN THE NETHERLANDS

### Introduction

Just one section in a report cannot do justice to the history and dynamics of any national police system. It would take several new studies and a summary of various books, articles and reports to give an adequate account of the police system in the Netherlands. Hence, the text below is merely meant to provide a contextual account which enables the reader to identify developments concerning international police cooperation and the creation of national facilities. What follows is a brief account of the main characteristics of the Dutch policing system on the one hand, and the complementary relationship between regional police forces and central coordination on the other.

### A System of Dual Control

The police organisation used to be subjected to a system of dual control by the Ministry of Justice and the Minister of the Interior, but the Ministry of the Interior recently gained responsibility for managerial tasks concerning the National Police Agency (*Korps Landelijke Politiediensten* (KLPD)).[9] Historically, the Ministry of Justice has carried responsibility for the police since 1813. When the Ministry of the Interior acquired responsibility for the municipal authorities in 1931, this also entailed responsibility for the financing of the municipal police forces. The minister of Justice was "the" minister for police matters at least until 1940.

The Dutch police organisation should be characterised as a uniform, de-concentrated (or decentralised) police system, as it is subdivided in 25 regional police forces – each with their own managerial and budgetary responsibility – plus the twenty-sixth force (the above-mentioned KLPD) which carries national duties and responsibilities.

The police force acts under a single statute (same tasks and competencies, same uniform, same weapons), which should guarantee some uniformity. Its general management is centrally directed by the Ministry of the Interior, and its criminal investigation priorities and methods are subjected to the Ministry of Justice, the Code of Criminal Procedure and central guidelines issued by the Public Prosecution Service.[10] Critics[11] argue that in reality there are still two police forces in the Netherlands, as the *Marechaussee* (Royal Military Constabulary, which can be compared with the French *gendarmerie*) performs certain police tasks. Hence, the system could – with academic caution – be categorised as a dual policing system.

On 1 January 1998, the Dutch police service numbered 41382.7 full-time equivalent (fte) officers. The two largest regional police forces are: Amsterdam-Amstelland (5480.6), and Rotterdam-Rijnmond (4745.7). A recent report from the Dutch Ministry of Justice on the legal infrastructure in an international perspective shows that the number of personnel within the police service is relatively low. With an average of 270 police officers per 100,000 inhabitants, the Netherlands is comparable to countries like Denmark (248/100,000) and Canada (253/100,000). EU Member States like Italy (531/100,000), Spain (452/100,000), Greece (422/100,000), France (410/100,000), Belgium (406/100,000), Austria (360/100,000), and Ireland (348/100,000) however employ many more police personnel.[12]

## Centralisation and regionalisation

Paradoxically, perhaps, the "regionalisation" of the Dutch police service is regarded as a move towards centralisation. This certainly makes sense when viewed from a historical perspective: before 1993, several municipalities used to have their own police force, and they had to relinquish their force to the benefit of the newly established regional forces.[13] The regionalised landscape of the Dutch police organisation certainly amounts to a rather differentiated picture. A Parliamentary Evaluation Committee ("Kalsbeek"), which during 1999 screened the implementation of the recommendations of the Parliamentary Committee on special investigation methods ("Van Traa"), observed that reorganisations were rather diversified in the various regions, but this seemed to cohere with the philosophy "de-central[ise], unless...".[14] One of the latest reorganisations concerns the creation of regional information desks which responded to the need of an inter-regional information exchange, and which should encourage the regional and the national information exchange (including intelligence). In 1996, these information desks were implemented in 24 of the 26 forces. At this moment, all twenty-five regional forces, the Royal Military Constabulary and the *Rijksrecherche* have – within the information desk – access to the national VROS[15] system, which provides information on ongoing criminal investigations.[16]

Central coordination and operations within the police service are:
(1) The National Police Agency (twenty-sixth force; *Korps Landelijke Politiediensten*) by virtue of the 1993 Police Law. The core divisions of the National Police Agency (*KLPD*) are: a) the National Crime Intelligence Department (now *Directie Recherche*), which is the non-operational nexus in criminal investigation processes; b) the Transport Police (*Transportpolitie*); c) the Division of Executive Police Support (*Executieve Politie ondersteuning*); d) Management (*Beheer*).[17]
(2) In the course of the year 2000, the National Crime Squad (*Landelijk*

*Rechercheteam*; (LRT)) absorbed into the National Crime Intelligence Service under the name of Department of Criminal Investigations (*Recherche Onderzoeken*). The National Crime Squad was created in 1995 and used to function as the operational investigation arm of the KLPD. The main aim of the LRT was: delivering an adequate (inter-) national performance against organised crime in cooperation with the regions.[18] The focus of the LRT was: the investigation of crimes which, considering their seriousness, frequency or organised nature, seriously undermine the rule of law, and for which a high degree of expertise on financial and revenue issues is required; investigation in response to international mutual assistance requests; investigation of crimes committed in a national or international context necessitating the involvement of the LRT; and serious "horizontal" fraud cases.

Between January 1996 and December 1998, the LRT initiated 26 investigations into crimes, most of which had a financial component. The aim of the LRT was been to cooperate with the core squads (see below), the regional criminal investigation departments and the special investigation services (*bijzondere opsporingsdiensten*), both in terms of human resource as well as information capacity. The regional forces and the core squads argue they noticed little of this support, which was apparently due to a lack of capacity.[19] The office in Zoetermeer is responsible for information and networking tasks, and the office in Driebergen is responsible for supporting and autonomous tasks.[20]

## III.   THE PUBLIC PROSECUTION SERVICE IN THE NETHERLANDS

Like the Dutch police service, the Public Prosecution Service (*Openbaar Ministerie*) underwent a major reform process during the 1990s. The most important challenge was to transform the organisation from autonomously acting professionals to a more cohesive professional organisation. The findings of the Parliamentary Committee were a considerable blow to the service, and much has been done since to strengthen central supervision and accountability, in particular with regard to (international) organised crime investigations which often requires innovative policing techniques.

### Organisation and Structure of the Prosecution Service

The Public Prosecution Service is a national organisation. The Public Prosecution Service is not a governmental department like a Ministry:

together with the courts, it constitutes the judiciary, which is the authority responsible for the administration of justice.[21] Though hierarchically subordinate to the Minister of Justice, who is politically responsible, the Public Prosecution Service is a judicial organisation, together with the judiciary.

Despite the fact that the Public Prosecution Service has the status of a national organisation, there was a lack of unity. In the second half of the 1980s, a clearly recognisable national policy seemed absent. The Procurators General were captured in a vague structure, as it was for instance unclear where policy initiatives stemmed from.[22] Under former Minister of Justice Korthals-Altes, a proposal was launched to create an independent forum for the Procurators General, but the Minister of the Interior and the Secretary General turned it down. The compromise was to create a rather small agency, which was restricted to two officials from the Prosecution Service. Creating a single structure for the Public Prosecution Service would have consequences for the position of the Procurator General, as it would imply the abolition of this superior position in a group of districts.[23]

A recent, large-scale reorganisation of the Public Prosecution Service was undertaken on the basis of the "Donner report".[24] Mrs Sorgdrager, who was Minister of Justice at the time, declared in a letter on 14 December 1994 that she could largely accept the recommendations of the Donner Committee. She promised to elaborate this in an advice from the cabinet. In May 1995 a Plan of Action was published.[25] Implementation of the plan was delayed by the findings of the Parliamentary Inquiry Committee.

The reform process started in 1995 and was recently completed. The reorganisation was evaluated. The main conclusions of the evaluation were that:

- The Prosecution Service is indeed working more as one organisation, which is made clear in the autonomous management of means and facilities, an independent cycle of planning and accountability, an independent main office of the Board of Procurators General.
- It appears that the social orientation of the Prosecution Service has been strengthened, which means that the service is able to give a better contribution to the safety of citizens and the integrity of society (improvement of professional administrative capacity).
- The quality of the processing of cases is sufficient, but there is scope for improvement.
- The authority *vis-à-vis* criminal investigation has been improved; approximation of working processes of police and prosecution service.[26]

The reorganisation of the Public Prosecution Service was particularly difficult in view of the political influence.

In 1998, the service numbered 443 prosecutors. From an international perspective, this amounts to 3 public prosecutors per 100,000 inhabitants, which is low compared to other "benchmark" countries, such as Sweden (7.9), Canada (5.6), Denmark (10) and Germany (7.5).[27]

### Tasks and Functions of the Prosecution Service

The Public Prosecution Service decides whether an offender must appear before court and it prepares the indictment. It has sole discretion to decide whether a case should be prosecuted. The Service almost entirely works in the field of criminal law.[28]

The Public Prosecution Service carries ultimate responsibility for the criminal investigation: the police have to give account for their actions to a public prosecutor, the officer of the Public Prosecution Service. Every investigation is carried out under the instructions of a public prosecutor, who ensures that the police observe all rules and procedures laid down by law. This is of particular importance in the case of a serious offence, where the public prosecutor will be in direct charge. The Public Prosecution Service is also responsible for supervising investigations carried out by other authorities, such as the municipal social services, the Fiscal Intelligence and Investigation Service (FIOD), and the Economic Investigation Service (ECD).[29]

Coordination by the Public Prosecution Service of the police can be undertaken by virtue of national public prosecutors at the National Public Prosecutor's Office, who are mandated to carry responsibility for certain forms of criminality (organised crime, smuggling of migrants, terrorism, environmental offences, money laundering and fraud). The 20 Chief Public Prosecutors are organised in the form of a Council (*OM-Beraad*), which deals with important questions relating to administrative, organisational and content matters, in order to achieve a speedy and uniform point of view on behalf of the top members of the Public Prosecution Service. Members of this Council are the members of the Board of Procurators General, the 20 Chief Public Prosecutors and the five Chief Advocates General of the Public Prosecution Departments. The Council also has to ensure a more effective and cohesive functioning of the Public Prosecution Service.[30] The Council replaces the supra-regional college of Chief Public Prosecutors. The organisation of the Public Prosecution Service corresponds to the various types of law court in the Netherlands. First there are the sub-district courts, followed by the district courts, the courts of appeal and finally the Supreme Court. The Public Prosecution Service has an office in each city with a court of law.

**Central Coordination Trends within the Public Prosecution Service**

First, we should mention the creation of a (national) **Board of Procurators General** (*College van Procureurs-Generaal*). The Board of Procurators General is the Public Prosecution Service's highest authority, and plays a key role in the determination of policy on investigation and prosecution. The committee and its staff form the department's head office. The Board of Procurators General meets with the Minister of Justice on a monthly basis (except for the month of August).[31] The meeting itself is not a decision-making forum, although it is the catalyst for decision making between the Ministry of Justice and the Public Prosecution Service.

The Board is composed of three to five Procurators General and is a Collegial Council which stands above the Public Prosecution Service. The Board is chaired by one of the Procurators General, and is appointed for a three-year term (this term can be renewed once). The powers of the Board include:
a)  giving general and specific orders to members of the Prosecution Service;
b)  collection of relevant information originating from the members of the Prosecution Service;
c)  subordination of district heads with regard to the performance of their duties.[32] This creates a legal condition for central, uniform policy implementation.

The Board of Procurators General concerns itself explicitly with supra-local matters: 1) the introduction of new policy requiring specific, national instruments; 2) crime at local level which is "not visible" (e.g. corruption); 3) crimes requiring a supra-local repressive or preventive approach; 4) international obligations.

The Board is in charge of prior approval of local plans of action, and exercises process evaluation on the basis of questions such as a) has the problem been made clear and is it based on a solid view of the environment?; b) is there a logical connection between the problem and the intervention strategy?; c) are agreements with external partners sufficient?; d) have agreements been effected in the internal management of the prosecution district?; e) is information available on law enforcement implementation? Hence, the emphasis is on quality evaluation rather than content.[33]

The board of Procurators General is advised by a – among others – serious crime committee (*CcZwaCri*), which fulfils an important function in policy-making concerning organised crime and which filters recommendations about organised crime control. The latter committee – consisting of Chief Public Prosecutors and Chief of Police and headed by one of the Procurators General – initiated a Public Prosecution guideline, e.g. a priority setting instruction for core squads in the national action against serious and organised crime. The CcZwaCri has been appointed as coordinating body in the context of Recommendation 20 of the High Level Group Action Plan against Organised Crime (1997). At the time of writing, the Dutch member of the Committee is Mrs J. Kuitert, teamleader International Affairs at the National Public Prosecutor's Office. She reports to the Title VI Multidisciplinary Group on Organised Crime about relevant developments in the EU in the area of CcZwaCri.

Second, we should consider the **National Public Prosecutors's Office** (*Landelijk Parket*), which had been under construction since 1995[34] and which acquired legal status on 1 September 1999. This office exercises judicial supervision of the National Police Agency (KLPD), in particular the national crime squad (LRT) and the national criminal intelligence service (*Directie Recherche*). Moreover, it cooperates closely with other prosecution bureaux, the six core squads (*kernteams*),[35] the core squad environmental crime, the regional criminal investigation departments, and foreign criminal investigation departments. Within the new structure of the Prosecution Service, the *Landelijk Parket* is one of the 25 offices (19 district offices, 5 *ressortsparketten*). The legal basis for the National Prosecution Public Prosecutor's Office can be found in Articles 134 and 137 of the law on legal organisation (*Wet op de Rechterlijke Organisatie*).

The *Landelijk Parket* prepares and drafts the national policy against organised crime for the College of Procurators-General, particularly through prioritising the activities of the core squads.[36] The National Public Prosecutor's Office also accommodates the secretariat of the Central Assessment Committee. A public prosecutor at the National Public Prosecutor's Office is competent to prosecute crimes of an (international) organised nature.

The Public Prosecutors of the *Landelijk Parket* direct the criminal investigations of the Department of Criminal Investigations, which is the operational arm of the National Police Agency. This means that the *Landelijk Parket* is the official competent authority for all matters related to international exchanges of information concerning organised crime cases. There is intensive cooperation between the National Public Prosecutor's Office and the national crime squad when it concerns the investigation of large, complex and international organised crime cases, for which specialist expertise is required in the area of financial investigation. An operational task of the *Landelijk Parket* is the coordination and performance of foreign requests for legal assistance.

On 16 April 1999, the National Public Prosecutor's Office accommodated the following portfolios: a) one Public Prosecutor (PP) for the LRT and three PP's for the LRT criminal cases; b) one PP charged with the "unusual" transactions unit and who is particularly responsible for the (inter-)national control of money laundering; c) one PP responsible for the criminal intelligence department of the KLPD and some special investigation services; d) one PP for the national coordination of infiltrations, witness protection, smuggling of migrants, terrorism and who liaises with the state intelligence office; e) one PP responsible for international mutual legal assistance; f) one PP for the criminal intelligence department of the General Inspection Service and deputy chief PP of the National Public Prosecutor's Office. The logic of these portfolios may have been affected slightly by the restructuring of the National Criminal Intelligence Service.

Third, we should consider the Central Assessment Committee (*Centrale Toetsings-commissie*). The CTC advises the Board of Procurators General on the employment of certain investigative techniques in certain specific cases. The CTC has been independent from the moment of its creation in 1994. Since then an advisory task has been added to its mandate as a result of the recommendations of the Parliamentary Inquiry Committee. At the moment, the CTC consists of two chambers, each of which has one chairperson, and about six members amongst whom some (national) public prosecutors and a police officer. Both chambers have a secretary who is seconded by the Ministry of Justice. The CTC secretariat is part of the National Public Prosecutor's Office.

The provisional guidelines, which date from the end of 1996, state that the next special investigation techniques are to be assessed by the CTC through the mediation of a chief public prosecutor: a) various forms of long-lasting and project-related infiltration and "store-fronts"; b) controlled release of damaging or dangerous goods; c) deals with criminal witnesses; d) requests for witness protection. The CTC requires the registration of a number of other special investigation techniques, such as controlled delivery and the use of cameras.[37]

With the entry into force of the new law on special police investigation techniques[38] on 1 February 2000, the role and tasks of the CTC have been reconsidered. On the one hand, it was expected that the new law has resulted in less work for the CTC, on the other hand new investigation techniques (such as direct bugging and the employment of infiltrators) may have resulted in more work.[39]

## IV. LAW ENFORCEMENT UNITS TO CONTROL ORGANISED CRIME

In the 1980s, the Dutch police service was still divided into a national police and several municipal police services. Regional squads were developing, and towards the end of the 1980s, the Interregional Crime Squad (IRT Utrecht–Noord-Holland) was created with a specific purpose to investigate organised crime cases. This development was paralleled by discussion about increasing the scale and use of investigation methods.

In this section, we will not draw a specific distinction between local and national anti-organised crime units. Against the background of the regionalised structure of the Dutch police service, most anti-organised crime units are based on a regional, rather than local level, and they interact directly with the national criminal investigation service.

## Tactical Investigation Departments

Tactical investigation departments (*"tactische recherche"*) are responsible for the collection of evidence for concrete criminal court cases. They are mostly organised at three levels (basic units, districts, regions). Those that concern themselves with organised crime are predominantly situated at the regional level, whilst evidence concerning frequent crimes is gathered at local district level.[40] In the event of criminal investigations of organised crime, the regional units of the *tactische recherche* are mostly elaborate teams or units which focus on certain criminal organisations. These investigations are often elaborate and time consuming, which means that these teams usually do not handle more than 10 or 11 investigations annually.[41] For the employment of investigative techniques (such as interceptions of telephone communications) the *tactische recherche* and the criminal intelligence departments often make use of supportive services, namely the surveillance team (OT), the section technical support (STO), the police infiltration team (PIT),[42] and the apprehension team (AT).[43] The request for support requires a prior authorisation from the Public Prosecutor.

## Regional Criminal Investigation Squads

Following a strong lead by the Prosecution Service, the Regional Criminal Investigation Squads were created at the beginning of the 1990s.[44] There was a growing awareness among police and judicial services that organised crime was not being met with an appropriate response, and thus the regional forces in North Holland and Utrecht allocated 1% of their force to the creation of an Interregional Crime Squad (*Interregionaal Recherche Team* – IRT).[45] The action plan against organised crime (1992: *"Plan van Aanpak Georganiseerde Misdaad"*) led to the creation of five more interregional crime squads. The target of these squads is the supra-local (international) organised crime and organisational (white-collar) crime (*"organisatiecriminaliteit"*).

In 1993, then Procurator-General Gonsalves established that these

Interregional Crime Squads required central national coordination. A proposal to create a special portfolio "organised crime" for the direct management of the interregional crime squads was abandoned by the Procurators-General.[46] The Parliamentary Inquiry Committee was doubtful about the value of the interregional crime squads, but recommended they should remain.

## Core Squads

The seven (including the National Department of Criminal Investigations) squads are now generally referred to as "core squads" (*Kernteams*).[47] The tasks of the core squads include:
a) carrying out exploratory research
b) carrying out criminal investigations
c) crime prevention
d) providing support to the regional forces in the area of law enforcement.[48]

Even though the creation of the interregional core squads may be considered as a form of central coordination, the organisational structure of these core squads differs quite distinctly between the peripheral and the non-peripheral squads. The core squads "Randstad Noord en Midden", "Zuid and Noord-Oost Nederland" are identifiable, separate organisations for cases of supra-regional importance. The other three are more or less embedded within the regular criminal investigation structure of the regional forces. The Board of Procurators-General allocated a special domain to each core squad (e.g. the core squad Noord-Oost Nederland conducts investigations on east European crime, and the core squad of Rotterdam-Rijnmond mainly investigates south-east Asian crime).[49] The core squad Noord-Oost Nederland accommodates a special man-smuggling unit for a probationary period of four years. The core squads apply the whole range of special investigation techniques, including interception, camera surveillance, infiltration and pseudo purchases.

For the purpose of special investigations, they may use the support of a national technical support service (*Dienst technische operationele ondersteuning* – DTOO), which is part of the National Police Agency (KLPD), which for instance carries responsibility for placing tracking devices and video cameras.

There is still a concern about whether the six interregional core squads are regionally controllable. The functioning of these core squads has been subject of criticism: the tackling of organised crime is considered to be insufficient, notably because a "nodal" approach of criminal networks is lacking. The reason for this is that there is an absence of information: the information position of the National Criminal Intelligence Department on the basis of the existing information exchange with the regional police forces is regarded as insufficient, both in qualitative and quantitative terms.[50] Moreover, the temporary evaluation committee (successor to the Parliamentary Inquiry) observed that the cooperation between the core squads tends to be minimal, and recommended that the squads should be linked together.[51]

This view is however rejected by the current Director of the National Criminal Intelligence Department, Mr Van Gemert, who claims that the core squads have jointly appointed a policy official. Moreover, the heads of the core squads have coordination meetings with the participation of their public prosecutors. The serious crime committee (CcZwaCri) monitors the cohesion of their activities, and in large-scale operations the core squads are expected to offer mutual assistance, which is apparently given frequently. The Parliamentary Evaluation Committee recommended that each core squad acquires its own Criminal Intelligence Department (*Criminele Inlichtingendienst,* or CID), which would link it to the national register.[52] The core squads are currently the subject of an evaluation but have a permanent status.

Another squad – not formally a core squad but of national importance – is the **Serious Environmental Crime Squad** (*Kernteam "Zware Milieucriminaliteit"*), and is based in Krimpen a/d IJssel. The team was officially launched on the basis of a covenant which was signed at the end of 1995. The core squad used to be managed by the Rotterdam-Rijnmond Regional Police Force, and is a sub-department of the Regional Crime Squad (*Regionale Recherchedienst* (RRD)). The core squad is however a cooperation framework between different services. Its members are the Ministry of Housing, Planning and Environmental Affairs (VROM, members of the *Milieubijstandsteam*), the DRCI; Amsterdam-Amstelland Regional Police Force, Rotterdam-Rijnmond Regional Police Force, Zuid Holland-Zuid Police Force, and the Midden- and West-Brabant Police Force. The environmental crime squad is engaged in exploratory criminal investigations, cooperation with the regional police forces on the investigation of environmental crime cases, participation in environmental cases, execution of market exploratory research. Some of these activities are performed on a national level. The core squad also has an information group. In the course of 2000, the squad became a department of the National Police Agency (KLPD).

**Synthetic Drugs Unit**

A noteworthy specialised crime unit is the Synthetic Drugs Unit (USD), which is based in Brabant-Zuid-Oost (Eindhoven). In July 1996, the core squad "Zuid-Nederland" conducted an analysis of synthetic drugs. The researchers advocated the creation of a national unit. During that same year, the government decided that the trade and production of synthetic drugs deserved national priority, which led to the creation of the Synthetic Drugs Unit. The Unit is specialised in combating the trade in and the production of synthetic drugs, such as ecstasy (in particular MDMA), amphetamine and LSD.

The USD functions jointly with the core team "Zuid-Nederland". The Chief Public Prosecutor of the Den Bosch district exercises control and supervision, and the management of the Unit is in the hands of the regional police force Brabant Zuid-Oost. The Unit has offered assistance to the activities of the special investigation services, and has assisted in carrying out foreign requests for legal assistance.

The main tasks and objectives of the Synthetic Drugs Unit are:
(1) promoting and improving national coordination of information streams in the area of synthetic drugs and the operationalisation of that information
(2) improving the finalisation of legal assistance requests in the area of synthetic drugs
(3) supporting district *parquets*, core teams, police regions and special investigation services in criminal investigations on synthetic drugs
(4) carrying out national and international criminal investigations into organised crime.

At the time of writing, the Synthetic Drugs Unit had drawn officers from the police service (20), the Royal Military Constabulary (10), the customs service (4), the ECD (8), the FIOD (4), the National Criminal Intelligence Service (3), and 1 from the National Traffic Inspectorate (*Nationale Verkeersinspectie*).

The Unit is jointly financed by the Ministries of Justice, the Interior, Defence, Finance and Economic Affairs for the investigation services that are subjected to their competences. The largest synthetic drugs syndicate which was caught was thought to have generated NLG 264 million, but only NLG 15 million could be traced.[53] The Synthetic Drugs Unit featured in the media, as the Haaglanden regional force was apparently no longer prepared to second two chemists/laboratory experts to the Unit.[54]

The USD was evaluated during its third year of operation. An important question was whether the USD should be given national status, or whether it should be incorporated into a core squad on synthetic drugs. A future trend is likely to be a focus on the environmental and security component of the production of synthetic drugs. Many of the basic materials are dumped and the Fire Service in particular attaches great interest to the matter. The American Drug Enforcement Administration (DEA) gives courses on these issues. A new partner for the USD is VROM (the Dutch Ministry for Housing, Spatial

Ordering and Environment); together they in the process of preparing a protocol which obliges the perpetrator of environmental crimes through dumping to pay a fine.

The latest news on the control of synthetic drugs is that three or four new squads will be created, together comprising around 100 investigators. These squads are to become operational in the regions Amsterdam, Rotterdam and Limburg; the coordination will remain in the hands of the USD. The cooperation with the USA will be improved by the secondment of an embassy adviser and two liaison officers. A total of 41 million NLG has been reserved for the new anti-ecstasy strategy.[55]

## Other Specialised Squads

Furthermore, in the field of anti-organised crime units there are the following specialist squads that may or may not have relations with the fight against organised crime:

- **Fraud Squads**: There are currently four interregional fraud squads (*interregionale fraude teams* – IFTs). In the course of the year 2000, similar provisions were established in Amsterdam, Rotterdam and The Hague.
- **Football Vandalism**: Utrecht (Central Information Point). The issue of football vandalism gained wide political and media attention because of the preparations for the European Championships 2000. One regional chief constable was assigned with the portfolio of football vandalism in order to coordinate efforts.
- **Computer Crime:** Computer crime units (mostly with an interregional task) in: Groningen (*Bureau Computercriminaliteit Groningen*); Gelderland-Zuid (*Interregionaal Team Computercriminaliteit*); Amsterdam-Amstelland (*Productgroep Computercriminaliteit*); Haaglanden (*Interregionaal Team Computercriminaliteit*); Midden- en West-Brabant (*Interregionaal Bureau Computercriminaliteit*), Gerechtelijk Laboratorium (*Sectie Forensisch Computer Onderzoek*), and the CRI (*Afdeling Computercriminaliteit*).
- **Cybercrime Squad**: The National Police Agency is in the course of establishing a squad for the fight against Internet criminality. The squad will comprise 15 different investigating officers. It is expected that child pornography, illegal trade and credit card fraud will represent the bulk of the investigations.[56]

**Criminal Intelligence Departments**

It should be pointed out that all twenty-five regional police forces have a **(serious) organised crime branch** within their organisation.[57] Essential to the investigation of organised crime are the **Criminal Intelligence Departments** (CIDs), which are mostly subdivided into separate departments.[58] The Parliamentary Inquiry Committee argued that the CIDs were operating too much on an autonomous basis. The Parliamentary Evaluation Committee requested the government why there was still no precise normative description of the task of the CIDs. An Advisory Council for CIDs was created in 1995 and it issued guidance in 1999 about the organisational embedding of the CIDs within the general criminal investigation services of the police.[59]

## V.  PUBLIC PROSECUTION UNITS FOR THE CONTROL OF ORGANISED CRIME

The creation of the National Public Prosecutor's Office (*Landelijk Parket*) has not resulted from reforms proposed by EU legal instruments, but existed prior to the Action Plan on Organised Crime in a slightly different format. However, its coordinating tasks seem to be in line with the recommendation. As discussed under section III, national coordination centres have been created within the Prosecution Service to deal with organised crime, in particular the National Public Prosecutor's Office, the Board of Procurators General and the Central Assessment Committee.

In cooperation with the police service, "**intelligence desks**" (*informatie-knooppunten*) are to be established within the districts (*arrondissementen*), in accordance with the core squad structure. Each core squad and the relevant Chief Public Prosecutor are jointly responsible for one of these intelligence desks. They have to create an information platform in their specific field of attention. They are supposed to generate national intelligence within these particular fields. Information desks are currently being created in the police regions to support the intelligence desks.

Following the recommendations of the Parliamentary Inquiry Committee (1996), each district appointed an officer of investigations (*recherche-officier van justitie*). Most of the prosecution bureaux have a specialised unit within which officers focus on serious crime.[60] In 1998, the prosecution bureaux were requested to widen their attention for serious and organised crime cases.[61]

Except for the drugs trade, many other issues are looked at from a regional point of view: organised fraud, man smuggling and the trade in human beings, serious environmental crimes, civil service offences (corruption), large-scale burglary, suspicious concentrations of power within dance venues, bars, etc. Except for primary perpetrators, attention is devoted to the supporting criminal network (e.g. money launderers). In the drugs context, there is a particular focus on: synthetic drugs (all prosecution bureaux provide information to the Synthetic Drugs Unit); sale of hard drugs to school pupils; commercial production of marihuana plants; coffee shops.[62] In 1998, it was expected that nationally, 85 to 90 organised crime cases would be dealt with (this was the numerical goal). In reality, there were 150 cases in different investigation phases, and 33 cases under preparation. The National Bureau of Public Prosecution prepared 8 investigations in 1998, particularly in the field of large-scale fraud and international legal assistance. On 1 December 1998, the Man-smuggling Unit (part of the core squad North and East Netherlands) commenced its activities for a probationary period of 4 years.

## VI.  MULTIDISCIPLINARY INTEGRATED TEAMS

Most teams at the national and decentralised level in the area of organised crime have a multidisciplinary nature (Recommendation 20 of the High Level Group Action Plan on Organised Crime).

- First, it should be noted that the Department of Criminal Investigations (the former National Crime Squad) is a multidisciplinary integrated team.
- Second, the other six core squads (Section IV) comprise police inspectors as well as officers from the special investigation services (*"bijzondere opsporingsdiensten"*). There is increasingly experimentation with *ad hoc* cooperation, especially in the core squad *"Zuid Nederland"*.[63] Police officers are more or less seconded from the region to the squad: they return to the squad after a minimum of four years and a maximum of six years.[64] Almost every core squad includes or used to include an officer seconded by the FIOD, Military Constabulary or the Immigration and Naturalisation Service. A new regulatory guideline for the core squads (*"kernteamregeling"*) entered into force on 1 January 2000, which contains a further specification of their task. The squads are to be financed in a different way. The Minister of the Interior will decrease the budgets of the regional police forces proportionally and redistribute these funds directly to the core squads. The core squads have a mandate to conduct exploratory investigations, criminal investigations, prevent criminal acts and support the regional police forces in the field of law enforcement (all this within the framework of the combating of organised crime of national or international importance).[65]
- Certain core squads are specialised in certain forms of crime. This includes – as already discussed in Section IV – the Synthetic Drugs Unit

and the environmental crime squad, which engages in exploratory criminal investigations, cooperation with the regional police forces on the investigation of environmental crime cases, participation in environmental cases, and the execution of market exploratory research.

- Also the Computer Crime Units are multidisciplinary in nature as they cooperate with forensic experts of the judicial laboratory and the National Criminal Investigation Department.


**Financial Intelligence Units**

Also the financial intelligence units (as foreseen by article 6 of the 1991 Money Laundering Directive) are composed as multidisciplinary teams. There is not one central financial intelligence unit[66] in the Netherlands. However, there is a central notification desk for unusual transactions (*Meldpunt Ongebruikelijke Transacties* – MOT), which is based on a Dutch law (*Wet melding ongebruikelijke transacties*; entered into force on 1 February 1994).[67] The basis of the MOT law is to implement the EC Directive of 10 June 1991, and seven recommendations of the Financial Action Task Force on money laundering of 30 May 1990 in Dutch law. The complementary unit of the MOT is the *Bureau Landelijk Officier Meldpunt Ongebruikelijke Transacties* – BLOM, which is the Desk of the National Prosecutor for the Notification of Unusual Transactions. The BLOM – which could be compared to the financial units abroad – is situated within the National Criminal Intelligence Service (*Divisie Recherche*). The creation of a notification desk for money laundering is under discussion.

A choice was made for a notification/registration desk independent from the police. The rationale behind it was to create a buffer in order to prevent notifications of unusual – not necessarily "suspect" – data being inserted directly into the criminal investigation circuit. The Minister of Justice is responsible for the general management and organisation of the MOT.[68] A national public prosecutor (*Landelijk Officier van Justitie*), who is a member of the National Public Prosecutor's Office, was appointed to manage the information flows from and to the police organisation and to determine criminal investigation priorities (in line with the principle of expediency). The "MOT" prosecutor has been accountable to the Procurator General, with serious organised crime in his portfolio (who is also chairman of the interdisciplinary supervisory committee of the MOT[69]). The Title VI decision on financial intelligence units may have an impact on the Dutch system, which currently draws a distinction between suspect and unusual transactions (see also above).

The central objectives of the MOT are:

(1) Collection, registration, processing and analysis of data concerning unusual transactions which are notified by financial institutions on the basis of legally established indicators, to see whether these data are important for the prevention or the detection of criminal offences.
(2) Prevention of misuse of the financial system for money laundering and the control of money laundering.

The Dutch MOT cannot simply be compared with financial intelligence centres abroad, mainly because in other countries only *suspect* transactions are reported, while in the Netherlands unusual transactions are reported. There is regular exchange of notifications with the Belgian CFI (*Cel voor Financiële Informatieverwerking*). In 1998, 88 suspect transactions were notified to the Belgian authorities; the Belgians notified 95 transactions to the Dutch MOT (297 in 1997). The MOT takes part in an EU project which aims at assisting countries of central and eastern Europe to fight money laundering practices.

The number of notifications rose from 16974 in 1997 to 19303 in 1998. Except for regular notifications concerning unusual transactions, 5977 notifications were entered concerning unusual money transfers. Most notifications originate from currency change offices (11,913), followed by the banks (7,013), casinos (571) and credit card companies (494).[70] A special automated system was established in 1997 (MOTION), which allows the investigators at the notification centre to compile dossiers and to quickly retrieve suspect transactions. A pilot project was started with four regional police forces to send the notifications electronically.[71]

There is also a project on Financial Investigations (*Project Financieel Rechercheren*), which is a collective initiative from the College of Procurators General and the Council of Chief Constables (*Raad van Hoofdcommissarissen*). In order to intensify the fight against horizontal fraud, **four inter-regional fraud units** were created, which means that the prosecution districts (*arrondissementen*) and regional police forces cooperate in the fight against fraud. Also the National Crime Squad (LRT) accommodates a Fraud Team. A national bureau/desk for horizontal fraud (*"landelijk loket horizontale fraude"*) has been created in Rotterdam to encapsulate the inter-regional fraud teams.

A crucial actor in financial investigations is the **Fiscal Intelligence and Investigations Service** (FIOD – *Fiscale Inlichtingen – en Opsporingsdienst*), which is embedded within the National Revenue Office and which is subjected to the authority of the Ministry of Finance. This service is primarily responsible for the investigation of fiscal fraud offences. It contributes to the investigation of organised crime by taking part in cooperative ventures with police and other special investigation services, but only when there is a fiscal or customs element. Its expertise with financial investigations is regarded as crucially important in the criminal investigation of organised crime.[72] The FIOD cooperates on short-term investigations into drug transports, in the context of cooperative ventures with police, royal military constabulary and customs. At Schiphol Airport, the FIOD is frequently involved in the performance of controlled deliveries.[73]

The effectiveness of the implementation of money laundering legislation is evaluated by the Financial Action Task Force (FATF), which has concluded that the Netherlands adequately meets the international obligations and is even considered to be advanced in some respects.[74]

The FIOD cooperates with the core squads on a structural basis. Each year, a framework covenant is made up with the Public Prosecution Service for the cooperation with the police in fighting "communal" offences. At the time of writing around 15 FIOD officers were stationed within the core squads. Some were seconded, others remained functionally within the FIOD. Their competencies varied.[75]

It is hard to know with exactitude whether there are agreements or other arrangements with the view to improving their cooperation (as foreseen by the Council Resolution 96/C 375/01 of 29 November 1996). Examples are the annual covenant between FIOD and Public Prosecution Service concerning cooperation in core teams and cooperation with police to combat communal crimes (it is unknown whether this covenant was inspired by the 1996 EU resolution) and a directive concerning the cooperation between the National Taxation Office and the police and other investigation services (*Voorschrift inzake de samenwerking van de Belastingdienst met de politie – en andere opsporingsinstanties*). The FIOD cooperates with the customs service with respect to the criminal law aspects of drug transport uncovered by the customs service.

## VII. INTERNATIONAL COORDINATION AND CONTACT POINTS

The coordination function is in principle carried by certain branches/ departments within the National Police Agency (KLPD). The chief responsibility for the coordination of the flow of information between the Dutch police service and foreign or international police bodies is vested within the National Criminal Intelligence Department (*Directie Recherche*), which acts as the national contact point for Interpol, Europol, and Schengen/ SIRENE.

*Monica den Boer*

## The Reorganisation of the National Criminal Intelligence Service

The National Criminal Intelligence Department is based in Zoetermeer (near The Hague), and predates the recent police reforms and the Treaty of Maastricht. It has always been non-operational and has provided criminal investigation information, criminal analysis expertise to police, the judicial services and the special investigation services (*bijzondere opsporingsdiensten*); crime analyses for specific target groups; coordination and support of criminal investigations for the detection of criminal cases nationally and internationally. The newly acquired international coordination functions that flow from Recommendation 1 of the Action Plan have been added to its already existing functions.

As can be seen in the overview below, the coordination of international exchanges of information is predominantly within two departments of the National Criminal Intelligence Department, namely the Communications and Identification Department (BBI) and the Crime Intelligence Department.

The Communications and Identifications Department functions as the central contact point for foreign police services. It uses a "single counter" principle, which is meant to prevent that the relevant parties do not have to search the right desk for handling their message. The principle is meant to encourage uniformity, to avoid overlap and time loss. Either the Communications Department deals with the message itself, or it facilitates direct contact between the parties. In order to prevent translation problems, the service has its own translation unit (English, French, German and Spanish). The officers of the Communications and Identification Department provide daily advice to police and judiciary about investigation means in relation to legal assistance requests.

The Crime Intelligence Department delivers, on the other hand, services with regard to the investigation and detection of serious and organised crime. Its National Intelligence Coordination Unit provides analysed criminal intelligence to relevant investigation services, and seeks to give a concrete contribution to the determination of strategies, priorities and the establishment of the effectiveness of crime control. It also provides advice and coordination with regard to the coordination on embargo investigations and the national coordination of rewards for criminal information. Its Regional Exchange of Information Units (four) facilitate the exchange of intelligence between the 25 police regions and the various special Investigation Services in close cooperation with the regional "intelligence desks" (*informatieknooppunten*).

The **International Exchange of Intelligence Unit**, which is also part of the Crime Intelligence Department, explicitly functions as an intermediary between the Netherlands and foreign countries for international exchanges of information in the area of serious and organised crime. It concerns information flows with an operational character under the authority of the National Public Prosecutor's Office (*Landelijk Parket*). The unit has a number of geographical desks (Europe; East Europe; America; and Asia, the Middle-East and Africa combined in one desk). When contact is deemed necessary with a local police force abroad, liaison officers can be requested to initiate this contact. The National Criminal Intelligence Department is the national coordination centre for liaison officers. At the time of writing, it had seconded 36 liaison officers abroad, and also a number to the Dutch desk of Europol. They are responsible for international exchanges of information and the coordination of international operational activities. Except for the foreign liaison officers who are stationed at Europol in The Hague, at the time of writing there were around 37 foreign liaison officers (FLO's) seconded to the Netherlands. A special working group has been installed by the Minister of Justice to judge the necessity to tighten the rules for foreign liaison officers. The Military Constabulary and the Fiscal Intelligence and Investigation Office (FIOD) will second officers to the reorganized National Criminal Intelligence Department, which is supposed to facilitate horizontal connections between the different investigation services.

Also the Special Investigations Department has a number of international responsibilities. In particular the **National Infiltration Unit** (*Afdeling nationale coördinatie politiële infiltratie – ANCPI*) coordinates (inter-)national infiltration activities on the basis of foreign mutual assistance requests and requests for assistance from the Dutch police regions and special investigation services which do not have sufficient infiltration capacity. Furthermore, the department carries responsibility for witness protection (under the orders of the Minister of Justice and the Board of Prosecutors General) and provides facilities for and supervision of police infiltrators.[76]

Furthermore, the Department incorporates coordination centres for police infiltration (mostly with an international component) and cross-border surveillance.[77]

## Central Contact Points

The Communications and Identification Department acts as the central contact point and operates as a single desk for requests addressed to Schengen/SIRENE, Interpol and Europol. As already mentioned above, in the area of organised crime, the International Exchange of Intelligence Unit functions as an intermediary between the Netherlands and foreign countries for international exchanges of information in the area of serious and organised criminality; the department also acts as the contact point for Dutch liaison officers who are stationed abroad, foreign liaison officers who are stationed in the Netherlands and the Dutch desk at Europol.

Counterpart of the latter within the National Criminal Intelligence Department is the "Dutchdesk Europol". On the one hand it provides Europol with Dutch information, and on the other hand it facilitates the information flow from Europol to Dutch police services. The Netherlands has seconded four liaison officers (one from the Fiscal Intelligence and Investigation Office (*FIOD*)) to Europol. The liaison officers correspond with the national unit by means of a structured e-mail system (InfoEx system). The Europol national unit will have direct access to Europol's information system once the system becomes operational.[78] The desk processes 5,000 messages each year, 75% of which concern drugs.

Moreover, the national crime investigation division accommodates the SIRENE bureau, which employs around 30 officers. The Netherlands signals information about 700 people a year.[79]

Finally, the national crime investigation division accommodates the national central bureau of Interpol. Each year, the NCB Interpol receives about 80,000 messages (220 a day), which leads to 14,000 translations each year. Over 55,000 of these messages originate from West European countries.

Although functionally still separate, the Dutch desk Europol, the NCB Interpol and the Dutch SIS/SIRENE, can be consulted through one desk or counter. This fusion of information channels flows from Recommendation 19 of the High Level Group on Organised Crime. The fusion of information channels provides a single infrastructure and is expected to result in more efficiency, round-the-clock service, and independent message handling. It also provides a single translation service to all information channels. One respondent noted that quality control (legal and administrative procedures) can also be exercised more accurately. Moreover, a computer system called LIST makes it possible to consult all three systems through one computer (from within the Netherlands). About 140 of the 600 officials currently employed by the National Department of Criminal Intelligence are involved in international exchanges of information.

The central contact point also provides information to law enforcement agencies on national legislation, jurisdiction and procedures (Recommendation 19 of the High Level Group Action Plan). There are three main information systems that are supposed to answer legal or technical questions, namely the *Bureau internationale rechtshulp in strafzaken* (BIRS)[80] (judicial angle), the national bureau of public prosecution, and the KRIS (CD-ROM).

## Coordination Centres at Interregional Level

Eight regional International Coordination Centres (*Internationale Coördinatie-centra* – ICCs) and one national ICC (*Landelijk Coördinatiecentrum* – LCC) were created by the end of the year 2000 for the processing of international mutual (legal) assistance requests. The International Mutual Assistance in Criminal Matters Desk (BIRS) will be the tenth ICC. All ICCs will be using the LURIS system.[81] The regional police forces have been given a financial incentive (2.6 million NLG in total on an annual basis) to create an ICC. According to the agreement the regional forces have to establish a joint ICC together with the Public Prosecution Service (the relevant judicial authority). For example, an ICC has jointly been created by the regions of Groningen, Friesland and Drenthe in the north of the Netherlands. Similarly, the Amsterdam-Amstelland police force cooperates with Utrecht and Gooi-Vechtstreek. Not all ICCs are accommodated within the police service; the ICC Haarlem is situated within the Public Prosecution Service, for instance.

The creation of a national ICC (LCC) has been decided by in tripartite consultation within the National Police Agency (KLPD). It will be located within the National Criminal Intelligence Department and will take on all mutual assistance requests that require national expertise and/or intelligence. Like all other ICCs, the LCC will be supervised by the National Public Prosecution Service, in this case the National Public Prosecutor's Office. There is no hierarchical relationship between the national ICC of the National Criminal Intelligence Department and the regional ICCs. The *Directie Recherche* only offers expertise on demand from the regions.

The creation of the ICCs resulted from a recommendation of a special committee on international criminal law enforcement (*Commissie Internationale Strafrechtshandhaving*), chaired by Procurator General Mr. Dato Steenhuis, and consisting of members drawn both from the police forces and the Public Prosecution Service. The most important task of the ICCs is registration, which allows relevant authorities to supervise the execution of mutual legal assistance requests. Coordination and the development of expertise are also important aspects. The surplus value of the ICCs is their multidisciplinary composition (police officers and officials of the Public Prosecution Service),[82] their capacity to coordinate information flows concerning international mutual (legal) assistance requests, and their available knowledge and expertise (information desks for the police regions). The directors of the ICCs meet each other regularly. Currently, they are working on standardisation of working procedures and criteria for assistance requests.

The legal basis for the creation of the ICCs can be found in all relevant international cooperation frameworks, such as Schengen, Interpol and (Foreign) Liaison Officers.[83] The International Mutual Assistance in Criminal Matters

Desk (BIRS) at the Ministry of Justice filters all completed assistance requests before they are handed back to the requesting states. Formally, all international mutual assistance requests enter the Netherlands via the BIRS or the Interpol-desk at the National Criminal Intelligence Service (*Directie Recherche*) in Zoetermeer.

## Horizontal Linkages: Meetings, Liaison Officers, Mutual Legal Assistance and Interoperability

Concerning international law enforcement cooperation, there are several direct horizontal linkages, such as meetings, with foreign law enforcement services that are specialised in the fight against organised crime.

Meetings take place at various levels, namely at the level of policy-making, the operational level, the bilateral level and the expert level. There are many contacts, e.g. within or around Europol, Schengen, OLAF (the former UCLAF), Interpol and at the bilateral level.[84] Operational meetings are hosted by Europol, where actions subsequent to analysis results are being discussed. The Working Group SIRENE and the Interpol meetings are also mentioned as specific examples.

The Department on International Networks (*Dienst Internationale Netwerken*) was created within the National Criminal Intelligence Department.[85] This department will be the nexus between the Dutch and the foreign criminal investigation services, and will also be the national bureau for Interpol and Europol. The department will support the Dutch criminal investigation services by providing and maintaining international networks. The network includes Dutch liaison officers abroad, and foreign liaison officers in the Netherlands (see above).[86]

The Public Prosecution Service supports international requests for legal assistance, such as SIRENE. A special supporting system, called "LURIS" has been created for this purpose, in particular with the purpose to monitor deadlines. There is a general expectation to shorten the terms within which these requests for assistance can be processed.[87]

A new law on special police investigation techniques (*Wet bijzondere opsporingsbevoegdheden;* BOB) entered into force on 1 February 2000.[88] It is the intention of the Prosecution Service and the police service to provide structured information about the new law to countries with which the Netherlands undertakes regular investigations.[89]

## International Coordinators

Most regional forces employ a coordinator for international or European affairs. Their task is to advise senior staff on international cooperation issues, to coordinate contacts with other regions and the Department of the Interior.

## National Centre for International Police Cooperation

A national centre for international police cooperation (*Nederlands Centrum voor Internationale Politiesamenwerking;* NCIPS) has been established recently, and is integral part of the Dutch Police Institute (*Nederlands Politie Instituut; NPI*). Its principal task will be to provide coordination of non-operational police cooperation, to deliver policy support, to realise interregional coordination, and to generate joint policy recommendations on behalf of all police regions, e.g. *vis-à-vis* the developments in Title VI. NCIPS is co-supervised by an interdepartmental structure.

## VIII. INFORMATION EXCHANGE WITH OTHER BODIES

The police organisation does not and cannot work in splendid isolation from other investigation bodies in the public and private sphere. Moreover, over the last few years, a multidisciplinary approach to crime investigation has gained wide popularity within the Netherlands. The section below looks at formal and informal processes of information exchange with non-police bodies, with a strong focus on the cooperative ventures for the control of organised crime.

## The National Secret Service

Officially, the National Secret Service (*Binnenlandse Veiligheidsdienst =* BVD) has no competencies in the fight against organised crime. Its task is to protect core interests, namely the continuation of the democratic order, the security and other important state interests, and the preservation of social life. Hence, the target of the secret service consists of activities and developments that are considered to be harmful to these interests. In principle, the object of the investigations carried out by the BVD should always be activities of a structural character. The law on information and security services (1987) provides the rules for the cooperation between police and BVD.[90] At the time of writing a draft bill on the Information and Security Services was under debate in Parliament.[91]

The Parliamentary Inquiry Committee on special investigation methods saw a danger of overlap between the "secret teams" of the CIDs and the national secret service, and suggested that additional regulation on their boundaries would be necessary (this question has recently been repeated by members of parliament). In addition, the Parliamentary Evaluation Committee established a lack of coordination between the new law on special police investigation techniques (BOB) and the new bill, which regulates investigation techniques by the national security service. Contrary to the findings of the committee, the government replied that in fact there had been coordination. In addition, the government stated that the BVD's investigation techniques are not used in the criminal justice sphere, are by definition secret, and concern a completely different group of actors. If the BVD were to develop a focus on organised crime, it would look at it from the perspective of its own task-setting and it would employ its own mandate.[92] The Annual Report of the BVD over the year 2000 actually does state that aspects related to organised crime are being investigated by the BVD. This concerns cases in which the integrity has been breached or in suspected cases of 'offensive counter strategies' which can hinder the criminal investigation. The BVD maintains an additional value concerning those aspects of organised crime which pose a threat to the integrity of the public sector.

The national public prosecutor for the BVD – who is a member of the National Public Prosecution Bureau – is the recipient of messages from the BVD. The formal procedure implies that s/he forwards the information to the police. These messages usually concern "residual catches", e.g. when in the context of an investigation into terrorism hard drugs were found, or *vice versa*, when the police discovers a large arsenal of military weapons. In 1997/1998, the BVD forwarded 67 of these messages to the relevant national prosecutor. Prior to the transfer of these messages, a consultation takes place to judge whether the information is reliable, verifiable, etc.

On a regional level, the BVD performs its task in conjunction with the regional intelligence forces (RIDs). Formally there is a distinction between the two circuits, but in fact the information can be mixed. Within the police organisation, the opinion prevails that the BVD only plays a marginal role with regard to the investigation of organised crime. This opinion was adopted by the Parliamentary Evaluation Committee.[93]

Formally, the state security service and the regular police organisation do not exchange information on organised crime. On a regional level, however, the cooperation between the regular police service and the national security service has tended to contribute to the evaporation of borders which hitherto marked a clear distinction between the services. Concrete cases support this trend, because they reveal a considerable overlap in intelligence gathering processes between police and the BVD. An illustrative example is the case of

"Mink K.", who is allegedly the main figure behind the controlled release of 15,000 kilos of cocaine. According to *Vrij Nederland*,[94] intelligence about the presence of weapons was "accidentally" passed from the BVD to the Criminal Intelligence Department of the Amsterdam police force. The BVD was seemingly frustrated about the fact that it had to tone down its investigations in Mink K. (who is also suspected of corrupting administrators) because the national crime squad (LRT) claimed prime responsibility for the investigation.

In the near future, the BVD will be renamed as General Intelligence and Security Service (*Algemene Inlichtingen- en Veiligheidsdienst – AIVD*).

## Private Policing

Formally, information can be exchanged between the public (i.e. State) police bodies and private sector security providers. The formal basis for this information exchange is a special covenant signed in 1994 between the Council of Chief Constables (*Raad van Hoofdcommissarissen*) and the Association of Private Security Agencies (*Vereniging van Particuliere Beveiligingsorganisaties* (VPB)). This association acts as a general organisation for this sector, and imposes certain conditions on companies that seek to become a member (these conditions include commitment to a behavioural code and general labour conditions). Membership of the association is only allowed after a special license has been obtained from the Ministry of Justice. It is estimated that around 90% of the personnel in the private security sector are employed by companies that are affiliated with the association. The activities of these private security providers are based on a special law.[95] The cooperation agreements between police and private security providers emphasise the prime responsibility of the police for the management and direction of integral security plans.[96]

The Council of Chief Constables has sent a formal recommendation to the Minister of the Interior with regard to a stricter law for private investigation agencies (*particuliere recherchebureaus*). The police organisation is of the opinion that private investigators should have more access to police information, "because it cannot be the case that these private investigators take work off the hands of the police without getting anything back for it."[97] This type of cooperation should only be possible with qualified agencies. The value of this proposal is mainly seen in the area of fraud: financial investigators have been cooperating closely with accountants for years. Although the Association of Private Security Agencies has been pleading in favour of access to registers of Criminal Intelligence Departments, the Chief Constables have turned this down.

At the same time, financial experts are seconded to the Department of

Criminal Investigations by the Dutch Banking Association (*Nederlandse Vereniging van Banken* (NVB)) and the unusual transactions unit (MOT). There is also a special cooperation contract between the investigations division of the national police agency and a private computer firm to jointly develop investigation software for the Internet.

Private and public sector security providers maintain contacts regarding organised crime matters. Most of the employees of the private investigation agencies are ex-police officers. Although not formally arranged, private investigation agencies are frequently approached by regular police services to take over (parts of) complex investigations. Some of these investigations may concern organised crime or fraud. The competencies of the private investigation agencies are seldom subject to control. It should be noted that also large consultation firms (e.g. KPMG, Ernst & Young) are requested to participate in complex criminal investigations.

When viewed from an international perspective, the Netherlands employs relatively few people in the private security sector. Within the EU, the average is 160 private security agents per 100,000 inhabitants; in the Netherlands, the number is 132 per 100,000 inhabitants. These figures are low compared with the United States (582/100,000) and Australia (516/100,000). Within the EU, the United Kingdom scores reasonably highly with 275 private security agents per 100,000 inhabitants.[98]

## IX. RECENT OR UPCOMING REFORMS IN THE LAW ENFORCEMENT AGENCIES AND IN THE PUBLIC PROSECUTION SERVICE[99]

The police reform of 1993 implied the disappearance of the distinction between Municipal Police forces (*Gemeentepolitie*) and National Police (*Rijkspolitie*).[100] The fusion between these forces had already been facilitated by the creation of Regional Crime Squads at the beginning of the 1990s. One national police organisation was created, with 25 regional forces and a twenty-sixth force responsible for national tasks (*Korps Landelijke Politiediensten* (KLPD)). This twenty-sixth force accommodates, amongst others, the National Criminal Intelligence Service (*Directie Recherche*), which in turn accommodates national services such as Interpol, Europol and Schengen/SIRENE (see also *infra*). The reform – which by some was seen as a major compromise between national and local interests[101] – contained a major large-scale operation with an estimated expenditure of NLG 35 million.

## Rationale of the Reform

The most important reason for reforming the police organisation by virtue of the 1993 Police Act was the need to increase efficiency and effectiveness and to design a police organisation which was adequately equipped to deal with supra-local criminality.[102] Social unrest about the lack of safety, public order problems and the rise of criminality,[103] fragmentation, lack of internal efficiency and external effectiveness and a relatively high expenditure (hence the need for budgetary cuts) further infused the 1993 police reorganisation.[104] Regional police forces operating in the context of a uniform police organisation were regarded as the most suitable means to reach these objectives.

The call for more efficiency resulted in regionalisation and an enlargement of scale, and in more management of police working processes by the Prosecution Service. The increase in international and supra-local crime is mentioned as one of the chief rationales for enlargement of scale and regionalisation, but was definitely not the only reason to initiate a large-scale reform process.[105]

## Recent Recommendations

Although a major crisis in the criminal investigation system – triggered by the disbanding of an interregional crime squad – led to calls for a new police act, no drafting initiatives have since been undertaken.[106] The Parliamentary Inquiry Committee made a number of recommendations with regard to reorganisation. To facilitate the management of the implementation of these recommendations, both police ministers created a Steering Committee (*Stuurgroep* IPEO). The Steering Committee was disbanded when most of the decision points had been implemented. The management of the remaining project was embedded within the relevant directorates general of the two ministries (*DG Rechtshandhaving,* and *DG Openbare Orde en Veiligheid*). The blueprint that was used for the implementation turns out to be at odds with the regional police model.[107]

The Parliamentary Evaluation Committee established that many regions introduced many and far-reaching reorganisations, but noted that these reorganisations were implemented in a dissimilar manner. This is mainly due to the Police Law, which defers extensive autonomy to the regions and the lack of centrally formulated guidelines.[108] One police region ("Rotterdam-Rijnmond") decided to create a 'Van Traa' project-group to study the recommendations and their effect for the organisation of criminal investigation ("*recherche*"). In another region ("*Midden- en West-Brabant*") a reorganisation process was already ongoing, but the parliamentary recommendations helped to reinforce this process.

427

## The Reform Process within the National Criminal Intelligence Service

Looking at another, small-scale reform, the chief rationale for the reorganisation of the (National) Criminal Intelligence Service on 1 January 2000 lies within national demands rather than international ones. Generally, there is a need for more efficiency: avoidance of overlap and duplication; improvement of criminal intelligence exchange between the regional police forces; the improvement of the fight against organised crime; and flows from the evaluation of the 1993 Police Act. Furthermore, the Parliamentary Inquiry Committee and a rather critical report from the Dutch Court of Auditors (*Rekenkamer*)[109] have left their traces. The parliamentary inquiry committee emphasised the introduction of a system of checks and balances, and suggested that wider police competencies would have to be compensated with a more stringent system of control. Crime fighting could not remain untouched and there was pressure to change the culture into a more transparent one (e.g. better reporting procedures for liaison officers).

In line with this philosophy, the Committee recommended the establishment of one Criminal Investigations Department, and one Public Prosecutor responsible for these matters. The former Minister of Justice explicitly looked at organisational solutions. With regard to the reorganisation of the national criminal intelligence service, there has been an explicit choice not to create hierarchical relationships. In this philosophy, the (reorganised) National Criminal Intelligence Service delivers services to the whole country. The latest reform within the National Criminal Intelligence Service took place by means of "merging processes".

## Suggested Reforms within the Criminal Intelligence Departments

The temporary evaluation committee also devoted special attention to the CIDs (*criminele inlichtingendiensten*). The CIDs are regarded as a crucial nexus in criminal investigation: they collect crime information, e.g. through informants. Their emphasis is mainly on drug offences. Activities in the field of fraud or environmental crimes are developing slowly, mainly because these investigation purposes require entirely different networks of informants.[110] There is also a growing emphasis on man smuggling.

The Parliamentary Inquiry Committee concluded that these branches had a rather autonomous existence within the police regions.[111] Within most police regions, a reorganisation led to either a criminal intelligence department at regional level (under the direct responsibility of a RCID chief), or a criminal intelligence department which is formally organised at regional level, but which allows its detective officers to be stationed within the districts.[112]

**Impact of EU Legal Instruments on National Reforms**

The main reform that results from the High Level Group Action Plan to Combat Organised Crime is that Interpol NCB, Dutchdesk Europol and the national Schengen/SIRENE desk can be consulted simultaneously through one desk (fusion between information channels). The Dutch government notes that the European Judicial Network will have the task of supporting a structural information exchange about the criminal justice systems in the EU Member States.[113]

**No organisational reforms have thus far directly resulted from (the impact of) EU legal instruments.** The government notes that the developments concerning Europol do not affect an autonomous determination of criminal justice policies. In the view of the Dutch government, Article 30 of the Treaty on the European Union is not legally binding (i.e. the fact that Europol will be entitled to request information from national law enforcement authorities).

**Notwithstanding this marginal impact of European instruments on the domestic architecture of the Dutch criminal justice system, respondents acknowledge that the Europol Convention and the Schengen Agreement have an "institutional impact." These are regarded as "European impulses". However, centralised coordination no longer seems to be regarded as absolutely indispensable for international exchanges of information.** The standardisation of information flows and procedures is now regarded as a more successful cure for lacking efficiency. More emphasis will be laid on analysing the quality and quantity of information channels (such as Europol), in order to evaluate their output: to what extent can information acquired through international channels be considered as the key to the solution? Moreover, in the view of the respondents, there should be more attention for the informal processes of convergence: the harmonisation of organisational models or crime intelligence models tend to take shape during the negotiations about new Title VI instruments.

The respondents also note that the Dutch administration needs to reflect on the "translation" and implementation of Third Pillar instruments. The most important actors in this field are the Ministries of Justice and the Interior, and the National Criminal Intelligence Department. The latter is specifically requested to reflect strategically and pragmatically about matters related to, for instance, Europol.

**Reform Processes within the Public Prosecution Service**

A major reform of the **Public Prosecution Service** was effected by a law that entered into force on 1 June 1999.[114] The main aspects of the reform concern the organisational architecture of the Prosecution Service and its relation with the Minister of Justice. The most important change affects the structure of the Prosecution Service, notably by means of creating a Board of Procurators General (see above).[115] The Board has the authority to direct all members of the Prosecution Service (public prosecutors and advocates general), thereby dissolving the hierarchical relationship between public prosecutors and advocates general. A new office was created in the form of the National Public Prosecutor's Office, which is the leading authority for the National Crime Squad (LRT) and which looks after the prosecution of cases resulting from LRT investigations. Another important change concerns the position of the Procurator General in the Supreme Council, who will no longer be part of the Prosecution Service, but is independent and autonomous with his own tasks (mainly advice to the Supreme Council). The main rationale for this reform was the fact that daily practice was no longer in line with the rule of law. Moreover, Procurators General (each with a different portfolio) experienced double loyalties, as a tension grew between their national and district responsibilities. The Minister of Justice carries political responsibility for the Public Prosecution Service.

These decisions followed a previous reform, which was laid down in the *Plan van Aanpak voor de reorganisatie van het OM,*[116] which for a large part was based upon the report of the "Public Prosecution Service" Committee. The most important elements of this action plan concerned coherence, consistency and quality of the organisation and performance of the Prosecution Service. The main rationale for this reform was lack of efficiency.

Suggestions have been put forward recently about privatising the Public Prosecution Service,[117] which implies that lawyers could be hired to perform prosecutorial tasks. However, no serious attempts have been undertaken to translate these ideas into formal proposals.[118]

## Acceptance of the Reforms

The improvement of effectiveness and efficiency[119] was seen as a major objective of the 1993 police reform, but there was no specification at the time about the expected effectiveness of the fight against organised crime. Van Reenen argues that the success of the police reform could be difficult to establish, given the fact that neither efficiency nor effectiveness can be appropriately measured.[120] In fact, it seems that the moment of the police reform coincided with a window of opportunity (the time was right from a political-administrative perspective). The reform was mainly based on factors that were assumed to contribute positively to the increase of effectiveness and efficiency. Hence, the 1993 police reform rested on a policy theory, which provided the conceptual tools for a reform policy or reorganisation process.[121] Also the reorganisation of the National Criminal Intelligence Service in 2000 was inspired by the need for more effectiveness and efficiency.

Policy analysts note that the effectiveness of the police system has benefited considerably from the enlargement of scale.[122] However, one cannot really measure the increase in effectiveness, as the enlargement of scale and priority shifting were already on-going processes when the police reform was carried out. Hence, the expected effectiveness of the latest organisational reforms depends on the numerical parameters that were set out (80% basic police care, 20% of the police capacity to be used for the supra-local control of serious or organised criminality).[123]

One respondent noticed that although the current structure is more transparent, pseudo monopolies have remained. Ministries emphasised the creation of an improved information archive/storage, but conditions that apply to the exchange of information should also have been issued. A positive note about the police reform process is struck by a recent parliamentary document, which proposes the revision of some regional and local accountability structures. It summarises the benefits of the 1993 police reform as: the facilitation of flexible operationalisation of police personnel, improved support of operational tasks, and increased professionalisation of specialist functions.[124]

Except for the evaluations of the Parliamentary Inquiry Committee, the National Court of Auditors and the temporary Parliamentary Evaluation Committee, no explicit evaluations have been drawn up concerning the functioning of the coordination body, the central contact point and the multidisciplinary teams. Instead, the main observations of the temporary committee (published in the summer of 1999) may be summarised as follows:

a)   the national information archive/storage is insufficient, but may benefit from the new national index for ongoing investigations (VROS)

b)   the information exchange between the national criminal information exchange and the regional police forces has been sub-optimal but may be improved by the regional information desks[125]

c)   the linkage between intelligence and operations was insufficient; this situation has since been amended by the merger between the national criminal intelligence service (CRI) and the national crime squad (LRT) on 1 January 2000

d)   the engagement of officers from other law enforcement agencies in the core squads and the specialised teams is judged positively, but uncertainties are related to offhand (mostly temporary) secondment contracts.

## X.   ACCOUNTABILITY

The system of supervision and control is probably one of the most complex aspects of any organisation, let alone a police and public prosecution organisation that functions in a rather differentiated context. Although the section below contains some information on overall aspects of accountability, the analysis is restricted to national anti-organised crime mechanisms.

### Internal Accountability Systems

The investigation of criminal cases by the police service is carried out under the judicial supervision and administrative directorship of the Public Prosecution Service. In official terms, the hierarchical relationship implies that the lowest ranking official within the Public Prosecution Service is superior to the highest-ranking official in the police service. This formal rule tends to be ignored in practice. Moreover, the authority of the Public Prosecutor tends to be limited when it concerns operational investigations. The authority pertains to a difference between responsibilities.

In the recent past, much criticism has been ventured about the considerable autonomy within the police service and a weak supervision in the area of proactive investigation methods by the Public Prosecution Service.

The Parliamentary Inquiry Committee established in 1996 that the Chief Constables (*korpschefs*) did not exercise sufficient authority and that they were badly informed. Hence, the Parliamentary Inquiry Committee implicitly criticised the weakness of the internal accountability system. There was a plea for the restoration of the administrative authority of the Public Prosecution Service, particularly in view of the employment of proactive investigation techniques in the investigation of organised crime cases. The criticisms of the Committee resulted in increased awareness by the regional police chiefs of the employment of (special) investigation techniques and investigations of (international) organised crime. However, it depends on the size of the regional force and the regional priorities (not always organised crime) to what extent the regional police chiefs are involved. The chiefs who are in charge of criminal investigations ("*divisiechef recherche*") usually have most operational insight into criminal investigations.[126]

### Dual System of Control

Administratively, the police organisation is accountable to two authorities: the public prosecutor and the mayor, the Queen's Commissioner and the

Procurator General, and the Minister of Justice and the Interior. Compared with the previous 1957 Police Law, the municipalities have lost their own police forces and management over these forces.[127] Their managerial task has effectively been taken over by a Regional Management Board (*bestuurscollege*), which implies that the management of the police rests on the principle of divided power.

The basic construction is a "triangular authority" in each police region, consisting of the relevant Chief Constable (*korpschef*), Chief Public Prosecutor (*hoofdofficier van justitie*), and Mayor (*burgemeester*) of the largest town in that region.[128] These three actors meet in a regional board (*regionaal college*). This construction, which shows gaps particularly *vis-à-vis* mayors of smaller municipalities, has led to discussions concerning the democratic accountability of the mayor in the investigation of (organised) crime cases.

Hence, the political-administrative embedding of the police service has been problematic from the very moment the Police Act of 1993 was designed: there is no provision for direct accountability to a democratically chosen body. The accountability *vis-à-vis* the mayors does not respond to this need, as the mayors themselves are appointed instead of being democratically elected.[129] In addition, the administrative border lines of the police regions do not coincide with those of the twelve provinces, which are administrative entities directed by a Queen's Commissioner and a Provincial Senate. This implies that administratively, police regions are floating entities. A large-scale administrative reform of the provinces has not taken place.

Democratic control of criminal investigation aspects tends to be absent, and is being delegated to the Public Prosecution Service. The Parliamentary Inquiry Committee recommended that the relevant mayors should carry much more responsibility, but the Prosecution service and the mayors themselves expressed objections. The managerial responsibility for the regional police forces is usually (implicitly or explicitly) delegated to the Chief Constables. To rebalance this situation, a new Police Act could be considered. Others have strongly argued against this, as it would make responsibility for the investigation of organised crime cases (even) fuzzier. The Council of State (*Raad van State*) objected to the 1993 Police Bill that it lacked democratic control over the regional police forces, as the municipal councils would lose a lot of their impact. The Ministers of Justice and the Interior announced an adaptation of the 1993 Police Bill to amend the democratic and administrative deficiencies that have been outlined above.[130]

Although the police service has its own Inspectorate, it is subjected to a national inspection service/National Police Internal Investigation Department (*Rijksrecherche*). This latter service is located within the Dutch police service, but at an official level it is the only investigation service which has remained subject to the authority of the Ministry of Justice, and directly to the

Board of Procurators General. It is a small but highly specialised investigation service. The main objective of the *Rijksrecherche* is to guarantee the integrity of the criminal investigation. Its mandate covers law enforcement organisations (regular police service and the Royal Military Constabulary), the special criminal investigation services, the judiciary (including the Prosecution Service), and staff employed by municipal, provincial and central authorities. The inspection service investigates criminal offences like fraud, corruption, breach of confidentiality and competencies.

**Prosecution Service**

The Chief Public Prosecutor has a role in management (*"beheer"*) as well as in the judicial supervision of the police service. The managerial task is new, and it has been observed that the Prosecution Service is gradually getting used to its new task. Within the regional college, the regional triangle and the district triangle, the Prosecution Service is able to correct the criminal justice priorities: national and regional priorities are of great importance in this regard (including priorities with regard to the detection and investigation of organised crime cases).[131] According to police officers and mayors, the Prosecution Service is dominated too much by national priority setting. The guidelines of the Board of Procurators-General prevail in this respect.[132]

With regard to organised crime, the Procurators General, National Public Prosecutors, and National Public Prosecution Bureau carry principal responsibility for the supervision of investigations into (international) organised crime.

The Parliamentary Inquiry Committee established that the Public Prosecution Service did not exercise sufficient authority and was badly informed. Criticism had been expressed a few years prior in the so-called *"Donner Report"* (1994). Police officers often complain that since the Parliamentary Inquiry, the permission for the employment of proactive investigative techniques has become a lot more bureaucratic ("accumulation of written orders").[133]

The Public Prosecution Service itself is accountable to two separate authorities. On the one hand, the courts review the conduct of the Prosecution Service and the police services. The Minister of Justice carries simultaneous political responsibility for the Department's conduct and performance, and s/he may be requested to render account to both houses of the Dutch parliament. Policy is therefore always on the agenda in consultations between the Public Prosecution Service and the Minister. The responsibility of the Minister includes general policy on investigation and prosecution. Only rarely does s/he intervene in individual cases, although s/he may issue instructions to the

Public Prosecution Service officers after consulting the Board of Procurators General.[134] The Central Assessment Committee is responsible for the evaluation of special investigative techniques.

### *Juge d'instruction*

The *"juge d'instruction"* (*rechter-commissaris*) is responsible to the extent that he supervises the execution of coercive measures or rogatory commissions. S/he is not responsible for the authorisation of special investigation techniques. However, the new law on special police investigation techniques allows the *rechter commissaris* more insight into the criminal investigation, as the employment of these techniques will have to be recorded in writing.[135]

### Competent Ministries

As explained above, the Dutch police service is subjected to a dual ministerial responsibility. In general terms, the Minister of Justice is responsible for criminal investigations performed by the police, whilst the Minister of Interior carries final managerial responsibility (finances, personnel matters, resources, etc.).[136] The supervision of the National Police Agency (KLPD), which includes the national criminal intelligence service and the national crime squad, was recently transferred from the Ministry of Justice to the Ministry of the Interior,[137] mainly for logistic reasons.

As far as the accountability of local and regional actors to the relevant Minister is concerned, they hardly perceive the necessity to give account to the Queen's Commissioner or the Minister of the Interior.[138] Regional autonomy is a highly valued commodity within the Dutch policing context.

The Parliamentary Inquiry Committee on special investigation methods recommended that the Ministries of Justice and the Interior needed to sharpen their management of the police organisation. In the aftermath of the IRT crisis, the then Minister of Justice (Ernst Hirsch Ballin) and the Minister of the Interior (Ed van Thijn) resigned. The Parliamentary Committee established that the Minister of Justice had been ignorant of uncontrolled drug releases by the Rotterdam and The Hague police services.

A Minister of Justice is held responsible for authorising sensitive, costly and radical (proactive) investigation methods, such as long-term infiltration and the controlled release of drugs onto the market. The Kalsbeek Committee – responsible for evaluating the implementation of the recommendations of the Parliamentary Inquiry Committee – established that the current Minister of Justice (Mr. Benk Korthals) remained ignorant of several transports of cocaine (with an estimated total amount of 15,000 kilos released onto the Dutch market), which allegedly took place before he was appointed as Minister. However, the Second Chamber (Parliament) accepted the explanations of the Minister. A research group which was guided by Professor Fijnaut established early July 2001 that the truth was hard to reconstruct, and thus that the accusations about cocaine releases would remain a mystery. In the meantime, a special squad has been created to investigate these large-scale imports of cocaine. The responsibility for the investigation is in the hands of the National Crime Squad (LRT). The special LRT squad has temporarily been extended with 12 detectives from other core squads.

## Second Chamber

The Parliament or Second Chamber (*Tweede Kamer*) carries formal responsibility to control the supervisory activities and authorisations given by the Ministers. Ministers were held to account on their authorisation of payments to criminal informers (Sorgdrager) and/or the employment of radical, costly and sensitive proactive investigation techniques (Hirsch Ballin, Van Thijn, Sorgdrager, Korthals) on a number of occasions. Furthermore, the Dutch Parliament has repeatedly debated the situation within the Prosecution Service and the criminal justice system – mainly with regard to the control of organised crime – on the basis of reports of parliamentary inquiries or press releases.

## National Data Protection Authority

As a national body of control, the Dutch Data Protection Authority (*Registratiekamer*) is an independent supervisory authority that monitors the application of the legislation concerning the processing of personal data. It is competent to exercise supervision over the National Criminal Intelligence Service and its liaison officers. In that capacity, the *Registratiekamer* has access to all data that are entered by the Netherlands into the Europol system. The *Registratiekamer* is able to establish an opinion about the validity and correctness of this data input, exchange and analysis on the basis of the Europol Convention and Dutch law. A Dutch citizen can request the *Registratiekamer* to check whether his/her data are stored within Europol. In the event of refusal by the *Registratiekamer*, a citizen may appeal to the Joint Control Authority. The Dutch state is responsible for damage as a result of illegal or incorrect entry of data into the Europol system.[139] The functioning of the National Schengen Information System (NSIS) was the subject of a report drawn up by the *Registratiekamer*, and it was rather critical of it.[140] The president of the *Registratiekamer* (Peter Hustinx) is the Dutch representative in the Joint Control Authority for the Schengen Information System. Following the new law on the protection of personal data, the Registratiekamer adopted a new name on 1 September 2001: *College Bescherming Persoonsgegevens (CPB)*.

## National Ombudsman

The National Ombudsman is a Senior Institution of State (*Hoog College van Staat*), a position created in 1982. The National Ombudsman investigates complaints concerning behaviour of representatives of the state, the police, etc. After a decision about the admissibility of the written complaint, the director of the regional police force (*korpsbeheerder*) is able to react to the complaint. This can involve several stages. Civil servants can be interrogated as witnesses. The National Ombudsman can also decide to conduct a local investigation. After the investigation, a public report is usually published, with the findings, the judgement, a conclusion and possibly recommendations about new measures.

## Services Specialised in the Area of Organised Crime

One form of accountability which is imposed on the National Police Agency (KLPD) is in the form of the Council for the National Police Force (*Raad voor het Korps Landelijke Politiediensten*). According to Article 39 of the 1993 Police Act, the tasks of this Council include:
a) annual determination of the organisation, formation, budget, annual budget, policy plan and annual report of the force
b) provision of information to Ministers of Justice and/or the Interior
c) execution of tasks delegated to it by the Minister of Justice.

The National Criminal Intelligence Service is subjected to another, special Council (*Raad voor de Divisie Centrale Recherche Informatie*), which issues recommendations on strategic aspects of the cooperation between the National Criminal Intelligence Service and other segments of the Dutch criminal justice system. The supervision and control of the judicial activities are in the hands of the Public Prosecution Service, in particular the National Bureau of Public Prosecution (*Landelijk Parket*).

## XI.  FINAL OBSERVATIONS

- New developments that have been signalled include the establishment of international coordination centres and a special department of international networks within the National Criminal Intelligence Department.
- Another development that has been signalled in the framework of nationalisation is that all special investigation services (BODs) will be fused into four large investigation services: one in the field of finance and economics, one in the area of agriculture, one in the area of social security, and one in the area of public housing and the environment. The government regards these fused services as a third force next to the regular police service and the special intelligence force. It also supports the tendency of gradual enlargement and the development of national structures.
- The development of information and communication technologies (ICT) and their application within the Dutch police service has been given considerable attention.[141] The most important issues are: the introduction of a national mobile communication system C2000; further development and implementation of the perspective *Basis Infrastructuur Politie*; renewal of work places in a large number of regional police forces; development of views with regard to renewal of systems; stimulation and coordination of innovative developments; improvement of access to management and accountability data. These developments require more cooperation between the forces and the police departments. A joint platform ICT has been created, and it will look specifically into supra-regional functionalities of the ICT infrastructure.[142]
- One respondent noted that as Title VI instruments increasingly often become binding instruments, it is more important to anticipate the possible impact of these instruments on Dutch legislation.
- The Schengen Implementation Agreement has been responsible for the introduction of a new article in Dutch criminal procedure law (Article 552i), which allows police forces direct contacts with foreign law enforcement authorities. This article also allows direct exchange of police intelligence, e.g. concerning the investigation of organised crime. The article resulted in a significant decline of mutual assistance requests that were centrally addressed to the Ministry of Justice.
- Interestingly, because of the fact that the (first) High Level Group Action Plan against organised crime was authored by Dutch civil servants during the Dutch Presidency, the document undeniably carries the traces of the Dutch law enforcement model. Hence, it is anticipated that along with the implementation of the recommendations, elements of the Dutch model might be "exported" to the law enforcement systems of other EU Member States.

- The Research and Documentation Centre of the Dutch Ministry of Justice has recently argued that annually, 200 criminal groups and/or networks should be included in criminal investigation. The current average of 1000 criminal investigators needs to be doubled, according to the report, with another 1,000, 700 of whom should become active on the local and regional level, and 300 on the national level.[143]

**NOTES**

1.  For the translation of the Dutch terminology into English (particularly with regard to the units within the National Criminal Intelligence Division), I have made use of the translation list which was produced by the Documentation and Publications Unit in cooperation with the Translations Unit of the National Criminal Intelligence Service (*Divisie Recherche*).
2.  These criteria are summed up in the document "Prioriteitenstelling bij het landelijke optreden tegen georganiseerde misdaad", which can be found at http://www.openbaarministerie.nl/publikat/geocrim/prioriteit.htm.
3.  See report *Georganiseerde criminaliteit in Nederland*, 1999 (WODC).
4.  The predecessor of the serious crime committee was the Coordinating Policy Forum (*CBO*), which was defined as an advisory body of the Board of Procurators General. Similar to its predecessor, the serious crime committee offers (amongst other things) advice on priorities in criminal investigations into national or international organised crime.
5.  Enquêtecommissie opsporingsmethoden, *Inzake opsporing*, Den Haag, SDU, 1996, p. 25.
6.  Marc van Erve, "Toekomst bestrijding zware, georganiseerde criminaliteit, belicht vanuit het perspectief van de Hoofdofficier van Justitie IRT", in *Greep op de misdaad*, 1997, pp. 19-23, on p. 19.
7.  "Prioriteitstelling bij het landelijke optreden tegen georganiseerde misdaad", http://www.openbaarministerie.nl/publikat/geocrim/ prioriteit.htm.
8.  "Strategy against alien smuggling", http://www. openbaarministerie.nl/english/ reports/smuggle.htm.
9.  Wijziging van de Politiewet 1993 in verband met de concentratie van beheersbevoegdheden op rijksniveau met betrekking tot de regionale politiekorpsen bij de minister van binnenlandse zaken en koninkrijksrelaties (bijl. Hand. II, Z. 1999-2000, 26 813, Nos. 1-3); Kamerstukken II 1998-99, 26 461, Nos. 1-3.
10. The parliamentary "Kalsbeek" committee, which was responsible for the follow-up and evaluation of the recommendations that were made by the Parliamentary committee on special police investigation methods ("Van Traa") noted that most regions had come to extensive reorganisations, but that the differences were still sizeable. The differences are mainly due to the Police Law, which attaches greater autonomy to the regions, but on the other hand the central level has not formulated starting points or directives which could have supported the reorganisation process. It is obvious that these latter reorganisations were not due to European influences, but were triggered by an internal crisis in the criminal justice system. From: Tijdelijke Commissie evaluatie opsporingsmethoden, *Opsporing in uitvoering*, Tweede Kamer, vergaderjaar 1998-99, 26 269, Nos. 4-5, p. 5, 93.
11. P. van Reenen, "Het zwevende politiebestel", in *Justitiële Verkenningen*, jrg. 19, No. 4, 1993, pp. 7-36, on p. 24.
12. Statistics quoted from table 1, *Criminaliteitsbeheersing. Investeren in een*

*zichtbare overheid*, 2001.

13. U. Rosenthal, "Reorganisatie van de politie: over democratie en politiecratie", in A.Cachet en U. Rosenthal (eds.), *Reorganisatie van de politie: een tussenbalans*, Arnhem, Gouda Quint, 1992, p. 82.

14. Tijdelijke Commissie evaluatie opsporingsmethoden, *Opsporing in uitvoering*, Tweede Kamer, vergaderjaar 1998-99, 26 269, Nos. 4-5, p. 93.

15. *Verwijsindex Recherche Onderzoeken en Subjecten*, which is a fusion of three indicative indexes (started May 1999).

16. Tijdelijke Commissie evaluatie opsporingsmethoden, *Opsporing in uitvoering*, Tweede Kamer, vergaderjaar 1998-99, 26 269, Nos. 4-5, p. 96.

17. A reorganisation was implemented on 1 January 2000, which is discussed in section IX *infra*; see also below and footnote 13.

18. Tijdelijke Commissie, Tweede Kamer, vergaderjaar 1998-99, 26 269, Nos. 4-5, p. 129.

19. Tijdelijke Commissie, Tweede Kamer, vergaderjaar 1998-99, 26 269, Nos. 4-5, p. 130.

20. Zoetermeer: National analysis of organised crime, information centre, expertise and notification centres, fingerprint analysis, research and development, innovative products, accounting function regions, publications, temporary programmes, Interpol, Europol, Schengen, Liaison, Internal Policy Advice; Driebergen: Technical Support, Surveillance-innovation, witness protection, infiltration, intervention, technical development, forensic accountancy, international legal assistance, fraud, national interest cases, transport criminality, war crimes, anti-terrorism.

21. From: "Plan van aanpak Reorganisatie Openbaar Ministerie", http://www.openbaarministerie.nl/pubikat/hetom/plva_reorg.htm.

22. See also: Jo Horn, "Gesloten ministerie", in *Publiek Management*, 2000, p. 43.

23. Ex-procurator General Gonsalves in an interview with Kuipers, 1997, p. 18.

24. Commissie Openbaar Ministerie, *Het functioneren van het openbaar ministerie binnen de rechtshandhaving. Rapport van de Commissie Openbaar Ministerie*, Den Haag, 1994.

25. *Plan van aanpak Reorganisatie Openbaar Ministerie*. See: Cyrille Fijnaut, Dirk van Daele and Raf Verstraeten, "De hervorming van het openbaar ministerie. Een rechtsvergelijkend commentaar op de totstandkoming, inhoud en draagwijdte van het Octopus-Akkoord", in Cyrille Fijnaut and Dirk van Daele (eds.), *De hervorming van het openbaar ministerie*, Leuven, Universitaire Pers Leuven, 1999, pp. 271-350, on p. 289.

26. Annual Report 1998, p. 7; see also http://www.openbaarministerie.nl/persberi/p990406.htm.

27. From: Directie Algemene Justitiële Strategie, *Juridische infrastructuur in internationaal perspectief. Criminaliteitsbeheersing*, Den Haag, 2000, p. 42.

28. From: "Plan van aanpak Reorganisatie Openbaar Ministerie", http://www.openbaarministerie.nl/pubikat/hetom/plva_reorg.htm.

29. From: "Plan van aanpak Reorganisatie Openbaar Ministerie", http://www.openbaarministerie.nl/pubikat/hetom/plva_reorg.htm.

30. Source: http://www.openbaarministerie.nl/persberi/2000/p000309.htm.
31. *Kamerstukken* I, 1998-99, 25392, No. 46c, pp. 6 and 7.
32. Van der Flier, 1999, p. 742.
33. Fijnaut, Van Daele & Verstraeten, 1999, p. 307.
34. Originally under the name *Landelijk Bureau Openbaar Ministerie (LBOM)*.
35. Noord-Oost-Nederland; Randstad-Noord en Midden; Rotterdam; Haaglanden; Amsterdam-Amstelland / Gooi-Vechtstreek; Zuid-Nederland.
36. Note that this policy is also heavily influenced by the priorities that are lined up by the serious crime committee – *Cczwacri*.
37. Tijdelijke Commissie evaluatie opsporingsmethoden, *Opsporing in uitvoering*, Tweede Kamer, vergaderjaar 1998-99, 26 269, Nos. 4-5, p. 170-174.
38. BOB = bijzondere opsporingsbevoegdheden (special investigation competencies).
39. Bijlage 2, aanbiedingsbrief bij het kabinetsstandpunt inzake het rapport Opsporing in uitvoering, 31 August 1999 (Antwoorden op de vragen van de vaste commissies van Justitie en BZK inzake het rapport van de Tijdelijke Commissie evaluatie opsporingsmethoden, gesteld aan het kabinet bij brief van 13 juli 1999), http://www.minjust.nl/c_actual/rapport/kalsbeek.htm.
40. Tijdelijke Commissie evaluatie opsporingsmethoden, *Opsporing in uitvoering*, Tweede Kamer, vergaderjaar 1998-99, 26 269, Nos. 4-5, p. 104.
41. Tijdelijke Commissie evaluatie opsporingsmethoden, *Opsporing in uitvoering*, Tweede Kamer, vergaderjaar 1998-99, 26 269, Nos. 4-5, p. 104-105.
42. There are currently six police infiltration teams in the Netherlands. They deliver facilitatory services to the regional forces and are organised at a supra-regional level.
43. Tijdelijke Commissie evaluatie opsporingsmethoden, *Opsporing in uitvoering*, Tweede Kamer, vergaderjaar 1998-99, 26 269, Nos. 4-5, p. 108.
44. Lars Kuipers, "De prijs die je betaalt voor duidelijkheid", in Voorlichting Openbaar Ministerie, *Greep op de Misdaad*, 1997, pp. 10-18, on page 16.
45. Jan Wilzing, "De crisis in de opsporing en de toekomst van de criminaliteitsbestrijding", in *Greep op de misdaad*, 1997, pp. 28-39, on p. 30.
46. Ex Procurator General in an interview with Kuipers, 1997, on p. 17.
47. Region Brabant-Zuid-Oost however still has an Interregional Crime Squad: *Interregionaal Recherche Team* South-Netherlands, which accommodates the Synthetic Drugs Unit .
48. Tijdelijke Commissie evaluatie opsporingsmethoden, *Opsporing in uitvoering*, Tweede Kamer, vergaderjaar 1998-99, 26 269, Nos. 4-5, p. 112.
49. Tijdelijke Commissie evaluatie opsporingsmethoden, *Opsporing in uitvoering*, Tweede Kamer, vergaderjaar 1998-99, 26 269, Nos. 4-5, p. 113-114.
50. Marc van Erve, "Toekomst bestrijding zware, georganiseerde criminaliteit, belicht vanuit het perspectief van de Hoofdofficier van Justitie IRT", in *Greep op de misdaad*, 1997, pp. 19-23, on p. 20.
51. The temporary parliamentary evaluation committee recommended that the interregional core squads should have their own special branch. Tijdelijke Commissie, Tweede Kamer, vergaderjaar 1998-99, 26 269, Nos. 4-5, p. 116.

52. Tijdelijke Commissie evaluatie opsporingsmethoden, *Opsporing in uitvoering*, Tweede Kamer, vergaderjaar 1998-99, 26 269, Nos. 4-5, p. 116, 118.

53. From: Stand van zaken Unit Synthetische Drugs, Den Bosch, 25 March 1997, which can be found at: http://www.openbaarministerie.nl/publikat/drugs/syndrugs/htm.

54. *Netwerk*, d.d. 25 November 1999.

55. *De Volkskrant*, 9 May 2001.

56. *De Volkskrant*, 5 October 1999.

57. Clearly identifiable regional organised crime units are to be found in: Groningen, Twente (*Afdeling Georganiseerde Criminaliteit*), Utrecht (*BECRO – Bestrijding Criminele Organisaties*, division of the Investigation Service), Kennemerland (*Afdeling Zware/Georganiseerde Criminaliteit*), Amsterdam-Amstelland (*Georganiseerde criminaliteit en drugs, projectvoorbereiding*, part of the Central Investigation Service), Rotterdam-Rijnmond (Regional Crime Squad) *Regionale Recherche Dienst; Zware/Georganiseerde Criminaliteit*), Zeeland (*Regionaal Recherche Team Zware Georganiseerde Criminaliteit*), Midden- en West-Brabant (*Divisie Georganiseerde Criminaliteit*), Region Brabant-Zuid-Oost (Interregional Crime Squad: Interregionaal Recherche Team Zuid-Nederland, which accommodates the Synthetic Drugs Unit, and Organised Crime Investigations – *Recherche Georganiseerde Criminaliteit*), Limburg-Zuid (Division on Organised Crime (*Georganiseerde Criminaliteit*), which includes a Financial Investigation Desk and a Regional firearms and Ammunition Desk).

58. The *Dutch Police Handbook* does not always show whether or not there is a CID in place in every police region; however Limburg Noord has its own Regional CID.

59. Bijlage 2, aanbiedingsbrief bij het kabinetsstandpunt inzake het rapport Opsporing in uitvoering, 31 August 1999 (Antwoorden op de vragen van de vaste commissies van Justitie en BZK inzake het rapport van de Tijdelijke Commissie evaluatie opsporingsmethoden, gesteld aan het kabinet bij brief van 13 juli 1999), http://www.minjust.nl/c_actual/rapport/kalsbeek.htm.

60. Tijdelijke Commissie evaluatie opsporingsmethoden, *Opsporing in uitvoering*, Tweede Kamer, vergaderjaar 1998-99, 26 269, Nos. 4-5, p. 146.

61. Annual Report 1998, p. 14.

62. Annual Report 1998, p. 14.

63. Marc van Erve, "Toekomst bestrijding zware, georganiseerde criminaliteit, belicht vanuit het perspectief van de Hoofdofficier van Justitie IRT", in *Greep op de misdaad*, 1997, pp. 19-23, on p. 21.

64. Tijdelijke Commissie, Tweede Kamer, vergaderjaar 1998-99, 26 269, Nos. 4-5, p. 112-113.

65. Tijdelijke Commissie, Tweede Kamer, vergaderjaar 1998-99, 26 269, Nos. 4-5, p. 112.

66. In some Member States the financial intelligence unit may be known as the irregular transactions unit.

67. The Notification Desk on Exceptional Transactions started on 1 February 1994 (Wet Melding ongebruikelijke transacties; 16 december 1993, Stb.705, gewijzigd

bij Wet van 9 maart 1994, Stb.252).

68. Rick Smid, "Gezag en sturing ter zake MOT, Corpus Alienum in de informatieketen", in Voorlichting Openbaar Ministerie, *Greep op de Misdaad,* Den Haag, 1997, pp. 46-50, on p. 46.

69. Its members are: representatives from the Ministry of Justice, the Ministry of Finance, notifying companies from the private sector or their supervisors, the Economic Inspection Service (Economische Controledienst), the Public Prosecution Service and the police organisation.

70. Press release 27 April 1999, http://www.minjust.nl/c_actual/persber/pb0420.htm.

71. Press release 24 April 1998, http://www.minjust.nl/c_actual/persber/pb276.htm.

72. Tijdelijke Commissie, Tweede Kamer, vergaderjaar 1998-99, 26 269, Nos. 4-5, p. 133.

73. Tijdelijke Commissie, 1999, p. 135.

74. Press release 27 April 1999, http://www.minjust.nl/c_actual/persber/pb0420.htm.

75. Tijdelijke Commissie, 1999, p. 134.

76. Brochure "Korps Landelijke Politiediensten – Divisie Centrale Recherche Informatie (CRI)".

77. LIPO = *Landelijk informatie punt observatie.* Cross-border surveillances are carried out by one of the five Schengen teams. In: Tweede Kamer, vergaderjaar 1998-99, 26 269, Nos. 4-5. p. 137.

78. "Wat is en wat doet Europol?", in *Algemeen Politieblad*, No. 17, 28 augustus 1998, p. 6-10.

79. "Nationaal Schengen Informatie Systeem", in *Algemeen Politieblad*, No. 23, 21 november 1998, p. 12.

80. The *Bureau internationale rechtshulp in strafzaken* is based within the Ministry of Justice and is the central authority for the Netherlands in relation to the Vienna Treaty. The temporary committee considers that the Ministry of Justice and the Public Prosecution Service need to be tuned to each other in international cases (Tijdelijke Commissie, Tweede Kamer, vergaderjaar 1998-99, 26 269, Nos. 4-5, p. 136).

81. National Uniform Registration System Mutual Legal Assistance.

82. In the future, it may be possible that members from other law enforcement forces join the ICCs.

83. For an overview of the Dutch participation in international police cooperation frameworks, see M.G.W. den Boer, "Internationale Politiesamenwerking", in C.J.C.F.Fijnaut, E.R. Muller & U. Rosenthal (eds.), *Politie. Studies over haar werking en organisatie*, Alphen a/d Rijn, Samsom, 1999, pp. 577-617, on pp. 584-588.

84. Mainly: Great Britain, Germany and France.

85. This reorganisation was offered a new momentum by a critical report of the national court of auditors (*Rekenkamer*). The reorganisation process had already started, but was momentarily annulled because of the report then subsequently changed and rapidly implemented. (Algemene Rekenkamer, *Uitwisseling van recherche-informatie tussen CRI en politieregio's*, 24 September 1998 (Tweede Kamer 1998-99, 26 215).

86. Dutch liaison officers are stationed in: Asia (Thailand, Pakistan, Turkey); South America (Dutch Antilles, Venezuela, Colombia); eastern Europe (Poland, Hungary and Russia); and West Europe (France, Spain). Foreign liaison officers: 37 police officers from 13 different countries.

87. Annual Report 1998, p. 18.

88. *Staatsblad*, 27 January 2000, No. 32.

89. Brief aan de Tweede Kamer (Persbericht), 31.08.99, "Kabinet neemt vrijwel alle aanbevelingen over van de Tijdelijke Commissie evaluatie opsporings-methoden" (http://www.minjust.nl/c_actual/persber/pb0469.htm).

90. Nic van Helten, "BVD legt nieuwe banden met politie", in *Algemeen Politieblad*, No. 21, 30 October 1993.

91. Voorstel Wet op de Inlichtingen- en Veiligheidsdiensten.

92. Bijlage 2, aanbiedingsbrief bij het kabinetsstandpunt inzake het rapport Opsporing in uitvoering, 31 August 1999 (Antwoorden op de vragen van de vaste commissies van Justitie en BZK inzake het rapport van de Tijdelijke Commissie evaluatie opsporingsmethoden, gesteld aan het kabinet bij brief van 13 juli 1999), http://www.minjust.nl/c_actual/rapport/kalsbeek.htm.

93. Tijdelijke Commissie, 1999, p. 131 and 132.

94. *Vrij Nederland*, 8 January 2000.

95. *Wet Particuliere Beveiligingsorganisaties en Recherchebureaus.*

96. A.A. Sels, "Veiligheidsconvenant op lokaal niveau. Samenwerking tussen politie en particuliere beveiligers", in *Bestuursforum*, mei 1998, 133-136, on p. 133.

97. "Politie wil commerciële recherche informeren", *Volkskrant*, 10 September 1999.

98. From: Directie Algemene Justitiële Strategie, *Juridische infrastructuur in internationaal perspectief. Criminaliteitsbeheersing*, Den Haag, 2000, p. 40.

99. Much of the information contained in this chapter is a repetition of information elaborated in previous chapters.

100. For a description of these forces in English, see e.g. Trevor Jones, *Policing and Democracy in the Netherlands*, London, Policy Studies Institute, 1995, pp. 50-55; Monica den Boer, *The Police in the Netherlands and European Cooperation*, Working Paper series "A system of European police cooperation after 1992", Edinburgh, University of Edinburgh, 1992.

101. Trevor Jones, 1995, p. 72.

102. P. van Reenen, "Het zwevende politiebestel", in *Justitiële Verkenningen*, jrg. 19, No. 4, 1993, pp. 7-36, p. 8.

103. See: A. Cachet en J.M. de Blaey, "Reorganisatie van de politie: de zin van permanente discussie", chapter 1 in A. Cachet & U. Rosenthal, *Reorganisatie van de politie: een tussenbalans*, Crisis Onderzoek Team, Arnhem, Gouda Quint, 1992, p. 3.

104. Van Reenen (1993: 9) criticises the lack of a solid analysis of these problems: "... de Memorie van Toelichting bij het wetsontwerp geeft geen nader antwoord op de vraag wat nu precies de actuele problemen zijn, wat daarvan de oorzaken zijn en op welke wijze en in welke mate juist de gekozen oplossing het probleem

verkleint of zelfs helemaal doet verdwijnen. [...]Wat wordt hier bedoeld met ondoelmatigheid, waaruit blijkt deze, wat zijn de oorzaken ervan en hoe preceis kan de politie doelmatiger worden gemaakt, zo moet men zich afvragen. Overigens was het blijkbaar ook in het verleden niet gemakkelijk een goede analyse te presenteren; het wetsontwerp voor een provinciale politie van 1980 kent evenmin een probleemanalyse; men moet teruggaan naar het voorontwerp *Herziening politiewet* van 1969 voor een soort probleemanalyse." See also Cachet and De Blaey, 1992, p. 4.

105. A.C. Zijderveld, "Schaalvergroting en cultuurconflict", in A. Cachet & U. Rosenthal, *Reorganisatie van de Politie: een tussenbalans*, Arnhem, Gouda Quint bv, 1992, 99-106, on p. 103. See also: J.M.M. Polman, "Een veilige schaal voor de politie?", in *Bestuurskunde*, jrg. 7, No. 1, 1998, pp. 10-18, on p. 14.

106. "Noch bij het politie-apparaat zelf, noch bij de politiek, noch bij commentatoren bestaat thans animo voor een nieuwe structuurwijziging van de politie-organisatie na die van begin jaren negentig; voorts is het politieke en bestuurlijke draagvlak voor provinciale politie vrijwel geheel afwezig." From: J. Burkens, review of J. Koopman, De democratische inbedding van de regionale politie, in *RM Themis* 1999/6, p. 196.

107. Bijlage 2, aanbiedingsbrief bij het kabinetsstandpunt inzake het rapport Opsporing in uitvoering, 31 August 1999 (Antwoorden op de vragen van de vaste commissies van Justitie en BZK inzake het rapport van de Tijdelijke Commissie evaluatie opsporingsmethoden, gesteld aan het kabinet bij brief van 13 juli 1999), http://www.minjust.nl/c_actual/rapport/kalsbeek.htm.

108. Tijdelijke Commissie evaluatie opsporingsmethoden, *Opsporing in uitvoering*, Tweede Kamer 1998-99, 26 269, Nos. 4-5, p. 5.

109. *Uitwisseling van recherche-informatie tussen CRI en politieregio's*, Algemene Rekenkamer, 24 September 1998 (Tweede Kamer 1998-99, 26 215).

110. Tijdelijke Commissie evaluatie opsporingsmethoden, *Opsporing in uitvoering*, Tweede Kamer, vergaderjaar 1998-99, 26 269, Nos. 4-5, p. 102.

111. Tijdelijke Commissie evaluatie opsporingsmethoden, *Opsporing in uitvoering*, Tweede Kamer, vergaderjaar 1998-99, 26 269, Nos. 4-5, p. 97.

112. Tijdelijke Commissie evaluatie opsporingsmethoden, *Opsporing in uitvoering*, Tweede Kamer 1998-99, 26 269, Nos. 4-5, p. 99.

113. Aanbevelingsbrief 31 August 1999 (Response to question 127).

114. Wet van 19 april 1999 (*Stb.* 194) tot wijziging van de Wet op de rechterlijke organisatie, het Wetboek van Strafvordering, de Politiewet 1993 and other laws.

115. See e.g. P.J. van der Flier, "De wetgeving inzake de reorganisatie van het openbaar ministerie", AA 48 (1999), 10, pp. 740-745. The Board of Procurators General was created on the basis of article 130 Wet RO.

116. *Kamerstukken* 1994/1995, 24034, No. 3.

117. Idea stemming from ex-top civil servant Sweder van Wijnbergen, later positively discussed in the media by Chief Prosecutor Vrakking (Amsterdam).

118. Ybo Buruma, "Privatisering van het Openbaar Ministerie", in *Nederlands Juristenblad*, 12 November 1999, issue 40, pp. 1886-1889. In an interesting commentary, Paul Kapteyn signals a trend of internationalisation and increasing

policy competition; reorganisation cycles create new centres of power. The internationalisation of criminality, he argues, shifts the working terrain of the Prosecution Service to foreign territory, away from national parliamentary and judicial control. The consequence is that central management is becoming more powerful. (*NRC*, 1 September 1999).

119. Van Reenen (1993: 26); "Landelijke taaktoedeling is soms efficiency-verhogend, hoewel rekening moet worden gehouden met frictieverliezen wanneer regionale korpsen onvoldoende meewerken of tegenwerken. Of ook de effectiviteit wordt gediend, hangt af van de effecten van de grote afstand tot de bevolking die wordt gecreëerd." ... "De bepaling van de doelmatigheid (effectiviteit) van de politie is altijd problematisch geweest. Zoals gezegd, is niet bekend wat de effectiviteit van de politie is en welke factoren die effectiviteit beïnvloeden. ... Wel is het zo dat efficiencyverbetering mogelijkheden geeft voor effectiviteitsverbetering; de capaciteit neemt immers toe. Bovendien is in ieder geval de redenering plausibel, dat wanneer de schaal van een probleem toeneemt ook de schaal van een organisatie moet groeien. *Die redenering gaat in ieder geval op voor een aantal vormen van georganiseerde criminaliteit. Daar staat tegenover dat de georganiseerde criminaliteit veelal sterk gebonden blijft aan een specifiek crimineel milieu, dat vaak nog het jachtgebied is van de lokaal ingevoerde rechercheur (Van Duijne e.a., 1990).*"

120. Van Reenen (1993: 9): "Effectiviteitswinst is niet na te gaan omdat onbekend is of en in welke mate de gestelde beleidsvraagstukken door de politie kunnen worden opgelost. Of regiovorming inderdaad zal leiden tot een betere bestrijding van de bovenlokaal georganiseerde criminaliteit, de internationale criminaliteit en de onveiligheidsgevoelens is een open vraag."

121. Van Reenen, 1993, p. 11.

122. K. de Ridder, "De externe besturing van de politie: over belemmeringen voor een integrale besturing van de regiokorpsen", in: *Beleidswetenschap*, No. 3, 1999, pp. 232-259, on p. 235.

123. Van Reenen, 1993, p. 11.

124. Tweede Kamer, vergaderjaar 1998-99, 26 661, No. 1, p. 3.

125. In a reaction to a report on anti-firearms strategy (*Aanpak illegaal wapenbezit en –geweld*, bijl. Hand. II, Z. 1999-2000, 26 494, No. 2), the two "police ministers" supported recommendations to improve the information exchange between the regions and the *CRI*. Moreover, they welcomed initiatives to create operational and pragmatic cooperation structures between the different European countries in the area of firearms. From: *Delikt en Delinkwent*, 29 (1999), afl. 10, p. 1032.

126. Tijdelijke Commissie evaluatie opsporingsmethoden, *Opsporing in uitvoering*, Tweede Kamer, vergaderjaar 1998-99, 26 269, Nos. 4-5, p. 97.

127. L.Cachet, A. van Sluis, E.J. van der Torre, U. Rosenthal & E.M. Muller, "Een nieuwe Politiewet, maar geen nieuw begin. Ontwikkelingen in de relatie politie, bevoegd gezag en gemeenteraad.", in *Justitiële Verkenningen*, jrg. 19, No. 4, 1993, pp. 37-68, on p. 43. The authors note a political-administrative vacuum in the regionally organised parts of the police organisation which are responsible

for the fight against supralocal and international forms of organised crime. This is an aspect which falls beyond the scope of the mayor and the municipal council.

128. For an overview of tasks and mandates of the *korpsbeheerder, korpschef* and *hoofdofficier van justitie*, see: D.J. Elzinga, "De bestuurlijke inbedding van de regionale politiekorpsen", in *Justitiële Verkenningen,* jrg. 19, No. 4, 1993, pp. 69-90.

129. Universitair consortium politie-onderzoek, *Evaluatie Politiewet 1993*, VUGA, Den Haag, 1998, p. 12.

130. "Regionaal politiebestel", Tweede Kamer, vergaderjaar 1998-99, 26 661, No. 1.

131. Universitair consortium politie-onderzoek, *Evaluatie Politiewet 1993*, VUGA, Den Haag, 1998, p. 204.

132. Universitair consortium politie-onderzoek, *Evaluatie Politiewet 1993*, VUGA, Den Haag, 1998, p. 205.

133. Tijdelijke Commissie evaluatie opsporingsmethoden, *Opsporing in uitvoering*, Tweede Kamer, vergaderjaar 1998-99, 26 269, Nos. 4-5, p. 149.

134. From: "Plan van aanpak Reorganisatie Openbaar Ministerie", http://www.openbaarministerie.nl/pubikat/hetom/plva_reorg.htm.

135. Aanbevelingsbrief kabinet, 31 August 1999.

136. "Artikel 53 geeft de ministers van Justitie en van Binnenlandse Zaken een aanwijzingsbevoegdheid. Artikel 53 lid 1 van de Politiewet bepaalt dat de minister van Justitie in bijzondere gevallen, na overleg met de minister van Binnenlandse Zaken, aan een korpsbeheerder de nodige aanwijzingen kan geven ten aanzien van personeel en middelen ten behoeve van de strafrechtelijke handhaving van de rechtsorde en andere taken ten dienste van justitie. De minister van Binnenlandse Zaken kan hetzelfde doen, indien het belang van het beheer van de politie dit eist (art. 53 lid 2)." From: Universitair consortium politie-onderzoek, *Evaluatie Politiewet 1993*, VUGA, Den Haag, 1998, p. 22.

137. This required a change in the 1993 Police Law (*Kamerstukken II 1998-99, 26 461, Nos. 1-3*).

138. Universitair consortium politie-onderzoek, *Evaluatie Politiewet 1993*, VUGA, Den Haag, 1998, p. 224.

139. Myriam Gijzen, "Wat is en wat doet Europol?", in *Algemeen Politieblad*, nummer 17, 28 augustus 1998, p. 9.

140. See also: Algemene Rekenkamer, Nationaal Schengen Informatie Systeem, 30 January 1997, Tweede Kamer, vergaderjaar 1996-97, 25 200, Nos. 1-2.

141. *Beleidsplan Nederlandse Politie 1999-2002*, bijl. Hand. II, Z. 1999-2000, 26 345, No. 19.

142. *Delikt en Delinkwent* 29 (1999), afl. 10, p. 1029.

143. Nota *Criminaliteitsbeheersing. Investeren in een zichtbare overheid"*, 2001, on p. 59.

**BIBLIOGRAPHY**

Boer, M.G.W. den, "Internationale Politiesamenwerking", in C.J.C.F. Fijnaut, E.R. Muller & U. Rosenthal (eds.), *Politie. Studies over haar werking en organisatie*, 1999, Alphen a/d Rijn, Samsom, 1999, pp. 577-617.

Boer, M.G.W. den, *The Police in the Netherlands and European Cooperation*, Working Paper series "A system of European police cooperation after 1992", 1992, Edinburgh, University of Edinburgh.

Burkens, J., Review of J. Koopman, De democratische inbedding van de regionale politie, in *RM Themis* 1999/6, p. 196.

Buruma, Y., "Privatisering van het Openbaar Ministerie", in *Nederlands Juristenblad*, 12 November 1999, issue 40, pp. 1886-1889.

Cachet, A. and De Blaey, J.M., "Reorganisatie van de politie: de zin van permanente discussie", Chapter 1 in A. Cachet & U. Rosenthal, *Reorganisatie van de politie: een tussenbalans*, Crisis Onderzoek Team, Arnhem, Gouda Quint, 1992, p. 3.

Cachet, A., Van Sluis, A., Van der Torre, E.J., Rosenthal U., and Muller, E.M., "Een nieuwe Politiewet, maar geen nieuw begin. Ontwikkelingen in de relatie politie, bevoegd gezag en gemeenteraad.", *Justitiële Verkenningen*, jrg. 19, No. 4, 1993, pp. 37-68.

Directie Algemene Justitiële Strategie, *Juridische infrastructuur in internationaal perspectief. Criminaliteitsbeheersing*, Den Haag, 2000.

Elzinga, "De bestuurlijke inbedding van de regionale politiekorpsen", in *Justitiële Verkenningen,* jrg. 19, No. 4, 1993, pp. 69-90.

Erve, M. van, "Toekomst bestrijding zware, georganiseerde criminaliteit, belicht vanuit het perspectief van de Hoofdofficier van Justitie IRT", in *Greep op de misdaad*, Voorlichting Openbaar Ministerie, Den Haag, 1997, pp. 19-23.

Fijnaut, C., Van Daele, D. and Verstraeten, R. "De hervorming van het openbaar ministerie. Een rechtsvergelijkend commentaar op de totstandkoming, inhoud en draagwijdte van het Octopus-Akkoord", in C. Fijnaut and D. van Daele (eds.), *De hervorming van het openbaar ministerie*, Leuven, Universitaire Pers Leuven, 1999, pp. 271-350.

Flier, P.J. van der, "De wetgeving inzake de reorganisatie van het openbaar ministerie", *AA* 48, 1999, 10, pp. 740-745.

Gijzen, M., "Wat is en wat doet Europol?", *Algemeen Politieblad*, nummer 17, 28 August 1998, p. 9.

Helten, N. van "BVD legt nieuwe banden met politie", *Algemeen Politieblad*, No. 21, 30 October 1993.

Horn, J., "Gesloten ministerie", *Publiek Management*, February 2000, p. 43.

Jones, T., *Policing and Democracy in the Netherlands*, London, Policy Studies Institute, 1995.

Korsten, A.F.A., and J.L.M.L. Soeters, "Parlementaire enquête opsporingsmethoden. Resultaten, beoordelingen en debatten", *Bestuurskunde*, jrg. 5, No. 2, 1996, pp. 50-65.

Kuipers, L., "De prijs die je betaalt voor duidelijkheid", *Greep op de Misdaad*, Voorlichting Openbaar Ministerie, Den Haag, 1997, pp. 10-18.

Leijten, J.C., "De crisis in de opsporing na Van Traa. Enkele gedachten", *Bestuurskunde*, jrg. 5, No. 2, 1996, pp. 97-99.

Naeyé, J. en T. Schalken, "Commissie-Van Traa en de crisis in de opsporing", *Nederlands Juristenblad*, 9 February 1996.

Polman, J.M.M., "Een veilige schaal voor de politie?", *Bestuurskunde*, jrg. 7, No. 1, 1998, pp. 10-18, on p. 14.

Reenen, P. van, "Het zwevende politiebestel", *Justitiële Verkenningen*, jrg. 19, No. 4, 1993, pp. 7-36, on p. 24.

Reijntjes, J., "Wat vertel ik mijn baas? De paradoxen van het toezicht", *Bestuurskunde*, jrg. 5, No. 2, 1996, pp. 100-104.

Ridder, K. de, "De externe besturing van de politie: over belemmeringen voor een integrale besturing van de regiokorpsen", in: *Beleidswetenschap*, No. 3, 1999, pp. 232-259.

Rosenthal, U., "Reorganisatie van de politie: over democratie en politiecratie", in A.Cachet en U. Rosenthal (eds.), *Reorganisatie van de politie: een tussenbalans*, Arnhem, Gouda Quint, 1992.

Sels, A.A., "Veiligheidsconvenant op lokaal niveau. Samenwerking tussen politie en particuliere beveiligers", in *Bestuursforum*, mei 1998, 133-136.

Smid, R., "Gezag en sturing ter zake MOT, Corpus Alienum in de informatieketen", *Greep op de Misdaad,* Voorlichting Openbaar Ministerie, Den Haag, 1997, pp. 46-50.

Universitair consortium politie-onderzoek, *Evaluatie Politiewet 1993*, VUGA, Den Haag, 1998.

Wilzing, J., "De crisis in de opsporing en de toekomst van de criminaliteitsbestrijding", in *Greep op de misdaad*, Voorlichting Openbaar Ministerie, Den Haag, 1997, pp. 28-39.

Zijderveld, A.C., "Schaalvergroting en cultuurconflict", in A. Cachet & U. Rosenthal, *Reorganisatie van de Politie: een tussenbalans*, Arnhem, Gouda Quint bv, 1992, 99-106.

**LIST OF RESPONDENTS**

- Wil van Gemert, Director, National Criminal Intelligence Department, Zoetermeer, also referee of the Falcone-project
- Hans Holthuis, National Public Prosecutor, National Public Prosecution Bureau (*Landelijk Parket*), Rotterdam (now at the International Criminal Tribunal for the former Yugoslavia in The Hague)
- Harm Trip, Director International Affairs, National Criminal Intelligence Department, Zoetermeer
- Ab van Stormbroek, Director, National Intelligence Coordination Unit, National Criminal Intelligence Department, Zoetermeer
- Mascha Toussaint, Policy Development Adviser, National Criminal Intelligence Department, member of several Title VI Working Groups (Police Cooperation, Europol, Schengen, Multidisciplinary Group), Zoetermeer
- Peter Reijnders, Director Synthetic Drugs Unit, Eindhoven

## APPENDIX: GLOSSARY*

| Dutch expression | Dutch abbreviation | English translation |
|---|---|---|
| Afdeling Dactyloscopie | | Fingerprints Unit |
| Afdeling Documentatie & Publicaties | | Documentation and Publications Unit |
| Afdeling Getuigenbescherming | | Witness Protection Unit |
| Afdeling Infiltratie (also: Afdeling nationale coördinatie politiële infiltratie) | ANCPI | National Infiltration Unit |
| Afdeling Innovatie Programma's | | Innovation Programmes Unit |
| Afdeling Internationale Inlichtingen-Uitwisseling | | International Exchange of Intelligence Unit |
| Afdeling Kerntaken | | Infiltration Support Unit |
| Afdeling Meldpunten | | Disclosure Desks Unit |
| Afdeling Monitoring | | Suspect Monitoring Unit |
| Afdeling Nationaal Inzicht | | National Intelligence Coordination Unit |
| Afdeling Onderzoek en Analyse | | Research and Analysis Unit |
| Afdeling Ontwikkeling Recherche Technologie | | Crime Investigation Technology Development Unit |
| Afdeling Recherche Advisering | | Crime Investigation Advisory Unit |
| Afdeling Recherche Informatiebureaus | | Regional Exchange of Information Unit |
| Afdeling Terrorisme | | Anti-terrorism Unit |
| Arrestatie Team | AT | Apprehension Team |
| Berichtenbehandeling | | Communications Unit |
| Bestuurscollege | | Regional Management Board |
| Bijzondere Opsporingsdienst | BOD | Special Investigation Service |
| Binnenlandse Veiligheidsdienst | BVD | National Secret Service |
| Bureau Landelijk Officier Meldpunt Ongebruikelijke Transacties | BLOM | Desk of the National Prosecutor for the Notification of Unusual Transactions |
| Centrale Commissie Zware Criminaliteit | CcZwaCri | Serious Crime Committee |
| Centrale Toetsingscommissie | CTC | Central Assessment Committee |

---

\* Not all the Dutch terms included in the list below remained in the text when it was edited for the purposes of publication.

| | | |
|---|---|---|
| (College van) Procureurs Generaal | PG-college | Board of Procurators General |
| Coordinerend Beleidsorgaan | CBO | Coordinating Policy Forum |
| Criminele Inlichtingendienst | CID | Criminal Intelligence Department |
| (Dienst) Berichtenbehandeling en Identificatie | BBI | Communications and Identification Department |
| Dienst Bijzondere Recherche Zaken | | Special Investigations Department |
| Dienst Centrale Recherche Informatie | (D)CRI | National Criminal Intelligence Service |
| Dienst Internationale Netwerken | | International Networks Department |
| Dienst Nationaal Recherche Informatie Knooppunt | | National Crime Intelligence Coordination Centre |
| Dienst Recherche Advies en Ontwikkeling | | Crime Research and Advice Department |
| Dienst Recherche Informatie | | Crime Intelligence Department |
| Dienst Specialistische Recherche Toepassingen | | Special Applications to Criminal Investigations Service |
| Dienst Technische Operationele Ondersteuning | DTOO | National Technical Support Service |
| DG Openbare Orde en Veiligheid | | Directorate General Public Order and Security (Ministry of the Interior) |
| DG Rechtshandhaving | | Directorate General Law Enforcement (Ministry of Justice) |
| Divisie Koninklijke en Diplomatieke Beveiliging | | Royal and Diplomatic Protection Division |
| Divisie Logistiek | | National Logistics Division |
| Divisie Mobiliteit | | National Mobility Division |
| Divisie Ondersteuning | | National Support Division |
| Directie Recherche | | National Criminal Intelligence Service |
| Economische Controle Dienst | ECD | Economic Investigation Service |
| Fiscale Inlichtingen- en Opsporingsdienst | FIOD | Fiscal Intelligence and Investigation Service |
| Gemeentepolitie | | Municipal Police Forces |
| Hoofdofficier van Justitie | HOvJ | Chief Public Prosecutor |
| Hoog College van Staat | | Senior Council of State |
| Informatieknooppunten | | Intelligence desks |
| Inlichtingen- en Veiligheidsdiensten | IVD | Intelligence and Security Services |

| | | |
|---|---|---|
| Internationaal Coördinatie Centrum | ICC | International Coordination Centre |
| Bureau Internationale Rechtshulp in Strafzaken | BIRS | International Mutual Assistance in Criminal Matters Desk |
| Interregionaal Fraude Team | IFT | Interregional Fraud Squad |
| Kernteams (interregionale teams) | (IRT) | Core Squads (Interregional Crime Squad) |
| Kernteam Zware Milieucriminaliteit | | Serious Environmental Crime Squad |
| Koninklijke Marechaussee | | Royal Military Constabulary |
| Korpsbeheerder | | Director of the Regional Force |
| Korpschefs | | Chief Constables |
| Korps Landelijke Politiediensten | KLPD | National Police Agency |
| Landelijk Bureau Openbaar Ministerie | LBOM | National Public Prosecution Bureau |
| Landelijk Loket Horizontale Fraude | | National Desk for Horizontal Fraud |
| Landelijk Officier van Justitie | LOvJ | National Public Prosecutor |
| Landelijk Parket | | National Public Prosecution Bureau |
| Landelijk Rechercheteam | LRT | National Crime Squad |
| Landelijk Uitvoeringssysteem Rechtshulp in Strafzaken | LURIS | National Uniform Registration System Mutual Legal Assistance |
| Message Achieve Routing System | MARS | Message Achieve Routing System |
| Meldpunt Ongebruikelijke Transacties | MOT | Central Notification Point for Unusual Transactions |
| Ministerie van Binnenlandse Zaken en Koninkrijksrelaties | BZK | Ministry of Interior |
| Ministerie van Justitie | MvJ | Ministry of Justice |
| Ministerie van Volkshuisvesting, Ruimtelijke Ordening en Milieu | VROM | Ministry of Environmental Affairs |
| Nationaal Schengen Informatie Systeem | NSIS | National Schengen Information System |
| Nederlands Politie Instituut | NPI | Dutch Police Institute |
| Nederlands Centrum voor Internationale Politiesamenwerking | NCIPS | Dutch Centre for International Police Cooperation |
| Nederlandse Vereniging van Banken | NVB | Dutch Banking Association |
| Observatieteam | OT | Surveillance team |

| | | |
|---|---|---|
| Openbaar Ministerie | OM | Public Prosecution Service |
| Organisatiecriminaliteit | | White collar crime |
| Parlementaire enquêtecommissie | PEC | Parliamentary Inquiry Committee |
| Particuliere recherchebureaus | | Private investigation agencies |
| Politie Infiltratie Team | PIT | Police Infiltration Team |
| Raad van Hoofdcommissarissen | | Council of Chief Constables |
| Raad van State | | Council of State |
| Raad voor de Divisie Centrale Recherche Informatie | | Council for the National Criminal Intelligence Service |
| Raad voor het Korps Landelijke Politiediensten | | Council for the National Police Force |
| Recherche-officier van justitie | | Officer of Investigations |
| Rechercheteam Transport & Logistiek | RT&L | Transport and logistics investigation squad |
| Rechter-commissaris | | Investigating Judge (*juge d'instruction*) |
| Registratiekamer | | National Data Protection Protection Authority |
| Regionaal college | | Regional board |
| Regionale Recherchedienst | RRD | Regional Crime Squad |
| Rekenkamer | | Court of Auditors |
| Rijkspolitie | | National Police |
| Rijksrecherche | | National Police Internal Investigation Department |
| Sectie Technische Ondersteuning | STO | Section Technical Support |
| Stafeenheid Informatiebeheer &Kwaliteitszorg | | Data Management Unit |
| Stafeenheid Ondersteuning Management | | Management Support Unit |
| Stafeenheid Vertalingen | | |
| Stuurgroep IPEO | | Steering Committee |
| Tactische recherche | | Tactical investigation departments |
| Tweede Kamer | | Parliament (Second Chamber) |
| Unit Synhetische Drugs | USD | Synthetic Drugs Unit |
| Vereniging van Particuliere Beveiligingsorganisaties | VPB | Association of Private Security Agencies |
| (Wet) Bijzondere Opsporingsbevoegdheden | BOB | (Law on) Special Investigation Techniques |
| Wetenschappelijk Onderzoeks- en Documentatiecentrum | WODC | Research and Documentation Centre (Ministry of Justice) |

455

# Portugal

## Monica den Boer[1]

**INTRODUCTION**

With around 10 million inhabitants, Portugal counts as one of the smaller countries within the European Union. It acceded the EU in 1985 and has since been one of the staunchest pro-integrationist Member States. Like the Netherlands, Belgium and Greece, it currently enjoys 5 votes within the European Council (this will go up to 12 as of 1 January 2005). Portugal shares one internal border with another EU Member State, namely Spain. The two countries are known to have a longstanding pragmatic form of law enforcement collaboration at their joint border, and have even established joint commissariats for this particular purpose. Given its geographical position on the outer fringes of the European mainland, Portugal is seen as an important gateway country for Latin American cocaine entering the European market. Moreover, it is regarded as a location for transhipment of hashish from North Africa to Europe. Compared to other EU countries, the number of asylum requests is relatively low.

**ORGANISED CRIME IN PORTUGAL**

Portugal has witnessed an increase in the international dimension of organised criminality. Some expansion of Mafia-activities from the former Eastern Bloc has been noticeable. Their business mainly consists of the use of extortion in the immigrant communities which originate from these countries and who are mainly active in the construction industry. At least two murders have been reported recently within this scene. Moreover, financial crime, the narcotics trade and raids have risen lately. In its annual situation report on organised crime in 1997, Portugal also includes other organised crime categories, such as trade in human beings and prostitution, stolen art, forgery of documents, trade in stolen vehicles, and kidnappings.

Drug trafficking operations take place in the country. In the northern part of the country, in the area around Porto, a large quantity of heroin was seized, sufficient to prepare over 64,000 individual doses, during an operation called CONCHA.[2] Also cocaine transports have been intercepted by the Portuguese police: after more than 6 months of investigation, a quantity of cocaine was seized which was reported to be sufficient for 300,000 individual doses.[3] The cocaine was hidden aboard a plane from Caracas, Venezuela. In this case, criminal contacts were exploited with an official of Lisbon airport who had privileged access to air cargo, and who could thus facilitate the import of the drugs. Another case, which involved seizure of heroin sufficient for the production of around 190,000 individual doses, was intercepted on 21 July 2001 after an investigation which had commenced in March 2000. From the five individuals who were arrested, three were of Portuguese nationals, one was Spanish and another Russian. The heroin had been imported in Spain and was distributed from there to Portugal, in particular the region of the Algarve. Finally, an international criminal organisation was dismantled which trafficked cocaine from Trinidad and Tobago via the Caribbean islands to Portugal; on 17 August 2001, an amount of cocaine – hidden in sacks full of rice – was intercepted sufficient to produce 600,000 individual doses.[4]

In 1999, Portugal issued a national strategy for the fight against drugs. According to statistics published by the Portuguese Institute for Drugs and Toxicants Dependence (IDPT), drugs import remains a rather pertinent problem for the law enforcement agencies (Appendix Table 1).[5] The total number of drugs seizures has almost doubled between 1993 and 1999 (Appendix Table 2). In 1997, around 27% of all the drugs apprehended in Portugal originated from Thailand, Asia. Other drugs, such as hashish, mainly originate from Morocco. Brazil, Venezuela and Colombia are the main countries of origin for cocaine (Appendix Table 3). Globalisation is seen as one of the main underlying patterns of drugs trade and drugs consumption. Traffickers benefit from improved means of transport and communication; the Internet is increasingly used as a vehicle for the production and commercialisation of illicit drugs, and also to store illegally obtained capital in so-called 'tax havens'.

The concern in Portugal about international organised crime has been considerable and has contributed the proposal of a new law which introduces a new legal regime for covert investigations for the prevention of (organised) crime. The bill proposes and legalises the employment of covert agents and police infiltrators who are officers within the Judicial Police (see below).[6] These means of investigation are allowed for various organised crime-related categories, such as criminal associations, trafficking of drugs and psychotropic substances, corruption, fraud, economic-financial infractions committed in an organised form and/or of an international or transnational character, counterfeiting, and also terrorist organisations and acts of terrorism. A magistrate of the Public Ministry (Public Prosecution) and the Central Investigation Department have to give prior authorisation for the employment of covert techniques.

Moreover, a new law for the means of investigating organised crime and financial economic crime has been proposed (*Proposta de Lei no 94/VIII*), which gives the examining magistrate more possibilities in investigating crimes of a financial nature (in particular through lifting certain conditions under which professional secrecy can be guaranteed). Again, the latter applies only in a limited number of crime categories, among which drugs trafficking, passive and active corruption, criminal associations, contraband and arms trafficking. Also the domestic law on corruption has been amended, this time to bring it in line with international legislation, issued by the Council of Europe and the European Union; this regime will apply to officials in the public and private sector.[7]

## LAW ENFORCEMENT AGENCIES

The **Judicial Police** (*Polícia Judiciária*) is the main law enforcement organisation in Portugal. It was established in 1945, and has since been subject to the authority of the Ministry of Justice. It is organised in a hierarchical manner and has the mandate to assist in the administration of justice. In practice it has the mandate to investigate serious, complex and organised crime cases. From this it follows that also the investigation of criminal associations resides under the competence of this force. Lately, there has been a change of the Organic Law on the Judicial Police, mainly with the aim to make its investigations more efficient.[8]

The Judicial Police has a number of central directorates, some of which have a special mandate in the area of organised crime policing:
- The **DCITE** (*Direcção Central de Investigação do Tráfico de Estupefacientes* or Directorate General for the Investigation of Drug Trafficking), which investigates drug trafficking offences, trade in psychotropic substances and narcotics crimes.[9]
- The **DCCB** (*Direcção Central de Combate ao Banditismo* or Central Directorate to Combat Banditry) has a special competence in preventing and investigating crimes such as crimes against peace and humanity, terrorist organisations, crimes against the state, and the production of arms.
- The **DCICCF** (*Direcção Central de Investigação da Corrupção e Criminalidade Económica e Financeira* or Central Directorate for the Investigation of Corruption and Economic and Financial Crime), which

is responsible for staging a large-scale preventive operation on forgery of the Euro.

Another police force is the **National Republican Guard** (*Guarda Nacional Republicana*). The National Republican Guard is a security force of a military character and is organised in four different branches, namely territorial brigades, specialist brigades, instruction, and reserve. It encompasses four territorially based brigades (2, 3, 4 and 5).[10] The main ambit of the National Republican Guard relates to public order policing, within the context of respecting the constitutional rights, liberties and guarantees. Its mission also includes the protection of citizens in the event of danger, the assistance of the criminal police and the execution of other law enforcement tasks, such as the control of Portuguese nationals and foreigners.[11] Two specialist brigades include: the *Brigada de Trânsito*, which has a coordinative function in the regional territories, and in the Portuguese capital Lisbon; and the Fiscal Brigade (*Brigada Fiscal*), which includes numerous control units, which are mainly situated at the external border, the Portuguese islands (e.g. Madeira), and some at the internal EU-border with Spain.

The National Republican Guard was originally established in 1801 under the name *Guarda Real Da Polícia* along the lines of other gendarmerie forces in Europe (like in France and Belgium). The Guarda Real was disbanded in 1834, and replaced by a Municipal Guard (*Guarda Municipal*), originally first only in Lisbon, later also in Porto. By decree in 1910, the Guarda Real became extinct and was replaced by the National Republican Guard. The authority for the National Republican Guard is partly in the hands of the Ministry of Internal Administration (recruitment, administration and execution of mission), and partly in the hands of the Ministry of Defence (military doctrine, equipment and armament). Due to the accession of Portugal to the European Community, the exercise of the force's mandate was reviewed in 1993, in particular with regard to the control of persons. Under "international cooperation" of the force it is mainly understood activities and operations in Timor and Angola. Since 1993, there has also been is an institutionalised multilateral arrangement with foreign security forces with a military statute. This arrangement between France, Italy and Spain and Portugal functions under the name FIEP, and is meant to step up coordinative efforts against international crime, principally through the sharing of information. Also armed security forces in Morocco, Turkey and the Netherlands participate in this project Since 1998 the association is called *Associação de Forças de Polícia e Gendarmerias Europeias e Mediterrânicas com Estatuto Militar*.[12]

Except for the national directorates of the Judicial Police, which have already been mentioned above, it is worth mentioning that the Judicial Police accommodates a special section for the investigation of informatics and telecommunications crime. It is called the SICIT (*Secção de Investigação de Criminalidade Informática e de Telecomunicações*), which consists of two investigation brigades. In September 1998, the *Brigada de Investigação de Criminalidade Informática* – BICI – which was created in January 1995, was replaced by the SICIT. It has a national competence for investigating informatics crime, comprising criminal offences such as sabotage through informatics, illegitimate access ("sniffing"), illegitimate interception (e.g. through "hacking"), illegal reproduction of protected programmes, and the production and distribution of pornographic images.

The **Public Security Police** (*Polícia de Segurança Pública*) is a force which is active in the urban areas of the continent and the Autonomous Regions of Madeira and the Azores. A principal objective, along with the National Republican Guard and to some extent also the Municipal Police, is to keep policing close to the citizen (*"policiamento de proximidae"*). One of its projects concerns the role of victims of crime (project INOVAR).

The **Municipal Police Service** is functionally an administrative police service which corresponds with the territorial boundaries of municipalities. The Service cooperates with the national security forces in maintaining public order and in protecting local communities in the respective municipal area. The Service controls the execution of municipal regulations, exercises vigilance in public open spaces, protects public buildings, and takes care of traffic duties and the organisation of the files on transgressions for administrative procedure. The organisation of this Service is under the direct supervision of the Mayor.

The Portuguese **Customs Service** (*Alfândegas*)[13] plays an active role in the control of certain aspects of international organised crime, in particular the (cooperation with the Judicial Police in the) interception of illegal drug transports. The DGAIEC (*Direcção-Geral das Alfândegas e dos Impostos Especiais sobre o Consumo*) is a service under the authority of the Ministry of Justice, which controls the external borders of Portugal and which controls infringement of various offences (fiscal, economic), also in the domain of public health.

## THE PUBLIC PROSECUTION SERVICE

The Public Prosecution Service (*Ministério Público*) is the State body entrusted with representing the State, prosecuting, as well as defending the democratic legality and any other interests that the law determines. As such it takes part in the enforcement of the criminal policy. The Public Prosecution

Service acts as an autonomous service,[14] independent of bodies of central, regional or local power. In exercising its functions, the Public Prosecution Service is assisted by justice officers and by officers from the criminal police (Judicial Police). The Public Prosecutor in general, as a judiciary authority, controls Police activity in criminal proceedings, and plays the main role in the execution of the institutional criminal policy.

As a judicial body, the Service is structured by the courts in a uniform manner. The powers of the Public Prosecution Service cover the criminal prosecution, that is: to direct the criminal investigations; to promote the legality; to represent the State, as well as the disabled persons and those without permanent residence; and to perform advisory functions. Nowadays the Service is organised as a branch of the Magistracy that is autonomous in two senses: non-interference by the political power as regards the criminal prosecution; the concept of the Public Prosecution Service as a separate branch of the Magistracy, guided by a principle of separation and parallelism in relation to the Judiciary.

The Public Prosecution Service has a pyramidal structure. The Attorney-General is known as the *Procurador-Geral da República*, who is appointed by the President of the Republic for 6 years. The Attorney General's office has a Division for Judicial Cooperation (*Divisão de Cooperação Judiciária*). The pyramidal structure of the Prosecution Service is as follows:

- Attorney General and
  Vice-Attorney General — operate on the national level
- Deputy Attorney General — represents personally the Attorney-General at the Supreme Courts
- District Attorney-General
  – Appeals Court — operates at the Judicial District Level
- Prosecutor of the Republic — operates at the Circunscription Court (known as *Círculo Judicial*)
- Deputy Prosecutor — operates at the sub-Circumscription Court (known as the *Comarca Judicial*)

The judicial system in Portugal is divided in 4 judicial districts: each judicial district is subdivided into *círculos judiciais*, and each of those is subdivided into *comarcas judiciais*. The basic members of the Public Prosecution Service are deputy prosecutors, who work in counties or groups of counties.

In a recent circular letter,[15] the members of the Prosecution Service have been informed about the creation of a provisional Unit for Judicial Cooperation (Pro-Eurojust[16]). The Portuguese Public Prosecution Office has seconded a deputy procurator general: *Lic. José Lopes da Mota*. The competence for Portuguese participation in Eurojust runs via the Attorney General's office;

its member functions as a National Magistrate (*Magistrado Nacional*). Before that, a circular letter[17] had been sent about the European Judicial Network (EJN), which was established on the basis of a joint action adopted by the JHA Council on 29 June 1998: each DIAP[18] (Investigation and Penal Action Department) in Lisbon, Porto, Coimbra, and Evora has appointed a judicial contact; another one has been added to the Division for Judicial Cooperation at the Attorney General's Office. These judicial contact points can be contacted for the execution of a mutual judicial assistance request, the execution of rogatory commissions, or obtaining judicial authorisation from foreign courts.

## INTERNATIONAL COOPERATION AND CONTACT POINTS

Recently the Portuguese Parliament approved of the EU Convention on Mutual Assistance in Criminal Matters, which had been adopted by the Justice and Home Affairs Council during the Portuguese Presidency of the European Union on 29 May 2001. The approval i.e. ratification of the Convention took place on 21 May 2001 and with this, Portugal is one of the first EU Member States to have ratified that Convention. In connection with this, the Law on International Legal Cooperation (*Lei da Cooperacão Judiciária Internacional*) had been adapted. When the bill was presented to Parliament, the Minister of Justice had argued that globalisation and improved means of communication had created new conditions for the criminal investigation of transnational crime. In this context, he also referred to the UN Convention for the Combating of Organised Crime, which had been signed in Palermo about six months before.

The Portuguese Ministry of Justice incorporates a special cabinet which has a mandate to engage itself international and European relations and cooperation (*Gabinete para as Relações Internacionais, Europeias e de Cooperação*). The website[19] of this cabinet refers to several issues related to Justice and Home Affairs matters within the European Union, such as updates on the Schengen, the state of play concerning the implementation of the EU Action Plan on Organised Crime and proposals concerning the protection of the Community's financial interests. The competences and objectives of the cabinet include the coordination of external relations and policies regarding judicial cooperation, without prejudice to the competences of the Ministry of Foreign Affairs. The cabinet fulfils the following functions:
* Assists the Minister of Justice in defining and executing policies in the area of justice related to the European Union, foreign governments and international organisations;

- Conducts legal cooperation policies, in particular with other Portuguese speaking countries;
- Coordinates the representatives of the Portuguese state in international justice bodies;
- Accompanies and encourages international policy of the Portuguese state in the area of justice;
- Coordinates the representation of Portugal in international committees, reunions, conferences or similar organisations active in the field of justice;
- Studies the norms of international law and their impact for domestic Portuguese law;
- Promotes studies on legislative harmonisation in the field of justice matters;
- Assists international delegations present in Portugal in the participation of Government initiatives;
- Promotes, coordinates and encourages means of judicial cooperation with other states.

In the area of international police cooperation, the Central Department of International Cooperation DCCI (*Departamento Central de Cooperação Internacional*) – which is part of the Judicial Police – should be regarded as a principal actor in the field of international cooperation. Its mandate includes several tasks and functions, such as the receipt and examination of requests for provisional detention in extradition cases; guaranteeing the working of mechanisms of international police cooperation (Interpol, Europol, and other international organisations with a similar ambit); develop, supervise and analyse processes, projects and missions at the level of international and institutional cooperation with other states, in particular with Portuguese-speaking countries; coordinate the participation of the Judicial Police in competent institutions in the field of European police cooperation; proceed in the secondment of Portuguese liaison officers abroad or foreign liaison officers in Portugal.

The UNE (*Unidade Nacional Europol*) is the National Europol Unit within the Judicial Police and the DCCI in particular. Based in Lisbon, it functions as the *exclusive* liaison unit between Europol and the competent services in Portugal. Any general information or request for information can – in principle – be submitted to the UNE, such as the identification of individuals, vehicles and telephone, criminal antecedents, but also specific information relating to certain criminal investigations. Also information considered to be relevant for foreign countries can be submitted. For SIRENE, there is the Gabinete Nacional SIRENE. Data relating to vehicles are – for instance – first verified by the latter SIRENE unit.

**DATA PROTECTION**

An essential component of the accountability situation with regard to international information exchange is the creation of the National Data Protection Commission (*Comissão Nacional de Protecção de Dados*), which is a national independent authority with powers to monitor and supervise compliance with the requirements of the law and regulations in the field of personal data protection. Significant changes were introduced by means of the Personal Data Protection Law (Law no. 67/98, of 26 October).[20] According to this law, the National Data Protection Commission (CNPD) has assumed new powers of investigation and inquiry, power of authority and of participation in decision-making processes, which is mainly done by issuing recommendations on data processing. Within the field of international police and judicial cooperation in criminal matters, the CNDP participates in European forums (Joint Supervisory Authority Europol and Schengen).

Monica den Boer

**NOTES**

1. The author wishes to thank António Bernardo Colaço, Deputy General Attorney. She has benefited enormously from his suggestions and expert knowledge. The responsibility for the contents of this chapter rests, however, solely with the author.
2. Press release, 16 August 2001: http://www.policiajudiciaria.pt/index.htm.
3. Press release, 27 July 2001: http://www.policiajudiciaria.pt/index.htm.
4. http://www.policiajudiciaria.pt/index.htm.
5. http://www.ipdt.pt/; Explanatory footnotes have been removed from this table.
6. Proposta de Lei nº 76/VIII; Regime Jurídico das acções encobertas para fins de prevenção e investigação criminal (Proposta de Lei).
7. Altera o regime jurídico dos crimes de tráfico de influência e corrupção; Proposta de Lei nº 91/VIII.
8. Alteração da Lei Orgânica da Polícia Judiciária; http://www.mj.gov.pt/ ?article=797&visual=1&id=1.
9. Exemplified in Articles 21º, 22º, 23º, 27º e 28º of Decree-Law nº 15/93, of 22 January 1993.
10. An organisation chart can be seen in: http://www.gnr.pt/organizacao_1.htm.
11. http://www.gnr.pt/organizacao_1.htm.
12. http://www.gnr.pt/cooperacao_2.htm.
13. http://www.dgaiec.min-financas.pt/sitedgaiec.nsf.
14. The autonomy of the Public Prosecution Service was performed during the second constitutional revision (1989). The Superior Council of the Public Prosecution Service began to include members appointed by Parliament. The principles approved in this revision were incorporated afterwards in Act nº 23/92, of the 20th of August.
15. Circular 04/2001: http://www.pgr.pt/english/index.htm.
16. *Official Journal* no. L 324, 21 December 2000, on p. 2.
17. Number 06/2000; http://www.pgr.pt/english/index.htm.
18. DIAP = *Departamento de Investigaçao a Acção Penal*, which deals with criminality in general. The DCIAP (=*Departamento Central de Investigaçao a Acção Penal*) is the Central Investigation and Penal Action Department and only has an office in Lisbon. The latter resides under the authority of the Attorney-General, who is specifically appointed for the direction of investigations and prevention of violent, highly organised, or particularly complex criminality.
19. See: http://www.gde.mj.pt/.
20. This Act transposes into the internal legal system of Portugal Directive 95/46/EC of the European Parliament and of the Council of 24 October 1995 on the protection of individuals with regard to the processing of personal data and on the free movement of such data.

# Appendix: Drugs Seizures

## Table 1:
### *Drugs Apprehended, by Year, Type and Drugs*
### *1991-1999*

| Type of Drugs/Year | 1991 | 1992 | 1993 | 1994 | 1995 | 1996 | 1997 | 1998 | 1999 |
|---|---|---|---|---|---|---|---|---|---|
| Heroin | 61,805 | 41,371 | 92,034 | 89,038 | 65,507 | 46,697 | 57,389 | 96,666 | 76,417 |
| Cocaine | 1,094,197 | 1,860,039 | 216,102 | 1,719,413 | 2,115,835 | 811,568 | 3,162,638 a) | 624,949 | 822,560 |
| Hashish | 7,629,972 | 11,711,941 | 52,483,552 | 40,392,698 | 7,333,287 | 5,324,091 | 9,621,188 | 5,574,794 | 0,636,075 i) |
| Cannabis | 123,462 | 8,462 | 43,806 | 32,694 | 159,892 | 35,971 | 72,256 | 7,115 | 65,766 |
| Other | 615 | | | | 2,967 | 7,875 | 14,348 | 23,792 | 6,955 |

## Table 2:
### *Number of Seizures, According to Year, Type of Drug and Seized Quantity*
### *1993-1999*

| Type of Drug – Quantity / Year | 1993 | 1994 | 1995 | 1996 | 1997 | 1998 | 1999 |
|---|---|---|---|---|---|---|---|
| **Total** | **3,892** | **3,467** | **4,614** | **6,185** | **6,314** | **7,190** | **8,475** |
| **Heroin** | **2,458** | **2,128** | **2,828** | **·3,787** a) | **·3,476** c) | **·3,750** e) | **·4,058** h) |
| < 10 g | 2,190 | 1,850 | 2,554 | 3,428 | 3,143 | 3,422 | 3,652 |
| > 10 g e < 100 g | 196 | 217 | 218 | 277 | 246 | 227 | 319 |
| > 100 g | 72 | 61 | 56 | 71 | 69 | 73 | 74 |
| **Cocaine** | **613** | **570** | **872** | **1,162** | **1,234** | **·1,377** f) | **·1,691** i) |
| < 10 g | 492 | 448 | 663 | 946 | 1,023 | 1,154 | 1,447 |
| > 10 g e < 100 g | 54 | 58 | 79 | 86 | 105 | 117 | 164 |
| > 100 g | 67 | 64 | 130 | 130 | 106 | 105 | 79 |
| **Hashish** | **744** | **686** | **746** | **1,106** | **1,463** | **1,917** | **·2,539** j) |
| < 100 g | 642 | 623 | 656 | 1,024 | 1,372 | 1,824 | 2,414 |
| > 100 g e < 1000 g | 52 | 34 | 44 | 55 | 61 | 62 | 79 |
| > 1000 g | 50 | 29 | 46 | 27 | 30 | 31 | 45 |
| **Cannabis** | **77** | **83** | **168** | **·130** b) | **·141** d) | **·146** g) | **·187** k) |
| < 100 g | 63 | 71 | 130 | 81 | 89 | 96 | 136 |
| > 100 g e < 1000 g | 6 | 3 | 11 | 10 | 7 | 7 | 9 |
| > 1000 g | 8 | 9 | 27 | 5 | 9 | 2 | 2 |

467

## Table 3:
### Drugs Apprehended, by Country of Origin and Type
### 1999

| Country of Origin/ Type of Drug | Heroin | Cocaine | Hashish | Cannabis |
|---|---|---|---|---|
| 1998 | 96,666 | 624,949 | 5,574,794 | 7,115 |
| Total General | | | | |
| 1999 | 76,417 | 822,560 | 10,636,075 | 65,766 |
| South Africa | .. | .. | .. | 45 |
| Angola | .. | .. | .. | 44,385 |
| Antilles | .. | 14,335 | .. | .. |
| Brazil | .. | 77,446 | .. | .. |
| Canada | 161 | .. | .. | .. |
| Colombia | .. | 5,856 | .. | .. |
| Costa Rica | .. | .. | .. | 2 |
| Ecuador | .. | 2,351 | .. | .. |
| Spain | 11,767 | 11,008 | 308,739 | .. |
| EUA | .. | .. | .. | 40 |
| France | .. | .. | 22 | .. |
| The Netherlands | 13,404 | 804 | 3,211 | 22 |
| Morocco | .. | .. | 6,339,550 | .. |
| Panama | .. | 265,000 | .. | .. |
| Paraguay | .. | 1,101 | .. | .. |
| Portugal | .. | .. | 127 | .. |
| Switzerland | .. | .. | .. | 34 |
| Venezuela | .. | 391,934 | .. | .. |
| Unknown | 51,085 | 52,725 | 3,984,426 | 21,238 |

# Spain

## *Óscar Jaime-Jiménez and Laia Moreno*

### 1. ORGANISED CRIME IN SPAIN

The political situation of Spain during the 1970s and 1980s deeply influenced the initial stages of the evolution of the organised crime in the Spanish territory. The first indicators appeared with tourism on the Mediterranean coast and the emergence of drug trafficking at small scale, which was quite stable until the 1980s. This decade was characterised by an increase of drug trafficking from South America. Spain became a principal route for introducing different kinds of drugs through the Galician coast. The state realised that more measures needed to be taken because the resources allocated to face such kinds of crimes were insufficient. Therefore the *Plan Nacional sobre Drogas* (National Plan against Drugs) was created in order to coordinate all the state measures against drug dealing, putting pressure on the supply and demand.

This perspective changed radically at the beginning of the 1990s. The new international context characterised by the fall of the regimes in communist countries and appearance on the Mediterranean coast of unknown organised gangs trying to establish themselves in the areas of drugs and laundering money in the local and national economy focused the attention of the state authorities. Some criminal organisations moved to the Spanish coast, creating a specific "know how" and maintaining the original internal structures. The outcome was the definitive establishment of gangs in Spain which had permanent links with countries of origin.

In the current Spanish organised crime arena, there are two main different powerful groups. The oldest and most integrated gangs are focused on cocaine trafficking inside Spain and from Spain to other areas of Europe. They are established in large cities like Madrid or Barcelona, because in such places the Colombians and North Africans avoid attracting the attention of the population and the police agencies. The increasing number of Latin American immigrants and their cultural similarities to Spain allow them to integrate partially into Spanish society. On the other hand, there are new criminal organisations from east Europe established on the Mediterranean coast. The high number of tourists in this area allows them to take on a tourist identity. The social and economical structure of this region allows them to launder money in tourist enterprises and at the same time enjoy a luxurious life on the *Costa del Sol*. The Mafia from Marseilles and Italy follow very similar patterns. During the present decade foreign organised crime has discovered new investment opportunities in different economic areas in Spain. These gangs have also discovered some legal "loopholes" which allow them to perform stable and profitable businesses without breaking the law.

The gangs established themselves permanently in Spain for different reasons. One of the most important is the political and economic stability of the country. The investment opportunities in a stable environment facilitate the transfer of money from their unstable political and economic context. The main economic structure of Spain, based on the construction and tourist sectors, which facilitate money laundering, is another factor that triggered this establishment. Lastly, the highly developed internal banking framework, properly connected with the international banking system, and with a close "Mafia and money laundering paradise" like Gibraltar, allows the quick transfer of large sums of money, avoiding any kind of effective control by the Spanish authorities. The conclusion is that Spain is one of the countries in which money laundering has penetrated deeply; nevertheless it is extremely difficult to offer figures.

The foreign criminal organisations which have settled in Spain have not penetrated the social fabric, because they try to keep themselves isolated from the environment. They have established contacts with the Spanish population only on professional basis. In order to maintain their structure they need the support and assistance of young liberal professionals and entrepreneurs to protect their investments against state surveillance.

The Colombians and Italians intensely use the highly developed Spanish banking system for money laundering, avoiding all kind of confrontation with the banks and following the national and international rules. The east European gangs follow very different rules based in some cases on threats and confrontation with the aim of influencing the banking system.[1]

Although there is not a legal definition of "organised crime" as such in the Spanish legal texts, we can develop criteria of what is meant by "organised crime" by looking at laws dealing or regulating other penal matters. These criteria corresponds to the European Union definition, although they are much more limited and, therefore leave greater scope for the location of organisations. The definition used by the police forces is also difficult to assess, but with the creation of the UDYCOs (see below) it seems that the EU definition is also being used in a wider sense, replacing the concepts used until now in the sphere of the police.

The CNP has traditionally used the concept produced in Interpol's framework and, more recently, the one derived from the Title VI activities on drugs and organised crime. Anyhow, the CNP uses from years ago in its analysis tasks an instrument called *"Cuestionario sobre Delincuencia Organizada"*[2] in which the definition of such kind of crime is divided in 11 items or criteria, in order to establish different levels of criminal organizations. These criteria are:

(1) Involvement of two or more people.
(2) Division of labour.
(3) Activity for a long or indeterminate period of time.
(4) Use of some kind of discipline or control.
(5) Rational suspicion of the performance of crimes which are of considerable importance.
(6) To be operative in an inter-regional or international level.
(7) Use of violence or intimidation.
(8) Use of commercial or business structures.
(9) Money laundering.
(10) Use of political influences, mass-media, public administrations or judicial or police structures.
(11) Pursuit of benefit and power.

Organic law 5/99, which modified the Law of Criminal Prosecution in order to improve investigation activities, in its Article 282 bis 4 – referring to the regulation covering covert agents – offers specific criteria about organised crime. The concept assumes three principles:

(1) Three or more associated people.
(2) Activities which are permanent or repeated.
(3) The carrying out of certain types of criminal behaviour.

The first two requirements were established traditionally by the Spanish doctrine in the construction of the concept of "organisation". In addition the new penal code has moved towards regulating the specific way in which police informers are dealt with in respect to drug dealing in Article 376, and crimes of terrorism in Article 579, which uses the same terms.

Other legal instruments from which it is possible to extract a definition of organised crime are, for instance: some legal texts on terrorism; the 5/1988 Law on the creation of special tax regime for drugs; the LO 8/92 which introduces a new article in the *Ley Cri* on entries into monitored areas; the 19/1993 Law on the fight against money laundering (which respond, in turn, to the Directive 91/308 of the CE); the LO 5/95 on the Jury; and many other.[3] Some sentences of the Supreme Court of Justice, such as, for example, sentences 5-2-88, 17-3-93 or 12-2-93 also give a good idea about how organised crime is defined.[4] Finally, we must remark the fact that in many legal provisions relating to the organisation of prisons we can find elements distinguishing organised crime from other forms of crime.[5]

## 2. THE LAW ENFORCEMENT AGENCIES IN SPAIN

The national Spanish police system (*Fuerzas y Cuerpos de Seguridad del Estado*, (FCSE)) is today formed by two central forces: the *Cuerpo Nacional de Policía* (CNP), a fully civilian police agency, and the *Guardia Civil*, under a military statute. During the 1980s, other forces which have competence in the Autonomous Communities (*Comunidades Autónomas*) and are under control of the regional governments were added to this traditional scheme: the Basque police (*Ertzaintza*) and the Catalan police (*Mossos d'Esquadra*). Both of them have as their main goal the assumption of the FCSE competences. Other Autonomous Communities have made a request to the central government to control some units of the national police forces. This process is still under way, but will probably finish in the next few years. At local level there are the local police, whose competences have been growing steadily during the last decades. Finally, there is the *Servicio de Vigilancia Aduanera* (SEVA), which comes under the Ministry of Economy; its main task is the fight against contraband trade.

In fact, there is not a police model, but a police system. The political transition after the dictatorship adopted the form of an "agreed split with the dictatorship". It meant, on the one hand, that the political rules changed radically, political parties and trade unions were legalised, and a parliament was established that could foster a western-style of democracy; on the other hand, the monarchy remained and the administrative structures were left practically untouched. The state bureaucracy, including the army, and the old security structures and agencies, remained virtually unchanged, with the same human resources and police ethos.

In 1977, a general political agreement among the most important political parties known as *Pactos de la Moncloa*, provided the impetus for a vague reform of the police, although this lacked specific far-reaching goals. The main and immediate aim of the political opposition was the expulsion of those members of the police forces who had taken part in political repression. Nevertheless, almost the entire structure and personnel remained with some "minor" structural changes. Only a few officials involved in the struggle against political opposition were actually dismissed.

The new police legislation was to a great extent the outcome of agreements among different political sensibilities. However, the influence of the military sector and of – for the most part the conservative – members of parliament was a decisive factor in holding back and postponing the restructuring of the police forces. Changes were introduced slowly and without great conviction since there was no defined model of what a police force should be in a democratic environment. In the new legislation, innovative elements were combined with others that served merely to perpetuate the characteristics of a militarised police force. This resulted in the drafting of legal texts that were difficult to understand or, in many cases, contradictory.

The Police Law, passed in 1978, was the immediate outcome of the Moncloa agreements.[6] The influence of the army on the police structure decreased, but it was still very important. Before this basic reform, most of the officers of the *Policía Armada* (renamed in 1978 as *Policía Nacional*, and in 1986, *Cuerpo Nacional de Policía*) came from the army. The military officers stayed on as members of the armed forces and received only a brief training. After the 1978 law, most of the new officers came from a specific police academy, and only a few military officers selected by the Ministry of the Interior were allowed to join the police. However, training continued to be largely of a military type and given by army personnel. The most immediate significant change was that military courts no longer dealt with activities relating to the freedom of speech, and the police forces ceased to be protected by military legislation. In 1986, new police legislation, the *Ley Orgánica de Fuerzas y Cuerpos de Seguridad del Estado (LOFCSE)* – State Police Law – was approved. Finally, thanks to this law, the non-paramilitary police forces rationalised their organisation. But one of the most important outcomes of this new law was that the *Cuerpo Nacional de Policía* (CNP) became a fully civil corps, abandoning its undermined military status.[7] A few years later, in 1992, the Public Order Law of 1959 was abolished by applying the *Ley de Protección de la Seguridad Ciudadana* – Protection of Public Safety Law.

The current police system is the outcome of the lack of a political willingness to apply structural solutions. The creation of the *Ertzaintza* and the political weakness of central governments in respect to the Basque Country and Catalonia, have hindered the design of a consensual police model. The maintenance of a stable situation was the priority, instead of trying to increase the levels of police efficiency. The final outcome was the superimposition of structures without effective functional and territorial coordination.

Despite the 1986 *LOFCSE*, many crucial problems there still remain and these have increased during recent years. This law established the CNP's dependence on the Ministry of Interior and the *Guardia Civil's* double dependence on the same ministry and the Ministry of Defence. Despite the fact that the functions assigned to each of the forces are clearly indicated in the legal text, there are mutual accusations of meddling and conflicts over many and different issues. There took place an expansion of the *Guardia Civil* activities since the 1980s into areas traditionally assigned to the CNP or the SEVA. This conflict affects organised crime because the *Guardia Civil* has important competences in the fight against smuggling and has created important anti-drug units. The presence of terrorism in Spain during the political transition and consolidation, strongly influenced the security agenda. Most of resources have been invested in this area, leaving in second place topics such as public safety, drugs and organised crime. It was the decline of terrorist activity which stimulated the slow change in the priority given to the internal security agenda.

Nowadays, many of the original problems are still present, for instance, the current democratic regime has still not defined the real military or civil status of the *Guardia Civil.*[8] Few changes have been introduced. The confusion is still prompted by its double dependence on the Ministry of Defence, for administrative and organisational issues, and the Ministry of the Interior for operational activities. Only the practical and operational changes are significant, but the essential structure, organisation and decision-making procedures have remained essentially unaltered despite the fact that the General-Director is a civilian and the general staff is formed by officers of the agency. In 1995, the Ministry of Justice and Interior tried to impose substantial structural changes at an organisational level, but the critical political situation and the resistance of the organisational structure of the paramilitary agency did not allow for far-reaching reforms.

The structure of the CNP, like the *Guardia Civil*, was militarised during the Franco period and was part of the armed forces. After the political transition, this force changed its name to *Policía Nacional* – National Police – and the 1978 Police Law introduced provisions which formed the basis of its future evolution. In 1986, the police agency structure was transformed. The plain clothes police agency known as the *Cuerpo Superior de Policía* – Higher Police Force – which was in charge of the direction and coordination of police services, intelligence and investigations, was merged with the uniformed patrolling agency of the *Policía Nacional* whose main functions were to assist the *Cuerpo Superior de Policía* and to maintain and re-establish public order, in order to form the *Cuerpo Nacional de Policía* or CNP.

The coordination between the two most important state security forces, the CNP and the *Guardia Civil*, were established at the highest level in the Ministry of the Interior. In 1994, before the radical transformation of the structure of the Ministry – i.e. the merging of the Ministries of the Interior and Justice[9] – the State Secretary of Security, a high-level political appointee, was in charge of the *Director-General of the Policía Nacional* and *Guardia Civil*. At a provincial level, the *Gobernador Civil* – Civil Governor – (today called *Subdelegado del Gobierno*) was in charge of the coordination and he was the commander of both forces.

After Franco's regime, two of the historical territories (Autonomous Communities), the Basque Country, from the very beginning, and then Catalonia, were willing to assume internal security functions.[10] The Basque political establishment thought that the first and main step towards solving the terrorist problem was to form a Basque police agency, which was close to the community and able to better understand the problems and points of view of the population. For the Basque government, this was one of the main aims and they wanted the transfer of competences in this area to be accomplished as soon as possible. In 1981, the first graduation took place. During the following years, the number of Basque police forces quickly increased, until in 1995 there were 7,000 policemen. The aim of the autonomous government was for 8,500 policemen to graduate and to assume most of the conventional police functions on its territory, except for those related to the frontiers' surveillance and controlling smuggling. At the beginning, the Basque police agency was not very willing to assume competences for public order because this could have damaged the public image of the government, but finally such competences were exercised with toughness.

The Catalan police force, *Mossos de Esquadra*, faced fewer problems than the Basque police agency. Like the Basque Government, they wanted to perform most of the police functions but they were not very willing to exercise those related to the maintenance of public order. Nevertheless, their first action in this area took place in 1983, although it was much criticised because of its toughness in repressing students and farmers. Coordination with the state agencies was based on the *Junta de Seguridad* – Security Council – whose main function was to perform as a joint committee.

Whereas the number of autonomous police agents increases every year, the number of state police agents is increasing as well. In 1993 the *Cuerpo Nacional de Policía* had 51,109 agents, the *Guardia Civil* 75,346, the autonomous police forces 15,000 and the municipal police 40,000.[11] Since Franco's regime, the number of state police officers has been very high in comparison with the European standards. In 1975, the rate was 1 per 320 inhabitants, in 1986 it was 1 per 300 and currently it is approximately 1 per 315, but if we take into account the municipal and autonomous police, the rate increases to 1 per 214.[12] Nevertheless, according to public opinion there is a lack of police agents and the police officers claim that the security forces need more personnel. This situation is the logical outcome of a lack of coordination, because all the different police agencies perform almost the same functions in the same territory. Therefore, to the problems which emerged with the presence of the autonomous police forces must be added the traditional coordination problems between both state police agencies. Another problem that needs to be faced in the future is the definition of the *Guardia Civil* as a paramilitary structure, and specific militarised aspects of the CNP that are vestiges of Franco's Regime, which should be removed in order for the CNP to be a part of the European police system.

*Functions of the two state police forces (CNP and Guardia Civil)*

1. Common functions: both police forces must protect citizen's rights and liberties and public safety.
2. But the LO 2/86 establishes a territorial division between the forces (a):
   - the CNP performs common functions in provincial capitals and municipalities and urban areas determined by the government.
   - The *Guardia Civil* acts in the rest of the territory and at sea.
3. Following this clear distinction the law establishes exceptions for both forces: the CNP is able to exert some functions in the whole territory and the *Guardia Civil*, when necessary makes investigations in the same area.
4. Both forces are supposed to inform one another of any action outside their legal, territorial ambit.
5. On the other hand, not only when efficiency requires it, but also when the Public Prosecutor or a judicial mandate requires it, the national police forces act outside their territories.
6. When there is a case of a conflict of competences, the force which has carried out the initial procedures is the one to follow them, until the Civil Governor or the Ministry of the Interior resolves the matter.
7. Finally, the Ministry of the Interior can ask any of the forces to act in an area outside their normal jurisdiction.
8. The second (b) division established by law is a functional division.
   - CNP: passports and national identity cards; control on the entrance to and exit from the national territory by foreigners and nationals; all the functions related to "alien status" (asylum and refugees, extradition, expulsion, emigration and immigration); law enforcement in gambling matters; investigation and fight against drug-related crimes; collaboration with other police forces, under direction of the Ministry; control over private security agencies and other functions which can legally be attributed to the CNP.
   - The GC has competence in the field of weapons and explosives legislation; it is the *"resguardo fiscal del estado"* (fiscal defender of the state) and will prevent and prosecute contraband offences; and carry out surveillance of frontiers, (airports, coast...); it also has functions related to the and other functions contemplated by legal texts: protection of the environment; transportation of prisoners and taking care of individuals arrested between cities;
9. The police forces are obliged by law to cooperate.

## 3. THE PUBLIC PROSECUTION SERVICE IN SPAIN

The structure of the judicial system is organised under two main principles:
(1) Material criteria: civil, penal, contentious-administrative and social.
(2) Territorial criteria: the adaptation was quite slower than the evolution of

the social context.
- Courts of first instance and courts for instituting proceedings.
- Penal, social courts in the provincial courts (provincial level).
- High Courts of the Autonomous Communities.
- Special division of the Supreme Court *Audiencia Nacional*.

The pyramidal structure of the judicial system[13] in Spain starts with the Local Courts; they are located in the municipalities where there are not *Juzgados de Instrucción y Primera Instancia* (Courts of first instance and the institution of proceedings). They deal with penal and civil processes and with the civil register, and they are elected by the *Sala de Gobierno* of the Superior Tribunal. In 1988, the *Juzgados de lo Penal* (criminal courts) were established in order to follow the constitutional doctrine.

The other level are the *Audiencias Provinciales* (provincial courts), in provincial capitals. They act by *Salas* (divisions dealing with different types of crimes) and can also create sections. The judicial organisation at the level of the Autonomous Communities culminates in the *Tribunales Superiores de Justicia* (High Courts); for matters in the Autonomous Communities they are last appeal organs. They have penal, civil, contentious-administrative and social sections.

Finally, we can find the *Audiencia Nacional* and the *Tribunal Supremo* (Supreme Court of Justice). The first was created in 1977 and its jurisdiction is the whole Spanish territory; its seat is in Madrid. It deals with penal, contentious-administrative and with crimes against the king, the queen and the prince and against other high institutions of the state. Its competence also covers economic crimes, falsification, fraud and network-based crimes (terrorism, organised crime, etc.). Inside the *Audiencia Nacional* there are the *Juzgados Centrales de Instrucción* (central courts); which are competent to investigate the cases corresponding to the *Penal Sala* (criminal division) of the *Audiencia*.

The *Tribunal Supremo* (Supreme Court of Justice) has jurisdiction in the whole territory and is the highest jurisdictional organ in all areas (except constitutional guarantees, which are dealt with by the Constitutional Court: (*Tribunal Constitucional*)). It is also divided in divisions: civil, penal, contentious-administrative, social and military (specific legislation), which can be organised in sections.

If judges exert jurisdictional authority, the Public Prosecutor is the institution which must carry it out. It also has to guarantee the tribunals independence. The Public Prosecutor works according to the principles of unity and hierarchical dependence. The personnel of the public prosecutors' offices are independent from judges and magistrates, and are supposed to be completely independent from the government, and their relationship with the

Ministry of Justice is one of collaboration (in this sphere we should mention the special relationship between the prison administration and the Ministry of Justice).

The Spanish judicial structure is traditionally characterised for its dispersion, fragmentation, lack of means, and the performance of a highly autonomous power. The senior ranks of the judicial system are appointed by the Parliament. The law protects the independence of the judges through the implementation of different measures, but its real independence is permanently put at stake, because the different judicial associations show a strong ideological character and, at the same time, it is possible for an individual to shift from the political life to the judicial structure and vice-versa.

The Constitution has established a dual structure at the top of the judicial hierarchy; the High Court (*Tribunal Supremo*) and the General Council of the Judicial System *(Consejo General del Poder Judicial,* (CGPJ)). The Ministry of the Interior has only administrative competences, managing the human and economical resources. The presidency of the CGPJ is elected by the members of the Council, as well as by the head of the High Court. This measure aims to prevent confrontation between both of them. The CGPJ is not under political control.

The main functions of the CGPJ are:

a) The election of members of other high state institutions.

b) The organisation and governance of judges professional careers.

The competence of the Ministry is actually quite diminished. The Autonomous Communities have the competence to organise the judicial structure at an administrative level in their territories.

Currently a profound reform of the judicial structure is being discussed between the government and the main opposition party. It has been reached agreement on some crucial and important questions, a consensus that had never been achieved before and which is completely necessary. These reforms should be completed within a period of maximally eight years. Some of its main points are included in the drafting of a new *Ley de Enjuiciamiento Criminal* (which will include all the Constitutional Tribunal jurisprudence on popular and private accusation, protection of victims, prisons reform and other relevant issues), the study of the possibilities of public prosecutors assuming the criminal process and a role for judges as warrants of fundamental rights, a new formula to elect the CGPJ, an increase in competences for the Autonomous Communities which already have them and facilitation of assuming them for the rest, a new judicial map and a new Act on Judges and Magistrates. This reform is supposed to resolve many of the problems that have been identified and it will follow criteria such as acceleration, modernisation, de-politicisation or de-centralisation.

## 4. LAW ENFORCEMENT UNITS TO FIGHT ORGANISED CRIME

Only in the mid-1980s did the FCSE begin to focus its attention on organised crime. It was the above-mentioned increase in foreign tourism in the Mediterranean coast (*Costa del Sol*) and the increasing drug-related crimes in this area which convinced the administration to face the problem through new means. Some units marked by a partially specialised character were created, but they were just concerned with drugs; organised crime as such was initially not considered.

The *Plan Nacional sobre Drogas* (PNSD)[14] is of great importance in Spain in the fight against drugs.

On 27 October 1984, the Spanish parliament asked the government for the creation of an interdepartmental plan against drugs. The Council of Ministers created then an interministerial working group in which all departments affected by the problem took part. From this initiative, a Royal Decree 1677/ 85 was created and with it the Interministerial Group for the National Plan on Drugs whose secretariat function is carried out by a government representative.

The fact that it was necessary to emphasise the police role in the fight meant that the National Plan on Drugs moved in December 1993 to the Ministry of Interior (RD 2314/1993). The government office is then an organ of the State's Central Administration which must develop an integrated policy. The functions and competences of the post are regulated by RD 1885/ 1996 (which concerns the Ministry's structure).

Under the government representative are four Sub-directorates: *Subdirección General del plan Nacional sobre Drogas* (The general sub-direction for the National Plan on Drugs); *Subdirección General de Gestión y Relaciones Institucionales* (the sub-directorate for administration and international relations), the *Gabinete de Evaluación* (evaluation office) and the *Gabinete de Coordinación* (coordination office). These two separated offices are the political organs. When the governmental office for the plan was assigned to the Ministry of the Interior, the government representative was given the task of coordinating the State Police forces with competency for dealing with drug crimes and associated money laundering, particularly those crimes committed by criminal organisations, those crimes which fall within the competence of the *Audiencia Nacional*. That was the way in which the two offices appeared in the general structure.

This heavy participation in a structure like the government office for the plan has an important effect on the operative capacity of the police forces. The government representative's has the task of coordinating investigations. In these cases a "coordination summit" is held to design the strategy, assign resources, and so on. In general terms, we have here a forum in which the highest ranks and the members of the different police forces sit together and share techniques, data, etc.

In the normative field it has provided the stimulus for new legislation (the broadening of the concept of controlled delivery to substances used to produce drugs and to money; prosecution in relation to money obtained through these operations; the creation of a general register on classified chemical substances, etc.); at the police level, the better function of the special units, the creation of new ones (UDYCOs, EDOAs), the formation plans for police staff and initiative for international cooperation. The new "*Estrategia 2000-2008*" (Strategy 2000-2008), presented ideas such as legislation on informers, the extension of the judicial intervention to survey suspect electronic mail, the creation of a register on boats, an so on.

Moreover, the likelihood of an increase in drug smuggling activities in Spain (which became an important point on some international routes) and the recommendations made by the EU (Action Plan 1997) made the Spanish administration establish a basis for the development of specialised police structures in combating organised crime. A priority for these new structures was the fight against money laundering related to drug trafficking.

In January 1997, the *Unidades de Droga y Crimen Organizado* (UDYCOs, units for drugs and organised crime) were created inside the CNP. These units were centralised in the *Comisaría General de Policía Judicial* (Central Division of Judicial Police) of the CNP and their main goal is the fight against organised crime as defined by the EU indicators. The idea is to establish UDYCO units where necessary, that is to say, in "high-risk" territories (the Mediterranean coast, Galicia and Madrid, among others). There was no significant resistance to their creation, which was promoted by the *Plan Nacional sobre Drogas,* which in term was created to coordinate the fight against drug smuggling, and its effects at different levels of social life.

The initial deployment of the UDYCOs took place in accordance with a "situation report", which is issued every year and reflects the geographical distribution of the different types of crime. The deployment was performed in two stages: first, the most important, high-risk and criminal points on the map were covered; only in a second phase was the scope of the unit expanded to cover the whole affected territory.

The number of policemen forming the UDYCOs is about 1,000. They are selected because they are qualified in the area of organised crime: there are special training programmes. The UDYCOs units are provided with sound technical equipment and they are permanently being modernised.

At the top of the hierarchical structures there are the *Unidades y Servicios Centrales de la Comisaría General de la Policía Judicial* (units and central services of the central division of the Judicial Police). There is also a Regional Coordinator – or a provincial one, if the unit has a provincial range. "*Antenas Informativas*" (passive information receivers) are located in some especially sensitive points; their function is merely informative and they depend on the provincial UDYCOs.

The UDYCOs work is organised according to three main tasks: analysis, which is carried out autonomously by members of the unit with the assistance, sometimes, of the *Grupo de Análisis y Tratamiento de Información* (GATI-Analysis and Information Processing Group); the parallel investigation of the economic implications of every crime carried out by a specialised unit in order to give the judge as much information as possible; and finally, the collection of information in the field by operational groups on the streets. The collected information about the cases and the evidence are brought to the juridical organs and prosecution services.

The *Guardia Civil* created similar units with the same goals one year later. The EDOAs *(Equipos de Investigación de Delincuencia Organizada y Antidroga* – the investigative team on organised crime and drugs) have focused their attention also on organised crime (national and transnational) and in particular on those crimes that require, in order to be investigated, a specialised training or technical skills. Initially the *Guardia Civil* did not regard organised crime as a main threat because this agency is mainly deployed in rural areas, and organised crime is an urban phenomenon. The units are still quite undeveloped.

There are ten EDOAs and the recruiting sources are the Judicial, Anti-fraud Units, the Investigation Group for Organised Crime and the Information Service of the *Guardia Civil*. These EDOAs are functionally dependent on the central unit of the Judicial Police, which is in the central headquarters in Madrid. The three main investigation areas are: financial and economic crime; fraud; and internal affairs and drug trafficking. The deployment of the units will take place in two stages: first the units in Madrid, Sevilla, Málaga, Valencia, Alicante, Barcelona, La Coruña, Baleares and Las Palmas; in a second stage, Cádiz, Granada, Almería, Murcia and Tenerife. In fact, this was the initial idea, but it seems that the deployment of the units has not been completed within the planned period. Therefore, there will also be several peripheral EDOAs and a central one, in Madrid. When a peripheral EDOA has to face a problem which exceeds its capacity, the case is transferred to the central one. These peripheral units have relative independence, which means they broke with the tradition of the *Guardia Civil* having a strongly centralised internal structure. At the same time, the *Guardia Civil* is aiming for a wider international presence and tries to move the central points for international cooperation, officially situated in the CNP, to other more "neutral" institutions in the Ministry of the Interior.

There are other units focused on the fight against the effects of organised crime such as money laundering. Once the 1991 EC money laundering directive was adopted, the national law against money laundering was approved. Then the *Servicio Ejecutivo de Prevención de Blanqueo de Capitales* (SEPBLAC – Executive Service to Prevent Smuggling of Capital) was created in the national central bank. It files all the information about suspicious operations. The *Brigada de Delitos Monetarios y Blanqueo de Capital* (special squad created to fight financial crimes and money laundering) is inside this structure and it performs proactive investigations to determine whether or not there is enough evidence to continue the investigation. If there is enough evidence, all the information is transferred to the national security agencies (*Guardia Civil* or CNP). The SEPBLAC is probably one of the European financial intelligence units with more competences: it is in fact an administrative unit with inspection capacity and the authority to develop preventive activities, which are carried out by its own operative unit.

Inside the main army intelligence agency CESID, (*Centro Superior de Información de la Defensa*), there are some units focused on organised crime. These have been strengthened in recent years, although the terrorist issue in Spain will for the moment remain the main worry of the army as regards internal security affairs. There are not formal processes for the exchange of experiences or information. If there is an exchange of this kind, it takes place through the Ministry of Interior and not directly with the police units. The fact that CESID and *Guardia Civil* have the same military roots probably facilitates the exchange of information on different topics.

Private security companies in Spain do not play any role in the fight against organised crime. The law is very clear on this point and it obliges them to transmit any information they obtain to the police services. This information is, in any case, channelled through the *Unidad Central de Seguridad Privada* of the *Comisaría General de Seguridad Ciudadana* (Central Unit of Private Security, which under the Central Division of Public Safety) and it sends the information to the competent units.

## 5. PUBLIC PROSECUTION UNITS TO FIGHT ORGANISED CRIME

At the judicial level a different response to serious crimes (differentiated from responses to ordinary crimes) such as terrorism, organised or financial crime has been established. In 1977 the Court which had fought political opposition during the dictatorship (*Tribunal de Orden Público* – court for public order), was transformed to deal with the most serious crimes. The new court was the abovementioned *Audiencia Nacional*. Taking into account the lack of experience, more complex structures have not yet been created, because, so far, terrorism is still considered the main threat. Moreover, and as mentioned above, there is not a definition of organised crime *per se* in Spain, although the meaning of the concept can be derived from some legal instruments.

In relation to the structure of Public Prosecution, the *Memorias of the Fiscalía General del Estado*[15] point to the need of structuring the system in order to make it capable of dealing with organised crime, while recognising the scarce resources and structural possibilities of the Spanish judicial system.

The Judicial Police[16] in Spain is regulated by four main laws: the Constitution, LO 6/1985 on Judicial Power, LO 2/86 on the state police forces and RD 769/1987 on the Judicial Police. The Constitution limits their function to penal issues and establishes their dependence on the judges, tribunals and the Public Prosecutor. Although it is not as specific as other European constitutions on this matter, it establishes a clear link to the judicial power. The law regulating the judicial power provides that judicial police units are dependent on the judicial authorities and the Public Prosecutor, something which is made concrete by *Juzgados*, Tribunals and the Public Prosecutor leading the criminal investigation functions. Organic dependence is established in LO2/86. Judicial Police units are organised by the Interior Ministry and their personnel regime is common to that of the national police forces in general. The functional dependence is also strengthened by this law.

Actually, the tasks of investigation of these criminal activities began to bear fruits. There are more than fifty penal cases for money laundering in relation to drugs trafficking which have gone through or are going through the judicial organs of the *Audiencia Nacional*. Twenty of those have been the subject of verdicts (with 16 sentenced and 4 not guilty verdicts), the other fifteen are pending trial or are in the instruction phase, and the other twenty are in the investigation phase. In the investigations performed by the CNP and *Guardia Civil*, between 1994 and 1999, money, monetary instruments, property, vehicles, and other goods and effects whose total value reached 38,000 million pesetas were confiscated.

## 6. MULTIDISCIPLINARY INTEGRATED TEAMS

Permanent multidisciplinary teams integrated by the agents of different forces and with a regular existence have not been created. But, at the judicial level, there are some mixed teams which are organised – and based on an *ad hoc* philosophy – to carry out a specific investigation. They are integrated by agents from the central forces and occasionally by members of the SEVA or the Central Bank or the Ministry of Economy. They do not have a defined and stable relation with the coordination point or the central contact point. Recently an informal cabinet was formed by state police agents, judges and prosecutors and in which different propositions for reform and internal changes in the state's structures are discussed, but its character is informal.

On the other hand, as we have said above, also under the Government

Delegation for the *Plan Nacional sobre Drogas* some mixed teams have been established.

## 7. INTERNATIONAL CONTACT POINTS

The unified treatment of information for international cooperation has been focused, so far, mainly on drug-related issues through the *Centro Nacional de Comunicaciones Internacionales* (CENCI – National Centre for International Communications). The different services are centralised: Interpol, Europol, OCN drugs and liaison offices. There is also a crisis unit whose task is to evaluate and adopt quick decisions at key moments. This structure has been mainly dealing with narcotics, but it expects to assume more competences.

As regards the central body of coordination, in accordance with the Action Plan to Combat Organised Crime, the Spanish Ministry of Interior has given the *Secretaría Técnica de la Comisaría General del Policía Judicial* (Technical Secretariat of the Central Division of the Judicial Police of the CNP) the role of being the coordination point at the national level, coordinating the CNP, the *Guardia Civil*, the *Ertzaintza*, the *Mossos d'Esquadra*, and sometimes, in specific cases, the SEPBLAC. The *Gabinete de Coordinación de la Secretaría de Estado para la Seguridad* of the Ministry of Interior (Cabinet for Coordination of the Security Secretariat of the Ministry of Interior) has paradoxically a similar function. This means that there are in fact two coordination points, which indicates the lack of consensus on this issue. This problem is a consequence of pressure exerted by the *Guardia Civil*, which wants a coordination point that is outside the CNP and directly dependent of the Ministry. The CNP considers that, by law, they are responsible for the international relations of the Spanish security framework, and therefore the international link should remain attached to the civil police agency.

This coordination activity is not an operational function as such, but it involves drawing up the main objectives and lines of action, with the idea of supporting FCSE activity. It has become the most important information exchange resource, via a common database for all forces. The last goal is to add to this scheme the organisation of the judicial structure in a similar way, something which has not been possible for the moment. It is explicitly recognised that there are many aspects of the coordination organs and their activity which must still be defined.

No direct links between the UDYCOs/EDOAs and Europol has been established, although there is an indirect link, because both, UDYCOs and the office responsible for Europol are located at the *Comisaría General de Policía Judicial* (Central Division of the Judicial Police). This common location makes it easier for any UDYCO unit to ask for information. Information flows both ways. The link with SIRENE is of a different nature, because SIRENE only performs consultation functions. There is some discrepancy within the CNP about the functions which SIRENE should carry out. The relationship with OLAF is permanent and close.

The *Guardia Civil* uses ordinary channels when collaboration is needed (Europol, Interpol). There are also international inter-force relationships (FIEP, militarised police forces), which stress informal contact between officers and agents as being a very important way of getting things done. These kinds of relations are considered very useful in order to advise politicians to take the necessary steps in formal forums.

## 8. SUPERVISION AND CONTROL

Judges and magistrates check the police activity through ordinary channels. A prosecutor or judge has no control over police as such, although the prosecution service against drugs coordinates more complex and important procedures in this area. Inside the UDYCOs there is only a hierarchical control performed internally. The National Ombudsman, finally, has no real power over police.

The control that is really relevant in relation to this matter is the hierarchical one, the control exerted on every policeman by his superior. This chain ends in the Minister, who is at the same time responsible to the parliament. The parliament exerts control through questions to the government, and the public discussions.

Inside the CNP a global supervision and control system has been devised, but it is still not in force in the organised crime units. It is called *"Policía 2000"* which focuses on evaluation techniques mainly (the plan also implies some degree of decentralisation). The idea is to establish new forms of control over efficiency and productivity managed by the police itself. The *Unidad de Planificación y Control* (Planning and Control Unit) located at the *Secretaría Técnica* (Technical Secretariat) is the organ that periodically measures the levels of efficiency, but the figures are not published.

## NOTES

1.  See, Carlos Resa, "La delincuencia organizada en España", *Cuadernos de la Guardia Civil. Revista de Seguridad Pública*, 21 (1999), pp. 31-47.
2.  Ángel de Miguel Bartolomé, in Gutiérrez-Alviz, Conrado, *La Criminalidad Organizada ante la Justicia*, Universidad de Sevilla, Sevilla, 1996.
3.  Faustino Gutiérrez-Alviz Conradi ed., *La Criminalidad Organizada ante la Justicia*, Universidad de Sevilla, Sevilla, 1996.
4.  Ángel de Miguel Bartolomé , in Gutiérrez-Alviz, Conrado, *La Criminalidad Organizada ante la Justicia*, Universidad de Sevilla, Sevilla, 1996.
5.  Borja Mapelli Caffarena, in Gutiérrez-Alviz, Conrado, *La Criminalidad Organizada ante la Justicia*, Universidad de Sevilla, Sevilla, 1996.
6.  The real effects of this law have been discussed by Manuel Ballbé, Orden público y militarismo en España p. 471 ff.; Diego López Garrido, *El aparato policial en España*, Barcelona: Ariel, 1987; p. 14 and Ian R., Macdonald, "The Police System of Spain"; pp. 224 ff. in John Roach and Jurgen Thomaneck (eds.), *Police and public order in Europe*, London: Croom Helm, 1985.
7.  The *Cuerpo Nacional de Policía* continued, in part, to have a military nature even until 1985, since one in three posts in the police administration from the highest levels down were occupied by career soldiers. See Manuel Ballbé, ibid., p. 484.
8.  A broad reflection about the current status of the *Guardia Civil* has been exposed by Diego Lopez Garrido, *El aparato policial en España*, Barcelona: Ariel, 1987.
9.  In 1994 the socialist government merged the Ministries of Interior and Justice.
10. The development and evolution of the Basque police agency inside the Spanish police structure has been analysed by Gonzalo Jar Couselo, *Modelo Policial Español y Policías Autónomas*, Madrid: Dykinson, 1995.
11. Figures from Benyon, John *et al.*, *Police Cooperation in Europe: An Investigation*, Leicester: Centre for the Study of Public Order. University of Leicester, 1993, p. 265.
12. This information has been calculated on the basis of data provided by Gonzalo Jar Couselo, *Modelo policial español y policías autónomas*, Madrid: Dykinson, 1995; p. 502.
13. Sánchez de Dios, Manuel, "El Poder Judicial y la Jurisdicción Constitucional", in *Sistema Político Español*, MacGraw Hill, Madrid, 1995.
14. Robles Orozco, Gonzalo, "La Guardia Civil en la Delegación del Gobierno para el Plan Nacional sobre Drogas" en *Cuadernos de la Guardia Civil*, No. 21, 1999.
15. Faustino Gutiérrez-Alviz ed., *La Criminalidad Organizada ante la Justicia*, Universidad de Sevilla, Sevilla, 1996.
16. Blázquez González, Félix, *La Policía Judicial*, Tecnos, 1998, Madrid.

## LIST OF ABBREVIATIONS

| | | |
|---|---|---|
| CGPJ: | Consejo General del Poder Judicial | General Council of the Judicial System |
| CNP: | Cuerpo Nacional de Policía | National Police Agency |
| FCSE: | Fuerzas y Cuerpos de Seguridad del Estado | State Security Forces |
| EDOA(s): | Equipos de Investigación de Delincuencia Organizada y Antidroga | Organised Crime Investigation Units |
| Ertzaintza: | Policía Autonómica Vasca | Autonomous Basque Police |
| LOFCSE: | Ley Orgánica de Fuerzas y Cuerpos de Seguridad del Estado | State Police Law |
| Mossos d'Esquadra: | Policía Autonómica de la Generalitat de Catalunya | Autonomous Catalan Police |
| SEPBLAC: | Servicio Ejecutivo de Prevención de Blanqueo de Capitales | Executive Service for Money Laundering Prevention |
| SEVA: | Servicio de Vigilancia Aduanera | Customs Service |
| UDYCO(s): | Unidades de Droga y Crimen Organizado | Narcotics and Organised Crime Units |

# Sweden

## Janne Flyghed[1]

### 1. ORGANISED CRIME IN SWEDEN

There is no official description or definition of organised crime in Sweden. However, the eleven criteria adopted by the EU are used as the constitutive elements of the operational definition at the National Criminal Intelligence Service. In this sense, Sweden can be said to have an official definition. If the police find it necessary they have the possibility to adopt a different one. The Ministry of Justice in Sweden has not judged it necessary to introduce a formal definition of organised crime, since the legislation in Sweden is not based on this concept. Definitions are considered to have threshold effects for the police.[2] The absence of a formal definition allows the police a wider scope for action. A strict definition limits their possibilities.

Within the Ministry of Justice, intensified efforts to control organised crime were initiated in 1997. A group comprised of participants from different authorities (the RPS and Customs authority) is currently investigating and gathering information about organised crime in Sweden (*Kartläggning av den organiserade brottsligheten i Sverige – ObiS*).[3] The purpose of the project is to elaborate concrete methods that may serve as a basis at the national level for investigation and evaluation of organised crime and possibly also other kinds of serious criminality. An information system will be created in order to gather information and knowledge about organised crime. KOBS is a project with a connection to Europol in relation to the creation of a register containing descriptions of several types of organised crime.

### 2. LAW ENFORCEMENT AGENCIES IN SWEDEN

The police in Sweden form a national organisation, which means that there are no municipal police forces. The Swedish police was nationalised in 1965. Furthermore, the police system is a decentralised civil system organised at the local, regional and central level. Consequently, it does not have any features of a military police. The base of the police is the local police organisation with 177 police districts. At the regional level Sweden is divided into 24 counties and there is a large amount of independence from the central level of the organisation.[4] The board of the County, which is an administrative body that can be compared to a regional government, is also responsible for the police and decides on the division of the county into police districts and prepares the budget for the police organisation in that county. The National Police Board (*Rikspolisstyrelsen* – RPS) is the highest authority. It is responsible for certain administrative issues and supervision. The Police Academy, the National Criminal Investigation Department (*Rikskriminalpolisen* – RKP) and the National Security Service (*Säkerhetspolisen* – *SÄPO*) are all parts of the National Police Board. Connected to this Board is also the National Laboratory of Forensic Science (*Statens Kriminaltekniska Laboratorium*). The Police are subjected to the authority of the Ministry of Justice, which carries the political responsibility for the police force but is not operationally responsible.

The police force comprises in total 27,000 employees of whom 16,600 are trained police officers. This means that Sweden has 282 police officers per 100,000 inhabitants. Today, the sanction for more than 80% of all crimes and offences is a summary fine that is imposed by police officials or prosecutors.

Criminal investigation units exist at all levels in the police organisation. At the local level, there is, as a rule, a specific criminal department in every police district. At the county level, regional investigation units exist for narcotic and economic crimes, as do technical units. Within the RPS, the RKP carries out investigations at the national level of international crimes and of certain categories of narcotic and economic crimes.

In addition to the regular police service there are, at all levels, special law enforcement agencies which are vested with rights to detect and investigate a restricted category of offences. Here the Customs agencies and the Coast Guard that investigate crimes relating to drugs and illegal immigrants, for example, can be mentioned. The Financial Inspectorate (*Finansinspektionen*), an agency at the national level that oversees the performance of banks and insurance companies is one unit that carries out the fight against economic crimes. Other agencies are the Competition Authority (*Konkurrensverket*) and the Environment agency (*Naturvårdsverket*). The latter investigates crimes relating to the environment together with the boards of the County and the local boards of health (*hälsovårdstyrelserna*).[5]

## 3.  THE PUBLIC PROSECUTION SERVICE IN SWEDEN

As is the case with the organisation of the police and the court system, the Public Prosecution Service is nationally organised and is a hierarchical organisation under the authority of the Ministry of Justice. The Public Prosecution consists of 1,300 employees, of whom 650 prosecutors. Organisationally, the Public Prosecution Service is divided into 13 regions. These regional authorities have prosecutors for certain types of crime, in particular economic crimes. At the local level, the Public Prosecution Service is divided into 86 local districts. The regional authorities supervise 83 of these local districts, whereas the districts of the three largest cities of Sweden, Stockholm, Gothenburg and Malmö are independent from the regional organisation.

The Attorney General (*Riksåklagaren – RÅ*) leads and is responsible for the administration of the Public Prosecution Service. He also has the task of being the prosecutor when the Supreme Court considers a criminal case. It is also of importance that he does not need to be granted leave for appeal by the Court. The office of the RÅ employs 50 persons. Lastly, there is an authority responsible for economic and other crimes committed in more than one region (*Statsåklagarmyndigheten för speciella mål*).

The main task of the public prosecutors is naturally the prosecution of crimes, including the investigation of alleged crimes. Pre-trial investigations can be initiated either by the police or the public prosecutor. If the police have initiated the investigation, the public prosecutor shall take over as soon as someone is "reasonably suspected" (*skäligen misstänkt*) of having committed such a crime.[6] Recent reforms that have taken place include, for example, a development unit being created at the Office of the RÅ in 1995, which was initiated by the central government. The development unit deals with the aims of the organisation and different groups of cases and working methods. It has been stated by the government that organised crime will receive priority, together with economic crime, drug trafficking and crimes against women. The public prosecutor service was subjected to reform in 1996. The main direction of the reform was that the operational responsibility should be with the local districts of the prosecution service.[7]

## 4.  LAW ENFORCEMENT UNITS TO CONTROL ORGANISED CRIME

### 4.1 National Law Enforcement Units

At the national level the National Criminal Investigation Department (*Rikskriminalpolisen – RKP*) is divided organisationally into three sections:

the National Criminal Intelligence Service, the National Policing Section, and the Investigations/Surveillance/Operational Support. The section dealing with intelligence is called KUT (*Kriminalunderrättelsetjänsten – KUT*) and was set up in 1995. It was then created as a separate service dealing only with the analysis of intelligence, which meant that Sweden conformed to the system in many other EU Member States.[8] KUT has approximately 140 agents. At the regional level, there are in total about 125 agents, most of them in the districts of Stockholm, Gothenburg and Malmö, who collaborate with the intelligence service. KUT works as the gate in and out of the Swedish system and has a very important role in the fight against organised crime. Information is obtained, for example from Interpol, Europol and Schengen, and processed there. Information is also transferred to the authorities in Sweden about current trends and tendencies. As regards the exchange of information there is therefore a clear centralisation.[9] Within KUT there is a department called the National Liaison Office (*Nationella Samarbets Kontoret – NSK*) with a number of smaller sub-units dealing respectively with Interpol, Europol, SIS/Sirene, BDL (*Bureau de liaison*), Baltic Sea and the Coordination of Records. KUT is still in a phase of building up its structure and organisation. Mechanisms for storing, analysing and exchanging data are being created in order to establish permanent channels for the exchange of information with the rest of the Schengen and Europol countries. Information will be shared and sent to databases in other countries. Sweden is also expected to report annually to Europol about the control of organised crime at the national level. Hence, structures are in the process of being established to allow for the collection of information required both at the national and the regional level.

Within KUT there is also a department that deals with the collection of criminal intelligence. It consists of five units. The first four units comprise the Drugs Unit, the Illegal Immigration Unit, the Environmental Crime Unit and the Financial Intelligence Unit. The fifth is quite a large unit called the Special Objects or Special Issues Unit. It consists of a number of smaller groups that deal with different kinds of crime. It has a very flexible structure and task forces can be set up for a shorter or longer period of time. The kind of crimes dealt with has often been dependent on public opinion and on which issues have attracted attention lately. If a certain category of crime is discussed in the Parliament, the Ministry of Justice will be made aware of the situation and subsequently the National Police Board will be told to do something about it. Money is then granted by the parliament and ends up in this unit in order to fight the category of crimes in question.[10] Different groups that exist today within the Special Objects Unit are groups dealing with child pornography, crimes committed in connection with motorcycle gangs and criminality originating in eastern Europe and Russia.

One of the units of the Criminal Intelligence Collection – the Financial

Intelligence Unit (FIU) – works within the framework of KUT. FIU was set up in 1993 as a response to the EC Money Laundering Directive of 1991. Until 1997, FIU was a unit directly under RPS but was organisationally united with the Financial Police in 1998 (*Finanspolisen – FIPO*). Today, FIU and FIPO are consequently one unit dealing with economic crime and economic intelligence. FIPO was established in 1994 because of the influence of the G7 and their Financial Action Task Force (FATF). According to the recommendations of the FATF a central unit should be established that receives information from the banks and gives guidelines as to how the banks should behave towards their customers.[11] The FIPO started their work in 1995 and at that time dealt exclusively with money laundering. According to a specially created computer system, certain kinds of bank transactions could be registered. This means that people can be registered who for the time being are not suspected of having committed any crimes, but these data are considered as potentially useful in the future. FIPO is solely an intelligence unit both as regards money laundering and economic intelligence. FIPO work closely with the Economic Crimes Authority (*Ekobrottsmyndigheten – EBM*) and are their primary source of information. If suspicions of a crime already committed are established by the FIPO, the EBM is often contacted and deals with the case.[12] The FIPO are also in contact with OLAF for an exchange of information. The merger with FIU meant that the Financial Police today also deal with economic intelligence. FIU are working according to its own specific and detailed rules and their work is characterised by a very high degree of secrecy. They have their own direct links for example with the Ministries of Justice and Finance.

A third department within KUT is an Analysis Unit, which deals with strategic and operational analysis in order to inform the decision-makers, such as the Swedish government and parliament and the EU (Westfelt 2001).

Within the RKP there are several interregional crime squads with special tasks that can be sent out to support the police at the local level. These squads are specialised in certain categories of crimes. Examples of such squads are a "profiler group" (a group working on criminal/crime profiles), a homicide squad, and a squad dealing with serial criminality.

The customs authorities can also be mentioned as taking part in the fight against organised crime since they also have an intelligence service. An informal exchange of information also takes place between private companies and the police on ad hoc basis.[13]

Possible reform plans for the future that are currently being discussed include a change in the distinction between the RKP and the National Security Service (*Säkerhetspolisen – SÄPO*) in order to combat organised crime more efficiently. Furthermore, the creation of a central authority for the control of organised crime is under discussion. This authority would coordinate the work of the police, the customs and the public prosecution. There is a certain political will for the creation of such a body.[14] In March 2000 a Swedish Government Official Report (SOU 2000:25) suggested an amalgamation of the National Security Service and the National Criminal Investigation Department. The report was heavily criticised and did therefore not lead to any government bill. But only a couple of months later, the matter was on the agenda again, when the government mandated the National Police Board – with the purpose to strengthen the fight against serious organised crime – to overhaul the possibilities to change the distinction between the RKP and the National Security Service. The National Police Board delivered its report in June 2001 and reached, maybe not too surprisingly, the conclusion that the creation of a new operational unit – that is, an amalgamation of the NCID and the NSS – will promote the efficiency of organised crime control.[15]

## 4.2 Regional Law Enforcement Units

Since 1995, so-called "Regional Criminal Intelligence Units" (*länskriminalunderrättelserotlar*) have been created at the regional level (the borders of these regions correspond with the administrative borders of the regions). Their tasks are the same as those of the KUT, which are to analyse intelligence and assist the other units of the organisation with information and provide a basis for organised crime control. As regards narcotic crimes and child pornography, there are special units dealing with these crimes in many police districts. There is, however, no central structure that corresponds to these tasks.

Sweden has also cultivated a culture of interregional cooperation, but this was not established with the specific purpose to control organised crime, even though it is often used to deal with this kind of crimes. This cooperation is a more practical solution established by the police rather than the result of directives from the government or another body at a higher level. Examples of such cooperation that takes place are between the Swedish region Skåne and Denmark, Skåne and Schleswig-Holstein, Skåne and Mecklenburg. (Schleswig-Holstein and Mecklenburg are both regions in the northern part of Germany). There is also cooperation between Skåne and the north of Poland and between the Swedish region Västra Götaland and Schleswig-Holstein. In contrast to the abovementioned cooperation, a specific task force has been established in order to tackle organised crime in the Baltic Sea Region.[16] This will be described further below.

## 4.3 Local Law Enforcement Units

"Neighbourhood policemen" (*Närpoliser*) might be mentioned here as a measure to prevent organised crime. Their work is pro-active and consists of gathering information about a certain area as regards the population and the activities going on. With this information at hand it is potentially easier to anticipate and to prevent organised crime.[17]

## 5. PUBLIC PROSECUTION UNITS TO FIGHT ORGANISED CRIME

A reform currently in progress is the establishment of specialist prosecutors. In every local public prosecution authority there will be two specialist prosecutors that deal with organised crime. A system has been initiated where prosecutors are to be given further training within their respective specialist fields. They attend academic courses and take part in a training programme over three years.[18] This means that at the local level there are certain special units but not at the central level. There is no organised coordination between the specialist prosecutors at the local level in the different parts of the country. It is, however, possible that once the reform is completed this will be established. Furthermore, something that has been discussed for a long time is the creation of prosecutors working on a national level to fight organised crime.[19]

A special prosecution office with an original statute has been set up in the field of economic crime. The Economic Crimes Authority (*Ekobrottsmyndigheten* (EBM)) was set up in January 1998 and started its operative work in June the same year. It is a kind of public prosecution authority composed of prosecutors, policemen and economists. The setting up of this organ was contrary to the basis of the Swedish law system where police and prosecutors are separate and have different roles. Because of this, there was initially much resistance against this new authority. As it was not possible to create an integrated unit, the policemen are agents of the RKP and seconded to the EBM.

In the EBM there is one head of the police and one head of prosecution. In the practical work they are however integrated. The police officers investigate the cases they either receive from the FIPO or discover on their own. The tax authorities also report many cases. When they have sufficient evidence during the investigation procedure they can go directly to a prosecutor at the same authority. EBM is directly subordinate to the government, which means that it is not subordinate to the administration of, for example, the police, the public prosecution service or the tax authorities.[20] It coordinates the fight against economic crime of all kinds, regardless of definitions. EBM has also the task of analysing threats and providing information to the state authorities, creating and participating in international networks and being the coordinating unit for proactive work. They also provide the government with information about how the relevant legislation works, analyse the legislation and initiate changes to this legislation.

EBM has, apart from the office in Stockholm, regional offices in Gothenburg and Malmö, which are the second and third largest towns in Sweden. The regional offices also include investigators and public prosecutors. Furthermore, the regions Halland and Gotland belong to the EBM in Gothenburg and Stockholm respectively, whereas the cases in other parts of Sweden normally remain within the ordinary public prosecution system. The public prosecutors in other parts of Sweden may however request EBM to adopt the case if the economic crime in question is very complex, if it has international connections, or extends to large areas of the country. From January 2000, EBM took over the contact with OLAF and is the representative of Sweden in this respect.[21]

At the regional level, the motorcycle task force in Malmö led by a chief prosecutor should be mentioned. He/she deals with criminality related to the motorcycle gangs in the southern part of Sweden. At the local level, there is for example a special commission regarding "raves" in Stockholm.

## 6. MULTIDISCIPLINARY INTEGRATED TEAMS

EBM was created in 1998 and is the only pure example of a multidisciplinary integrated team in Sweden. It is, however, likely that a similar unit will be created in the future within the area of environmental crimes. EBM consists of policemen and prosecutors working together. Even though the police officers formally still belong to the police authority, it is in practice a unit where organised crime control is carried out in teams. The main field of work of this authority is the fight against economic crime. There is, however, no definition of economic crimes, which means that all crimes that in one way or the other are economic can be included in the activities of EBM.[22] This comprises tax crimes, crimes against company legislation and insider legislation. The latter kind of crime may be reported also by the Financial Inspection. EBM has, however, a general responsibility for coordination of the fight against economic crime also within the other prosecution authorities in Sweden. This means for example supervision of how public resources are used and the assurance of a high competence throughout the country. An economic council (*Ekoråd*) has been set up which consists of all heads of the authorities that are active in connection with EBM. The Council is chaired by the RÅ. Other participants are the head of the National Police Board and the heads of the tax and customs authorities and the Financial Inspection. The head of the Council for Crime Prevention (*Brottsförebyggande rådet – BRÅ*) also takes part in Ekorådet. In addition representatives of the Patent Office and the agricultural authority are present.

Within the police there are task forces where the customs authority, the coast guards, the immigration authority (for example as regards illegal immigration) and the tax authority take part. These groups are, however, created if there is a need for them in a specific case. The network between the authorities is permanent but the operative groups are formed on an *ad hoc* basis.

Some members of the police force have requested to intensify the operationalisation of multidisciplinary teams. This is motivated by the impression that the most serious forms of criminality are becoming increasingly heterogeneous in character. All areas that are expected to be profitable are interesting for the persons committing serious crimes. In order to analyse these forms of criminality the traditional structures have to be abandoned.[23]

Within the public prosecution service, the RÅ has given orders to the public prosecution authority in Malmö to look for new working methods and develop new organisational solutions in order to improve cooperation with the police, the custom authorities and the coast guards.

As mentioned above, the creation of a central authority for the fight against organised crime is under consideration in Sweden. It would be considered as a multidisciplinary integrated authority since it would coordinate the work of the police, the custom authorities and the prosecution service.

## 7. INTERNATIONAL COORDINATION AND CONTACT POINTS

The National Criminal Investigation Department (RKP) was designated by the Swedish government to function as the body of coordination as foreseen by Recommendation 1 of the EU Action Plan. KUT, one of its divisions, has coordinating competencies in the policy field, whereas RKP can be said to also have the operational coordination competencies. Together they are coordinating the work of the police force, the customs authority and the coastal guards.

At the level of the law enforcement agencies there is no Central Contact Point for all authorities according to Recommendation 19 of the EU Action Plan. Within the police the NSK (National Liaison Office) is the central contact point for exchange of information. The NSK fulfils Recommendation 19 to some extent, with the exception that it does not function as a national centre for information as regards the administration of justice and organised crime.

Consequently the coordination body and the central contact point in Sweden can be said to belong to the same structure. NSK is a part of KUT, which in its turn is a sub-unit of RKP. NSK, as the central contact point for the Swedish authorities, includes the national central bureau of Interpol, the Europol national unit and the SIRENE desk. NSK is therefore the gate in and out of the Swedish system and all information passes through there.

At the level of the judiciary RÅ can be said to have the function of a central contact point. There are reforms taking place under which every prosecution authority will nominate two specialist prosecutors for the fight against especially serious and cross-border crime. These specialist prosecutors will work in close cooperation with the operational units of the police. Thus far however, no organised coordination has been taking place between these special prosecutors in different local districts.

Other forms of international cooperation that can be mentioned are the Baltic Sea Cooperation and the cooperation that takes place between the Nordic countries. Police cooperation is very developed between the Scandinavian countries. It is based on the Nordic Police Agreement from 1968. The police in Sweden may contact their colleagues in another Scandinavian country without any formal barriers and procedures. The involvement of national authorities is not needed. In the context of organised crime the Police and Customs Cooperation in Scandinavia (*Polis och tullsamarbete i Norden* (PTN)) is relevant and important. This cooperation dates back to 1982 when a political agreement was established between the Nordic countries to mutually combat drug crimes. PTN includes cooperation in practice and the exchange of information and also a corps of Nordic liaison officers abroad with competence to act on behalf of all Nordic countries. At present there are 34 of these liaison officers working for the police and customs authorities. Every police district may then contact the liaison officers abroad. The mandate has since 1996 been extended to cover all forms of international cross-border crime. Police officers from one country can also travel without hindrance and bureaucracy to another of the Nordic countries in order to carry out investigations.

Sweden is also participating in police cooperation in the Baltic Sea Region. In 1996 a task force on organised crime was created at the Baltic Sea States Summit when the respective heads of government concluded that there was an urgent need for direct and concerted action to combat organised crime. A task force was therefore established in order to elaborate measures for the implementation of regional cooperation in this field and other concrete proposals to reinforce it. The measures of the task force include exchange of information, joint action, judicial cooperation and special surveys and training.[24] As regards the exchange of information special contact points have been created that are staffed 24 hours. A communication system, BALTCOM, has also been established on the basis of the already existing X-400 Interpol communication system. Joint concrete and operative measures have been carried out in the fields of drugs, illegal migration, stolen vehicles and highly taxed goods and within the field of money laundering. However, such regional cooperation existed independently even before Sweden joined the EU, especially the cooperation between Sweden and the other Nordic countries. The Baltic Sea cooperation is also not an EU project, but the fact that Sweden joined the EU encouraged and increased international cooperation. Furthermore, informal contacts have become formalised.[25]

## 8.   ACCOUNTABILITY

### 8.1 Institutions and Methods

As regards internal control services the police naturally have a system for internal control and revision. Revision of the police organisation is constantly taking place. The public prosecution service is also controlled by its own (internal) hierarchy. The work of the public prosecutors is supervised in the first place by prosecutors at a higher level. A suspect or victim can appeal a decision to prosecute or not to prosecute to the regional prosecutor or the RÅ.

The Public Prosecutors supervise the law enforcement organisation during the pre-trial investigations. The public prosecutor is always entitled to take over an investigation from the police. A suspect can also initiate such a take over.

The control that can be exercised by a competent ministry is subjected to the principle of independence of the administrative agencies, which is laid down in the Swedish Constitution. This principle means that the government, the parliament and government ministers are unable to interfere in an individual case dealt with by an authority/agency. The Parliament and the government have a general responsibility to supervise the work of the authorities but cannot interfere in an individual case. They can only supervise by changing the legislation or the budget as regards the question at issue.

The Data Protection Authority (*Datainspektionen*) supervises the handling of personal data and gives permission to set up databases. They do however not have the authority to prosecute in order to sanction infringements of data protection rules.

The Judicial Ombudsman (*Justitieombudsmannen* (JO)) supervises public prosecutors and the police on behalf of the Swedish people. He has the right to press charges against policemen and prosecutors. This can also be done by the Judicial Chancellor (*Justitiekanslern* (JK)). The JK exercises supervision of the authorities on behalf of the Swedish government. The JO, the JK and the Data Protection Authority may carry out inspections of the activities of the police without prior notice. They are for that purpose allowed to enter the premises and demand access to documents of any kind.[26]

Another body of control is the Swedish National Audit Office (*Riksrevisionsverket* (RRV)). This authority is an independent institution for central government auditing and it examines the accounting and performance of all government agencies. Other bodies that are subjected to its control are public enterprises and certain state owned companies and foundations.

Recent reforms that have taken place regard the legislation concerning police data systems. Before this reform, the police had to consult and ask permission from the Data Protection Authority before creating a database. This procedure has now been facilitated. According to the new legislation, the police can make their own evaluation as to whether a new database fits the legislative framework. They do not have to ask for permission by the Data Protection Authority.

## 8.2 Proactive Policing

Even though its been widely discussed and subject for a couple of Swedish Government Official Reports through the years, "bugging" is not allowed in Sweden.[27] In 1998 it was concluded in an Official Report that bugging was necessary to make the police efforts to control crime more effective. According to the report, the evidence for its effectiveness was so overwhelming that the protection of integrity and privacy had to stand back.[28] The Committee therefore suggested that bugging should be allowed only when there is a suspicion of serious criminality against someone that is "reasonably suspected" (*skäligen misstänkt*). The suspicion will have to be in connection with a crime that can give rise to a minimum of 4 years in prison. It was also suggested that, if bugging should be introduced by law, the need for some kind of ombudsman to protect the rights of suspects should be considered. The Ombudsman might be given the right to interfere and appeal against a decision of the court, since the suspect may be unaware of the activities carried out by the police, and therefore is unable to defend his interests himself. The Report was criticised – no hard empirical evidence was for instance presented concerning actual threats or concerning the efficiency of bugging operations. The Government never presented any proposal, apparently because there was uncertainty about whether it would the proposal to introduce bugging would achieve a majority. For the moment it seems like the new minister of justice has referred the proposal to the shelf.

Telephone tapping and television surveillance is provided for in Swedish legislation but the execution of this is subject to approval by a court decision.[29]

The public prosecutors may file a request to the court, which can be a court of any kind in the hierarchy. The police therefore have to go by way of the public prosecution service if they consider making use of these kinds of methods. The new legislation concerning the police data system will however facilitate the situation since the police will be allowed to build up a permanent criminal intelligence database with information also about non-suspects.[30]

The shift towards proactive, more intelligence-led, policing and the amalgamation of the secret police and the open police can be illustrated by the following figures. "Proactive" refers to actions taken by the police before a crime is committed; and "reactive" to actions taken after a crime is committed. "Repressive" measures include violations of integrity (privacy), while the category "non-repressive" does not.

*Typology of Police-activities* before *the introduction of the Criminal Intelligence Service*

|  | Proactive | Reactive |
| --- | --- | --- |
| **Repressive measures** | Secret police (SÄPO) | Open Police/Secret Police |
| **Non repressive measures** | Open police/Secret Police | Open Police |

*Typology of Police-activities* after *the introduction of Criminal Intelligence Service.*

|  | Proactive | Reactive |
| --- | --- | --- |
| **Repressive measures** | Secret police (SÄPO) Criminal Intelligence Service Community Policing | Public Police/Secret Police |
| **Non repressive measures** | Public police/Secret Police | Public Police |

With the creation of Criminal Intelligence Units, there has been an increased emphasis on proactive repressive measures within the public police; measures which formerly were connected with the Secret Police. The Criminal Intelligence Service can be seen as a hybrid police organisation, crossing over the traditional, public police and the secret police. It breaks up the distinction between two formerly separate types of policing, which can be regarded as an innovation in Swedish policing.

## 9. CONCLUSION

The most important organisational changes within the police and prosecution service that have taken place as a consequence of the fight against organised crime are the creation of a National Criminal Intelligence Service (KUT) and a National Liaison Office (NSK) in 1995. These organisational changes are not due to Sweden joining the EU, but due to the collapse of communism. As a consequence of the latter, organised crime is deemed to have increased in other countries, such as USA and Germany. Sweden was not so attractive for organised crime but has adapted anyway to the increased threat.[31] The KUT represents a more intelligence-oriented way of working for the police, which prior was only characteristic of the National Security Service. It might also be because of this orientation that the current discussion on changing the distinction between the RKP and the National Security Service is taking place. A reform that is discussed at present is also the creation of a central authority for the coordination of organised crime control.

On the level of the public prosecution it is very interesting that the nomination and education of prosecutors specialised in organised crime is currently taking place. It will however take a few years before the reform is fully carried out and the consequences can be evaluated.

It has been stated that the most important change that has occurred as a consequence of intensified efforts against organised crime is the forging of multi-agency relationships. There is closer cooperation between the police, the public prosecutors and the customs authority that is taking place nowadays, especially the cooperation between KUT and EBM.

This closer cooperation has manifested itself in EBM, which was created as a multidisciplinary unit and is composed of policemen, prosecutors and customs officials. EBM is the only example of a permanent multidisciplinary integrated team in Sweden. This might however change in the future since it seems to be recognised that organised criminality stretches across traditional borders and might be easier to control by these kinds of units, for instance in the context of environmental crime.

**NOTES**

1. The author wishes to thank Lisa Westfelt, MA in Criminology, for the excellent research-assistance she provided.
2. Interview with Christer Ekberg, Jan Garton and Fredrik Wersäll.
3. Interview with Lennart Berg, EBM.
4. Interview with Christer Ekberg, Head of the National Criminal Intelligence Service.
5. The facts in this chapter are taken from Bo Svensson, *Criminal Justice in Sweden*, BRÅ-report 1995:1.
6. The facts of this chapter have been taken from Bo Svensson, *Criminal Justice in Sweden*, BRÅ-Report 1995:1.
7. Other consequences of the reform were a reduction in personnel and that a new data system was introduced.
8. Even before 1995 KUT existed, but it was a very small unit directly under RKP and not comparable to the KUT in its present form.
9. Interview with Jan Garton, Senior Analyst at KUT.
10. Interview with Christer Ekberg.
11. Interview with Sune Jansson, at the Financial Police.
12. Interview with Sune Jansson.
13. Interview with Jan Garton.
14. Interview with Jan Garton.
15. NPB-report, VKA-120-5802/00.
16. The countries taking part in this are Denmark, Estonia, Finland, Germany, Iceland, Latvia, Lithuania, Norway, Poland, Russia and Sweden.
17. Interview with Christer Ekberg.
18. Interview with Ewa Nyhult, Senior Administrative Officer at the General Attorney.
19. Interview with Jan Garton.
20. In its prosecutor function, EBM is subordinate to RÅ.
21. The contacts with OLAF were previously dealt with by FIPO. The customs authorities were also in contact with OLAF.
22. Interview with Lennart Berg, EBM.
23. Interview with Jan Garton.
24. Fact Sheets concerning the Task Force on Organised Crime in the Baltic Sea Region.
25. Interview with Peter Strömberg, Assistant Under-Secretary at the Ministry of Justice.
26. Interview with Christer Ekberg.
27. It was however allowed before 1975 when the law was changed.
28. SOU 1998:46, p.343.
29. See the Procedural Code: *Rättegångsbalken* (SFS 1942:740), chapter 27.
30. Interview with Fredrik Wersäll.
31. Interview with Christer Ekberg.

**BIBLIOGRAPHY**

Fact-sheets concerning the Task Force on Organised Crime in the Baltic Sea Region
Flyghed, Janne (2000) (ed): *Brottsbekämpning – mellan effektivitet och integritet* (Crime-control – between efficiency and integrity) Lund: Studentlitteratur.
SOU (1998), *Om buggning och andra hemliga tvångsmedel* (The Swedish Governments Official Report: Bugging and other secret coercive means)
SOU (2000), *Den centrala polisen* (The Swedish Governments Official Report: The central police)
Svensson, Bo (1995), *Criminal Justice in Sweden*, BRÅ-report.
Westfelt, Lisa (2001), *Organisatoriska förändringar inom svensk polis under 1990-talet med avseende på kampen mot organiserad brottslighet* (Organisational changes in the Swedish Police during the 1990s with the purpose to control organised crime) Department of Criminology, Stockholm University, Report 2001:1.

**RESPONDENTS**

* Christer Ekberg, Head of KUT
* Ewa Nyhult, Senior Administrative Officer at the Attorney General
* Jan Garton, Senior Analyst at KUT
* Peter Strömberg, Assistant Under-secretary at the Ministry of Justice
* Fredrik Wersäll, Assistant Under-secretary at the Ministry of Justice
* Sune Jansson, The Financial Police
* Lennart Berg, The Economic Crimes Authority

## ABBREVIATIONS

- **NCIS** – The National Criminal Intelligence Service = (*KUT* – *Kriminalunderrattelsetjansten*)
- The Economic Crimes Authority = (*EBM* – *Ekobrottsmyndigheten*)
- The Attorney General = (*RÅ* – *Riksåklagaren*)
- **EU** – European Union
- The Judicial Ombudsman = (*JO* – *Justitieombudsmannen*)
- The Judicial Chancellor = (*JK* – *Justitiekanslern*)
- The Financial Police = (*FIPO* – *Finanspolisen*)
- **FIU** – Financial Intelligence Unit
- **OLAF** – Office de Lutte Anti-Fraude – European Anti-Fraud Office
- The National Criminal Investigation Department = (*RKP* – *Rikskriminalpolisen*)
- The National Police Board = (*RPS* – *Rikspolisstyrelsen*)
- The Council for Crime Prevention = (*BRÅ* – *Brottsförebyggande rådet*)
- The National Security Service = (*SÄPO* – *Säkerhetspolisen*)
- Police and Custom Cooperation in Scandinavia = (*PTN* – *Polis och Tullsamarbete i Norden*)
- The National Liaison Office = (*NSK* – *Nationella Samarbetskontoret*)
- Swedish National Audit Office = (*RRV* – *Riksrevisionsverket*)

# United Kingdom

## James Sheptycki

### INTRODUCTION

Policing in the United Kingdom has historically been territorially decentralised. Policing services have different cultural histories in each of the three separate jurisdictions of England and Wales, Scotland and Northern Ireland. There are at present 43 separate constabularies in England and Wales, 8 in Scotland and 1 in Northern Ireland. The system of prosecution in the UK takes place under the common law and is enacted through the adversarial system. In England and Wales the police had responsibility for the prosecution of offences until 1986 when the Crown Prosecution Service was created for this purpose. In Scotland the office of the Procurator Fiscal has undertaken prosecutions since before the inception of the modern police. In the contemporary period there is some convergence of policing practice north and south of the border and this is especially evident in relation to the policing of organised crime.

There have been significant changes in the architecture of the policing system in the UK over the course of the last decade and this has been, in substantial part, because of the identification of organised crime as a significant social problem. The National Criminal Intelligence Service (NCIS) emerged in 1992 as the principal institutional hub for coordinating the national response to organised and serious crime. The NCIS defines organised crime as "any enterprise, or group of persons, engaged in continuing illegal activities which has as its primary purpose the generation of profits, irrespective of national boundaries". Evidence reviewed in this report suggests that between 47% and 66% of criminal cases that come to the attention of police which conform to this definition are connected with drug trafficking. Changes in the architecture of policing in the UK subsequent to the identification of organised crime as a significant social problem have tended to centralise the system while preserving the appearance of administrative fragmentation. This has been accomplished by a move towards intelligence-led policing and information sharing across the variety of police agencies operating within the

UK. The dominant focus in policing organised crime has been on law enforcement rather than crime prevention. It is not clear how effective the new measures have been in responding to the problems posed by organised crime.

**PRELIMINARIES – A SHORT DESCRIPTION OF THE POLICING AND PROSECUTION SYSTEM IN THE UNITED KINGDOM IN ITS HISTORICAL CONTEXT**

Criminal Justice in the United Kingdom is based on a common law tradition. Historically, the police service has had the responsibility of preparing the case for the prosecution in England and Wales.[1] It was only in 1986 that the Crown Prosecution Service (CPS) was established as an independent institution in the criminal process. In contrast, the legal system in Scotland has historically maintained the Office of the Procurator Fiscal (roughly akin to the *Juges d' Instruction* in the continental system) and decisions about prosecution have never rested directly with the police. The relatively late introduction of the CPS into the criminal justice system and the existence of a common law tradition mark significant differences that underpin the culture of criminal justice in England and Wales compared with continental Europe. Despite the Procurator Fiscal, Scotland shares the common law tradition with her southern neighbour and the possibility of "judge made law" sets both jurisdictions apart from the continental model.

The history of policing in England and Wales is conventionally dated from 1829, with the foundation of the London Metropolitan Police. Police forces for the rest of the country were established from 1856 with the passage of the County and Borough Police Act. There was an earlier police tradition, but it was the formation of the "new" police from 1829 that marked the establishment of the institution of the British Bobby (constable) that is recognised as the symbol of policing in Britain today (Reiner, 2000). The system that was set up during the nineteenth century shared similar features with the police system that was established in the Netherlands during the latter part of that century. It was parochial and a great deal of decision-making power over policing remained in the hands of local élites. The reason for this is that, historically, there has been resistance to a police system centrally controlled by the national government. There were some 259 police forces in England and Wales by 1860. The subsequent history of these is one of gradual amalgamation and centralisation. It is possible to understand the creation of the National Criminal Intelligence Service (NCIS) and the National Crime Squad (NCS) in the final decade of the twentieth century as the latest phase of this long historical trajectory.

Initially the Treasury paid one-quarter of the operating expenses of these police forces and undertook efficiency checks by annual inspection undertaken through the offices of three Inspectors of the Constabulary. The police system that grew up across the country in the wake of this act was a patchwork quilt and, as Stallion and Wall (1999) have documented, each patch in the quilt was virtually unique unto itself. Initially, since most of the funding came from the local government, what external control over the police there was remained largely in the hands of provincial élites in the form of "watch committees" and the office of Justice of the Peace. Some historians argue that chief officers were largely autonomous from local governmental oversight (Bunyan, 1976). Chief constables of county forces have been characterised as particularly autocratic, running their forces as individual fiefdoms (Brogden, *et al*, 1988). It is generally agreed that there was virtually no inter-force cooperation and the largest force, the London Metropolitan Police, provided something of a national police body, if only on an ad hoc basis. It was about 1875 that the central government began to pay 50% of the cost of county and borough forces and from about that time statistical returns became more detailed. Most historians agree that by the 1880s central government, through the Home Office, was becoming more important as the institution of governmental oversight than local borough or county government (Emsley, 1997a).

However, it was the First World War that provided the great watershed. The war of 1914-1918 created a new perception of the need to coordinate the actions of chief constables under central guidance. A number of more or less abortive police strikes in 1919 led to the setting up of the Desborough Committee and then to the Police Act in that year. The Police Act standardised pay and conditions across the country and "introduced the new concept of a centrally guided and largely uniform system of local police forces" (Critchley, 1978, p. 194). Gradual amalgamation of the many small police forces had been taking place over the course of the first century of the "new" police. By 1939 there were 183 police forces, in the 1964 there were 125, but in that year an acceleration of force amalgamations began. Also in that year the Regional Crime Squad system for coordinating inter-force criminal investigations was put in place. There had been some discussion of developing a "national police force" at that time but "regionalisation" was seen as a more logical progression (Whitaker, 1964, p. 88). At that time nine regional crime squads were superimposed on top of the existing force structure. Amalgamations continued until, by the 1970s, the present territorial division of 41 provincial forces in England and Wales, plus the City of London and the London Metropolitan Police, was set.[2]

The police system in Scotland is somewhat different. There the establishment of the modern police dates from the establishment of the Glasgow police in 1800, followed by Edinburgh in 1805, Paisley (1806), Gorbals (1808), Perth (1811), Aberdeen (1818), Calton (1819), Airdire

(1822), and Dundee (1824). Police forces in Scotland were thus confined to areas of high population concentration. The subsequent development of policing in Scotland was piecemeal and control and direction of day-to-day policing was mainly at a local level. In 1857 the Inspectorate for the Constabulary of Scotland was established and a modicum of central state control dates from that period. The consolidation of Scottish police forces during the course of the twentieth century was marked: in 1945 there were 49, in 1950 there were 33 and in 1968 there were 22. The most important stage in centralisation came with the reorganisation of Scottish local government in May 1968 when the number was reduced to the present 8 (Gordon, 1980).[3] A Regional Crime Squad for the whole of Scotland was formed in the following year. With Scottish Devolution in 1999 this means that there is, in all but name, a national crime squad for Scotland. It should be noted that the offices of the Procurators-fiscal assumed at least some of the responsibilities of a public prosecutor from the mid-eighteenth century – long before the "new police". Since 1907 this office has been centrally appointed by the Lord Advocate and since 1927 the Procurators-fiscal have been civil servants. As previously mentioned, unlike the police of England and Wales, in the Scottish system, decisions to prosecute have never rested with the police. Rather, decisions to invoke the criminal process have been seen to be matters of public policy pursued in the public interest and this has, in important respects, made *law enforcement* in Scotland more of a centrally discharged function.

Policing in Northern Ireland is a subject which resists easy summation. The Royal Ulster Constabulary (RUC) is the fourth title for the state policy agency in the region in the past 170 years (Brogden, 1995, p. 6). The Peace Preservation Force, became the Irish Constabulary, which became the Royal Irish Constabulary which became the RUC. In the contemporary period the RUC is again undergoing considerable reform, but the historic situation in the province means that this transformation is proceeding from a basis of a considerable build-up of state policing capacity. In the mid-1990s Northern Ireland had three times more officers per capita than England and Wales (1:135 in Northern Ireland as opposed to 1:445 in England and Wales). In addition, at roughly £600 million per annum in the mid-1990s, per capita spending on police in the province was roughly three times higher than in England and Wales (Weitzer, 1996, p. 28). Due to the political situation in Northern Ireland, it has been estimated that terrorism and public order duties consume 80% of police resources and time (ibid. p. 29). The RUC is responsible to a Police Authority, the members of which are appointed by the government. Brogden reports that "there is a rejection of the institutions which structure police-community relations" including the Police Authority for Northern Ireland (PANI) (op cit. P. 6). Weitzer (1996) reports that the PANI's limited powers over the RUC help to explain why the Authority has not intervened more frequently in matters of controversy and instead has concentrated on technical and administrative matters (p. 34-35). The low levels of reported crime in the province have been linked to the tensions arising out of the political situation. Practices of 'informal' or 'popular' justice which circumvent the formal criminal justice apparatus have been documented (Hillyard, 1993, Morrissey and Pease, 1982). These may account for the low official crime figures.

Currently there are efforts to demilitarise policing in the province and attempts are being made to construct a model of democratically accountable, community-oriented policing. Brogden (1995) suggested that the move to community policing must necessarily come after an intermediate stage, which he refers to as the "bandit-catching" phase. In his words:

> In a community that regards the state police as illegitimate, there has to be a progressive gaining of trust. Truces have to be negotiated [and] effectiveness demonstrated before the consent intrinsic to community policing is achieved. While clearly effective crime-fighting policing is often underpinned by community support, the latter must be earned incrementally... the new community peace structures must be accommodated by police commitment to prove themselves competent as crime fighters. A negotiated local Policing by Objectives strategy provides the one mechanism of transition from military-style policing through bandit-catching or crime fighting to community policing (ibid. p. 18-19).

Efforts to transform the RUC will inevitably be affected by broader changes to the legal context of policing. It is beyond the capacity of this report to deal in detail with such matters. However, it can be stated that changes to the legal context of policing in Northern Ireland principally concern changes in legislation that is peculiar to Northern Ireland, legislation that has been devised both at the level of the Courts and at the level of police powers that aim to deal with the perceived threat to social and political stability. The RUC have wielded extensive powers under two main emergency laws – the Emergency Provisions Act (EPA) and the Prevention of Terrorism Act (PTA), which allow for preventative detention for up to seven days, house searches, exclusion orders and "Diplock-Court" trials (special non-jury trials for terrorist cases with exceptional rules of evidence). It was reported in 1996 that over the previous 20 years over 60,000 people had been arrested, interrogated and released without charge (Weitzer, 1996, p. 30). Clearly a political settlement acceptable to all parties is inextricably tied to the project of transformation and the democratic legitimation of policing in Northern Ireland. However, this process is extremely fraught, not least because of the practice of "popular justice" (Hillyard, 1993). Observing the semi-formalised nature of popular justice, some criminologists have conceptualised these often violent community reactions to crime and disorder as "the black criminal justice system" (Morrissey and Pease, 1982). Informal justice in the province bears some considerable resemblance to the historic form of "committees of vigilance" on the frontier of the United States during the nineteenth century. Both the formal and informal systems of policing use the issue of crime and its control as a vehicle in the struggle for political legitimacy. In such circumstances it is very difficult to draw easy distinctions between policing, vigilantism, protection rackets and organised crime. At the time of writing a settlement has yet to be achieved and the policing situation in the province remains in considerable flux.


## ORGANISED CRIME IN THE UNITED KINGDOM

The term organised crime is not a fixed category and there is considerable debate about the scope of its meaning. Given that the organised crime problematic has implications for the national architecture of policing in the United Kingdom, it is worthwhile looking at how the term has come to be used in police and policy making circles during the recent past.

According to the National Criminal Intelligence Service (NCIS) memorandum to the Home Affairs Committee (1994) "many well informed commentators and academics maintain that organised criminal activity *per se* is a myth. They are wrong, but time and again we come back to that illusive quest of (sic) a working definition..." (p. 140). Attempts to define the problem have been, invariably, only partial and all parties seem to agree that the definition of "organised crime" is problematic. It seemed obvious to police practitioners that too stringent a definition would lead to artificial parameters on policing responses to societal problems. Academics pointed out that too loose a definition would mean that everything becomes organised crime. In spite of terminological difficulties, the British police consolidated a definition of "organised crime" which has become the official one proffered by NCIS. It states:

> Organised crime constitutes any enterprise, or group of persons, engaged in continuing illegal activities which has as its primary purpose the generation of profits, irrespective of national boundaries (Home Affairs Committee, 1994, p. 141).

According to Dorn *et al* (1991) "the argument for the reorganisation of the police has moved from unpublished internal police reports, through the specialist policing magazines and journals, to appear as overt pressure for change, expressed through chief officers and Members of Parliament" (p. 95). As they saw it "explicit assumptions underpinning thinking in this area of policy are that terrorism and drug trafficking typify "serious crime", that they go hand-in-hand, and that they are increasingly organised on a national or international level." Thus many in policing circles concluded *a fortiori* "policing should therefore be reorganised on national or international levels to meet this challenge" (p. 92). NCIS produced key documents in the 1990s that illustrate this process (NCIS, 1992, 1993, 1994) and, further, show both the elasticity and the narrowness of the concept of organised crime.

The first of these is the official statement of purpose and objectives of the NCIS. It begins by noting that "the idea of a national tier of criminal intelligence is not new; it has been discussed in the police service for nearly 20 years" (1992, p. 4). The reason for this long-held pre-occupation was the "increasing sophistication and mobility of major criminals" which led to an "ACPO [Association of Chief Police Officers] inspired proposal for a National Criminal Intelligence Service" (*ibid.* p. 4). The intention was to concentrate policing efforts on "the top echelon of criminal activity" and this was to be done by focusing on "major criminals" and "serious crime". The former were "persons, organisations or corporate bodies who are currently active in or suspected of serious crime" which was understood to fall under specific headings. This list is an interesting litany of crime types: 1) murder and attempted murder; 2) kidnapping, abduction and attempts; 3) blackmail and extortion; 4) serious sexual offences, rape, buggery and attempts; 4) robbery – aggravated, with intent to rape, artifice, of specific regional/ national importance, of firearms dealers or of explosives; 5) theft of high-value loads; 6) serious or organised fraud; 7) counterfeit currency or forgery; 8) theft of heavy goods vehicles and plant; 9) offences of regional special interest/significance (e.g. serious sexual assaults).

This "shopping basket" approach to defining organised crime leaves the academic criminologist with the problem of how to interpret an absence, that absence being drug trafficking. The omission is all the more glaring since the Parliamentary Home Affairs Committee which considered the problem of organised crime noted that NCIS statistics revealed that roughly 50% of organised criminal activity related to drug trafficking (Home Affairs Committee, 1994, p. 6). Moreover, and even more alarming, "between 50 and 70% of all crime in this country is drugs related" (ibid. p. 38). The NCIS statement of aims (NCIS, 1992) made mention of the capacity to undertake crime pattern analysis (CPA) using sophisticated new databases and information technology. CPA was focused on six specific crime categories: 1) murder and attempted murder; 2) kidnapping, abduction and attempts; 3) blackmail and extortion; 4) serious sexual offences; 5) robbery offences where there was evidence of a firearm; 6) offences of a regional, special interest/significance. While the final "catch-all" category may obviously include drugs, the issue of drug law enforcement was invisible in this document. It seems reasonable to suggest that the NCIS was, in this initial phase, anxious to project itself as offering a generalist policing service of use to the local constabularies across the entire range of issues.

The occasion of the *NCIS Threat Assessment Conference* in May of 1993 was an important moment in the refinement of the functional logic for restructuring the police system (NCIS, 1993). It was at this conference that the essence of organised crime as defined by NCIS was distilled from a long list of potential crime types that were thought to comprise it. The document that resulted from the conference is the product of many voices and defining its central point is a difficult task. A Detective Superintendent working for the NCIS did so by noting that "organised crime is a reality not imaginary", it is the product of "organised crime groups [who] are in the market place for any commodity or service in which they can satisfy their greed". He advocated "disruption as opposed to arrest and conviction" as "the way forward" and noted that "a weakness of organised crime groups is in their financial dealings, in particular their endeavours to launder their illicit gains" and urged that "we must focus our attention in this area of vulnerability" (p. 62). In his summary remarks he echoed strongly the earlier contribution of the Assistant Director of the FBI who advocated the "enterprise theory" of organised crime investigation. According to the FBI Assistant Director, "under the Enterprise Theory, prosecution is sought of the criminal organisation's leadership for all of the enterprise's criminal activities. Assets generated by the criminal organisation are also identified through this process so that they can ultimately be seized and forfeited to the government" (ibid., p. 40). The head of the organised crime unit at NCIS, who opined that the term "organised crime" was misleading (ibid. p. 5), also pursued the theme of "enterprise crime". He was keen to look at "criminal enterprises" and "criminal entrepreneurs" and to try " to understand how they organise themselves to make a profit out of their criminal enterprises by looking their market behaviour" (ibid. p. 5). He advocated that "by using every lawful means at our disposal, often clandestinely, [we should] seek to limit, inhibit, or block the capacity to carry out criminal enterprise operations successfully" (ibid. p. 7).

In summing up the 1993 NCIS Threat Assessment Conference, Anderson noted that "most of the accounts . . . were either based on stereotypical definitions of organised crime [or were] heavily influenced by older American analyses of the problem." Further, "they gave an overall impression of a global threat which required a coordinated response both nationally and internationally." This in turn "suggested an enhanced role for NCIS because effective international cooperation could not take place without efficient national coordination of anti-organised crime measures (Anderson, 1993, p. 302). In Anderson's analysis, UK policy formation had to be understood in the context of the international system of which it is a part. He noted that its history and geography had "allowed Britain to maintain a certain distance from European arrangements" (p. 303) but that "the general influence of the United States on thinking about multilateral law enforcement cooperation is considerable" (p. 305). Pressures from without and favourable domestic political conditions meant that "as long as any agreements and arrangements can be represented as intergovernmental, and therefore not in breach of British sovereignty, the UK government has a strategic stance in which British cooperation is almost guaranteed." He concluded, accurately as it turned out, that "international cooperation against what might be termed "organised crime" has had a high priority on the government's agenda and there is little reason to suppose that this would alter if the political complexion of the government changed after a general election" (p. 307).

In spite of interminable definitional quibbles the notion of "organised crime" was gradually gaining a concrete and practical focus in operational policing circles in the UK. The new rubric of "enterprise crime" was most evident in the NCIS *Outline Threat Assessment,* issued less than one year after the Threat Assessment conference (NCIS, 1994). The purpose of the briefing document was to "give an overview of the threat posed to our society by Criminal Groups who have organised themselves to embark upon "Enterprise Crime" to the detriment of the public, commerce, financial institutions and ultimately, our system of administration" (from the Introduction). Although some mention of fraud and white collar crime was made, this document focused largely on drug trafficking. It noted an increase in the scale of organised crime since the 1970s and suggested that "the prospects of considerable financial returns from drug trafficking . . . prompted the growth in organised crime." Further, "the need for complex logistics for financing, transportation and distribution saw the development of rather more structured organisational arrangements established, it is believed, by a small number of experienced criminals, some of whom are in contact with organised crime groups abroad" (p. 1). The report proceeded under a number of headings, many of which referred to criminal groups by geographical origin. Thus, Chinese Triads, the Italian Mafia, Russian and other east European groups, Jamaican Yardies, Israeli, Turkish and outlaw Biker groups were each given analysis in turn. Some other crime categories were tangentially considered, including criminal acquisition of firearms, counterfeiting, criminal infiltration of the toxic waste industry and, lastly, casinos and gambling. The main focus was, however, clearly on drug-related crime and associated money laundering and most of the attention was on "non-indigenous crime groups".

The functional logic that appeared as the driving force behind greater centralisation of the system of public policing in the UK thus came to settle on the problem of enterprise crime and the vast majority of criminal enterprises were understood to be involved in illicit drug markets. Thus, "as surely as night follows day, centralisation leads to concentration" (Stelfox, 1999). Earlier shopping basket approaches to defining organised crime, where police simply listed a variety of crime types that exhibited temporal sustainability, were gradually displaced by a focus on illicit trafficking in drugs and the problem was increasingly seen to be one emanating from "non-indigenous sources". Beare and Naylor (1999) argued that discourses on "organised crime" produce two "classes of criminal"; a class of career criminals and a class of legitimate citizens who may stray into illegality from time to time. In American discourses on organised crime the image of the career criminal has been fused with discourses relating to immigrants and the centrality of the Sicilian Mafia is the paradigm case. They go on to note, however, that "any truth that may have existed in notions of ethnic succession on the crime ladder, or layers of society trapped in a traditional crime culture, have surely lost much of their relevance in more recent years with greater social, geographic and inter-cultural mobility. Yet locked into the old mind set, many criminological experts studying "organised crime" and police specialising on chasing it have simply expanded the list of ethnic groups. To the ranks of Italian "organised crime", they have now added Nigerian, Vietnamese, Chinese, Japanese, Aboriginal, Russian and Aboriginal (*sic*). Biker gangs become an "ethnic equivalent" categorisation based on the presumed rationalisation that bikers are so offensive a species as to rank as a separate ethno-cultural identity!" (p. 32).

The definition of organised crime as it has come to be used in British police circles has two levels of meaning: denotative and connotative. At the denotative level, organised crime has been constructed so as to point to crimes associated with the "illicit economy" and drug market is the *sine qua non* of this. At the connotative level, organised crime has come to be associated with foreign contagion. The denotative and connotative levels of meaning act in combination producing a powerful control response. Understanding of the term also takes shape in relation to its sister concept "Serious Crime". Kidnappings, murders and other serious crimes continue to come to the attention of the national policing apparatus as will be revealed below. The concept of "serious crime" served to carry the residue of the earlier shopping basket of crimes which did not come under the crimes of the clandestine economy. What tends to disappear in these discourses about "organised crime" are "economic crimes". This is evident in the segregation of the topics of "white-collar crime" and "organised crime" in academic criminology in the UK. The authoritative text in British criminology is the *Oxford Handbook of Criminology* and both the first and second editions of this compendious book (published in 1995 and 1997) contain separate chapters on each of these topics. The difference in the two discourses is significant. The accumulated wisdom of academic criminologists on white-collar crime, fraud and other crimes of the powerful is that the control response is, in David Nelken's (1997, p. 911-921) turn of phrase "ambivalent" (see also: Box, 1983; Levi, 1991; Levi and Nelken, 1996; Nelken, 1997; Pearce, 1976; Pearce and Woodiwiss, 1993, Tupman, 1999). The bugbear of organised crime does not illicit an ambivalent response, as is revealed below.

## THE CROWN PROSECUTION SERVICE IN ENGLAND AND WALES

The origins of the Crown Prosecution Service (CPS) for England and Wales date from 1986. The establishment of this institution was based on recommendations of the Report of the Royal Commission on Criminal Procedure, chaired by Sir Cyril Philips. In brief, the report concluded that it was undesirable for the police to both investigate and prosecute crime. It was also concluded that standardisation of prosecution practice across England and Wales was both necessary and could only be achieved by the development of a more robust system of public prosecution. Philips advised that the functions of investigation and of deciding whether to charge a person with an offence should remain with the police, but that from that point onwards the conduct of the prosecution should be the responsibility of a new, *locally based* prosecuting service with some national features. Instead, the government established a national Prosecution Service headed by the Director of Public Prosecutions and under the supervision of the Attorney General, that is, one which was accountable at the national level and not to any local body. The CPS was legislatively embodied with the passage of Prosecution of Offences Act 1985 and commenced operations in 1986. Currently the CPS is organised into 13 areas which are in control of 93 branches and this system is controlled through two CPS headquarters offices, one for London and one in York. Branches are required to operate in highly standardised ways and instances of particularly serious crime may be forwarded to the Central Casework Unit.

This new institution occupies a position between the police and courts. The police continue to be responsible for deciding on the charge and for preparing a case file for the CPS. The CPS role is one of reviewing cases passed to it by the police after they have charged a defendant in order to decide whether the evidence justifies the charge. CPS lawyers may choose to proceed with a prosecution, downgrade the offence to a lesser charge or discontinue the prosecution altogether. It is not uncommon for the CPS to send papers back to the police to ask for clarification, additional statements or, in some instances, request that the police undertake further enquiries. Reportedly, there has been tension between the police and the CPS, but the new institution has not markedly affected the workings of the court (Glidewell, 1998). The CPS employs approximately 6,000 personnel about one third of whom are lawyers and the rest administrative support staff. By the late 1990s this service managed about 1.3 million cases a year, of which 120,000 were serious enough to be tried in a Crown Court. The vast majority of this work is routine and involves relatively minor offences but the CPS is responsible for "serious crime" including complex cases which might be said to fall under the heading of "organised crime".

The CPS has little control of its workload. Case files arrive from the police who have already agreed the date of the first hearing in court. About 12% of cases advanced by the police are discontinued and this is the source of some friction. According to some police managers, police officers no longer feel the sense of ownership over routine cases that they once did (personal communication to author). After assembling the file, officers pass it on and subsequently only revisit it at the behest of CPS lawyers. Cynicism about the prosecution service on the part of rank and file police officers may emanate from an awareness of discontinuances and/or the downgrading of offences, which suggests a lingering sub-cultural reluctance to drop the "traditional" police role of prosecutors and adopt the "new" role of impartial evidence gatherers on behalf of the "true" prosecuting authority: the Crown Prosecutor. Statistically the highest discontinuance rates and downgrading of offences are associated with charges of violence against the person and criminal damage, while the lowest are associated with motoring offences.[4] A plausible explanation for this is that it is relatively easy for the CPS to down-grade offences associated with violence (Grievous Bodily Harm to Actual Bodily Harm, Actual Bodily Harm to Common Assault, etc.). According to Glidewell (1998) this is a matter for concern, but there is no research evidence to suggest why this pattern has come about (p. 5). Some operational police officers have suggested that this is symptomatic of plea bargaining.

The CPS memorandum of evidence to the Home Affairs Committee of Inquiry into Organised Crime (Home Affairs Committee, 1994) emphasised that the police in England and Wales are responsible for the investigation of crime and the CPS for conducting the prosecution. However, it also pointed out that, under section 3(2)(e) of the Prosecution of Offences Act 1985, it is the duty of the Director of the CPS to give advice on all matters relating to criminal offences. This was taken to suggest that in lengthy and complex investigations the CPS might be involved at the pre-charge stage, but only at the request of the police service. Such involvement was said to be with regard to sufficiency of evidence requirements and an evaluation of matters relating to the public interest. The memorandum states: "it is recognised that there is a fine dividing line between advice on evidence and on the legal and evidential effect of investigative techniques, on the one hand, and advice on the tactics and day-to-day handling of a police enquiry, on the other" (p. 112). Moreover, "the CPS considers it imperative that this distinction does not prevent the police from requesting and receiving full advice in cases of major crime, where evidential pitfalls may have the gravest implications for a successful prosecution." (p. 112). Nevertheless,

> This division of responsibility is of particular importance and difficulty in relation to participating informants. Organised crime groups are difficult for the police to investigate and undercover methods may be necessary. Whilst the CPS wishes to give as much advice as possible about the legal effects of police actions, it cannot enter into the area of directing operations or sanctioning criminal offences (ibid. p. 112).

The 1998 review of the Crown Prosecution Service touched upon the relationship between CPS lawyers and the new National Crime Squad (about which more below). Although far from specific the Review seemed to echo the above position (Glidewell, 1998). The review recommended that these cases be handled through central casework management structures based at the CPS headquarters and, further noted "the need for highly skilled Crown Prosecutors able to provide prompt and detailed legal advice to operational officers engaged on complex trans-national investigations. Familiarity and close liaison with foreign law enforcement and judicial authorities will also be essential" (ibid. p. 149). It was recommended that special case work groups be established in close proximity to the regional offices of National Crime Squads – it was envisaged that the protocol would require that officers of NCS and cooperating Special Caseworkers would inform the Chief Crown Prosecutor when cases were in the early stages of development. Direct approaches by NCS to casework lawyers was not precluded in the recommendations, in other words: the prosecutors were envisaged as a resource for law enforcement (ibid. p. 150).

The CPS is not in a hierarchical relationship with the police and is not understood to be a source of external monitoring of the construction of criminal cases. Crucially, the relationship between the CPS and the police service must be understood in the context of the adversarial system. The prosecution file that the CPS receives is not intended to be an objective basis for judgement over guilt or innocence. It is an unofficial aid to the prosecution's oral presentation of its case. As Field *et al.* explain (1995), because of the strongly competitive relationship between the prosecution and defence, lawyers acting on behalf of an accused person (the defence) are not prepared to reveal any aspects of their case, since it is in their interests to hold back as much information as possible from the prosecution until court proceedings thereby maximising the element of surprise. This fact, combined with the absence of investigating judges as, for example, are found in the system for criminal prosecution in the Netherlands, means that the CPS is heavily dependent on the information it gets from the police who construct the case against the suspect. Nor is the prosecution obliged to seek out exculpatory evidence. Field *et al.* (1995) also note that a central feature of the adversarial system is that there is no non-partisan party whose duty it is to establish the veracity and consistency of files pertaining to the case for the prosecution and, further, suggest that it is this that has led to a number of miscarriages of justice. A particularly tragic instance of this noted by Reiner (2000, p. 66) is the case of Stefan Kiszko who served sixteen years in prison for a murder which evidence suppressed by the police showed he could not have committed.

To date there has been no scientific empirical study that considers precisely how the police and CPS work in the context of criminal investigations pertaining to organised or other serious crime. One study of the prosecution process in England and Wales (McConville *et al.*, 1991) argued that every criminal case – embodied in a file – is "constructed". This empirical study showed how the information presented to the prosecutor is controlled and shaped by the police in such a way that the report received by the prosecutor is not an objective account of a crime, but rather is geared to producing the outcome the police wish to secure. This view provoked a sustained debate within British academic criminology regarding the appropriate balance to be reached between considerations of efficiency and the need to respect civil liberties in efforts to repress criminal conduct (Duff, 1998, p. 612-613). Although there has been some considerable research on "intelligence-led policing" in Britain (Sheptycki, 1999), which considers in almost equal proportions questions pertaining to efficiency/effectiveness and police ethics, this has not included substantive analysis of the involvement and role of the CPS in pro-active police investigations. Journalistic accounts, however, reveal that there is considerable scope for problems. In 1996, the journalist David Rose reported on a police operation conducted in 1992 which involved police entrapment. According to him a top CPS official, the director of headquarters case-work in London, gave permission for the police first to obtain and then to attempt to supply a group of suspected criminals with counterfeit American Express travellers cheques. Rose reported that the CPS official promised that if the undercover officers involved had to commit offences to trap the individuals under investigation they would be given immunity from prosecution. Further, the CPS official "made no attempt to verify any of the police claims being made about the value of this operation" and "with the customary "hands-off" CPS approach, he took what he was told at face value" (Rose, 1996, p. 203). Such action is in direct contravention of Home Office guidelines which state that:

No public informant should counsel, incite or procure the commission of a crime. When an informant gives the police information about the intention of others to commit a crime in which they intend he shall play a part, his participation should be allowed to continue only where (i) he does not actively engage in planning and committing the crime; (ii) he is intended to play only a minor role; and (iii) his participation is essential to enable the police to frustrate the principal criminals and to arrest them.... [T]he police must never commit themselves to a course which, whether to protect an informant or otherwise, will constrain them to mislead a court in any subsequent proceedings (quoted in Levi, 1995, p. 200).

What this indicates is that pro-active investigations against organised crime groups are not constrained much by external oversight. The dominant view within the criminal justice system seems to be that it is necessary to smooth the path of police investigations. As one academic observed, contemporary crime control efforts mean that "rights are increasingly bestowed upon and embedded in the system itself, enabling it to produce, distribute and use whatever knowledge is deemed necessary" (Ericson, 1994, p. 113). The CPS is to be an active agent in furthering this process. The 1998 review of the CPS noted that it was necessary for the prosecution service to be organised to cope with serious crime and that CPS lawyers would need to be able to advise the police at an early stage in the investigation process. "This will involve some CPS lawyers and caseworkers in working closely with police teams" and this "will probably also involve international cooperation". There was therefore a requirement "that there should be in the CPS both lawyers and caseworkers with particular expertise in these areas of crime". Further, "in many cases it will be important that the prosecutor should be well versed in the protection of the identity of undercover officers and in the handling of sensitive evidence and in the present law relating to advance disclosure" (Glidewell, 1998, p. 149).

## THE ROLE OF THE LORD ADVOCATE AND THE OFFICES OF THE PROCURATOR-FISCAL IN SCOTLAND

The situation with regard to the role of Scottish prosecution service requires separate treatment. As previously mentioned, the role of Procurator-fiscal in the routine management of the system of public prosecution is historically entrenched in the Scottish system. The Scottish prosecution service is headed by the Lord Advocate and his deputy, the Solicitor General, both of whom are government appointees. The Lord Advocate appoints several members of the

Scottish Bar to act as Advocates Depute, these senior law officers being known collectively as the Crown Counsel. They both prosecute in the High Court (where most serious cases are heard) and provide advice to local prosecutors about the categorisation of cases. In routine cases, proceeded against in Sheriff or District Courts, the Lord Advocate acts through the Procurators-fiscal, that is the local prosecutors, of which there are currently 49, most of whom have one or more deputies. It is usual that in cases of serious crime advice will be taken from the Crown Office in Edinburgh.

In a somewhat anodyne article pertaining to the Annual Report of the Scottish Chief Inspector of Constabulary in 1996, *The Scotsman* newspaper (Aug. 30, 1996) reported that John Boyd, the then Chief Inspector of Constabulary for Scotland, had expressed some concern regarding the establishment of an office of the National Criminal Intelligence Service (NCIS, about which more below) in Scotland. According to that newspaper:

> Government and Scottish Office ministers know the constitutional arrangements in Scotland are different from England. It's important that [NCIS] operate within the confines of the responsibilities chief constables have in Scotland and within the Scottish criminal system under the Lord Advocate.

At issue was the possibility that the opening of an NCIS office in Scotland would mean that an English chief constable might assume some jurisdiction in Scotland and, perhaps, undermine the proper supervisory role of the Lord Advocate. This is not a matter of nationalist pride. Referring to the establishment of the Scottish NCIS offices Neil Walker (1999) observed that "the decision to locate the UK-based Scottish NCIS and Customs and Excise alongside the Scottish-based Scottish Crime Squad in the same purpose built accommodation near Glasgow raises questions about their interrelationship and the adequacy of the accountability mechanisms..." (p. 111). Walker was observing the complexity of information flows within a variegated ("multi-tier") policing system and the problem of asserting a modicum of democratic control in a system that had grown increasingly complex through a process of "incremental drift". In Scottish criminal procedure responsibility for the investigation of crime rests with the police under the control and guidance of the public prosecutor who, according to Christopher Gane, "certainly enjoys greater discretionary powers than are enjoyed by his counterparts in any system in continental Europe" (Gane, 1999, p. 67).

The Scottish prosecution service, under the directorship of the Lord Advocate and his deputy the Solicitor General (both of whom are government appointees), operates under the principle of "expediency" (i.e. with levels of high discretion) and in what they consider to be the public interest. Peter Duff

(1999) characterised this as "a broad catch-all notion which allows them considerable freedom of action" (p. 118). However, while the *dirigiste* powers of the Crown Counsel are great on paper, research carried out by Moody and Tombs (1982) indicates that, like the situation south of the border, the role of the police is crucial in the supply of information to the Procurators-fiscal. Citing a raft of research pertaining to decisions to divert from prosecution, either to social work or psychiatric interventions, Peter Duff (1999, p. 119) concluded that "in essence, therefore, the police, as the main source of information for the prosecution service, do exercise a considerable measure of control over the progress of criminal cases". It seems reasonable to assume, although none in the academic research community in Scotland has yet sought to verify such an hypothesis, that the police service in Scotland has great latitude in shaping the case for the prosecution in instances what might be said to come under the rubric of "organised crime" as well and that the wide discretionary powers of the Lord Advocate and Crown Counsel are facilitative of decisions made. Wide powers of discretion and the consequent great flexibility of the system would explain how the potential jurisdictional difficulties attendant with the cross-border relations between the Scottish NCIS and NCIS in England and Wales have been elided. Operational officers at NCIS headquarters in London have indicated that cross-border police operations have been mounted between English and Scottish police and that, on occasion, such operations have been, to all intents and purposes, lead by English officers.

## THE SYSTEM OF PUBLIC PROSECUTION AND THE POLICING OF ORGANISED CRIME IN THE UK

To date no systematic academic research has been undertaken into the interface between the police service and the system of public prosecution in Great Britain as it pertains to the control of organised crime. What evidence there is suggests that, in general, criminal investigations, including (indeed, perhaps especially) "pro-active" ones, are shaped largely by the perceived needs of the police investigators. This gives rise to questions about the extent to which police investigations are governed by the rule of law. A symptom of this, as has already been mentioned, are the problems that surround the so-called rules of disclosure. Briefly, such rules require that the defence have access to all the information amassed by the investigators in the preparation of the case for the prosecution. Case law has developed in such a manner in England and Wales whereby all statements made by witnesses and suspects during the course of an investigation and all investigators" notes have to be disclosed to the defence (Levi, 1995, p. 199-200). Importantly, disclosure rules pertain to any information provided to the police by informants, including undercover police and participating and non-participating informants and it has been suggested that a significant number of cases have been withdrawn from prosecution or not proceeded against in order to protect the identity of such persons. From the point of view of a defence counsel which is in a structurally weak position in the adversarial courtroom battle, this is the best method of uncovering the use of *agents provocateurs* and one of their most potent weapons in cases of this sort. From the point of view of control agencies responsible for dealing with organised crime, however, such rules are extremely problematic. Rose (1996) suggests that 10% of such cases are withdrawn rather than risk bringing to light the identities of informants (p. 189). He also points to an unquantified number of "cracked trials" where proceedings have been discontinued rather than risk the consequences of such disclosure. The factually guilty have walked free as a result of the disclosure rules. At the same time, rare instances of unethical or unscrupulous law-enforcement action have made it clear that, in the absence of any non-partisan external review of the construction of the case for the prosecution, defence lawyers labour against a potentially oppressive juggernaut. This would suggests that there is a need to clarify the scope of acceptable investigative methods in cases of "organised crime" (Ashworth, 1994, p. 96) and to improve the system of oversight for police operations of this type (Saunders, 1997, 1080-84). The CPS in England and Wales and the Crown Counsel in Scotland might be the institutions through which the latter can be achieved, and a more robust Code of Practice "for all to see" (as recommended by Ashworth) could go some way to achieving the former. However, what is required most are sustained empirical investigations into the backstage areas where police and public prosecutors conduct their strategy sessions since legal accountability is inevitably limited by the low visibility and high discretion of investigative work (cf. Reiner, 1997, p. 1027). This is especially true of the infrastructure for policing "high level", "serious", or "organised" crime in Great Britain.

What is certain is that the system of criminal justice in Britain is rather different from her near neighbours on the continent. In England and Wales, case construction has historically been the province of the police and the introduction of the CPS has only marginally changed this. In no sense does the CPS direct the conduct of criminal investigations. In Scotland the historical position is different. There the tradition is more akin to the continental model. However, it does seem that police have become more directive of investigations and this seems especially likely in the case of pro-active police investigations that are associated with organised crime control. The implication of this is that, when European criminal justice agents cooperate with their counterparts in Britain in operational matters relating to the investigation of organised crime, they are likely to find themselves dealing, in the first instance with police officers and only latterly with officials from the Crown Prosecution Service. Technically cross-border operational police activity requires authorisation from the UK Central Authority based in the Home Office.

## ORGANISATIONAL CHANGE IN UK LAW ENFORCEMENT WITH RESPECT TO POLICY CONSIDERATIONS REGARDING ORGANISED CRIME

As was mentioned in the opening sections, the system of policing in Great Britain established in the first part of the nineteenth century was very parochial and it was only over time that it gained a modicum of centralised authority. Indeed, in the 1960s it was clear that policing in most of the country was largely a matter of local concern and, with 125 separate constabularies in England and Wales, it seemed indisputable that there was a need to rationalise the system. The Royal Commission report of 1962 did not recommend anything more than amalgamations of police forces, so that by the 1970s that number had been reduced to the present 43 forces of England and Wales, the 8 forces in Scotland and the RUC in Northern Ireland. It is seldom recalled that there was a minority report published alongside the official report of the Willink Commission, penned by one Dr Arthur Goodhart, which argued for a national police system. The minority report suggested that liaison across force boundaries could not be as effective as a command relationship. It was also noted that detective officers were frequently reluctant to share information about active criminals when such privileged knowledge, and the related potential for making "good arrests", might be instrumental in achieving promotion. However, the Royal Commission Report that was put together under the auspices of Sir Henry Willink did not pursue this. It was deemed politically infeasible. Ben Whitacker observed at the time:

> It is a debatable point whether it is the duty of a Royal Commission to advocate only what is politically possible, or whether it should advance an ideal solution even though it believes it is unattainable. Dr. Goodhart obviously subscribes to the latter view. Perhaps he was conscious of the development of organized crime in his home country of America; perhaps he was less blinkered by tradition . . . but the other members of the Willink Commission who signed the majority report, in deciding to work from the old rather than to build a new system, were not just being British or preoccupied by history. They may have been canny enough to realise that, if they compromised, some very necessary reforms would make their way into a Police Bill" (Whitacker, 1964, p. 82)

Compromise characterises the development of the modern police in Britain from its inception. We must not forget that Peel established the original "new" police in the face of sustained political opposition – fear of a centralised police establishment loomed large in this and such sentiments are still extant, if muted. The changes in the police system during the period of the 1960-70s were conditioned by the same sort of pragmatism that Peel exhibited. As was mentioned at the beginning of this report, what was feasible then was a system of regional crime squads superimposed on top of the territorially based police constabularies. The regional crime squads provided the infrastructure for inter-force criminal investigations until the 1990s when the National Criminal Intelligence Service (about which more below) came into being. The absence of a single national police force means that there is a complicated system of policing that bares some considerable attention. But before outlining the various institutions that comprise the system as a whole it would do to describe the system of the political and legal accountability of the police in Great Britain.

Debates about the governance of the police in the UK have tended to focus on the "tripartite arrangement for police accountability" which was most clearly formulated in the Police Act (1964) (Reiner, 1985) and which underwent some marginal adjustments as a result of the Police and Magistrates' Courts Act (1994) (Jones and Newburn, 1995; 1997). The broad outline of this constitutional arrangement is clear enough; three actors undertake the system of governance for the police: local government (through the Police Authorities), central government (through the Home Office) and the Chief Constables. This is so for all public police in Great Britain with the exception of the Metropolitan Police where the source of external accountability is parliament, through the office of the Home Secretary, there being no police authority for London. This peculiarity of the Metropolitan Police's accountability structure has been facilitative of its quasi-national role during earlier periods of British police history. At the present juncture it is seen as something of an anomaly and a police authority for London may be in place in the not too distant future. This would give London something like the same tripartite structure as prevails in the rest of the country.[5] However, the degree to which this structure delivers accountability to local communities is moot. This is because the tripartite relationship is girded with the "doctrine of constabulary independence". The principle holds that the police are ultimately accountable to the law itself and, in operational matters, the chief constable is the guiding authority. This doctrine has been upheld in case law (*Fisher vs Oldham Corporation, 1930*; *R vs Metropolitan Police Commissioner ex parte Blackburn*, 1968). In the former case it was ruled that there was no "master-servant" relationship between the authority and the chief constable and that, because constables have their legal authority conferred directly upon them, they are not subject to the directions or control of their paymasters. In the latter case it was held that the authority of the office is constable "is original, not delegated and is exercised at his own discretion, by virtue of his office" (quoted in Sheptycki, 1991, p. 181). Further, Lord Denning held that a chief constable

> is not a servant of anyone save the law itself. No minister of the Crown can tell him that he must, or must not, keep observation on this place of that; or that he must, or must not, prosecute this man or that one. Nor can any police authority tell him so. The responsibility for law enforcement lies on him. He is answerable to the law and the law alone (ibid. p. 214).

This has led to the observation that the Chief Constables of the 43 police forces of England and Wales "claim both a legal and a moral mandate to act according to their consciences" (Reiner, 1989, p. 208-09; see also Reiner, 1991). At the same time, since the Home Office is the more significant paymaster, and since Her Majesty's Inspectorate of Constabulary (HMI) undertakes efficiency inspections that may negatively impact on budget allocations, the guiding hand of central government on the actions of chief constables is significant. In their analysis of the Police and Magistrates Courts Act (1994), Jones and Newburn argue, somewhat contradictorily, that "a major shift in the tripartite structure has yet to occur", but also that the position of Chief Constables "has been strengthened" and, further, that operational and policy decisions are conditioned in important ways by "new managerialism" (1997, pp. 222-223). While they remained hopeful that local authorities would learn to assert what power they have, the changes brought about as a result of the 1994 Act "are clearly intended to tip the balance further towards central control" (1995, p. 458). In commenting on the Police Act (1996) (which consolidated the Police Act (1964); the Police and Criminal Evidence Act (1984) Part IX; and the Police and Magistrates Courts Act (1994)), Robert Reiner argued that the centralising trend had become clear (1997, p. 1030) even though it was "officially represented by the government itself as doing precisely the opposite" (ibid., p. 1032). The main focus of attention in these debates was on the effects of the new managerialism and the nexus of control over the constabularies, right down to the level of basic command units, that was afforded by its associated auditing procedures. One feature of the new managerialism is the devolution of budgets giving local commanders a degree of fiscal control and responsibility that they historically never had. At the same time, the development of "intelligence-led policing" (Sheptycki, 1999), with its focus on the consolidation and analysis of "criminal intelligence" has been a palpable centralising force. There is thus a paradoxical development whereby policing is being perceptibly centralised while at the same time responsibility is being devolved down to the local level.

527

In light of the above, it is especially interesting to examine the infrastructure for policing organised and serious crime that have arisen in the recent past. Despite, or perhaps because of, the fragmentation of the British police, there is a requirement for some level of police service provision at the national level. This has been achieved in the first instance by the development of national intelligence, collation and dissemination bodies and, with less fanfare, the development of a national operational capability. The police organisations that achieve this are firstly the National Criminal Intelligence Service (NCIS) which was formed to coordinate national intelligence gathering. Secondly, there are three coordinating bodies within Special Branch: the National Joint Unit, the European Liaison Section and the National Ports Unit. Additionally, there is one new national policing body with an operational role, the National Crime Squad (NCS), established in April 1998. Also, it should not escape mention that various parts of the security service have also been drafted into the "fight against organised crime".

**The establishment of the National Criminal Intelligence Service**

Prior to the inception of NCIS in 1992 national intelligence coordination had been achieved through the *ad hoc* establishment of several small initiatives mainly based within the headquarters of the Metropolitan Police at New Scotland Yard. The quasi-national role of the Metropolitan Police is an historical one stemming partly from its particular constitutional position. It also held this *de facto* national role because, in the absence of central funding or a national police organisation, the London Met, by far the largest force in the UK, was best able to meet the cost. Recent earlier initiatives include the National Drugs Intelligence Unit, the Regional Criminal Intelligence Offices, the National Football Intelligence Unit, the National Office for the Suppression of Counterfeit Currency, the Public Sector Corruption Index, the Paedophile Index, and elements of the Research Unit of the Stolen Vehicle Squad and Criminal Intelligence Branch. New Scotland Yard also housed the ICPO-Interpol NCB for the UK. The presence of these national units within the "Met" contributed much to the international reputation of New Scotland Yard, but also fuelled provincial resentment of the pre-eminence of London on as the global conduit for British policing communications and, arguably, contributed to an ignorance of transnational police issues among some of the provincial police forces. On the other hand, some constabularies with pressing needs, for example Kent, developed cross-border policing arrangements of their own because the "Metropolitan conduit" was unsuitable for their needs (Sheptycki, 1998).

As has been explained, perceptions of the need for a national policing capability for Britain dates back at least to the 1960s. This was given more impetus during the 1970s when concerns about terrorism in Europe began to take hold leading to the constitution of the TREVI group (Anderson, *et al*, 1995). The publication of a report by the Home Affairs Committee (Home Affairs Committee 1990) persuaded the then Home Secretary, Douglas Hurd, to begin the process which eventually led to the establishment of the National Criminal Intelligence Service (NCIS). The establishment of NCIS also included the establishment of five regional offices based upon the former Regional Criminal Intelligence Offices, plus one office for the whole of Scotland. It currently has about 590 staff, 300 of whom work at the headquarters in London (NCIS 1999, p. 43).[6] About 270 of NCIS staff are police officers, approximately 50 are officers from HM Customs and Excise Service and approximately 260 are Home Office, civil and support staff, the most important of which are the tactical and strategic crime analysts. NCIS headquarters also houses the financial intelligence unit which coordinates the handling of suspicious transactions reports (Sheptycki, 2000). Most of the NCIS staff are on temporary secondment from their parent organisations. In view of its international role NCIS is the base of the UK Europol Liaison Officers and Interpol and will house the Schengen Information System (SIS) when the UK opts into the treaty. Recently NCIS has worked with the Security Service (MI5) following governmental directives in which the latter was given a role in the fight against terrorism and organised crime. Although this is not mentioned in NCIS annual reports it is thought that two MI5 personnel are presently posted to NCIS headquarters (personal communication to author). The accompanying organogram shows the structure of NCIS as it was in 1998, but it should be pointed out that the institution is in a perpetual state of flux and its internal organisation is subject to almost constant revision. During a visit to NCIS one manager showed me a breakdown of the personnel under his supervision using an office chart to illustrate his points. He did so after pointing out that the three week old chart was already out of date.[7]

In view of the debates about accountability in policing it would do to mention the establishment of the Service Authority for the NCIS, which was established on 1 April 1998 and reported for the first time in 1999. The Service Authority was established as a requirement of Section 5 of the Police Act (1997), which charged it with "providing strategic direction and accountability to NCIS as well as ensuring that the organisation runs efficiently". In order to provide this, "the Authority and the Home Secretary agree a series of service objectives each year and monitor the performance of NCIS against them" (NCIS, 1999, p. 6). The objectives for its first year of operation were listed in a series of appendixes to the annual report, they were:
(1) To improve the quality of criminal intelligence available to combat serious and organised crime within the United Kingdom;

(2) To improve the quality of criminal intelligence available to overseas about criminals engaged in serious and organised transnational crime which impacts on the United Kingdom;

(3) To maintain the focus of the organisation in its work in combating the activities of major criminals and their organisations;

(4) To enhance the gathering and coordination of overseas intelligence by NCIS;

(5) To provide strategic intelligence assessments on serious and organised crime impacting upon the interests of the United Kingdom;

(6) To provide quality criminal intelligence on specialist areas of criminal activity;

(7) To provide services to operational teams and enhance the coordination and development of criminal intelligence;

(8) To provide corporate support to enhance the coordination and development of criminal intelligence.

In seeking to audit the services provided by NCIS the Service Authority noted that it "was mindful of the difficulties associated with developing meaningful ways of measuring performance in the area of intelligence" (NCIS, 1999, p. 6). While "not an exact science" it was thought that the figures cited demonstrated "a significant and genuine improvement in NCIS's output for the year 1998-99" (ibid. p. 6). For example, it was noted that "the Authority asked NCIS to achieve a 5% increase in the number of intelligence reports disseminated that fall within the highest two levels of the quality matrix" [objective 1] and that "this target was exceeded" (ibid. p. 6). It seems clear that the Service Authority is not so much a body for political or even legal accountability; rather it was established to provide "accountability". The term accountability is used deliberately. The Service Authority ostensibly performs an auditing function intended to assess efficiency and effectiveness, but the degree to which either efficiency or effectiveness can be gauged by reference to opaque measurements such as those relating to object 1 cited above is questionable. It was also reported in this document that "five full Authority meetings were held during the year, including the Annual meeting, which took place in June. All of these meetings were open to the public, with exempt or confidential issues being dealt with at the close of the public session" (ibid., p 7). The establishment of the Service Authorities for the NCIS and NCS could thus be characterised as a further development of what Rod Morgan (1989) conceptualised as "legitimating the doctrine of policing by consent". The Service Authorities draw on the constabulary Police Authorities for civilian representation at the national level. Meetings of local police consultative committees were described by Morgan in an earlier period as "cosy ritualistic affairs that achieve little practically and have no discernible impact on what the police do" (Morgan, 1989, p. 232). In view of the historic resistance to the idea of a centrally controlled police system in the United Kingdom, the low visibility afforded by the Service Authority oversight could be viewed as a crucial element for the preservation of the image of policing by consent. The preservation of this image in the contemporary period is being undertaken in the context of a gradually emerging national police system where the mechanisms for establishing and maintaining police accountability to the civilian population are becoming increasingly attenuated and where accountability is made with reference to criteria which are themselves increasingly opaque. Be that as it may, the practical point to be established in this report is that NCIS does act as a point from which the British police can communicate criminal intelligence nationally and internationally.

## Special Branch and international police communications

Special Branch also provides a national policing infrastructure for the United Kingdom as a whole, and one with an established pedigree (Bunyan, 1976). Importantly the SB also has a capability to communicate internationally. Although it has historically been limited to the tasks associated with policing terrorism and related issues, in view of the perceived fusion of terrorism and organised crime (and the fact the Europol has competence in these matters) the SB belongs within the ambit of consideration in this report. Special Branch is organised at the constabulary level and is accountable within the tripartite structure discussed above as is any other specialist unit within the police service. Having said that, there are three units within the Special Branch structure which coordinate activity at the national level. These are the National Joint Unit, the National Ports Office and the European Liaison Section. The precise role of the National Joint Unit, based at New Scotland Yard, is somewhat obscure. The following facts are in the public domain (Statewatch 1991 Vol. 1 No. 5). Each of the fifty-two constabularies within the United Kingdom (*nota bene*) has its own Special Branch section, and it is the role of the seventeen staff of the National Joint Unit to coordinate the intelligence activities of these sections. It maintains a central database of records, and provides advice to the Constabularies relating to the prevention of terrorism. In the event of an application for exclusion order made under this act, it is this unit which prepares the casework for submission to the Secretary of State.

The National Ports Office, based at Heathrow Airport, was set up in 1968 to coordinate anti-terrorist liaison between the fifty-one police forces involved in the National Ports Scheme. It is concerned with managing and collating statistics on such matters as passenger arrests, passenger movements, etc., but it also has a role coordinating Special Branch activities at ports under the Prevention of Terrorism Acts. It should be emphasised that Special Branch officers are, along with Customs and Immigration service, responsible for routine control at ports of entry into the United Kingdom as a whole. The SB NPO maintains a database on wanted persons and children sought under the Hague Convention. Also included within the Special Branch structure, although not part of the NJU, is the Trevi founded European Liaison Section (ELS) based within the Metropolitan Police at New Scotland Yard. This unit, staffed by multi-lingual personnel, has a national remit in that it undertakes on behalf of the constabulary Special Branches the international contact that Interpol was forbidden from dealing with by virtue of its constitution. The Metropolitan Police Special Branch has other national roles in coordinating the activities of the constabulary Special Branches, undertaking financial investigations and maintaining the Animal Rights National Index (ARNI). Information on any of the SB databases is disseminated on a "need to know basis" only.

An illustration of the process of incremental drift is that the United Kingdom has been slowly moving towards an aggregated national policing system. As noted above, the NCIS was established in 1992 and it was partly an amalgam of earlier national intelligence units existing within the London Metropolitan Police. The National Football Intelligence Unit (NFIU) was a high profile acquisition for the new agency, due to the significant amount of media attention being paid to the issue of "football hooliganism". More recently a National Public Order Intelligence Unit (NPOIU) has been established to coordinate the policing of all public order situations nationally. Interestingly, the NCIS refused the invitation to house this new unit on the grounds that its terms of reference did not, strictly speaking, relate to *criminal* intelligence. The new unit had to be housed somewhere and the Metropolitan Police SB was considered the only other likely place. At present the NCIS deals with football hooliganism and the newly established NPOIU deals with all other types of "non-sporting related hooliganism". Within these arrangements it is not clear who would lay claim to "cricket hooliganism" should that sport begin to create a significant public order problem.

**The National Crime Squad and international police communications**

The newest addition to the panoply of police agencies in Britain is the National Crime Squad. This agency officially came into being on 1 April 1998 and was established through an amalgamation of the six previously existing regional crime squads of England and Wales. Like the NCIS, it is accountable to a Service Authority – of which nine members are elected members from local

Police Authorities nominated by the Association of Police Authorities, three are Chief Constables and the remainder are Home Office appointees.[8] Again like NCIS, the National Crime Squad works to objectives set by the Service Authority, the most important of which are with regard to the total number of arrests affected by NCS operations and, the number of "disruptions" of criminal networks. In both instances, NCS is to target "core nominals", that is: serious offenders. The NCS is able to draw on the intelligence capabilities of the NCIS, the Scottish Crime Squad and the NCIS office in Scotland as well as the security and intelligence agencies. It inherited the staff, premises, equipment and workload of the previous RCS system and, as of 1999 was staffed by 1,450 police officers seconded from police forces in England and Wales plus 380 civilian support staff. It has its own intelligence and surveillance capabilities and can run pro-active police investigations using its own personnel. What the NCS offers that NCIS cannot, is the operational power of arrest. The National Crime Squad targets criminal organisations committing serious or organised crime which transcends national and international boundaries. Although none of the literature currently available on the NCS indicates that it engages in international communications, it should be assumed that this is the case.

**The Security Services and Organised Crime**

Lastly, it should be mentioned that in 1994 the House of Commons Intelligence and Security Committee concluded in 1995 that "the Security Service can bring a distinct package of skills to this arena (intelligence acquisition, processing, assessment and exploitation)" and, further that "its approach would be characterised by long-term investigation and analysis aimed at gaining a strategic advantage over organised crime threats" (King, 1995, p. 3). Several years earlier the Home Affairs Committee had inquired into the accountability of the Security Service (Home Affairs Committee, 1992). At that time the Home Secretary stated that "the holder of his office had always been accountable for the Security Service to the House" (Parliament). However, "it had never been the practice to answer questions about the operation of the Security Service" and that "he did not believe that it would be right to make the Security Service accountable to a Select Committee of this House" (p. v). After extensive examination of accountability mechanisms elsewhere the committee concluded that:

> The Home Secretary raised the bogy of a secret service that was not secret. The Committee wants no such thing. The work done by the Security Service is delicate, and much of it is necessarily of the highest

533

confidentiality. We do no believe that there is any general right or need to know what the service does on a day-to-day basis. But we do believe that *establishing a form of parliamentary scrutiny of the service would meet an important public interest and help to protect against any possible future abuse of power*" (p. xi, emphasis in original).

On 14 October 1996 new legislation extended the Security Services statutory remit to include supporting the law enforcement agencies in work on serious crime. This change reflected the government's intention to step up action in this field. It was reported that the Service's work in this area was to be financed from existing resources – perhaps indicating some diminution of work in the more traditional areas of the Security Service's remit (terrorism, subversion and related matters). It is of interest to note that the government provided NCIS with a budget in the region of £25 million, for the establishment of a headquarters in 1992, which caused them to rent office accommodation within an industrial estate in Lambeth. In 1999, it was revealed that, at the same time as NCIS was establishing its headquarters, MI6 was provided with purpose-built accommodation less than 400 yards away at a cost of £80 million, while across the river MI5 spent more than £200 million, well over three times the original estimate, refurbishing Thames House, its new headquarters (Norton-Taylor, 1999).

The 1996 legislation left primary responsibility for work in the organised crime area with the police, but fostered closer working ties between them (especially NCIS) and the Security Service. Under the legislation the Security Service is tasked to take on crime-related investigations on a case-by-case basis where it is agreed that its particular skills, knowledge or capabilities are likely to help the investigation (Security Service Booklet, 1998, p. 18). The law of disclosure as contained in the Criminal Procedure and Investigations Act (1996) is particularly relevant here. The Security Services gave evidence at nine trials between 1992 and 1998 (ibid. p. 26) all of which led to convictions. The duty of prosecutors to make material available to the defence in criminal cases is set out in the 1996 Act, which recognises that the duty of disclosure must also accommodate the need to protect sensitive information, the disclosure of which could damage those aspects of the public interest relating to national security. Intelligence gathered by these services in the context of investigations under the heading of organised crime is also potential evidence for the courts. Where an investigation leads to a prosecution the defence must be provided with material as required by the 1996 Act. In such instances it is Prosecuting Counsel who reviews the records of the security service and advises which are disclosable. If it is thought that disclosure would cause damage to the public interest (for example by compromising the identity of an agent or a sensitive investigative technique) the prosecutor may, having received the permission of the Home Secretary to do so, apply to a judge so that the material may be withheld under a claim of public interest immunity (PII).

It is evident that there is a degree of convergence between policing and security service work around the issue of organised crime. The result is that the Security Service has become open to more scrutiny than it has ever been, while certain aspects of police investigation have become more opaque. There are a considerable number of agencies empowered to undertake intrusive methods of investigation, surveillance and information gathering pertaining to organised or serious crime. Further, all of the abovementioned agencies have the capacity to communicate sensitive information both nationally and transnationally. Criminal intelligence channels are multiple. The result is that it is very difficult, if not impossible, to depict the investigative, surveillance and communications capacity of the policing infrastructure in Great Britain with an organogram. Simple organisational models of the paths of communications within and between these institutions belie the complexity of the policing complex that has been built up in the United Kingdom. But most transnational policing work is not at the high level that the Security Service or even the Special Branch, NCS or NCIS, operates.

## RULES AND PROCEDURES GOVERNING INTERNATIONAL POLICE COMMUNICATIONS

The fragmented and territorially based system of British Policing has had particular ramifications for the development of its transnational cooperation. As demands in this area grew, and the limitations of the Interpol system (Sheptycki, 1995) came to light, the functional needs obliged police to establish ad hoc structures to cater for increasing European police cooperation. The earliest examples of these include the European Association of Airport and Seaport Police (EAASP) set up in 1967, the appointment of a Kent County Constabulary European Liaison Officer in 1968 and the inauguration of the Cross Channel Intelligence Conference (CCIC) in 1970 (Sheptycki, 1998). In 1975, and again owing to problems within Interpol, the Metropolitan Police established an international liaison bureau for terrorist matters within Special Branch. This coincided with the setting up of the Trevi group, which took over the unit as the ELS. Subsequently the Single European Act and the Channel Tunnel prompted the establishment of ACPO's International Affairs Advisory Committee, the ACPO European Unit and the network of European Liaison Officers. In Kent at this time what had been a part-time European Liaison Officer post grew into a full-time European liaison unit with six personnel. The reader can thus appreciate the great profusion of arrangements for routine cross-border policing.

What rules govern how the British Police Service should cooperate with its colleagues abroad? This issue was clarified by Home Office Consolidated Circular 17/1989, which stipulated how contact with police forces in other countries were to be undertaken (Home Office 1989). Police officers wishing to initiate enquiries abroad were told that "As a general rule official channels, i.e. the ICPO-Interpol system, should be used". This circular paid little heed to the wide range of other means of communication available to the police in the UK. Home Office circular 17/89 was in effect a form of general advice and did not constitute a codified system of rules for transnational police contact. There are several reasons for this. In the first instance Interpol is perceived by local UK police constabularies as an inefficient conduit for communication. In higher policing circles there is some perception that the Interpol communications system may be too insecure to be used in certain cases of serious crime. (Sheptycki, 1998; also Gill, 2000).

This is certainly the case with regard to matters involving "national security". Deficiencies in the Interpol system left operational police officers with little alternative in the majority of cases but to communicate abroad as best they could. In relation to this, the most preferred route is contact via an officer abroad known personally to the requesting officer. There is a kind of professional *esprit de corps* among police officers, each having a common understanding of others' problems and purposes, and each wishing to be regarded as efficient and reliable. The historical development of the Kent County Constabulary's ELU is an example of this. In that territorial locale informal transnational communications grew in volume and importance until it was possible to speak of formalised informal communication (Sheptycki, 1999).

Historically then, poor communications between the police and the Home Office left the police to forge ahead and in the absence of government control the police made their own arrangements. There may be dangers in such a system, as Interpol has been wont to point out, and that is why transnational communications emanating from the KCC have not elided the formal and centralised channels altogether. This is considered "good practice" if only to avoid such obvious pitfalls as the possibility of two policing agencies working on the same case and inadvertently jeopardising each other's missions. Similarly, the ELU in Kent has always recognised that information held by the police in one country could be invaluable to a police service in another, and a central authority, with its own databanks, could have a very useful coordinating role. Lastly, it should be pointed out that since some, although certainly by no means all, transnational police communications result in law enforcement action, there has always been a necessity to liaise with the public prosecutor at crucial stages of such operations and this has also been documented

(Sheptycki, 1998).

The historical landmark of Home Office Circular 17/89 advised the use of the Interpol network, but the Home Office memorandum to the Home Affairs Select Committee on practical police cooperation in Europe put a slightly different interpretation on this:

(Interpol) provides a channel of communication between police forces which they may use *if they wish*. (emphasis added – Home Affairs Committee 1990: 4)

In recognition of recent developments in Europe, the Home Office circulated in the summer of 1995 a rewritten draft of Circular 17/89. Entitled "Home Office Circular xx/95: International Police Enquiries and Operations Overseas", this circular was intended to advise police officers and again recommended that "Interpol is the principal channel of communication between police forces throughout the world" but it did go some way to recognise the complexity of the arrangements that had evolved. For example, officers making drugs enquiries were advised to contact NCIS for a notification to be sent to the local drugs liaison officer (DLO), and officers conducting operations abroad were advised to contact the Foreign Office and Commonwealth Office. The draft circular recognises the existence of "special arrangements", such as Kent's ELU and Special Branch's ELS, as well as the existence of "Representatives of foreign law enforcement agencies (based) in the United Kingdom" who "occasionally make requests for assistance directly to forces by-passing the UK NCB." Acknowledging the existence of "long-standing informal agreements" that may result in a direct request for assistance, officers are advised that "the foreign officer or agency should be encouraged to liaise with the UK NCB." While acknowledging that there are multiple channels for communicating with police forces abroad (it identified six possible avenues of communication), the circular stated that "the UK NCB [located at NCIS] initiates all international police enquiries on behalf of all UK police forces and is the focal point for receiving enquiries in the United Kingdom from foreign law enforcement agencies." It is crucial to note that foreign enquiries requiring mutual legal assistance in criminal matters are ultimately directed through both Interpol and Dept. C2 at the Home Office.

Thus there is evidence of tendencies towards centralisation and decentralisation of police communications and structures in the UK and these are happening simultaneously. A sociological explanation for this might be that the new information and communications technologies tend to give rise to decentralisation, while at the same time the national-state attempts to (re)establish its sovereign authority in the face of 'Europeanisation' – or even more broadly 'globalisation'. Both tendencies are operating at the same time producing contradictory, although not necessarily inharmonious, effects. While the system of multiple channels for transnational communication in matters of day-to-day operational policing that has evolved cannot be stifled, it seems clear that any such communication that involves the transfer of evidence or other aspects of legal proceedings do get routed through this official conduit, even if such communications are also supplemented via informal channels.

Generally speaking, the UK government and police services have been keen to integrate into the systems of communication and data exchange for police cooperation at the European level. On March 12, 1999 the UK announced that it intended to apply to 'opt-in' to parts of the Schengen *acquis* (in the Treaty of European Union) and parts of the Free Movement Chapter (Title IV, Visas, Asylum, Immigration in the Treaty Establishing the European Communities) (House of Lords, 1999, p. 47). UK participation in the law enforcement and judicial cooperation elements of Schengen was approved by EU Justice & Home Affairs Ministers in May 2000. However, the UK only opted for those parts pertaining to the Schengen Information System (SIS), Police Cooperation, Drugs, and Judicial Cooperation and not for those parts pertaining to external/internal frontiers or visas. The official position was that the maintenance of strong frontier controls was considered the most effective way to control immigration. This supposition rested on the particularities of the UK's 'island geography'. As of this writing plans to implement Schengen in the UK were being drawn up. Although some legislation will be required, implementation of most of the provisions can be accomplished using administrative procedures.

With regard to Europol, the UK ratified the Convention which entered into force on October 1998. Europol itself was set to become 'operational' with its own 'joint investigative teams' within a year of that date. In this context 'operational' means actions such as information exchange, and intelligence analysis, but it also includes the possibility to undertake 'executive actions' (where specific powers have been granted by national law) such as surveillance, searches and arrests and even 'restricted executive powers' such as the interviewing of suspects (Statewatch, Vol. 10 No. 2, p. 18). The Europol Annual Report 1999, the most recent available as of this writing, reported that the United Kingdom was a substantive participant in one operation during the previous twelve months. It is perhaps significant this operation (Operation 'Samot') was not initiated by UK officers. It began when "Dutch law enforcement authorities started an investigation into an Iraqi organised crime group involved in the trafficking of human beings" (Europol Annual Report, 1999, p. 21). According to this report "the initial results of the investigations revealed that the organisation was arranging several trips of illegal immigrants from the Netherlands via Belgium and France to the United Kingdom" (p. 22).

The report continues:

"At the beginning of April 1999 an operational meeting was organised through Europol's liaison network between representatives of the Netherlands and the United Kingdom and information was exchanged with Belgium and France. As a result, the main target was arrested in the United Kingdom in mid April 1999. Subsequently, further information was exchanged between the investigating units through the Europol liaison network. Statements and additional evidence led to the arrest in May 1999 of nine members of the organisation in the Netherlands and two other members in the United Kingdom and France" (*ibid.* p. 22).

The United Kingdom was also mentioned in connection with 'Operation 'Page', but in this instance UK participation was much more limited as the focus of the investigation (of a criminal group involved in the smuggling of 'ecstasy') was on an Italian 'connection'. Some caution should be used when interpreting information disseminated in this report since it is obviously selected in order to show the 'best face' of the organisation. Nevertheless, it cannot escape mention that, of the six 'operations' reported, only one contained a substantial UK input, whereas the others showed a considerable effort by (in descending order of mention) Dutch, German, Belgian, Italian, French, Spanish and other European countries. This may be indicative of less active participation by UK police agents in Europol actions but, given the long history of police cooperation in joint task forces (Sheptycki, 1997; Sheptycki, 1998) it may be fair to suggest that the intensity of cooperation through Europol will increase over time.

The UK government has also ratified the convention relating to the operation of the Customs Information System, as of this writing one further ratification is needed in order for the Convention to come into force provisionally among eight Member States. With regard to EURODAC, the Home Office has noted that "the legal basis for [EURODAC has not] been agreed", but the Home Secretary stated on March 12, 1999 that the UK would seek to participate in all asylum measures to be adopted by the Community indicating an in-principle agreement that these control measures require a European level capability.

Lastly, with regard to Eurojust, the fledgling European Union public prosecution system, the UK's position has also been one of active, although perhaps somewhat distanced, participation. Initial meetings of the European Judicial Network, which began in 1998, were attended by six UK officials; two from the Home Office, two from the NCIS, and one each from the Her Majesty's Customs and Excise (HMCE) and the Crown Prosecution Service (CPS) (Statewatch, Vol. 10 No. 3/4, p. 29). A former Chief Crown Prosecutor for Sussex, Mike Kennedy was appointed the first British representative to Eurojust in early 2001 (*The Daily Telegraph*, March 20, 2001). At the time some British politicians expressed fears that the new institution was a 'legal Trojan horse' which would lead to the eventual creation of a centralised European justice department. On his appointment Kennedy explained that Eurojust would be a centralised information exchange for national prosecutors pursuing criminals in foreign jurisdictions. According to his view, rather than being the prototype for a European prosecutor, Eurojust would provide "an effective network of contacts between national prosecuting and investigating bodies, [thus] there will be no need for a prosecuting organisation with cross-border powers" (ibid.). Further, "Eurojust is not about putting people behind bars, it is for local prosecuting agencies to do that. We will help their investigation go effectively. It will be a persuasive authority. We won't have power, for example, to direct the French gendarmerie" (ibid.). Kennedy's statements, it may be presumed, are broadly reflective of official UK policy. On this view the UK is actively committed to Eurojust as an advisory and facilitative body.

In sum, British participation in international cooperation efforts against transnational organised crime is a matter of some considerable complexity. However, at every level of operations and intelligence gathering, from that of the local constabulary to the level of National Security, (including, it must be added, the quasi-police roles of the Immigration Service and the Customs Service) the British police complex has actively sought to network with European counterparts and beyond. At the level of formal policy the British government has been keen to foster such developments and has rarely, if ever, done anything to impede the policing capability. When it comes to organised crime, there seems to be agreement that strong measures are needed. The sense of mission with regard to this type of crime permeates the entire architecture of the police complex as well as the relevant policy circles in the UK government.

This brings us back to the discussion of the definition of 'organised crime' discussed in a previous section. What was shown there is that 'organised crime' in the UK is predominantly understood in terms of 'rounding up the usual suspects' (Gill, 2000). What tends to be left out of this discussion are types of crime described as 'white-collar', 'economic' or 'financial' crime. Given the changes evident in UK policing that are predicated on the assumptions built into the definition of the term 'organised crime', this leaves us with the question: how to we measure the effectiveness of law enforcement measures against it?

## EVALUATING LAW ENFORCEMENT EFFECTIVENESS AGAINST ORGANISED CRIME

Examining press-releases issued by the National Crime Squad for the period of October 1998 is revealing of what counts as success in police missions against organised crime.

**1 Oct. 1998**   **Motorcyclist drug dealer awaits sentence**
This case pertains to a man found in possession of weapons, ammunition and a large quantity of cannabis in April of 1998. The man was arrested by officers from NCS supported by the Dorset Tactical Firearms Unit

**15 Oct. 1998**   **Multi-million pound securities theft thwarted**
This case pertains to the arrest of two men believed to have been plotting to steal blank bankers cheques. One of the men arrested was an employee of the bank in question

**16 Oct. 1998**   **Contraband Cigarettes Seized**
Manchester NCS, together with Customs officials arrested 3 men and recovered 2 ½ million smuggled cigarettes

**28 Oct. 1998**   **Armed Robbery Foiled by Police**
Two men were arrested by NCS officers and a tactical firearms unit of the Greater Manchester Police. A third man escaped. One loaded shotgun was recovered. It was believed that the men had planned to intercept cash in transit.

**29 Oct. 1998**   **NCS trace man wanted for murder in Coventry**
Two men wanted in breach of bail in connections with drug trafficking offences were arrested by NCS officers. One of these individuals was wanted on a charge of Murder of a man on 26 March, 1998

**30 Oct. 1998**   **Twelve sentenced for exporting drugs and money**
Eleven men and one woman were arrested in connection with the export of amphetamine and MDMA (ecstasy) to Australia and charged with related money laundering offences. Nearly 200 cash transfers, with a total cash value of nearly £1 million were identified. This was a joint operation by the NCS and the National Investigation Service of HM Customs and Excise.

What these press-release stories[10] reveal is the presentation of a close cooperative relationship between the NCS and other elements of the British policing system; local firearms units, and customs in particular. The message crafted for media representation is that, although the police complex appears fragmented on paper, this does not impede multi-agency action. This is probably not all imagery. The police system in Britain, unlike for example the federal system of the USA, is territorial at its base and most police personnel working in national agencies are on temporary secondment (for a period of up to five years) from parent forces. NCIS and NCS do have core staff of there own – particularly civilian staff, which in the case of NCIS can be quite important since many of these people undertake crime analysis work and thus shape the priorities of the agency in important ways. But over all, despite the national agencies small core staffing, policing remains based in the local constabularies. Indeed, there has even been a periodic exchange of personnel between the Security Services and the police service (at least from Special Branch) (Bunyan, 1976, p. 154). NCIS, is principally staffed by police officers, but agents from Her Majesty's Immigration Service and also from Customs and Excise make up a growing proportion of the staff there. This movement of personnel between agencies fosters informal communication networks within the control system, the capacity of which is immeasurable.[11]

These press-releases also reveal the potential of pro-active policing; in two instances crimes were thwarted before they were carried out. It is important to stress that one of the NCS objectives is the "disruption" of criminal groups. Stopping armed robberies before they occur might be considered an instance of disruption. Stopping armed robberies before they occur might be considered an instance of this. However, in this regard it would do to note one press release emanating from the NCS (dated 10 Nov. 1999) in which Roy Penrose, its Director General, spoke in support of proposals to further enhance the laws on asset forfeiture to include civil forfeiture. He stated that the lower standard of proof required in civil proceedings (balance of probability *vs* beyond reasonable doubt) could be used to great effect against criminal groups since it would make it easier for the police to confiscate criminal assets. He stated that "many sophisticated 'super-fagin' criminals" avoid conviction by staying in the background and manipulating illicit dealing through "expendable lieutenants". The advent of civil forfeiture rules would allow for the targeting of criminal assets with or without attendant criminal proceedings. While such legislation has not been passed in Britain, such innovations have been undertaken in the United States. It is worth noting that in the UK context the proposal is for a National Confiscation Bureau, which would effectively insulate the policing system from the financial rewards of asset confiscation. This is not the case in the USA, where a cogent case has been argued that law enforcement agencies have become, in effect, addicted to the drug war because asset forfeiture has become such an important budgetary supplement (Worall, 1999; see also, Sheptycki, 2000). Disruption of criminal organisations is one of the primary aims of the NCS. This ill-defined term raises questions about the relationship between police operations and due process, since it is not altogether clear that police achievements in this manner would be the subject of judicial oversight.

On March 29, 1999 the NCS announced that in its first year of operations it had undertaken more than 425 operations and had made over 900 arrests. This is a powerful advertisement of the agency's success. There has been, as yet, no scientific evaluation on the workings of this agency and it is difficult to know precisely what these figures mean. Quantifying the press releases issued by the NCS by crime type gives some indication of what these numbers pertain to. This is laid out in the following table.

*A quantification of NCS press releases by crime type for the period 1 Oct. 1999 to 31 March 2000*

| TYPE | Drugs + | Drugs | Violent Crime | Other | Not Classed | |
|---|---|---|---|---|---|---|
| NUMBER | 7 | 22 | 2 | 7 | 6 | 44 |
| % of total | 16% | 50% | 4% | 16% | 14% | 100% |

Before commenting on the above table, it must be stressed that it is not being claimed that these figures represent a complete representation of the work undertaken by the NCS during the six month period between October 1998 and March 1999. Rather, this quantification of press releases represents an analysis of how the NCS represented itself to the public. For the most part these items, drafted for release in the nation's press, pertain to successful operations. They are the "best face" of the NCS.

The press releases counted under the "Not Classed" heading relate to those which either did not pertain to a criminal case or were "double hits", that is supplementary releases pertaining to cases already counted. As can be seen, most of the press releases pertained to successful operations that either resulted in arrests or convictions. For the purposes of the analysis being pursued here, what is most striking is that the great majority of cases (66%) pertain to drug trafficking. There are two sub-categories for drugs, since some instances also involved associated offences. Those cases classed as "Drugs+" should be seen as the more serious; five out of the seven included charges of weapons possession, while the other two also included associated charges of money laundering. The most serious weapons related case involved the seizure on 16 February 1999 of over 300,000 ecstasy tablets, 100 kilos of amphetamine paste, 1 kilo of cocaine, 3 Uzi sub-machine guns and one pistol. More typical is the case of the motorcyclist mentioned above who had in his possession a loaded .45 pistol. Another of these cases included, in addition to the drugs and weapon seizures, the discovery of 100 stolen credit cards. Press releases classed under the "Drugs" heading pertained to quite large quantities of drugs seized; the minimum seizure announced being for 1 kilo of cocaine, and more spectacular instances involving hundreds of thousands of ecstasy tablets, and, in one instance over 23 kilos of heroin. Clearly the NCS aims at large trafficking operations, not petty dealers. What these press releases also seem to reveal is that cross-over of criminal activity is a relative rarity. Most people involved in drug trafficking who were arrested by the NCS in this period (and whose cases were thought sufficiently interesting to warrant a press release) were arrested in connection with drug trafficking offences and no more. This might be taken to suggest that drug markets are sufficiently profitable in themselves so as to undercut the incentives of economic diversification. We might also pause to consider how few of these instances involve firearms, a possible reflection of the relative success of suppressing a cultural acceptance of gun ownership within the United Kingdom.

There are two cases from this sample of press releases that pertain to violent crime. The first of these was the armed robbery that was foiled by pre-emptive police action on 28 October 1998. The second of these involved one Keith Graham Rigby who was convicted at Manchester Crown Court in November of 1998 of Incitement to Murder his wife. According to the press release, this case came to NCS attention via a message received from the Special Investigations Branch of the Military Police in Germany. Following an undercover operation in which British police officers posed as would be assassins, the man was arrested and eventually sentenced to 12 years in prison. This case is one of the 12 that clearly included actual transnational police work. Accepting that many of these cases, especially the drug cases, are themselves transnational, it is remarkable that the majority appear to have been resolved without recourse to transnational policing per se. Fully 26 of the press releases pertaining to criminal cases (38 in total) *appear* to have required only action by British police agencies, that is 68%. Here again, it must be stressed that the data being analysed here offers only a partial view of these police operations.

Perhaps the more intrinsically interesting of these cases are those classed under the heading "Other". One of these pertains to cigarette smuggling, an illicit enterprise that exists purely because of the differentials in taxation for this commodity between Britain and her continental neighbours. The second case involved the recovery of two paintings stolen from the Museum of Fine

Arts in Poltava, Ukraine in 1997. These were recovered after a tip-off which led to an undercover NCS operation and returned, with some fanfare, to the Ukrainian ambassador on 14 December 1998. Four persons were sentenced as a result of this operation and proceedings were dropped in the case of a fifth person. Another of these cases pertains to the appearance in court on bail proceedings of eight men who had been arrested on 2 September 1998 as a result of "Operation Cathedral". This was a truly transnational police operation, involving police in Australia, Austria, Belgium, Finland, France, Germany, Italy, Norway, Portugal, Sweden and the United States and which concerned the distribution of child pornography on the Internet. Case four pertains to a person found in possession of a number of firearms and who was allegedly a procurer of firearms for organised crime. The fifth was a case involving the trial of four men on charges of counterfeiting currency and a sixth involved arrests under the 1994 Trademarks Act in connection with the counterfeiting of Compact Disks. The last of the cases classed as "Other", already mentioned at the beginning of this section, involved the recovery of blank banker's cheques.

The picture that these press-releases create of the actions of the NCS is that it is overwhelmingly dedicated to the pursuit of drug traffickers. Residual cases, classifiable under the heading of "serious crime", pertain to a range of crime types each unique enough to thwart attempts at classification. In trying to assess this picture it is useful to look at other studies that have sought to develop a view on the basis of actual police files. The most significant study on cross-border crime thus far undertaken was commissioned by the Association of Chief Police Officers and was stewarded by Colin Phillips, who was then an Assistant Chief Constable of Greater Manchester Police (Phillips, 1996). The statistics presented in the Phillips report, although more detailed and drawn from a bigger sample, are broadly in accord with the above picture. Thus, the national picture for Regional Crime Squad activity showed that: 45% pertained to international operations, 33% were strictly national, 15% crossed force boundaries and 7% were within the boundaries of a single force (p. 29). The picture of crime types is broadly in accord with the content analysis undertaken above, although given that Phillips and his team had access to a large sample of actual case files the clarity and specificity of the findings is greater. According to the Phillips Report: 47% of RCS (Regional Crime Squad – the precursor to the NCS) activity was related to drugs; serially related crimes accounted for 17.5%, firearms 9%, forgery for 8%, stolen lorry loads 5.5%, money laundering 4%, murder 1.5%, kidnap 0.5%, product contamination 0.5% and other 6% (p. 30). Broadly speaking, the Phillips Report suggested that it was indeed offences associated with the illicit market – drugs trafficking, to be sure, but also the sale of stolen goods, illegal firearms, counterfeit products, and smuggled tobacco – that constituted the "organised crime" that absorbed the attention of central police squads.

With this centralisation comes a concentration on a narrow section of criminals. The Report of Her Majesty's Inspectorate of Constabulary (1997) puts this succinctly:

> There was a clear commitment to target serious crime and major criminals, but originally it was hoped that wider levels of service could be provided, continuing in effect the role of the defunct Regional Criminal Intelligence Offices (RICOs). It soon become clear that there were simply too few resources to meet such wide ranging objectives. If NCIS was to succeed, it was vital to prioritise and resources were refocused on gathering intelligence to support operations against top tier criminality (HMIC, 1997, quoted in Stelfox, 1999).

These new national agencies, both NCIS and NCS, aim to target "core nominals", that is "quality" criminals. The image of the "Mr Bigs" of organised crime animates the shifts in policing architecture in Great Britain in the contemporary period. All the while academic criminologists have argued that the nature of these markets is one of diversity and fragmentation (Dorn et al, 1992). The picture that emerges is one of a complex market place where a variety of types of offender operate independently of each other (Hobbs, 1995, 1998). Further, a study of "criminal gangs" in Britain found that the overwhelming majority were composed of predominantly indigenous white members whose activities were largely limited in territorial ambit (Stelfox, 1996). It seems likely that the NCIS and the NCS can continue to produce annual figures pertaining to their law enforcement success that improves year on year. From that view, it is money well spent. However, "law enforcement has a limited capacity to prevent future offending other than for those few who it delivers to the criminal justice process" (Stelfox, 1999, p. 6). In his 1999 Police Foundation Lecture, Jürgen Storbeck, Director General of Europol, called for a shift of resources away from local policing in order to tackle the security threat posed to Europe by a rising tide of organised crime (Storbeck, 1999). In the UK significant resources are being shifted to the national level as NCIS continues to see favourable budgetary increases.

What has disappeared from the contemporary discourse on organised crime control in Britain, if, indeed, it ever existed, is any notion of crime prevention. That does not mean that there are not innovative ideas for preventing crimes of the illicit market, rather than retrospectively enforcing criminal law sanctions. Credit card fraud can be prevented by the introduction of personal identification numbers (PINs) at the point of sale, the marketing of stolen vehicles can be prevented by better regulation and inspection of used car dealerships and garages, commodity smuggling (tobacco and alcohol) can be prevented by harmonising "sin" taxes across Europe. There are many other facets of the "organised crime" phenomenon that might also be amenable to such controls. What is certain is that aggressive enforcement measures aimed at detection, seizure and confiscation of assets and prosecution of offenders will not change the circumstances that produced the problem in the first instance (Hicks, 1998). However, developments in the law relating to the confiscation of criminal assets are proceeding apace.

## LEGISLATION FOR THE CONFISCATION OF CRIMINAL PROCEEDS IN THE UK

The notion of targeting criminal money has come to be a significant new paradigm in law enforcement. Following the recommendations set down by the Financial Action Task Force and the EC Money Laundering Directive of June 1991, the United Kingdom has been at the forefront of international developments in this field. UK authorities have moved to criminalise money laundering, to develop systems for the tracing and confiscation of criminal assets, and have established systems to detect and prevent the proceeds of crime from being laundered through the banking system (Sheptycki, 2000). The United Kingdom has drug money laundering laws, crime money laundering laws, and terrorist money laundering laws (Home Office, 1997). While separate legislation exists for England and Wales, Scotland and Northern Ireland, international requests for assistance in matters relating to money laundering, asset freezing and confiscation are all processed by the UK Central Authority based at the Home Office. Section 9 of the Criminal Justice (International Cooperation Act) 1990, which enables Orders in Council to be made for the enforcement of external forfeiture orders, applies throughout the United Kingdom (ibid. p. 97). NCIS headquarters in London maintains the Financial Intelligence Unit (FIU), which receives notifications of suspicious transactions from UK banks, currently estimated to be approximately 18,000 disclosures per annum. Thus, according to Thony's typology (1996), the UK has adopted a "police centred model" for suspicious transaction reporting. The FIU is currently struggling to cope with the volume of reports as these are received in the form of paper records. Data input is a time consuming task and analysis of financial intelligence cannot proceed systematically prior to data entry. The sheer number of reports coming to the attention of the FIU probably retards the ability to make systematic use of the suspicious transaction reporting system (Sheptycki, 2000).

The move from targeting criminals and criminal activity to targeting criminal money has not developed to the same degree in the UK as it has in the United

States, where the criminal asset confiscation has come to be central to law enforcement efforts against "organised crime". How the further development of asset confiscation capabilities by the law enforcement apparatus will affect the development of policing efforts against organised crime is unclear at present. What seems certain is that the character of illicit markets and of policing are likely to be significantly shaped by these developments.

**CONCLUSION**

The British government indicated in March 1999 that it was interested in participating in the provisions of the Schengen *acquis* but it also indicated that this was to be on a limited basis. When former UK Home Secretary Jack Straw spoke at the Special European Council in Tampere on Justice and Home Affairs, he stated that he was unenthusiastic about creating a single judicial space for the European Union, but that he was in favour of developments such as "Eurowarrants" which would facilitate the arrest and transfer of suspects for trial across the territory of the EU. The UK government remains conscious of its sovereignty even while it is concerned to cooperate with its European partners in the enhancement of its own security. The development of state policing capacity in the UK for combating organised crime flies in the face of predictions made by adherents to a radical "globalisation thesis", which foresees a diminution in the power of the sovereign state. When considering crime control it is clear that the state capacities are being enhanced not eroded. This 'enhancement' of state capacities is multiplied as a result of transnational cooperation efforts like those underwritten by the European Union.

In recent years the policing architecture of England and Wales has undergone significant alteration. Despite the appearance of administrative fragmentation in UK policing, it seems clear that those structural changes are of a centralising nature. One curious anomaly is that two national police services have been created. The National Criminal Intelligence Service (NCIS) is the central hub of the police intelligence system while the National Crime Squad (NCS), a revamping of the already existing Regional Crime Squad System, represents the operational capacity of a nationalised policing system. It is possible that these organisations will be merged in the not too distant future. These institutional developments have taken place alongside the enhancement of the Security Service mission to include organised crime. At the same time, the position of Special Branch, historically focused on Irish terrorism, is becoming increasingly anomalous and it is unclear how it will be affected by the developing focus on organised crime. This trend towards centralisation seems undeniable, but at the same time the UK policing system still exhibits tendencies towards de-centralisation and fragmentation. These contradictions notwithstanding, it would do to point out that these developments (greater national purview over intelligence gathering and analysis, increased use of undercover police methods and the increase in involvement of the Security Service) are rather antithetical to the British police tradition, in particular the notion of local policing by consent (Loader, 1997).

Academic criminologists, particularly those of a sociological bent, have long pointed out that "organised crime" is embedded in the wider communities of civil society (Taylor, 1999). The British tradition of *policing* implies a wider responsibility than mere law enforcement – it is the "maintenance of the health of the social body" (Sheptycki, 1995). From the inception of the "new" police in Great Britain at the beginning of the nineteenth century, policing has been, first and foremost, about crime prevention (Reiner, 2000). The rise of a discourse about "organised crime", and especially "transnational organised crime", has displaced this way of thinking and replaced it with the more limited vision of policing as "law enforcement". In the contemporary period security and law enforcement agencies are competing for governmental resources and the rhetoric of "law enforcement against organised crime" has created the circumstances which ensure the eventual displacement of *policing* as a broad social practice. In making these observations it would do to recall the words of the conservative police historian Charles Reith:

> Whatever tends to loosen the bonds of the public's relationship with the police ... [such as] neglect of their principles by the police, or by the authorities who are responsible for them; or the ill-considered introduction of mechanical or other organisational changes which lessen the scope for contact between the individual citizen and the policeman on the beat must lessen, also, the power which the police derive from the public's appreciation of them. Any material decrease of this power will quickly lead to their increased dependence of the use of physical force; to the need, by central authority, of endowing them with despotic powers to enable them to fulfil their tasks; to police dependence, not on being liked by the people, but on being feared by them; and to the opening of a short road for the transference of their organisation into the only alternative form of police which is available (Reith, 1948, p. 112-113).

The need for enhanced European police cooperation in the fight against 'organised crime' goes hand-in-hand with national efforts. The justification for this partnership is, as Europol Director Jürgen Storbeck among others has stated, that by tackling the legal and procedural obstacles to cross-border investigations and by improving the intelligence gathering and dissemination system at the European level "we might stand a real chance to challenge the continuing growth of international crime and help preserve the security, not just of nations, but of local communities and of every citizen" (Storbeck, 1999, p. 13). This is an argument to continue a kind of organisational change which Reith warned against. It is evident that the term "organised crime" has underwritten changes in the policing system. It is also evident that an unintended consequence of this is the creation of an ever-widening gulf between the police and citizen, a gap that is being plugged by ever greater police surveillance powers. At first glance the need for enhanced policing power seems reasonable, since the threat of organised crime seems so plain. However, as the gulf between police and public grows the social harm that goes under the name of 'organised crime' may well be exacerbated. Perhaps then the first step in improving the security of the lives of individual citizens and of communities, not only in the United Kingdom but across the territory of the EU and beyond, would be to abandon the term "organised crime" altogether. But then, as Malcolm Anderson has observed, its "universal use in ordinary language as well as in professional law enforcement may make this an impractical recommendation" (Anderson, 1993, p. 308).

**NOTES**

1.   An office of the Director of Public Prosecutions was created by the Prosecution of Offences Act (1908) and this office could undertake prosecutions in particularly serious cases. But this was in practice rarely used. In the mid-1960s for example, it was estimated that only 2% of indictable offences were initiated by this office. The English tradition has been that the right of any person to institute offences and carry on criminal proceedings was inviolate and the system whereby police instituted criminal proceedings was, in theory, based on private prosecution (Reiss, 1976, p. 80-81).

2.   The 43 police forces of England and Wales are as follows: the Metropolitan Police, City of London Police, Avon and Somerset, Bedfordshire, Cambridgeshire, Cheshire, Cleveland, Cumbria, Derbyshire, Devon and Cornwall, Dorset, Durham, Dyfed-Powys, Essex, Gloucestershire, Greater Manchester, Gwent, Hampshire, Hertfordshire, Humberside, Kent, Lancashire, Leicestershire, Lincolnshire, Merseyside, Norfolk, Northamptonshire, Northumbria, North Wales, North Yorkshire, Nottinghamshire, South Wales, South Yorkshire, Staffordshire, Suffolk, Surrey, Sussex, Thames Valley, Warwickshire, West Mercia, West Midlands, West Yorkshire, and Wiltshire. The United Kingdom as a whole has several other police institutions that bear mention: the British Transport Police, which secure the railways and rail stations, and the 17 small police forces for various air and sea ports have been little studied. The Isle of Man, Guernsey and Jersey, have police forces which are part of the UK system. The Royal Parks Constabulary and the Royal Botanical Gardens Constabulary are responsible for patrolling the many small parks and gardens across the country. Lastly, there are several branches of military police: the Ministry of Defence Police, Royal Navy Regulating Branch, Royal Marines Police, Corps of Royal Military Police, Royal Air Force Police and the UK Atomic Energy Authority Constabulary.

3.   The police forces for Scotland are: Northern Constabulary, Grampian Police, Tayside Police, Central Scotland Police, Strathclyde Police, Fife Constabulary, Lothian and Borders Police and Dumfries and Galloway Constabulary.

4.   There are discrepancies in the statistics produced by the CPS, which show an increase in the proportion of cases in Crown Court resulting in a conviction, and those produced by the Court Service, which show the opposite. There is, as yet, no explanation as to why this is the case, but it may be symptomatic of the difficulties of introducing a new organisation into the criminal process that linger even now, a decade after the inception of the CPS.

5.   The Police and Magistrates Courts Act (1994) stipulated that the Home Secretary remains the Police Authority for London, but it also created an advisory body to act in support of the Home Secretary in relation to the effective and efficient running of the Metropolitan Police, but this falls short of a full-scale police authority for London (Jones and Newburn, 1997, p. 35)

6.   Personnel allocation for regional offices is as follows: North East, 40; North West, 37; Midlands, 34; South East, 95; South West, 36; Scotland, 12.

7.   This situation – of rapidly succeeding organisational innovations – resembles that in some other countries, like the National Criminal Intelligence Department in the Netherlands.
8.   There is some cross-over of personnel in the two SAs. Notably, the NCS and NCIS Service Authorities share representatives from the Police Authorities, which might be taken to be indicative of a future merging of the two bodies.
9.   There is some difficulty here, not least over the position with regard to Gibraltar (see House of Lords, 1999, p. 47).
10.  The reader should be informed that press releases themselves are much more detailed than the condensed versions displayed here.
11.  However, there is contrary evidence. According to *the Independent* (Oct. 1997) strong inter-institutional rivalry permeated the policing complex in Great Britain. This article is based on a leaked Home Office research study (which was reported to be based on 299 interviews with police and customs officers). One Regional Crime Squad officer said that he viewed the filing of information with NCIS as 'a waste of time': "I saw no value in it whatsoever for me as an operational manager".

**REFERENCES**

Anderson, M. (1993) "The United Kingdom and Organised Crime – The International Dimension", *European Journal of Crime, Criminal Law and Criminal Justice,* Vol 1, No. 4, pp. 292-308.

Anderson, M., den Boer, M., Cullen, P., Gilmore, W., Raab, C., and Walker, N. (1995), *Policing the European Union; Theory, Law and Practice,* Oxford: Clarendon.

Ashworth, A. (1994), *The Criminal Process; an evaluative study,* Oxford: Clarendon.

Beare, M. and Naylor, (1999), *Major Issues Relating to Organised Crime within the Context of Economic Relationships,* Nathanson Centre submission to the Law Commission of Canada, April 14, 1999.

Box, S. (1983), *Power, Crime and Mystification,* London: Tavistock.

Brogden, M. (1995), "An Agenda for Post-Troubles Policing in Northern Ireland – The South African Precedent", in *The Liverpool Law Review,* Vol. XVII(1), pp. 3-27.

Bunyan, T. (1976), *The Political Police in Britain,* London: Julian Friedmann.

Critchely, T. A. (1978), *A History of Police in England and Wales* (2nd ed.), London: Constable.

Dorn, N. Murji, K. and South, N. (1992), *Traffickers; Drug Markets and Law Enforcement,* London: Routledge.

Duff, P. (1998), "Crime Control, Due Process and 'The Case for the Prosecution': a problem of terminology?", *British Journal of Criminology,* Vol. 38, No. 4, pp. 611-616.

Duff, P. (1999), "The Prosecution Service; Independence and Accountability" in *Criminal Justice in Scotland,* P. Duff and N. Hutton (eds.), Aldershot: Ashgate.

Emsley, C. (1997), "The History of Crime and Crime Control Institutions", in R. Reiner, R. Morgan, and M. Maguire (eds.), *The Oxford Handbook of Criminology,* Oxford: Clarendon.

Ericson, R. V. (1994), "The Royal Commission on Criminal Justice System Surveillance" in *Criminal Justice in Crisis,* M. McConville and L. Bridges (eds.), Aldershot: Edward Elgar.

Field, S. Alldridge, P. and Jörg, N. (1995), "Prosecutors, Examining Magistrates and Control of Police Investigations" in *Criminal Justice in Europe; a comparative study,* C. Harding, P. Fennell, N. Jörg and B. Swart (eds.), Oxford: Clarendon.

Gane, C. (1999), "Classifying Scottish Criminal Procedure" in *Criminal Justice in Scotland,* P. Duff and N. Hutton (eds.), Aldershot: Ashgate.

Gill, P. (2000), *Rounding Up the Usual Suspects; developments in contemporary law enforcement intelligence,* Aldershot: Ashgate.

Glidewell, Sir Iain (1998), *The Review of the Crown Prosecution Service; summary of the Main Report with the Conclusions and Recommendations*, Cm 3972.

Her Majesty's Inspectorate of Constabulary (1997), *Inspection Report; The National Criminal Intelligence Service*, London: HMSO.

Hicks, D. (1998), Thinking About Organised Crime Prevention, *Journal of Contemporary Criminal Justice*, Vol. 14, No. 4, pp. 325-350.

Hillyard, P. (1993), "Paramilitary Policing and Popular Justice in Northern Ireland" in *Alternative Policing Styles*, M. Findlay and U. Zvekic (eds.), Deventer: Kluwer.

Hobbs. D. (1995), *Bad Business*, Oxford: Clarendon.

Hobbs, D. (1998), "Going Down to the Glocal; The local context of organised crime" *The Howard Journal*, Vol. 37, No. 4 pp 407-22.

Home Affairs Committee (1990), Practical Police Cooperation in Europe, London: HMSO, HC 363-2.

Home Affairs Committee (1992), *First Report on the Accountability of the Security Service*, London: HMSO, 265.

Home Affairs Committee (1994), *Organised Crime; Minutes of Evidence and Memoranda*, London: HMSO, 18-II.

Home Office, Organised and International Crime Directorate (1997), *Confiscation and Money Laundering: Law and Practice; a guide for enforcement authorities*, London: Her Majesty's Stationery Office.

House of Lords (1999), The Select Committee on the European Communities; European Union Databases, Session 1998-99, 23rd Report HL Paper 120, London: The Stationary Office.

Jones, T. and Newburn, T. (1995), "Local Government and Policing: Arresting the Decline of Local Influence", *Local Government Studies*, Vol. 21, No. 3, pp. 448-460.

Jones, T. and Newburn, T. (1997), *Policing After the Act; police governance after the Police and Magistrates Courts Act 1994*, London: Policy Studies Institute.

King, T. (The Rt. Hon.) (1995), *Intelligence and Security Committee Report on Security Service Work Against Organised Crime*, presented to parliament by the Prime Minister, Dec. 1995, London: HMSO 154.

Levi, M. (1991), "Fraudulent Justice? Sentencing the Business Criminal" in P. Carlen and D. Cook (eds.), *Paying for Crime*, Milton Keynes: Open University Press.

Levi, M. and Nelken, D. (eds.) (1996), The Corruption of Politics and the Politics of Corruption, *Journal of Law and Society Special Issue*, Vol. 23, No. 1.

Loader, I. (1997), "Policing and the Social: Questions of Symbolic Power", *British Journal of Sociology*, 48/1: 1-18.

McConville, M., Sanders, A. and Leng, R. (1991), *The Case for the Prosecution; police suspects and criminality*, London: Routledge.

Morgan, R. (1989), "Policing by Consent: Legitimating the Doctrine", in *Coming to Terms with Policing*, R. Morgan and D.J. Smith (eds.), London: Routledge.

Morrissey, M. and Pease, K. (1982), "The Black Criminal Justice System in West Belfast", *The Howard Journal*, Vol. 21, No. 3, pp 159-166.

National Criminal Intelligence Service (NCIS) (1999), *Annual Report*, 1998-99, London: Corporate Communications Branch.

NCIS (1992), *Aim, Statement of Purpose and Objectives of the NCIS*, London: National Criminal Intelligence Service, May 1992.

NCIS (1993), *Organised Crime Conference: A Threat Assessment*; a summary of the speeches presented at the Police Staff College, Hampshire, United Kingdom 24-26 May 1993, London: Office of International Criminal Justice.

NCIS (1994), *An Outline Assessment of the Threat and Impact By Organised/ Enterprise Crime Upon United Kingdom Interests*, Second Briefing Feb. 1994, London: NCIS Organised Crime Unit.

Nelken, D. (1997), "White Collar Crime", in R. Reiner, R. Morgan, and M. Maguire (eds.), *The Oxford Handbook of Criminology*, Oxford: Clarendon.

Norton-Taylor, R. (1999), "Security Spending Runs Out of Control" *The Guardian*, Friday, November 26, 1999.

Pearce, F. (1976), *The Crimes of the Powerful*, London: Pluto.

Pearce, F. and Woodiwiss, M. (eds.) (1993), *Global Crime Connections*, London: MacMillan.

Phillips, C. (1996), *International, National and Inter-Force Crime*, ACPO (unpublished).Reiner, R. (1989), "Where the Buck Stops: Chief Constables Views on Police Accountability", in R. Morgan, and D. Smith (eds.), Coming to Terms with Policing, London: Routledge.

Reiner, R. (1989), "Where the Buck Stops: Chief Constables Views on Police Accountability", in R. Morgan, and D. Smith (eds.), *Coming to Terms with Policing*, London: Routledge

Reiner, R. (1991), *Chief Constables*, Oxford: Clarendon.

Reiner, R. (1997), "Police and Policing" in *The Oxford Handbook of Criminology,* Oxford: Clarendon.

Reiner, R. (2000), The Politics of the Police (3rd Edition), Oxford: Oxford University Press.

Reiss, A. J. (1976), "Public Prosecutors and Criminal Prosecution in the United States of America; the Wilson Memorial Lecture", University of Edinburgh 1974; in *Lawyers in their Social Setting* D. N. McCormick (ed.), Edinburgh: W. Green and Son.

Reith, C. (1948), *A Short History of the British Police*, Oxford: Oxford

University Press.

Rose, D. (1996), *In the Name of the Law*, London: Jonothan Cape.

Saunders, A. (1997), "From Suspect to Trial" in *The Oxford Handbook of Criminology,* Oxford: Clarendon.

Security Service Booklet (1998), *The Security Service; an overview*, with a forward by the Home Secretary Jack Straw, London: HMSO 1998 ISBN 0 11 341184-7.

Sheptycki, J. W. E. (1991), "Deconstructing the 'Domestic Violence Incident'", in *Offenders and Victims; Theory and Practice,* S. Walklate and D. Waddington (eds.), Selected Papers of the 1991 BCC, Published by ISTD, London.

Sheptycki, J. W. E. (1995), "Transnational Policing and the Makings of a Post-modern State" *British Journal of Criminology,* Vol. 35, No. 4, pp. 613-635.

Sheptycki, J. W. E. (1997), "Faire la police dans la Manche: l'évolution de la coopération transfrontalière (1968-1996)" (*Cultures et Conflits,* Édition Spécial: *Contrôles: Frontières-Indentités Les enjeux autour de l'immigration et de l'asile,* Vol. 26/27, eté-automne 1997, pp. 93-123)

Sheptycki, J. W. E. (1998), "Police Cooperation in the English Channel Region, 1968-1996", in *The European Journal of Crime, Criminal Law and Criminal Justice,* Vol. 6, No. 3.

Sheptycki, J.W.E. (1999), "European Policing Routes; an essay on transnationalisation, policing and the information revolution", in *Public Safety in Europe*, H. Bruisma and J. G .A. van der Vijver (eds.), Twente: Twente Police Institute.

Sheptycki, J. W. E. (ed.) (1999), *"Intelligence Led Policing"*, Special Issue of Policing, Vol. 9, No. 4..

Sheptycki, J. W. E. (2000), "Policing the Virtual Launderette", in *Issues in Transnational Policing,* J. Sheptycki, (ed.), London: Routledge.

Stallion, M and Wall, D. (2000), *The British Police: Police Forces and Chief Officers*, 1829-2000, Bramshill: Police History Society.

Stelfox, P. (1996), *Gang Violence: Strategic and Tactical Operations,* London: Home Office Police Research Group.

Stelfox, P. (1999), "Transnational Organised Crime", a paper presented to the *ESRC Research Seminar on Policy Responses to Transnational Organised Crime,* Scarman Centre for Public Order, Dec. 12, 1999 (unpublished).

Storbeck, J. (1999), "Organised Crime in the European Union – the role of Europol in International Law-Enforcement Cooperation", *The 1999 Police Foundation Lecture*, London: Police Foundation.

Taylor, I. (1999), *Crime in Context*, Cambridge: Polity.

Thony, J-F. (1996), "Processing Financial Information in Money Laundering Matters: Financial Intelligence Units", *European Journal of Crime,*

*Criminal Law and Criminal Justice*, Vol. 4, No. 3, pp. 257-282.

Tupman, B. (1999), "The Sovereignty of Fraud and the Fraud of Sovereignty: OLAF and the Wise Men", *Journal of Financial Crime*, Vol. 7, No. 3, pp. 1-18.

Walker, N. (1999), "Situating Scottish Policing", in *Criminal Justice in Scotland*, P. Duff and N. Hutton (eds.), Aldershot: Ashgate.

Weitzer, R. (1996), "Police Reform in Northern Ireland", *Police Studies* Vol. 19, No. 2, pp. 27-41.

Whitacker, B. *The Police*, London: Penguin .

Worall, J. L. (1999), "Addicted to the Drug War? The Role of Civil Asset Forfeiture as a Budgetary Supplement in Contemporary Law Enforcement", a paper presented to the American Society of Criminology, Nov. 1999, Toronto, Canada (unpublished).

## ACRONYMS

| | |
|---|---|
| **ACPO** | Association of Chief Police Officers |
| **ARNI** | Animal Rights National Index |
| **C2** | UK Central Authority (Home Office) |
| **CCIC** | Cross Channel Intelligence Conference |
| **CPA** | Crime Pattern Analysis |
| **CPS** | Crown Prosecution Service |
| **DLO** | Drugs Liaison Officer |
| **EAASP** | European Association of Airport and Seaport Police |
| **ELS** | European Liaison Section |
| **ELU** | European Liaison Unit |
| **FBI** | Federal Bureau of Investigation (USA) |
| **FIU** | Financial Intelligence Unit |
| **HMCE** | Her Majesty's Customs and Excise |
| **HMIC** | Her Majesty's Inspectorate of Constabulary |
| **MI5** | The Security Service |
| **MI6** | The Secret Service |
| **NCB** | National Central Bureau (Interpol) |
| **NCIS** | National Criminal Intelligence Service |
| **NCS** | National Crime Squad |
| **NDIU** | National Drugs Intelligence Unit |
| **NFIU** | National Football Intelligence Unit |
| **NJU** | National Joint Unit |
| **NPO** | National Ports Office |
| **NPOIU** | National Public Order Intelligence Unit |
| **PII** | Public Interest Immunity |
| **RCIOs** | Regional Criminal Intelligence Offices |
| **RCS** | Regional Crime Squad |
| **RUC** | Royal Ulster Constabulary |
| **SB** | Special Branch |
| **SIS** | Schengen Information System |

**The UK Police System**

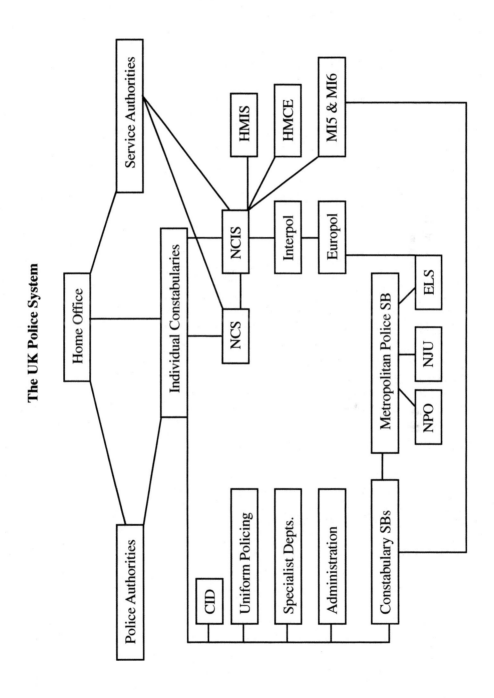

# Recent and Forthcoming EIPA Publications*

*All prices are subject to change without notice.*

**Organised Crime: A Catalyst in the Europeanisation of National Police and Prosecution Agencies?**
*Monica den Boer (ed.)*
EIPA 2002, approx. 556 pages: € **38.55**
(Only available in English)

**The EU and Crisis Management: Development and Prospects**
*Simon Duke*
EIPA 2002, 220 pages: € **27.20**
(Only available in English)

**The Dublin Convention on Asylum: Between Reality and Aspirations**
*Cláudia Faria (ed.)*
EIPA 2001, approx. 340 pages: € **11.35**
(Mixed texts in English and French)

**Civil Services in the Europe of Fifteen: Trends and New Developments**
*Danielle Bossaert, Christoph Demmke, Koen Nomden, Robert Polet*
EIPA 2001, 342 pages: € **36.30**
(Also available in French and German)

**Pouvoir politique et haute administration: Une comparaison européenne**
*Jean-Michel Eymeri*
IEAP 2001, environ 130 pages: € **27.20**
(Disponible en français uniquement)

**Meeting of the Representatives of the Public Administrations of the Euro-Mediterranean Partners in the Framework of the Euro-Mediterranean Partnership**
Proceedings of the Meeting; Barcelona, 7-8 February 2000
*Eduard Sánchez Monjo (ed.)*
EIPA 2001, 313 pages: € **36.30**
(Also available in French)

**Finland's Journey to the European Union**
*Antti Kuosmanen (with a contribution by Frank Bollen and Phedon Nicolaides*
EIPA 2001, 319 pages: € **31.75**
(Only available in English)

**Rethinking the European Union: IGC 2000 and Beyond**
*Edward Best/Mark Gray/Alexander Stubb (eds)*
EIPA 2000, 372 pages: € **36.30**
(Also available in French)

**EU Structural Funds beyond Agenda 2000: Reform and Implications for Current and Future Member States**
*Frank Bollen/Ines Hartwig/Phedon Nicolaides*
EIPA 2000, 236 pages: € **31.75**
(Only available in English)

**Schengen Still Going Strong: Evaluation and Update**
*Monica den Boer (ed.)*
EIPA 2000, 129 pages: € **27.20**
(Mixed texts in English, French and German)

**Negotiating the Future of Agricultural Policies: Agricultural Trade and the Millennium WTO Round**
*Sanoussi Bilal/Pavlos Pezaros*
Kluwer Law International 2000, 302 pages
(Only available in English)

**Umweltpolitik zwischen Brüssel und Berlin: Ein Leitfaden für die deutsche Umweltverwaltung**
*Christoph Demmke/Martin Unfried*
EIPA 2000, 248 Seiten: € **27.20**
(Nur auf Deutsch erhältlich)

**The Dublin Convention on Asylum: Its Essence, Implementation and Prospects**
*Clotilde Marinho (ed.)*
EIPA 2000, 413 pages: € **11.35**
(Mixed texts in English and French)

● **CURRENT EUROPEAN ISSUES SERIES**

**From Graphite to Diamond: The Importance of Institutional Structure in Establishing Capacity for Effective and Credible Application of EU Rules**
*Phedon Nicolaides*
EIPA 2002, 56 pages: € **15.90**
(Only available in English)

*Capacity Building for Integration*

\* **European Environmental Policy: The Administrative Challenge for the Member States**
*Christoph Demmke and Martin Unfried*
EIPA 2001, 309 pages: € **36.30**
(Only available in English)

\* **Managing EU Structural Funds: Effective Capacity for Implementation as a Prerequisite**
*Frank Bollen*
EIPA 2001, 44 pages: € **11.35**
(Only available in English)

---

\* A comprehensive list of EIPA's publications and order form can be found on EIPA's website at: http://eipa-nl.com/public/public_publications/default.htm

* **Organisational Analysis of the Europeanisation Activities of the Ministry of Economic Affairs: A Dutch Experience**
*Adriaan Schout*
EIPA 2001, 55 pages: € **15.90**
(Only available in English)

* **Effective Implementation of the Common Agricultural Policy: The Case of the Milk Quota Regime and the Greek Experience in Applying It**
*Pavlos D. Pezaros*
EIPA 2001, 71 pages: € **15.90**
(Only available in English)

* **Enlargement of the European Union and Effective Implementation of its Rules (with a Case Study on Telecommunications)**
*Phedon Nicolaides*
EIPA 2000, 86 pages: € **18.15**
(Only available in English)

**Between Vision and Reality: CFSP's Progress on the Path to Maturity**
*Simon Duke (ed.)*
EIPA 2000, 319 pages: € **31.75**
(Only available in English)

**L'égalité de traitement entre hommes et femmes**
*Sous la direction de Gabrielle Vonfelt*
IEAP 2000, 94 pages: € **18.15**
(Disponible en français uniquement)

● **CONFERENCE PROCEEDINGS SERIES**

**Increasing Transparency in the European Union?**
*Veerle Deckmyn (ed.)*
EIPA 2002, approx 250 pages: € **31.75**
(Only available in English)

**The Common Agricultural Policy and the Environmental Challenge: Instruments, Problems and Opportunities from Different Perspectives**
*Pavlos D. Pezaros and Martin Unfried (eds.)*
EIPA 2002, approx. 260 pages: € **31.75**
(Only available in English)

**Asylum, Immigration and Schengen Post-Amsterdam: A First Assessment**
*Clotilde Marinho (ed.)*
EIPA 2001, 130 pages: € **27.20**
(Mixed texts in English and French)